8/15

THE MAMMOTH BOOK OF **CULT COMICS**

EDITED BY **ILYA**

ROBINSON

RUNNING PRESS
PHILADELPHIA · LONDON

ROBINSON

First published in Great Britain
in 2014 by Robinson

A CIP catalogue record for
this book is available from the
British Library.

ISBN 978-1-47211-149-4
(trade paperback)

Typeset in FF Din
Printed and bound in Great
Britain by CPI Group CR0 4YY

Robinson
is an imprint of
Constable & Robinson Ltd
100 Victoria Embankment
London EC4Y 0DY

An Hachette UK Company
www.hachette.co.uk

www.constablerobinson.com

First published in the
United States in 2013
by Running Press Book
Publishers,
A Member of the Perseus
Books Group

Books published by Running
Press are available at special
discounts for bulk purchases
in the United States by
corporations, institutions, and
other organizations. For more
information, please contact the
Special Markets Department
at the Perseus Books Group,
2300 Chestnut Street, Suite
200, Philadelphia, PA 19103, or
call (800) 810-4145, ext. 5000,
or email special.markets@
perseusbooks.com.

US ISBN 978-0-7624-5468-6
US Library of Congress Control
Number: 2014940740

9 8 7 6 5 4 3 2 1
Digit on the right indicates the
number of this printing

Running Press Book
Publishers
2300 Chestnut Street
Philadelphia, PA 19103-4371

Visit us on the web!
www.runningpress.com

In loving memory of Andy Roberts
(1963–2005) and Steve Whitaker (1955–2008).
And for my dear brother, Simon (1963–2014),
with undying love – Ed.

Author and editor ILYA's comic strip stories
have been published internationally – in
America (Marvel, DC, Dark Horse), Japan
(Kodansha) and throughout Europe. Recent
book titles include the graphic novel
Room for Love, his daring adaptation of
Manga Shakespeare's *King Lear*, and noir
anthology *It's Dark in London* (all titles from
SelfMadeHero). Between 2006 and 2008
he masterminded three volumes of the
groundbreaking *Mammoth Book of Best
New Manga*. His virtual Rolodex bulges with
contacts from the world of comics, manga
and illustration.

CONTENTS

INTRODUCTION

The main purpose of this compilation is archival. The small press or independent comics scene – formerly an adjunct or alternative to the so-called "mainstream" but now existing largely in its own right – has been flourishing since the 1980s (earlier manifestations are largely referred to simply as "underground" or "comix"). What makes for a Cult Comic? Honest, heartfelt, homemade – self-published, stapled pamphlets, more often than not bundles of black and white photocopies with, if really pushing the boat out, handcoloured covers; or else short-run small and independent press printings, anywhere from a handful to a few thousand copies at one time.

These humble beginnings have nowadays morphed into a fantastic array of virtual art objects – sometimes literally so. Full-colour covers with black and white interiors, four-colour printing, two-colour, or by some other means colour throughout: lithographic, serigraphic (screen-printed), risographic; limitless variations of paper-stock and drop-ins and foil stamps and other special features to make them properly collectible and infinitely cherishable print artefacts. And then, at the opposite end of the scale, there's cyberspace – webcomics, be they one-off funnies or serials, available as downloadables, regularly posted and updated, or streaming direct to your choice of mobile device. Yes, excuse me if I yawn – these days we are spoilt for choice.

It wasn't always so.

Down to the limited circumstances of their first and often only appearances, many of the strips featured here are lost masterpieces that might otherwise never have seen the light of day again. And that would be too great a shame. As it is, many of the talented creators whose work fills these pages have long since moved on and no longer make comics. Even more sadly, a couple of them are no longer with us. Quite possibly, you won't have heard of many or any of them. This, of course, is no reflection at all on the merits of their work. By the nature of the form – small press, most often self-published – there exist no official records, few traces. When and where they do survive, these original publications are in the hands of private collectors. A few enthusiasts and aficionados may keep the flames alive in their online bulletins and listings (let us immediately refer you to: www.comics.edpinsent. com). But even among the proliferating numbers of independent creators that nowadays make this their trade or art form, awareness of what has come before is not always so very high. Fair enough, perhaps – more small-press "cult" comics are being made today than ever before, and of a high median quality. Still, if you have any interest in seeing where this wealth of activity all began – the wellspring it originates from – whether you want to relive some of the heights of the form or just to read some damn fine comics, here they are.

The following selection is, of necessity, confined to works first presented in the English language, when of course Cult Comics exist all over the world; fuel aplenty for further publications. As it is, within these pages we

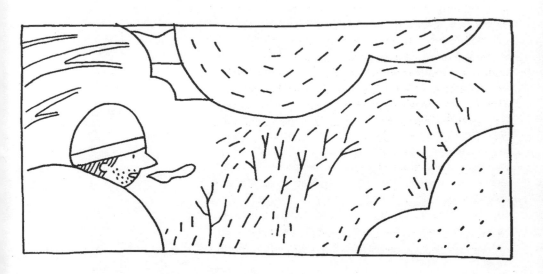

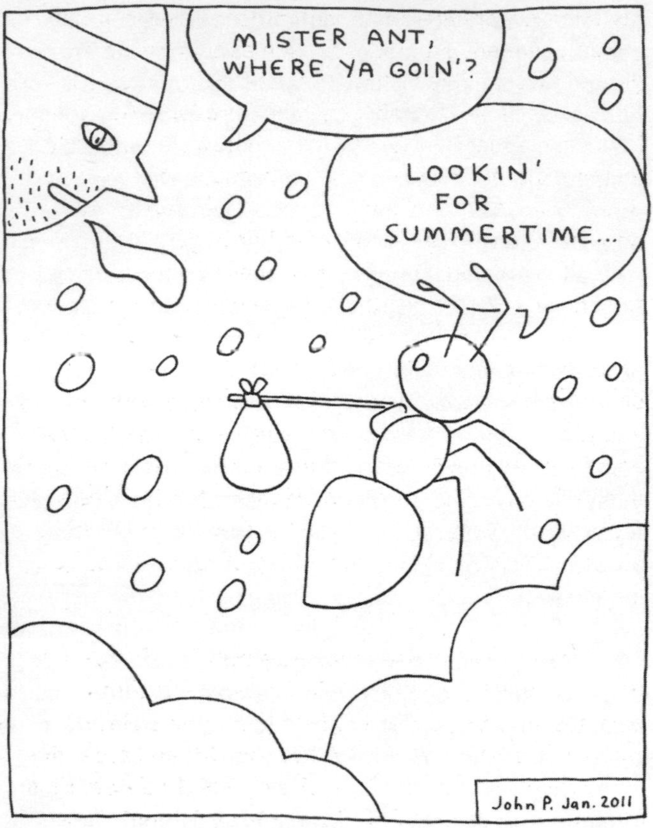
MISTER ANT, WHERE YA GOIN'?
LOOKIN' FOR SUMMERTIME...
John P. Jan. 2011

are proud to represent gems from creators based in the United States of America, the United Kingdom, New Zealand, Australia, and even Bosnia.

As with any gatherum of this type, there are of course notable exceptions. Many creators of Cult Comics have gone on to forge their own mainstream – Daniel Clowes, Craig Thompson, Gene Luen Yang, and their like – talents whose efforts have won them great recognition and success, and rightly so. They now have the chance to blaze their own trail. Gavin MacInnes, who once detailed myriad sexual misadventures within the photocopied pages of *Pervert*, went on to become founder of trendsetting Vice.com and its associated magazine; others work on, largely as independents to this day, leaders and legends: John (*King Cat*) Porcellino*, John (*Epoxy*, *Sublife*) Pham, Joe (*Silly Daddy*) Chiappetta – and you would do best to seek them out and show your support directly for their wares. Others, for whatever reason, have simply fallen away beyond record or recollection.

*The astute simplicity of Porcellino's stripped-back line artwork acts as a hotwire to the brain's storytelling centre, or narrative cortex. Proto-comics, or pure, clear and vital communication?
(Above and on previous page)

www.johnporcellino.blogspot.com

Female creators are not so very present. There simply weren't as many around back then as there are now. Annie Lawson, Lorna Miller, Rachael Ball, Kate Charlesworth, Myra Hancock, Megan Kelso, Cool Cheese, honourable mentions all, but for whatever reason not included here. I'd like to make particular note of Carol Swain, whose work absolutely would be represented were it not for the wide format of her pages. A more current snapshot of the scene would rightly reflect a ratio close to half. For that better sense of the current and future gender mix we refer you to a more prospective title, *The Mammoth Book of Best New Manga* (volumes one through three). Our content, meanwhile, necessarily and functionally dates back to before such enlightened and enriched times. As a gesture towards looking slightly ahead, however, we do round off with a few relatively more modern pieces, by Julia Gfrörer and Tom K, to indicate the state of play within this same Cult Comic arena now.

Other changes or trends that we simply could not track? Large-format newsprint comics, starting perhaps with Sirk's *Storeyville* in the US and David Hitchcock's *Whitechapel Freak* in the UK, and spreading like a rash ever since: *Ocular Anecdotes*, *Kuti Kuti*, *Cold Heat*, *Comics Comics*, *The Comic Reader*, *Adapt*, *Peter Arkle News*, and on and on. What's the attraction? To be determinatively different, most likely – something suggestive of "obsolescent" format or print technology, unreproducible in any other way; a hark back to the "funnies" of yore perhaps – a truly immersive large-scale reading experience that meanwhile, perversely, acknowledges the "throwaway" heritage and nature of the medium.

So what else can the past tell us? And what does the future hold?

There's much more use of colour now – rising stars Joe Sparrow, Robert Ball, Michel Fiffe with *Copra* and Tom Scioli with his subversive *Satan's Soldier* are all making work that very much relies on it as a crucial ingredient for impact. For this reason, among many others, the distinction of "mainstream" no longer really applies (at the same time negating "alternative" – alternative to what?).

The expectation might formerly have been that excellence in craft or notional popularity within a small-press incarnation would lead inexorably to offers of publication as a "proper" comic, or a publishing deal with the big boys – "selling out" in more ways than one. Equally so, much of the independent scene came into being not only in spite of mainstream comics, but explicitly so, to spite them, with an aesthetic approach and manner all their own. Such distinctions – perhaps, happily – hardly matter anymore. On the downside, at least in English language and culture, all comics these days can be termed "cult" – of limited, if feverish and enlightened, appeal.

Everybody is fringe nowadays, at least by the old standards. In music, art, television, books, comedy, philosophy, as in comics, the mass fractures into endless smaller pieces, the audience dividing and sub-dividing. The "mainstream" of comics has traditionally been taken to mean superheroes – even so, Marvel and DC superheroes. Despite conquering the cinema they nowadays subsist and glory within a ghetto of their own making. Truer mainstream appeal, appeal to the main flow of society, including any concomitant commercial potential, properly rests with the type of narrative found within these pages – whether introspective, ground level, meta-phorical, metaphysical, (ironically!) comical, romantic, horrific; even many or all of these things at once.

Breaking the fourth wall, dude (opposite). A clip from the seminal deconstruction comic *Summer Fun*, by Andy Roberts.

As with so many aspects of a properly popular comics culture, Japan shows us one possible future. Over there, a convention-style "Comic Market" (Comiket) is held twice a year, every August and December. The products sold there are Dojinshi – self-published – much of it fan fiction (unofficial versions of the most popular characters and series) but also wholly original manga, novels and graphic novels, games, fan-books, essays, dolls, etc. The first Comiket was held back in 1975. Thirty-two groups had their stalls and about 700 visitors came. By the winter 2008 Comiket 35,000 groups now had their stalls and about 560,000 visitors came to the summer 2009 event (held across three days). From 700 to over half a million, that's exponential growth by anyone's count (thanks to Kutsuwada Chie for the report on figures).

It begins to happen elsewhere – year by year, shows

such as Thought Bubble in the UK, and APE and MoCCA in the US, are expanding largely thanks to the presence of the latest Cult Comics and their creators, as well, of course, as the new hold that superheroes and their fantasy brethren have on popular culture. And, when it comes to fan fiction, especially slash fiction, sometimes they even come together. At one such recent gathering *Avengers* star Mark Ruffalo – screen alter ego of Marvel's Kirby Kreation The Incredible Hulk – was shown a series of drawings of his character getting it on with Robert Downey Jnr's Iron Man/Tony Stark (Kirby again). His reported response was, "I endorse [this art] 100 per cent. You know what it is? It's open-source creativity."

So there you have it. The playing field is very much levelled. Culturally speaking, everything and everyone is fair game. If we sell enough copies of this book to win a second volume, my aim is to prove that point with some stuff we didn't get to include this time . . .

ILYA, editor,
The Mammoth Book of Cult Comics (volume one)

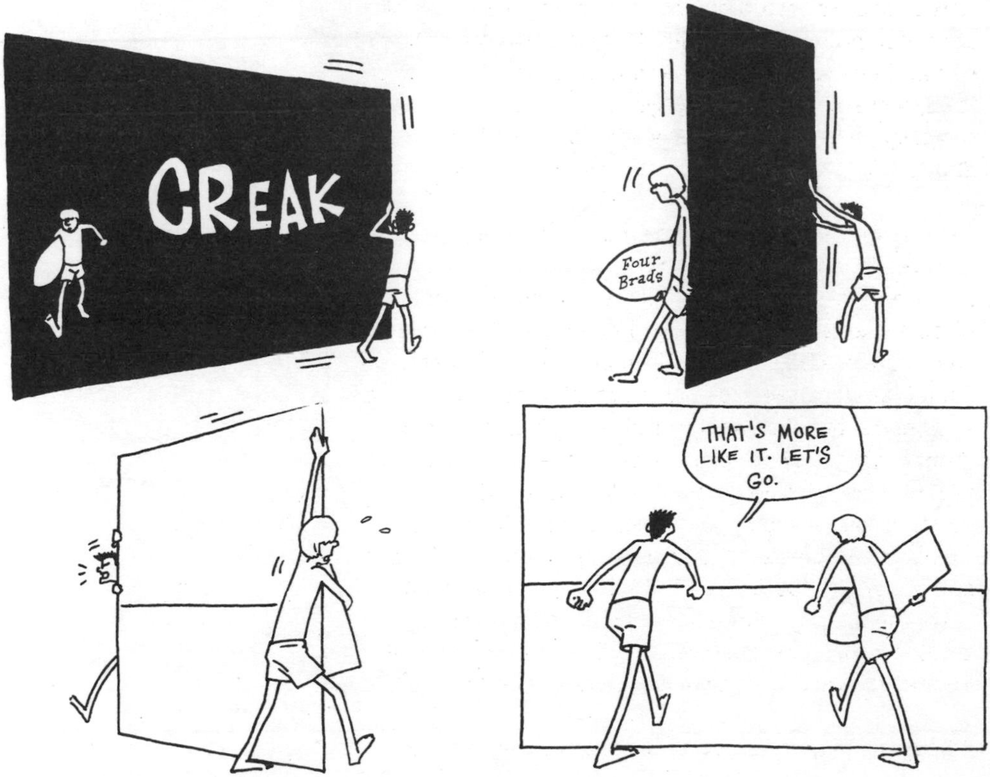
CREAK
Four Brads
THAT'S MORE LIKE IT. LET'S GO.

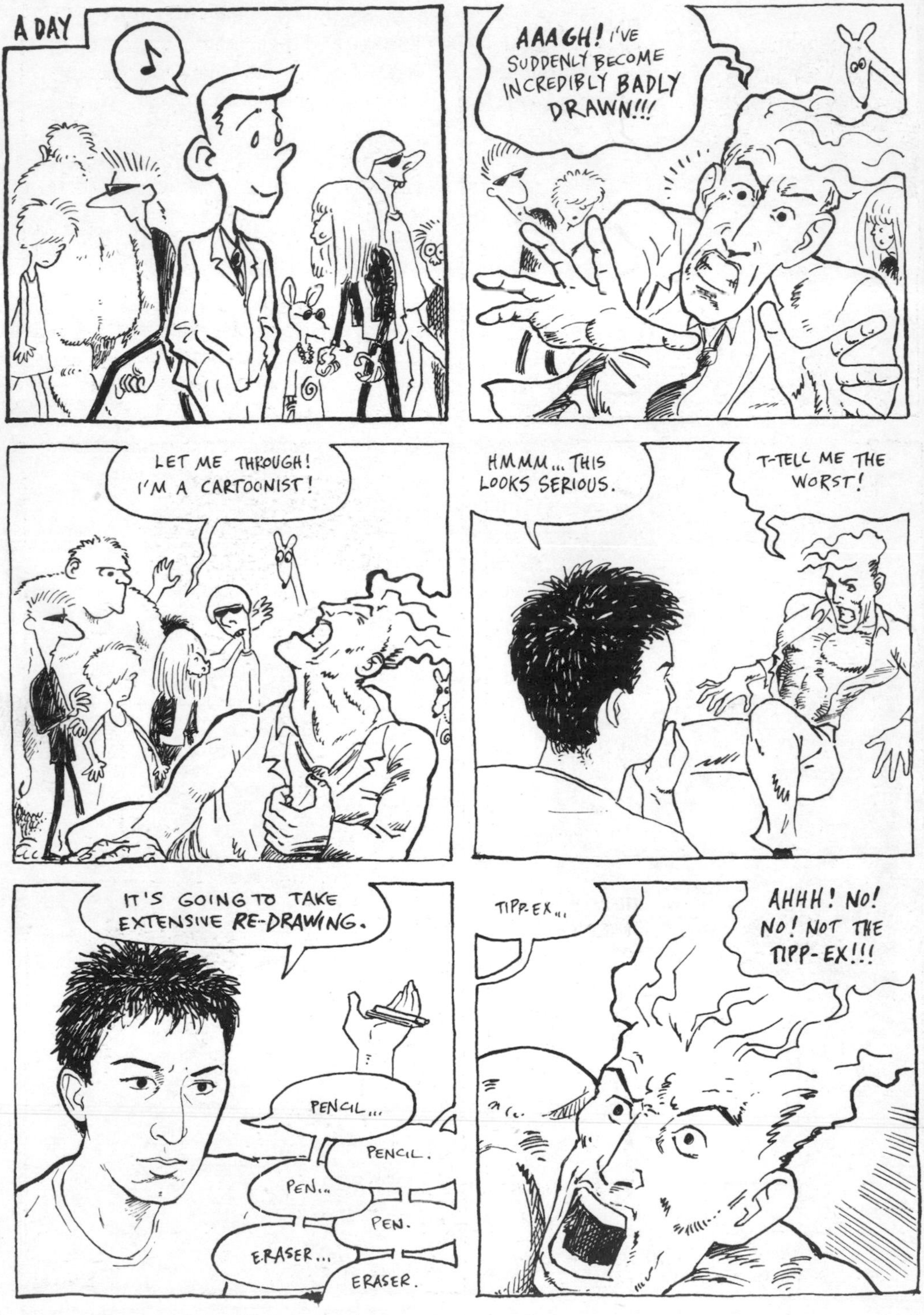
A DAY
AAAGH! I'VE SUDDENLY BECOME INCREDIBLY BADLY DRAWN!!!
LET ME THROUGH! I'M A CARTOONIST!
HMMM... THIS LOOKS SERIOUS.
T-TELL ME THE WORST!
IT'S GOING TO TAKE EXTENSIVE RE-DRAWING.
PENCIL...
PENCIL.
PEN...
PEN.
ERASER...
ERASER.
TIPP-EX...
AHHH! NO! NO! NOT THE TIPP-EX!!!

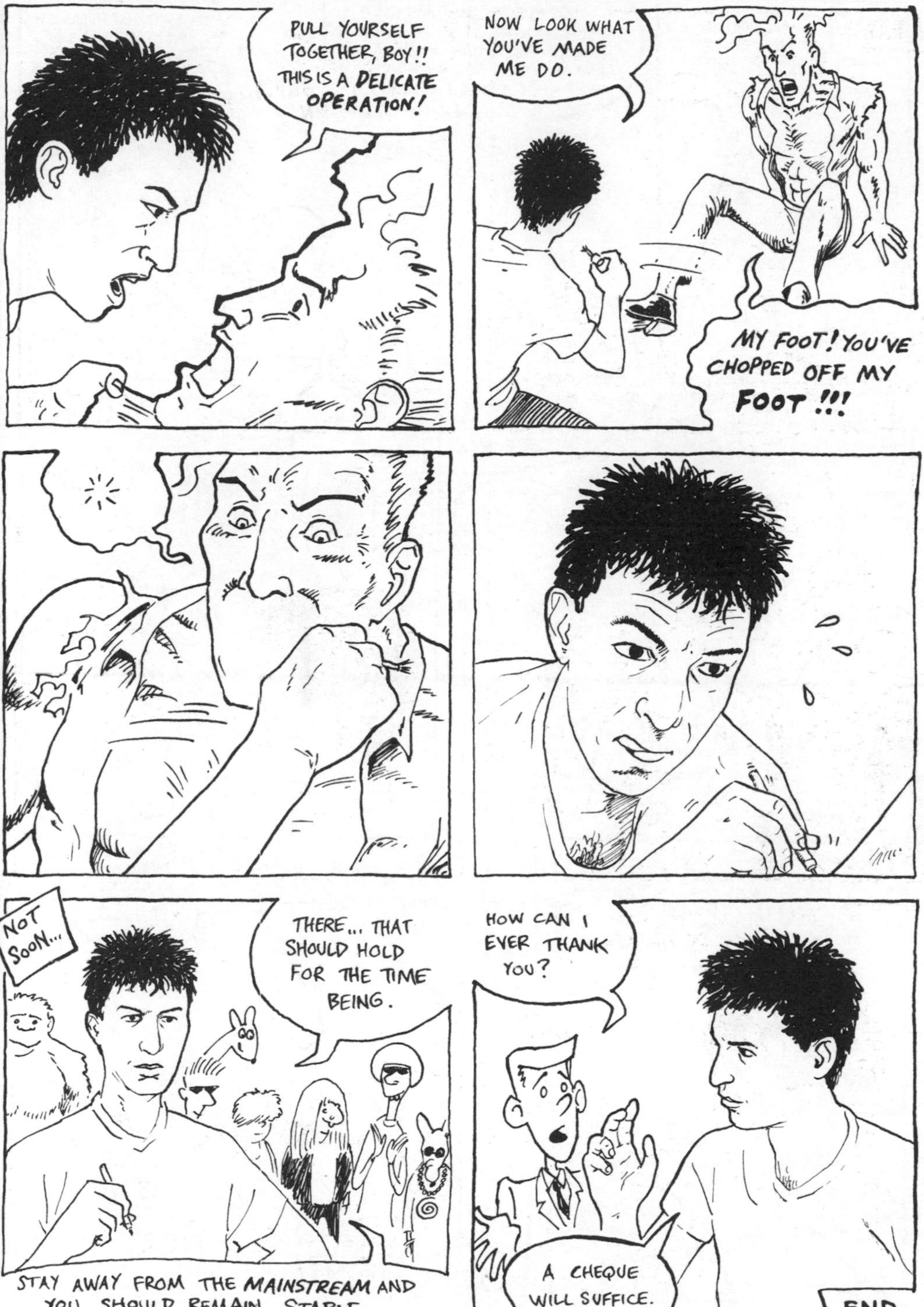
PULL YOURSELF TOGETHER, BOY!! THIS IS A DELICATE OPERATION!
NOW LOOK WHAT YOU'VE MADE ME DO.
MY FOOT! YOU'VE CHOPPED OFF MY FOOT!!!
NOT SOON...
THERE... THAT SHOULD HOLD FOR THE TIME BEING.
STAY AWAY FROM THE MAINSTREAM AND YOU SHOULD REMAIN STABLE...
HOW CAN I EVER THANK YOU?
A CHEQUE WILL SUFFICE.
END

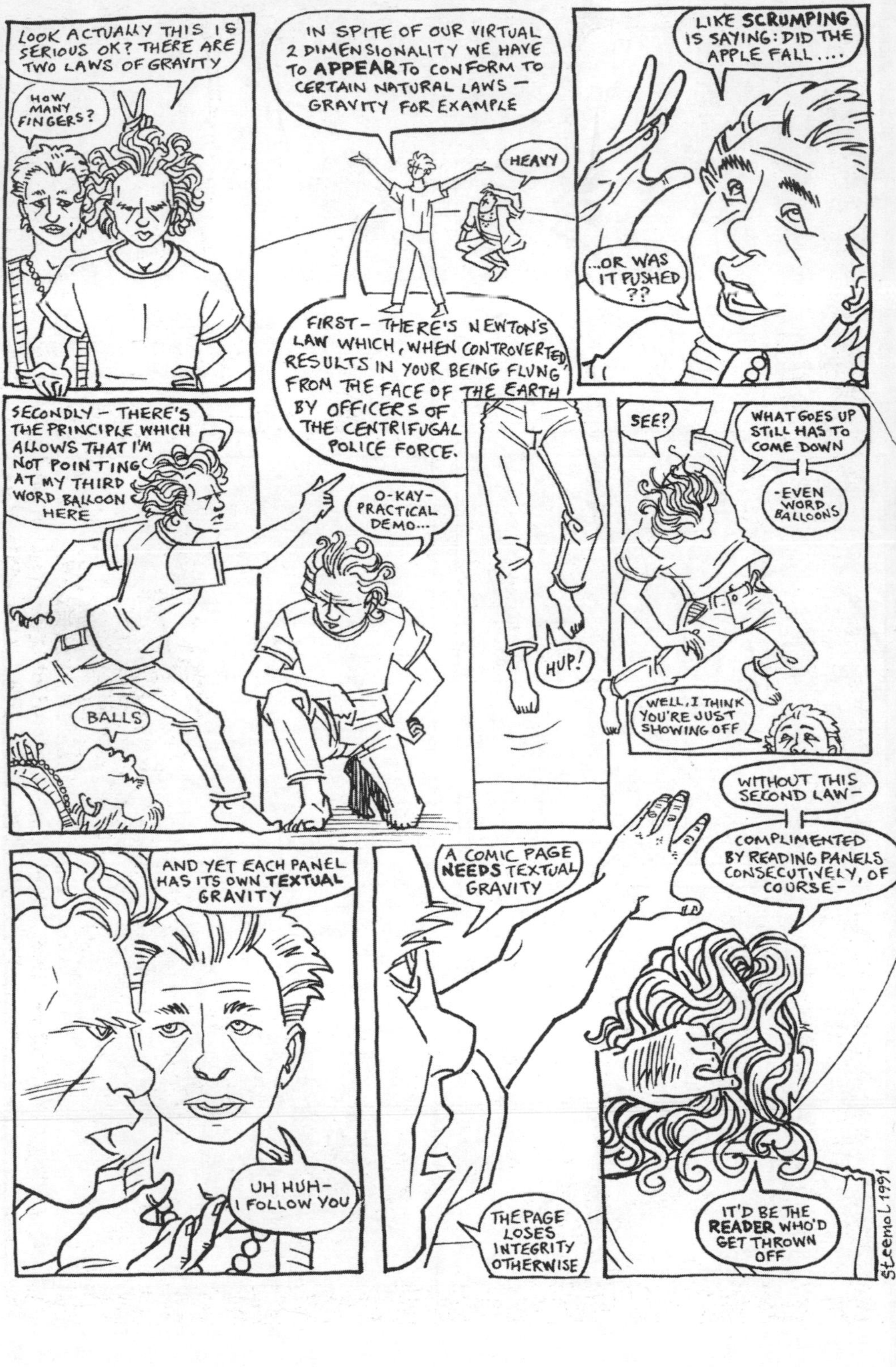
LOOK ACTUALLY THIS IS SERIOUS OK? THERE ARE TWO LAWS OF GRAVITY
HOW MANY FINGERS?
IN SPITE OF OUR VIRTUAL 2 DIMENSIONALITY WE HAVE TO APPEAR TO CONFORM TO CERTAIN NATURAL LAWS — GRAVITY FOR EXAMPLE
HEAVY
FIRST — THERE'S NEWTON'S LAW WHICH, WHEN CONTROVERTED RESULTS IN YOUR BEING FLUNG FROM THE FACE OF THE EARTH BY OFFICERS OF THE CENTRIFUGAL POLICE FORCE.
LIKE SCRUMPING IS SAYING: DID THE APPLE FALL....
...OR WAS IT PUSHED ??
SECONDLY — THERE'S THE PRINCIPLE WHICH ALLOWS THAT I'M NOT POINTING AT MY THIRD WORD BALLOON HERE
BALLS
O-KAY- PRACTICAL DEMO...
HUP!
SEE?
WHAT GOES UP STILL HAS TO COME DOWN
-EVEN WORD BALLOONS
WELL, I THINK YOU'RE JUST SHOWING OFF
AND YET EACH PANEL HAS ITS OWN TEXTUAL GRAVITY
UH HUH- I FOLLOW YOU
A COMIC PAGE NEEDS TEXTUAL GRAVITY
THE PAGE LOSES INTEGRITY OTHERWISE
WITHOUT THIS SECOND LAW-
COMPLIMENTED BY READING PANELS CONSECUTIVELY, OF COURSE-
IT'D BE THE READER WHO'D GET THROWN OFF
steemol 1991

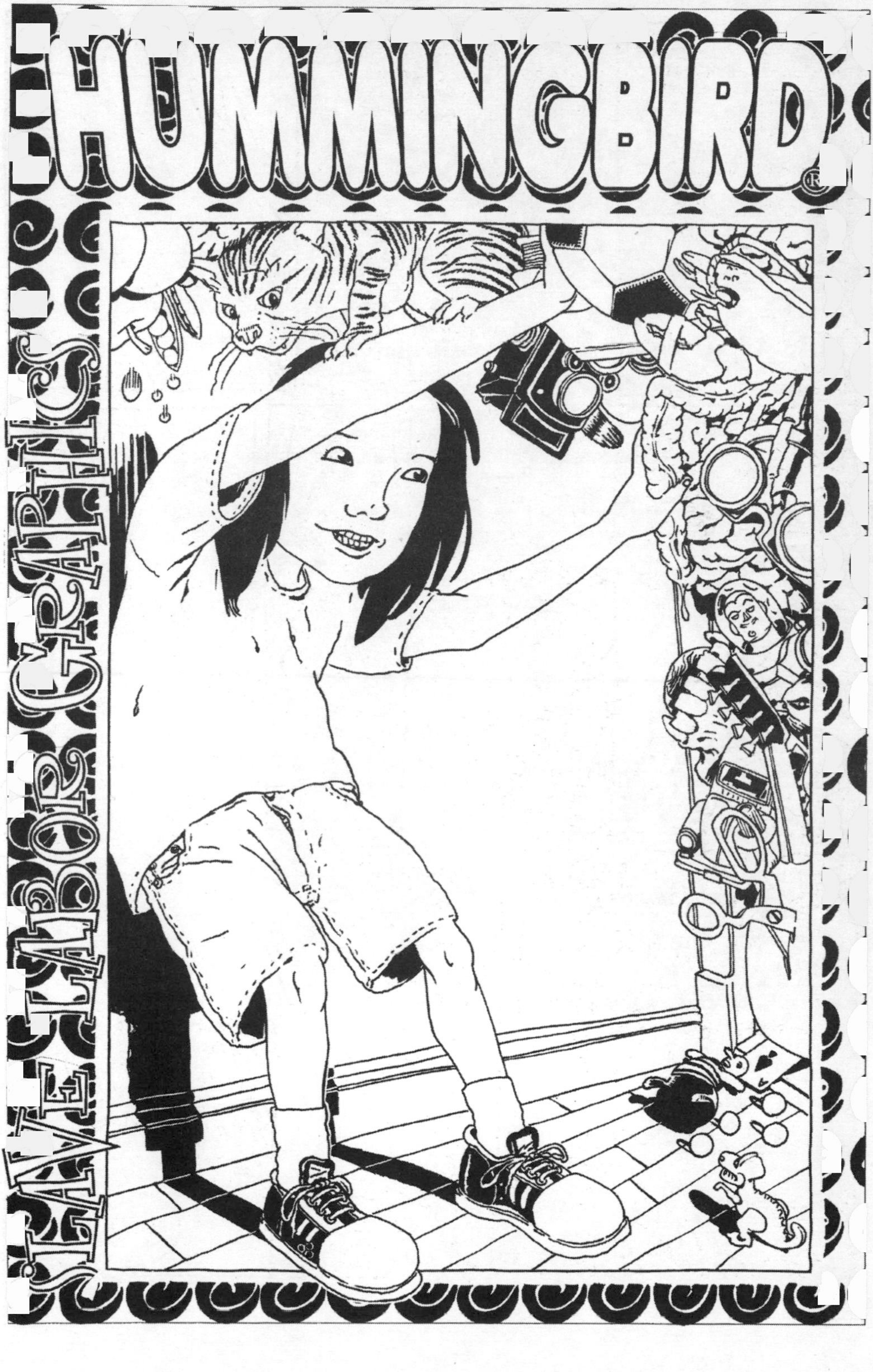

HUMMINGBIRD
SLAVE LABOR GRAPHICS

Gregory Benton

HUMMINGBIRD
Slave Labor Graphics, 1996

Gregory (Gory) Benton has been making comix since 1993. He cut his teeth on the political anthology *World War 3*, moving on to writing and drawing stories for Nickelodeon, Vertigo/DC Comics, *Disney Adventures*, Watson-Guptil and *Entertainment Weekly*, also contributing to numerous alternate-press comix anthologies.

This comic book was intended to be the first in a continuing series about a young girl reconciling with her estranged father in an unpredictable and violent world. It explores the universal theme of a child's realization that parents can be flawed and unreliable guardians. Pre-orders for a second issue were deemed not strong enough and the series was scrapped. Only the cover from issue two survives.

In April of 2013 Gregory's book *B+F* was awarded the Museum of Comic and Cartoon Art's inaugural Award of Excellence at MoCCA Fest 2013, an expanded version since published by Adhouse Books (USA) and Editions çà et là (France). He is currently working on the next volume, to be released early 2015. Additionally, Gregory is co-founder of Brooklyn NYC's Hang Dai Editions alongside fellow artist/writers Dean Haspiel, Seth Kushner and Josh Neufeld.

www.gregorybenton.com

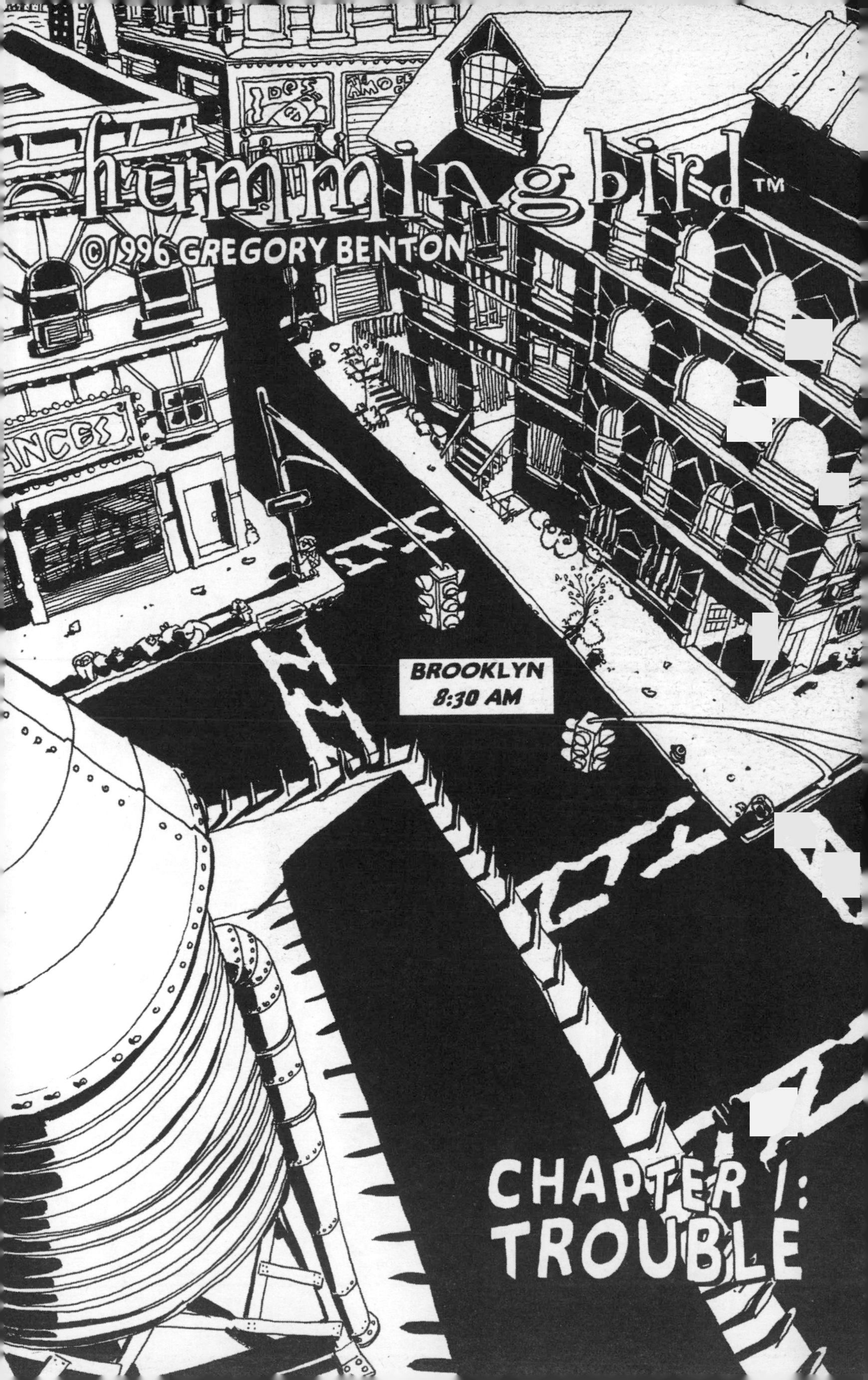
hummingbird™
©1996 GREGORY BENTON
BROOKLYN
8:30 AM
CHAPTER 1:
TROUBLE

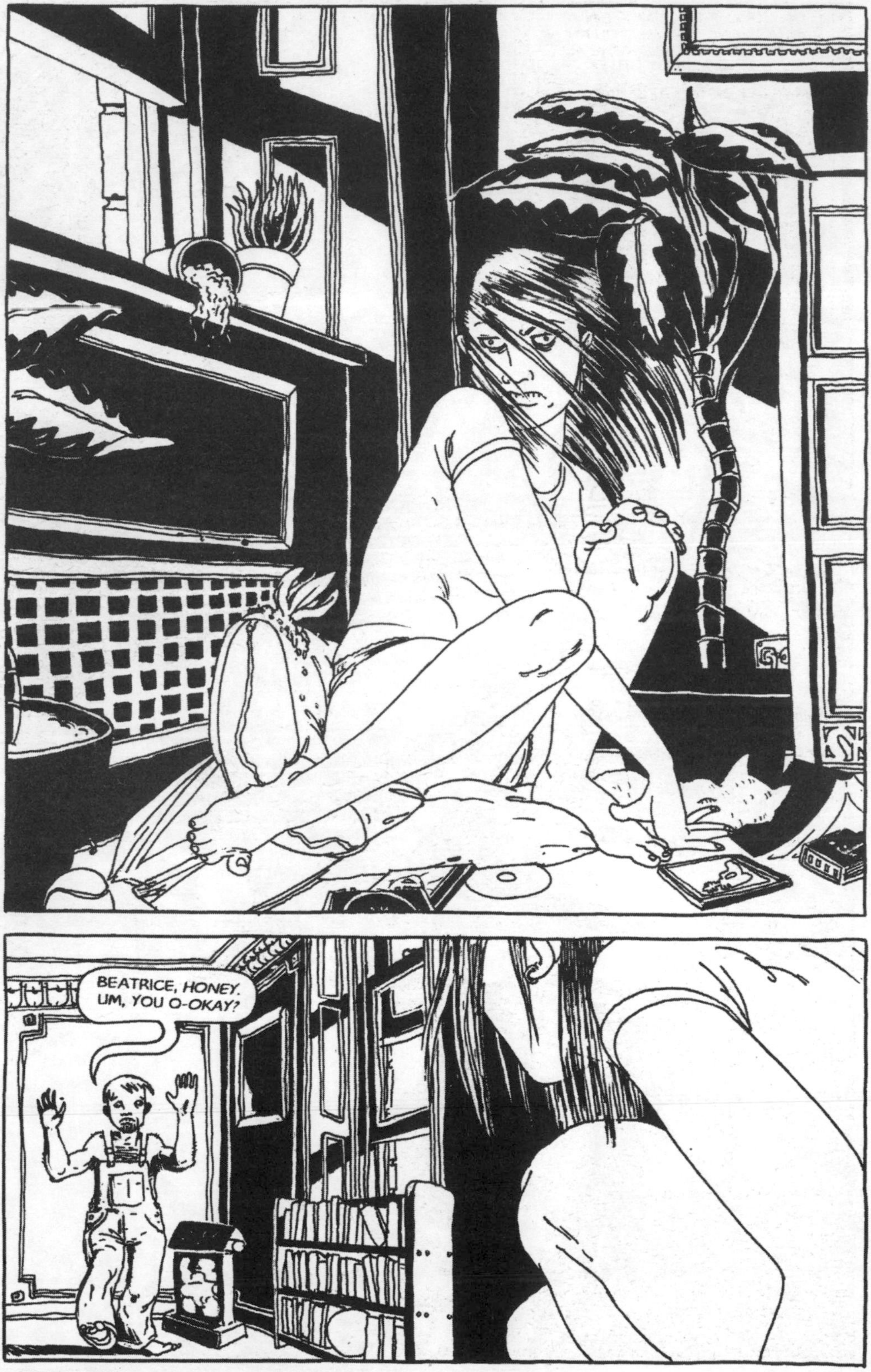
BEATRICE, HONEY. UM, YOU O-OKAY?

...I DIN'T MEAN *ENNYTHIN'* BY WHAT I SAID BEFORE, YOU KNOW, EARLIER? I MEAN, WE'RE ALL *CRAZY A LI'L*, 'KAY?

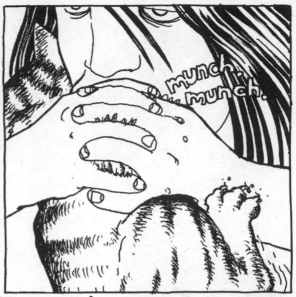

munch, munch.

SWOOO!

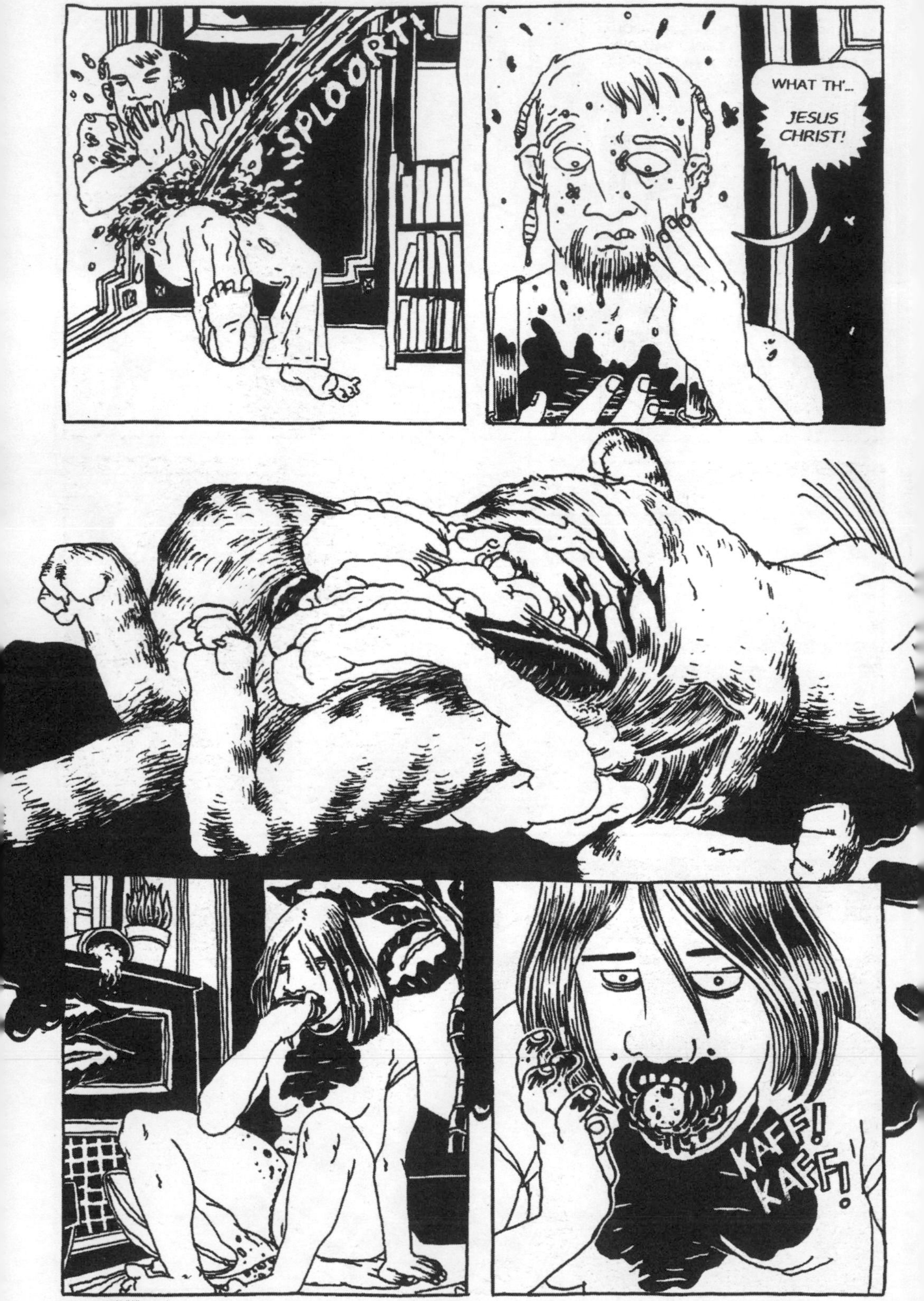
SPLOORT!
WHAT TH'...
JESUS CHRIST!
KAFF! KAFF!

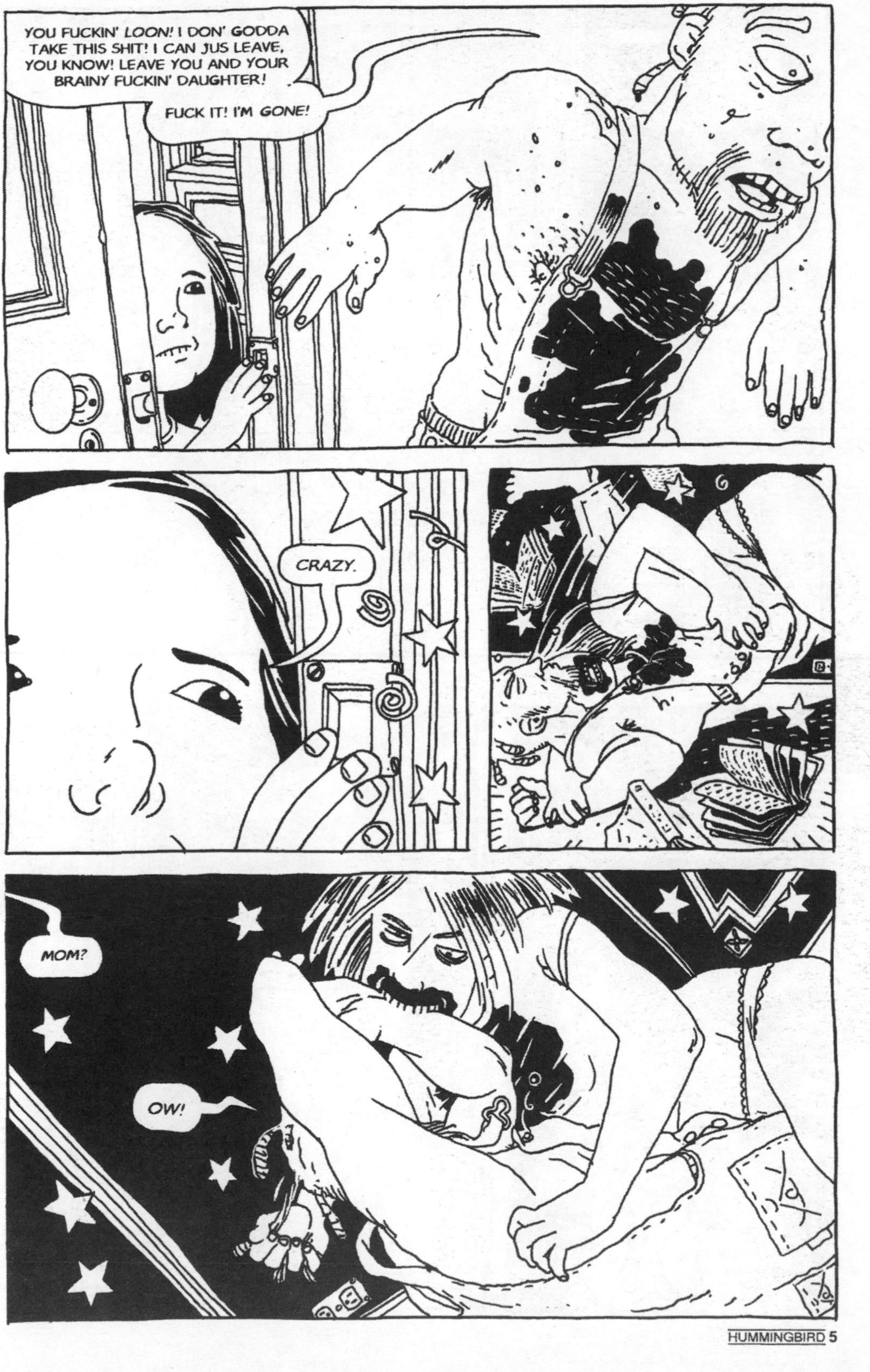
YOU FUCKIN' LOON! I DON' GODDA TAKE THIS SHIT! I CAN JUS LEAVE, YOU KNOW! LEAVE YOU AND YOUR BRAINY FUCKIN' DAUGHTER!
FUCK IT! I'M GONE!
CRAZY.
MOM?
OW!

HUMMINGBIRD!! DON'T JUST STAND THERE! CALL 911! -CALL 911!
POP!

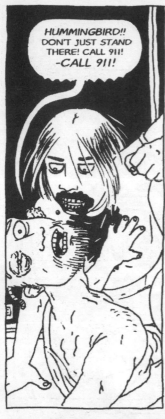

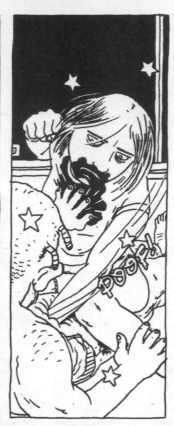

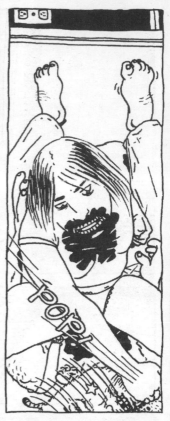

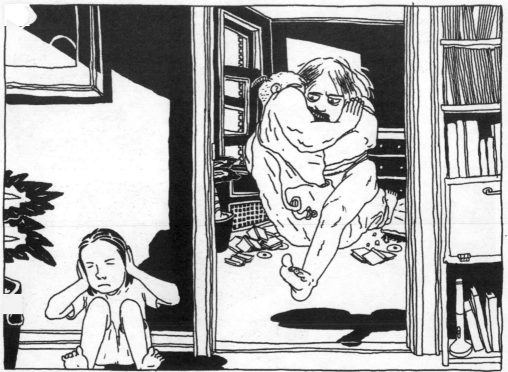

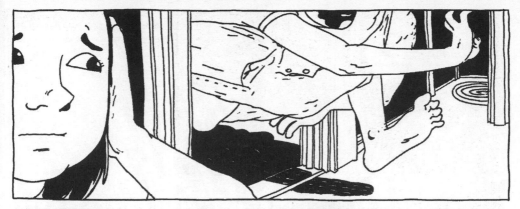

MOM?

BZZZZz

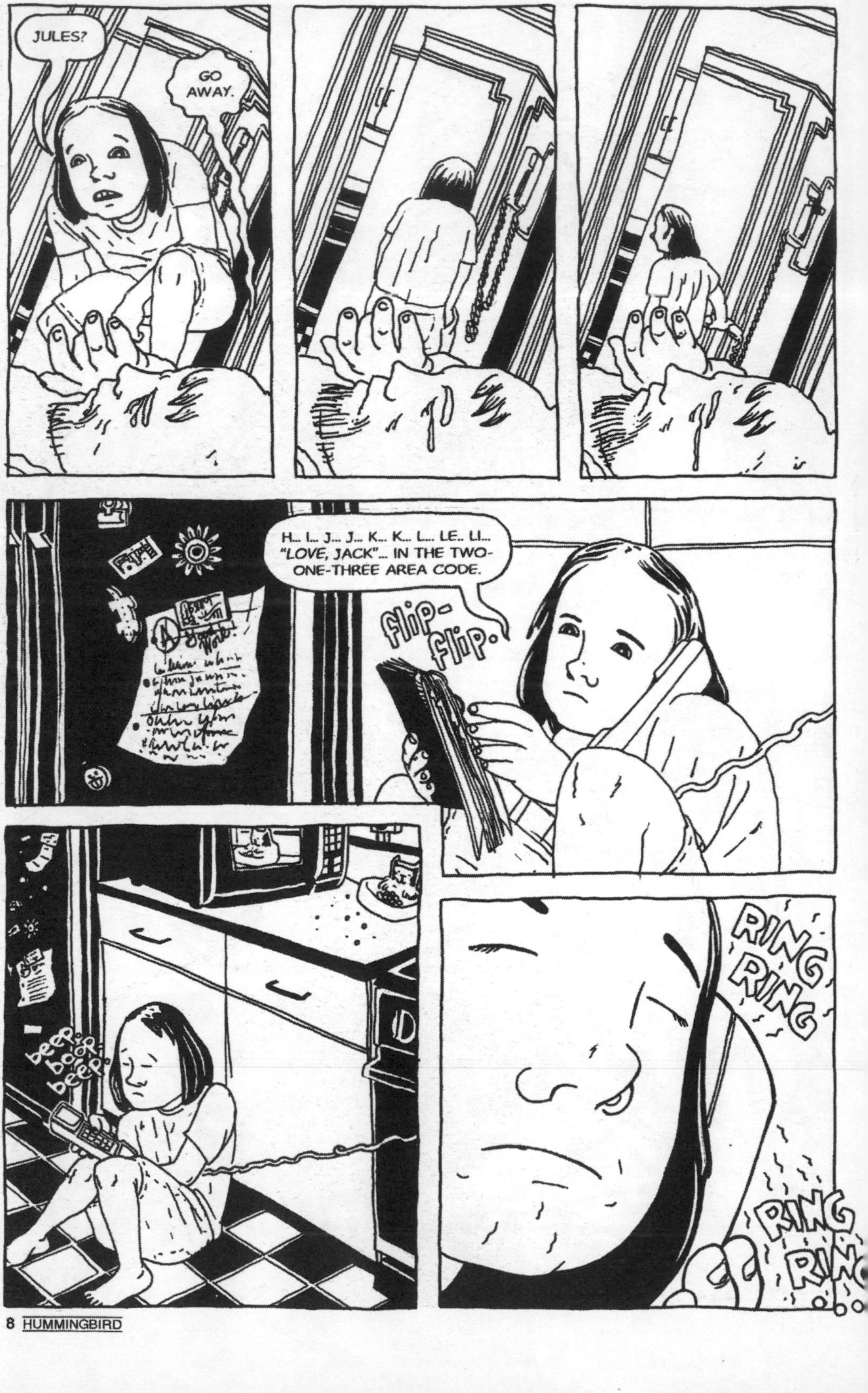
JULES?
GO AWAY.
H... I... J... J... K... K... L... LE.. LI...
"LOVE, JACK"... IN THE TWO-ONE-THREE AREA CODE.
flip-flip
beep-boop-beep
RING RING
RING RING

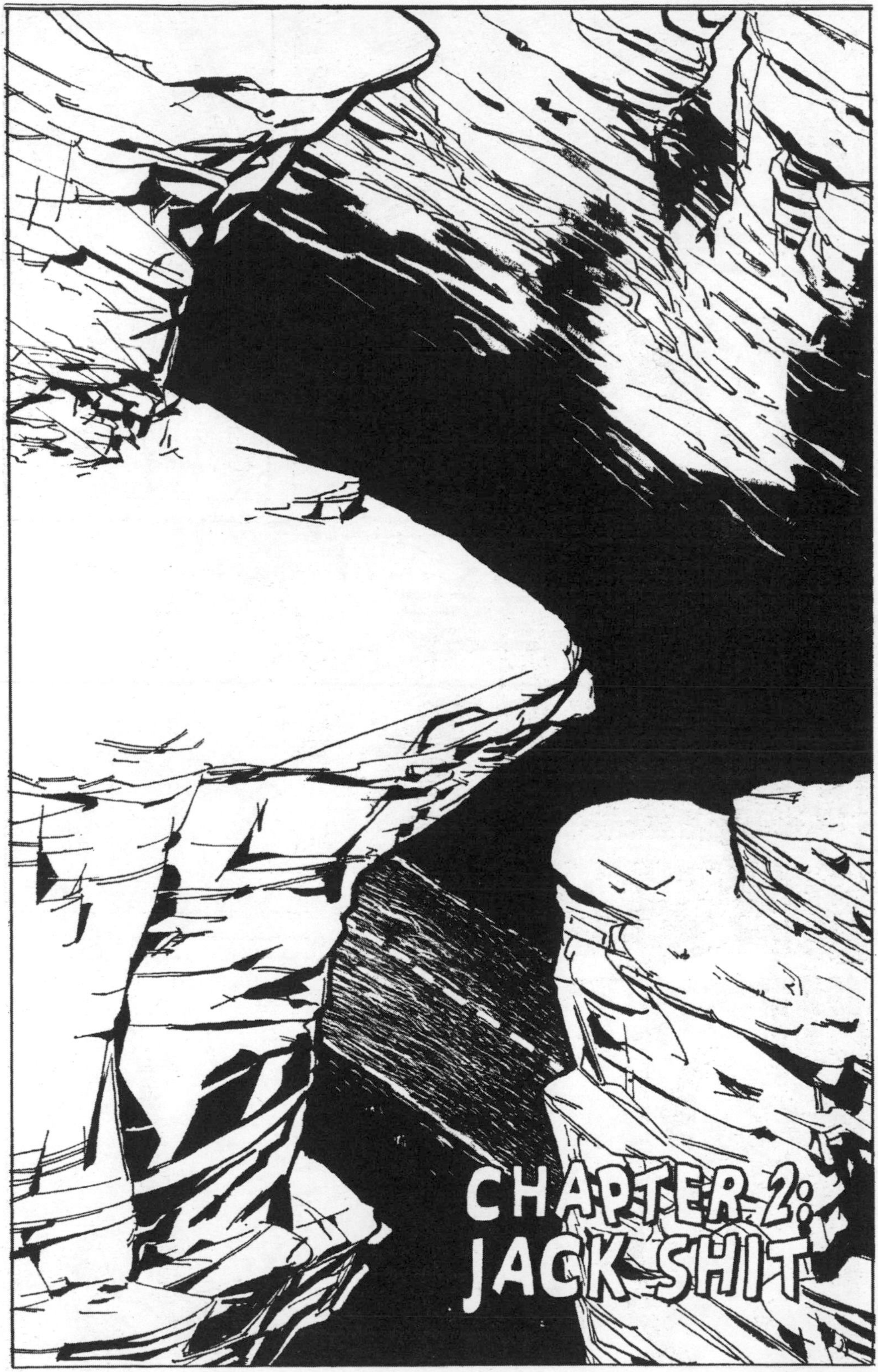
CHAPTER 2:
JACK SHIT

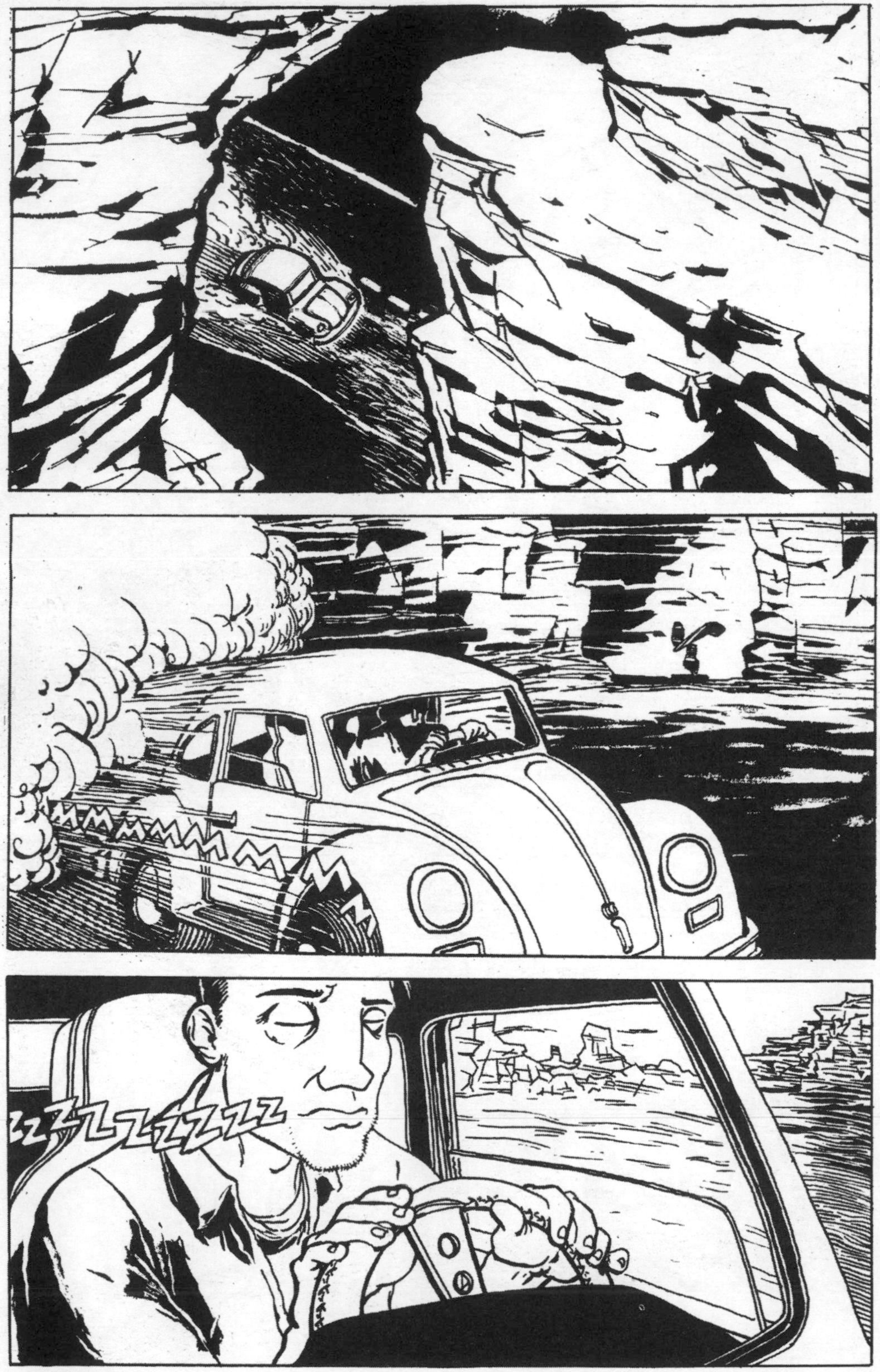
MMMMMMMM
ZZZZZZZZZZ

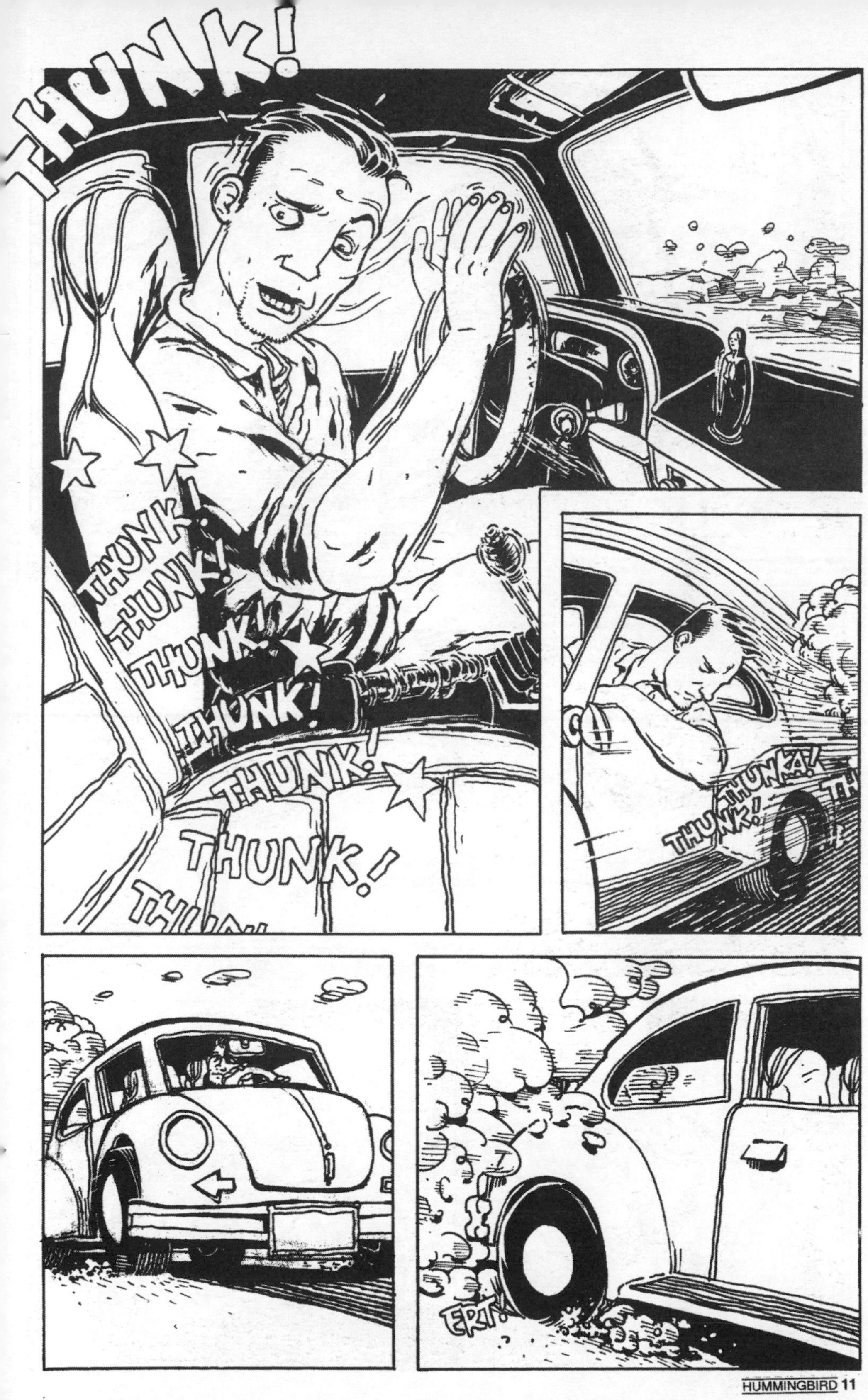
THUNK!
THUNK!
THUNK!
THUNK!
THUNK!
THUNK!
THUNK!
THUNK!
THUNKA!

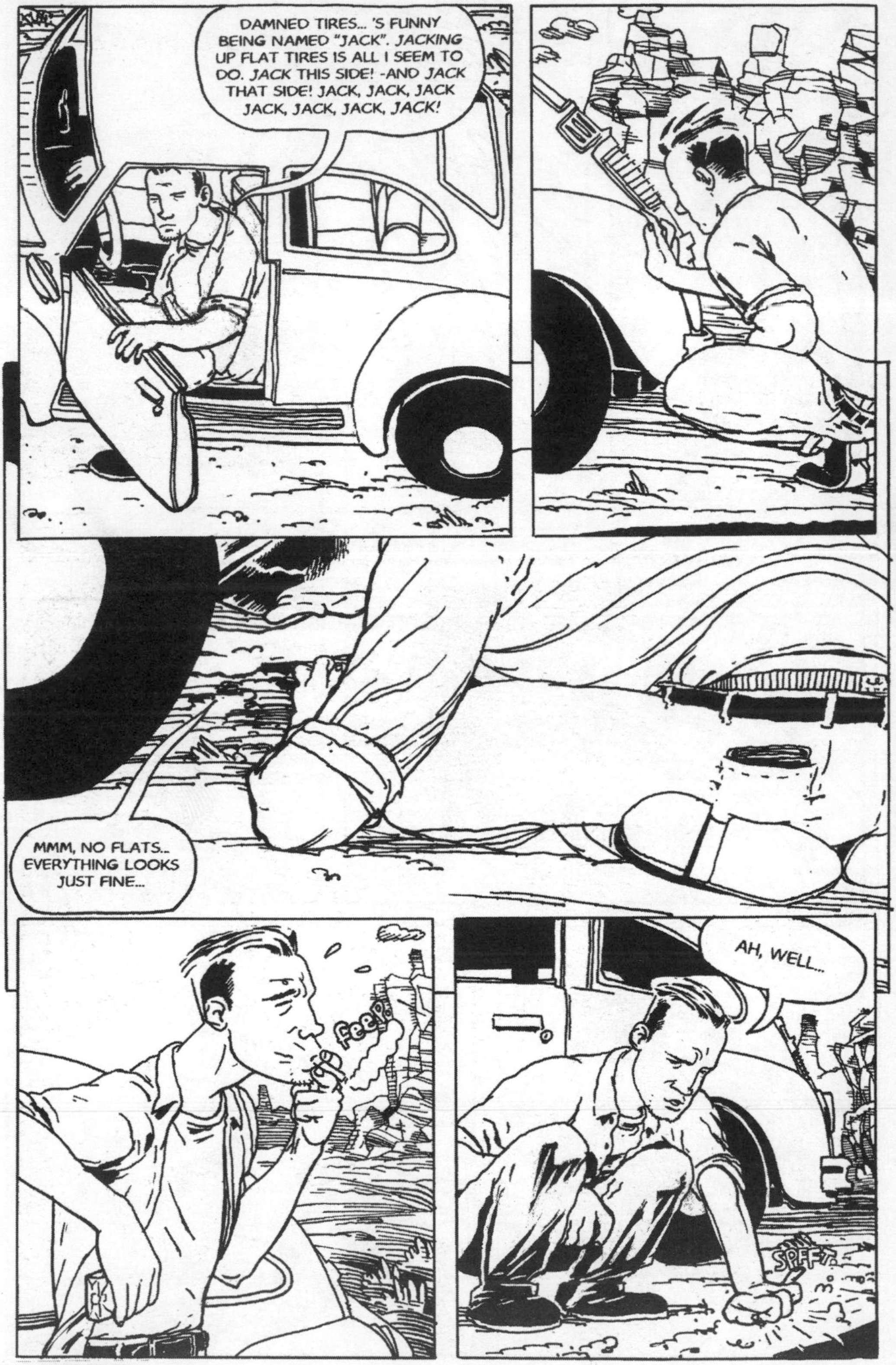
DAMNED TIRES... 'S FUNNY BEING NAMED "JACK". JACKING UP FLAT TIRES IS ALL I SEEM TO DO. JACK THIS SIDE! -AND JACK THAT SIDE! JACK, JACK, JACK JACK, JACK, JACK, JACK!
MMM, NO FLATS.. EVERYTHING LOOKS JUST FINE...
FEEP
AH, WELL...
SPFFT

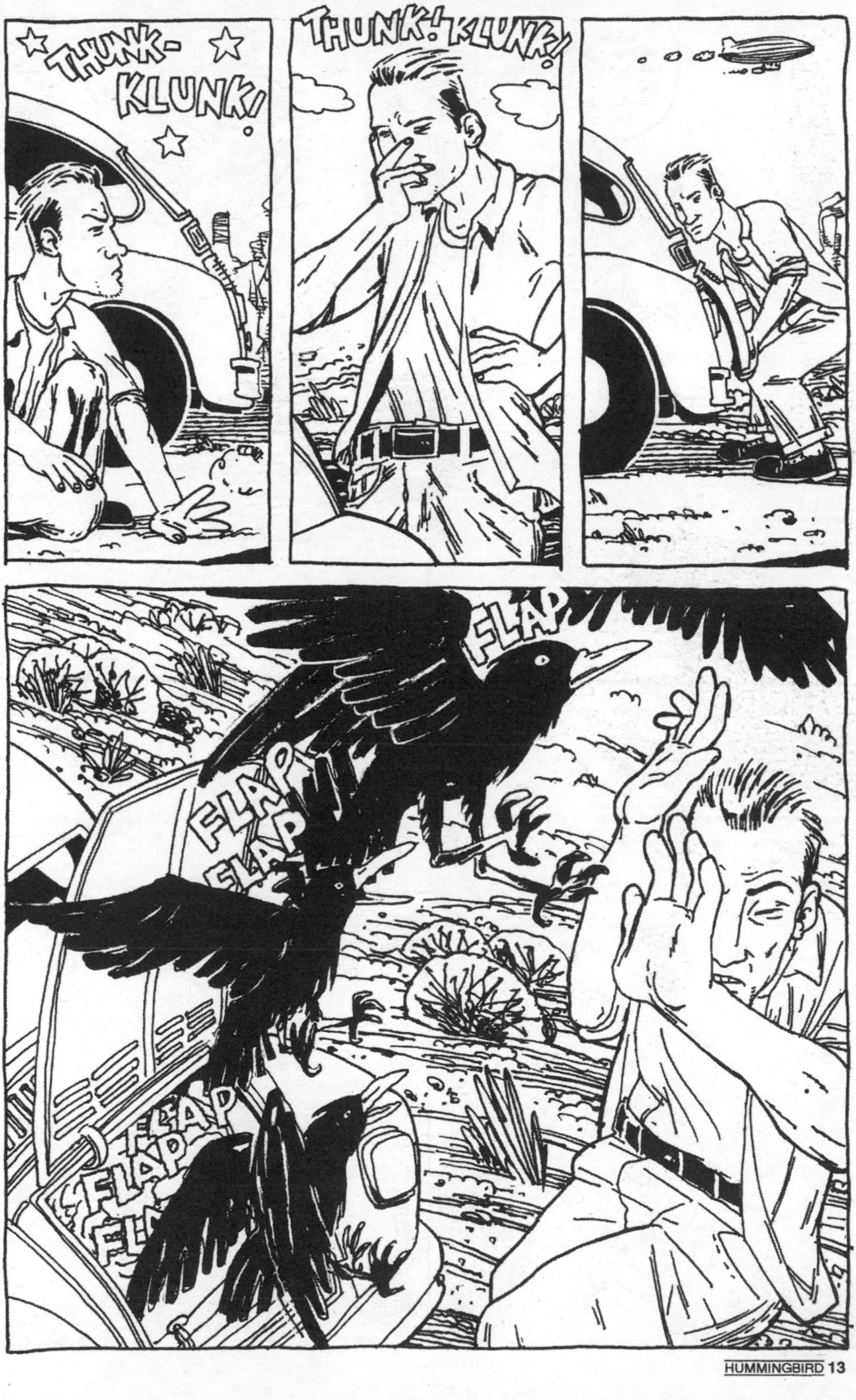
THUNK-
KLUNK!
THUNK! KLUNK!
FLAP
FLAP
FLAP
FLAP
FLAP
FLAP

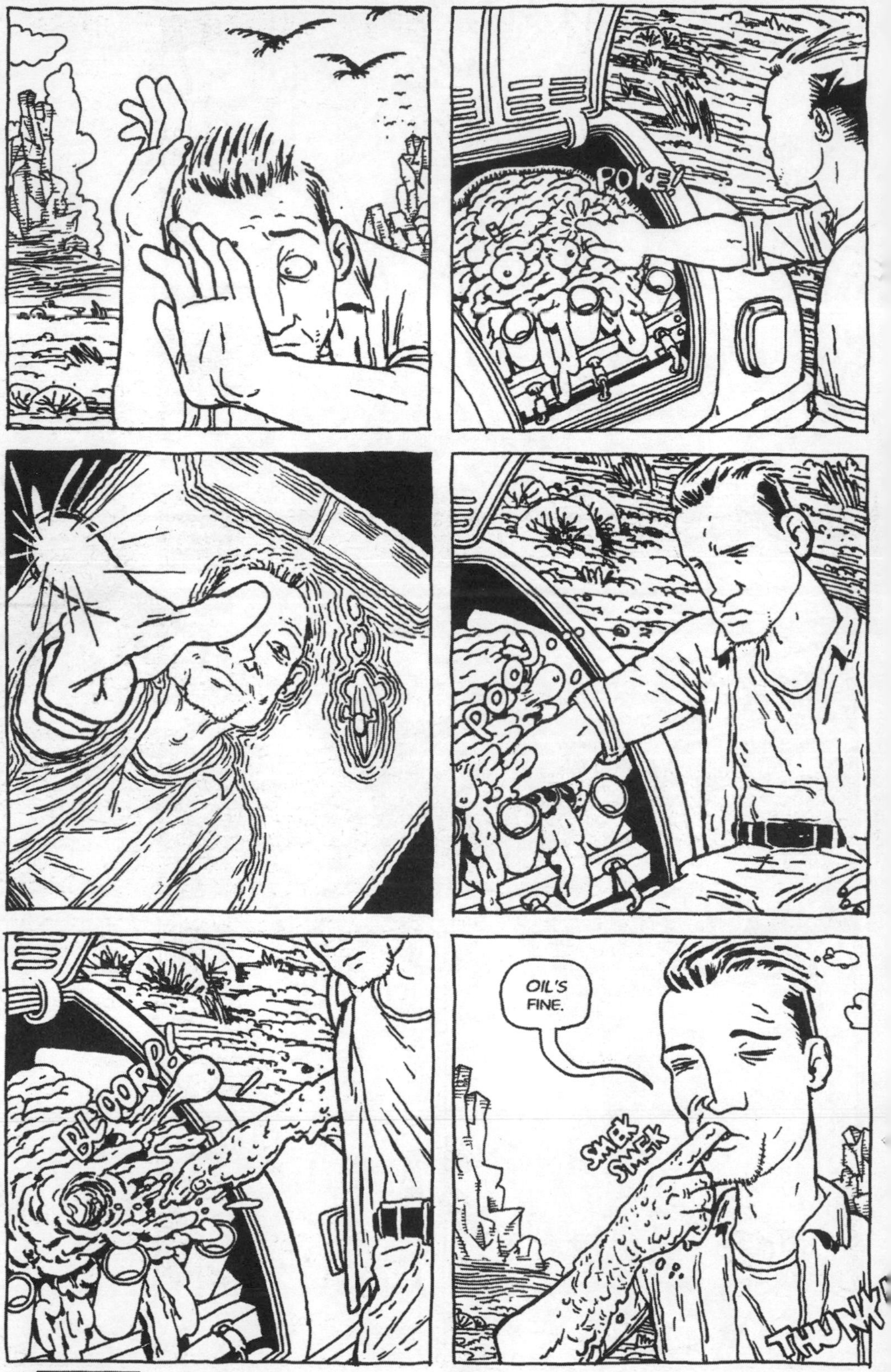
POKE!
POO
BLOORP!
OIL'S FINE.
SMEK SMEK SMEK
THUNK

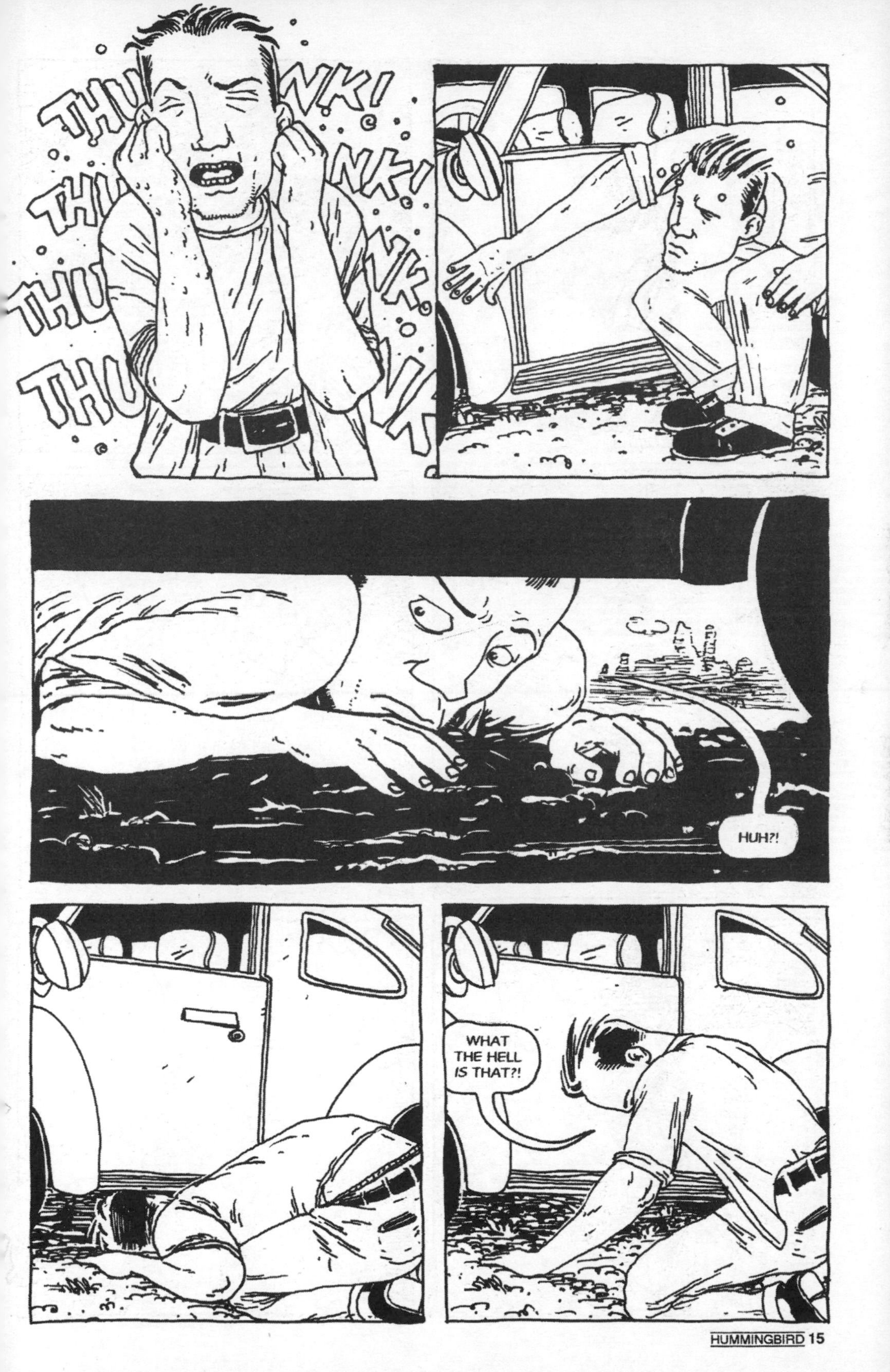
THU NK!
THU NK!
THU NK!
THU NK
HUH?!
WHAT THE HELL IS THAT?!

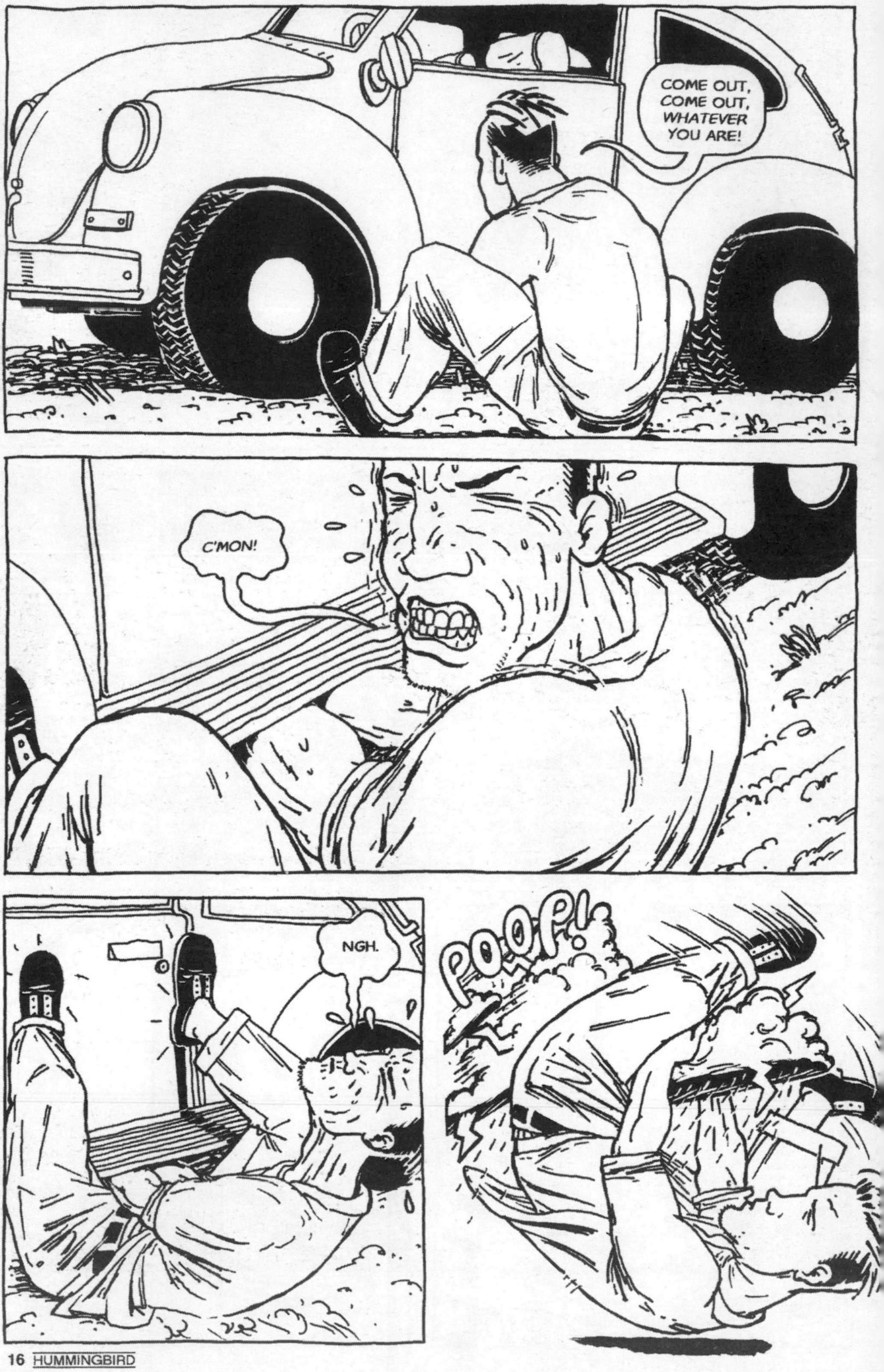
COME OUT, COME OUT, WHATEVER YOU ARE!
C'MON!
NGH.
POOP!

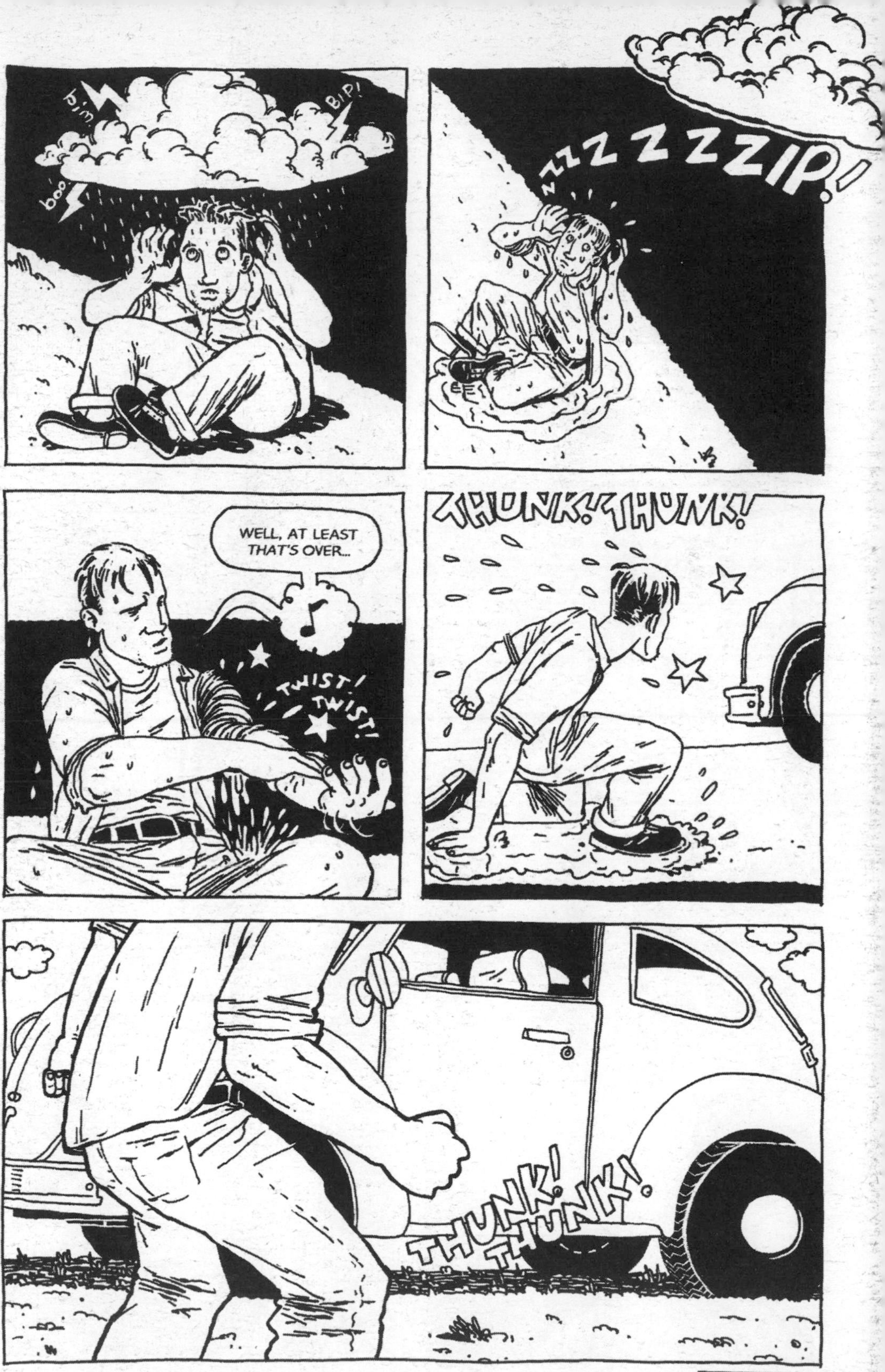
BIP!
boo
zzzZ Z Z ZZIP!
WELL, AT LEAST THAT'S OVER...
TWIST! TWIST!
THUNK! THUNK!
THUNK! THUNK!

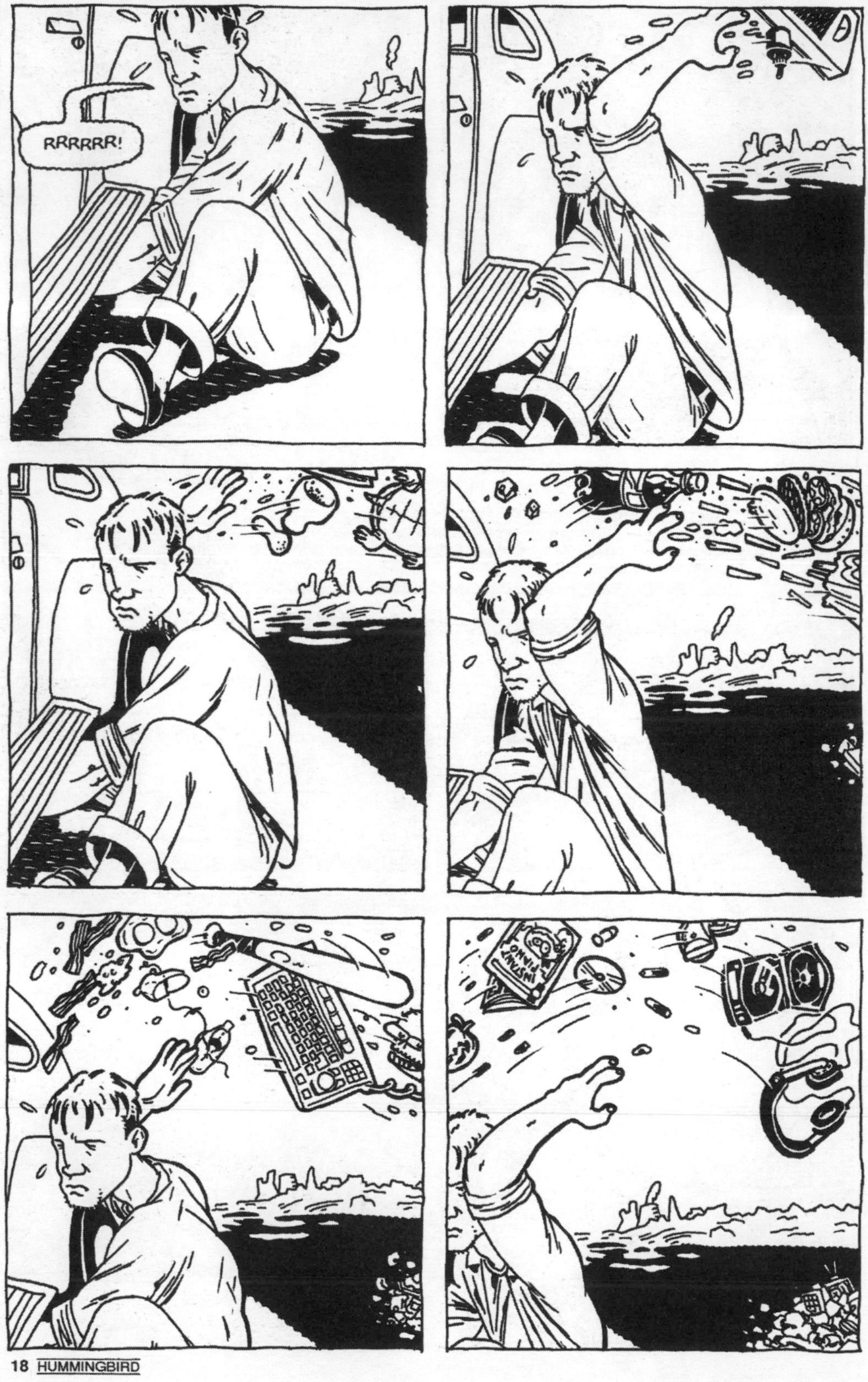
RRRRRR!

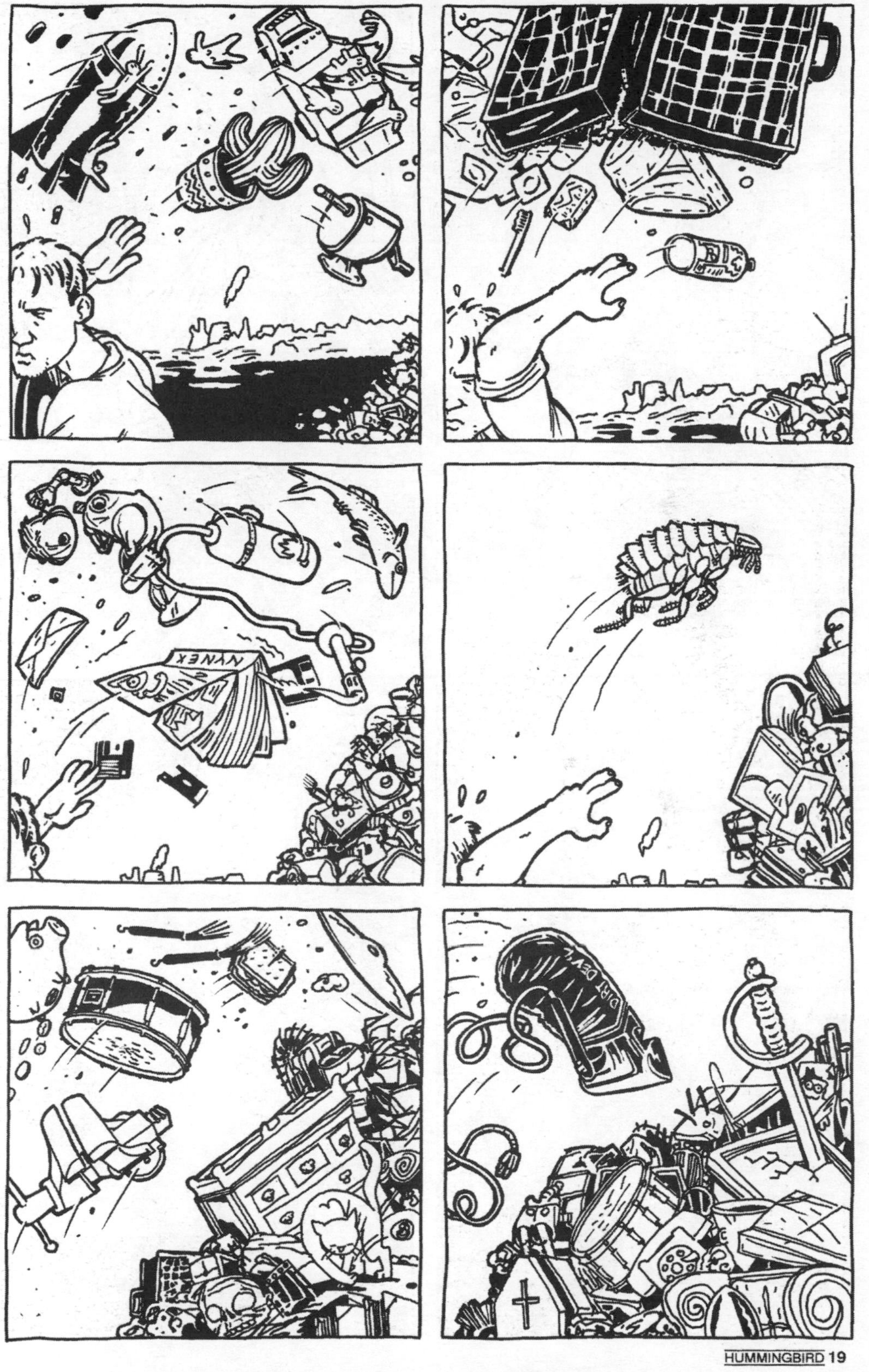
NYNEX
DIRT DEVIL

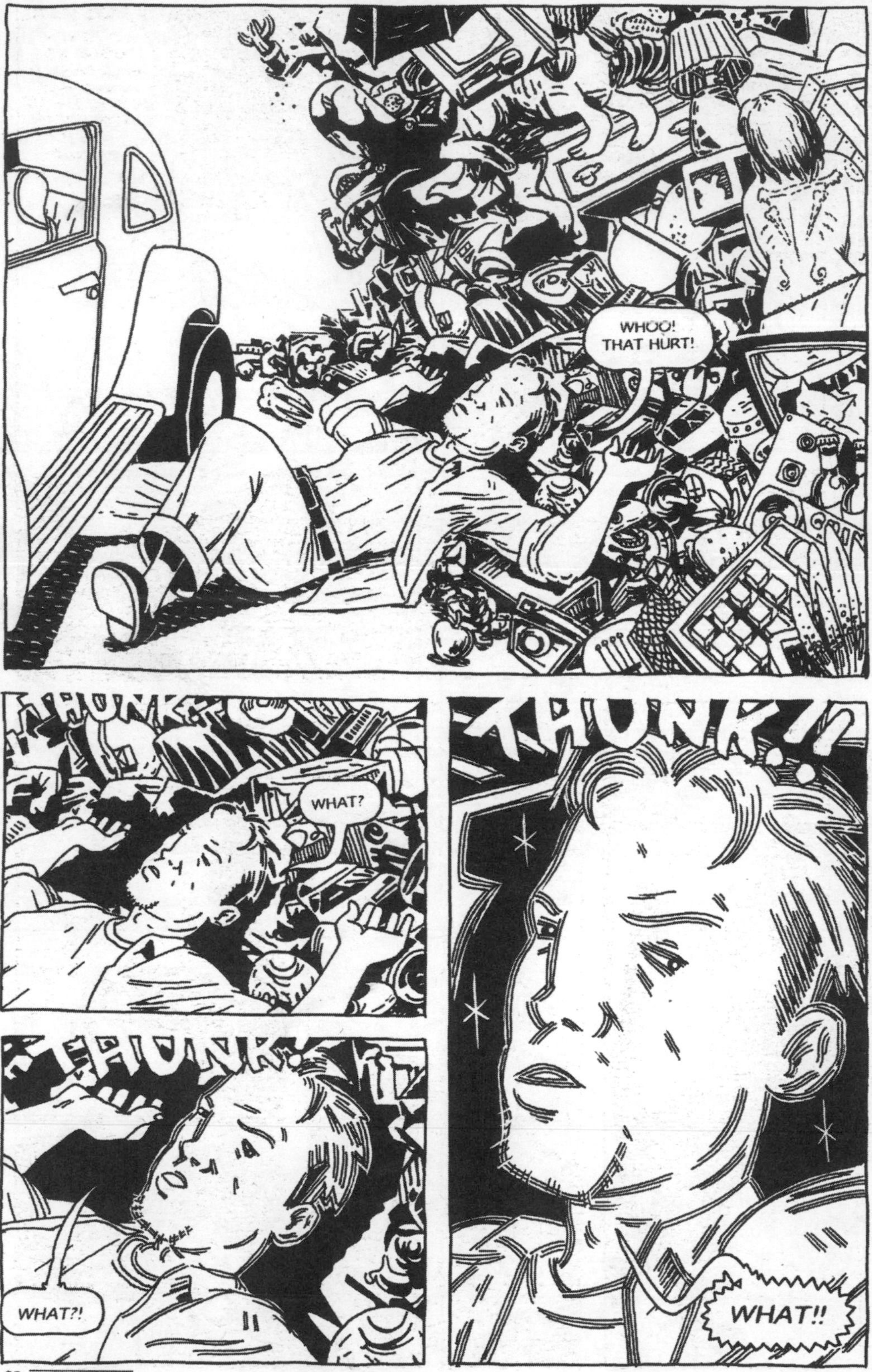
WHOO! THAT HURT!
THONK!
WHAT?
THONK!
WHAT?!
THONK!!
WHAT!!

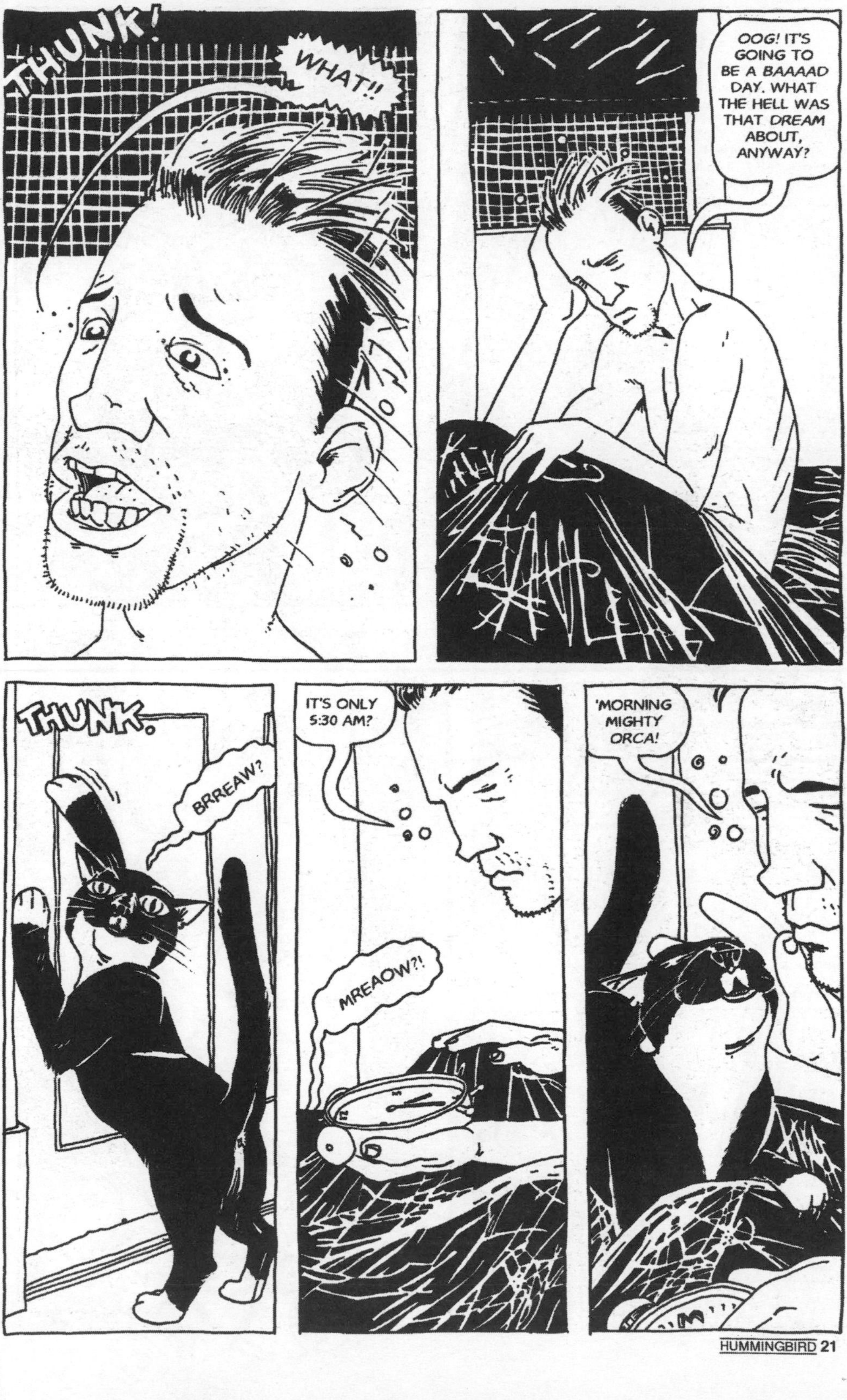
THUNK!
WHAT!!
OOG! IT'S GOING TO BE A BAAAAD DAY. WHAT THE HELL WAS THAT DREAM ABOUT, ANYWAY?
THUNK.
BRREAW?
IT'S ONLY 5:30 AM?
MREAOW?!
'MORNING MIGHTY ORCA!

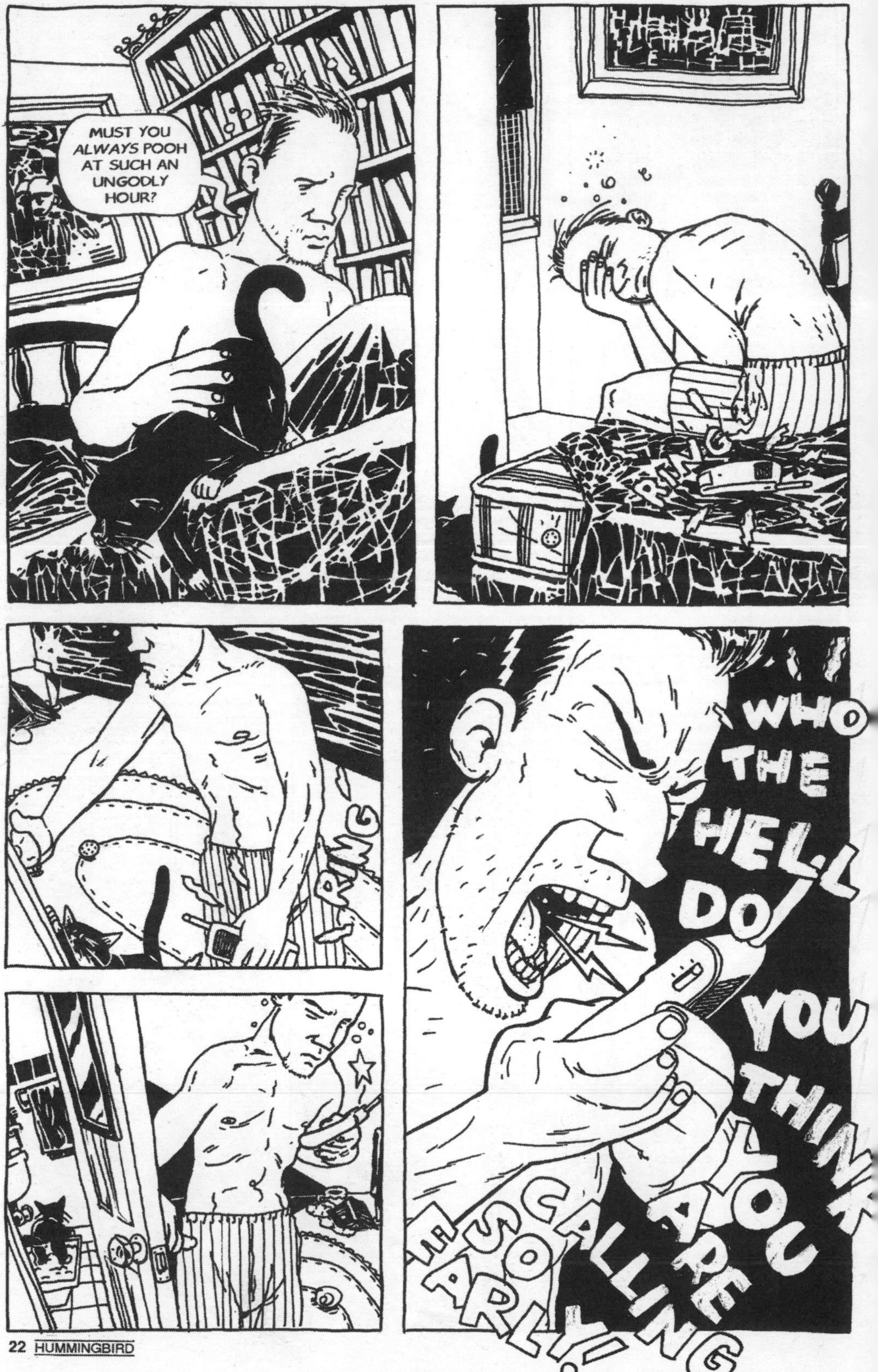
MUST YOU ALWAYS POOH AT SUCH AN UNGODLY HOUR?
RING
RING
WHO THE HELL DO YOU THINK YOU ARE CALLING SO EARLY?!

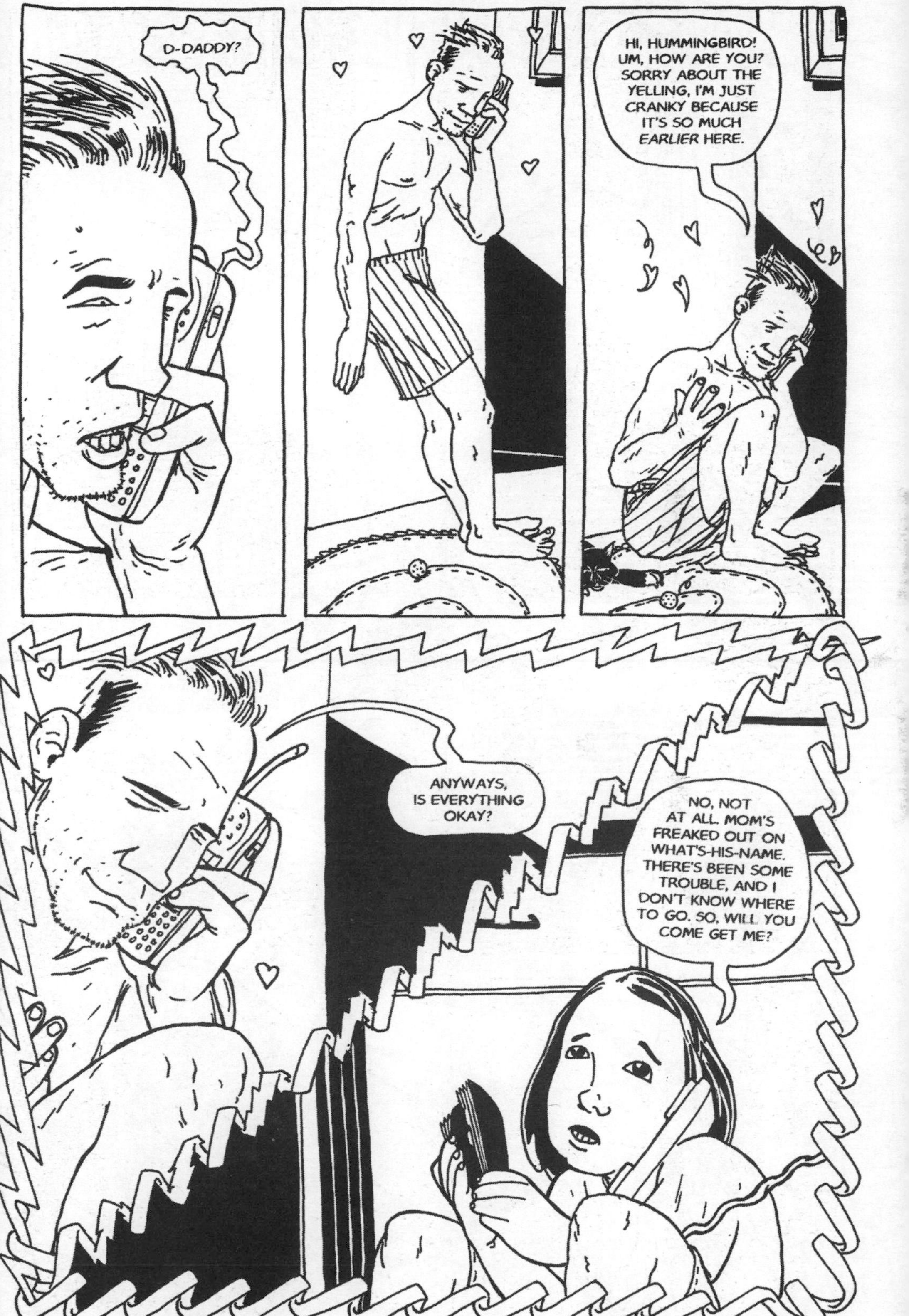
D-DADDY?
HI, HUMMINGBIRD! UM, HOW ARE YOU? SORRY ABOUT THE YELLING, I'M JUST CRANKY BECAUSE IT'S SO MUCH *EARLIER* HERE.
ANYWAYS, IS EVERYTHING OKAY?
NO, NOT AT ALL. MOM'S FREAKED OUT ON WHAT'S-HIS-NAME. THERE'S BEEN SOME TROUBLE, AND I DON'T KNOW WHERE TO GO. SO, WILL YOU COME GET ME?

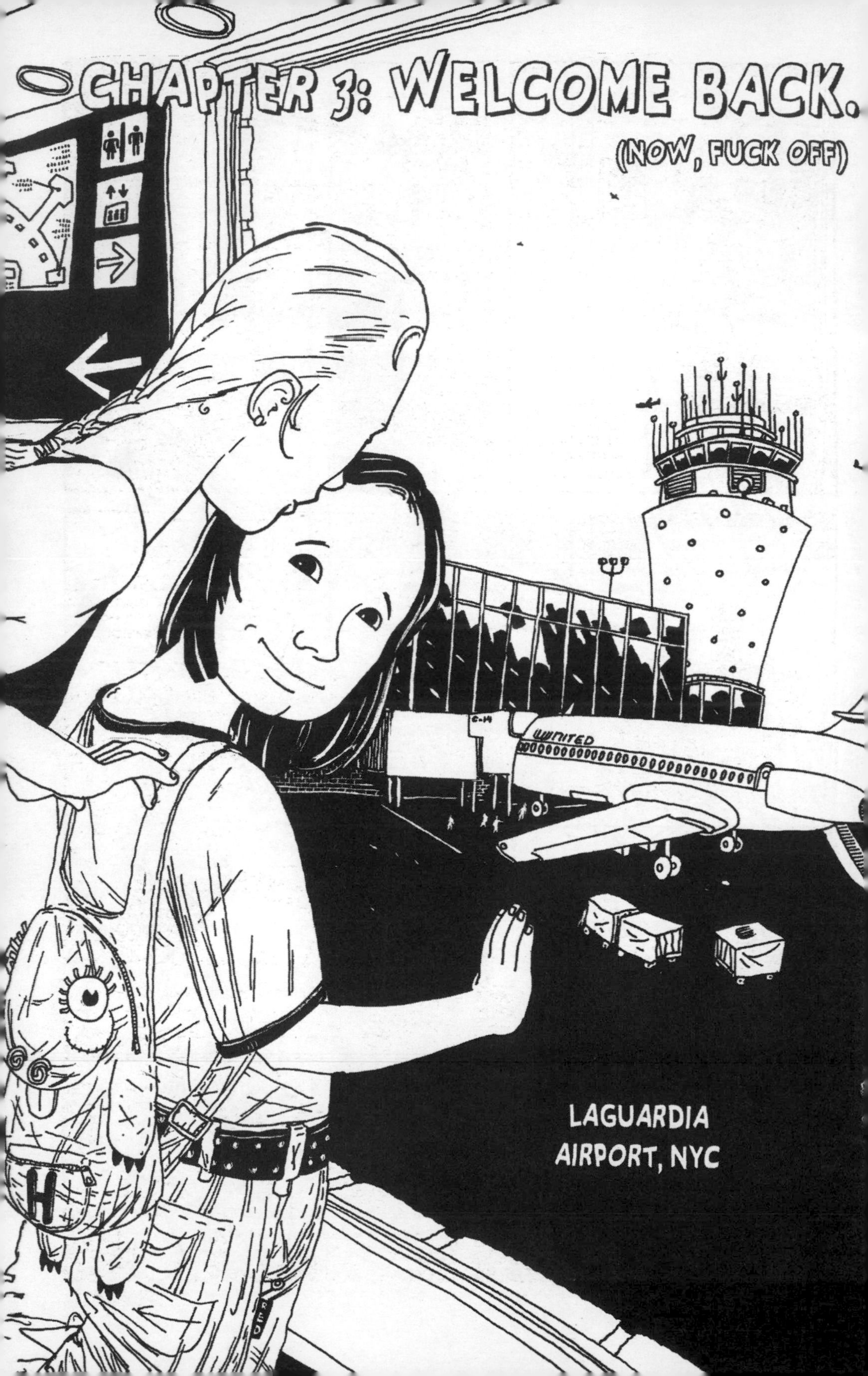
CHAPTER 3: WELCOME BACK.
(NOW, FUCK OFF)
UNITED
LAGUARDIA
AIRPORT, NYC

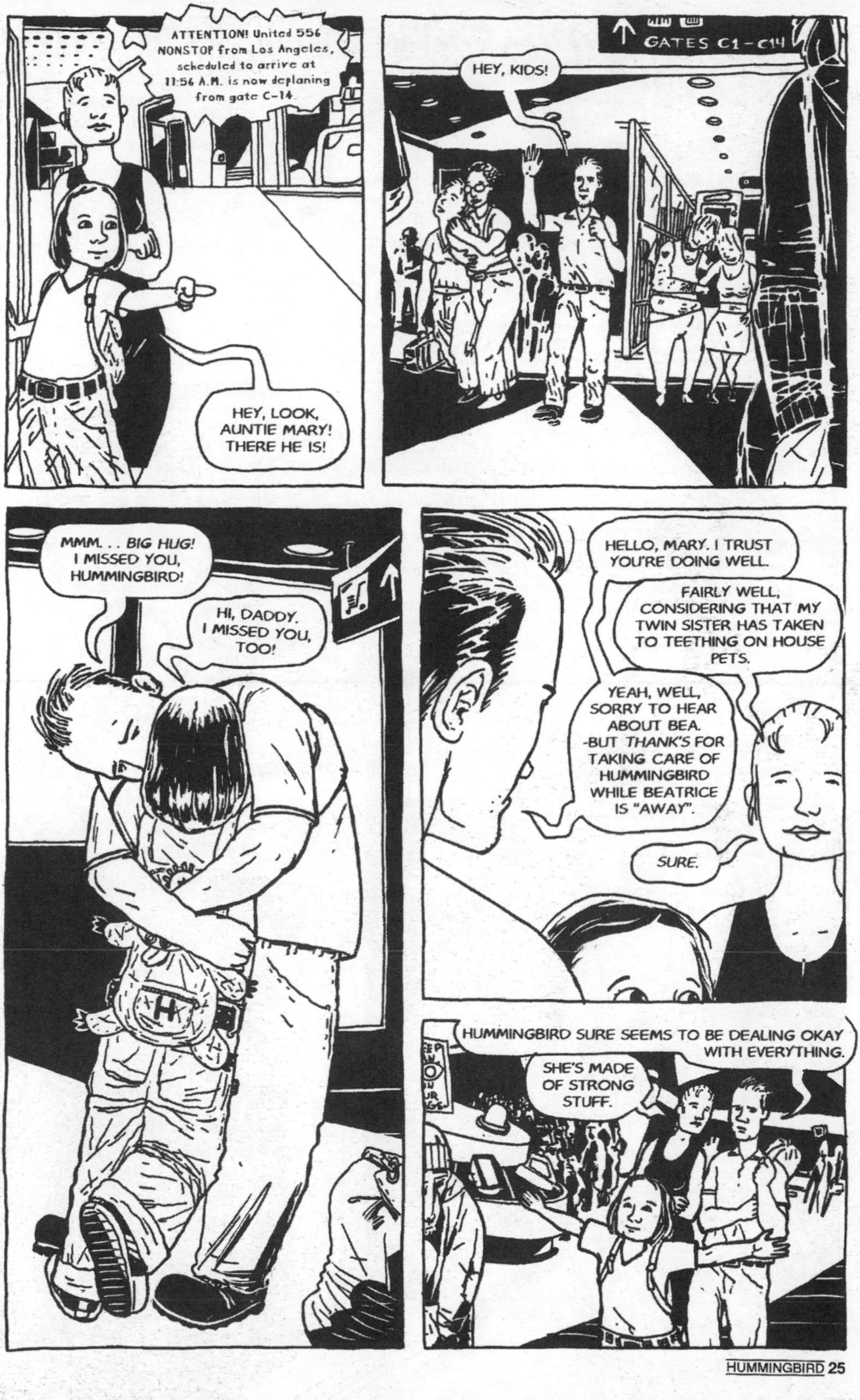
ATTENTION! United 556 NONSTOP from Los Angeles, scheduled to arrive at 11:56 A.M. is now deplaning from gate C-14.
HEY, LOOK, AUNTIE MARY! THERE HE IS!
GATES C1-C14
HEY, KIDS!
MMM. . . BIG HUG! I MISSED YOU, HUMMINGBIRD!
HI, DADDY. I MISSED YOU, TOO!
HELLO, MARY. I TRUST YOU'RE DOING WELL.
FAIRLY WELL, CONSIDERING THAT MY TWIN SISTER HAS TAKEN TO TEETHING ON HOUSE PETS.
YEAH, WELL, SORRY TO HEAR ABOUT BEA. -BUT THANK'S FOR TAKING CARE OF HUMMINGBIRD WHILE BEATRICE IS "AWAY".
SURE.
HUMMINGBIRD SURE SEEMS TO BE DEALING OKAY WITH EVERYTHING.
SHE'S MADE OF STRONG STUFF.

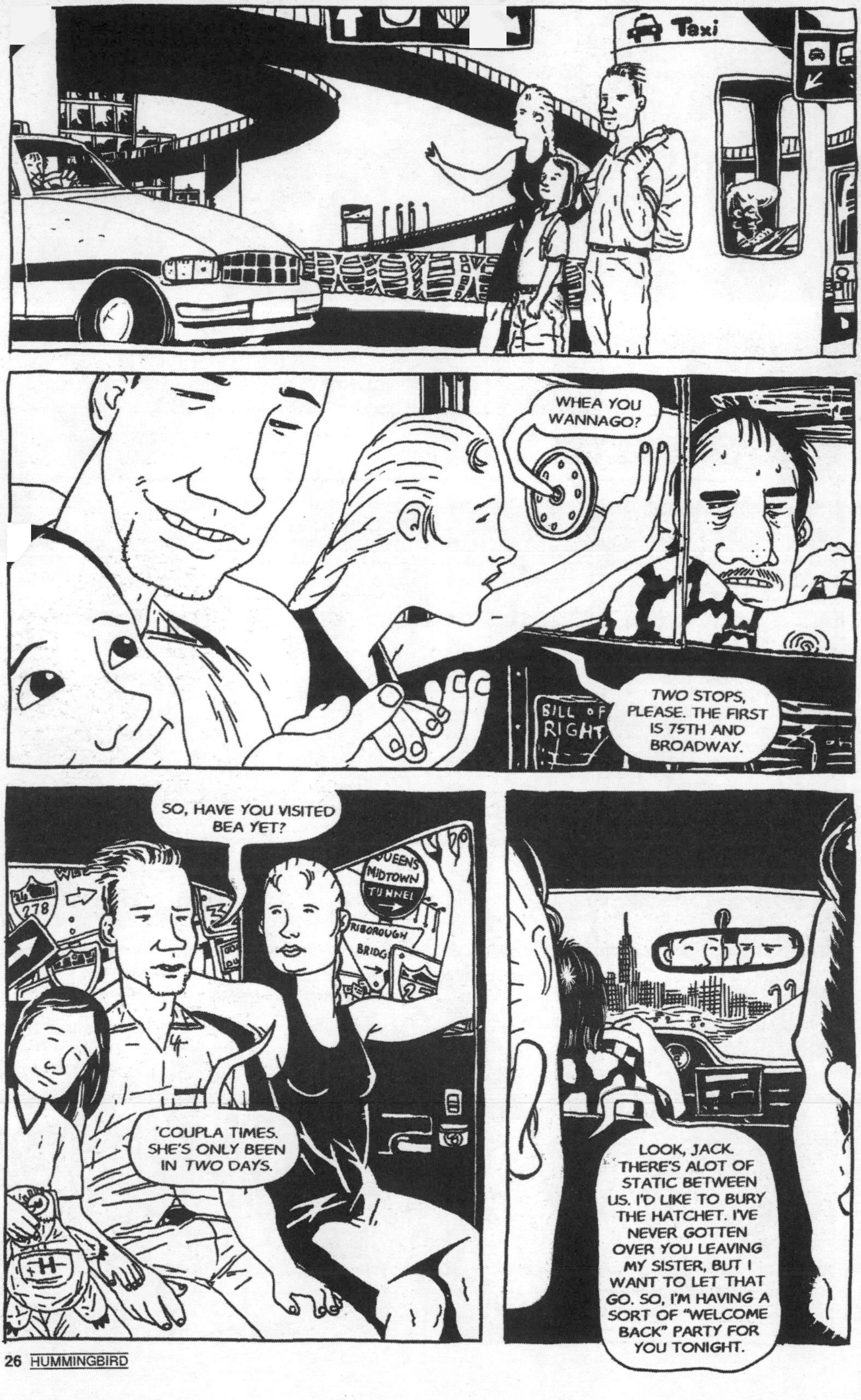
Taxi
WHEA YOU WANNAGO?
TWO STOPS, PLEASE. THE FIRST IS 75TH AND BROADWAY.
BILL OF RIGHT
SO, HAVE YOU VISITED BEA YET?
'COUPLA TIMES. SHE'S ONLY BEEN IN *TWO* DAYS.
QUEENS MIDTOWN TUNNEL
278
RIBOROUGH BRIDG
LOOK, JACK. THERE'S ALOT OF STATIC BETWEEN US. I'D LIKE TO BURY THE HATCHET. I'VE NEVER GOTTEN OVER YOU LEAVING MY SISTER, BUT I WANT TO LET THAT GO. SO, I'M HAVING A SORT OF "WELCOME BACK" PARTY FOR YOU TONIGHT.

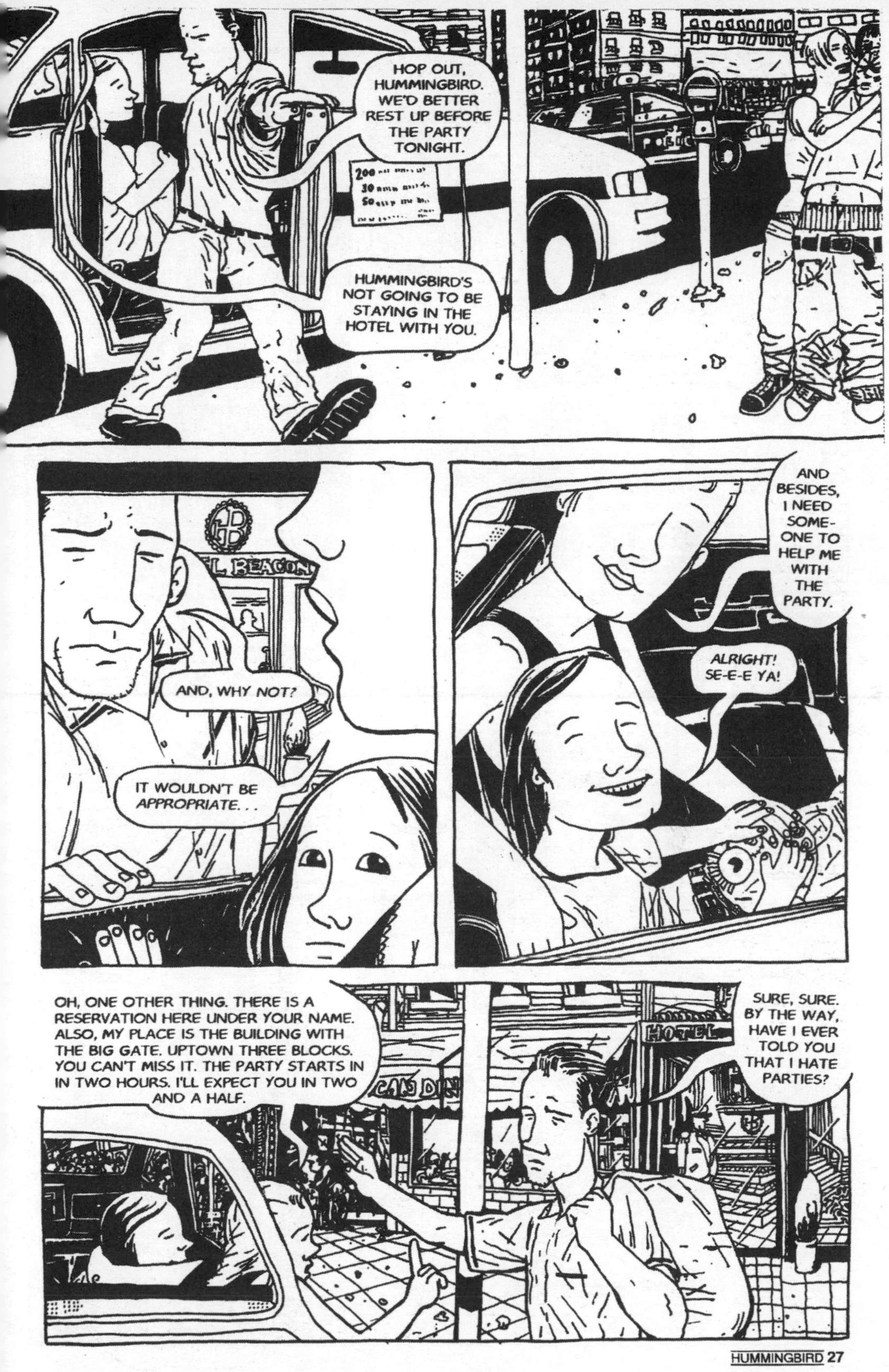
HOP OUT, HUMMINGBIRD. WE'D BETTER REST UP BEFORE THE PARTY TONIGHT.
HUMMINGBIRD'S NOT GOING TO BE STAYING IN THE HOTEL WITH YOU.
AND, WHY NOT?
IT WOULDN'T BE APPROPRIATE. . .
AND BESIDES, I NEED SOME-ONE TO HELP ME WITH THE PARTY.
ALRIGHT! SE-E-E YA!
OH, ONE OTHER THING. THERE IS A RESERVATION HERE UNDER YOUR NAME. ALSO, MY PLACE IS THE BUILDING WITH THE BIG GATE. UPTOWN THREE BLOCKS. YOU CAN'T MISS IT. THE PARTY STARTS IN IN TWO HOURS. I'LL EXPECT YOU IN TWO AND A HALF.
SURE, SURE. BY THE WAY, HAVE I EVER TOLD YOU THAT I HATE PARTIES?

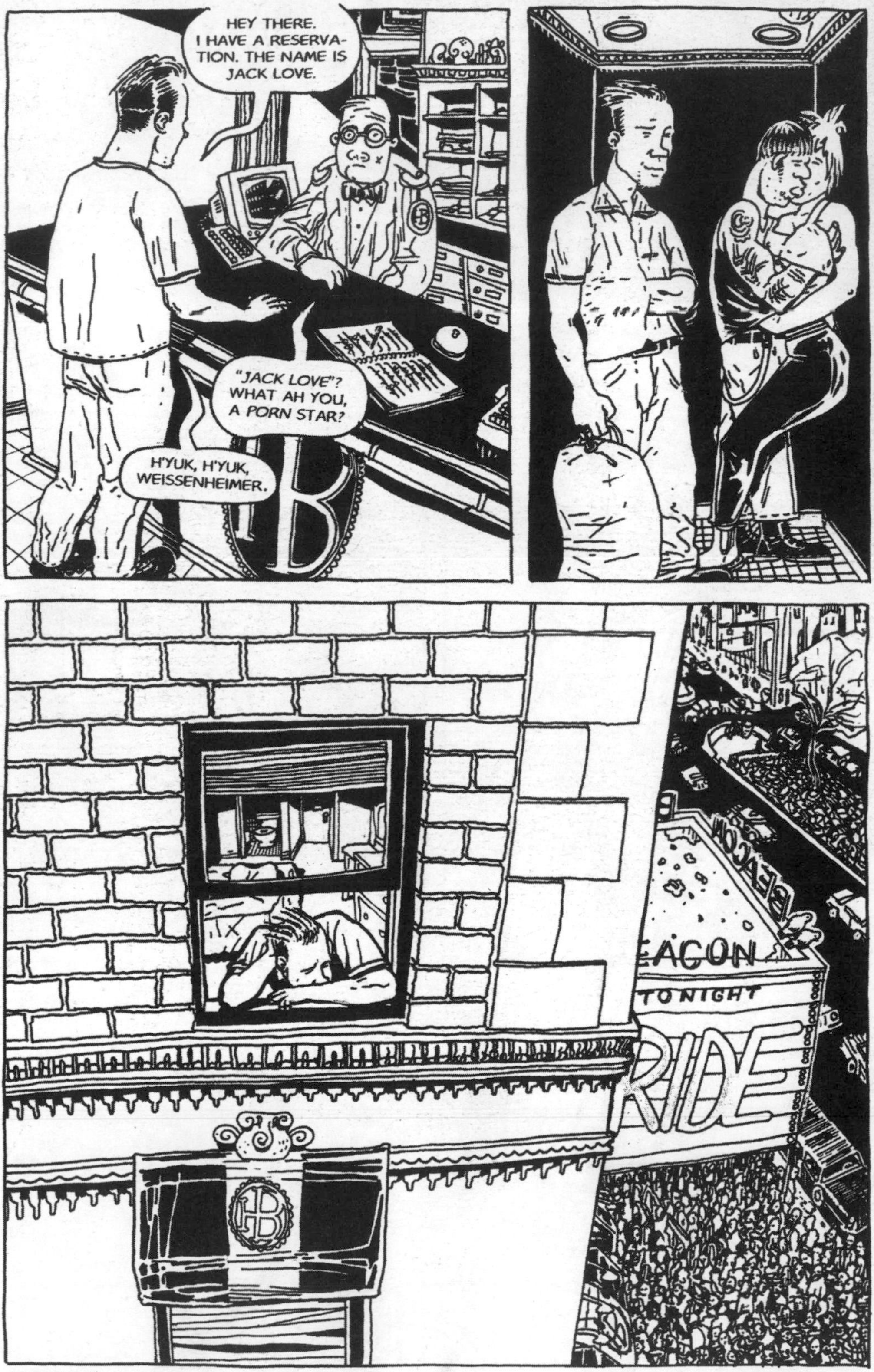
HEY THERE. I HAVE A RESERVATION. THE NAME IS JACK LOVE.
"JACK LOVE"? WHAT AH YOU, A PORN STAR?
H'YUK, H'YUK, WEISSENHEIMER.
BEACON
BEACON
TONIGHT
RIDE

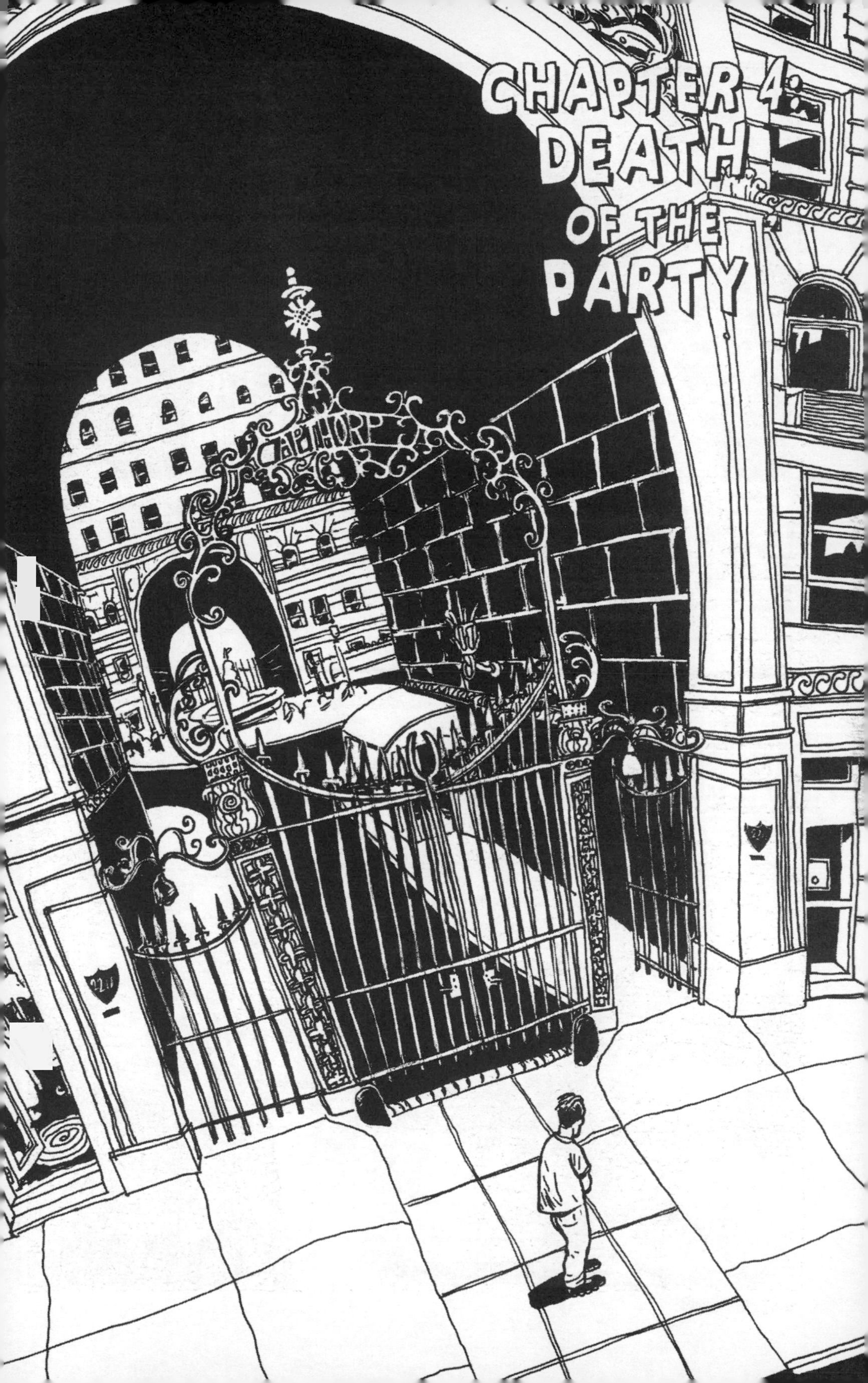
CHAPTER 4:
DEATH
OF THE
PARTY

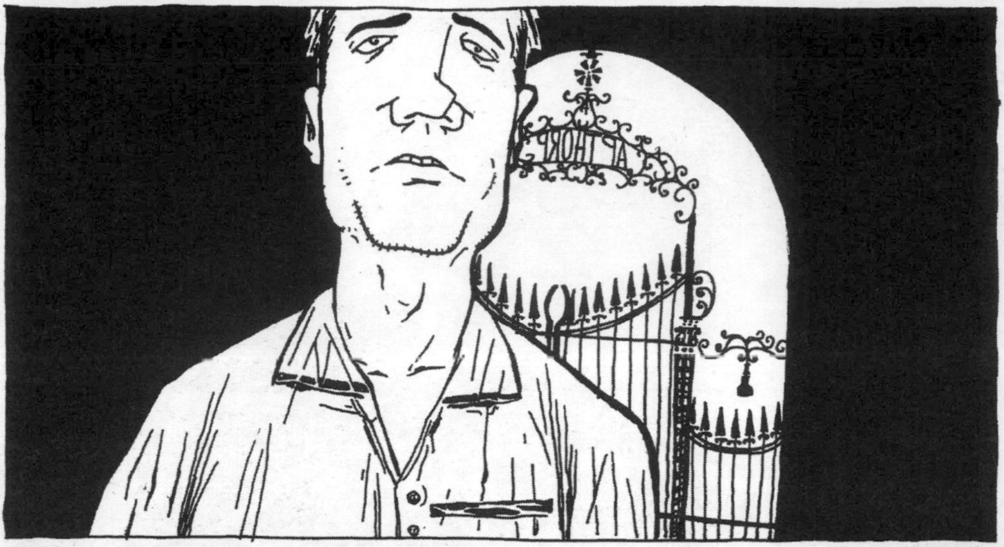

A'THORP

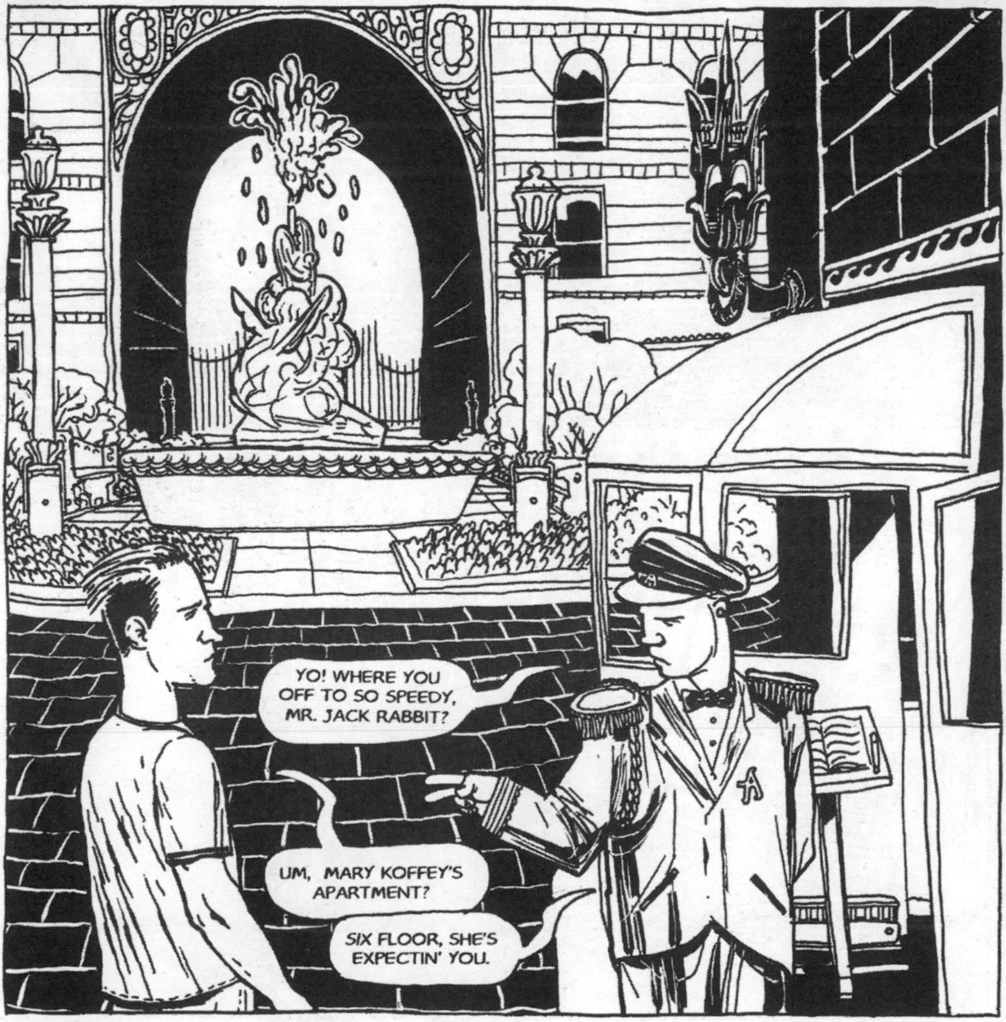

YO! WHERE YOU OFF TO SO SPEEDY, MR. JACK RABBIT?
UM, MARY KOFFEY'S APARTMENT?
SIX FLOOR, SHE'S EXPECTIN' YOU.

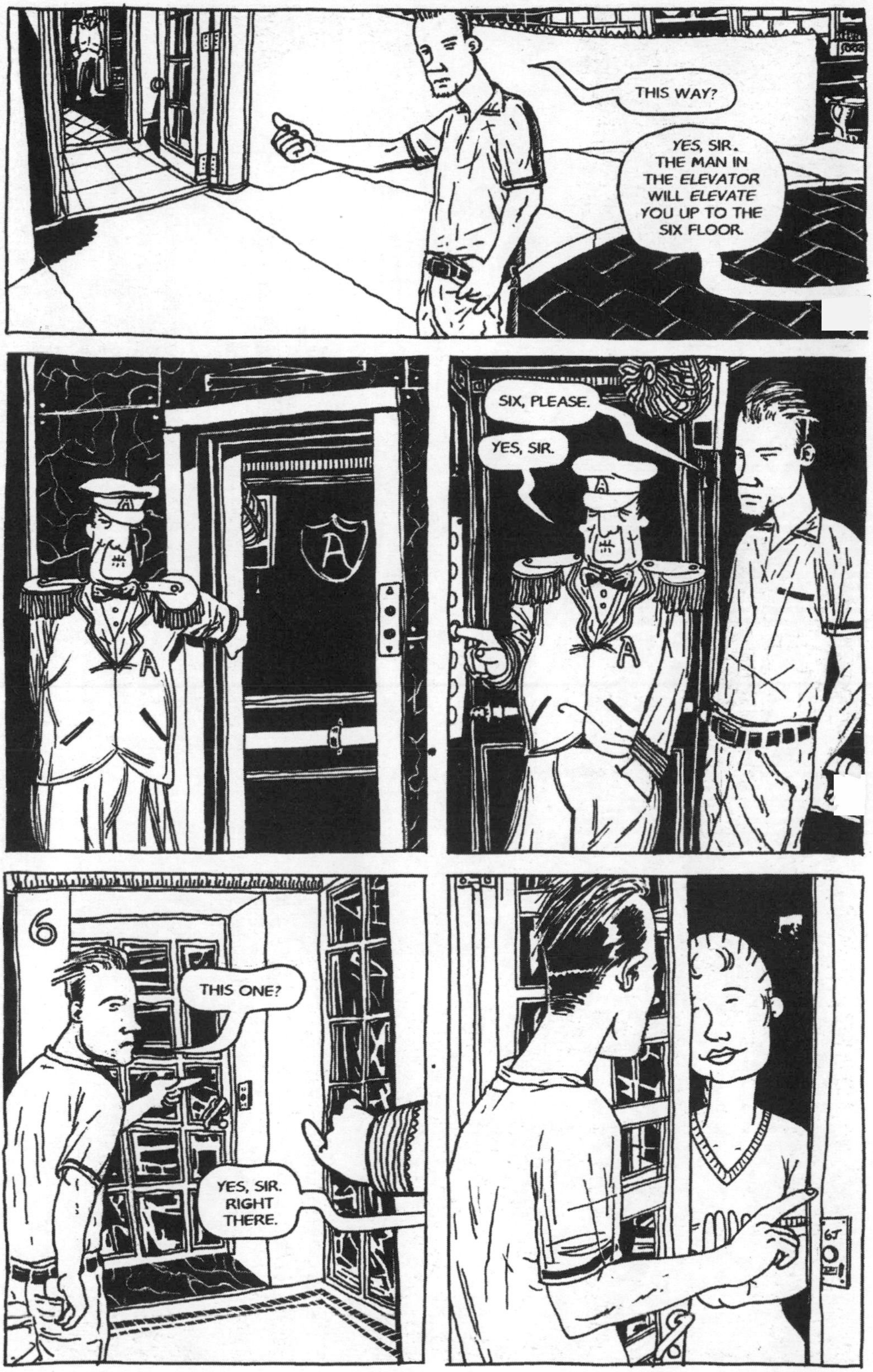
THIS WAY?
YES, SIR. THE MAN IN THE ELEVATOR WILL ELEVATE YOU UP TO THE SIX FLOOR.
SIX, PLEASE.
YES, SIR.
6
THIS ONE?
YES, SIR. RIGHT THERE.
6J

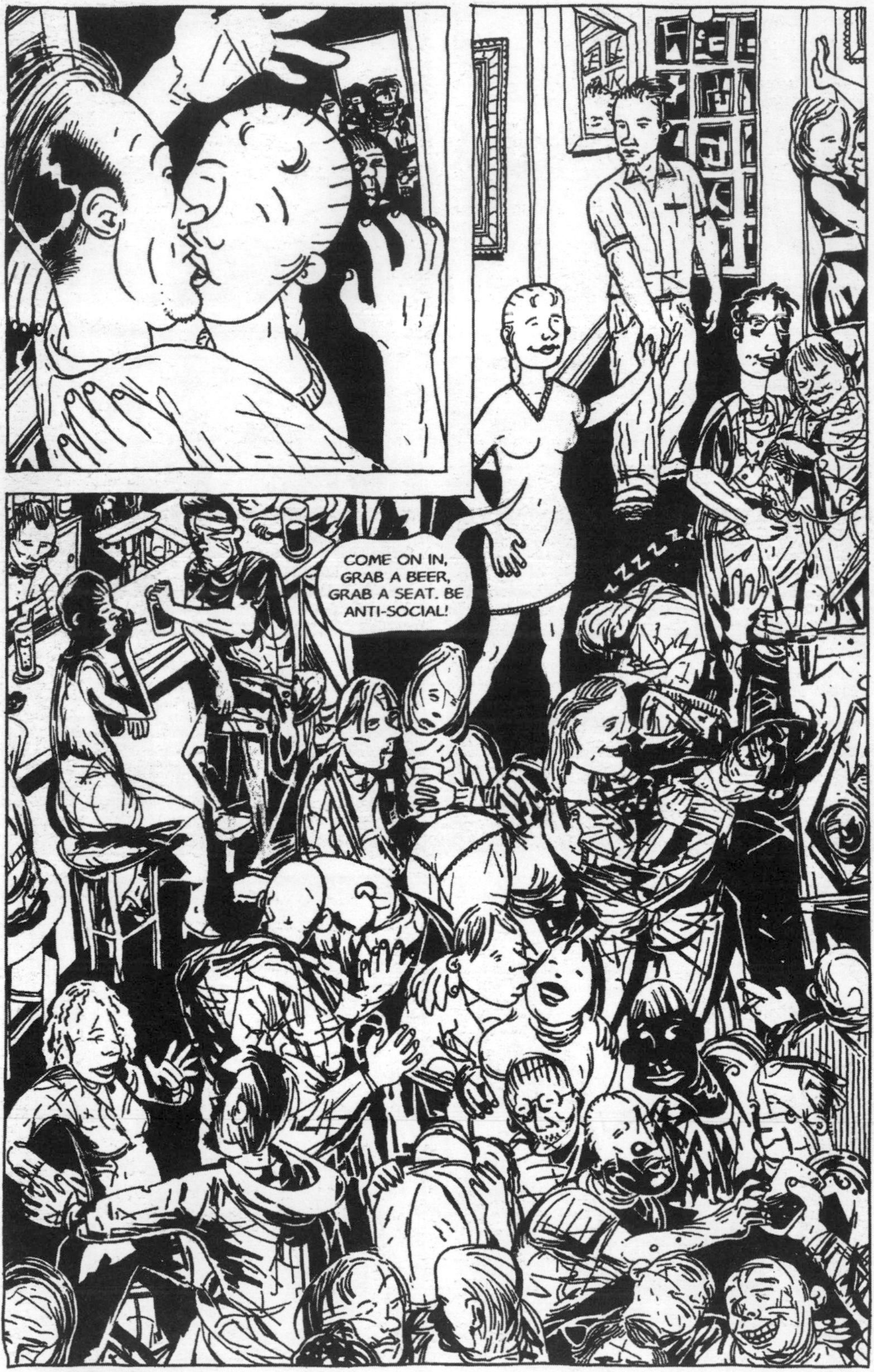
COME ON IN, GRAB A BEER, GRAB A SEAT. BE ANTI-SOCIAL!
ZZZZZZ

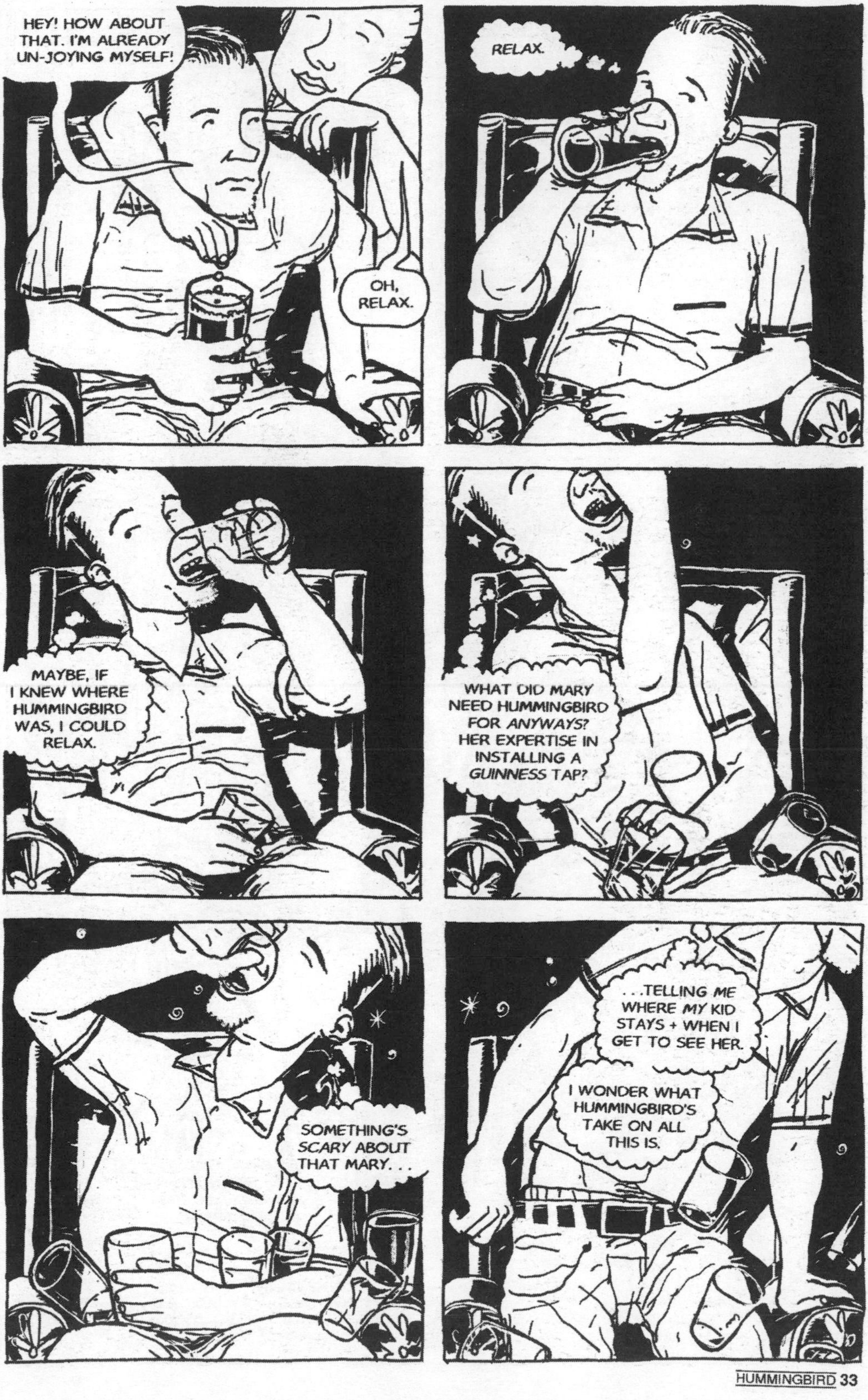
HEY! HOW ABOUT THAT. I'M ALREADY UN-JOYING MYSELF!
OH, RELAX.
RELAX.
MAYBE, IF I KNEW WHERE HUMMINGBIRD WAS, I COULD RELAX.
WHAT DID MARY NEED HUMMINGBIRD FOR ANYWAYS? HER EXPERTISE IN INSTALLING A GUINNESS TAP?
SOMETHING'S SCARY ABOUT THAT MARY...
...TELLING ME WHERE MY KID STAYS + WHEN I GET TO SEE HER.
I WONDER WHAT HUMMINGBIRD'S TAKE ON ALL THIS IS.

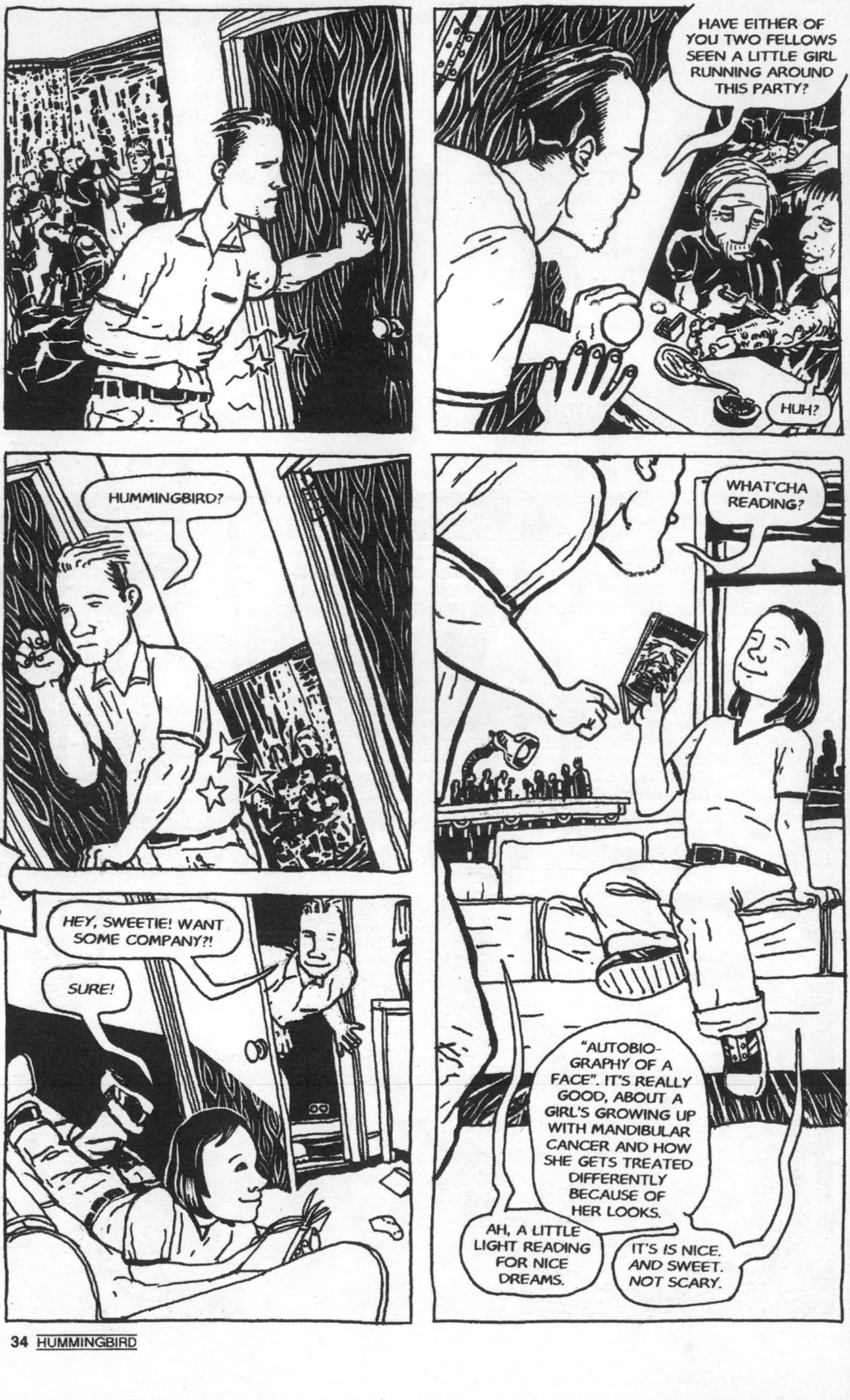
HAVE EITHER OF YOU TWO FELLOWS SEEN A LITTLE GIRL RUNNING AROUND THIS PARTY?
HUH?
HUMMINGBIRD?
HEY, SWEETIE! WANT SOME COMPANY?!
SURE!
WHAT'CHA READING?
"AUTOBIO-GRAPHY OF A FACE". IT'S REALLY GOOD, ABOUT A GIRL'S GROWING UP WITH MANDIBULAR CANCER AND HOW SHE GETS TREATED DIFFERENTLY BECAUSE OF HER LOOKS.
AH, A LITTLE LIGHT READING FOR NICE DREAMS.
IT'S IS NICE. AND SWEET. NOT SCARY.

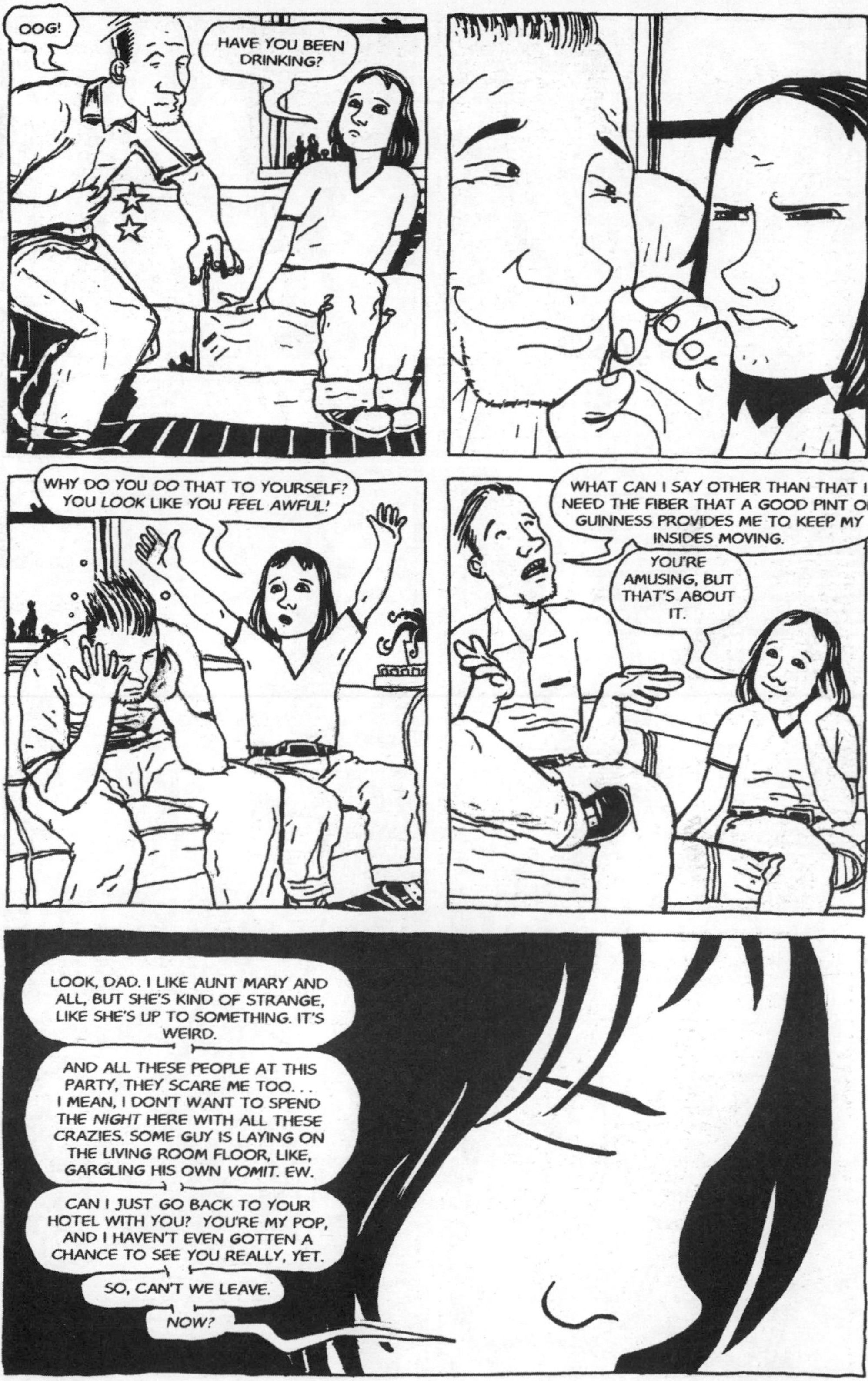
OOG!
HAVE YOU BEEN DRINKING?
WHY DO YOU DO THAT TO YOURSELF? YOU LOOK LIKE YOU FEEL AWFUL!
WHAT CAN I SAY OTHER THAN THAT I NEED THE FIBER THAT A GOOD PINT OF GUINNESS PROVIDES ME TO KEEP MY INSIDES MOVING.
YOU'RE AMUSING, BUT THAT'S ABOUT IT.
LOOK, DAD. I LIKE AUNT MARY AND ALL, BUT SHE'S KIND OF STRANGE, LIKE SHE'S UP TO SOMETHING. IT'S WEIRD.
AND ALL THESE PEOPLE AT THIS PARTY, THEY SCARE ME TOO... I MEAN, I DON'T WANT TO SPEND THE NIGHT HERE WITH ALL THESE CRAZIES. SOME GUY IS LAYING ON THE LIVING ROOM FLOOR, LIKE, GARGLING HIS OWN VOMIT. EW.
CAN I JUST GO BACK TO YOUR HOTEL WITH YOU? YOU'RE MY POP, AND I HAVEN'T EVEN GOTTEN A CHANCE TO SEE YOU REALLY, YET.
SO, CAN'T WE LEAVE.
NOW?

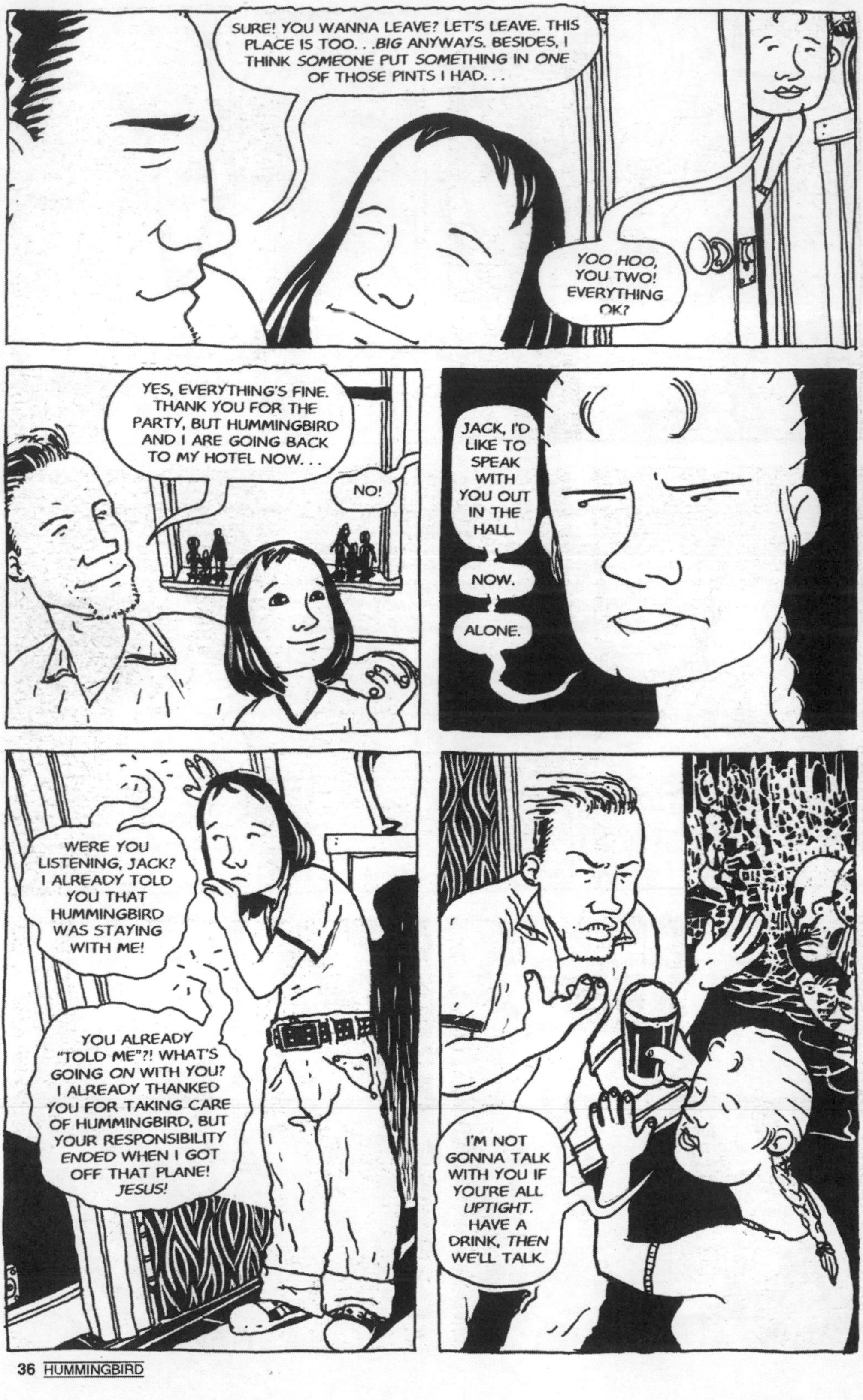
SURE! YOU WANNA LEAVE? LET'S LEAVE. THIS PLACE IS TOO. . .*BIG* ANYWAYS. BESIDES, I THINK *SOMEONE* PUT *SOMETHING* IN *ONE* OF THOSE PINTS I HAD. . .
YOO HOO, YOU TWO! EVERYTHING OK?
YES, EVERYTHING'S FINE. THANK YOU FOR THE PARTY, BUT HUMMINGBIRD AND I ARE GOING BACK TO MY HOTEL NOW. . .
NO!
JACK, I'D LIKE TO SPEAK WITH YOU OUT IN THE HALL.
NOW.
ALONE.
WERE *YOU* LISTENING, JACK? I ALREADY TOLD YOU THAT HUMMINGBIRD WAS STAYING WITH ME!
YOU ALREADY "TOLD ME"?! WHAT'S GOING *ON* WITH YOU? I ALREADY THANKED YOU FOR TAKING CARE OF HUMMINGBIRD, BUT YOUR RESPONSIBILITY *ENDED* WHEN I GOT OFF THAT PLANE! *JESUS!*
I'M NOT GONNA TALK WITH YOU IF YOU'RE ALL *UPTIGHT*. HAVE A DRINK, *THEN* WE'LL TALK.

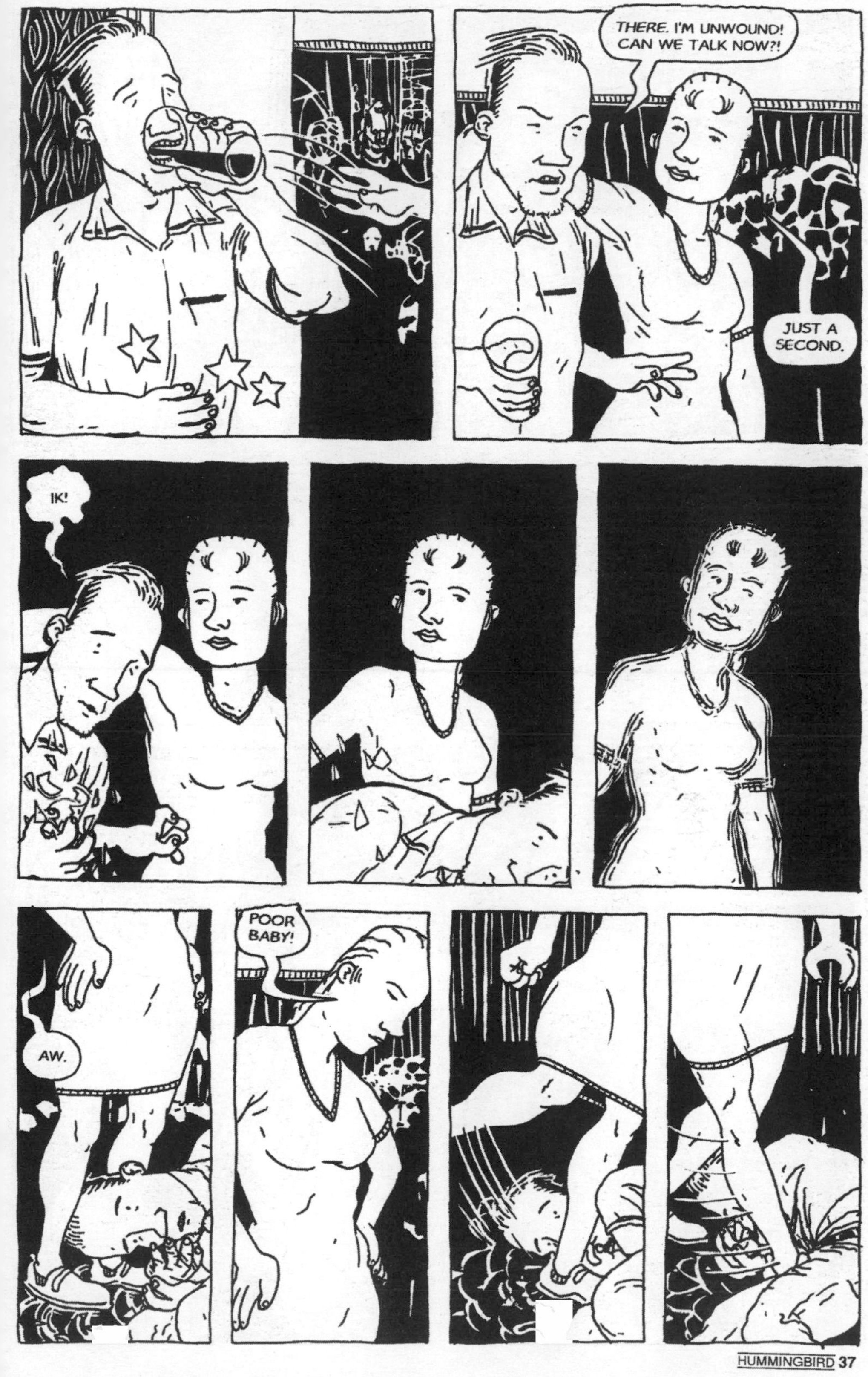
THERE. I'M UNWOUND!
CAN WE TALK NOW?!
JUST A SECOND.
IK!
AW.
POOR BABY!

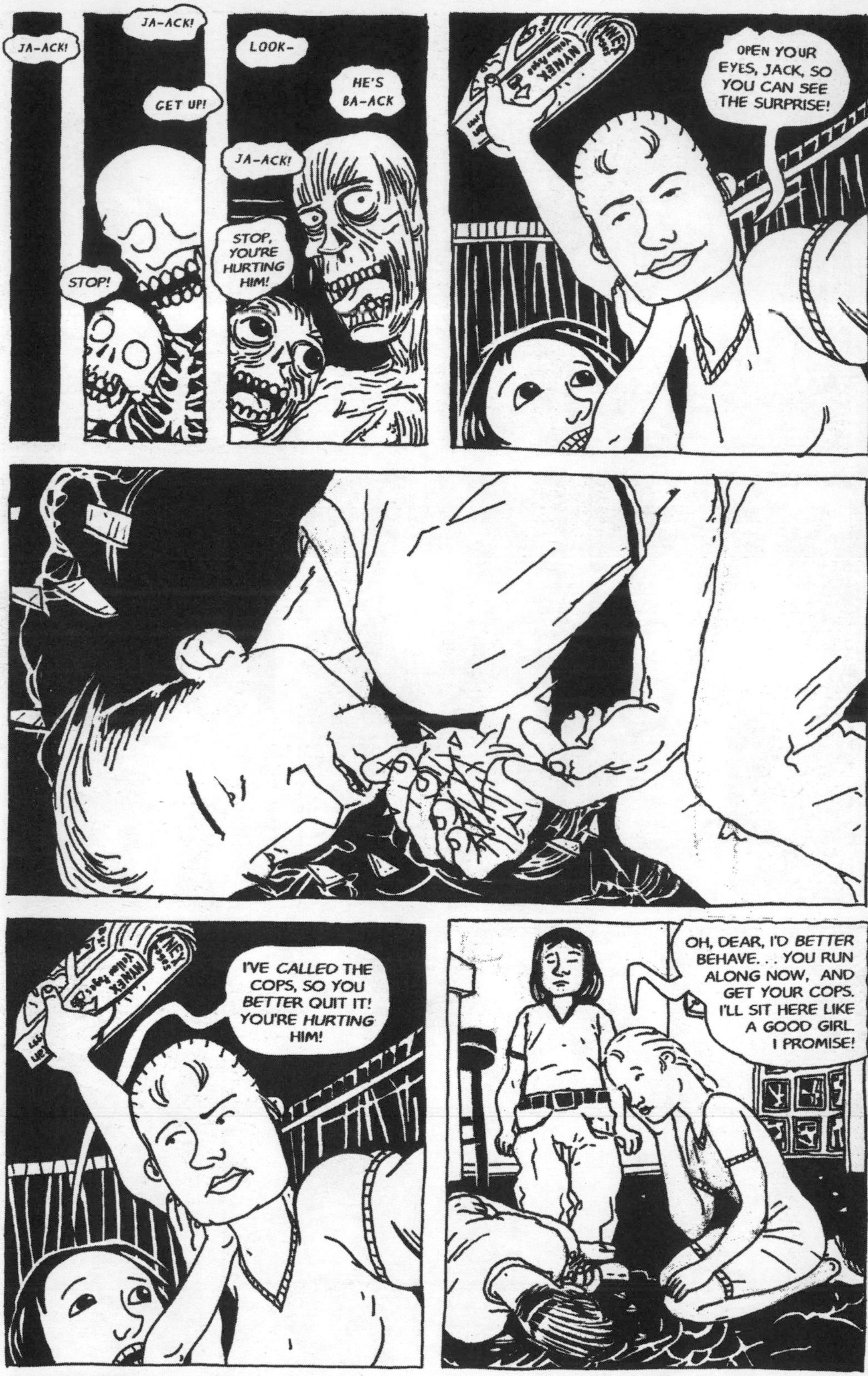
JA-ACK!
JA-ACK!
GET UP!
STOP!
LOOK-
HE'S BA-ACK
JA-ACK!
STOP, YOU'RE HURTING HIM!
OPEN YOUR EYES, JACK, SO YOU CAN SEE THE SURPRISE!
I'VE CALLED THE COPS, SO YOU BETTER QUIT IT! YOU'RE HURTING HIM!
OH, DEAR, I'D BETTER BEHAVE. . . YOU RUN ALONG NOW, AND GET YOUR COPS. I'LL SIT HERE LIKE A GOOD GIRL. I PROMISE!

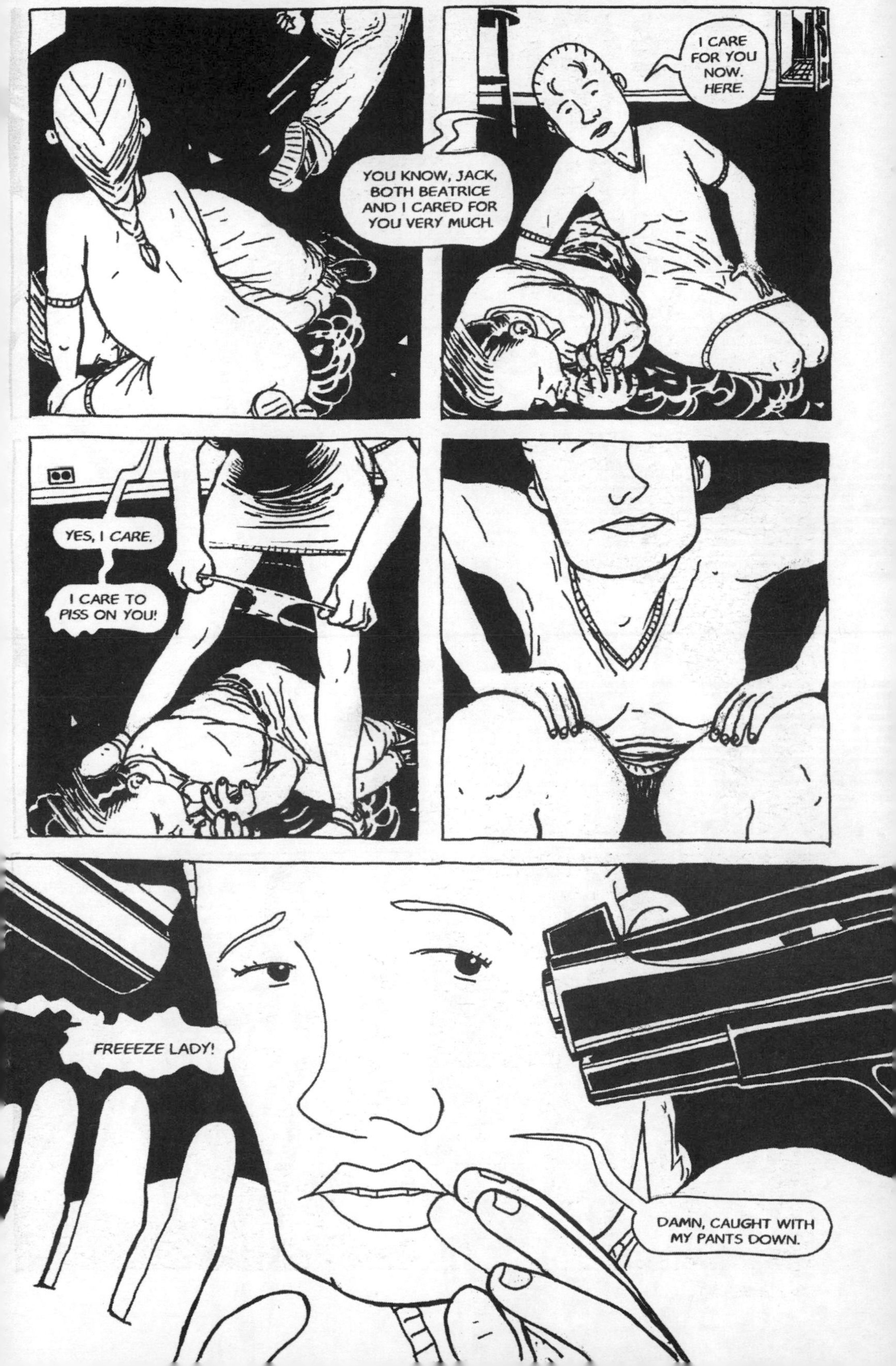
YOU KNOW, JACK, BOTH BEATRICE AND I CARED FOR YOU VERY MUCH.
I CARE FOR YOU NOW. HERE.
YES, I CARE.
I CARE TO PISS ON YOU!
FREEEZE LADY!
DAMN, CAUGHT WITH MY PANTS DOWN.

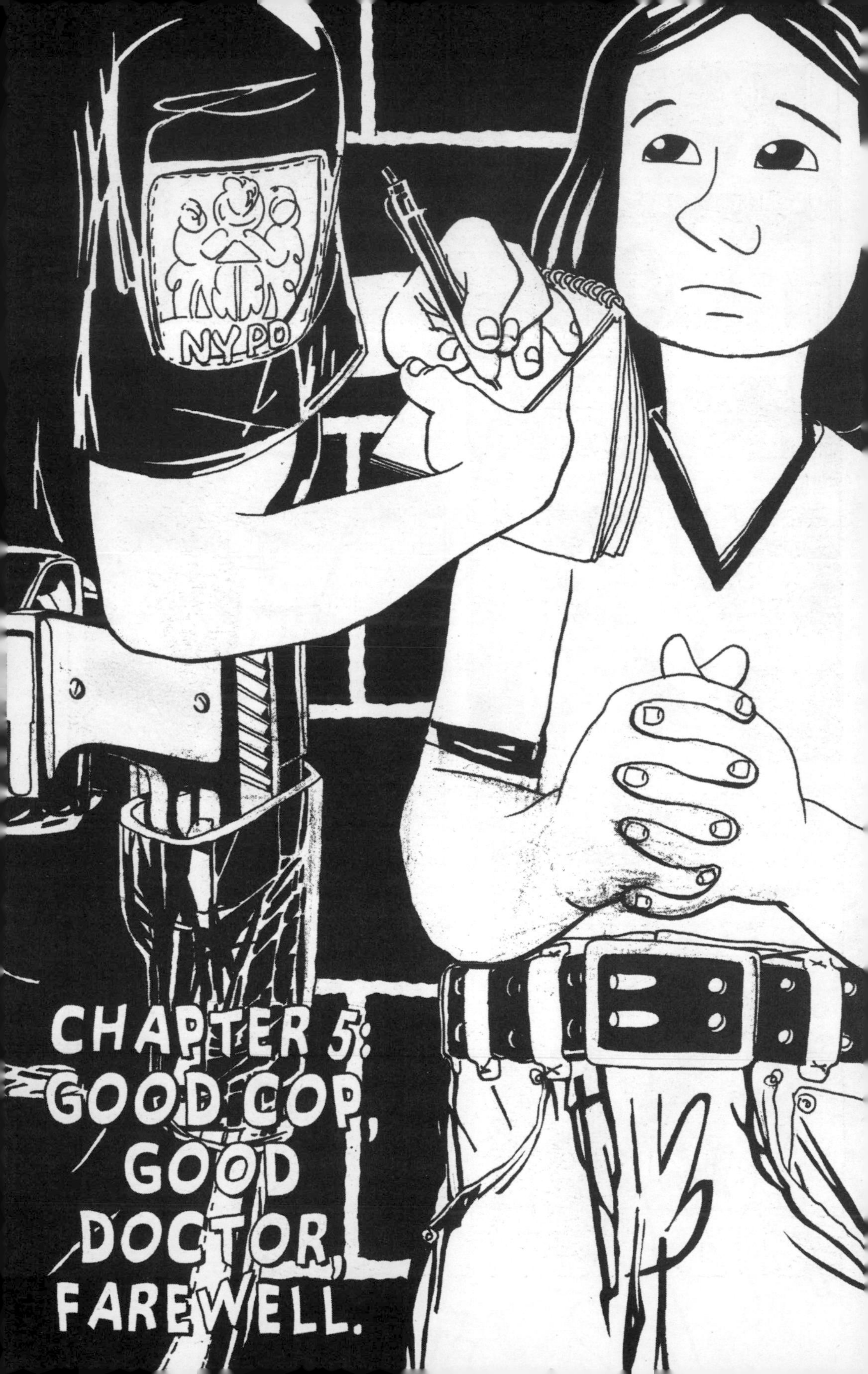
NYPD
CHAPTER 5: GOOD COP, GOOD DOCTOR, FAREWELL.

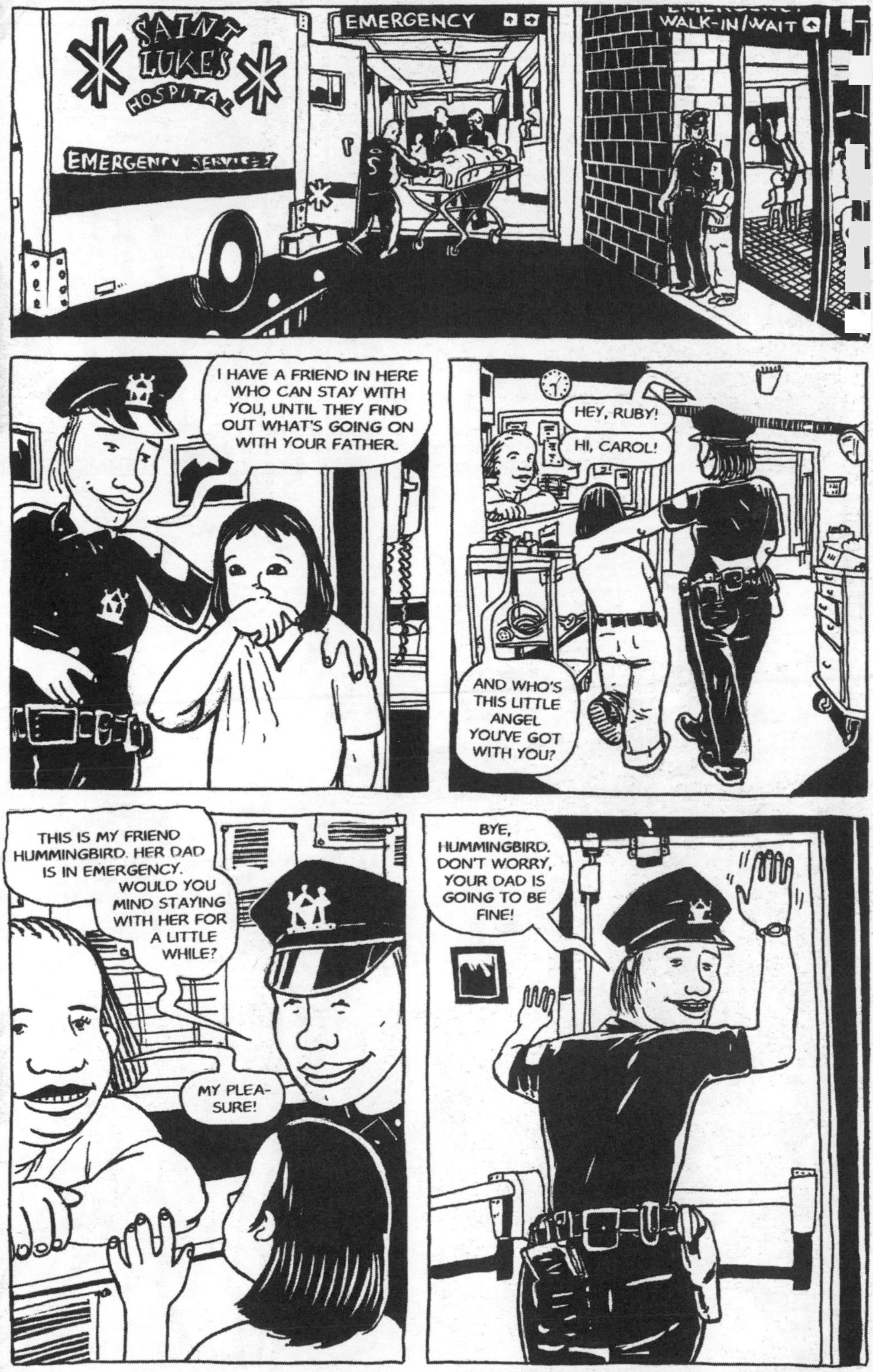
SAINT LUKE'S HOSPITAL
EMERGENCY SERVICES
EMERGENCY
WALK-IN/WAIT
I HAVE A FRIEND IN HERE WHO CAN STAY WITH YOU, UNTIL THEY FIND OUT WHAT'S GOING ON WITH YOUR FATHER.
HEY, RUBY!
HI, CAROL!
AND WHO'S THIS LITTLE ANGEL YOU'VE GOT WITH YOU?
THIS IS MY FRIEND HUMMINGBIRD. HER DAD IS IN EMERGENCY.
WOULD YOU MIND STAYING WITH HER FOR A LITTLE WHILE?
MY PLEA-SURE!
BYE, HUMMINGBIRD. DON'T WORRY, YOUR DAD IS GOING TO BE FINE!

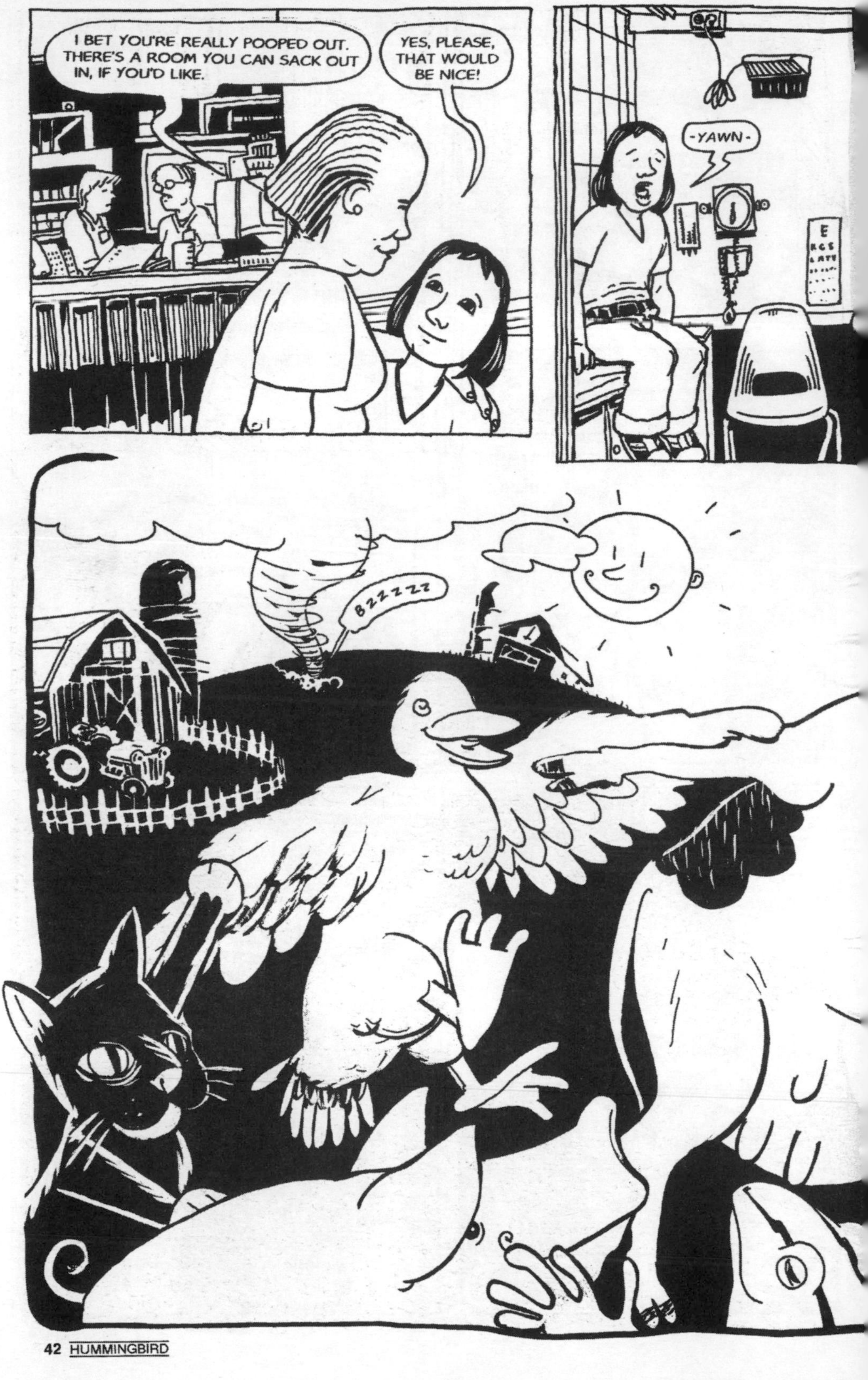
I BET YOU'RE REALLY POOPED OUT. THERE'S A ROOM YOU CAN SACK OUT IN, IF YOU'D LIKE.
YES, PLEASE, THAT WOULD BE NICE!
-YAWN-
BZZZZZ

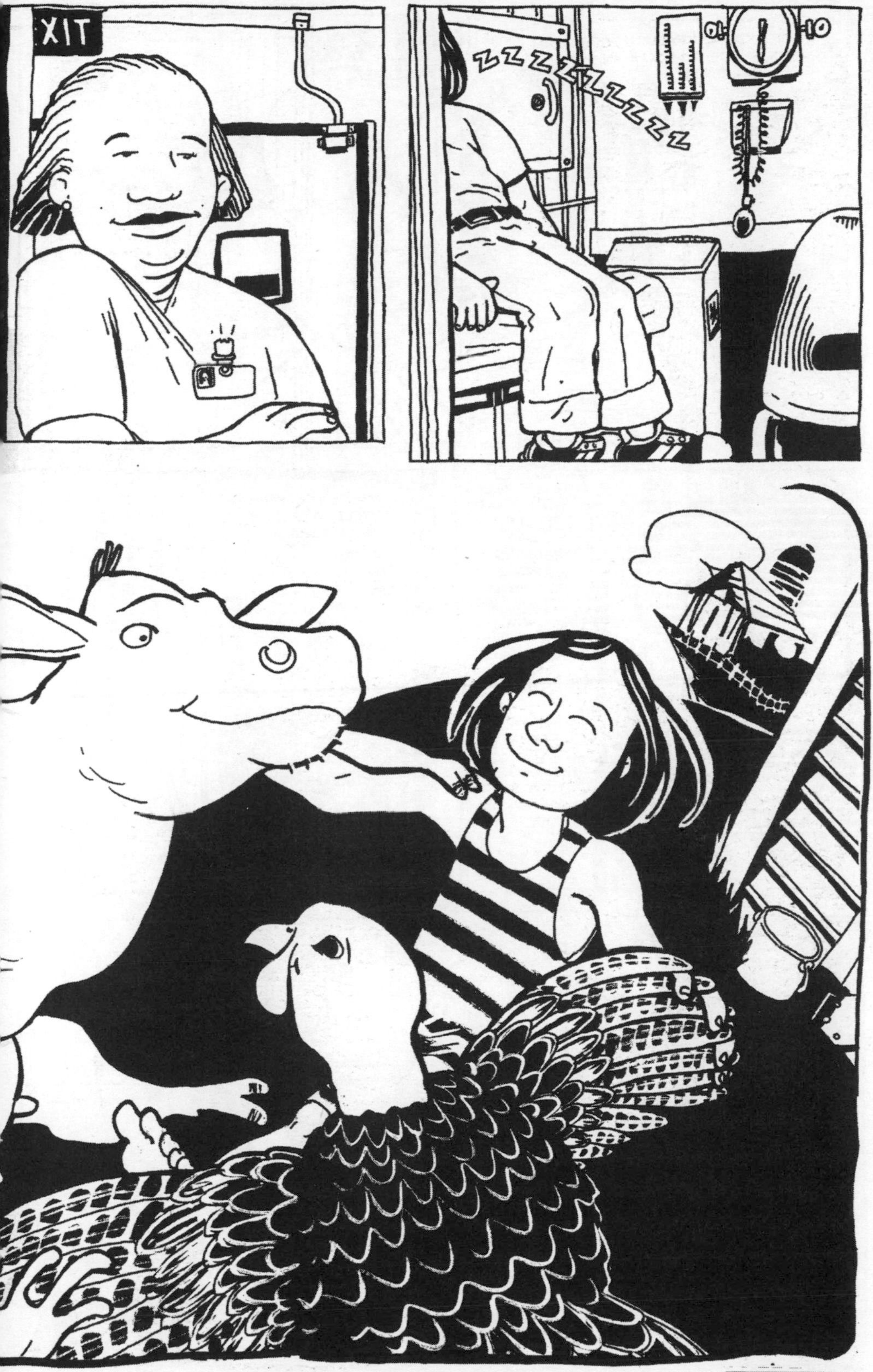
XIT
ZZZZZZZZZ

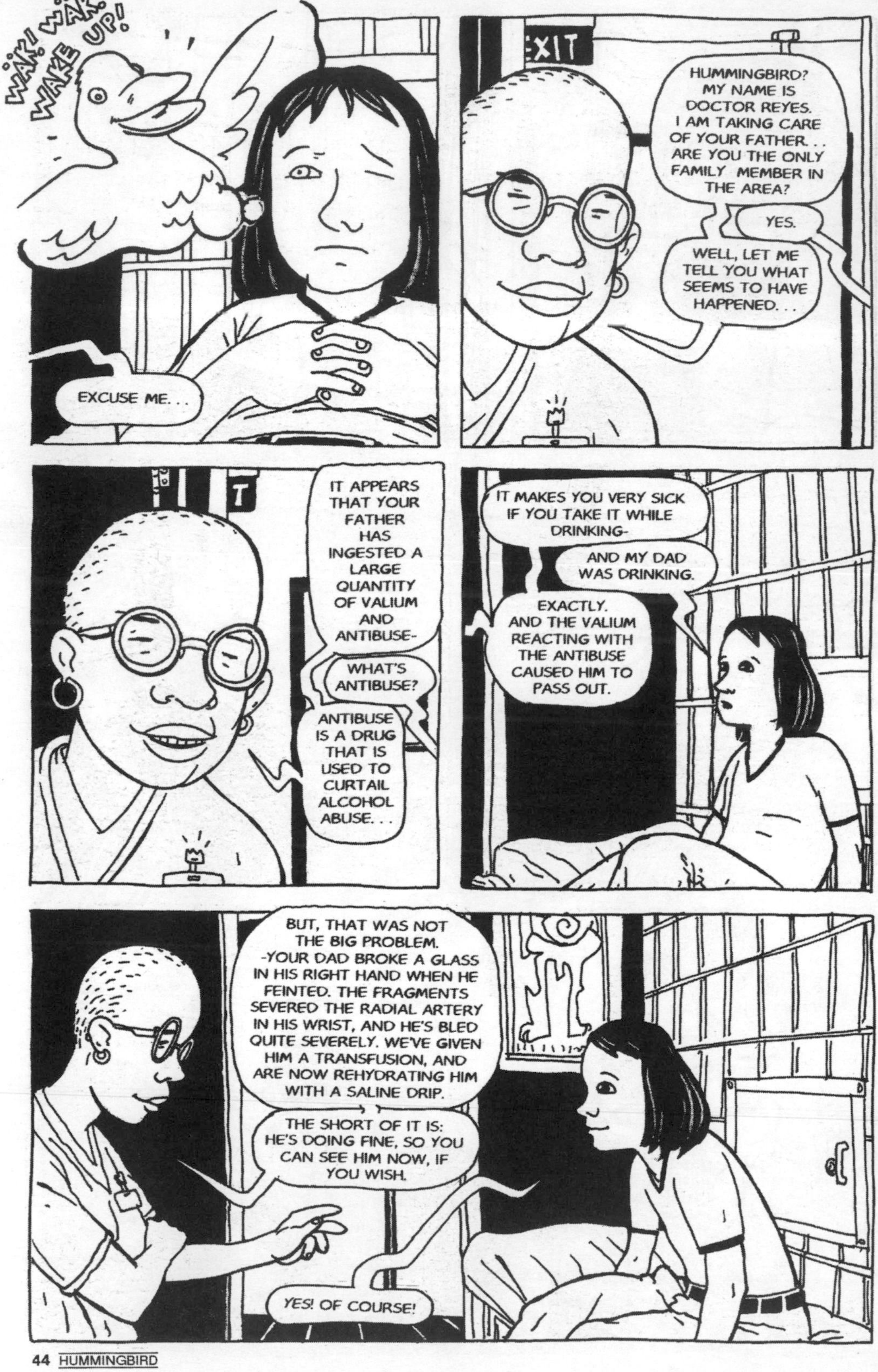
WÄK! WÄK! WAKE UP!
EXCUSE ME...
HUMMINGBIRD? MY NAME IS DOCTOR REYES. I AM TAKING CARE OF YOUR FATHER... ARE YOU THE ONLY FAMILY MEMBER IN THE AREA?
YES.
WELL, LET ME TELL YOU WHAT SEEMS TO HAVE HAPPENED...
EXIT
IT APPEARS THAT YOUR FATHER HAS INGESTED A LARGE QUANTITY OF VALIUM AND ANTIBUSE-
WHAT'S ANTIBUSE?
ANTIBUSE IS A DRUG THAT IS USED TO CURTAIL ALCOHOL ABUSE...
IT MAKES YOU VERY SICK IF YOU TAKE IT WHILE DRINKING-
AND MY DAD WAS DRINKING.
EXACTLY. AND THE VALIUM REACTING WITH THE ANTIBUSE CAUSED HIM TO PASS OUT.
BUT, THAT WAS NOT THE BIG PROBLEM. -YOUR DAD BROKE A GLASS IN HIS RIGHT HAND WHEN HE FEINTED. THE FRAGMENTS SEVERED THE RADIAL ARTERY IN HIS WRIST, AND HE'S BLED QUITE SEVERELY. WE'VE GIVEN HIM A TRANSFUSION, AND ARE NOW REHYDRATING HIM WITH A SALINE DRIP.
THE SHORT OF IT IS: HE'S DOING FINE, SO YOU CAN SEE HIM NOW, IF YOU WISH.
YES! OF COURSE!

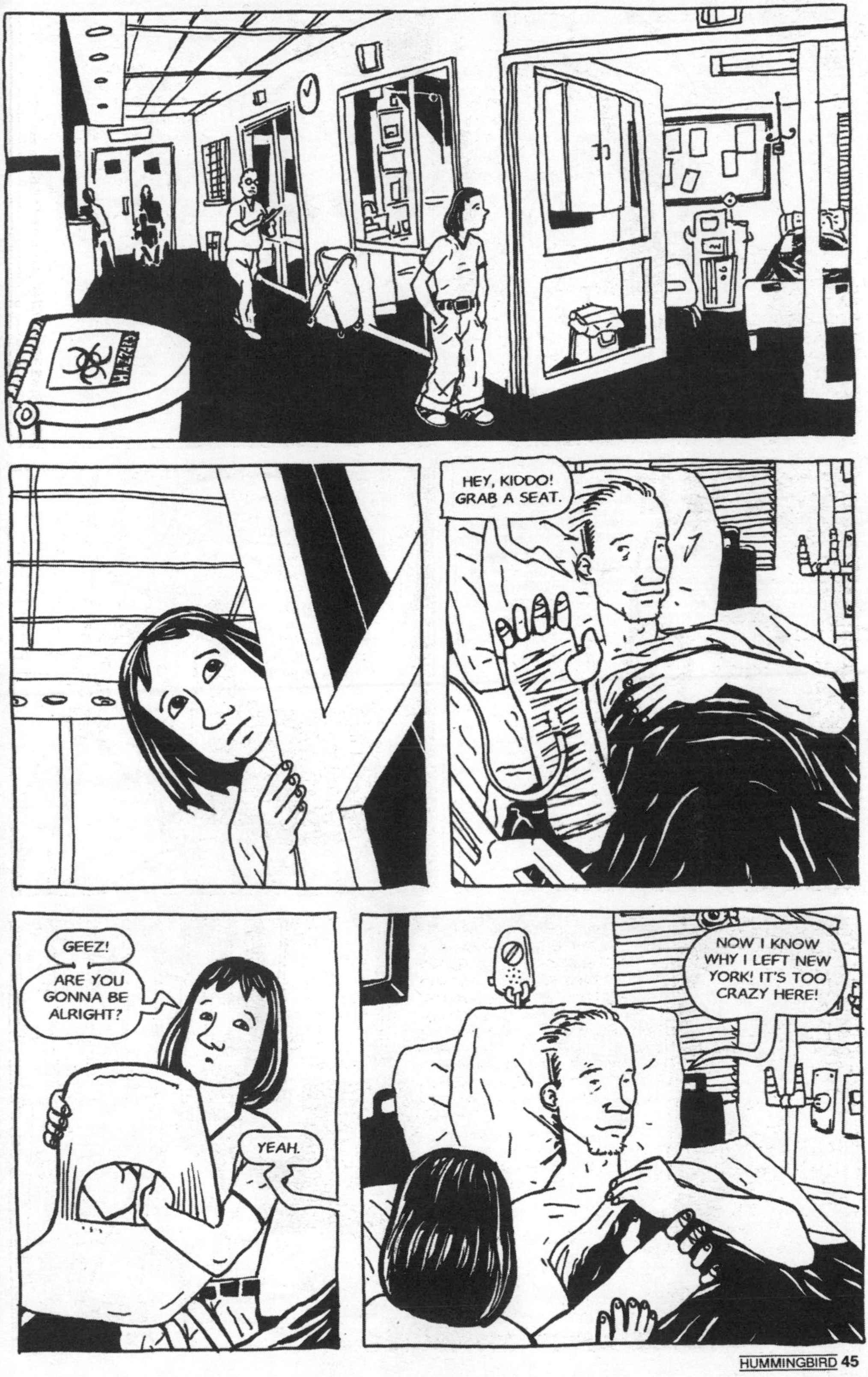
HAZARD
HEY, KIDDO! GRAB A SEAT.
GEEZ!
ARE YOU GONNA BE ALRIGHT?
YEAH.
NOW I KNOW WHY I LEFT NEW YORK! IT'S TOO CRAZY HERE!

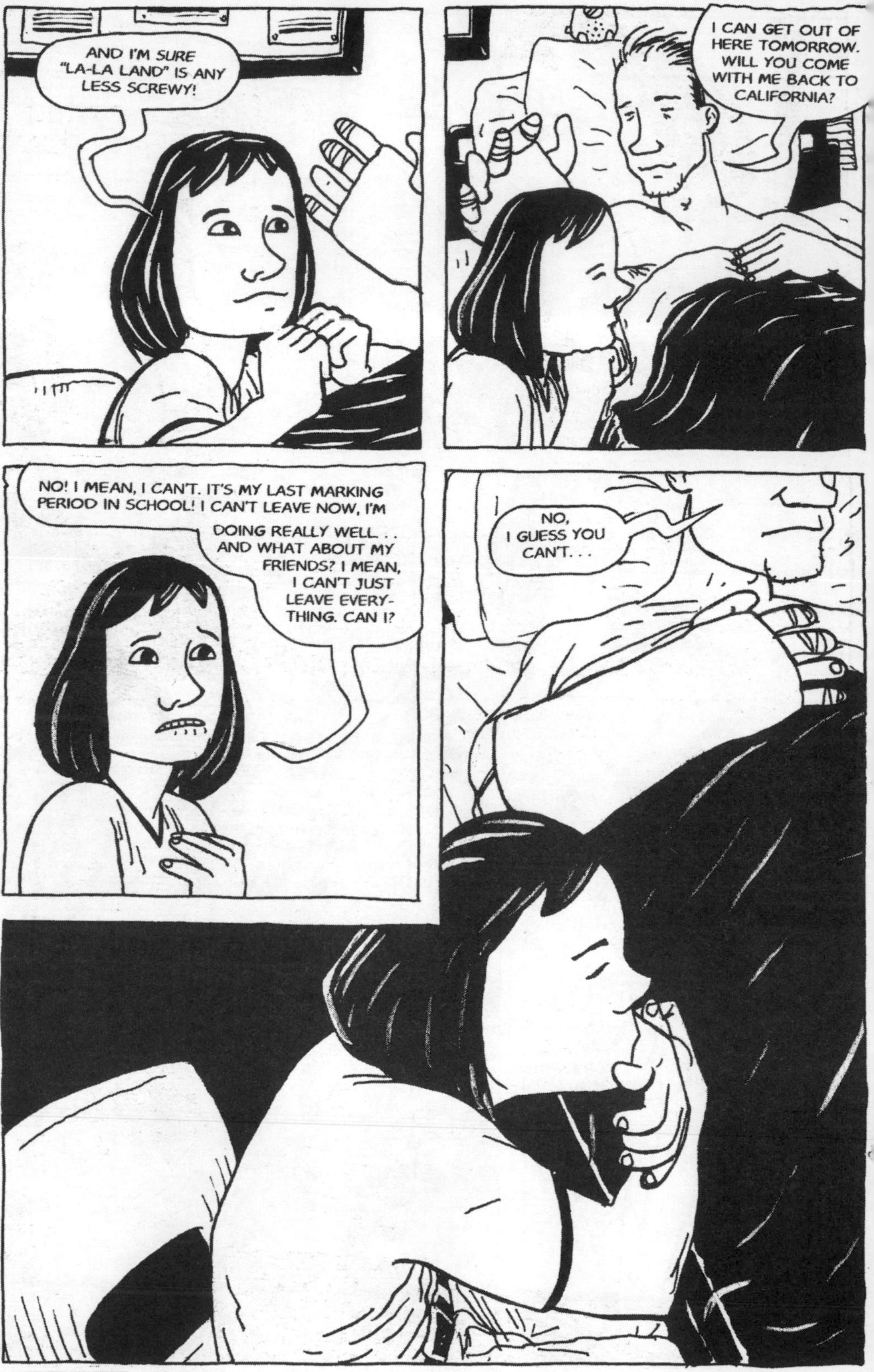
AND I'M SURE "LA-LA LAND" IS ANY LESS SCREWY!
I CAN GET OUT OF HERE TOMORROW. WILL YOU COME WITH ME BACK TO CALIFORNIA?
NO! I MEAN, I CAN'T. IT'S MY LAST MARKING PERIOD IN SCHOOL! I CAN'T LEAVE NOW, I'M DOING REALLY WELL. . . AND WHAT ABOUT MY FRIENDS? I MEAN, I CAN'T JUST LEAVE EVERYTHING. CAN I?
NO, I GUESS YOU CAN'T. . .

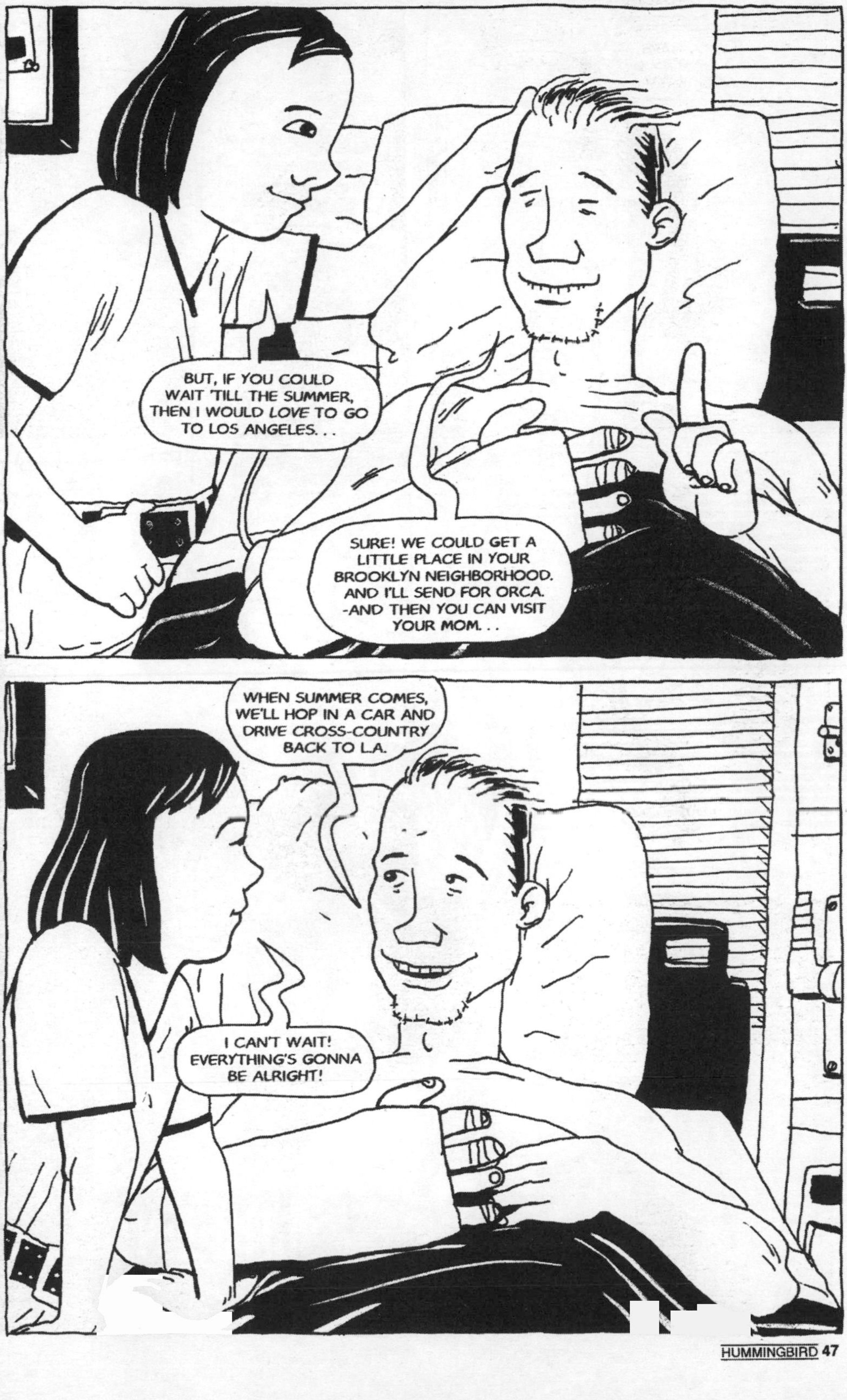
BUT, IF YOU COULD WAIT 'TILL THE SUMMER, THEN I WOULD *LOVE* TO GO TO LOS ANGELES. . .
SURE! WE COULD GET A LITTLE PLACE IN YOUR BROOKLYN NEIGHBORHOOD. AND I'LL SEND FOR ORCA. -AND THEN YOU CAN VISIT YOUR MOM. . .
WHEN SUMMER COMES, WE'LL HOP IN A CAR AND DRIVE CROSS-COUNTRY BACK TO L.A.
I CAN'T WAIT! EVERYTHING'S GONNA BE ALRIGHT!

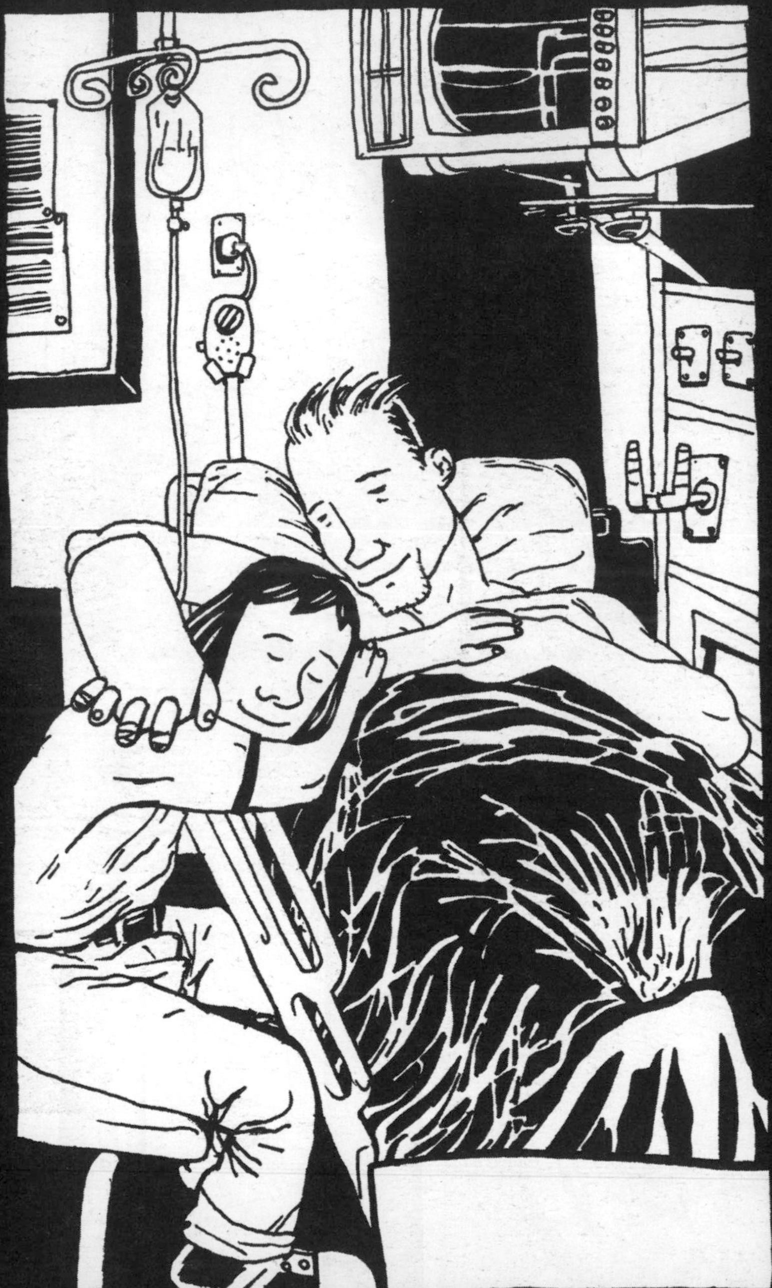

THE END

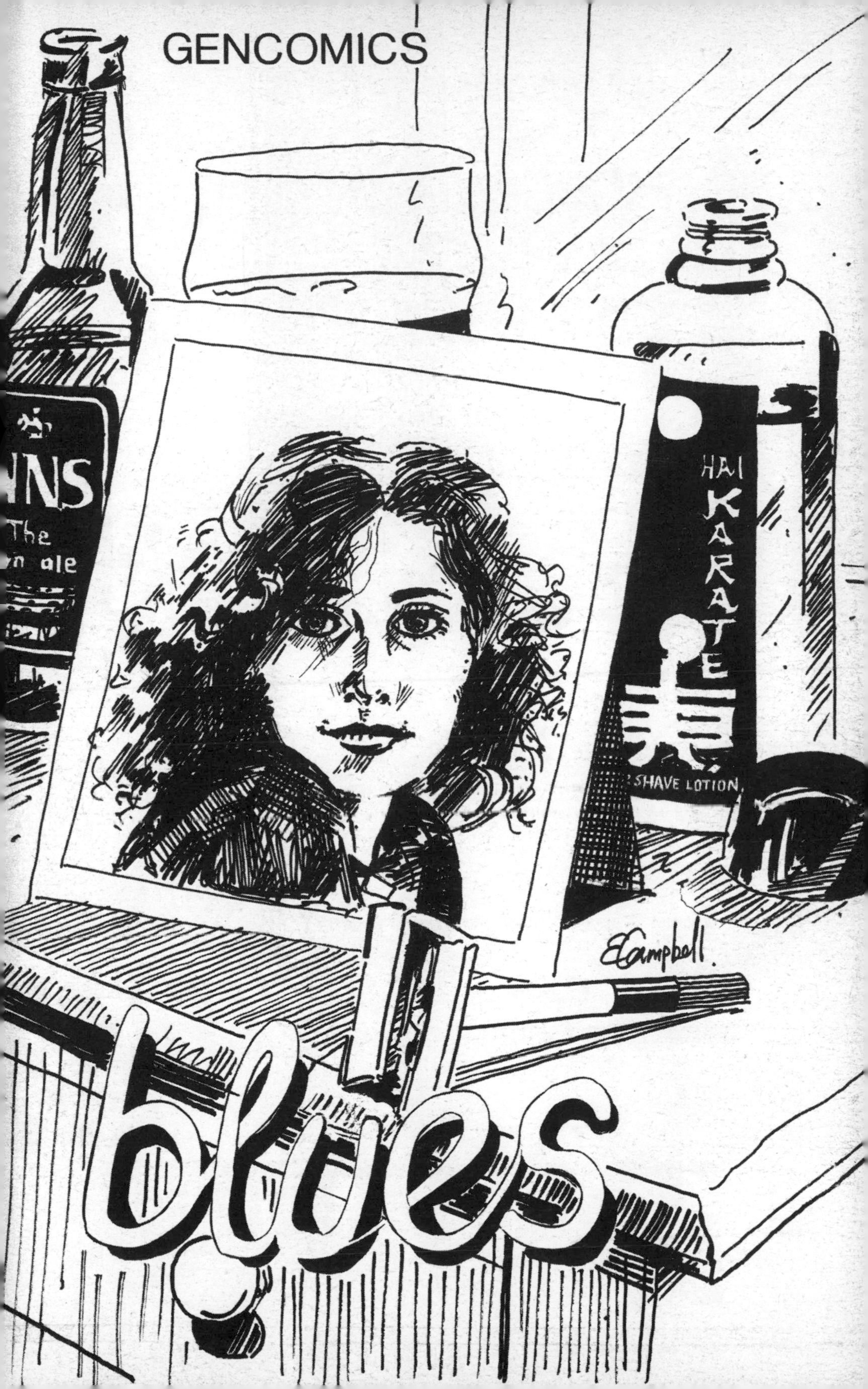
GENCOMICS
HAI
KARATE
SHAVE LOTION
E Campbell
blues

Eddie Campbell

BLUES
Gencomics #2, Co-publication with Ed Hillyer, 1983

"Jeezis, thirty-one years! Where did that go? And how did I get this far without substantially amending my masterplan? From doing this little very personal comic and getting yer current editor Ed Hillyer* to help me hand colour the cover of the booklet in which it first appeared, to the tune of 300 copies, I have managed to stick to my guns. If it tickles your fancy there's a huge big 600-page book of similar stuff titled *Alec: The Years Have Pants* (Top Shelf Comics, 2009). I'm tired now. I'm having a rest." – EC

aka ILYA. Don't ask, it gets confusing!

www.eddiecampbell.blogspot.com

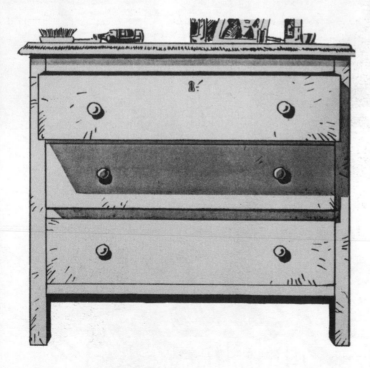

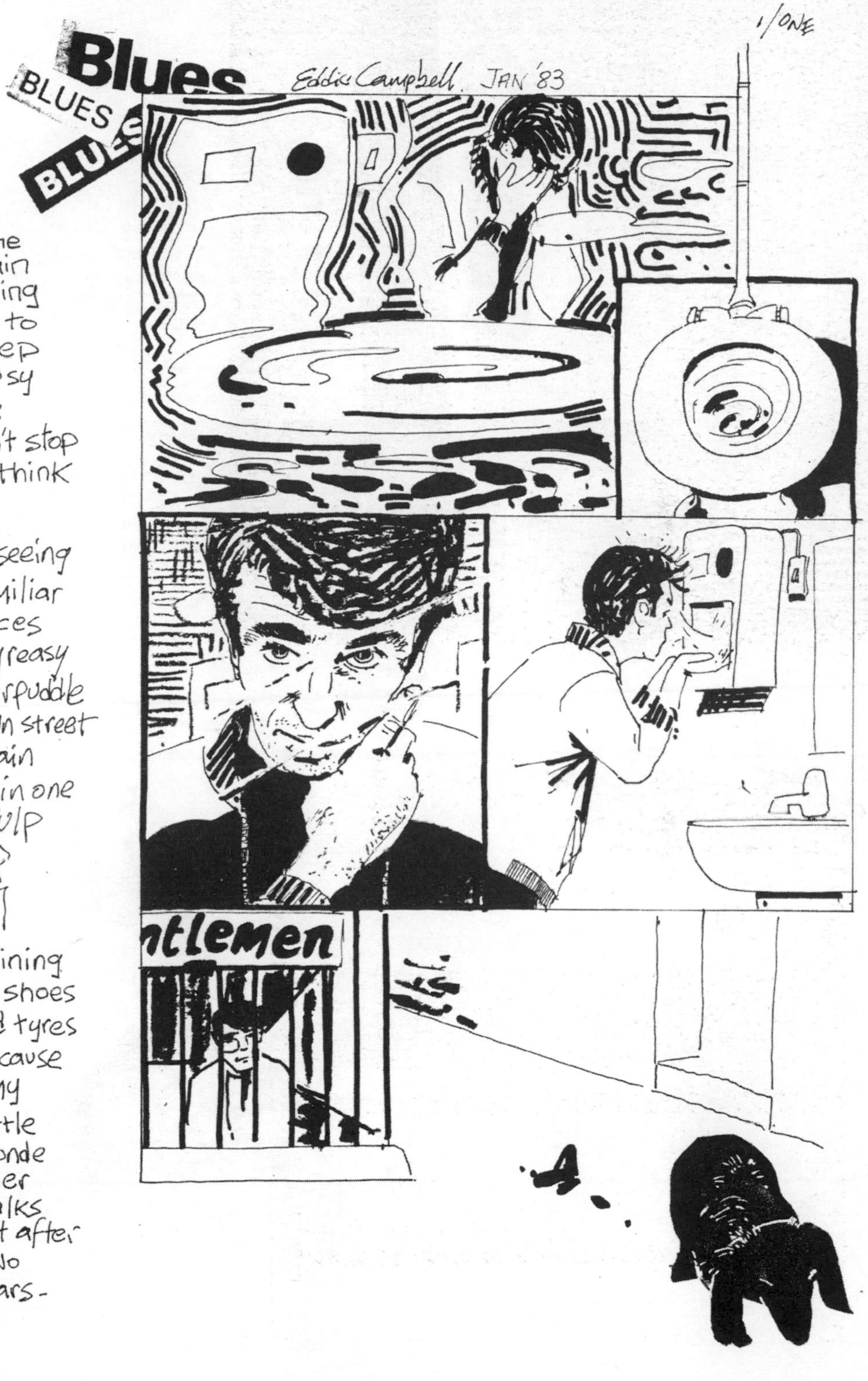
Blues
BLUES
BLUES
Eddie Campbell JAN '83
1/ONE
The main thing is to keep busy & don't stop to think
I'm seeing familiar faces in greasy beerpuddle down street drain all in one gulp
whining at shoes and tyres because my little blonde lover walks out after two years.
ntlemen

1/TWO

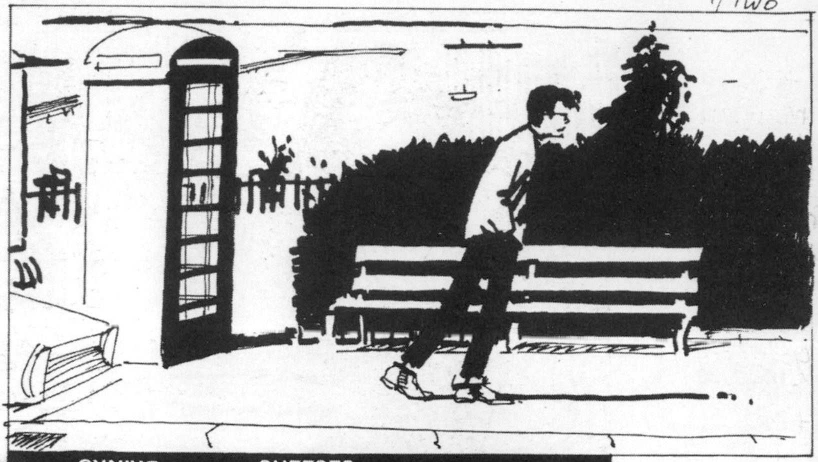

Just to confuse the situation that's my mood the night I ring George –

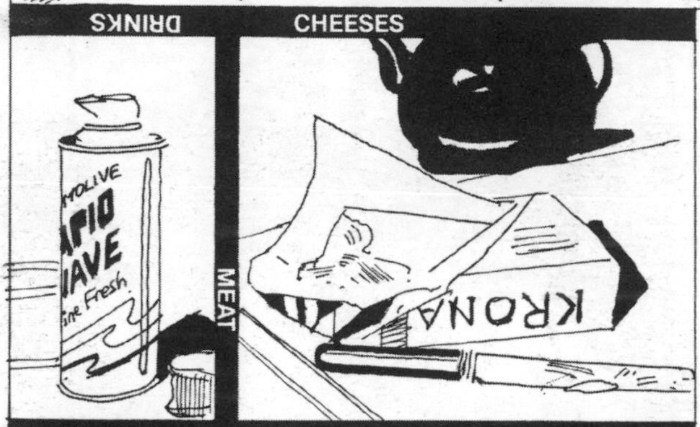

DRINKS
CHEESES
MEAT
KRONA

Maybe you've met George

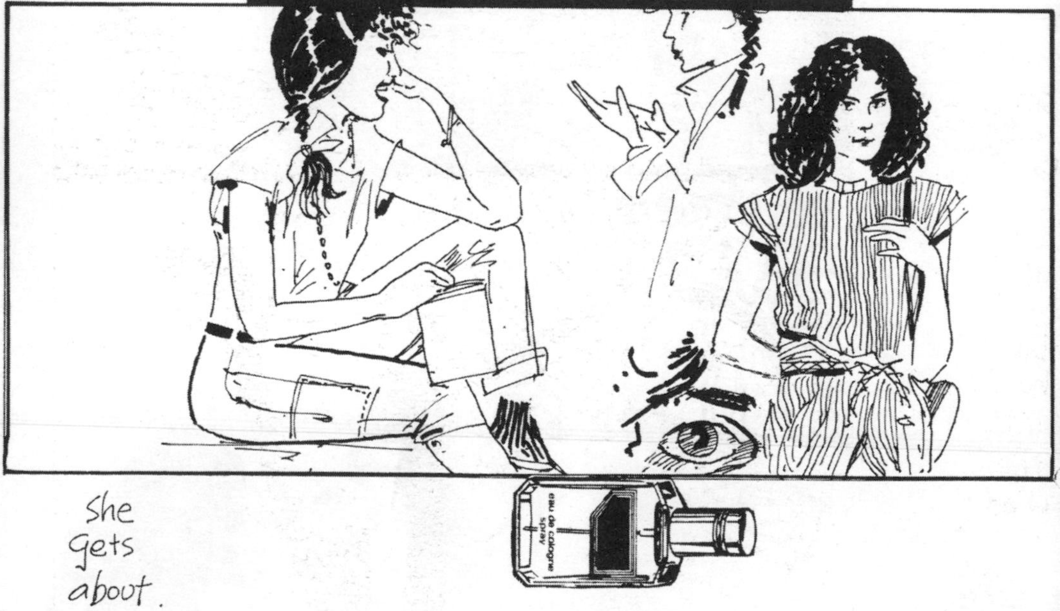

eau de cologne spray

She gets about.

In this manner I lurch into one razysituation the details of which I'll tell you some other time.

This guy's no longer me, this acheloin lumpthroat

sort of person

blunt head into the wind

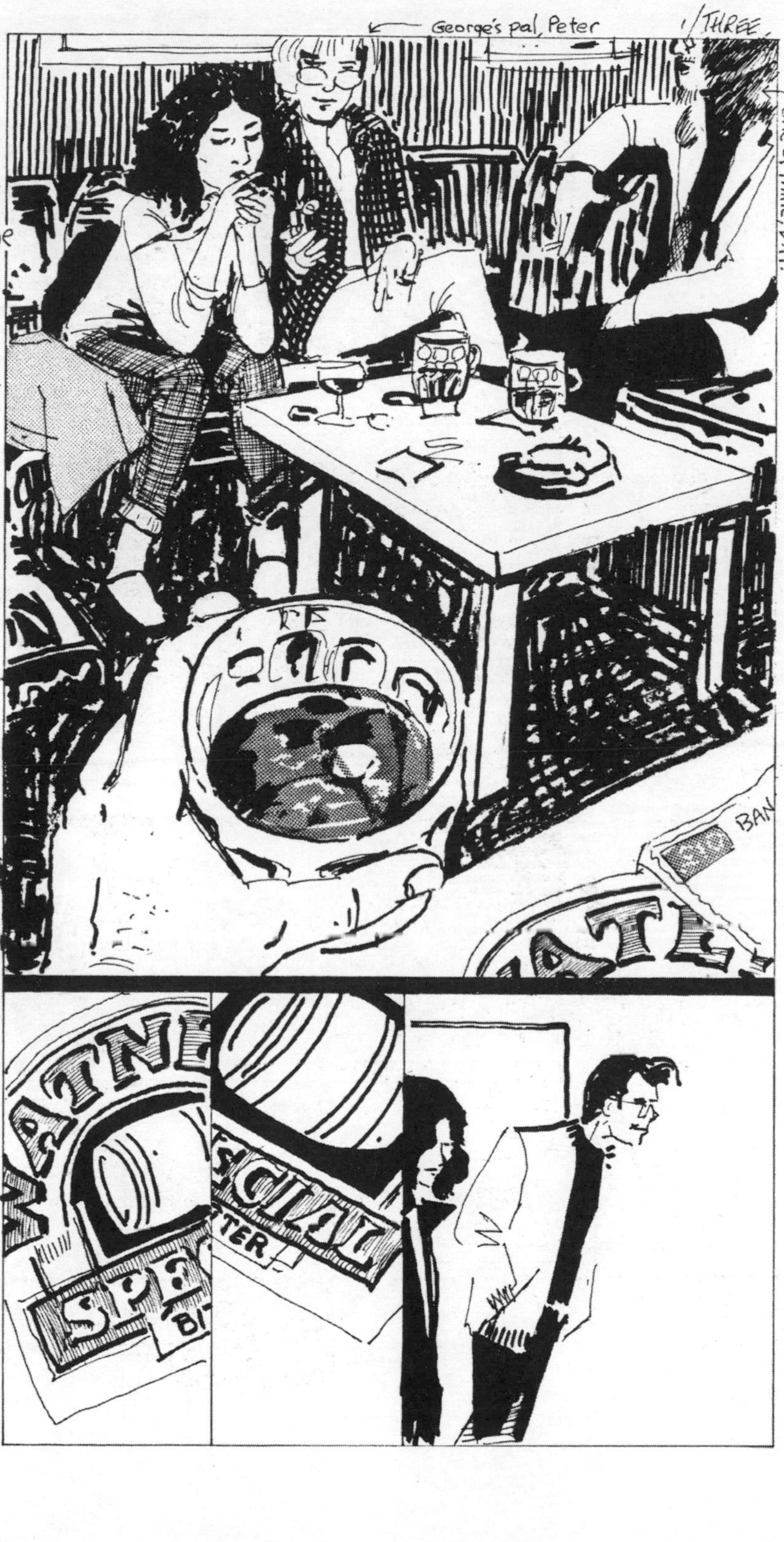
George's pal, Peter
THREE
one of mine, D.H.

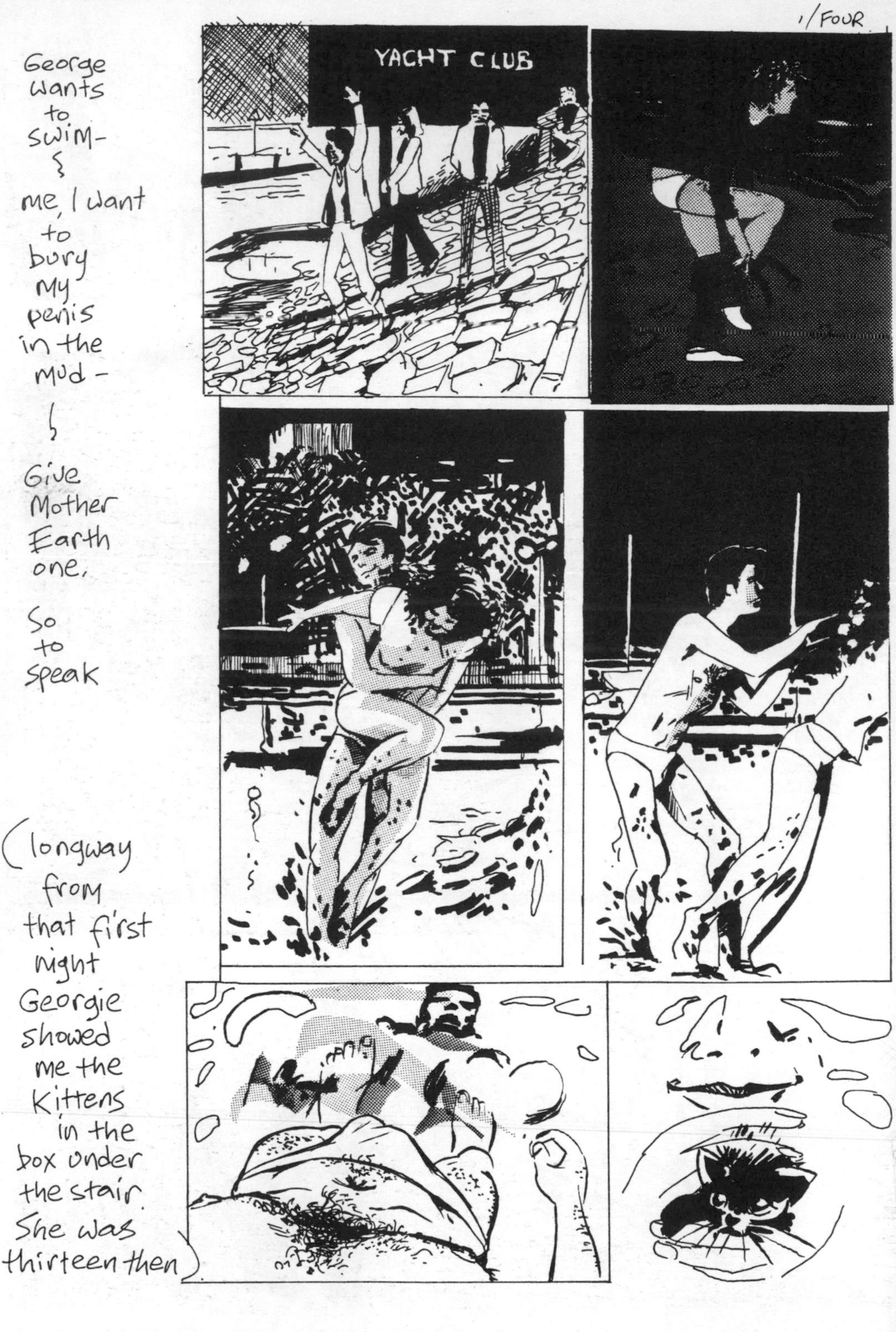
1/FOUR
YACHT CLUB
George wants to swim- & me, I want to bury my penis in the mud- & Give Mother Earth one, So to speak
(longway from that first night Georgie showed me the Kittens in the box under the stair. She was thirteen then)

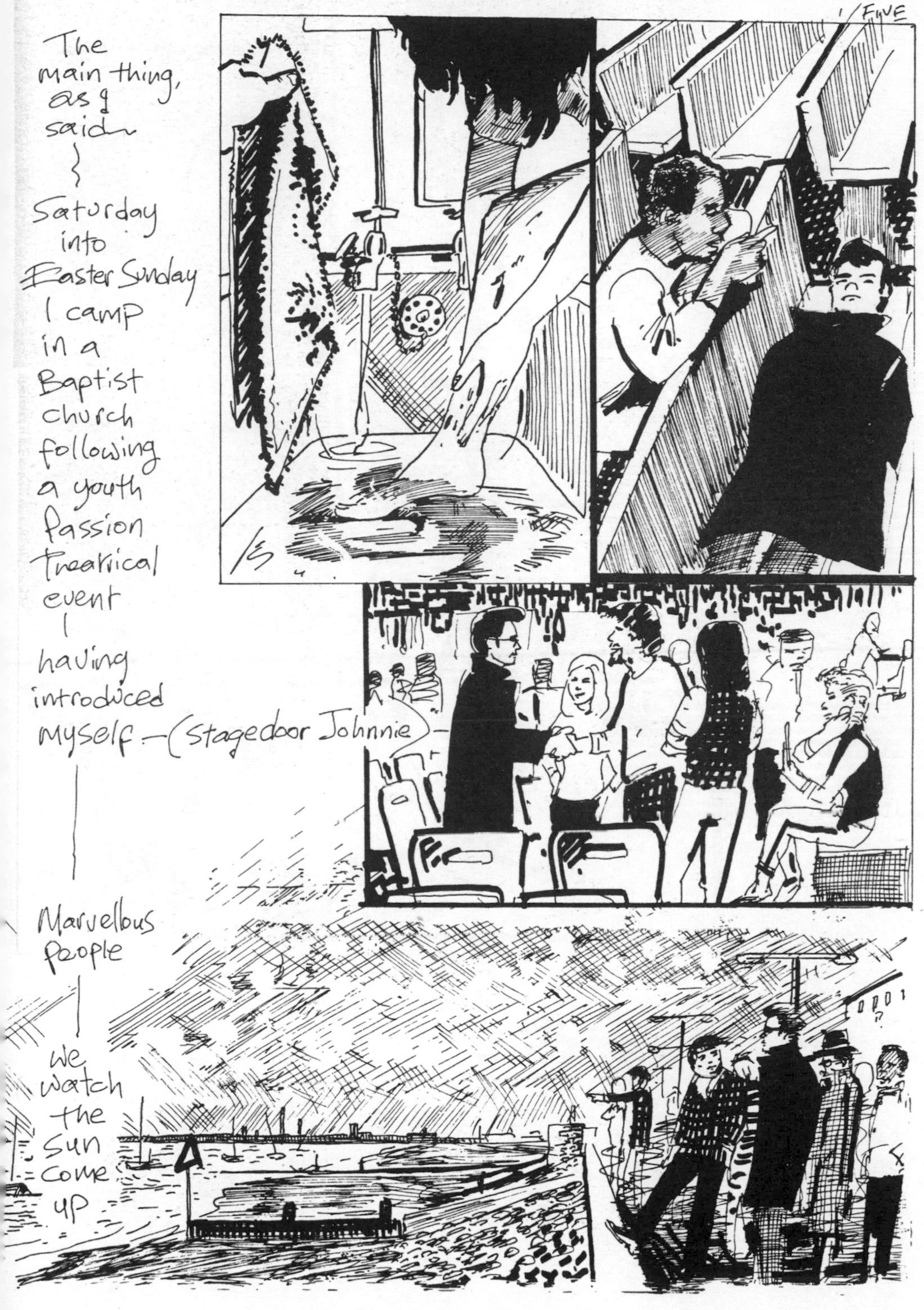
FIVE
The main thing, as I said
Saturday into Easter Sunday I camp in a Baptist church following a youth passion theatrical event
having introduced myself — (Stagedoor Johnnie)
Marvellous people
we watch the sun come up

Sunday Afternoon, then hitch-hiking from A to B I cross her scent_

I Track her down at the folk club

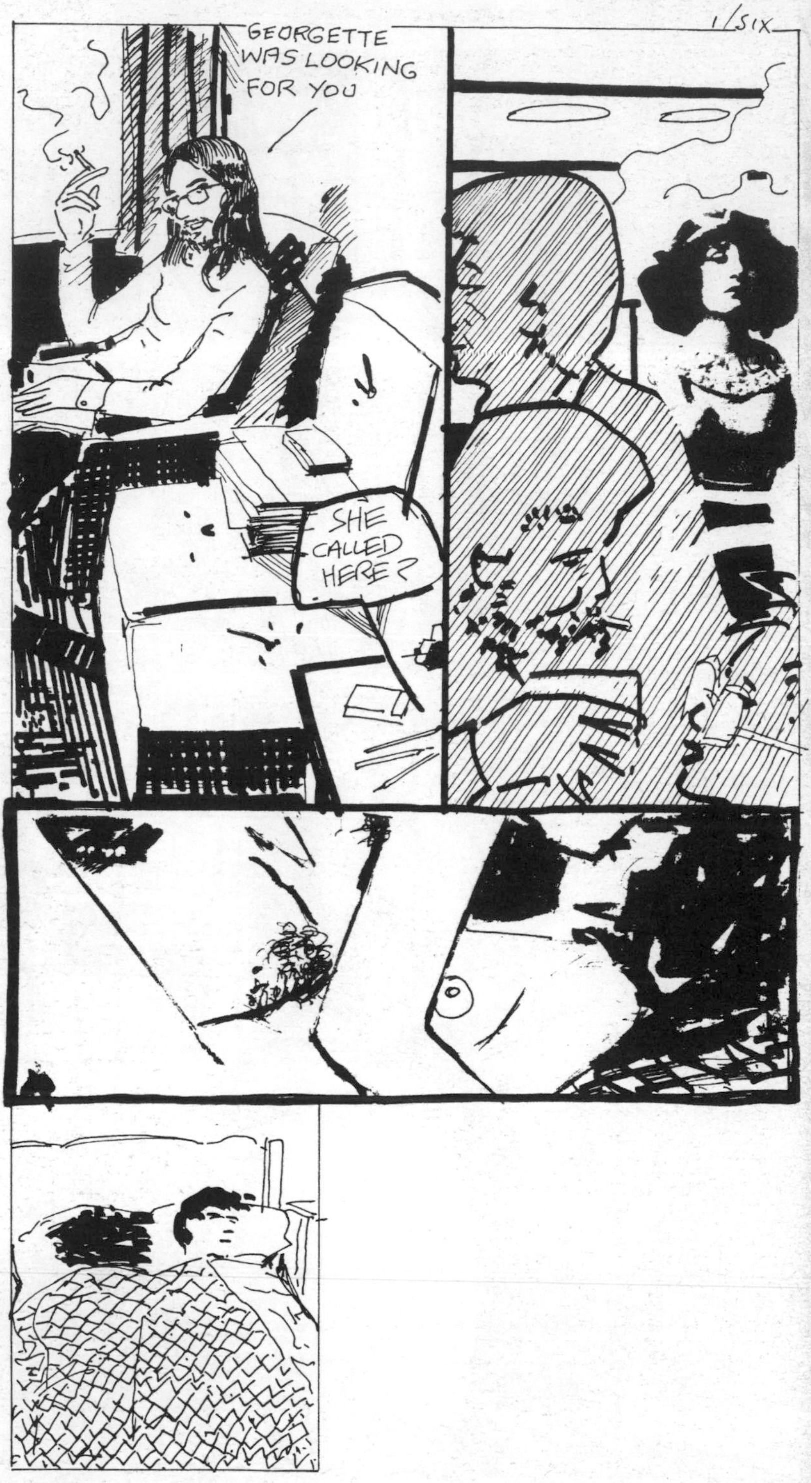
GEORGETTE WAS LOOKING FOR YOU
SHE CALLED HERE?

Night of soulless thrashing about that'll come to worse than nothing

my mouth's a paper bag

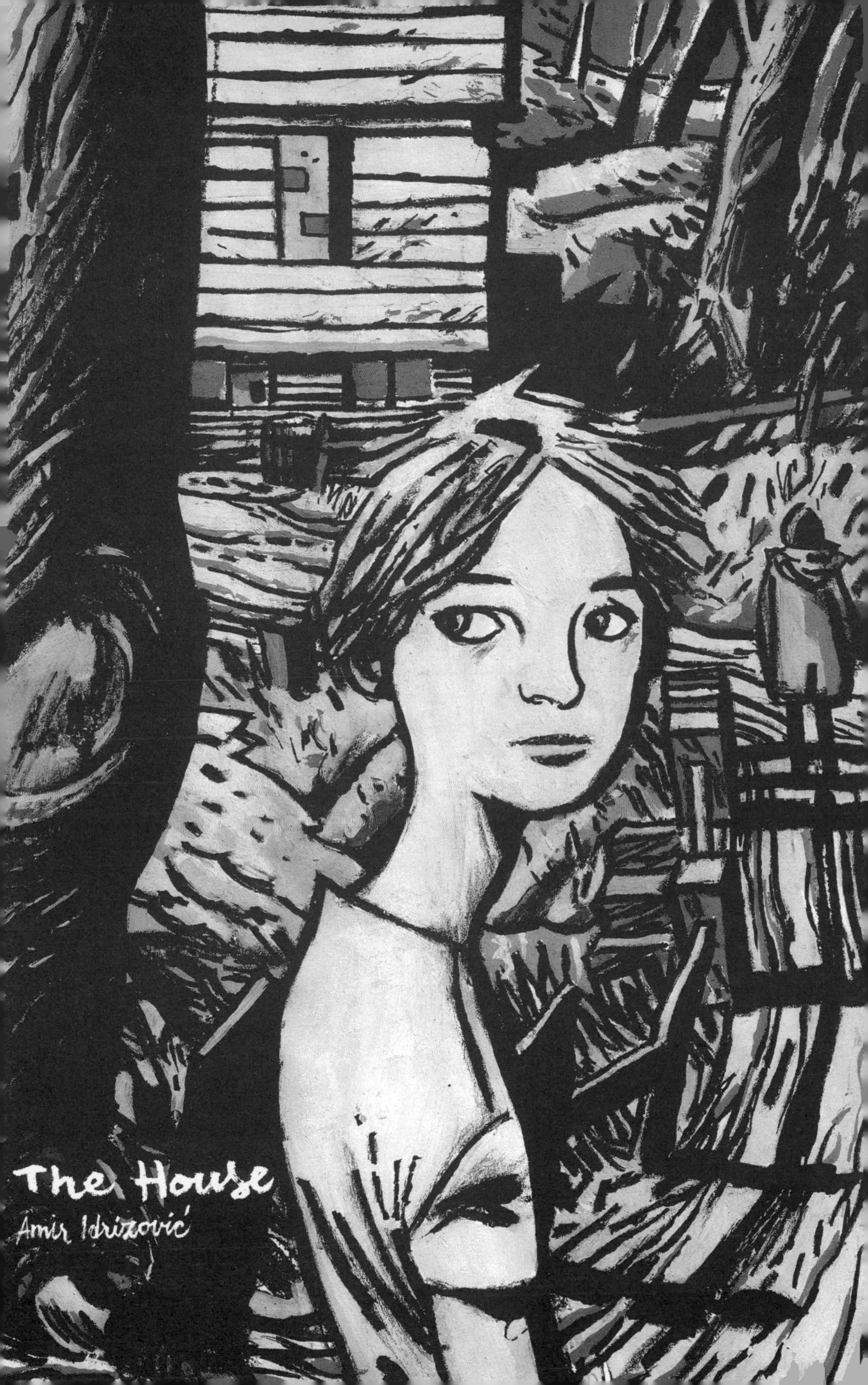
The House
Amir Idrizović

Amir Idrizovic

THE HOUSE
Forum Ljubljana, 2000

Born in Sarajevo, Bosnia, in 1975, Amir is a graduate of
the Sarajevo School of Applied Arts, and Art Academy.

The House first saw publication as part of *Miniburger*
(*Stripburger 28*) – one of twelve mini-comics from
different regional authors, printed separately and
collected in a neat cardboard box. As with other
Stripburger issues having international distribution,
it was printed in English. Exhibited as part of *Traits
Contemporains!* at 2002's Angouleme Festival, the strip
subsequently appeared – translated into French –
in *Bananas* magazine (2006).

"It was something I had started doing for myself
primarily. Finished over the course of several months, it
was an engaging and relaxing project, one of those you
feel good about.

"Since that time I've spent years in advertising, mainly
commercial animation, storyboarding and illustration.
Until only recently comics were no longer a part of my
work life, but I'm currently developing two separate
graphic novels. One of these, in collaboration with a good
friend I made at the Big Torino 2000 arts biennale in
Turin, Italy, will be *Dog Eat Dog*. Watch for it!" – AI

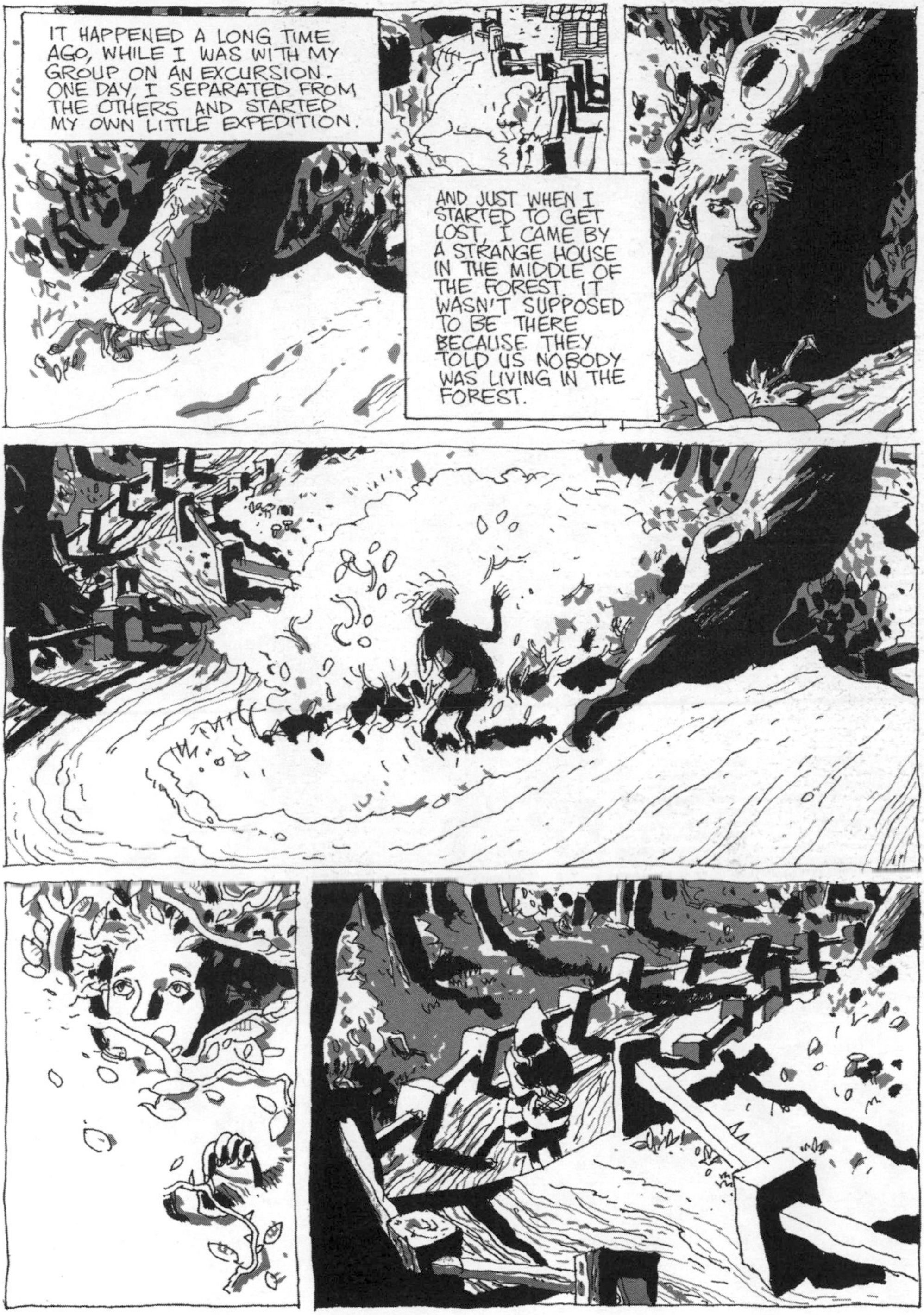
IT HAPPENED A LONG TIME AGO, WHILE I WAS WITH MY GROUP ON AN EXCURSION. ONE DAY, I SEPARATED FROM THE OTHERS AND STARTED MY OWN LITTLE EXPEDITION.
AND JUST WHEN I STARTED TO GET LOST, I CAME BY A STRANGE HOUSE IN THE MIDDLE OF THE FOREST. IT WASN'T SUPPOSED TO BE THERE BECAUSE THEY TOLD US NOBODY WAS LIVING IN THE FOREST.

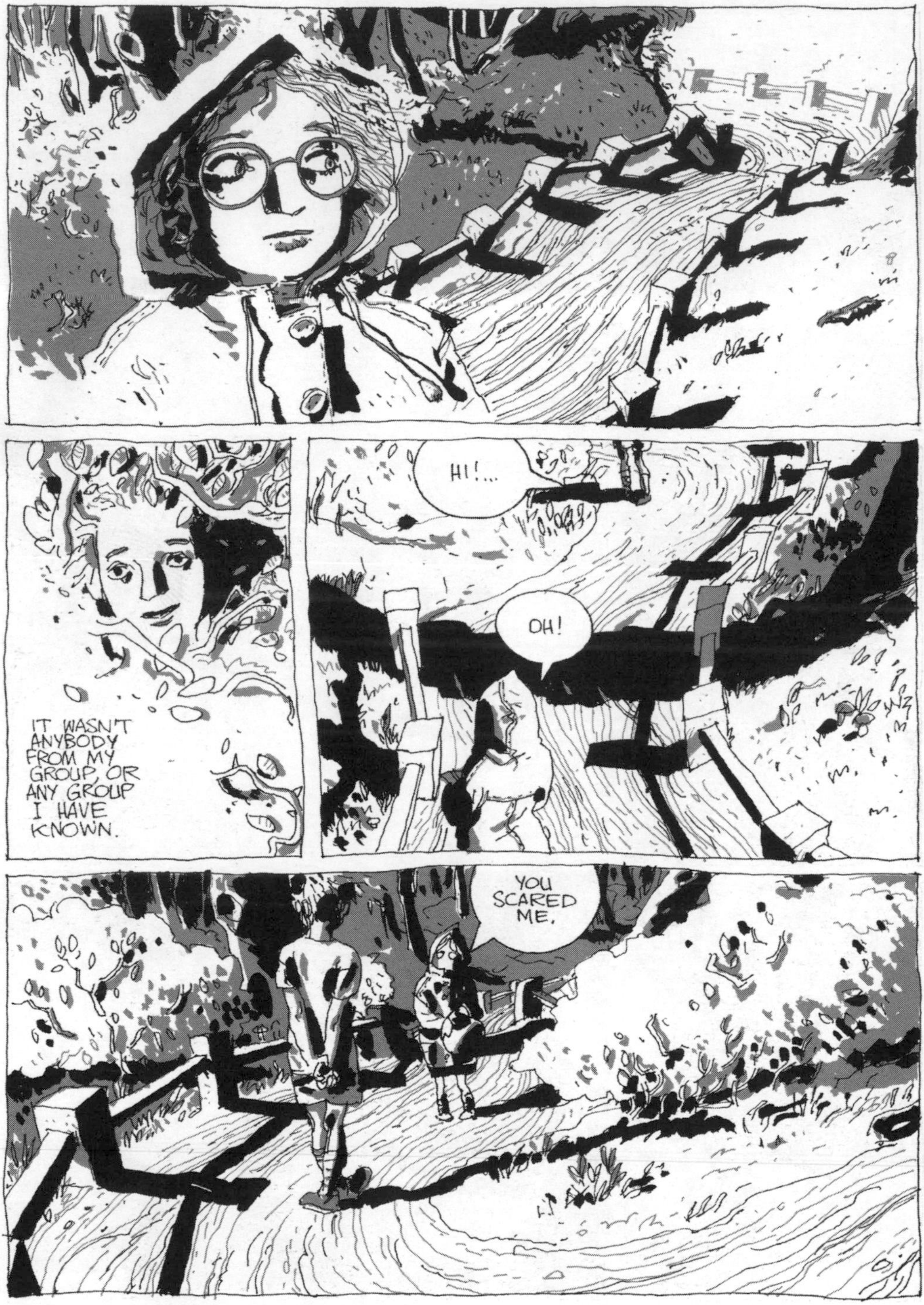
IT WASN'T ANYBODY FROM MY GROUP, OR ANY GROUP I HAVE KNOWN.
HI!...
OH!
YOU SCARED ME.

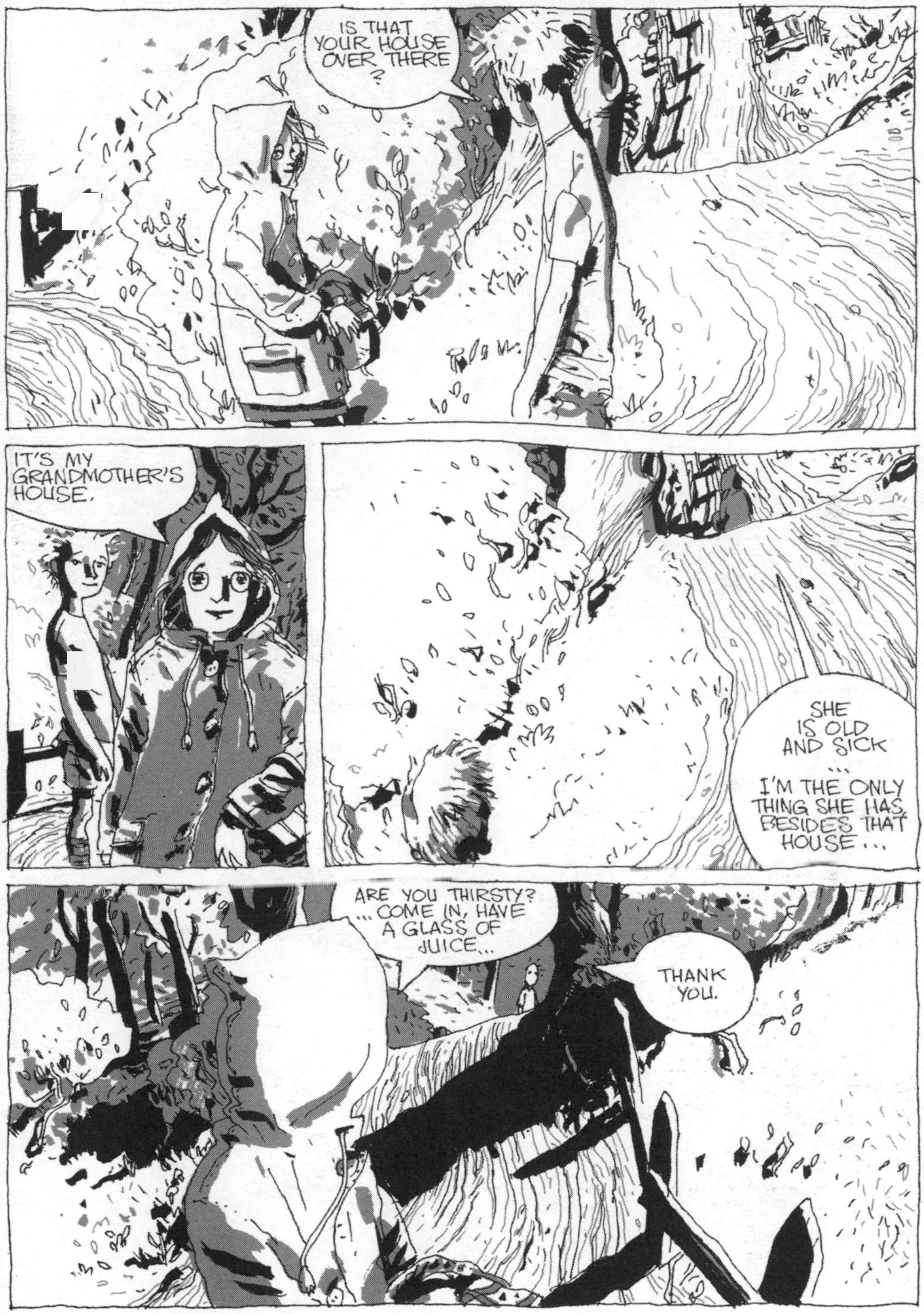
IS THAT YOUR HOUSE OVER THERE ?
IT'S MY GRANDMOTHER'S HOUSE.
SHE IS OLD AND SICK ... I'M THE ONLY THING SHE HAS BESIDES THAT HOUSE...
ARE YOU THIRSTY? ...COME IN, HAVE A GLASS OF JUICE...
THANK YOU.

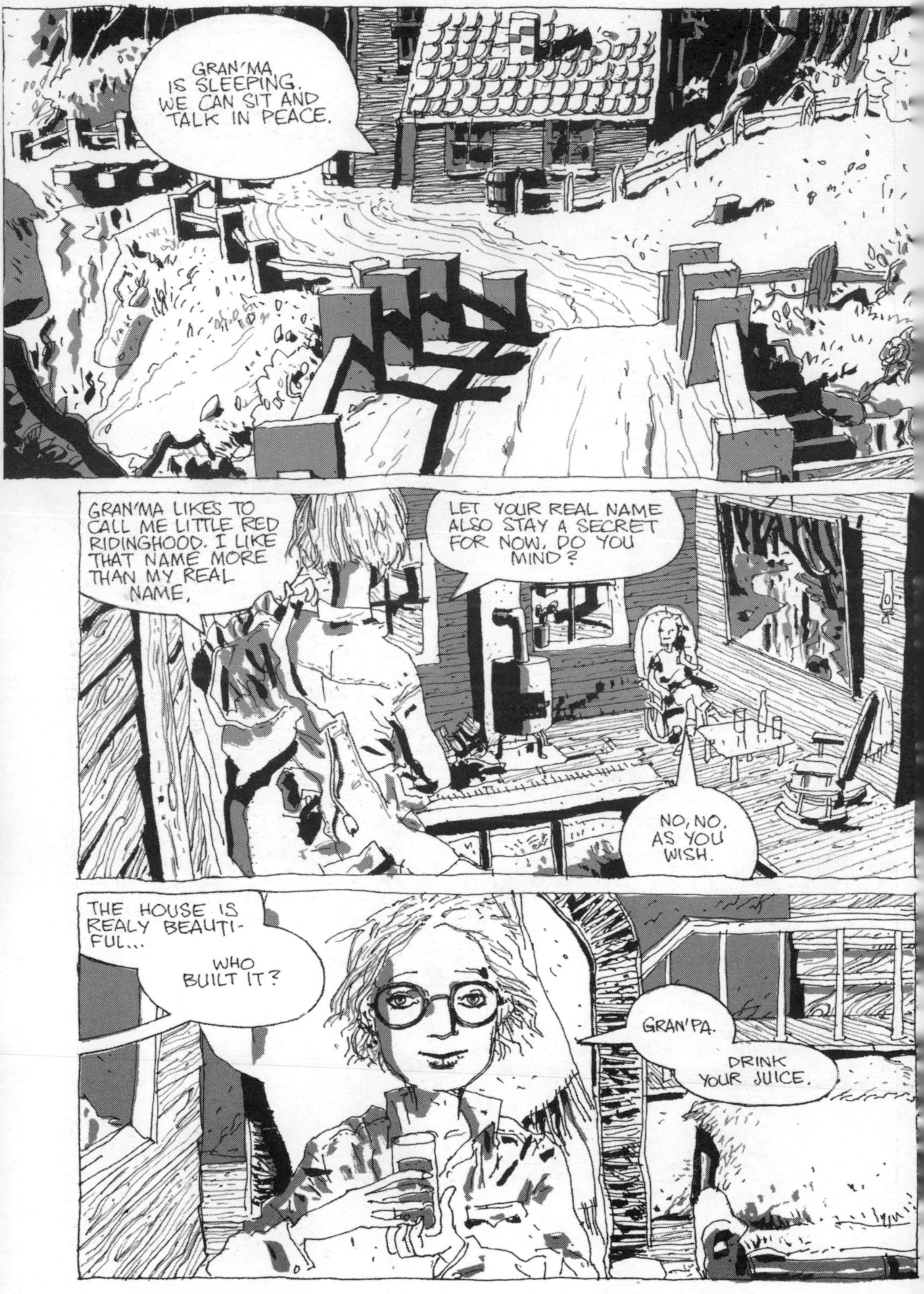
GRAN'MA IS SLEEPING. WE CAN SIT AND TALK IN PEACE.
GRAN'MA LIKES TO CALL ME LITTLE RED RIDINGHOOD. I LIKE THAT NAME MORE THAN MY REAL NAME.
LET YOUR REAL NAME ALSO STAY A SECRET FOR NOW, DO YOU MIND?
NO, NO, AS YOU WISH.
THE HOUSE IS REALY BEAUTI-FUL...
WHO BUILT IT?
GRAN'PA.
DRINK YOUR JUICE.

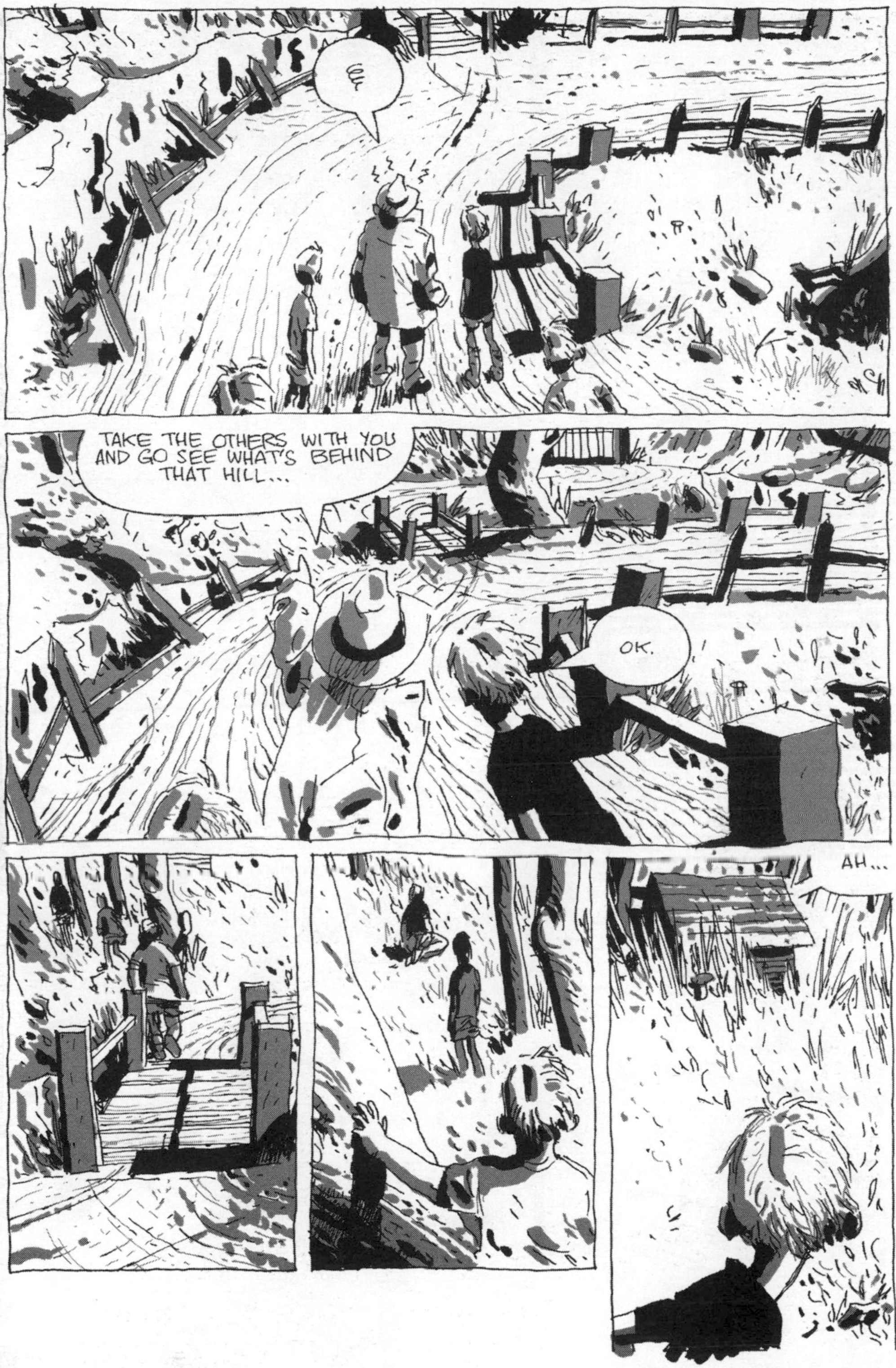
TAKE THE OTHERS WITH YOU AND GO SEE WHAT'S BEHIND THAT HILL...
OK.
AH...

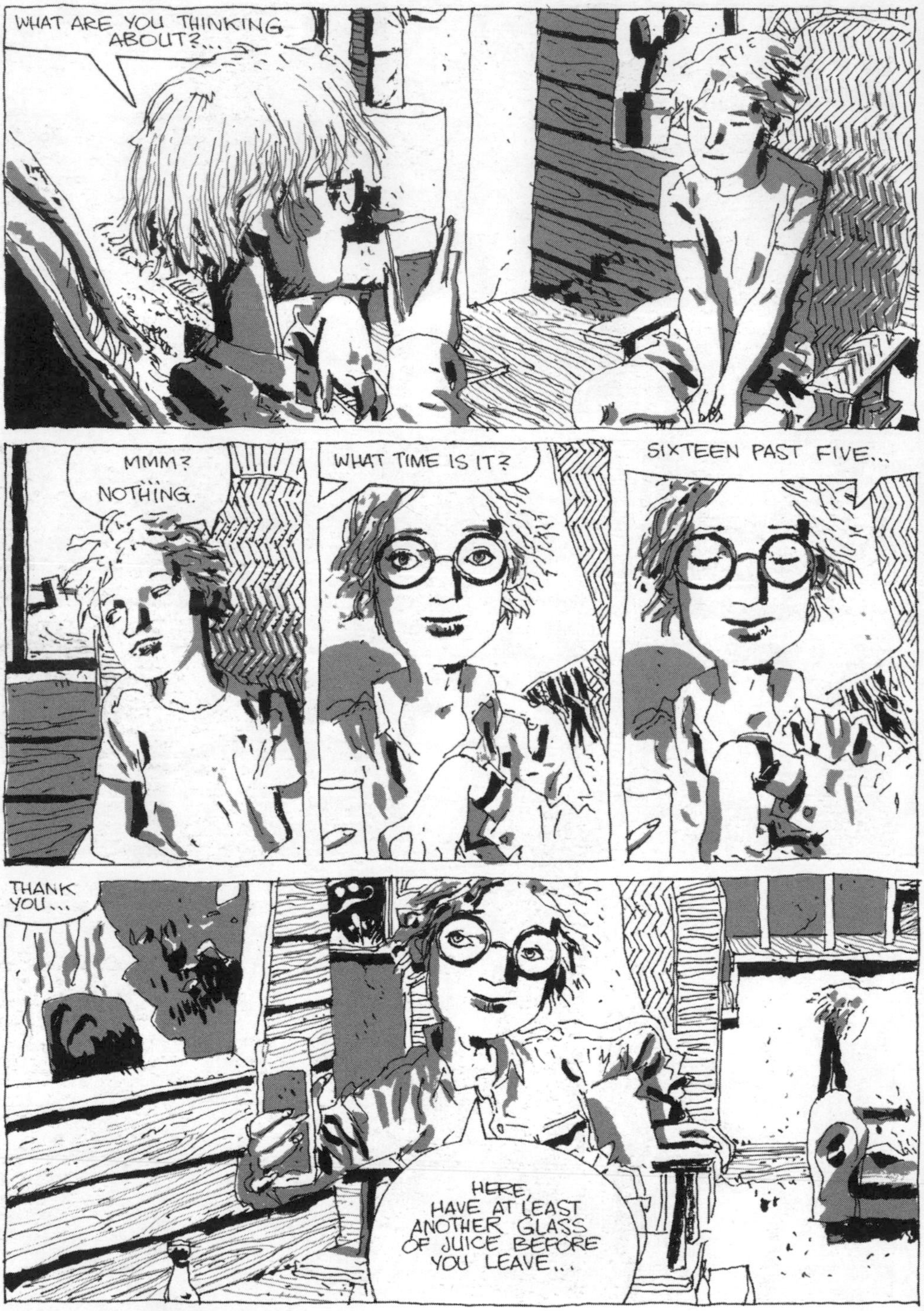
WHAT ARE YOU THINKING ABOUT?...
MMM? ... NOTHING.
WHAT TIME IS IT?
SIXTEEN PAST FIVE...
THANK YOU...
HERE, HAVE AT LEAST ANOTHER GLASS OF JUICE BEFORE YOU LEAVE...

WELL, I DON'T REALLY WANT TO GO BACK, BUT ...

SO DON'T.

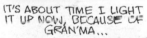

DO YOU MAKE FIRE IN IT?

YUP...

IT'S ABOUT TIME I LIGHT IT UP NOW, BECAUSE OF GRAN'MA...

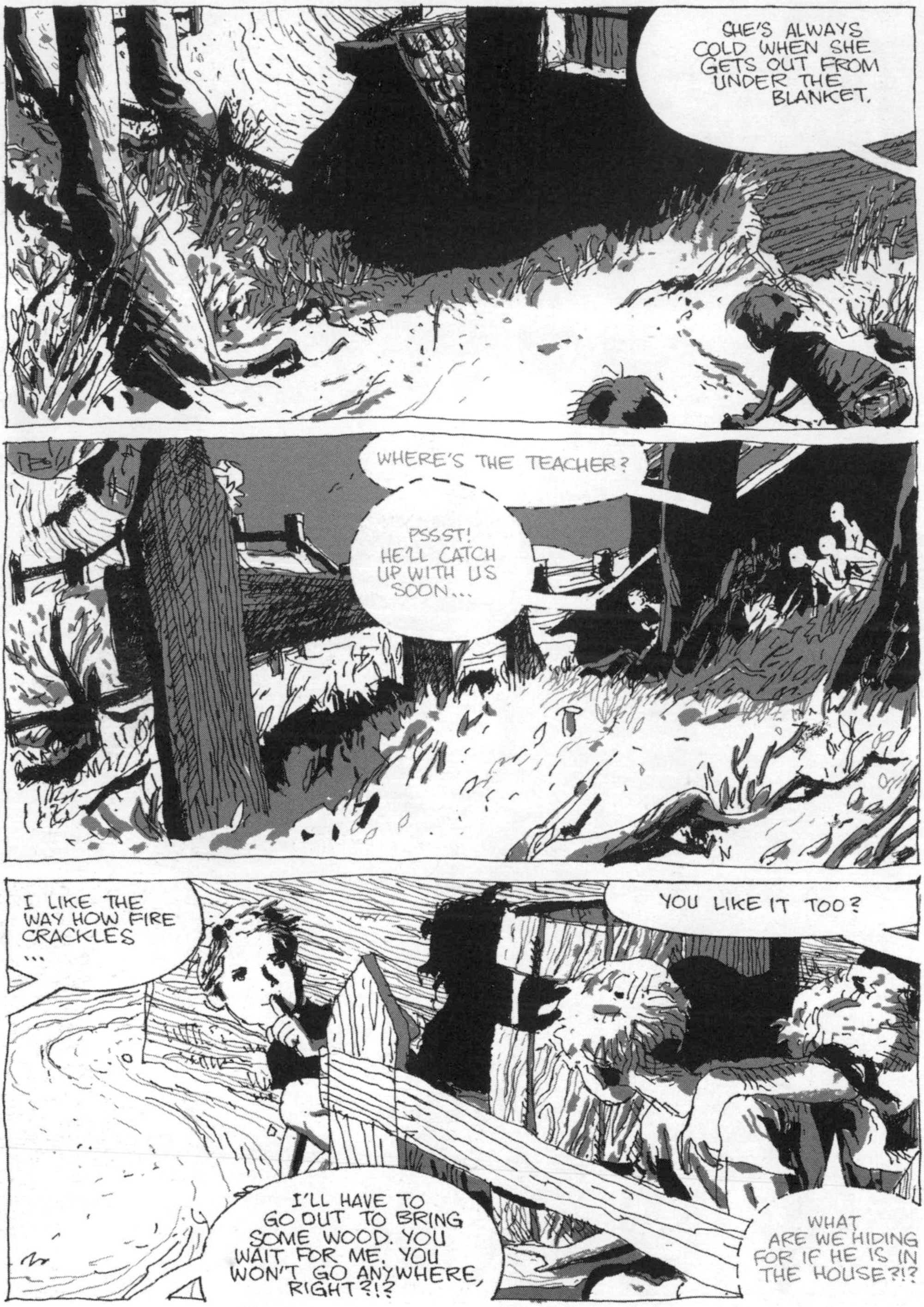
SHE'S ALWAYS COLD WHEN SHE GETS OUT FROM UNDER THE BLANKET.
WHERE'S THE TEACHER?
PSSST! HE'LL CATCH UP WITH US SOON...
I LIKE THE WAY HOW FIRE CRACKLES ...
YOU LIKE IT TOO?
I'LL HAVE TO GO OUT TO BRING SOME WOOD. YOU WAIT FOR ME. YOU WON'T GO ANYWHERE, RIGHT?!?
WHAT ARE WE HIDING FOR IF HE IS IN THE HOUSE?!?

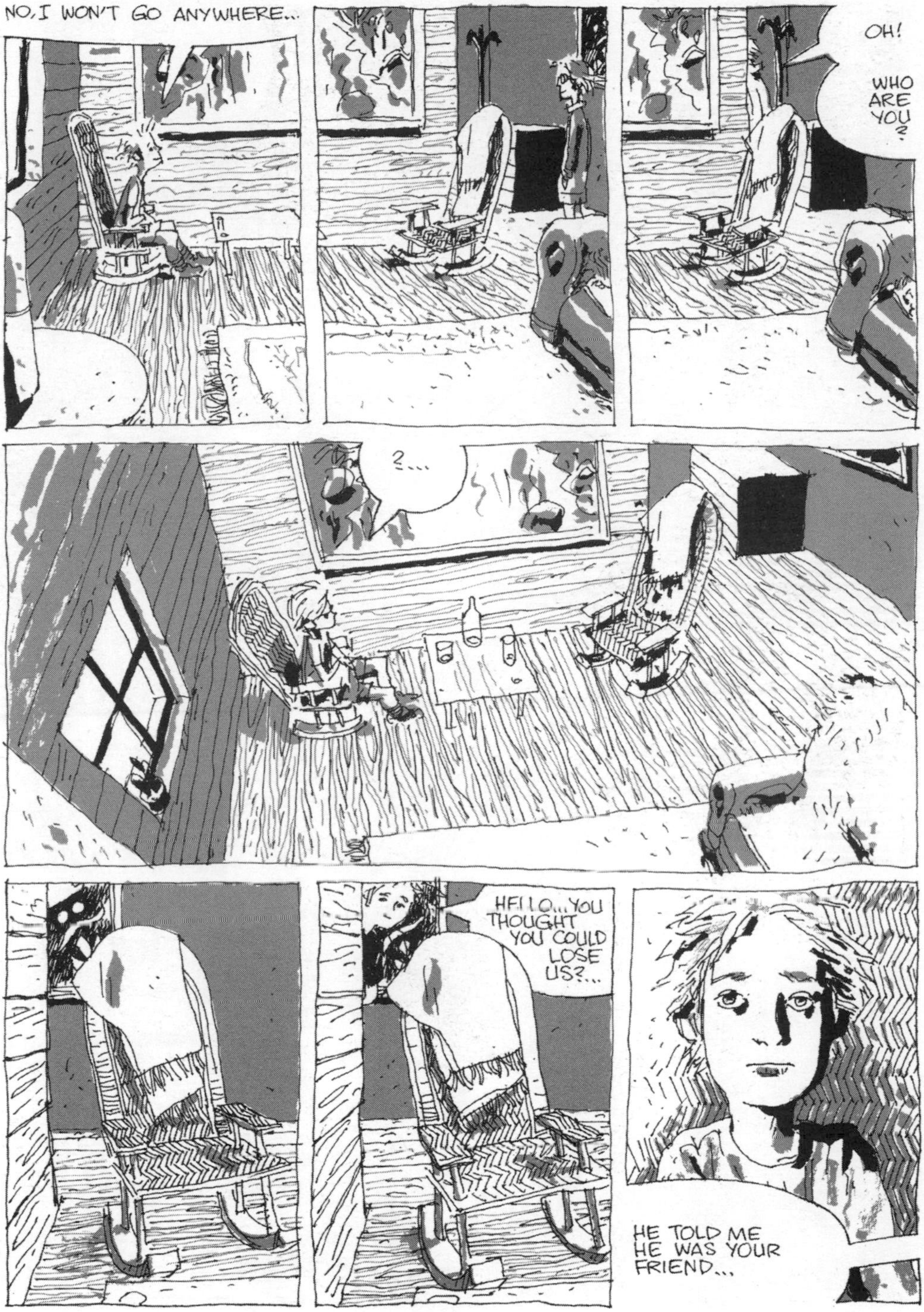
NO, I WON'T GO ANYWHERE...
OH!
WHO ARE YOU?
?...
HELLO... YOU THOUGHT YOU COULD LOSE US?...
HE TOLD ME HE WAS YOUR FRIEND...

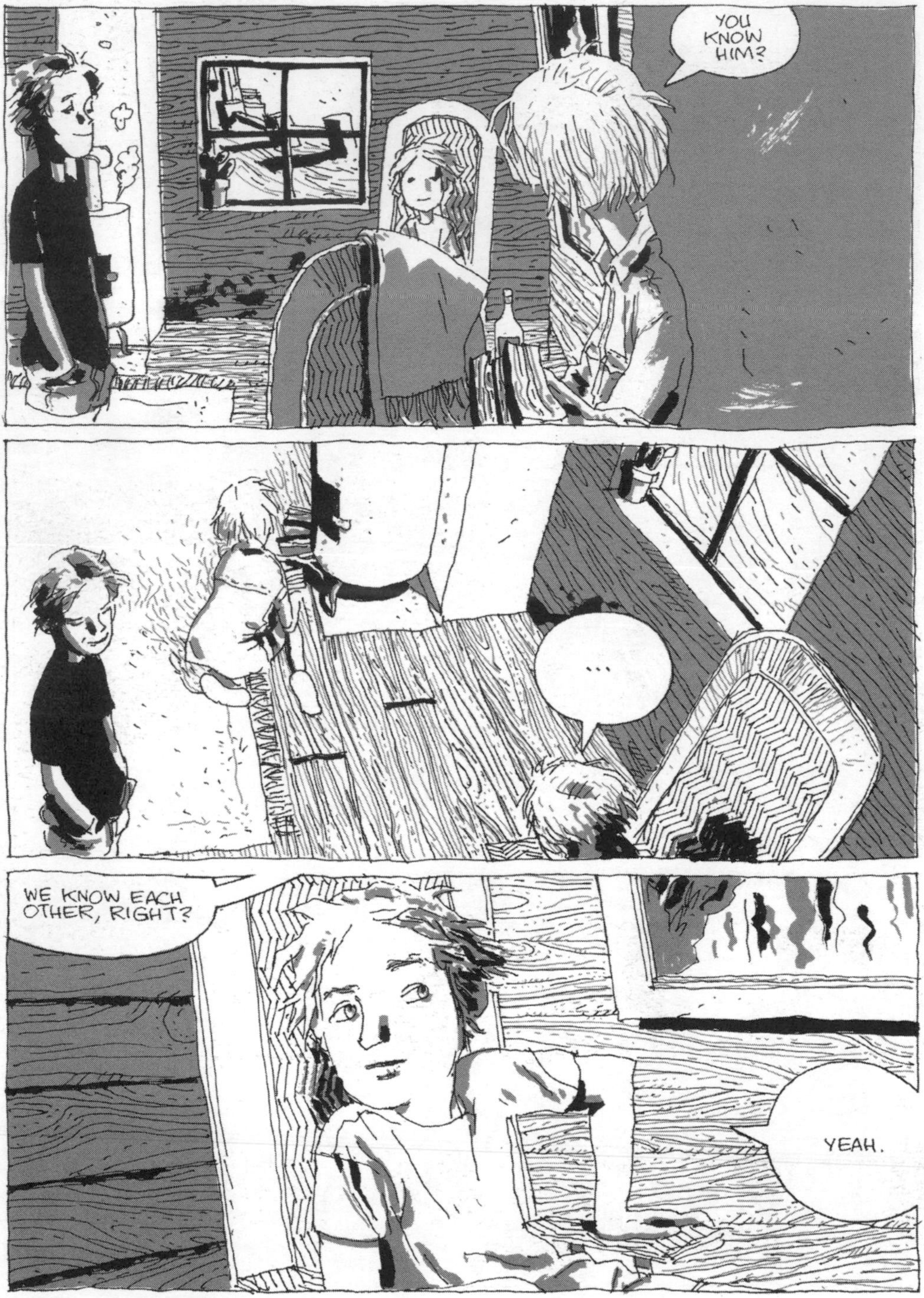
YOU KNOW HIM?
...
WE KNOW EACH OTHER, RIGHT?
YEAH.

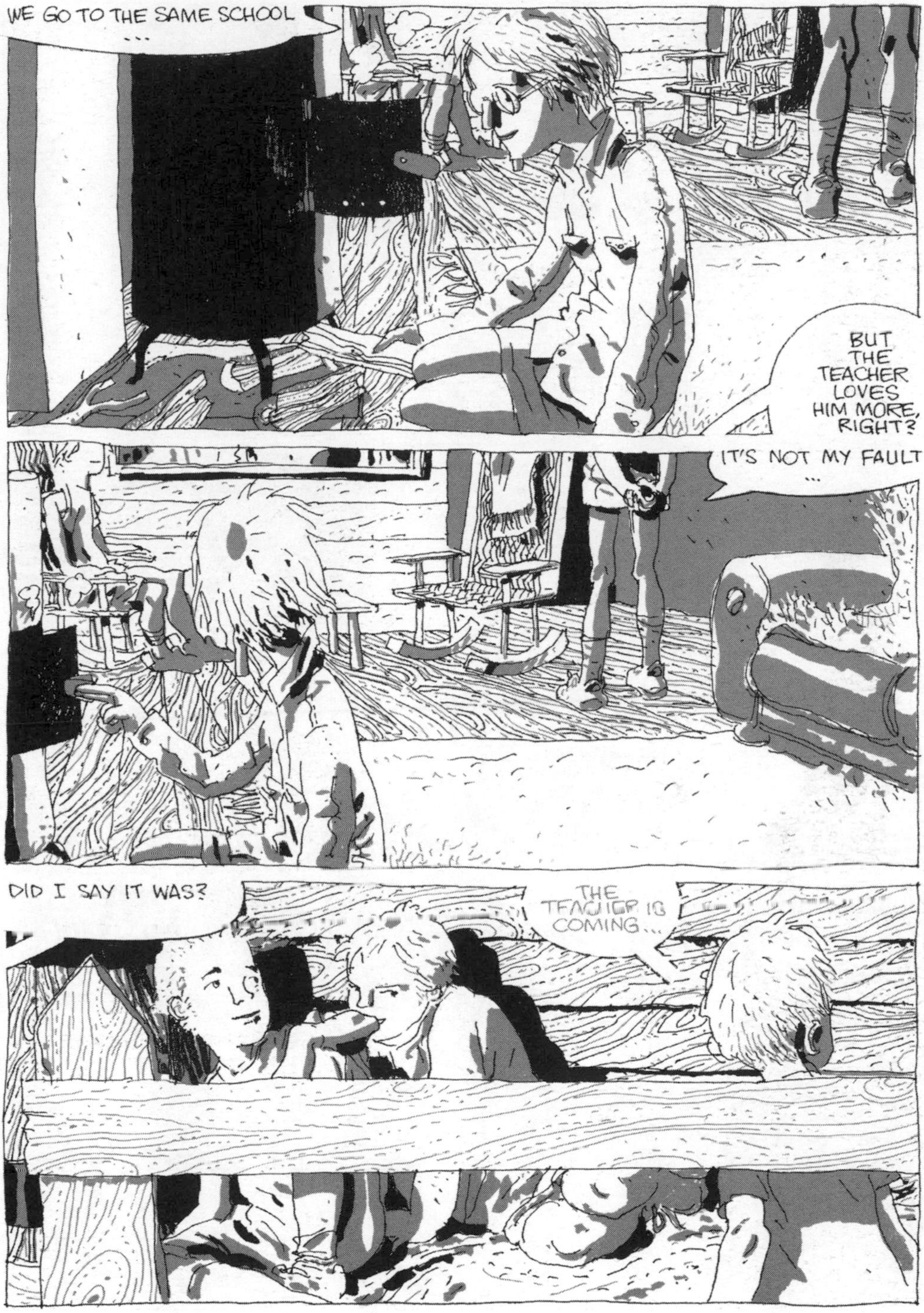
WE GO TO THE SAME SCHOOL ...
BUT THE TEACHER LOVES HIM MORE, RIGHT?
IT'S NOT MY FAULT ...
DID I SAY IT WAS?
THE TEACHER IS COMING...

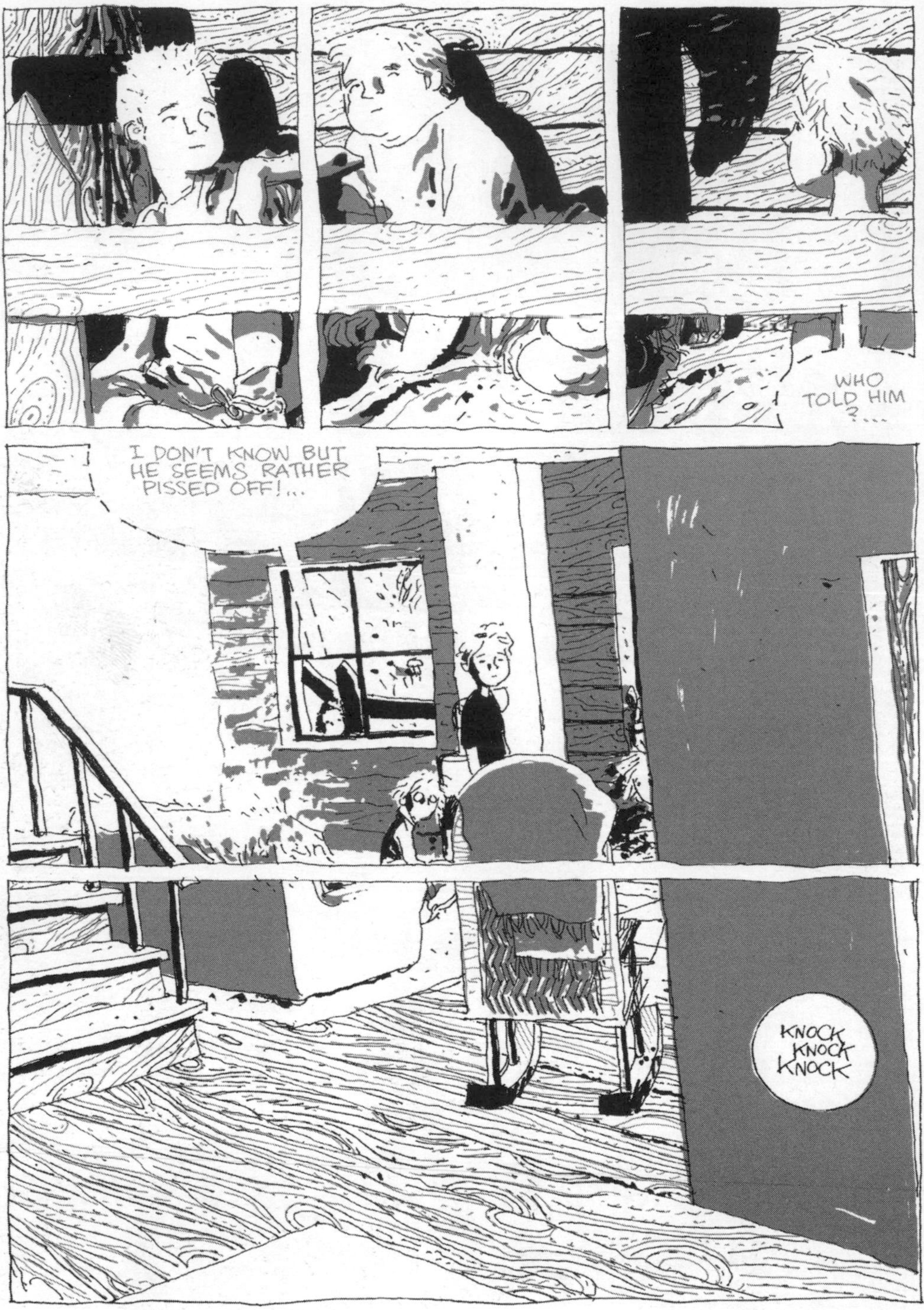
WHO TOLD HIM ?...
I DON'T KNOW BUT HE SEEMS RATHER PISSED OFF!...
KNOCK KNOCK KNOCK

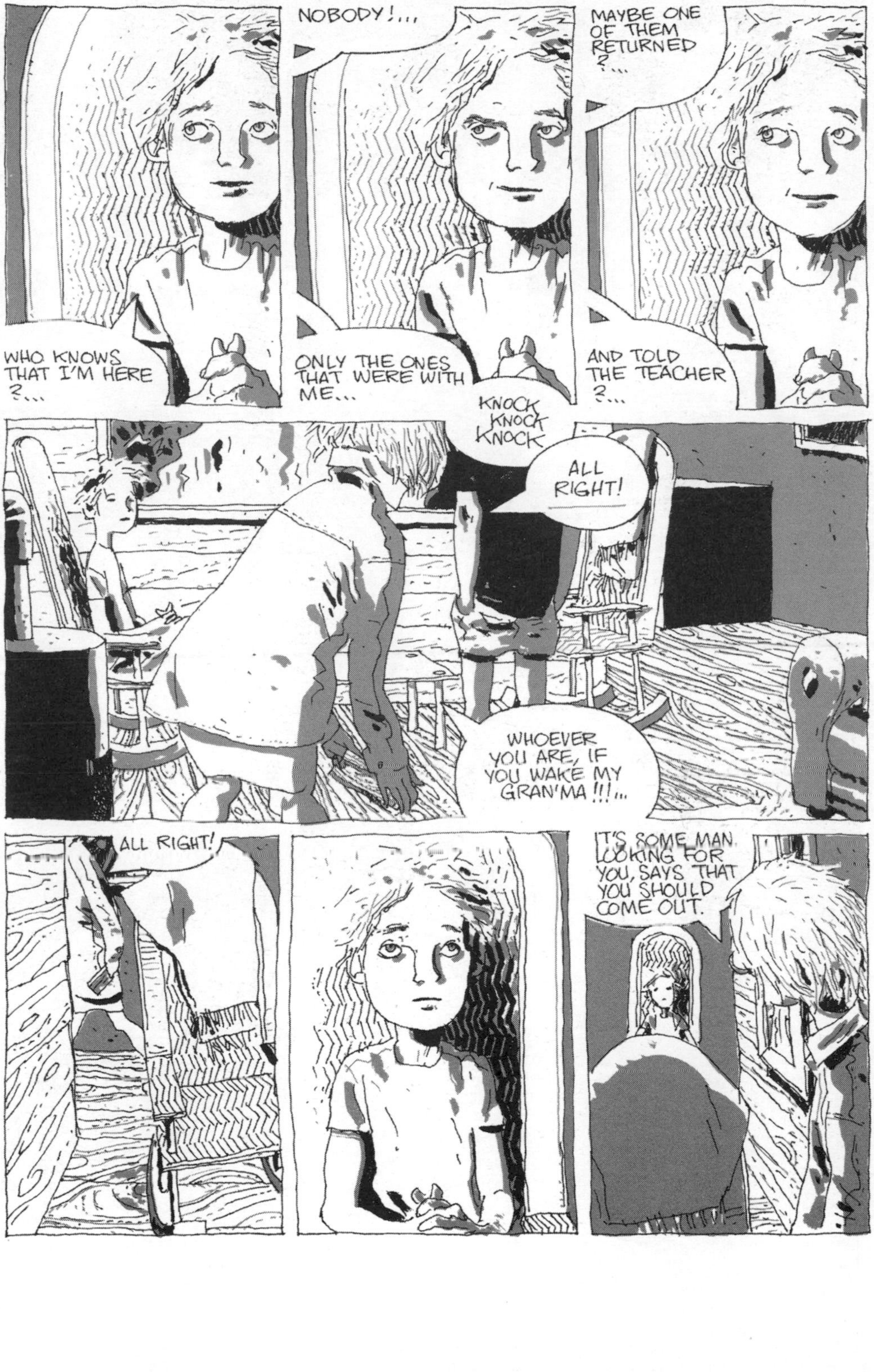
WHO KNOWS THAT I'M HERE ?...
NOBODY!...
ONLY THE ONES THAT WERE WITH ME...
MAYBE ONE OF THEM RETURNED ?...
AND TOLD THE TEACHER ?...
KNOCK KNOCK KNOCK
ALL RIGHT!
WHOEVER YOU ARE, IF YOU WAKE MY GRAN'MA !!!...
ALL RIGHT!
IT'S SOME MAN LOOKING FOR YOU, SAYS THAT YOU SHOULD COME OUT.

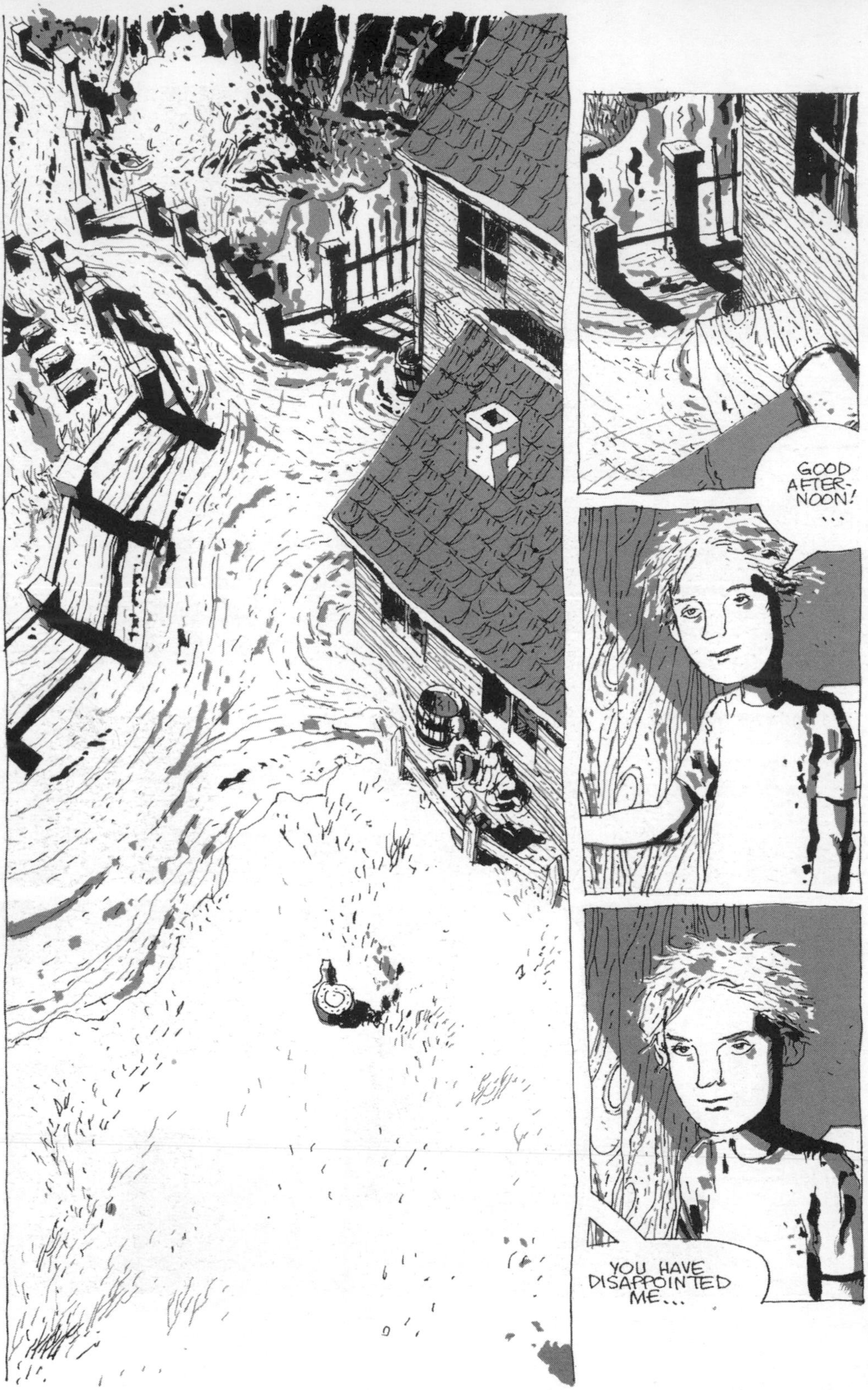
GOOD AFTERNOON! ...
YOU HAVE DISAPPOINTED ME...

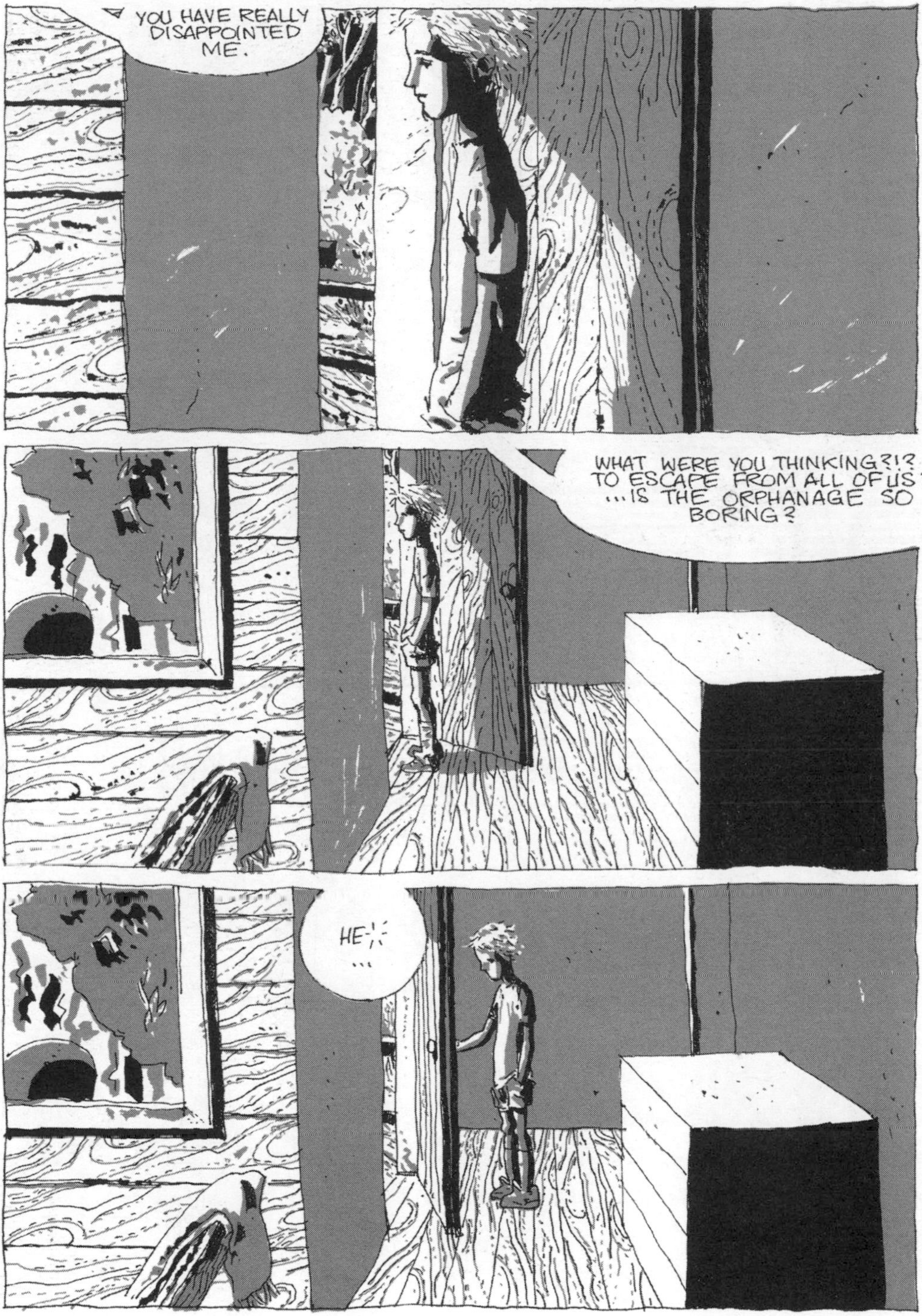
YOU HAVE REALLY DISAPPOINTED ME.
WHAT WERE YOU THINKING?!? TO ESCAPE FROM ALL OF US? ...IS THE ORPHANAGE SO BORING?
HE... ...

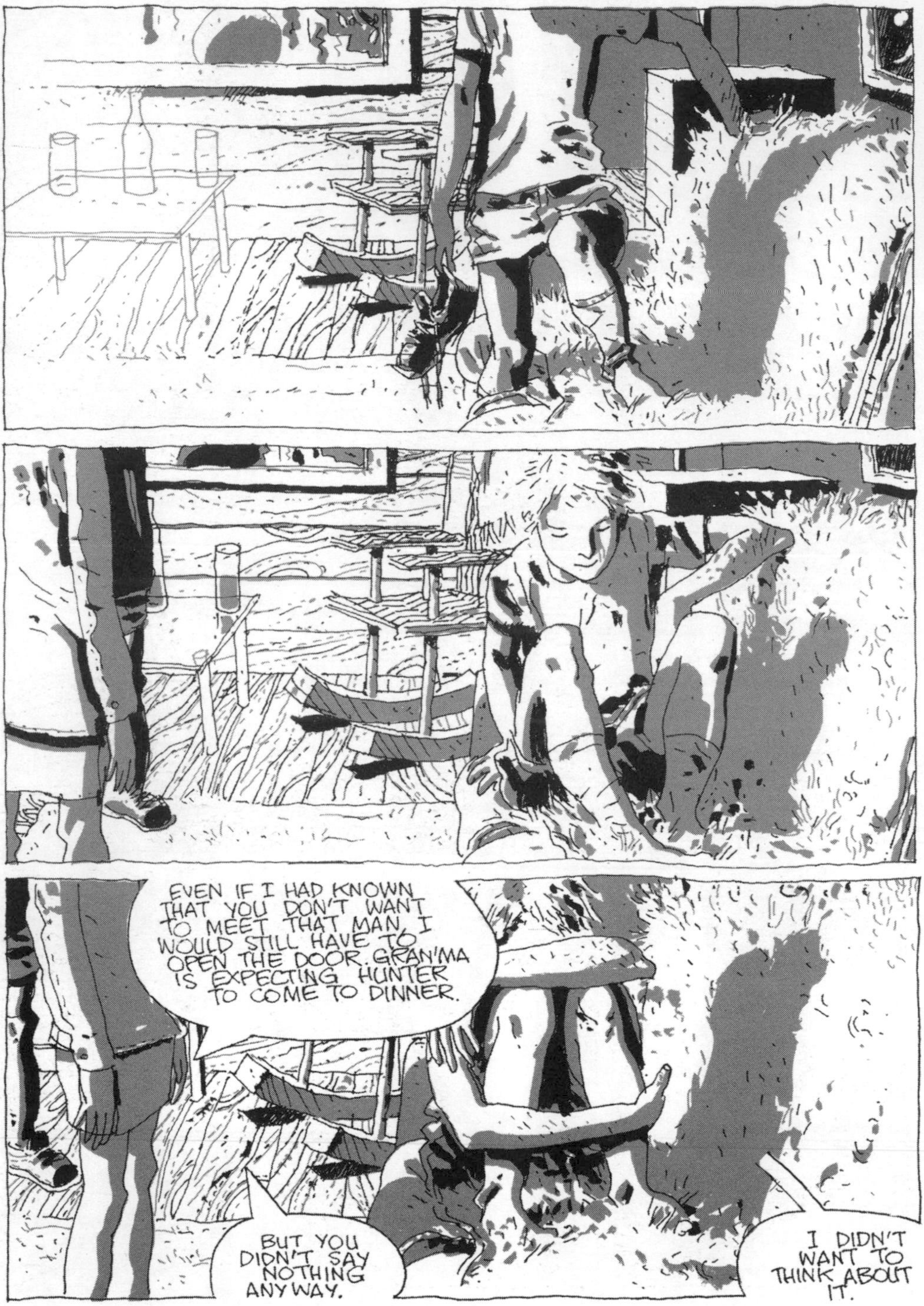
EVEN IF I HAD KNOWN THAT YOU DON'T WANT TO MEET THAT MAN, I WOULD STILL HAVE TO OPEN THE DOOR. GRAN'MA IS EXPECTING HUNTER TO COME TO DINNER.
BUT YOU DIDN'T SAY NOTHING ANYWAY.
I DIDN'T WANT TO THINK ABOUT IT.

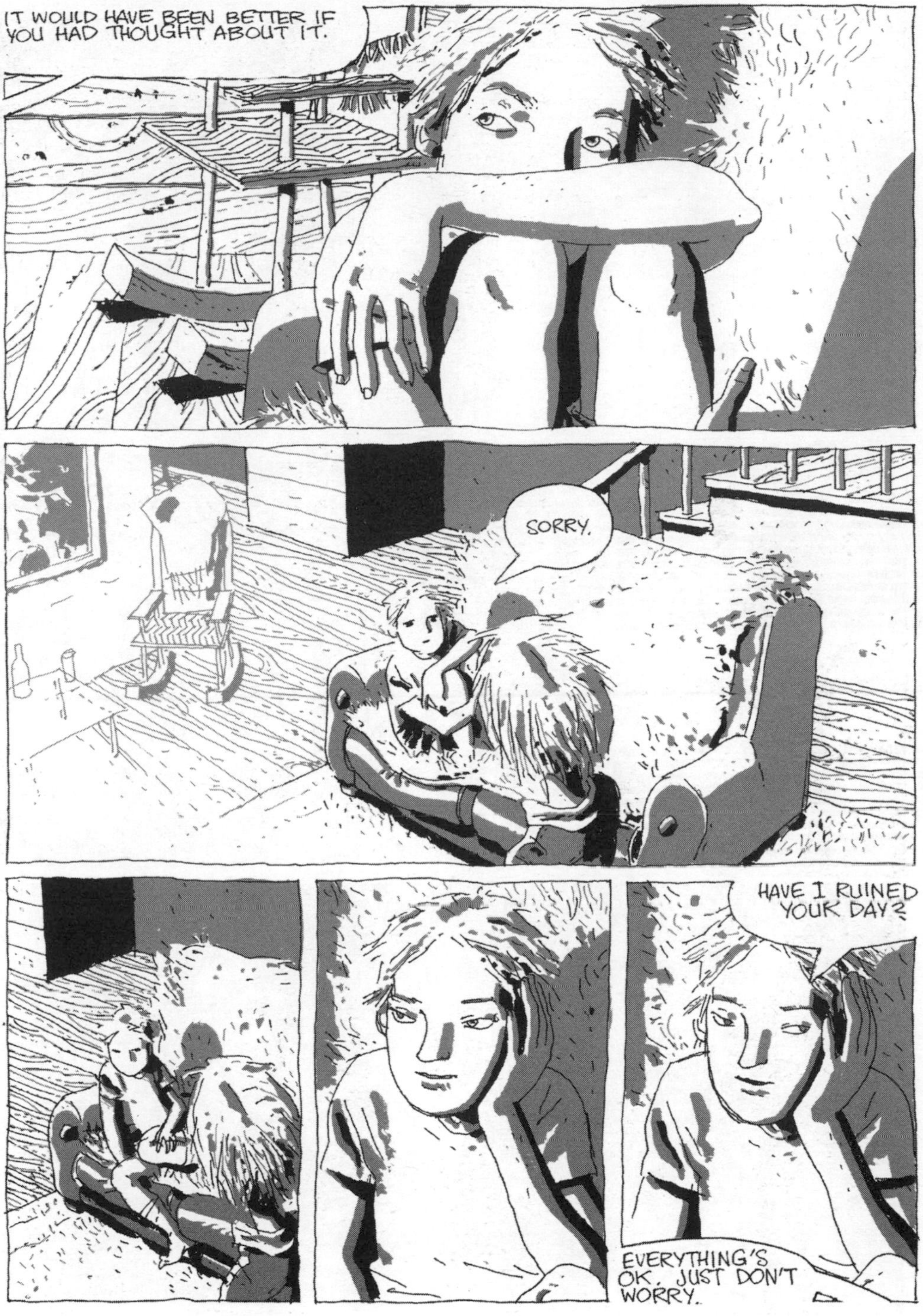
IT WOULD HAVE BEEN BETTER IF YOU HAD THOUGHT ABOUT IT.
SORRY.
HAVE I RUINED YOUR DAY?
EVERYTHING'S OK. JUST DON'T WORRY.

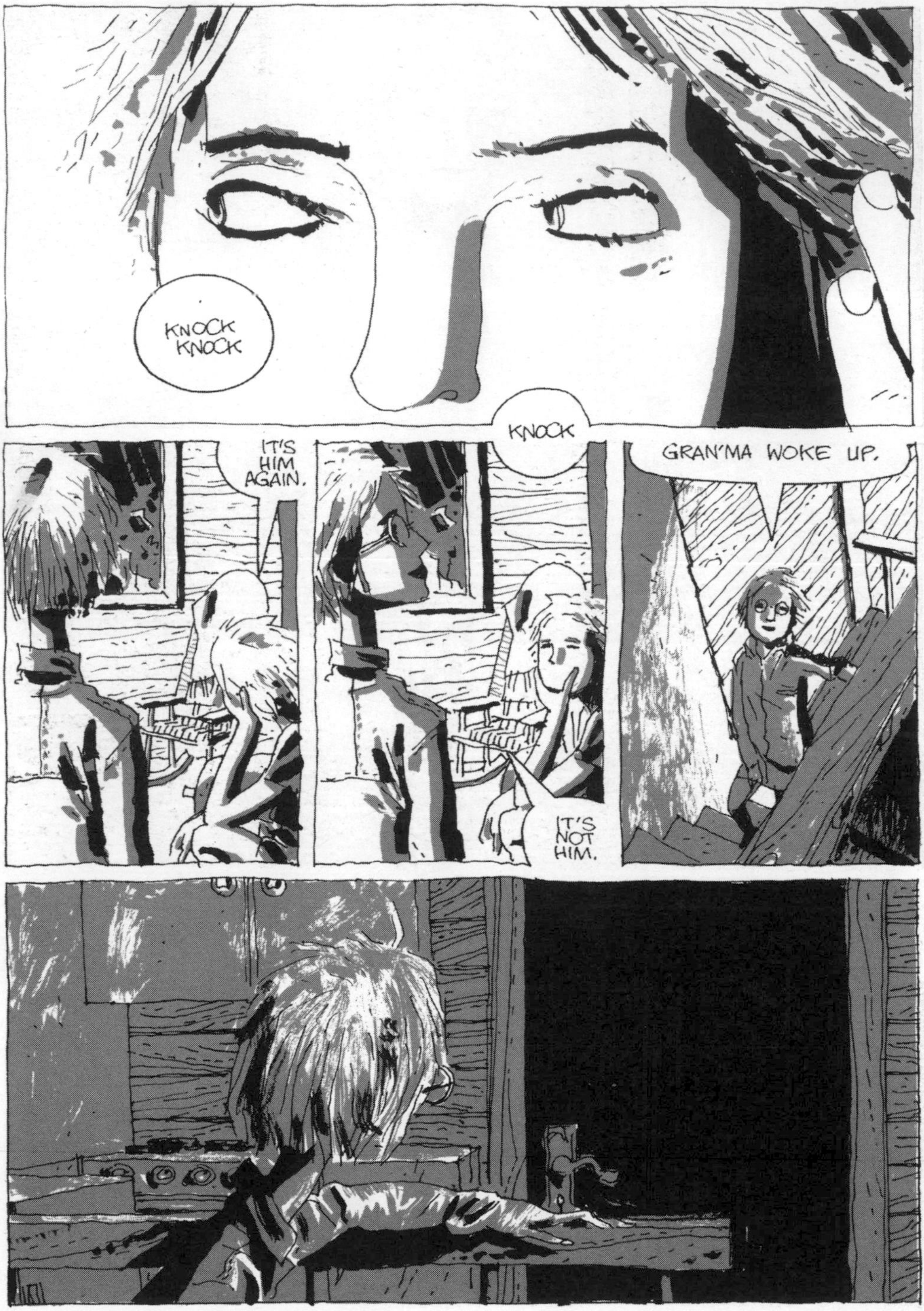
KNOCK KNOCK
IT'S HIM AGAIN.
KNOCK
IT'S NOT HIM.
GRAN'MA WOKE UP.

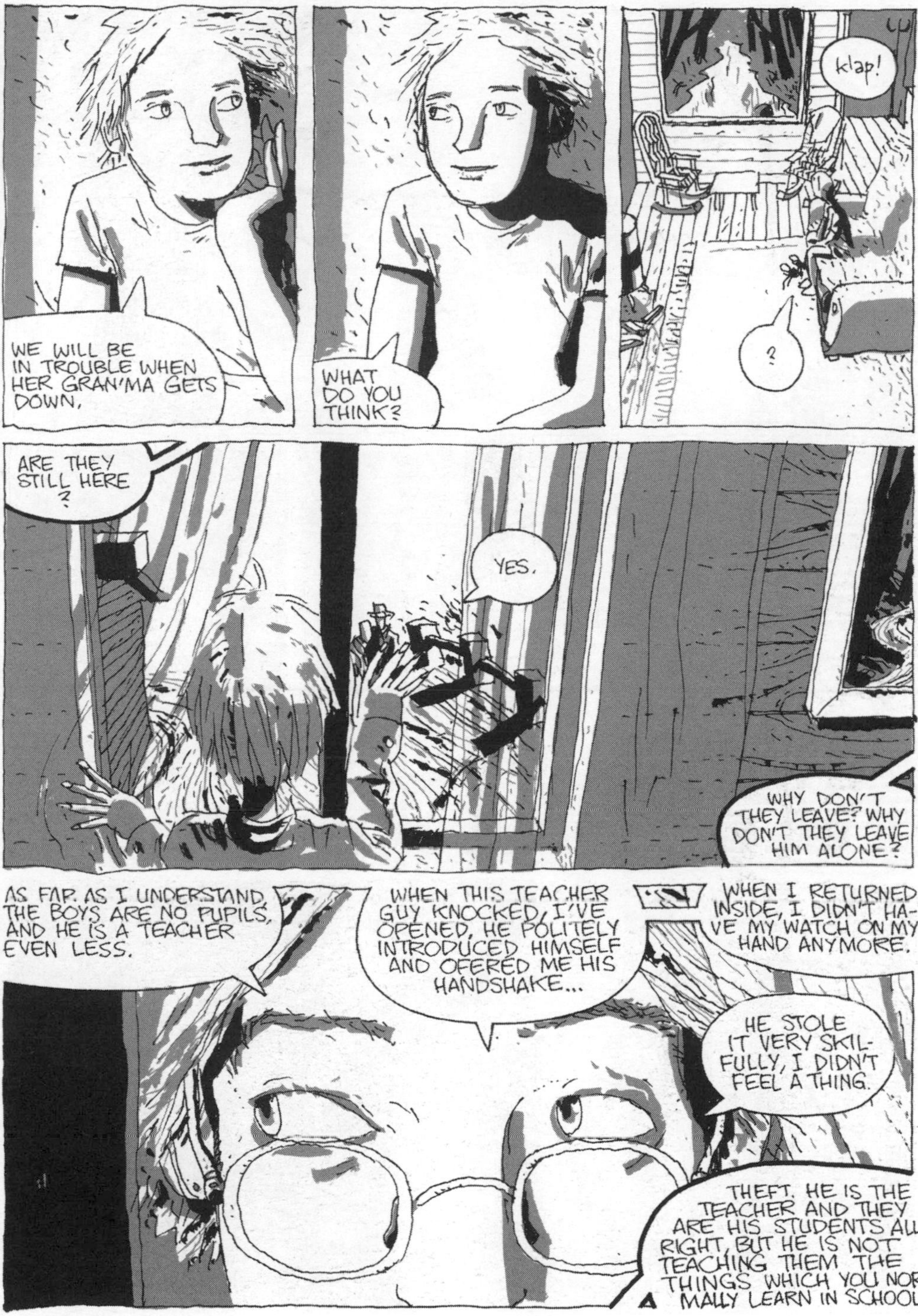
WE WILL BE IN TROUBLE WHEN HER GRAN'MA GETS DOWN.
WHAT DO YOU THINK?
klap!
?
ARE THEY STILL HERE ?
YES.
WHY DON'T THEY LEAVE? WHY DON'T THEY LEAVE HIM ALONE?
AS FAR AS I UNDERSTAND, THE BOYS ARE NO PUPILS, AND HE IS A TEACHER EVEN LESS.
WHEN THIS TEACHER GUY KNOCKED, I'VE OPENED, HE POLITELY INTRODUCED HIMSELF AND OFERED ME HIS HANDSHAKE...
WHEN I RETURNED INSIDE, I DIDN'T HAVE MY WATCH ON MY HAND ANYMORE.
HE STOLE IT VERY SKILFULLY, I DIDN'T FEEL A THING.
THEFT. HE IS THE TEACHER AND THEY ARE HIS STUDENTS ALL RIGHT, BUT HE IS NOT TEACHING THEM THE THINGS WHICH YOU NORMALLY LEARN IN SCHOOL.

eh...

I DON'T THINK THEY WILL STAY MUCH LONGER. I MENTIONED IN FRONT OF ONE OF THEM THAT WE ARE EXPECTING THE HUNTER TO COME TO DINNER.

THAT WAS THE FIRST THING THAT CROSSED MY MIND.

THEY ARE LOOKING UP.

I'M JUST ASKING.

AND THAT FIRST BOY?... DID YOU SHAKE HANDS WITH HIM TOO?

NO, I DIDN'T.

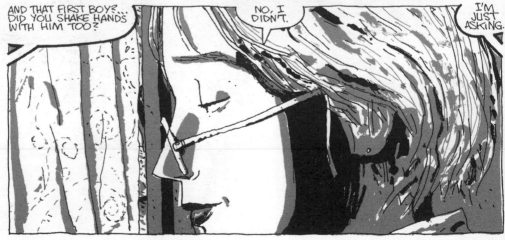

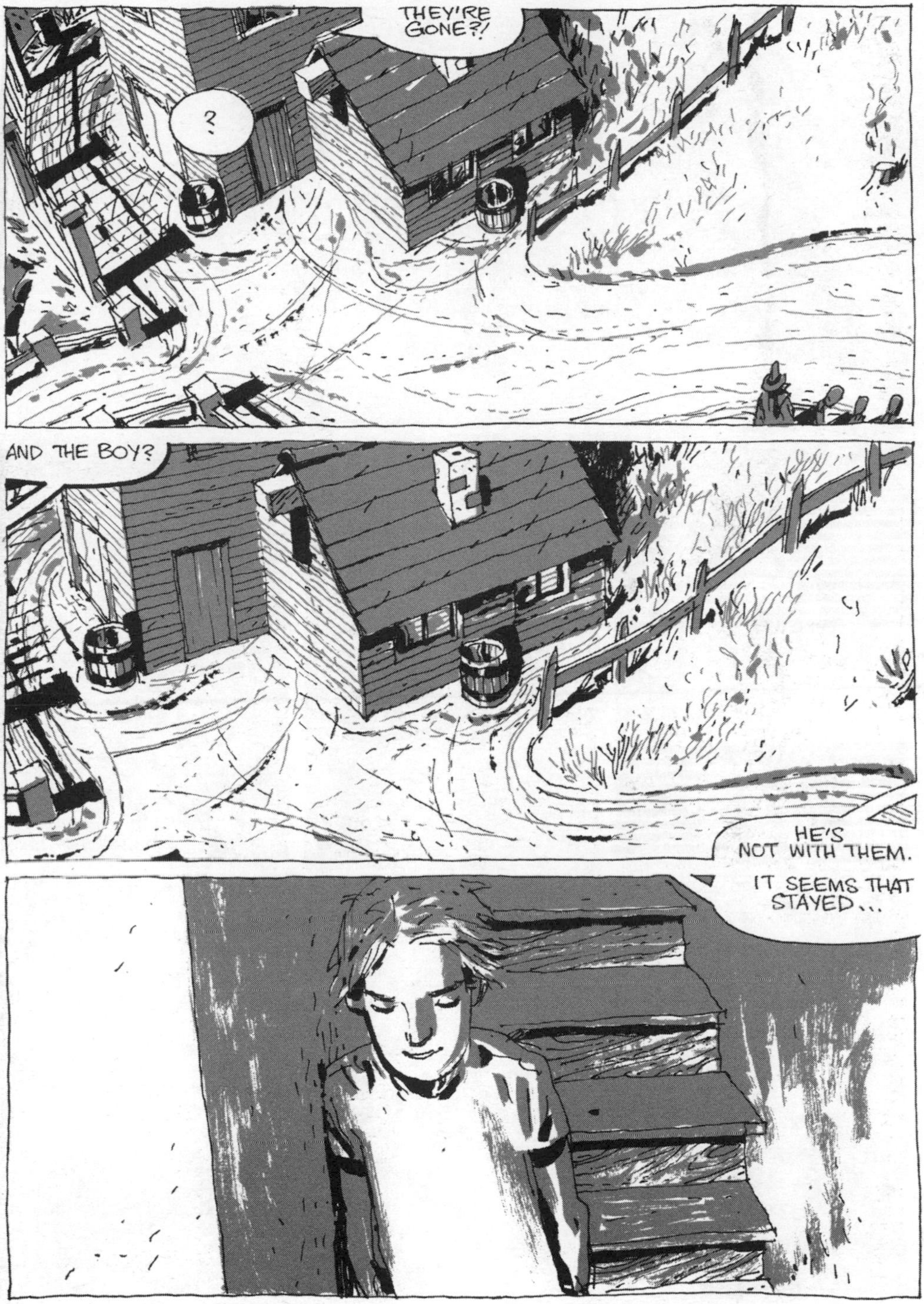
THEY'RE GONE?!
?
AND THE BOY?
HE'S NOT WITH THEM.
IT SEEMS THAT STAYED...

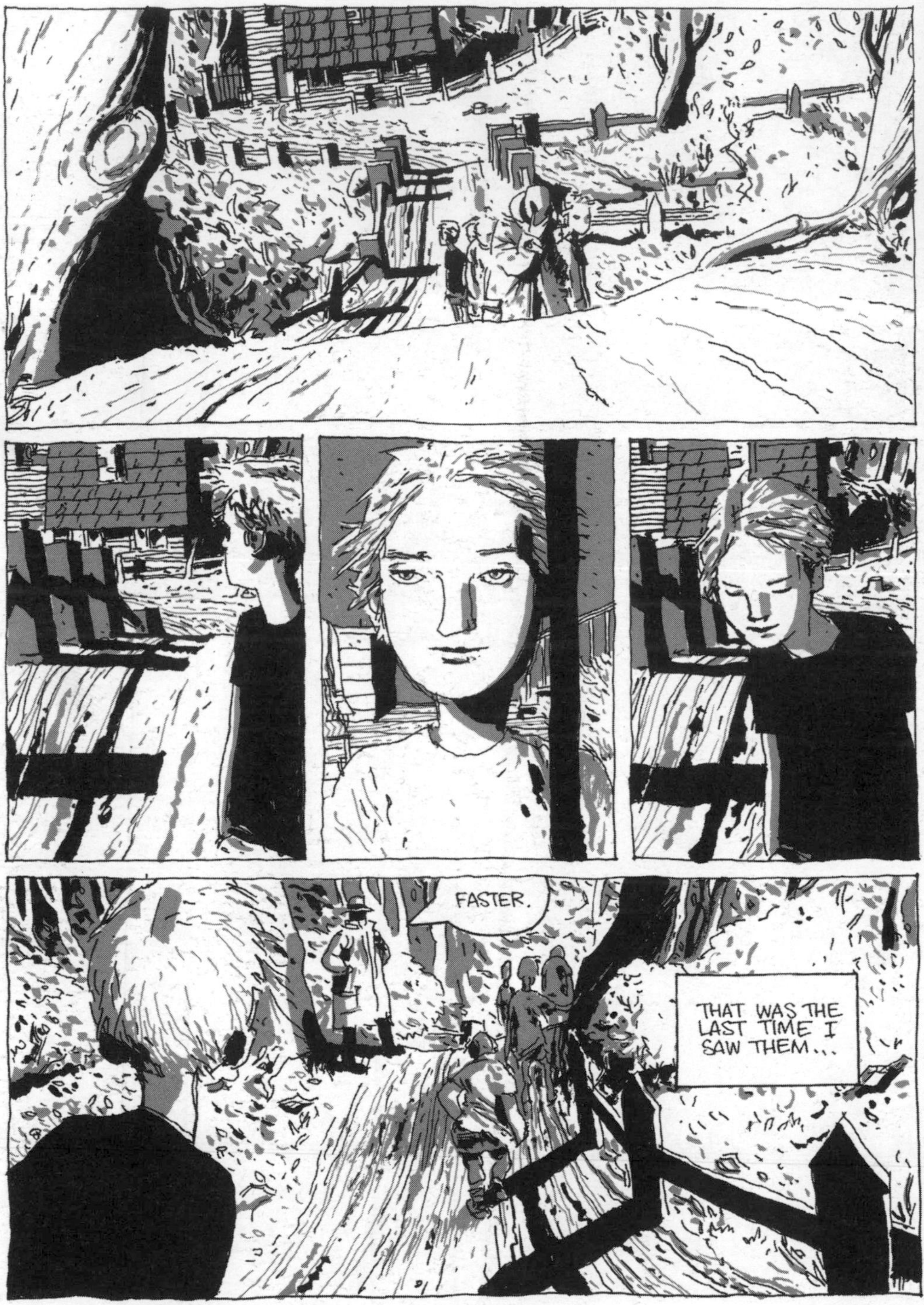
FASTER.
THAT WAS THE LAST TIME I SAW THEM...

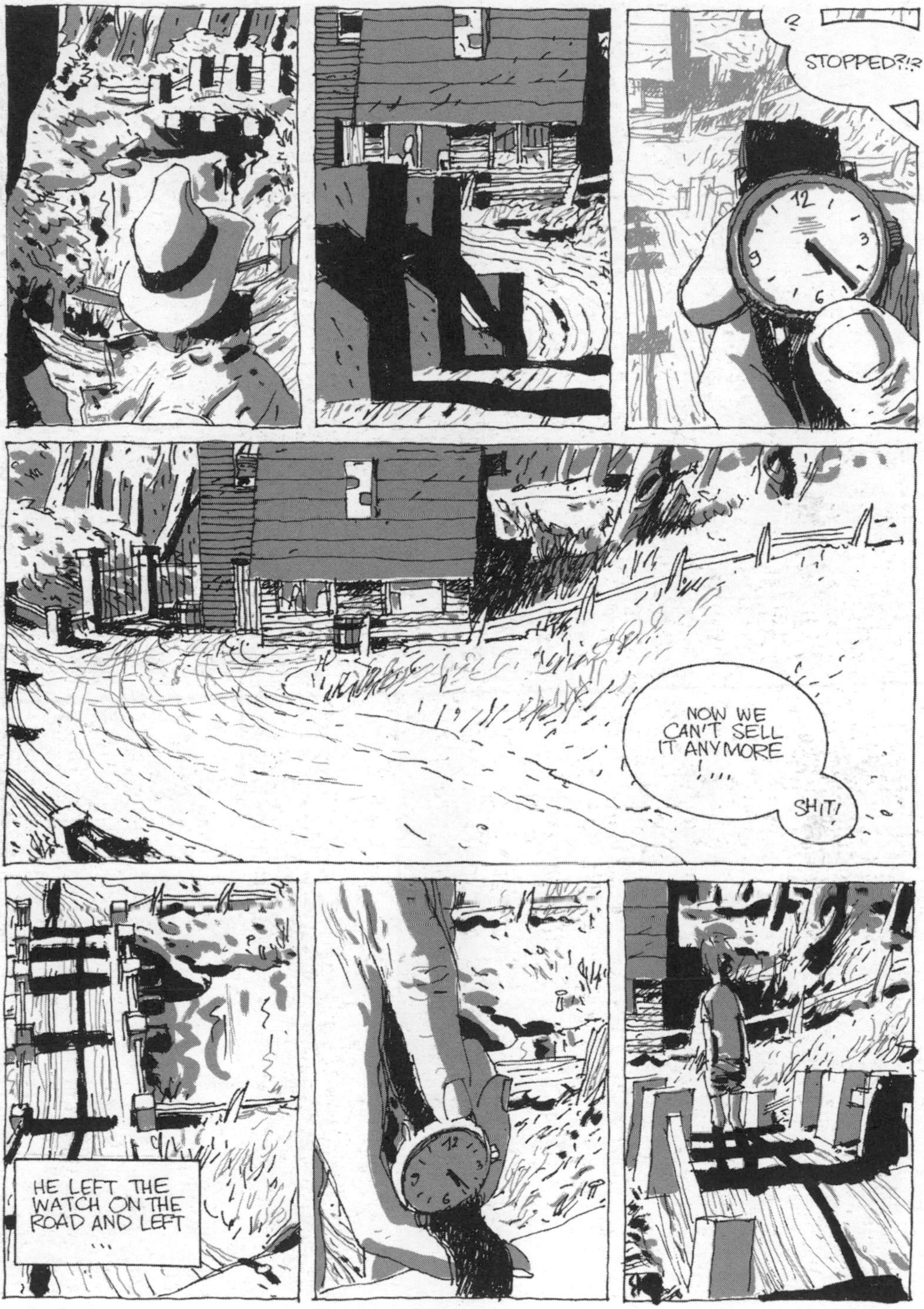
?
STOPPED?!?
NOW WE CAN'T SELL IT ANYMORE !...
SHIT!
HE LEFT THE WATCH ON THE ROAD AND LEFT ...

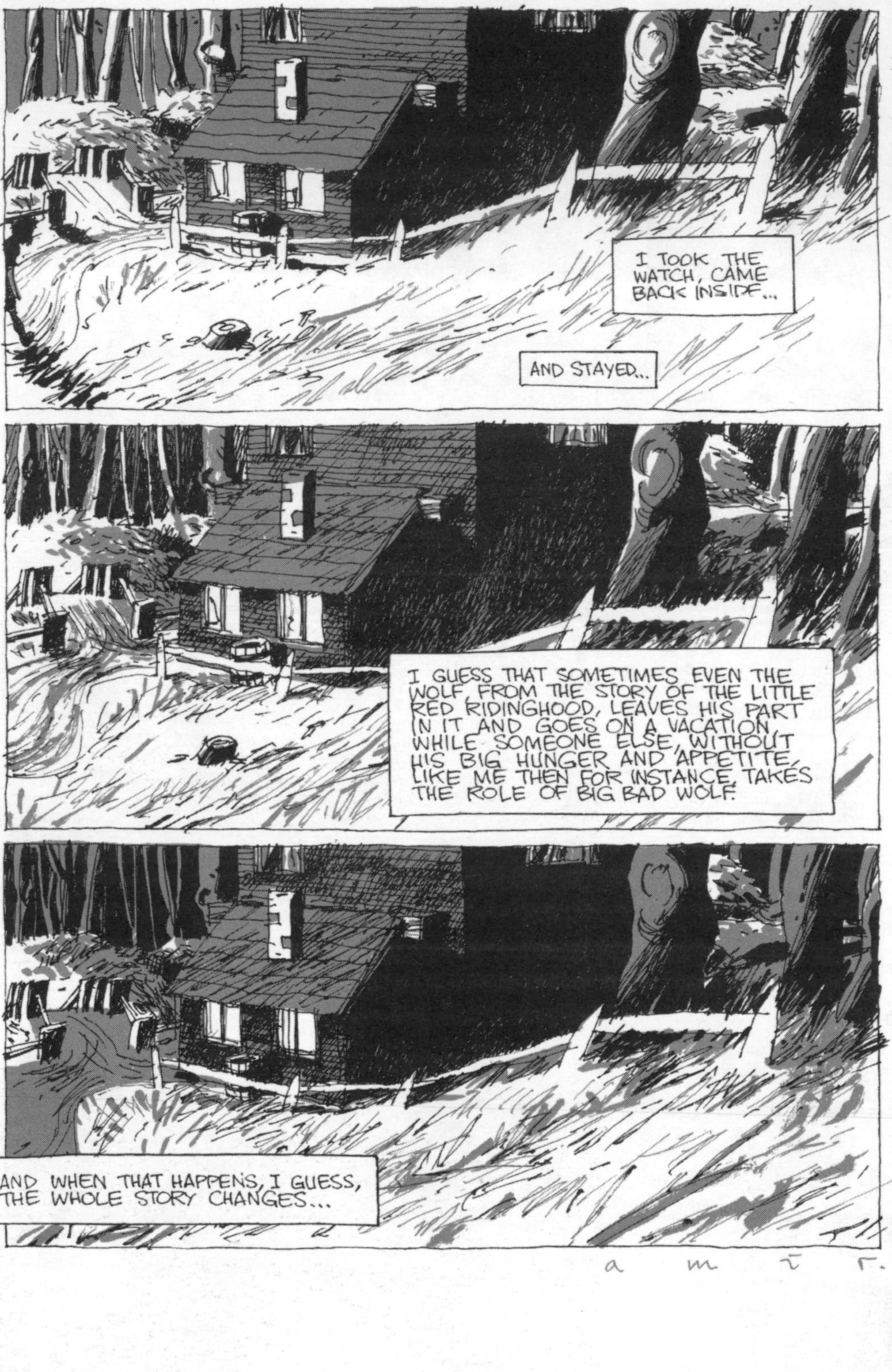
I TOOK THE WATCH, CAME BACK INSIDE...
AND STAYED...
I GUESS THAT SOMETIMES EVEN THE WOLF, FROM THE STORY OF THE LITTLE RED RIDINGHOOD, LEAVES HIS PART IN IT AND GOES ON A VACATION, WHILE SOMEONE ELSE, WITHOUT HIS BIG HUNGER AND APPETITE, LIKE ME THEN FOR INSTANCE, TAKES THE ROLE OF BIG BAD WOLF.
AND WHEN THAT HAPPENS, I GUESS, THE WHOLE STORY CHANGES...
a m i r.

Through the Habitrails

by Jeff Nicholson

$9.95
$13.50 in Canada
£5.95 in the UK

Jeff Nicholson

THROUGH THE HABITRAILS
Bad Habit, self-published, 1989–92

Nicholson was a major force in the so-called "B&W boom" of self- and small-press publishing in the 1980s, first with *Ultra Klutz*, and much later with his all-ages piratical adventure series *Colonia*. In between came the epic story you are about to read only highlights of – but oh, what highlights!

The job, the jar, the gerbils ... (shudder)

"When *Through the Habitrails* hit the scene in 1991 everything changed for me. In the late 1980s I had made a tenuous living from comics, but I had a cult audience and the general disdain of the comics press. This new work got me talked about and supported by the likes of comics greats Dave Sim, Stephen R. Bissette and Alan Moore. The audience grew, and ultimately good press happened as well. The tenuous living was still a reality but on those other levels I had 'made it'.

"The irony is that if my earlier work had been just a tiny bit more successful, I would not have had to take the day job that became the fuel for [my story], which then took me up a notch and let me quit the job that bore it. So take heart if your life imposes on your art: it will come back to serve you." – JN

www.fatherandsontoon.com

INCREASING
THE GERBILS

~

Story and Illustration
Jeff Nicholson

Lettering
Chad Woody

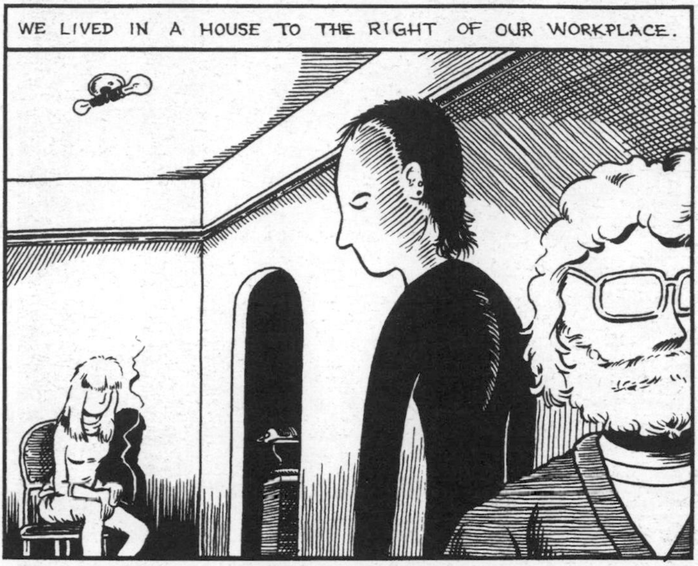
WE LIVED IN A HOUSE TO THE RIGHT OF OUR WORKPLACE.

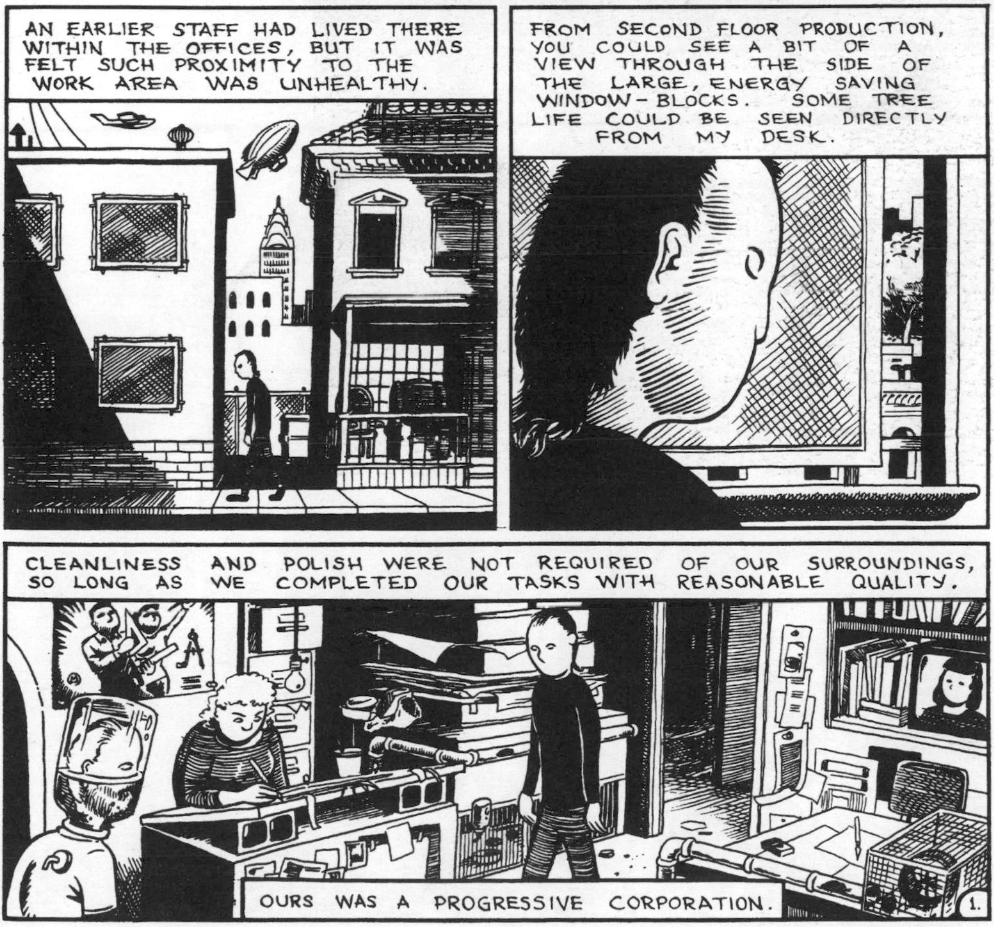
AN EARLIER STAFF HAD LIVED THERE WITHIN THE OFFICES, BUT IT WAS FELT SUCH PROXIMITY TO THE WORK AREA WAS UNHEALTHY.
FROM SECOND FLOOR PRODUCTION, YOU COULD SEE A BIT OF A VIEW THROUGH THE SIDE OF THE LARGE, ENERGY SAVING WINDOW-BLOCKS. SOME TREE LIFE COULD BE SEEN DIRECTLY FROM MY DESK.
CLEANLINESS AND POLISH WERE NOT REQUIRED OF OUR SURROUNDINGS, SO LONG AS WE COMPLETED OUR TASKS WITH REASONABLE QUALITY.
OURS WAS A PROGRESSIVE CORPORATION.

WE WERE CONSTANTLY REMINDED OF OUR STATION IN LIFE BY THE GERBILS, WHICH EXISTED THROUGHOUT THE BUILDING IN A VAST COMPLEX OF CLEAR TUBES AND GREY, UNKEMPT TIN CAGES.

THE GERBILS WERE A LIVING SYMBIOSIS BETWEEN OUR EMPLOYERS AND OURSELVES. WHILE THEY REMINDED US OF THE FUTILITY OF LIFE OUTSIDE THE COMPANY, THEY WERE ALSO RELEASED REGULARLY FOR THE BENEFIT OF THE STAFF. AFTER YEARS OF SUCH SPECIALIZED DOMESTICATION THEY HAD BECOME EMPATHS OF STRESS AND DESPAIR.

THE GERBILS WOULD ATTEMPT TO FLEE, AND DISPLAY UNCONTROLLED CRINGING AND SCHIZOPHRENIA. THE DESTRUCTION OF GERBILS WAS NOT FROWNED UPON, AS THEIR LIFE SPAN WITHIN THE OFFICE WOULD NOT EXCEED THREE WEEKS DUE TO THE BOMBARDMENT OF MISERY. THE GERBIL INDUSTRY WAS MASSIVE, AND THE SUPPLY COULD ALWAYS BE INCREASED.

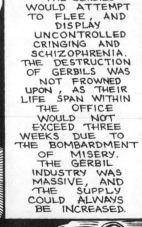

2.

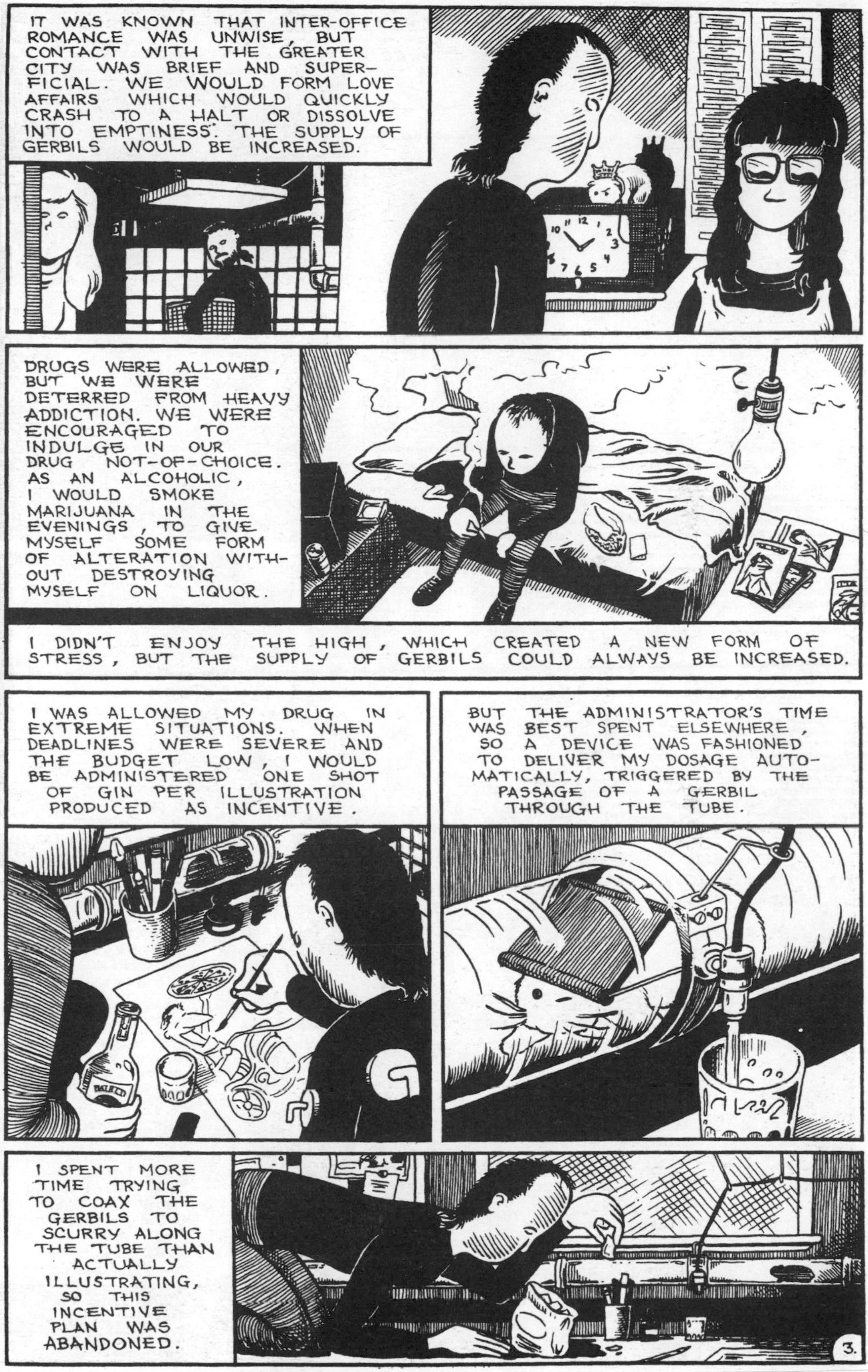

IT WAS KNOWN THAT INTER-OFFICE ROMANCE WAS UNWISE, BUT CONTACT WITH THE GREATER CITY WAS BRIEF AND SUPERFICIAL. WE WOULD FORM LOVE AFFAIRS WHICH WOULD QUICKLY CRASH TO A HALT OR DISSOLVE INTO EMPTINESS. THE SUPPLY OF GERBILS WOULD BE INCREASED.
DRUGS WERE ALLOWED, BUT WE WERE DETERRED FROM HEAVY ADDICTION. WE WERE ENCOURAGED TO INDULGE IN OUR DRUG NOT-OF-CHOICE. AS AN ALCOHOLIC, I WOULD SMOKE MARIJUANA IN THE EVENINGS, TO GIVE MYSELF SOME FORM OF ALTERATION WITHOUT DESTROYING MYSELF ON LIQUOR.
I DIDN'T ENJOY THE HIGH, WHICH CREATED A NEW FORM OF STRESS, BUT THE SUPPLY OF GERBILS COULD ALWAYS BE INCREASED.
I WAS ALLOWED MY DRUG IN EXTREME SITUATIONS. WHEN DEADLINES WERE SEVERE AND THE BUDGET LOW, I WOULD BE ADMINISTERED ONE SHOT OF GIN PER ILLUSTRATION PRODUCED AS INCENTIVE.
BUT THE ADMINISTRATOR'S TIME WAS BEST SPENT ELSEWHERE, SO A DEVICE WAS FASHIONED TO DELIVER MY DOSAGE AUTOMATICALLY, TRIGGERED BY THE PASSAGE OF A GERBIL THROUGH THE TUBE.
I SPENT MORE TIME TRYING TO COAX THE GERBILS TO SCURRY ALONG THE TUBE THAN ACTUALLY ILLUSTRATING, SO THIS INCENTIVE PLAN WAS ABANDONED.

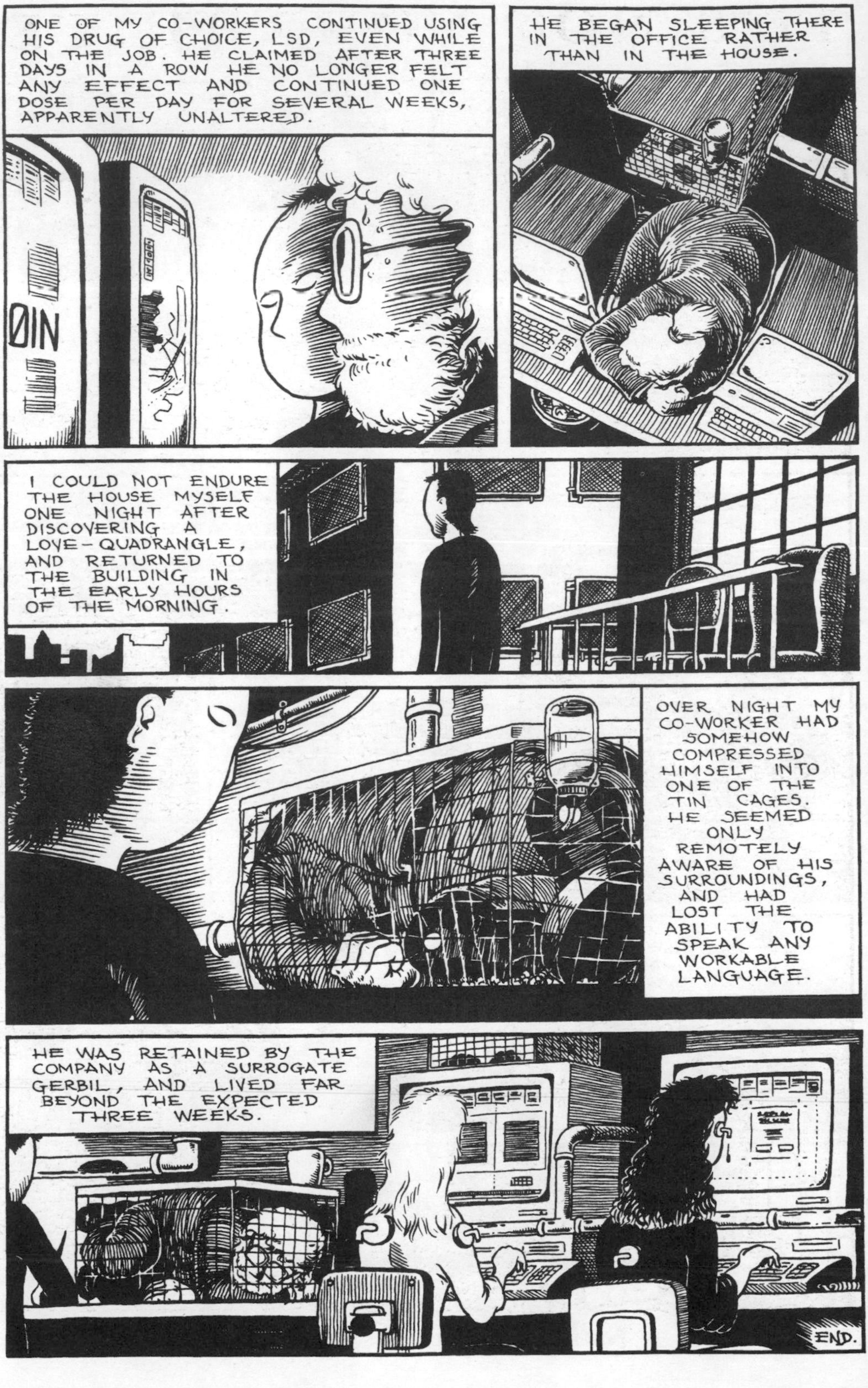
ONE OF MY CO-WORKERS CONTINUED USING HIS DRUG OF CHOICE, LSD, EVEN WHILE ON THE JOB. HE CLAIMED AFTER THREE DAYS IN A ROW HE NO LONGER FELT ANY EFFECT AND CONTINUED ONE DOSE PER DAY FOR SEVERAL WEEKS, APPARENTLY UNALTERED.
ØIN
HE BEGAN SLEEPING THERE IN THE OFFICE RATHER THAN IN THE HOUSE.
I COULD NOT ENDURE THE HOUSE MYSELF ONE NIGHT AFTER DISCOVERING A LOVE-QUADRANGLE, AND RETURNED TO THE BUILDING IN THE EARLY HOURS OF THE MORNING.
OVER NIGHT MY CO-WORKER HAD SOMEHOW COMPRESSED HIMSELF INTO ONE OF THE TIN CAGES. HE SEEMED ONLY REMOTELY AWARE OF HIS SURROUNDINGS, AND HAD LOST THE ABILITY TO SPEAK ANY WORKABLE LANGUAGE.
HE WAS RETAINED BY THE COMPANY AS A SURROGATE GERBIL, AND LIVED FAR BEYOND THE EXPECTED THREE WEEKS.
END.

IT'S NOT YOUR JUICE

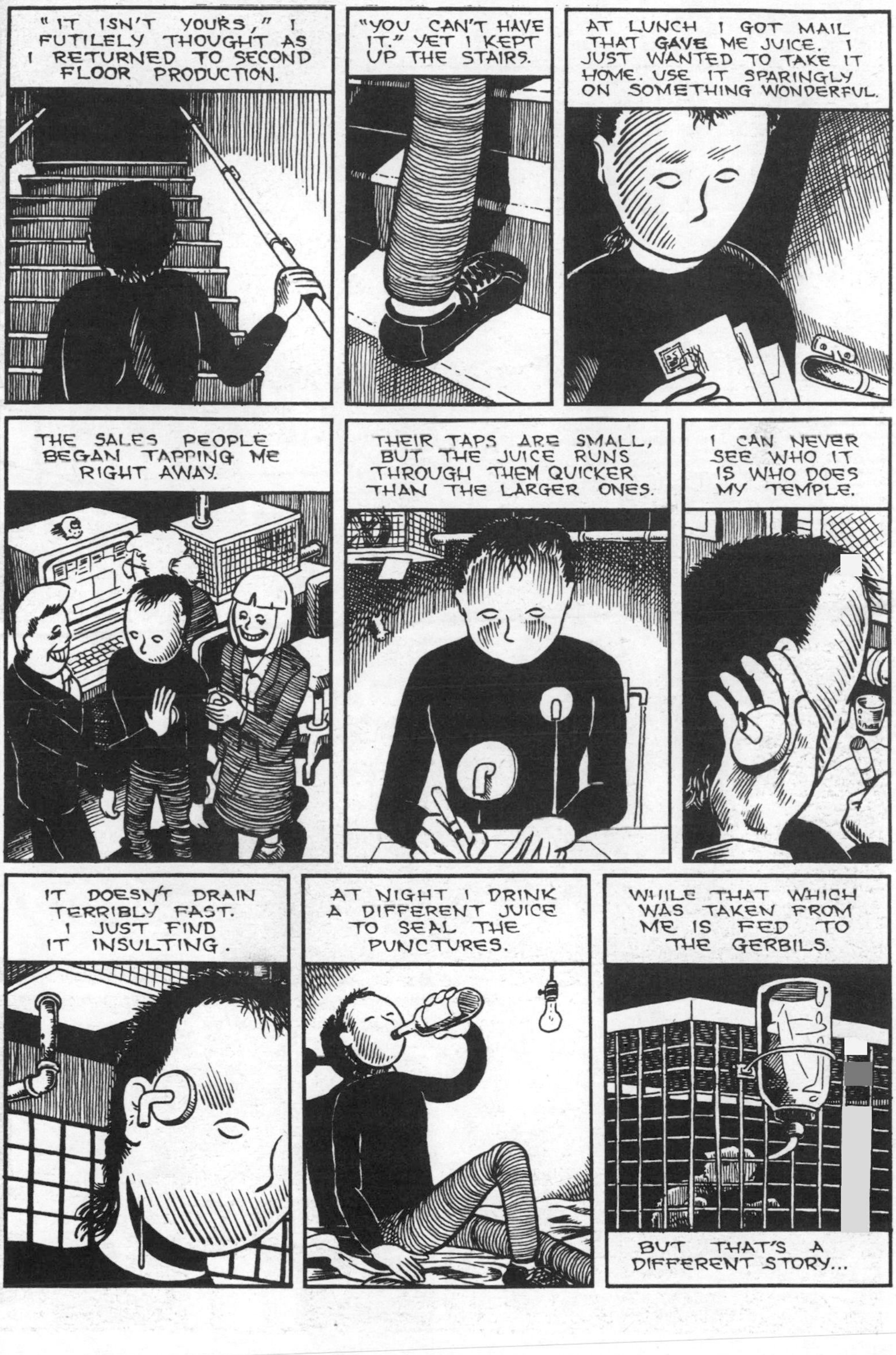
"IT ISN'T YOURS," I FUTILELY THOUGHT AS I RETURNED TO SECOND FLOOR PRODUCTION.
"YOU CAN'T HAVE IT." YET I KEPT UP THE STAIRS.
AT LUNCH I GOT MAIL THAT GAVE ME JUICE. I JUST WANTED TO TAKE IT HOME. USE IT SPARINGLY ON SOMETHING WONDERFUL.
THE SALES PEOPLE BEGAN TAPPING ME RIGHT AWAY.
THEIR TAPS ARE SMALL, BUT THE JUICE RUNS THROUGH THEM QUICKER THAN THE LARGER ONES.
I CAN NEVER SEE WHO IT IS WHO DOES MY TEMPLE.
IT DOESN'T DRAIN TERRIBLY FAST. I JUST FIND IT INSULTING.
AT NIGHT I DRINK A DIFFERENT JUICE TO SEAL THE PUNCTURES.
WHILE THAT WHICH WAS TAKEN FROM ME IS FED TO THE GERBILS.
BUT THAT'S A DIFFERENT STORY...

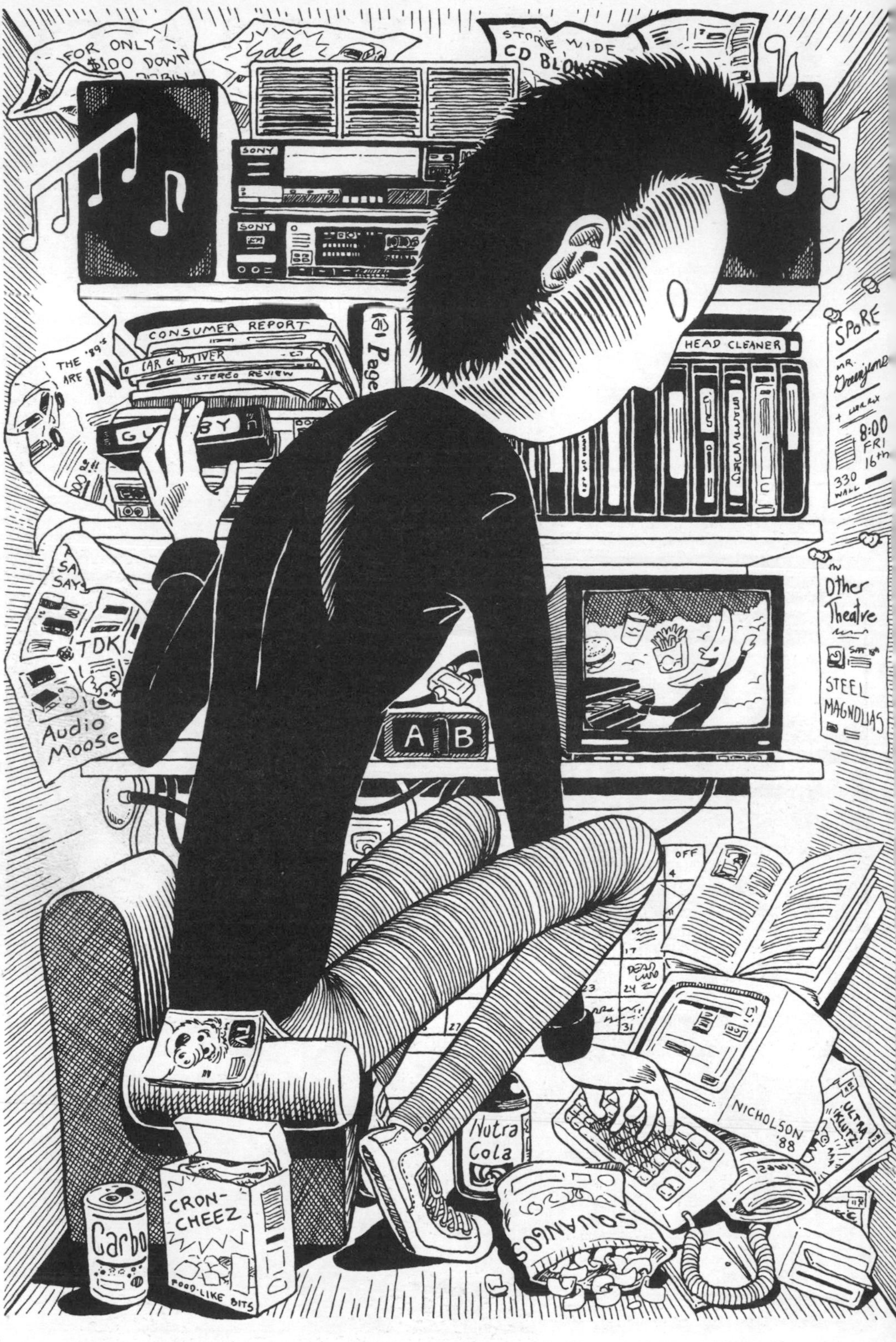

FOR ONLY $100 DOWN
Sale
STORE WIDE
CD BLOW
SONY
SONY
CONSUMER REPORT
CAR & DRIVER
STEREO REVIEW
THE '89'S ARE IN
HEAD CLEANER
SPORE
8:00
FRI
16th
330 WALL
Other Theatre
STEEL MAGNOLIAS
TDK
Audio Moose
A
B
OFF
NICHOLSON '88
ULTRA KLUTZ
Nutra Cola
CRON-CHEEZ
FOOD-LIKE BITS
Carbo
SQUANGOS

JAR HEAD

~

Story and Illustration
Jeff Nicholson

Lettering
Chad Woody

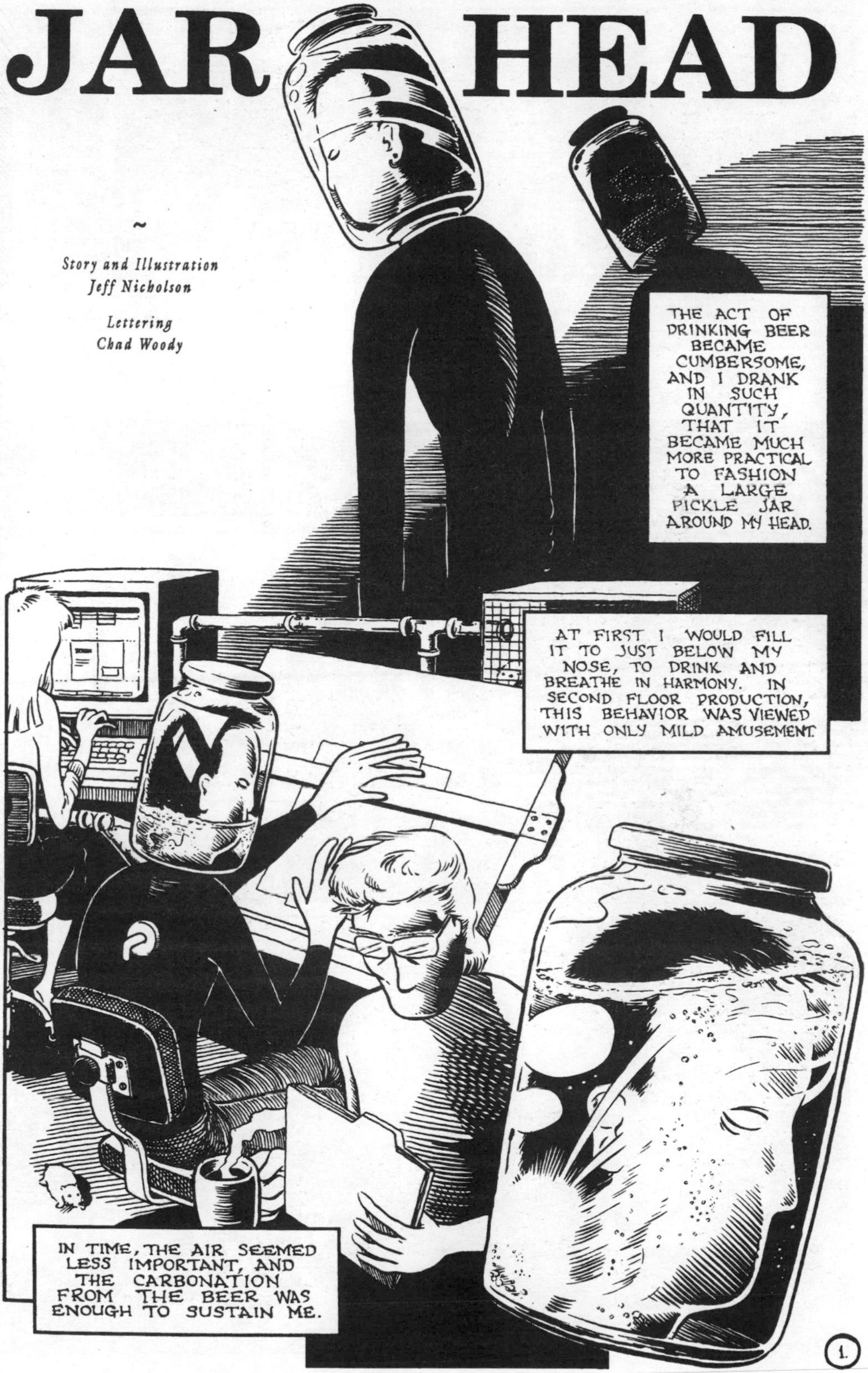

THE ACT OF DRINKING BEER BECAME CUMBERSOME, AND I DRANK IN SUCH QUANTITY, THAT IT BECAME MUCH MORE PRACTICAL TO FASHION A LARGE PICKLE JAR AROUND MY HEAD.
AT FIRST I WOULD FILL IT TO JUST BELOW MY NOSE, TO DRINK AND BREATHE IN HARMONY. IN SECOND FLOOR PRODUCTION, THIS BEHAVIOR WAS VIEWED WITH ONLY MILD AMUSEMENT.
IN TIME, THE AIR SEEMED LESS IMPORTANT, AND THE CARBONATION FROM THE BEER WAS ENOUGH TO SUSTAIN ME.

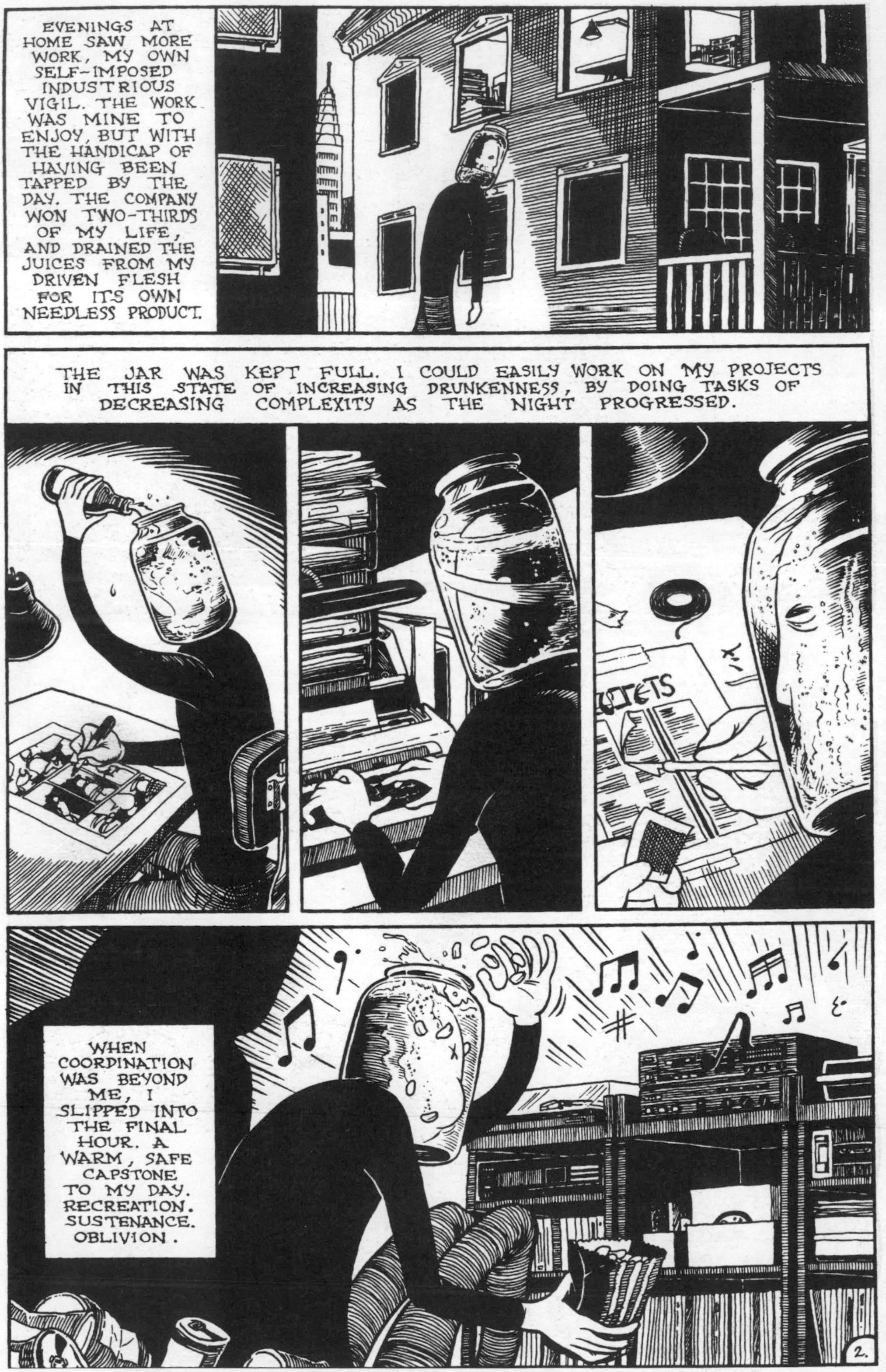
EVENINGS AT HOME SAW MORE WORK, MY OWN SELF-IMPOSED INDUSTRIOUS VIGIL. THE WORK WAS MINE TO ENJOY, BUT WITH THE HANDICAP OF HAVING BEEN TAPPED BY THE DAY. THE COMPANY WON TWO-THIRDS OF MY LIFE, AND DRAINED THE JUICES FROM MY DRIVEN FLESH FOR ITS OWN NEEDLESS PRODUCT.
THE JAR WAS KEPT FULL. I COULD EASILY WORK ON MY PROJECTS IN THIS STATE OF INCREASING DRUNKENNESS, BY DOING TASKS OF DECREASING COMPLEXITY AS THE NIGHT PROGRESSED.
WHEN COORDINATION WAS BEYOND ME, I SLIPPED INTO THE FINAL HOUR. A WARM, SAFE CAPSTONE TO MY DAY. RECREATION. SUSTENANCE. OBLIVION.

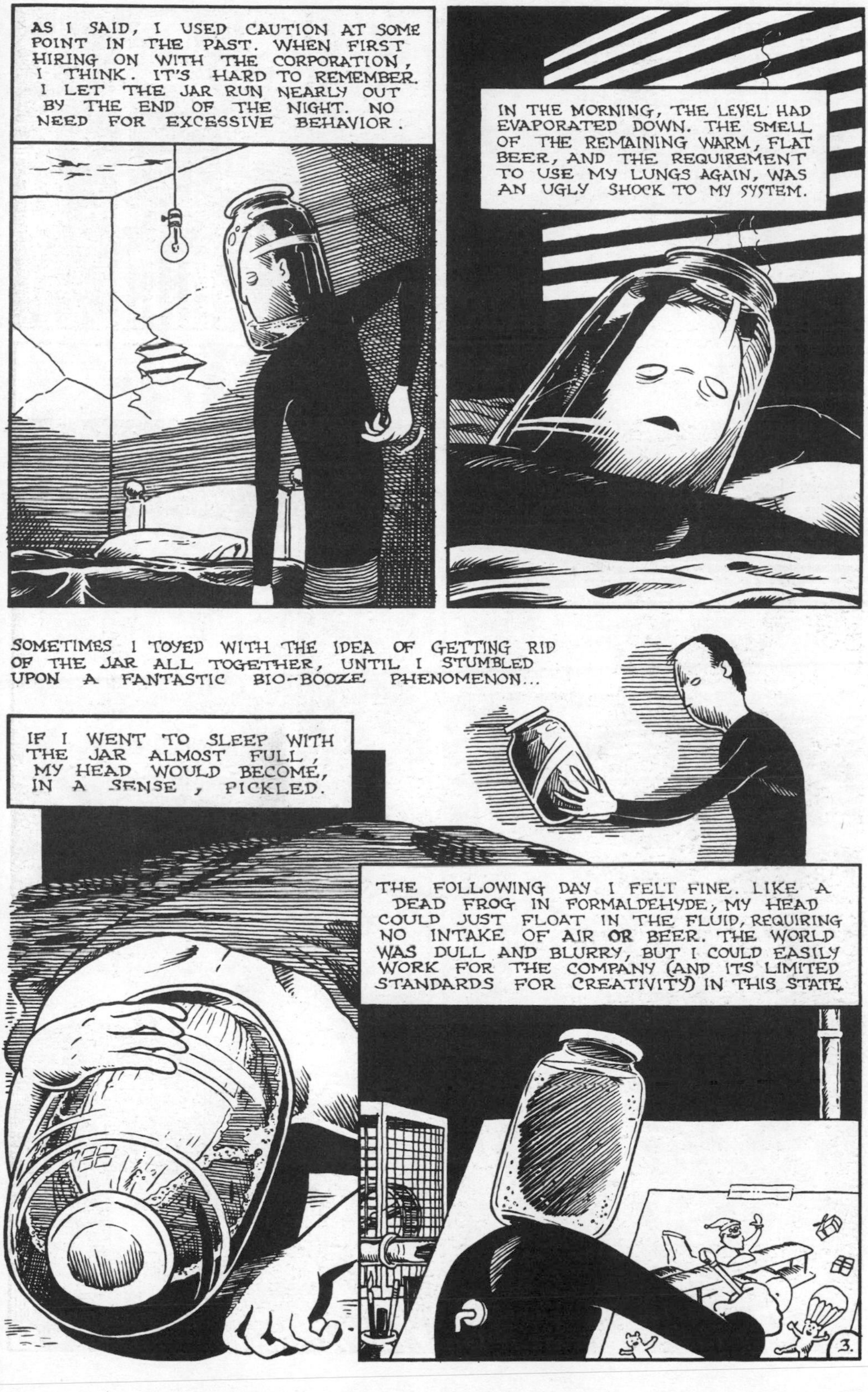
AS I SAID, I USED CAUTION AT SOME POINT IN THE PAST. WHEN FIRST HIRING ON WITH THE CORPORATION, I THINK. IT'S HARD TO REMEMBER. I LET THE JAR RUN NEARLY OUT BY THE END OF THE NIGHT. NO NEED FOR EXCESSIVE BEHAVIOR.
IN THE MORNING, THE LEVEL HAD EVAPORATED DOWN. THE SMELL OF THE REMAINING WARM, FLAT BEER, AND THE REQUIREMENT TO USE MY LUNGS AGAIN, WAS AN UGLY SHOCK TO MY SYSTEM.
SOMETIMES I TOYED WITH THE IDEA OF GETTING RID OF THE JAR ALL TOGETHER, UNTIL I STUMBLED UPON A FANTASTIC BIO-BOOZE PHENOMENON...
IF I WENT TO SLEEP WITH THE JAR ALMOST FULL, MY HEAD WOULD BECOME, IN A SENSE, PICKLED.
THE FOLLOWING DAY I FELT FINE. LIKE A DEAD FROG IN FORMALDEHYDE, MY HEAD COULD JUST FLOAT IN THE FLUID, REQUIRING NO INTAKE OF AIR OR BEER. THE WORLD WAS DULL AND BLURRY, BUT I COULD EASILY WORK FOR THE COMPANY (AND ITS LIMITED STANDARDS FOR CREATIVITY) IN THIS STATE.

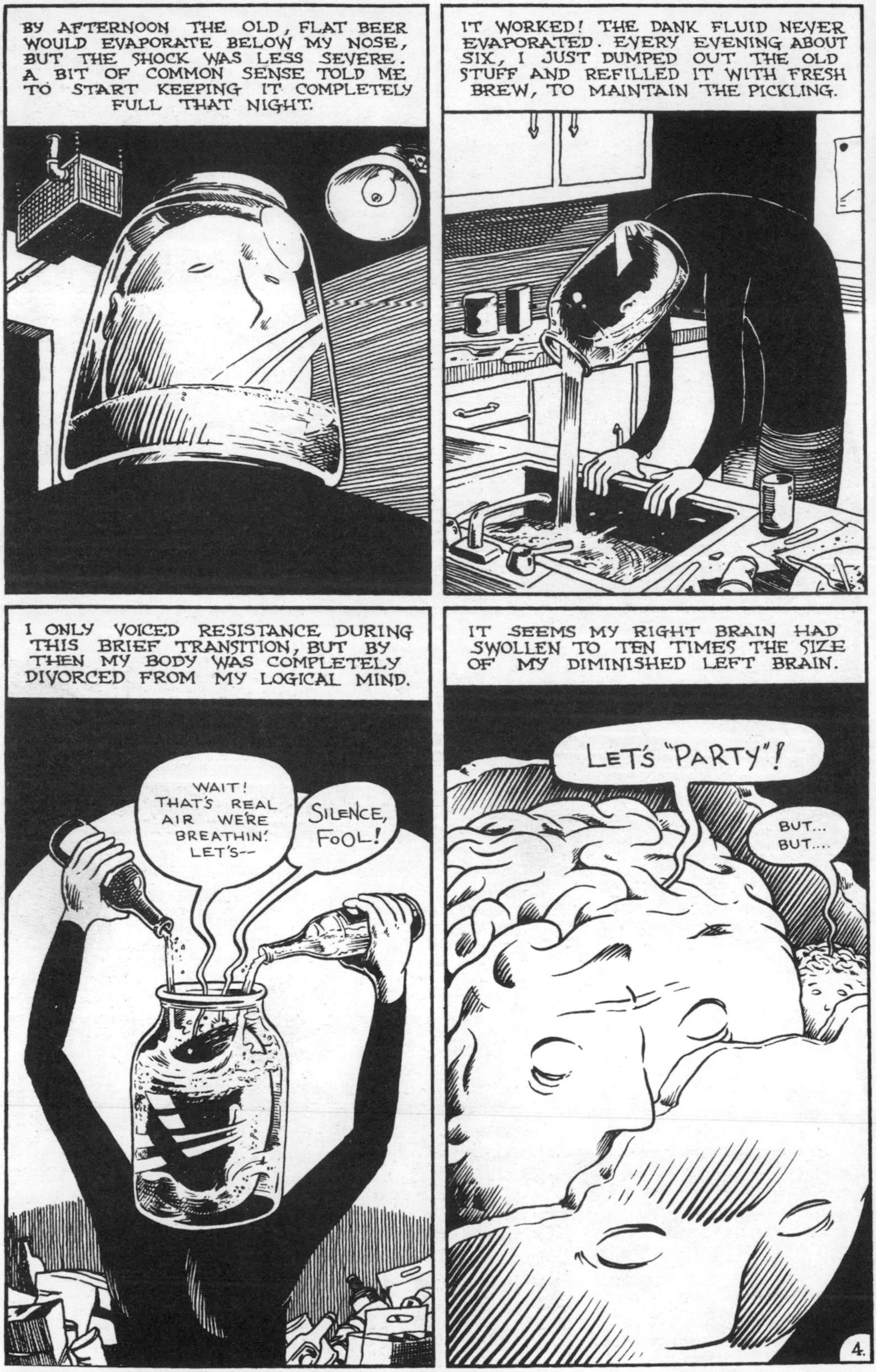

BY AFTERNOON THE OLD, FLAT BEER WOULD EVAPORATE BELOW MY NOSE, BUT THE SHOCK WAS LESS SEVERE. A BIT OF COMMON SENSE TOLD ME TO START KEEPING IT COMPLETELY FULL THAT NIGHT.
IT WORKED! THE DANK FLUID NEVER EVAPORATED. EVERY EVENING ABOUT SIX, I JUST DUMPED OUT THE OLD STUFF AND REFILLED IT WITH FRESH BREW, TO MAINTAIN THE PICKLING.
I ONLY VOICED RESISTANCE DURING THIS BRIEF TRANSITION, BUT BY THEN MY BODY WAS COMPLETELY DIVORCED FROM MY LOGICAL MIND.
WAIT! THAT'S REAL AIR WE'RE BREATHIN'! LET'S--
SILENCE, FOOL!
IT SEEMS MY RIGHT BRAIN HAD SWOLLEN TO TEN TIMES THE SIZE OF MY DIMINISHED LEFT BRAIN.
LET'S "PARTY"!
BUT... BUT....
4.

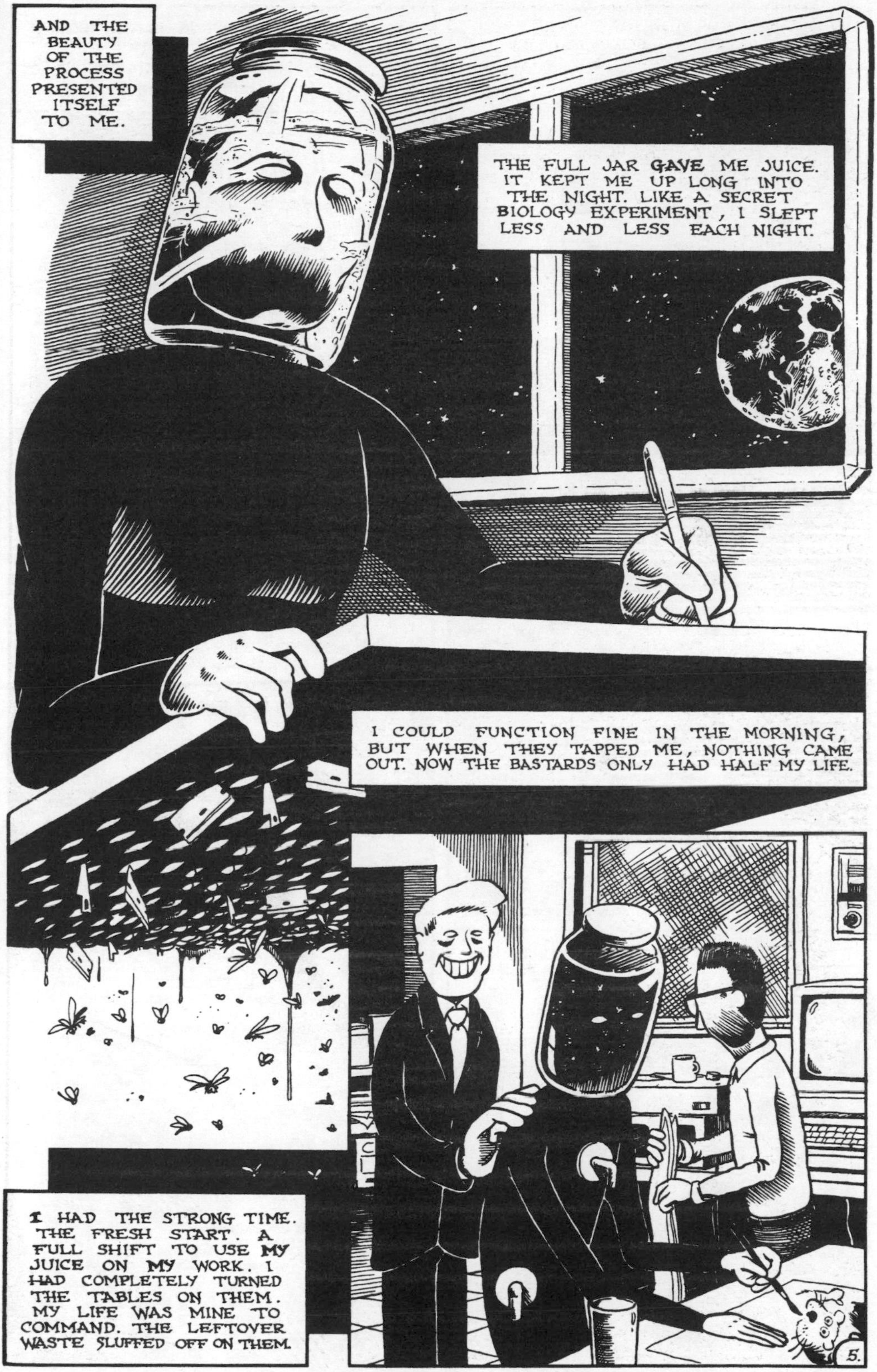
AND THE BEAUTY OF THE PROCESS PRESENTED ITSELF TO ME.
THE FULL JAR GAVE ME JUICE. IT KEPT ME UP LONG INTO THE NIGHT. LIKE A SECRET BIOLOGY EXPERIMENT, I SLEPT LESS AND LESS EACH NIGHT.
I COULD FUNCTION FINE IN THE MORNING, BUT WHEN THEY TAPPED ME, NOTHING CAME OUT. NOW THE BASTARDS ONLY HAD HALF MY LIFE.
I HAD THE STRONG TIME. THE FRESH START. A FULL SHIFT TO USE MY JUICE ON MY WORK. I HAD COMPLETELY TURNED THE TABLES ON THEM. MY LIFE WAS MINE TO COMMAND. THE LEFTOVER WASTE SLUFFED OFF ON THEM.
5.

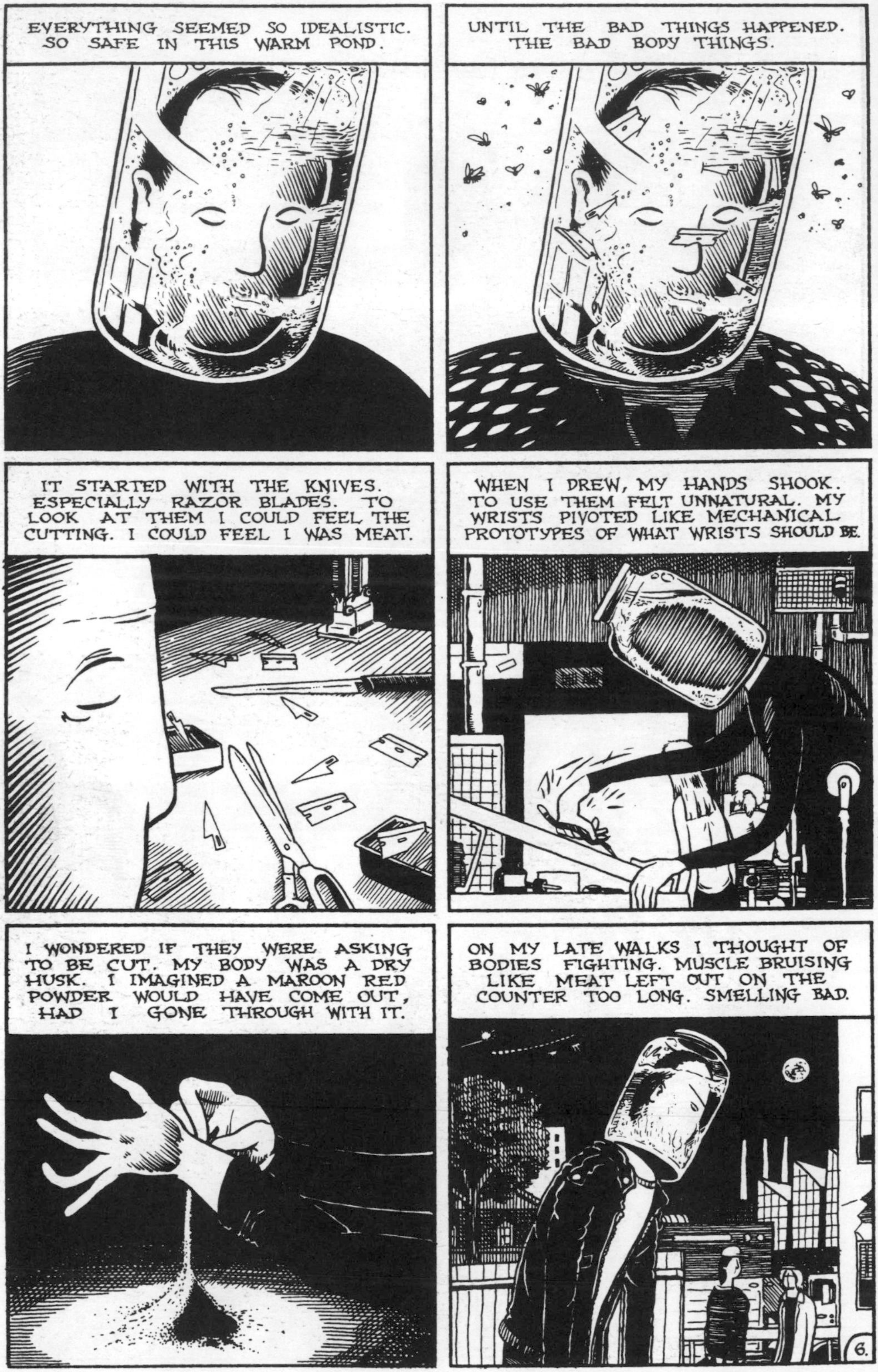
EVERYTHING SEEMED SO IDEALISTIC. SO SAFE IN THIS WARM POND.
UNTIL THE BAD THINGS HAPPENED. THE BAD BODY THINGS.
IT STARTED WITH THE KNIVES. ESPECIALLY RAZOR BLADES. TO LOOK AT THEM I COULD FEEL THE CUTTING. I COULD FEEL I WAS MEAT.
WHEN I DREW, MY HANDS SHOOK. TO USE THEM FELT UNNATURAL. MY WRISTS PIVOTED LIKE MECHANICAL PROTOTYPES OF WHAT WRISTS SHOULD BE.
I WONDERED IF THEY WERE ASKING TO BE CUT. MY BODY WAS A DRY HUSK. I IMAGINED A MAROON RED POWDER WOULD HAVE COME OUT, HAD I GONE THROUGH WITH IT.
ON MY LATE WALKS I THOUGHT OF BODIES FIGHTING. MUSCLE BRUISING LIKE MEAT LEFT OUT ON THE COUNTER TOO LONG. SMELLING BAD.
6.

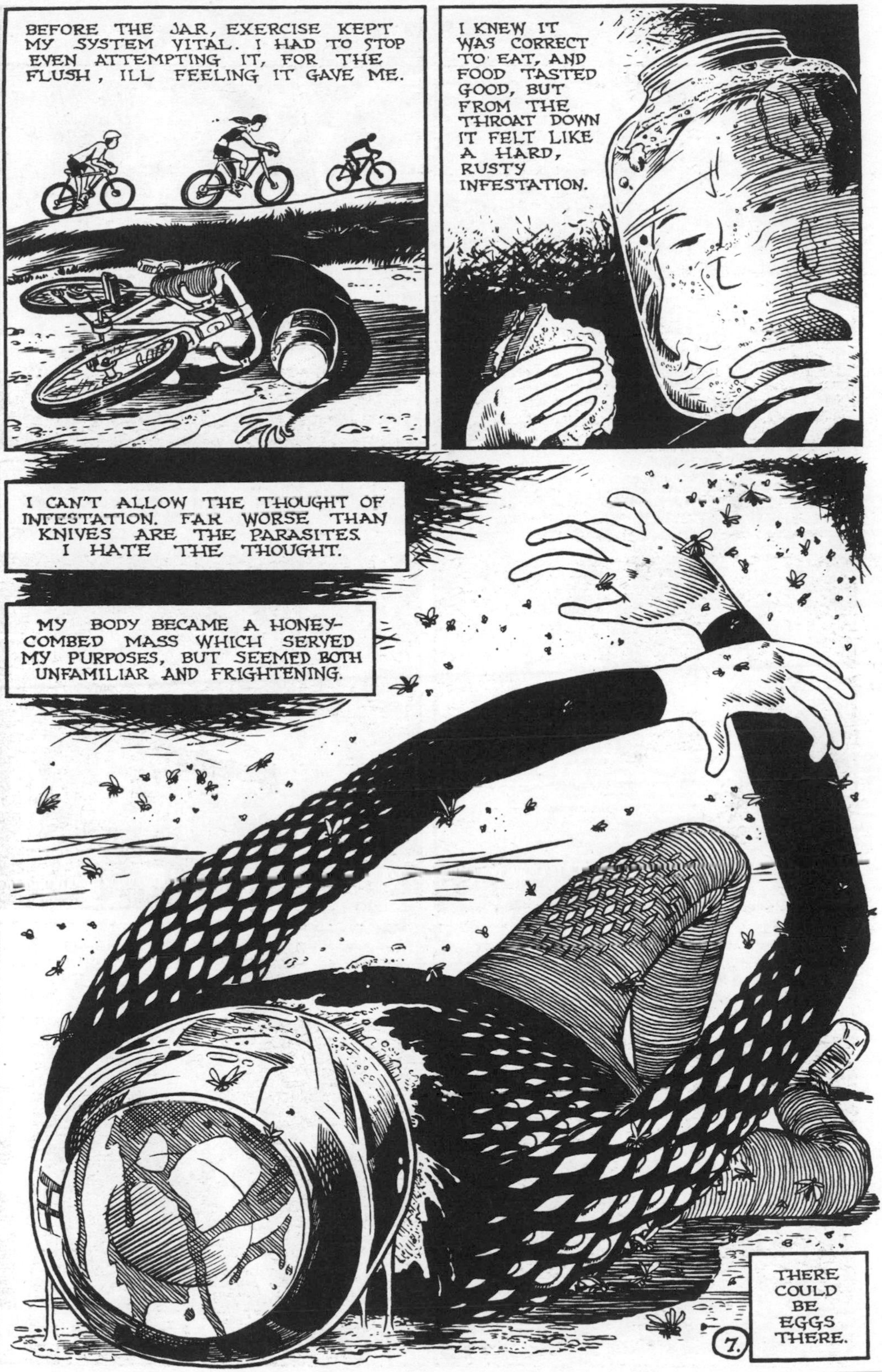
BEFORE THE JAR, EXERCISE KEPT MY SYSTEM VITAL. I HAD TO STOP EVEN ATTEMPTING IT, FOR THE FLUSH, ILL FEELING IT GAVE ME.
I KNEW IT WAS CORRECT TO EAT, AND FOOD TASTED GOOD, BUT FROM THE THROAT DOWN IT FELT LIKE A HARD, RUSTY INFESTATION.
I CAN'T ALLOW THE THOUGHT OF INFESTATION. FAR WORSE THAN KNIVES ARE THE PARASITES. I HATE THE THOUGHT.
MY BODY BECAME A HONEY-COMBED MASS WHICH SERVED MY PURPOSES, BUT SEEMED BOTH UNFAMILIAR AND FRIGHTENING.
THERE COULD BE EGGS THERE.

I USED DARKER ALES AND MALTS.

IT BECAME DIFFICULT TO DISTINGUISH REALITY FROM THE ODD REFLECTIONS THAT DARTED THROUGH THIS DARK, SEPIA LIQUID.

I BECAME COMPLETELY DISORIENTED, PACING WITH EMOTIONAL HALLUCINATIONS.

MY LIMBS WOULD MAKE SUDDEN MOVES OF THEIR OWN WILL.

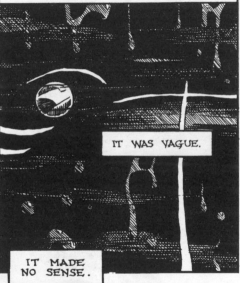

THE LIGHT CAST THROUGH THE GLASS AND BLACK BEER IN JUST SUCH A WAY, THAT AN IMAGE APPEARED ON THE INSIDE, DIRECTLY IN FRONT OF MY FACE

IT WAS VAGUE.

IT MADE NO SENSE.

IT WAS MY REFLECTION.

IT SCARED THE HELL OUT OF ME.

8.
END.

Escape #1: "El Muerte"

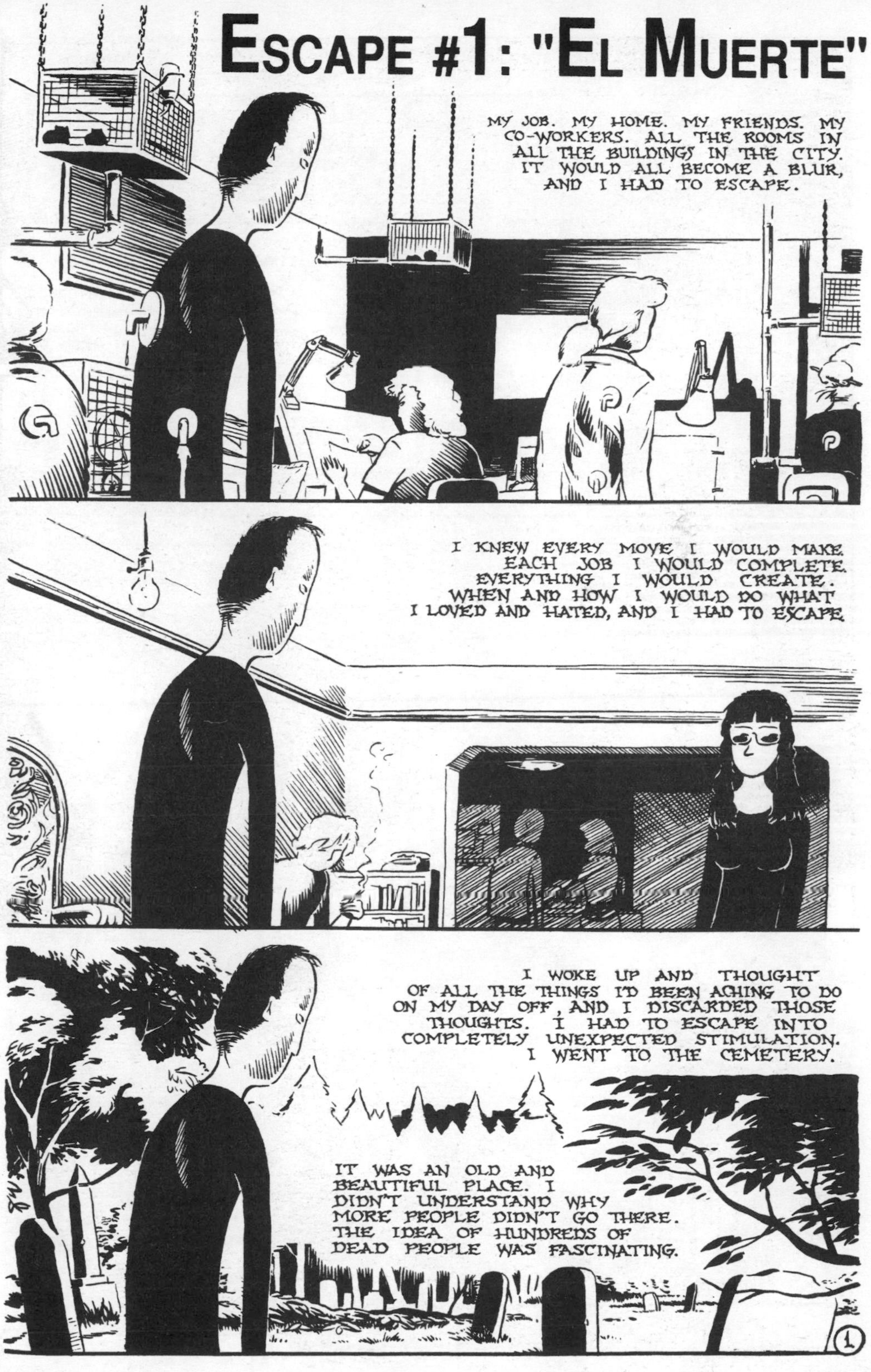
MY JOB. MY HOME. MY FRIENDS. MY CO-WORKERS. ALL THE ROOMS IN ALL THE BUILDINGS IN THE CITY. IT WOULD ALL BECOME A BLUR, AND I HAD TO ESCAPE.
I KNEW EVERY MOVE I WOULD MAKE. EACH JOB I WOULD COMPLETE. EVERYTHING I WOULD CREATE. WHEN AND HOW I WOULD DO WHAT I LOVED AND HATED, AND I HAD TO ESCAPE.
I WOKE UP AND THOUGHT OF ALL THE THINGS I'D BEEN ACHING TO DO ON MY DAY OFF, AND I DISCARDED THOSE THOUGHTS. I HAD TO ESCAPE INTO COMPLETELY UNEXPECTED STIMULATION. I WENT TO THE CEMETERY.
IT WAS AN OLD AND BEAUTIFUL PLACE. I DIDN'T UNDERSTAND WHY MORE PEOPLE DIDN'T GO THERE. THE IDEA OF HUNDREDS OF DEAD PEOPLE WAS FASCINATING.
1

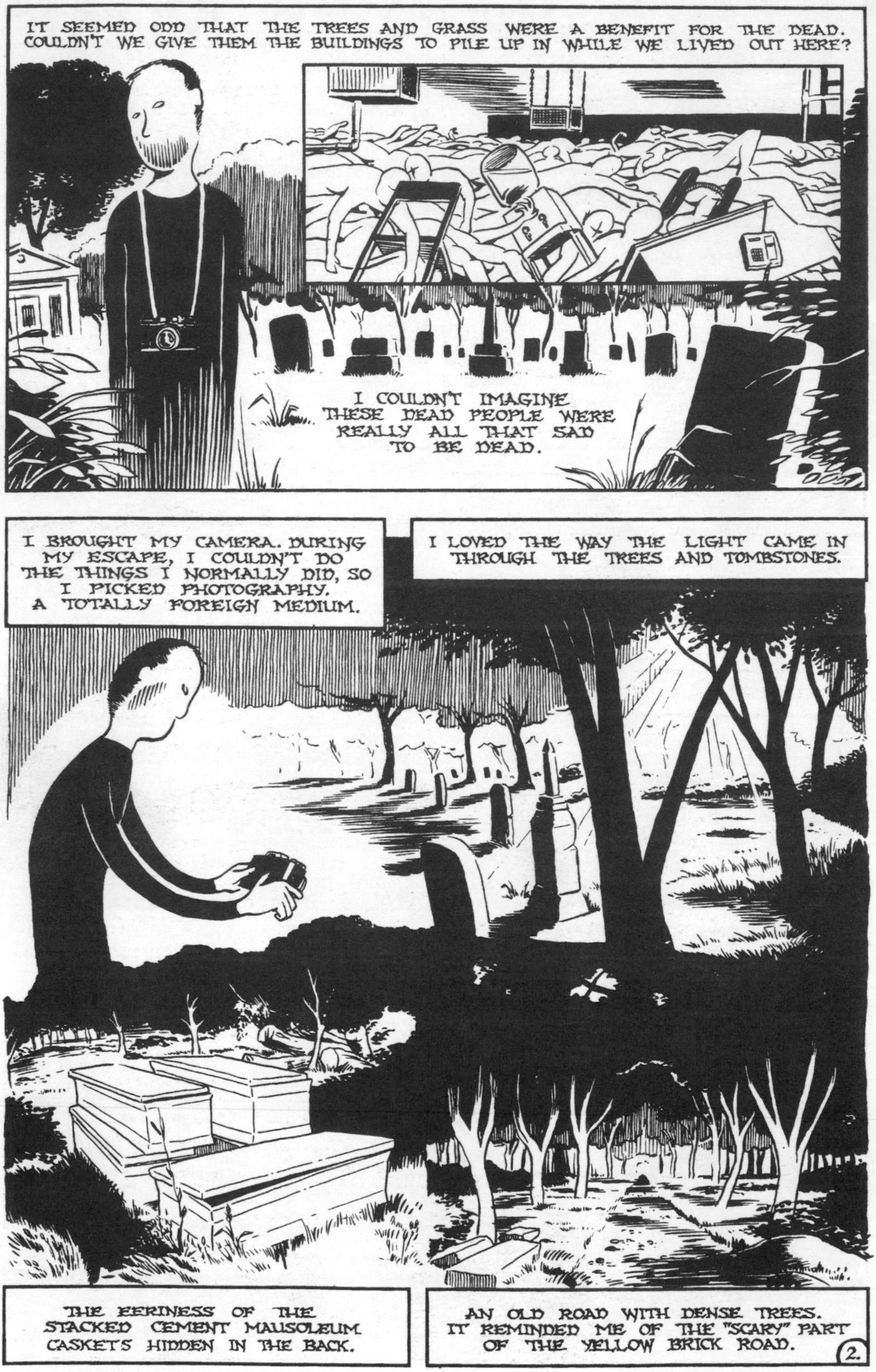
IT SEEMED ODD THAT THE TREES AND GRASS WERE A BENEFIT FOR THE DEAD. COULDN'T WE GIVE THEM THE BUILDINGS TO PILE UP IN WHILE WE LIVED OUT HERE?
I COULDN'T IMAGINE THESE DEAD PEOPLE WERE REALLY ALL THAT SAD TO BE DEAD.
I BROUGHT MY CAMERA. DURING MY ESCAPE, I COULDN'T DO THE THINGS I NORMALLY DID, SO I PICKED PHOTOGRAPHY. A TOTALLY FOREIGN MEDIUM.
I LOVED THE WAY THE LIGHT CAME IN THROUGH THE TREES AND TOMBSTONES.
THE EERINESS OF THE STACKED CEMENT MAUSOLEUM CASKETS HIDDEN IN THE BACK.
AN OLD ROAD WITH DENSE TREES. IT REMINDED ME OF THE "SCARY" PART OF THE YELLOW BRICK ROAD.
2.

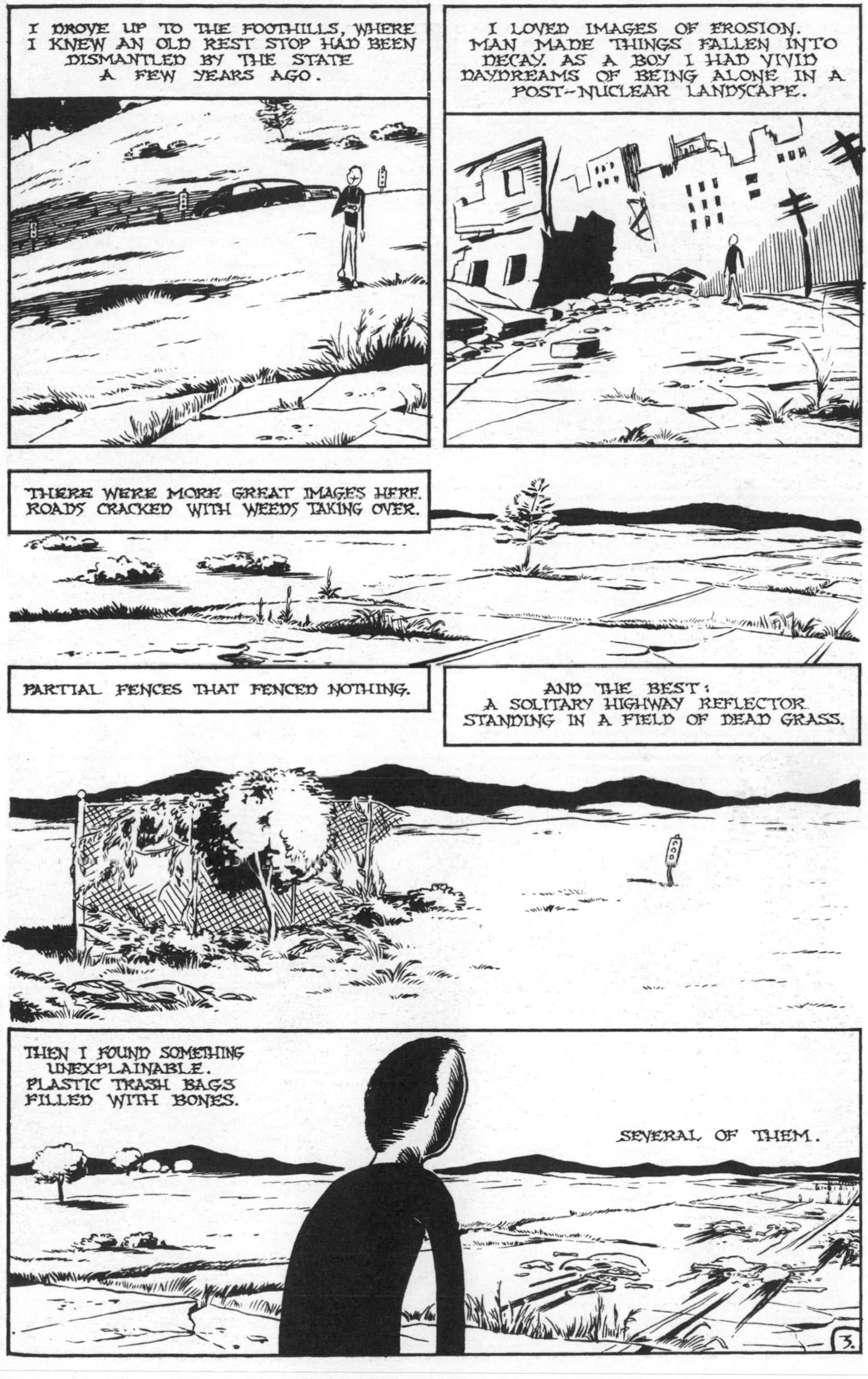
I DROVE UP TO THE FOOTHILLS, WHERE I KNEW AN OLD REST STOP HAD BEEN DISMANTLED BY THE STATE A FEW YEARS AGO.
I LOVED IMAGES OF EROSION. MAN MADE THINGS FALLEN INTO DECAY. AS A BOY I HAD VIVID DAYDREAMS OF BEING ALONE IN A POST-NUCLEAR LANDSCAPE.
THERE WERE MORE GREAT IMAGES HERE. ROADS CRACKED WITH WEEDS TAKING OVER.
PARTIAL FENCES THAT FENCED NOTHING.
AND THE BEST: A SOLITARY HIGHWAY REFLECTOR STANDING IN A FIELD OF DEAD GRASS.
THEN I FOUND SOMETHING UNEXPLAINABLE. PLASTIC TRASH BAGS FILLED WITH BONES.
SEVERAL OF THEM.
3.

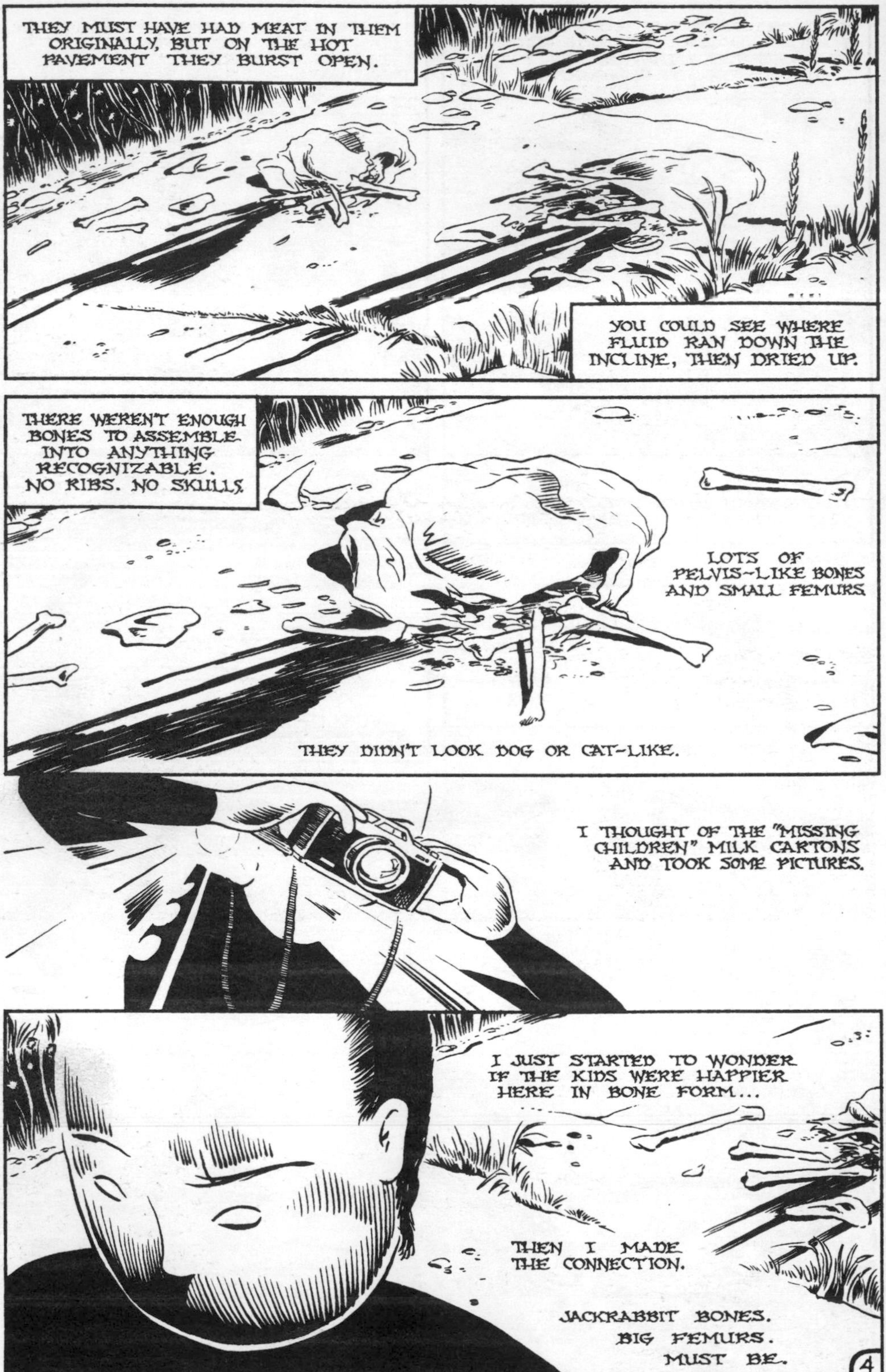
THEY MUST HAVE HAD MEAT IN THEM ORIGINALLY, BUT ON THE HOT PAVEMENT THEY BURST OPEN.
YOU COULD SEE WHERE FLUID RAN DOWN THE INCLINE, THEN DRIED UP.
THERE WEREN'T ENOUGH BONES TO ASSEMBLE INTO ANYTHING RECOGNIZABLE. NO RIBS. NO SKULLS.
LOTS OF PELVIS-LIKE BONES AND SMALL FEMURS.
THEY DIDN'T LOOK DOG OR CAT-LIKE.
I THOUGHT OF THE "MISSING CHILDREN" MILK CARTONS AND TOOK SOME PICTURES.
I JUST STARTED TO WONDER IF THE KIDS WERE HAPPIER HERE IN BONE FORM...
THEN I MADE THE CONNECTION.
JACKRABBIT BONES.
BIG FEMURS.
MUST BE.
4.

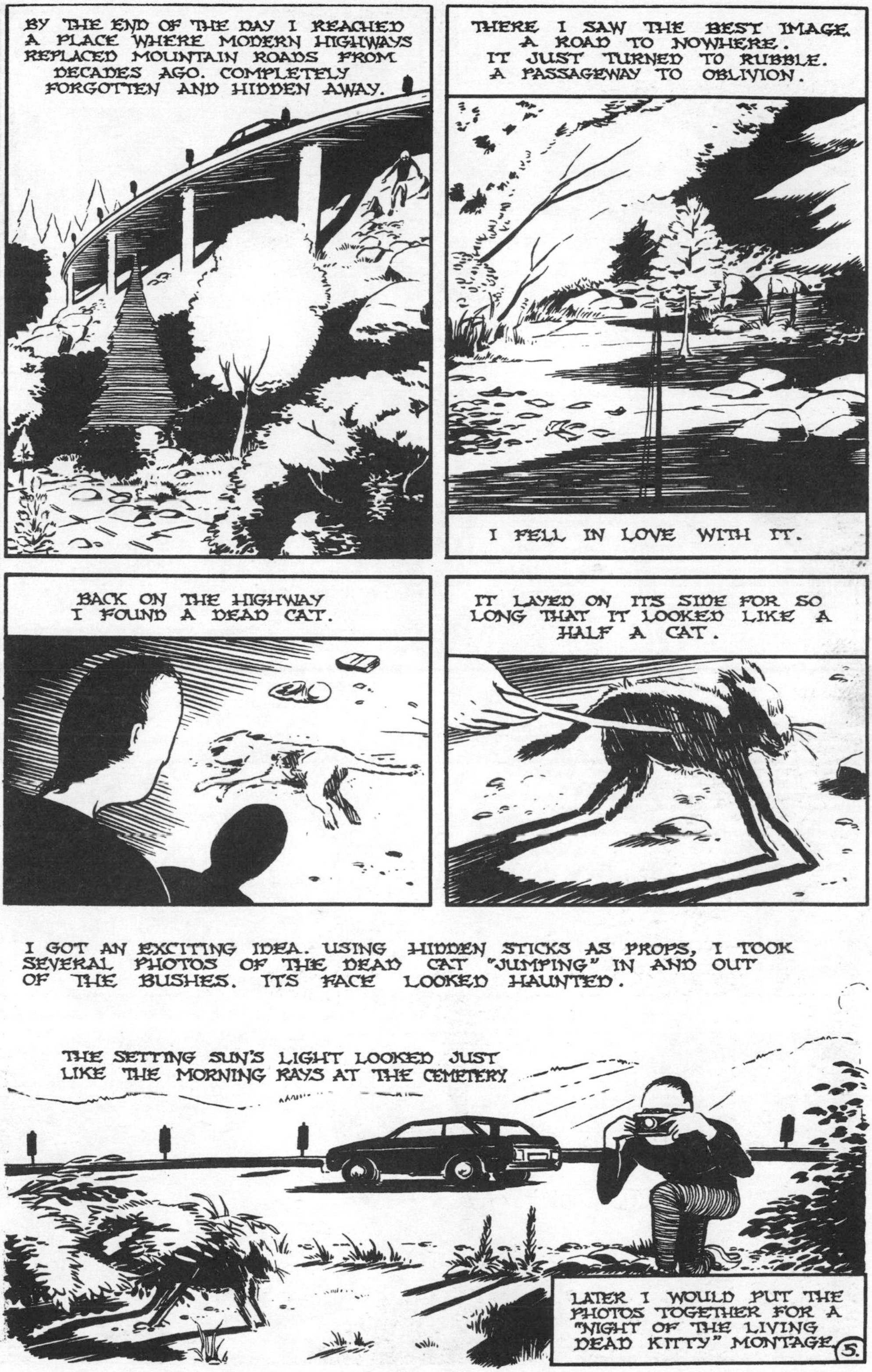
BY THE END OF THE DAY I REACHED A PLACE WHERE MODERN HIGHWAYS REPLACED MOUNTAIN ROADS FROM DECADES AGO. COMPLETELY FORGOTTEN AND HIDDEN AWAY.
THERE I SAW THE BEST IMAGE. A ROAD TO NOWHERE. IT JUST TURNED TO RUBBLE. A PASSAGEWAY TO OBLIVION.
I FELL IN LOVE WITH IT.
BACK ON THE HIGHWAY I FOUND A DEAD CAT.
IT LAYED ON IT'S SIDE FOR SO LONG THAT IT LOOKED LIKE A HALF A CAT.
I GOT AN EXCITING IDEA. USING HIDDEN STICKS AS PROPS, I TOOK SEVERAL PHOTOS OF THE DEAD CAT "JUMPING" IN AND OUT OF THE BUSHES. IT'S FACE LOOKED HAUNTED.
THE SETTING SUN'S LIGHT LOOKED JUST LIKE THE MORNING RAYS AT THE CEMETERY.
LATER I WOULD PUT THE PHOTOS TOGETHER FOR A "NIGHT OF THE LIVING DEAD KITTY" MONTAGE.
5.

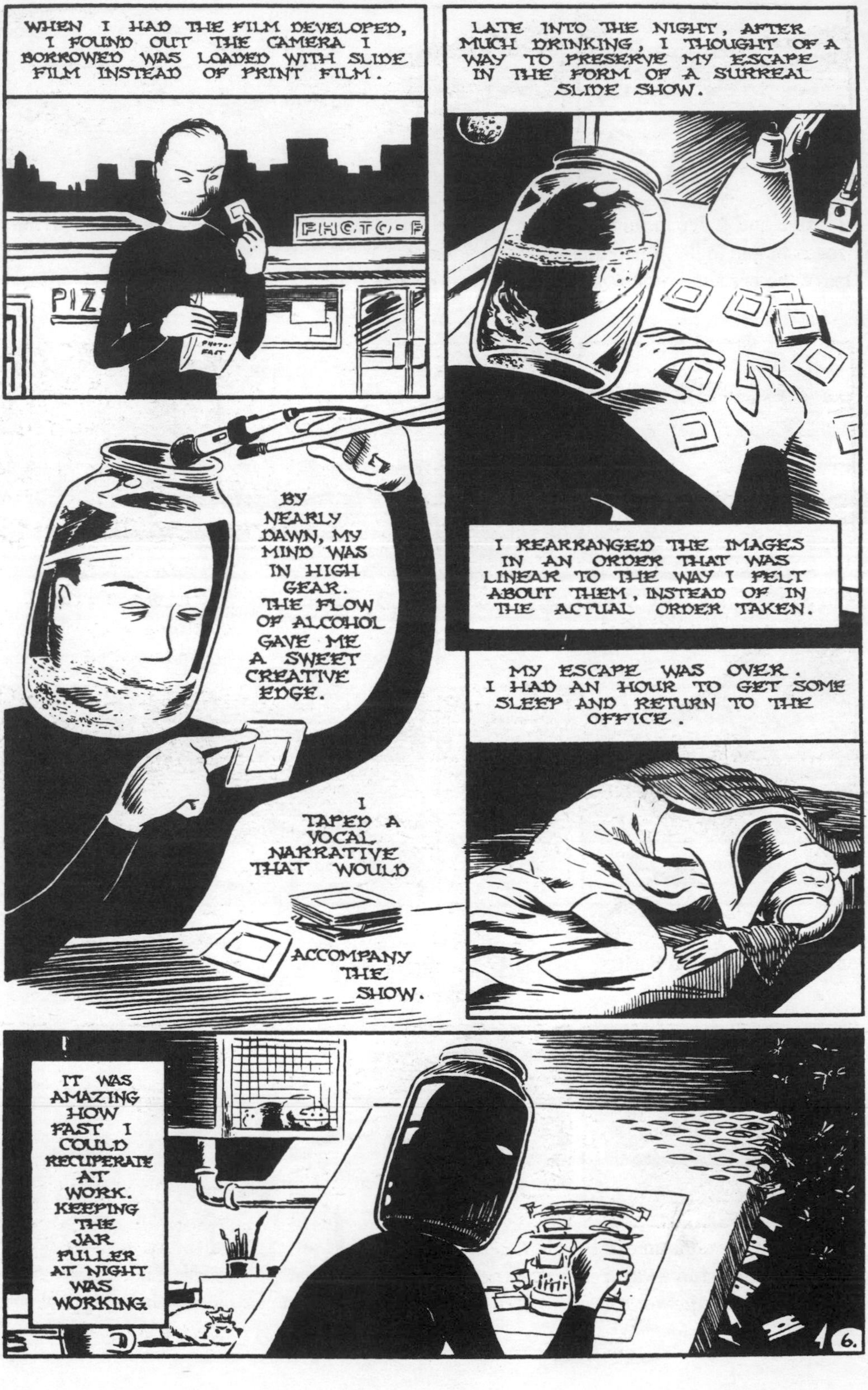
WHEN I HAD THE FILM DEVELOPED, I FOUND OUT THE CAMERA I BORROWED WAS LOADED WITH SLIDE FILM INSTEAD OF PRINT FILM.
PHOTO-F
PIZ
LATE INTO THE NIGHT, AFTER MUCH DRINKING, I THOUGHT OF A WAY TO PRESERVE MY ESCAPE IN THE FORM OF A SURREAL SLIDE SHOW.
BY NEARLY DAWN, MY MIND WAS IN HIGH GEAR. THE FLOW OF ALCOHOL GAVE ME A SWEET CREATIVE EDGE.
I TAPED A VOCAL NARRATIVE THAT WOULD
ACCOMPANY THE SHOW.
I REARRANGED THE IMAGES IN AN ORDER THAT WAS LINEAR TO THE WAY I FELT ABOUT THEM, INSTEAD OF IN THE ACTUAL ORDER TAKEN.
MY ESCAPE WAS OVER. I HAD AN HOUR TO GET SOME SLEEP AND RETURN TO THE OFFICE.
IT WAS AMAZING HOW FAST I COULD RECUPERATE AT WORK. KEEPING THE JAR FULLER AT NIGHT WAS WORKING.

I drove and drove, until the roads began to die. I had to leave the car and go on foot.

People have stumbled this way accidentally, but few came on purpose like I did.

Those who did try lay on the roadside. Their bodies failed them at that point.

I saw the last piece of civilization. I felt like I was really going to make it this time.

I could see it ahead. An ancient and beautiful place. So peaceful.

I was nearly there, then the light was obscured. Something unresolved was nagging at me.

Something hissing and horrible was there, heading me off through the bushes.

A cat! A mean, ugly, shrieking dead cat! I'm so much bigger but it scared me away.

I hate cats. Why was it ruining everything? It drove me down a dark passage to the side.

It mocked me and ran off. I hate cats that run away. I felt tricked and powerless.

It was too late. I could see signs of civilization again. A road grew out of the brush.

It led to my car. I had to go back. I'll have to get rid of some baggage before trying again.

I ALMOST FORGOT ABOUT THE SLIDE SHOW UNTIL AN OFFICE PARTY CAME UP. I THOUGHT IT WOULD MAKE GREAT ENTERTAINMENT, AND HUSTLED MY EQUIPMENT TOGETHER.

I DISPLAYED MY SHOW, BRIMMING WITH ENTHUSIASM.

MANY LEFT BEFORE ITS COMPLETION.

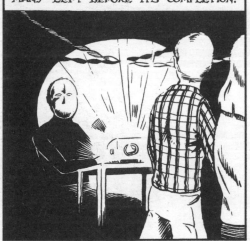

MANY MORE AFTER THE ENDING, WITH NO COMMENT GIVEN.

THEY DIDN'T SEE THE EDGE. THEY DISMISSED MY ESCAPE AS SILLY. OR SCARY. BUT IT WAS NEITHER.

NEXT TIME, I WOULD HAVE TO ESCAPE FARTHER.

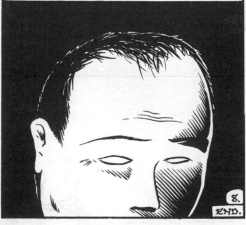

8.
END.

ESCAPE #2: The Dry Creek Bed

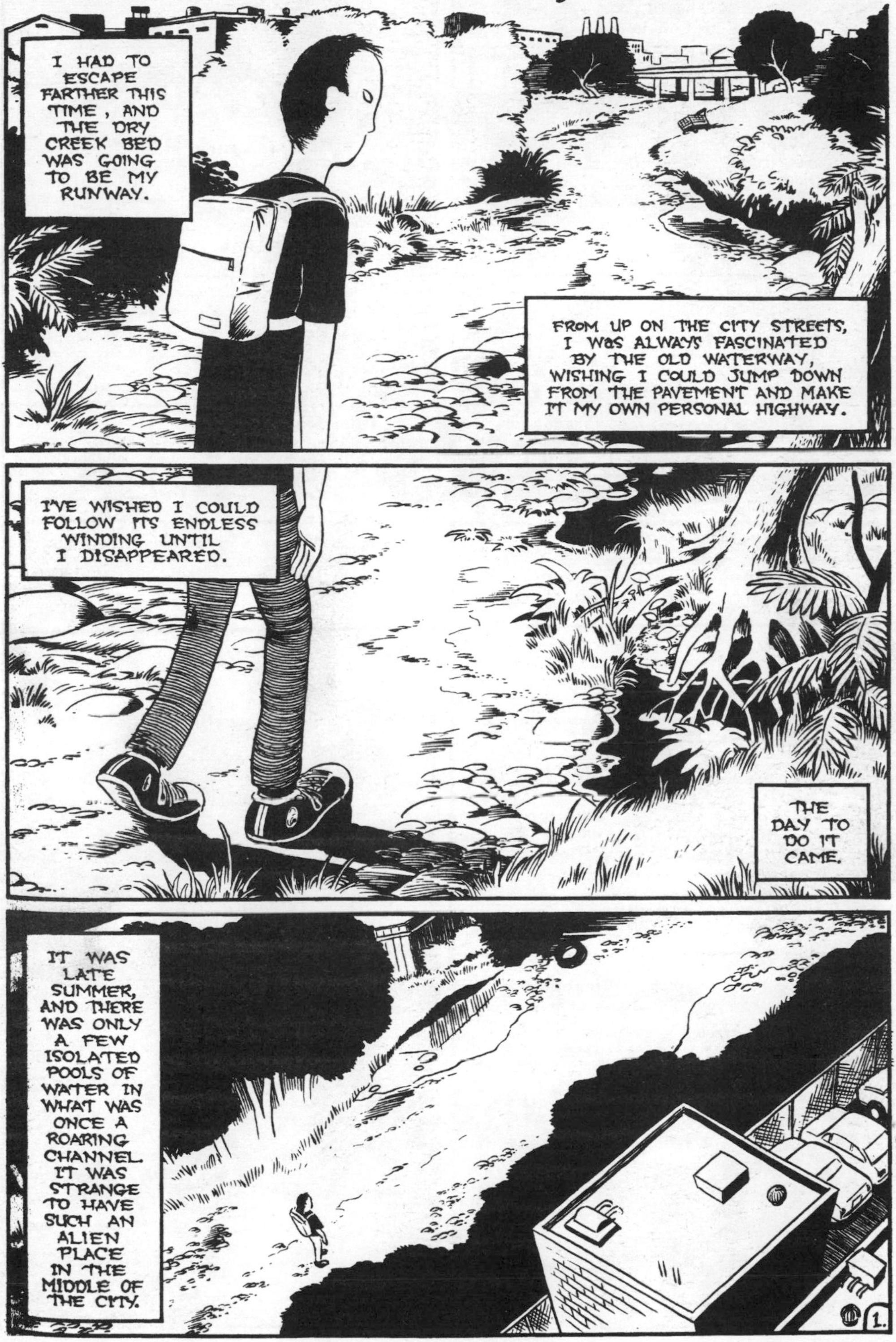
I HAD TO ESCAPE FARTHER THIS TIME, AND THE DRY CREEK BED WAS GOING TO BE MY RUNWAY.
FROM UP ON THE CITY STREETS, I WAS ALWAYS FASCINATED BY THE OLD WATERWAY, WISHING I COULD JUMP DOWN FROM THE PAVEMENT AND MAKE IT MY OWN PERSONAL HIGHWAY.
I'VE WISHED I COULD FOLLOW ITS ENDLESS WINDING UNTIL I DISAPPEARED.
THE DAY TO DO IT CAME.
IT WAS LATE SUMMER, AND THERE WAS ONLY A FEW ISOLATED POOLS OF WATER IN WHAT WAS ONCE A ROARING CHANNEL. IT WAS STRANGE TO HAVE SUCH AN ALIEN PLACE IN THE MIDDLE OF THE CITY.
1.

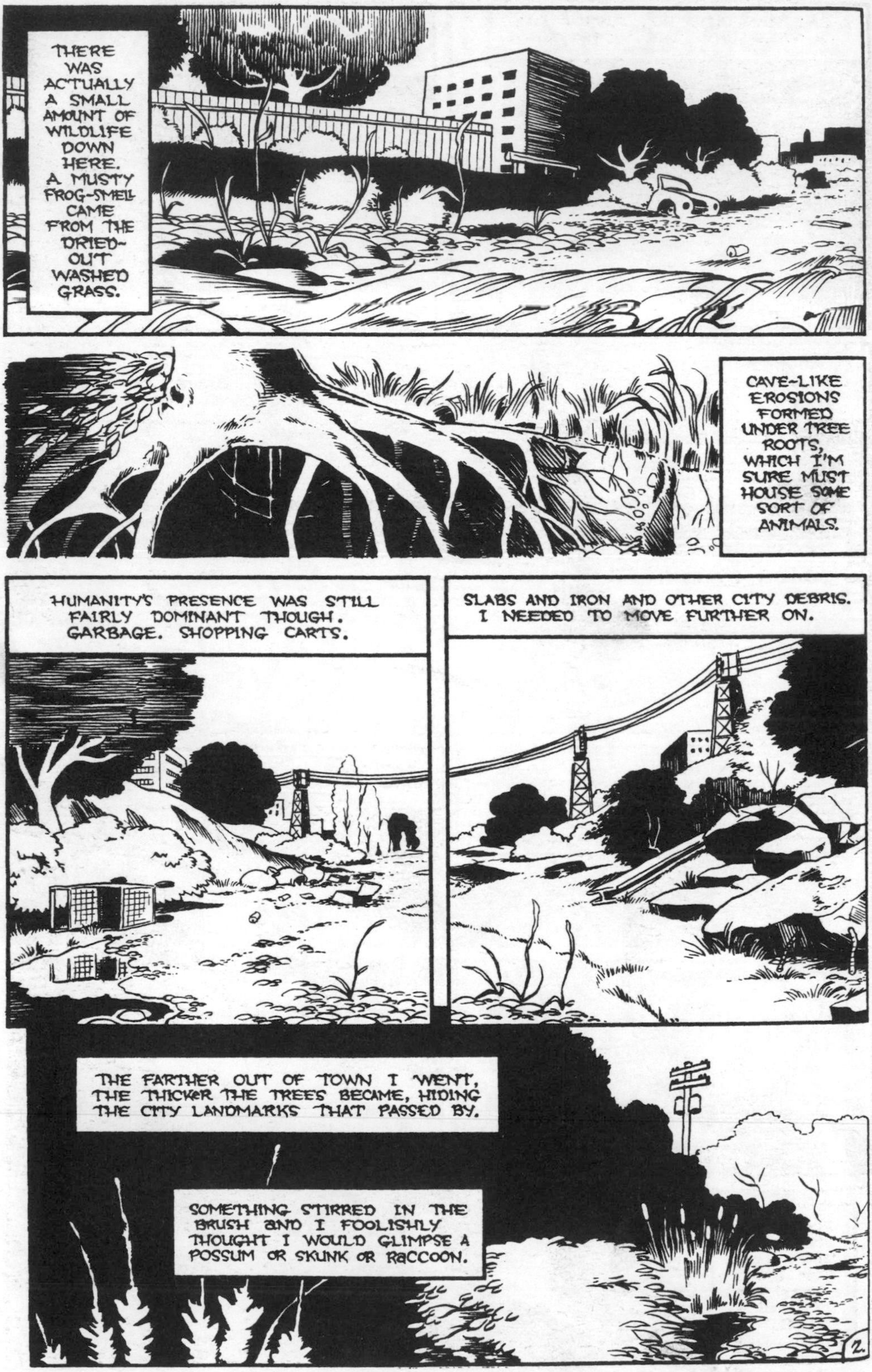
THERE WAS ACTUALLY A SMALL AMOUNT OF WILDLIFE DOWN HERE. A MUSTY FROG-SMELL CAME FROM THE DRIED-OUT WASHED GRASS.
CAVE-LIKE EROSIONS FORMED UNDER TREE ROOTS, WHICH I'M SURE MUST HOUSE SOME SORT OF ANIMALS.
HUMANITY'S PRESENCE WAS STILL FAIRLY DOMINANT THOUGH. GARBAGE. SHOPPING CARTS.
SLABS AND IRON AND OTHER CITY DEBRIS. I NEEDED TO MOVE FURTHER ON.
THE FARTHER OUT OF TOWN I WENT, THE THICKER THE TREES BECAME, HIDING THE CITY LANDMARKS THAT PASSED BY.
SOMETHING STIRRED IN THE BRUSH AND I FOOLISHLY THOUGHT I WOULD GLIMPSE A POSSUM OR SKUNK OR RACCOON.
2.

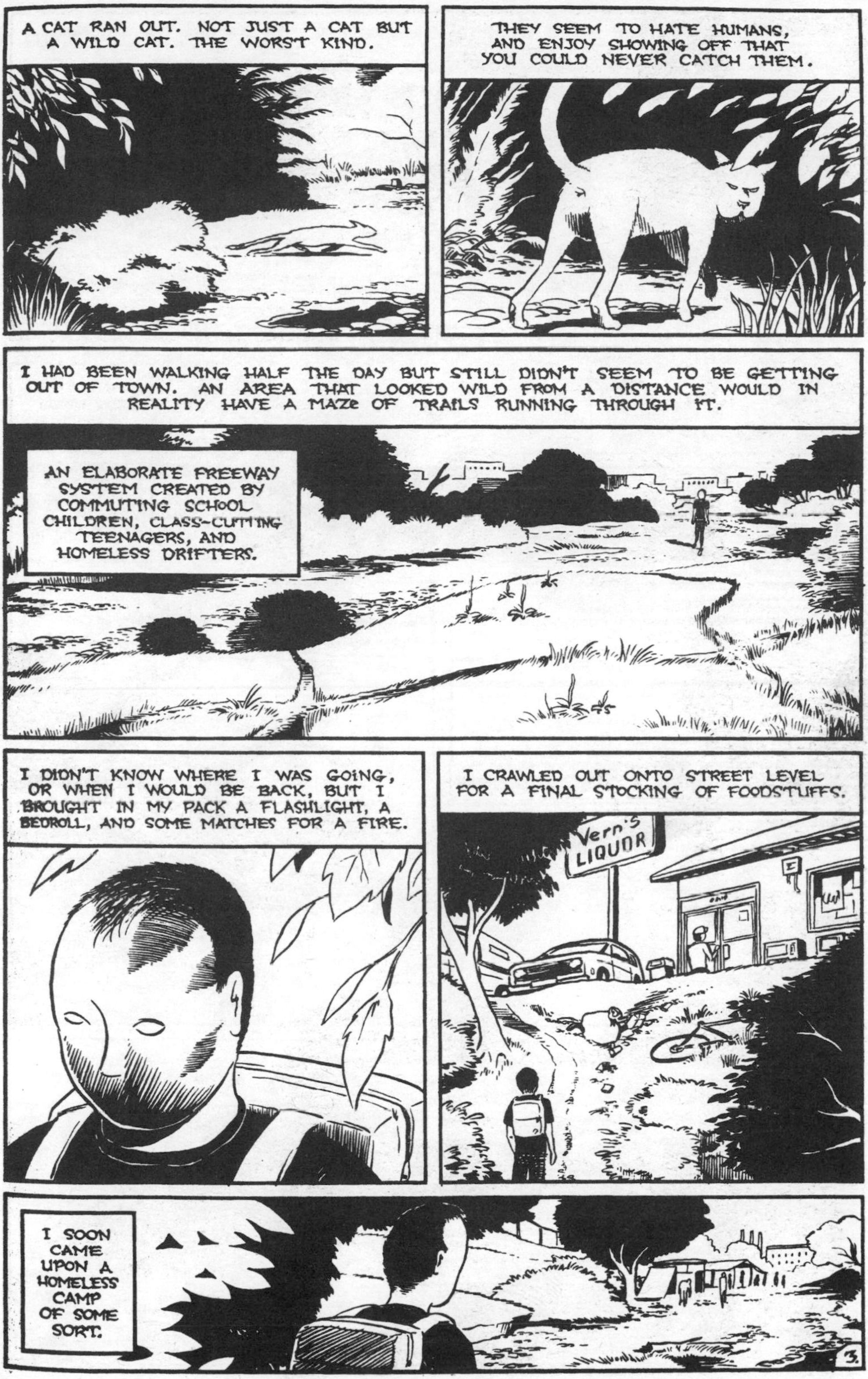
A CAT RAN OUT. NOT JUST A CAT BUT A WILD CAT. THE WORST KIND.
THEY SEEM TO HATE HUMANS, AND ENJOY SHOWING OFF THAT YOU COULD NEVER CATCH THEM.
I HAD BEEN WALKING HALF THE DAY BUT STILL DIDN'T SEEM TO BE GETTING OUT OF TOWN. AN AREA THAT LOOKED WILD FROM A DISTANCE WOULD IN REALITY HAVE A MAZE OF TRAILS RUNNING THROUGH IT.
AN ELABORATE FREEWAY SYSTEM CREATED BY COMMUTING SCHOOL CHILDREN, CLASS-CUTTING TEENAGERS, AND HOMELESS DRIFTERS.
I DIDN'T KNOW WHERE I WAS GOING, OR WHEN I WOULD BE BACK, BUT I BROUGHT IN MY PACK A FLASHLIGHT, A BEDROLL, AND SOME MATCHES FOR A FIRE.
I CRAWLED OUT ONTO STREET LEVEL FOR A FINAL STOCKING OF FOODSTUFFS.
Vern's LIQUOR
I SOON CAME UPON A HOMELESS CAMP OF SOME SORT.
3.

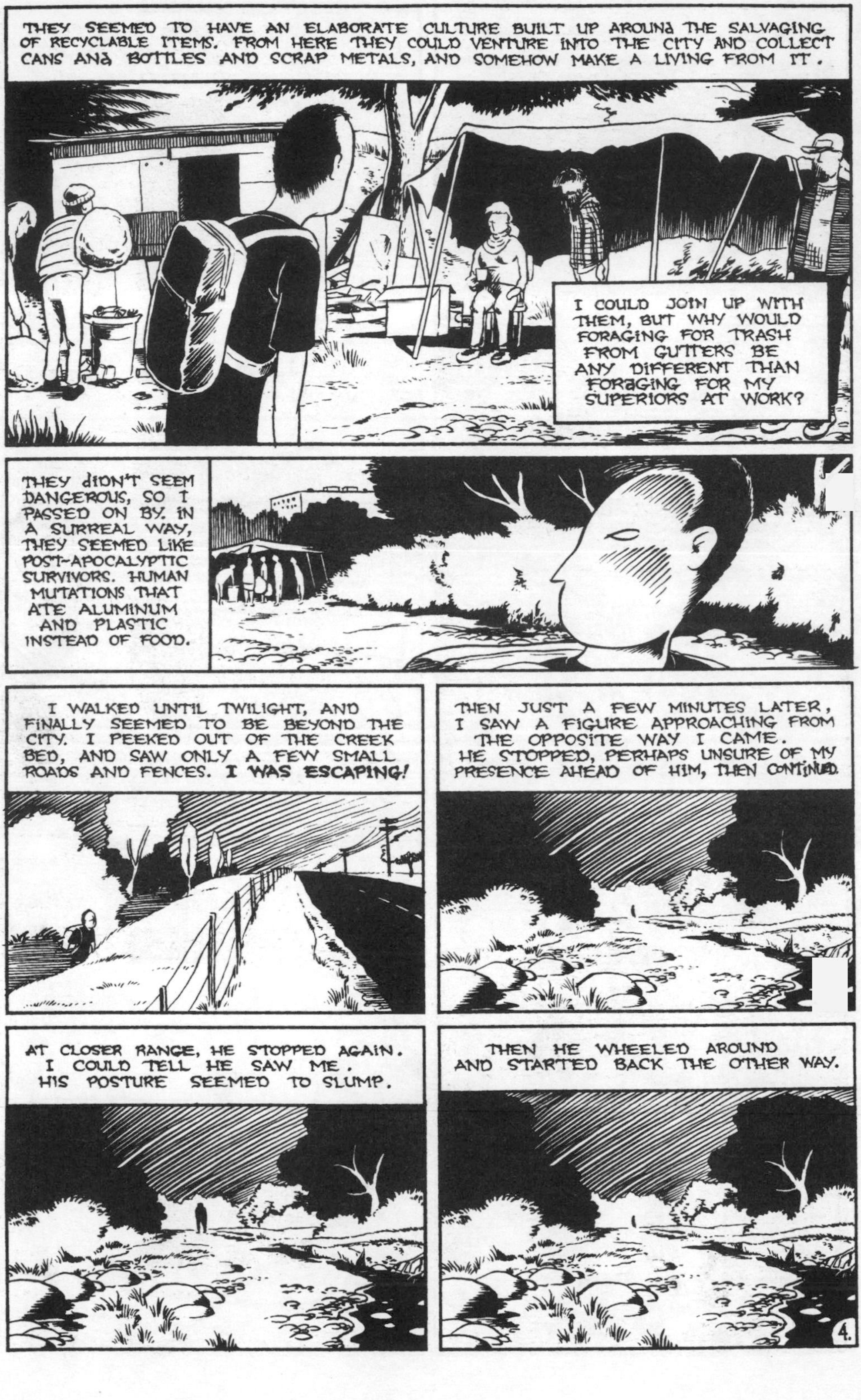
THEY SEEMED TO HAVE AN ELABORATE CULTURE BUILT UP AROUND THE SALVAGING OF RECYCLABLE ITEMS. FROM HERE THEY COULD VENTURE INTO THE CITY AND COLLECT CANS AND BOTTLES AND SCRAP METALS, AND SOMEHOW MAKE A LIVING FROM IT.
I COULD JOIN UP WITH THEM, BUT WHY WOULD FORAGING FOR TRASH FROM GUTTERS BE ANY DIFFERENT THAN FORAGING FOR MY SUPERIORS AT WORK?
THEY DIDN'T SEEM DANGEROUS, SO I PASSED ON BY. IN A SURREAL WAY, THEY SEEMED LIKE POST-APOCALYPTIC SURVIVORS. HUMAN MUTATIONS THAT ATE ALUMINUM AND PLASTIC INSTEAD OF FOOD.
I WALKED UNTIL TWILIGHT, AND FINALLY SEEMED TO BE BEYOND THE CITY. I PEEKED OUT OF THE CREEK BED, AND SAW ONLY A FEW SMALL ROADS AND FENCES. I WAS ESCAPING!
THEN JUST A FEW MINUTES LATER, I SAW A FIGURE APPROACHING FROM THE OPPOSITE WAY I CAME. HE STOPPED, PERHAPS UNSURE OF MY PRESENCE AHEAD OF HIM, THEN CONTINUED.
AT CLOSER RANGE, HE STOPPED AGAIN. I COULD TELL HE SAW ME. HIS POSTURE SEEMED TO SLUMP.
THEN HE WHEELED AROUND AND STARTED BACK THE OTHER WAY.
4.

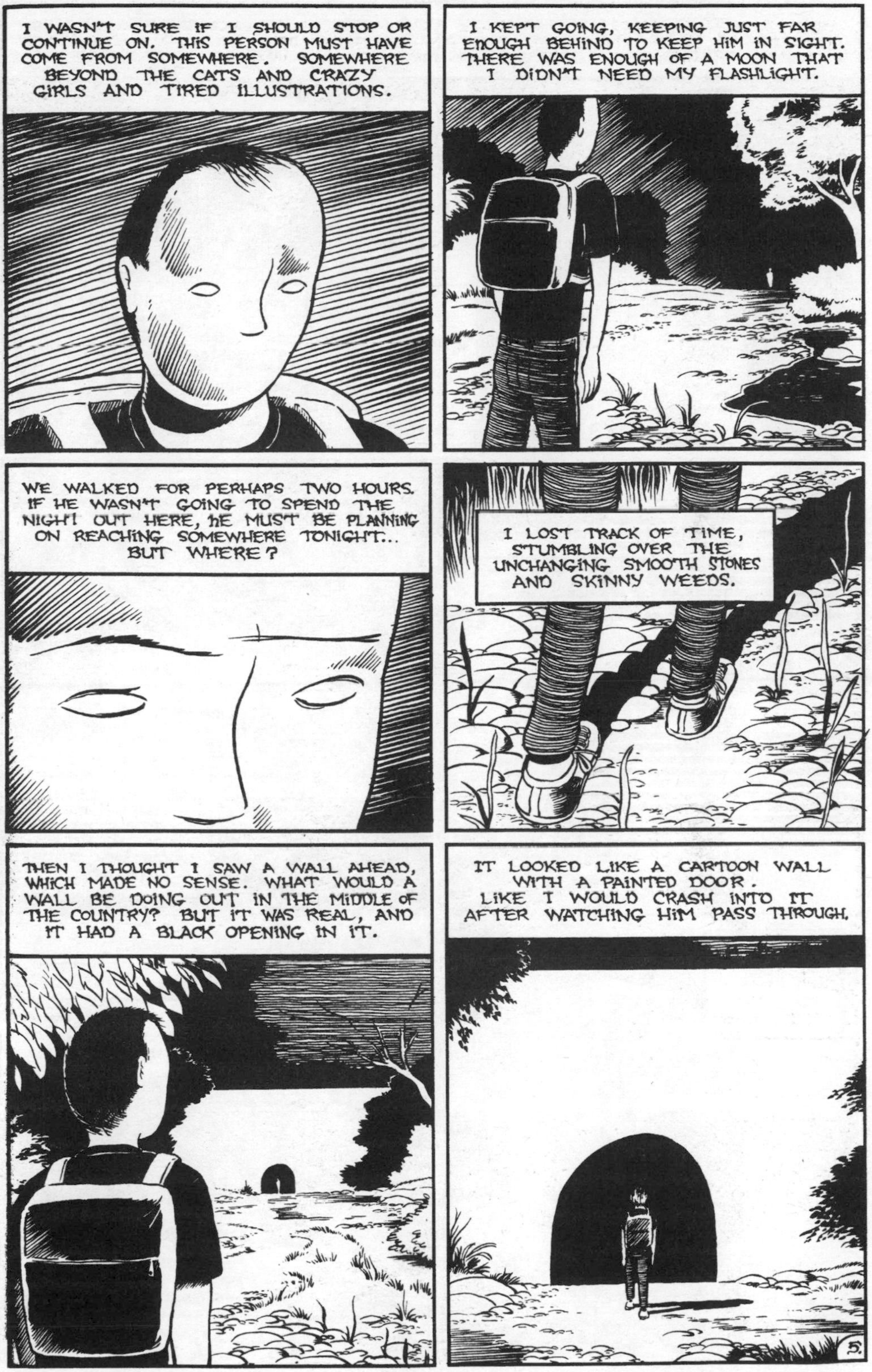
I WASN'T SURE IF I SHOULD STOP OR CONTINUE ON. THIS PERSON MUST HAVE COME FROM SOMEWHERE. SOMEWHERE BEYOND THE CATS AND CRAZY GIRLS AND TIRED ILLUSTRATIONS.
I KEPT GOING, KEEPING JUST FAR ENOUGH BEHIND TO KEEP HIM IN SIGHT. THERE WAS ENOUGH OF A MOON THAT I DIDN'T NEED MY FLASHLIGHT.
WE WALKED FOR PERHAPS TWO HOURS. IF HE WASN'T GOING TO SPEND THE NIGHT OUT HERE, HE MUST BE PLANNING ON REACHING SOMEWHERE TONIGHT... BUT WHERE?
I LOST TRACK OF TIME, STUMBLING OVER THE UNCHANGING SMOOTH STONES AND SKINNY WEEDS.
THEN I THOUGHT I SAW A WALL AHEAD, WHICH MADE NO SENSE. WHAT WOULD A WALL BE DOING OUT IN THE MIDDLE OF THE COUNTRY? BUT IT WAS REAL, AND IT HAD A BLACK OPENING IN IT.
IT LOOKED LIKE A CARTOON WALL WITH A PAINTED DOOR. LIKE I WOULD CRASH INTO IT AFTER WATCHING HIM PASS THROUGH.
5.

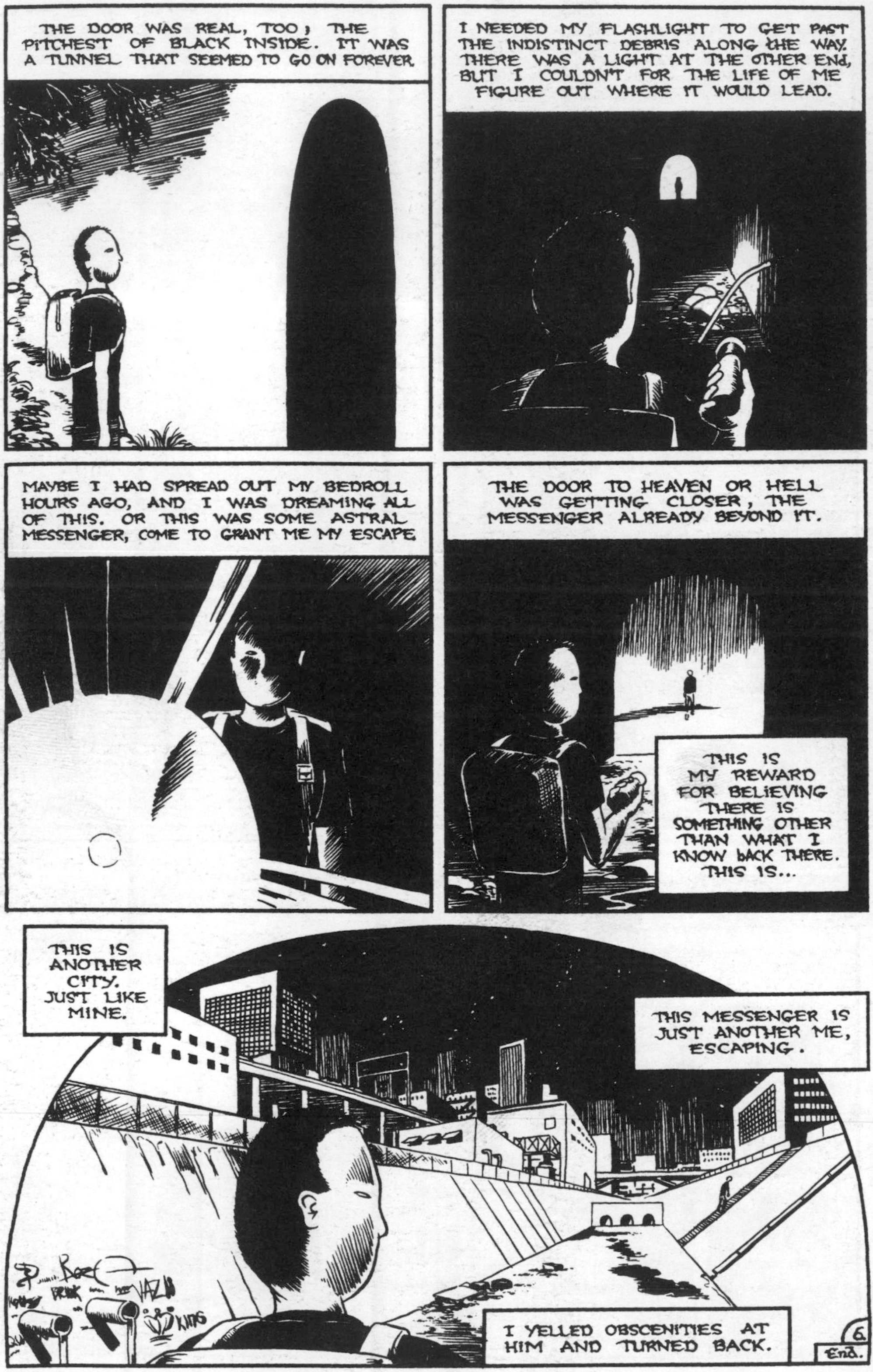
THE DOOR WAS REAL, TOO; THE PITCHEST OF BLACK INSIDE. IT WAS A TUNNEL THAT SEEMED TO GO ON FOREVER.
I NEEDED MY FLASHLIGHT TO GET PAST THE INDISTINCT DEBRIS ALONG THE WAY. THERE WAS A LIGHT AT THE OTHER END, BUT I COULDN'T FOR THE LIFE OF ME FIGURE OUT WHERE IT WOULD LEAD.
MAYBE I HAD SPREAD OUT MY BEDROLL HOURS AGO, AND I WAS DREAMING ALL OF THIS. OR THIS WAS SOME ASTRAL MESSENGER, COME TO GRANT ME MY ESCAPE.
THE DOOR TO HEAVEN OR HELL WAS GETTING CLOSER, THE MESSENGER ALREADY BEYOND IT.
THIS IS MY REWARD FOR BELIEVING THERE IS SOMETHING OTHER THAN WHAT I KNOW BACK THERE. THIS IS...
THIS IS ANOTHER CITY. JUST LIKE MINE.
THIS MESSENGER IS JUST ANOTHER ME, ESCAPING.
I YELLED OBSCENITIES AT HIM AND TURNED BACK.
6.
End.

"BE CREATIVE"

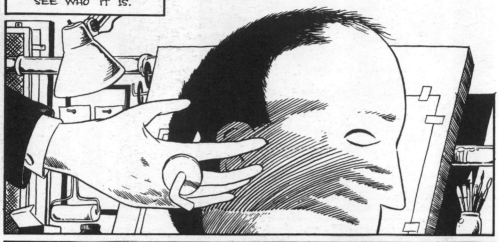

THERE IS A MAN, OR A WOMAN, WHO TAPS THE SIDE OF MY HEAD, AND I CAN NEVER SEE WHO IT IS.

THE TAP WOULD PUNCTURE MY TEMPLE WITHOUT WARNING.

I WOULD INSTANTLY FEEL A LITHIUM-LIKE EUPHORIA, AND IN THE TIME IT WOULD TAKE TO TURN MY HEAD AROUND, THEY WOULD BE GONE.

THE MANAGEMENT AND SALES PEOPLE TAP ME WITH NO SECRECY. IT IS MY JOB TO ACCEPT IT.

THE ONE WHO WANTS MY TEMPLE DOES NOT EVEN GRANT ME THE COURTESY OF A FACE-TO-FACE PLUNDERING OF MY JUICE.

SOMEDAY I WILL LEARN WHO THIS PERSON IS.

1.

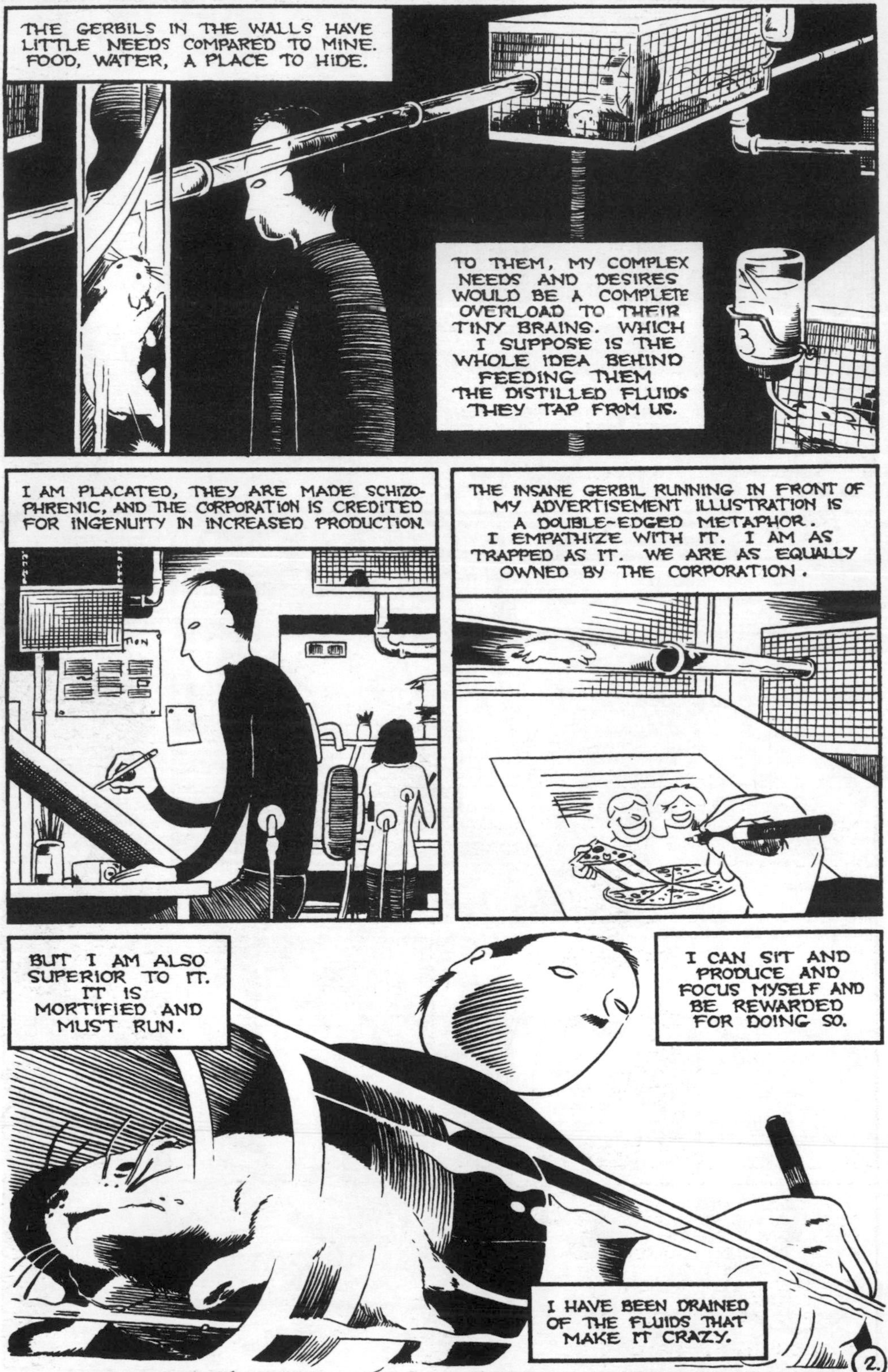
THE GERBILS IN THE WALLS HAVE LITTLE NEEDS COMPARED TO MINE. FOOD, WATER, A PLACE TO HIDE.
TO THEM, MY COMPLEX NEEDS AND DESIRES WOULD BE A COMPLETE OVERLOAD TO THEIR TINY BRAINS. WHICH I SUPPOSE IS THE WHOLE IDEA BEHIND FEEDING THEM THE DISTILLED FLUIDS THEY TAP FROM US.
I AM PLACATED, THEY ARE MADE SCHIZOPHRENIC, AND THE CORPORATION IS CREDITED FOR INGENUITY IN INCREASED PRODUCTION.
THE INSANE GERBIL RUNNING IN FRONT OF MY ADVERTISEMENT ILLUSTRATION IS A DOUBLE-EDGED METAPHOR. I EMPATHIZE WITH IT. I AM AS TRAPPED AS IT. WE ARE AS EQUALLY OWNED BY THE CORPORATION.
BUT I AM ALSO SUPERIOR TO IT. IT IS MORTIFIED AND MUST RUN.
I CAN SIT AND PRODUCE AND FOCUS MYSELF AND BE REWARDED FOR DOING SO.
I HAVE BEEN DRAINED OF THE FLUIDS THAT MAKE IT CRAZY.

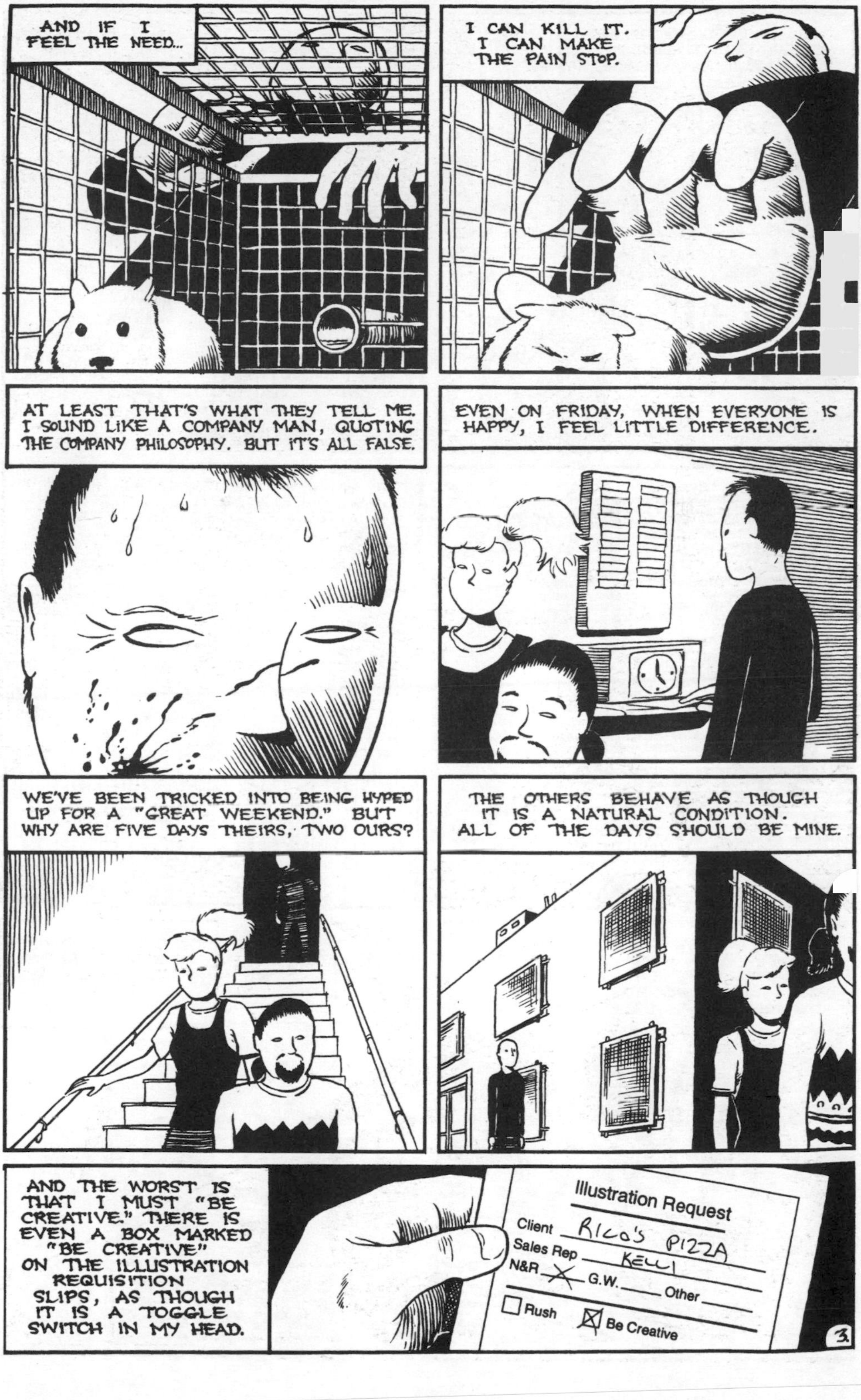
AND IF I FEEL THE NEED...
I CAN KILL IT. I CAN MAKE THE PAIN STOP.
AT LEAST THAT'S WHAT THEY TELL ME. I SOUND LIKE A COMPANY MAN, QUOTING THE COMPANY PHILOSOPHY. BUT IT'S ALL FALSE.
EVEN ON FRIDAY, WHEN EVERYONE IS HAPPY, I FEEL LITTLE DIFFERENCE.
WE'VE BEEN TRICKED INTO BEING HYPED UP FOR A "GREAT WEEKEND." BUT WHY ARE FIVE DAYS THEIRS, TWO OURS?
THE OTHERS BEHAVE AS THOUGH IT IS A NATURAL CONDITION. ALL OF THE DAYS SHOULD BE MINE.
AND THE WORST IS THAT I MUST "BE CREATIVE." THERE IS EVEN A BOX MARKED "BE CREATIVE" ON THE ILLUSTRATION REQUISITION SLIPS, AS THOUGH IT IS A TOGGLE SWITCH IN MY HEAD.
Illustration Request
Client RICO'S PIZZA
Sales Rep KELLI
N&R X G.W. Other
Rush
Be Creative
3.

I AM NEEDED TO THINK OF THINGS OTHERS ARE INCAPABLE OF, WHILE THOSE SAME PEOPLE ARE DRAINING THE JUICES NECESSARY TO DO IT.

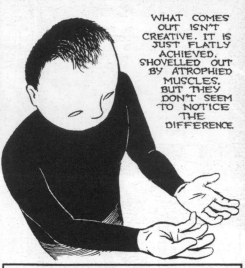

WHAT COMES OUT ISN'T CREATIVE. IT IS JUST FLATLY ACHIEVED, SHOVELLED OUT BY ATROPHIED MUSCLES. BUT THEY DON'T SEEM TO NOTICE THE DIFFERENCE.

SO MY DREAMS, THAT SCURRY AWAY THROUGH HABITRAIL TUBES, MUST BE WAYLAYED WHILE I FULFILL THE LIMITED DREAMS OF SALES REPRESENTATIVES.

BUT IT IS NOW THE "GREAT WEEKEND." LIKE A SCHIZOPHRENIC GERBIL, I RACE TO MY PLACE TO HIDE, AND TRY TO SUCKLE NOURISHMENT FROM THE JUICES I NEED.

BUT I AM SO DRIED INSIDE I WANT IT ALL IMMEDIATELY. I CAN'T PERCEIVE THAT THERE WILL BE HUNDREDS OF WEEKENDS AND AN ENTIRE LIFE AHEAD OF ME.

I COULD BE SMASHED LIKE THE THROWAWAY GERBIL AT ANY MOMENT. A WEEKEND WILL NEVER BE ENOUGH.

④

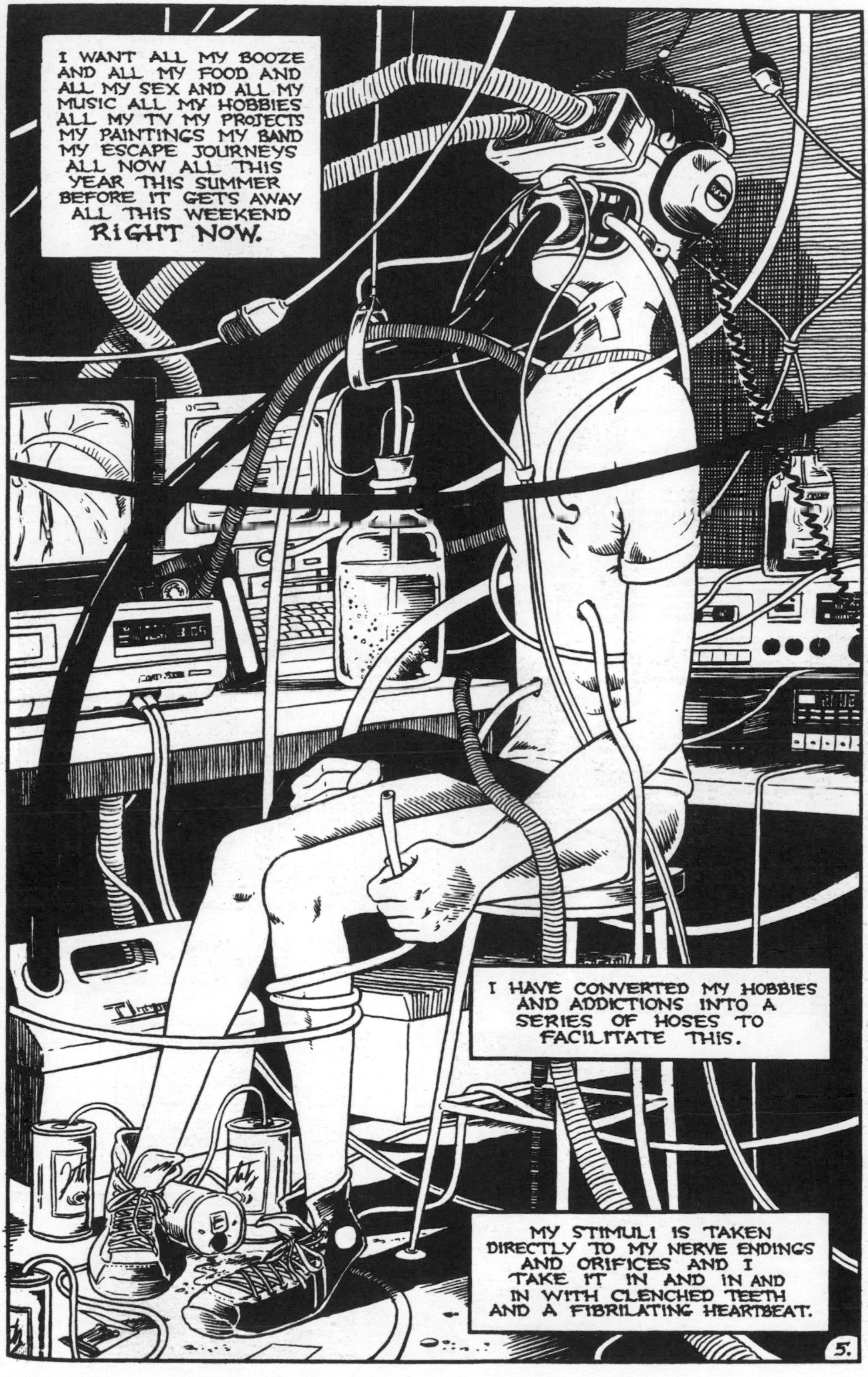
I WANT ALL MY BOOZE AND ALL MY FOOD AND ALL MY SEX AND ALL MY MUSIC ALL MY HOBBIES ALL MY TV MY PROJECTS MY PAINTINGS MY BAND MY ESCAPE JOURNEYS ALL NOW ALL THIS YEAR THIS SUMMER BEFORE IT GETS AWAY ALL THIS WEEKEND RIGHT NOW.
I HAVE CONVERTED MY HOBBIES AND ADDICTIONS INTO A SERIES OF HOSES TO FACILITATE THIS.
MY STIMULI IS TAKEN DIRECTLY TO MY NERVE ENDINGS AND ORIFICES AND I TAKE IT IN AND IN AND IN WITH CLENCHED TEETH AND A FIBRILATING HEARTBEAT.
5.

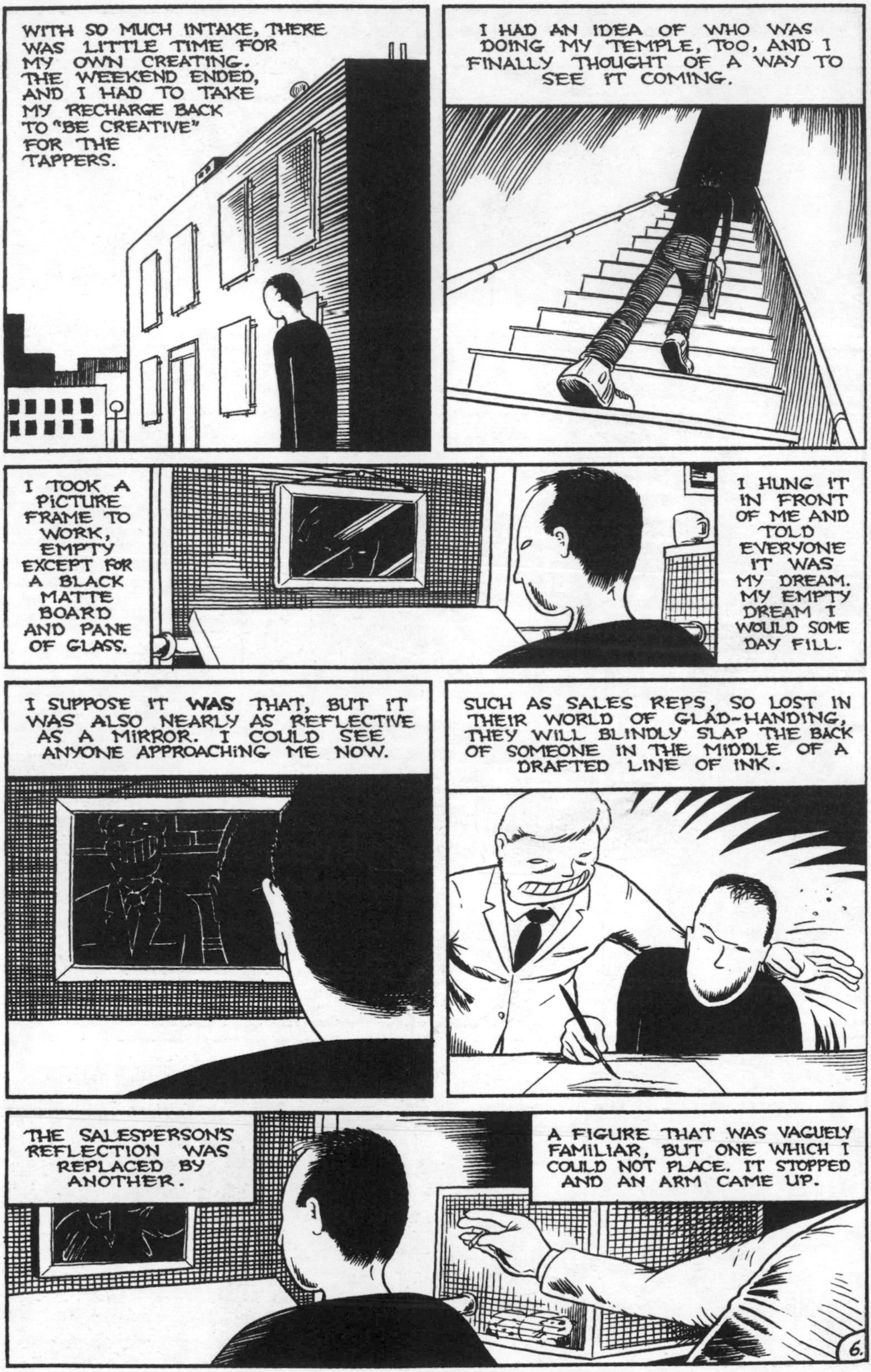
WITH SO MUCH INTAKE, THERE WAS LITTLE TIME FOR MY OWN CREATING. THE WEEKEND ENDED, AND I HAD TO TAKE MY RECHARGE BACK TO "BE CREATIVE" FOR THE TAPPERS.
I HAD AN IDEA OF WHO WAS DOING MY TEMPLE, TOO, AND I FINALLY THOUGHT OF A WAY TO SEE IT COMING.
I TOOK A PICTURE FRAME TO WORK, EMPTY EXCEPT FOR A BLACK MATTE BOARD AND PANE OF GLASS.
I HUNG IT IN FRONT OF ME AND TOLD EVERYONE IT WAS MY DREAM. MY EMPTY DREAM I WOULD SOME DAY FILL.
I SUPPOSE IT WAS THAT, BUT IT WAS ALSO NEARLY AS REFLECTIVE AS A MIRROR. I COULD SEE ANYONE APPROACHING ME NOW.
SUCH AS SALES REPS, SO LOST IN THEIR WORLD OF GLAD-HANDING, THEY WILL BLINDLY SLAP THE BACK OF SOMEONE IN THE MIDDLE OF A DRAFTED LINE OF INK.
THE SALESPERSON'S REFLECTION WAS REPLACED BY ANOTHER.
A FIGURE THAT WAS VAGUELY FAMILIAR, BUT ONE WHICH I COULD NOT PLACE. IT STOPPED AND AN ARM CAME UP.

I WHEELED AROUND BEFORE IT WAS TOO LATE. I BEAT HIM!

I LOOKED FLUSTERED, BUT THE MAN JUST LOWERED HIS EXTENDED ARM CALMLY, WITH NO INDICATION OF GUILT OR REMORSE.

"HOW ARE YOU, LAD?" HE ASKED. "FINE, SIR," MY RESPONSE.

"HOLD STILL FOR A MINUTE." "YES, SIR."

THIS MAN WAS NOT AFRAID TO CONFRONT ME. THIS MAN WAS THE OWNER OF THE CORPORATION. THIS MAN WAS TOO **BUSY** TO EVER HAVE SPOKEN TO ME.

I WAS TAPPED, AND WOULD RELAX. MY EMPTY DREAM WOULD WAIT.

ALL THESE TIRED DRAWINGS I DRAW TO SELL SOAP ARE ALL A PART OF THE GIANT DREAMS OF THIS MAN.

HE LIVES THE BENEFIT OF ALL THAT I DO, AND ALL THAT I DON'T.

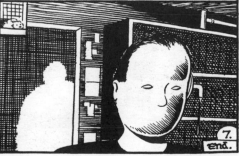

7. END.

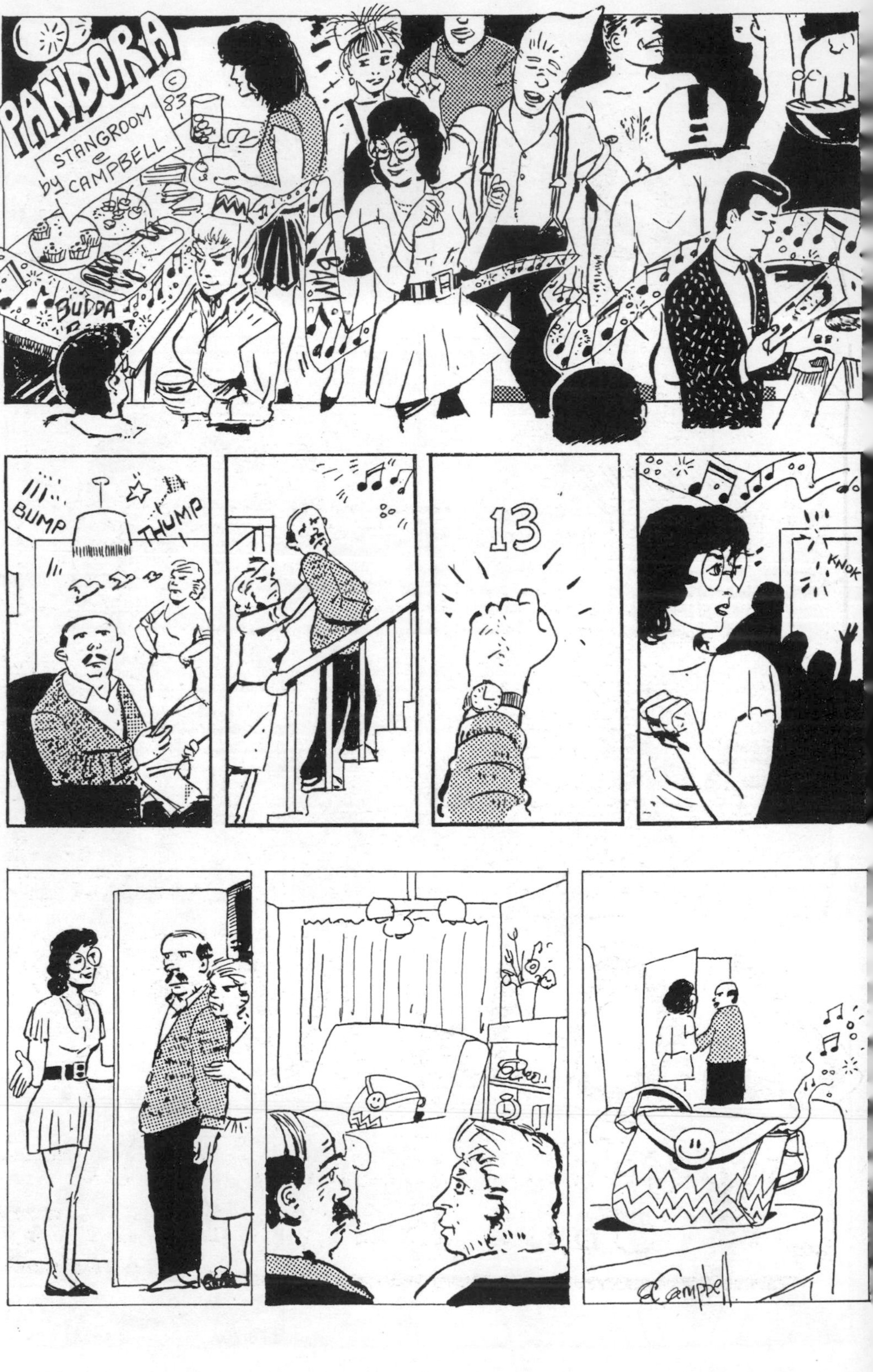
PANDORA
© 83
STANGROOM & CAMPBELL
by
BUDDA
BAM
BUMP
THUMP
13
KNOK
Campbell

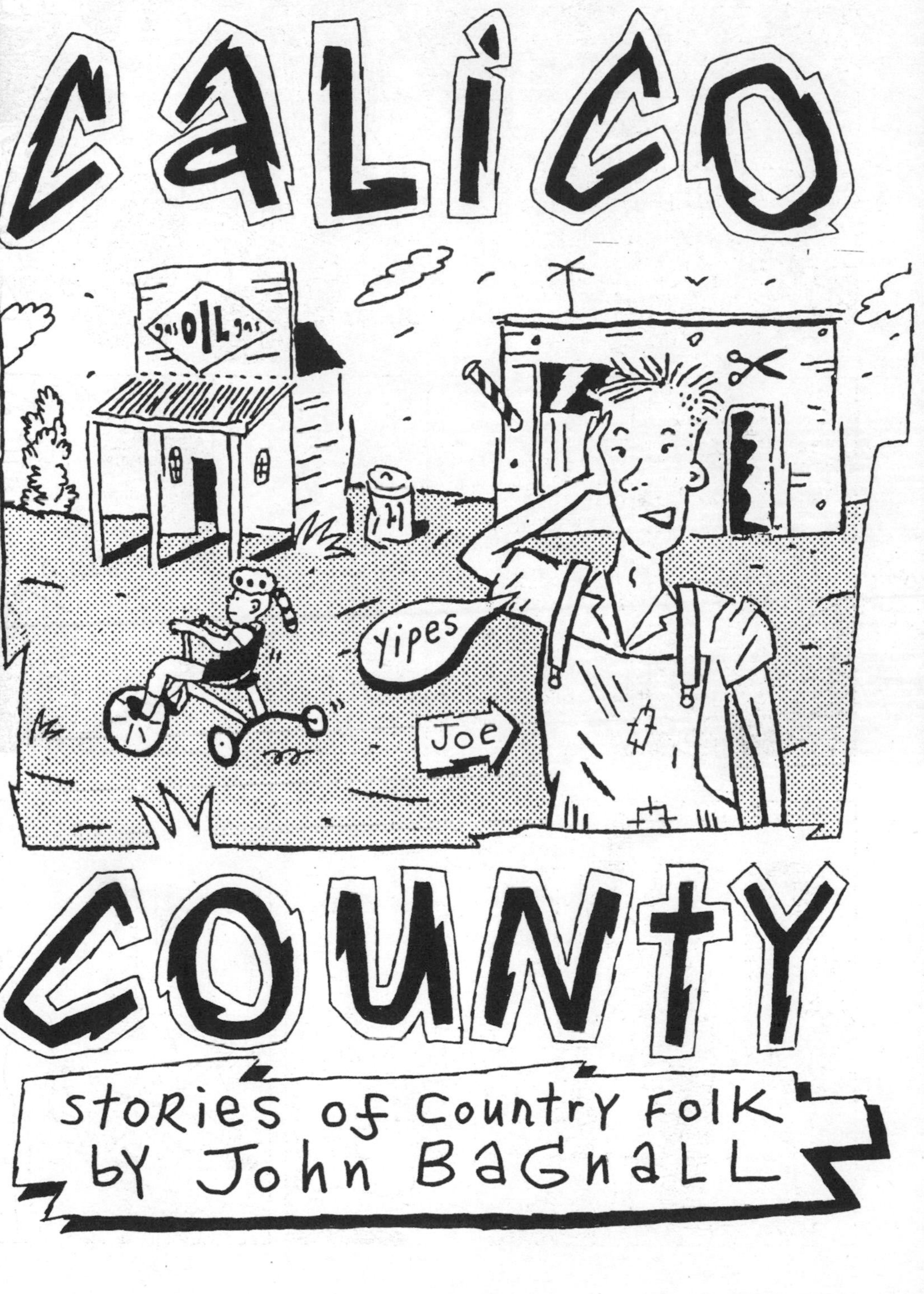
Calico
gas OIL gas
yipes
Joe
County
stories of Country Folk
by John Bagnall

John Bagnall

CALICO COUNTY
Self-published, 1984–85

In the mid-1980s, in his hometown of Liverpool, John Bagnall met with some like-minded comics enthusiasts and together they self-published a comics anthology called *Trashcan*. This garnered a rave review in the music paper *NME* (*New Musical Express*), and from this, he soon became acquainted with various other UK small-press creators who were receiving some attention. His strips started to appear in the now legendary early anthology, *Fast Fiction*.

"These *Calico County* stories are among the first comic strips I ever drew. I've drawn comics periodically ever since, between illustration and painting, my subject matter gradually becoming more overtly English and nostalgic, but still with a humorous bent. Book collections representative of this more recent work are *Don't Tread on my Rosaries* (Kingly Books, 2003) and *Knitting with Coalsmoke* (Lulu Books, 2013)." – JB

www.bagnallsretreat.blogspot.com
www.lulu.com

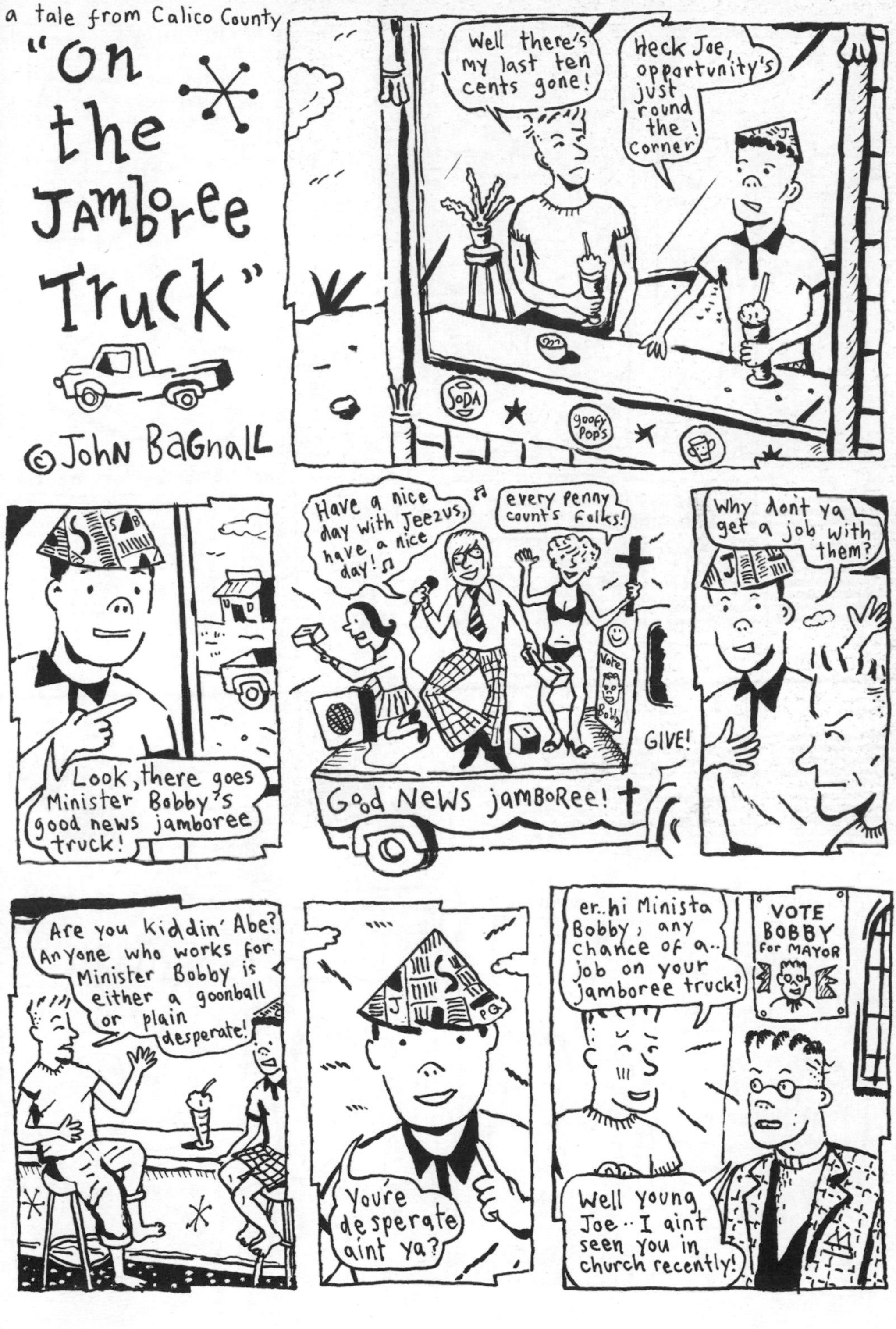
a tale from Calico County
"On the Jamboree Truck"
© John Bagnall
Well there's my last ten cents gone!
Heck Joe, opportunity's just round the corner!
SODA
goofy pop's
Look, there goes Minister Bobby's good news jamboree truck!
Have a nice day with Jeezus, have a nice day!
every penny counts folks!
Vote Bobby
GIVE!
Good NEWS jamboree!
Why don't ya get a job with them?
Are you kiddin' Abe? Anyone who works for Minister Bobby is either a goonball or plain desperate!
You're desperate aint ya?
er.. hi Minista Bobby, any chance of a.. job on your jamboree truck?
VOTE BOBBY for MAYOR
Well young Joe.. I aint seen you in church recently!

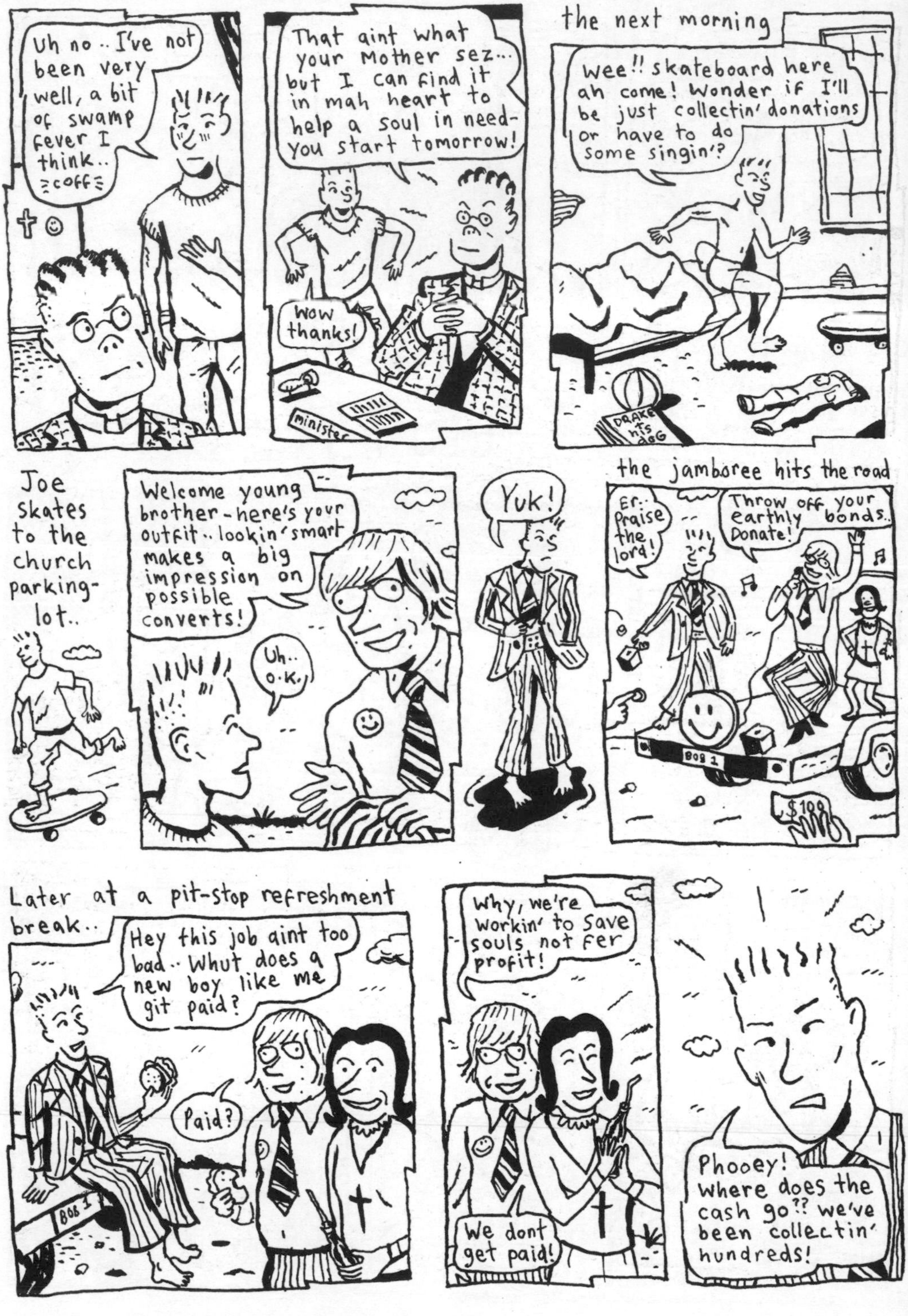
Uh no.. I've not been very well, a bit of swamp fever I think.. coff
That aint what your Mother sez... but I can find it in mah heart to help a soul in need- You start tomorrow!
Wow thanks!
minister
the next morning
Wee!! skateboard here ah come! Wonder if I'll be just collectin' donations or have to do some singin'?
DRAKE hits doG
Joe skates to the church parking-lot..
Welcome young brother - here's your outfit.. lookin' smart makes a big impression on possible converts!
Uh.. O.K.
Yuk!
the jamboree hits the road
Er. Praise the lord!
Throw off your earthly bonds.. Donate!
BOB 1
$100
Later at a pit-stop refreshment break..
Hey this job aint too bad.. Whut does a new boy like me git paid?
Paid?
BOB 1
Why, we're workin' to save souls not fer profit!
We dont get paid!
Phooey! where does the cash go?? we've been collectin' hundreds!

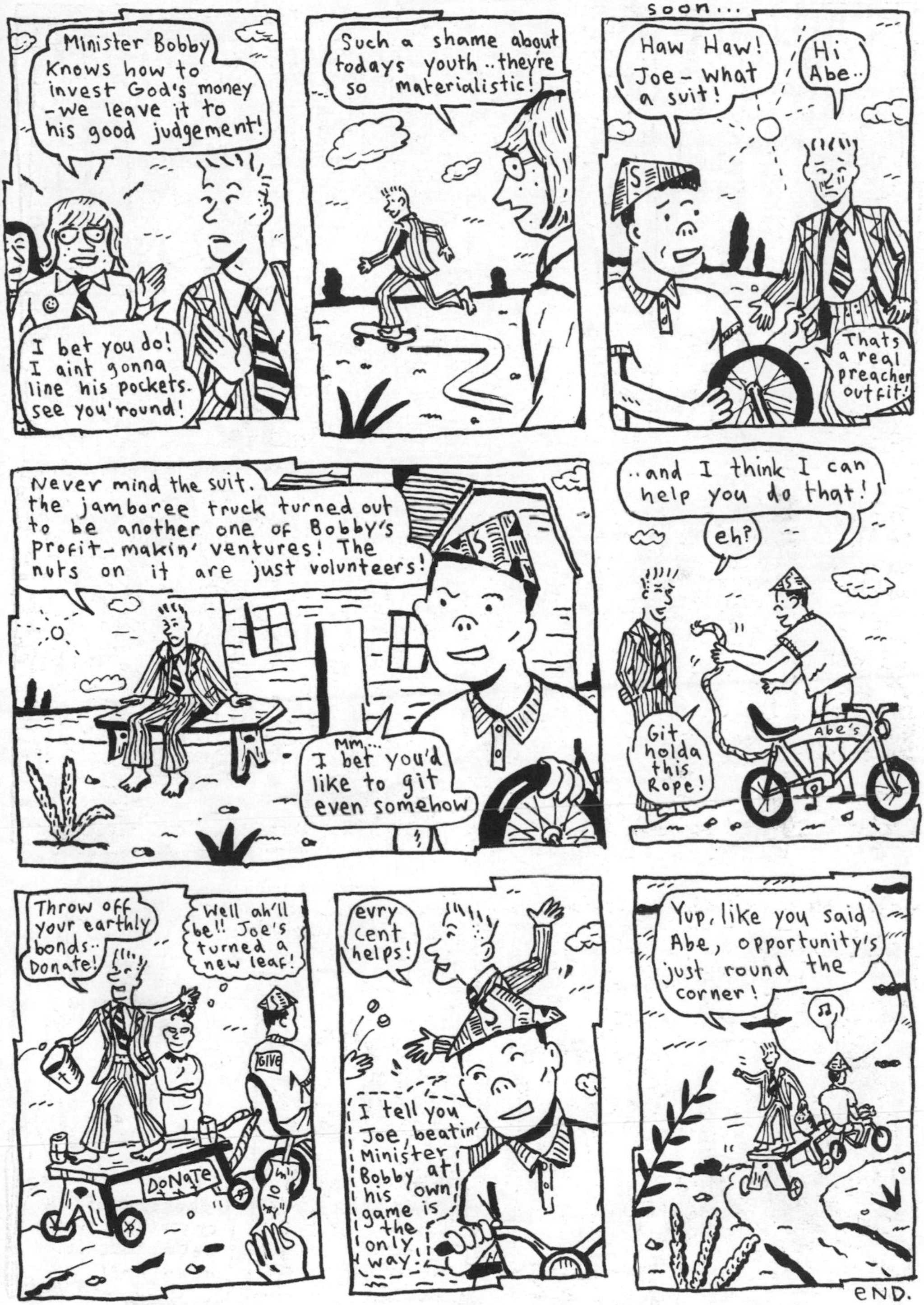
Minister Bobby Knows how to invest God's money - we leave it to his good judgement!
I bet you do! I aint gonna line his pockets. see you'round!
Such a shame about todays youth .. they're so materialistic!
soon...
Haw Haw! Joe - what a suit!
Hi Abe..
Thats a real preacher outfit!
Never mind the suit. the jamboree truck turned out to be another one of Bobby's profit-makin' ventures! The nuts on it are just volunteers!
Mm... I bet you'd like to git even somehow
..and I think I can help you do that!
eh?
Git holda this Rope!
Abe's
Throw off your earthly bonds.. Donate!
Well ah'll be!! Joe's turned a new leaf!
GIVE
DONATE
evry cent helps!
I tell you Joe, beatin' Minister Bobby at his own game is the only way!
Yup, like you said Abe, opportunity's just round the corner!
END.

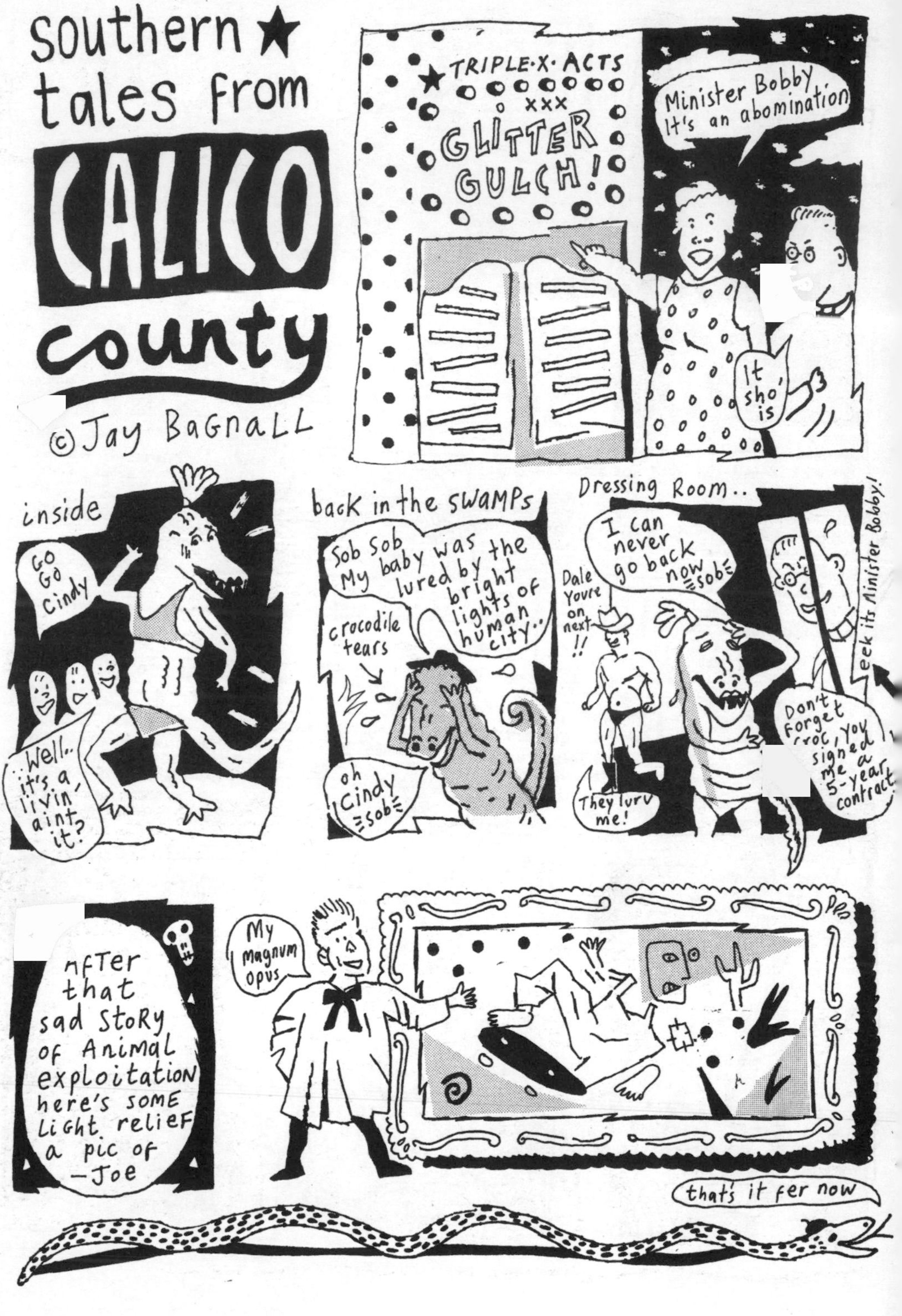
southern ★ tales from
CALICO
county
©Jay Bagnall
★ TRIPLE·X·ACTS
XXX
GLITTER GULCH!
Minister Bobby It's an abomination
It sho' is
inside
GO GO Cindy
Well.. it's a livin' aint it?
back in the SWAMPs
Sob Sob My baby was lured by the bright lights of human city..
crocodile tears
oh Cindy sob
Dressing Room..
I can never go back now sob
Dale Youre on next!!
They lurv me!
eek its Minister Bobby!
Don't forget croc, You signed me a 5-year contract!
After that sad Story of Animal exploitation here's SOME Light relief a pic of —Joe
My magnum opus
that's it fer now

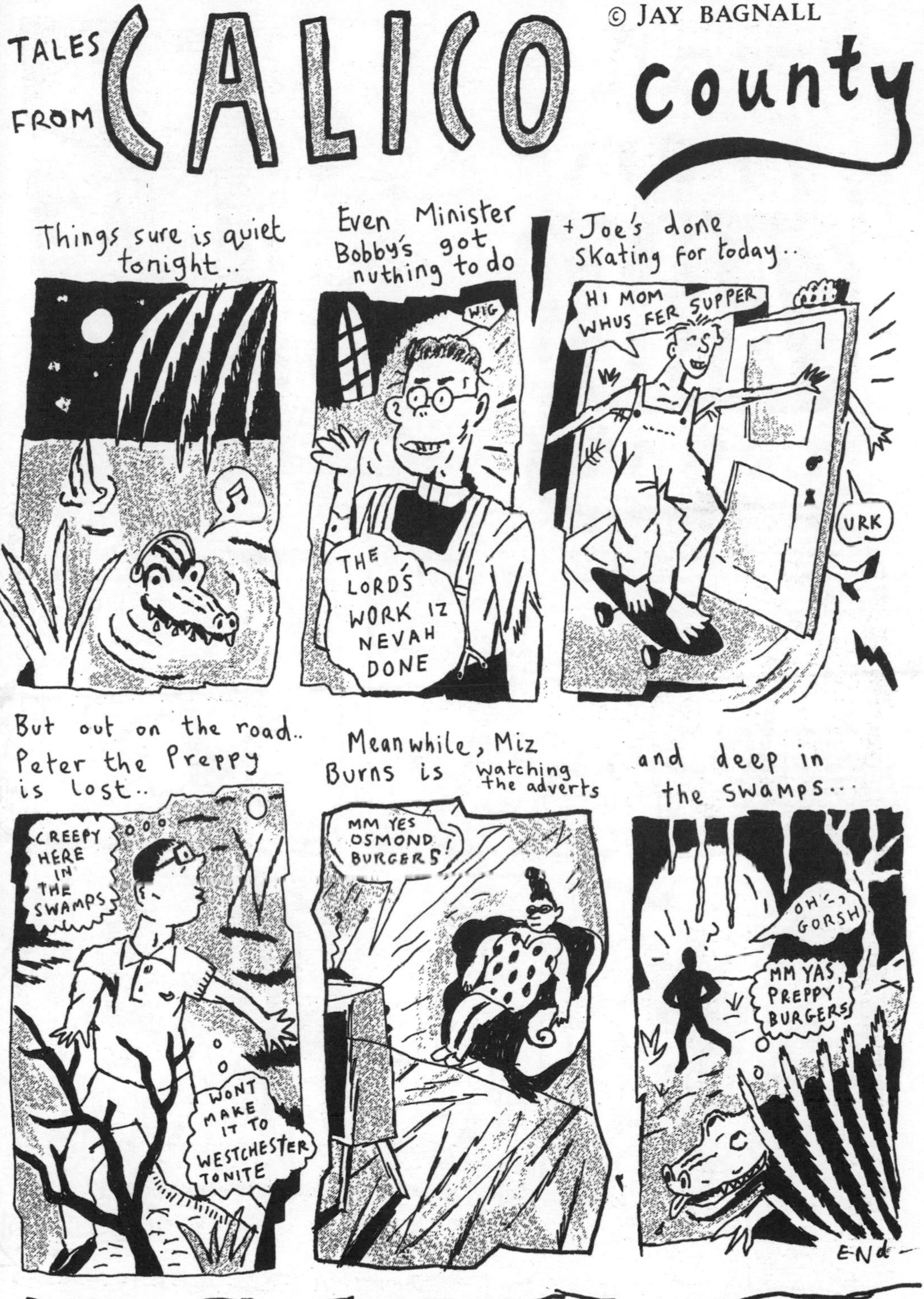

TALES FROM CALICO county
© JAY BAGNALL
Things sure is quiet tonight..
Even Minister Bobby's got nuthing to do
WIG
THE LORD'S WORK IZ NEVAH DONE
+ Joe's done Skating for today..
HI MOM WHUS FER SUPPER
URK
But out on the road.. Peter the Preppy is lost..
CREEPY HERE IN THE SWAMPS
WONT MAKE IT TO WESTCHESTER TONITE
Meanwhile, Miz Burns is watching the adverts
MM YES OSMOND BURGERS!
and deep in the swamps...
OH GORSH
MM YAS, PREPPY BURGERS
END

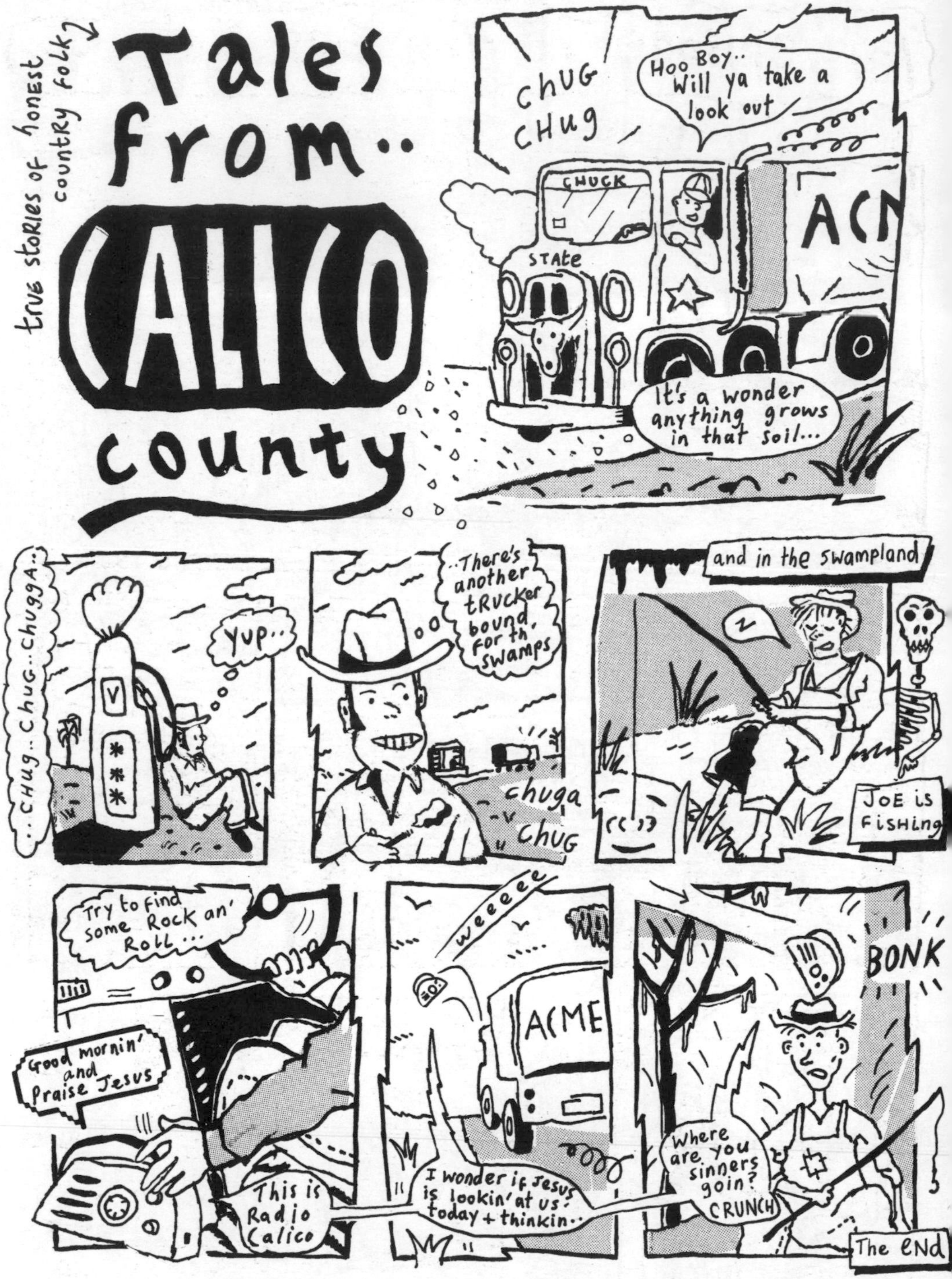
true stories of honest country folk
Tales from..
CALICO county
CHUG CHUG
Hoo Boy.. Will ya take a look out
CHUCK
STATE
ACN
It's a wonder anything grows in that soil...
..CHUG..CHUG..CHUGGA..
V
YUP..
..There's another TRUCKer bound for th SWAMPS
chuga CHUG
and in the swampland
Z
JOE is FISHING
Try to find some Rock an' Roll...
Good mornin' and Praise Jesus
This is Radio Calico
weeeee
ACME
I wonder if Jesus is lookin' at us today + thinkin..
BONK
Where are you sinners goin?
CRUNCH
The END

WIND-SHIELDED, Gas-o-Lined + Drawn © Jay BAGNALL.

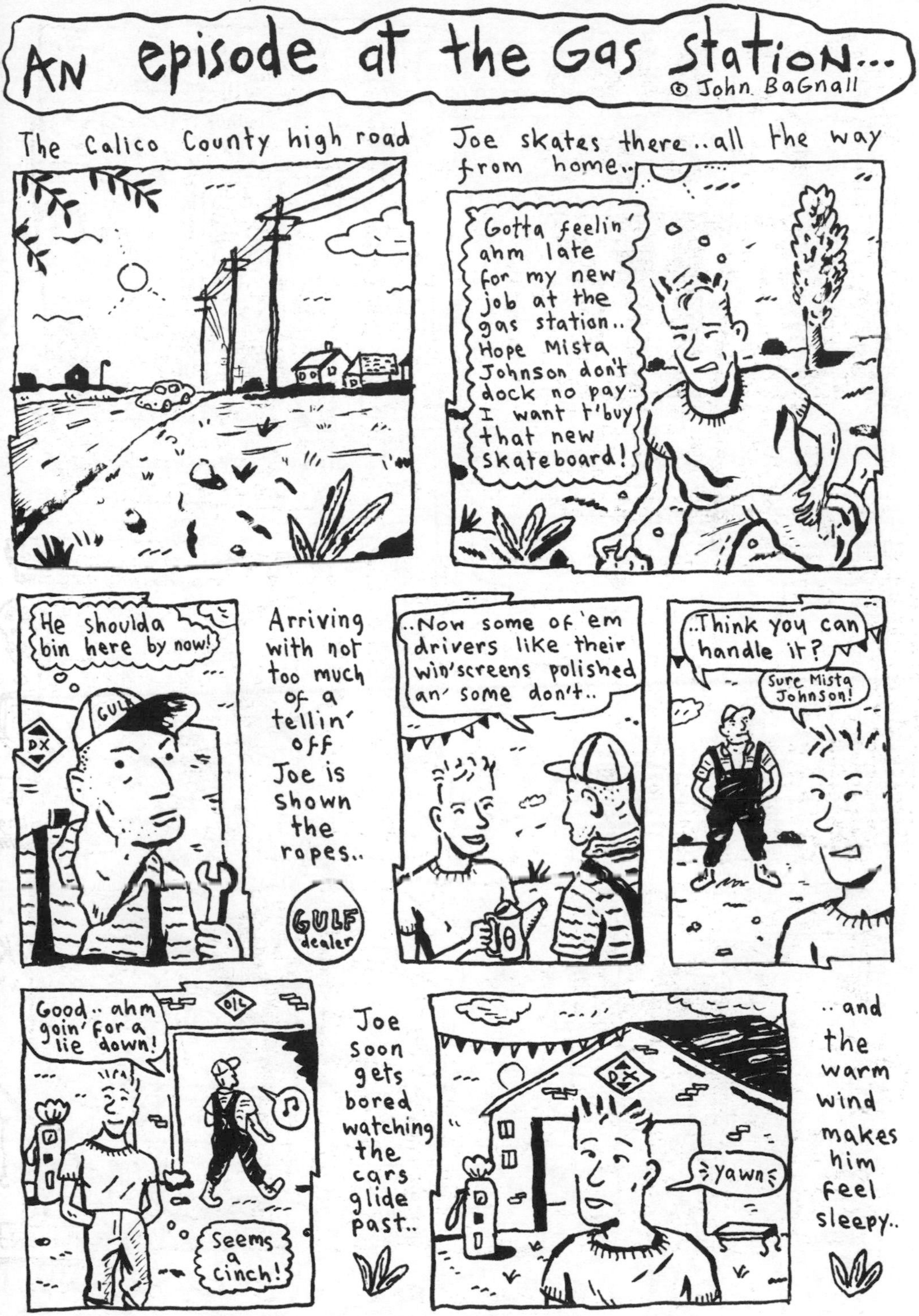
An episode at the Gas Station...
© John BaGnall
The Calico County high road
Joe skates there.. all the way from home..
Gotta feelin' ahm late for my new job at the gas station.. Hope Mista Johnson don't dock no pay.. I want t'buy that new skateboard!
He shoulda bin here by now!
GUL
DX
Arriving with not too much of a tellin' off Joe is shown the ropes..
GULF dealer
..Now some of 'em drivers like their win'screens polished an' some don't..
..Think you can handle it?
Sure Mista Johnson!
Good.. ahm goin' for a lie down!
OIL
Seems a cinch!
Joe soon gets bored watching the cars glide past..
DX
yawn
.. and the warm wind makes him feel sleepy..

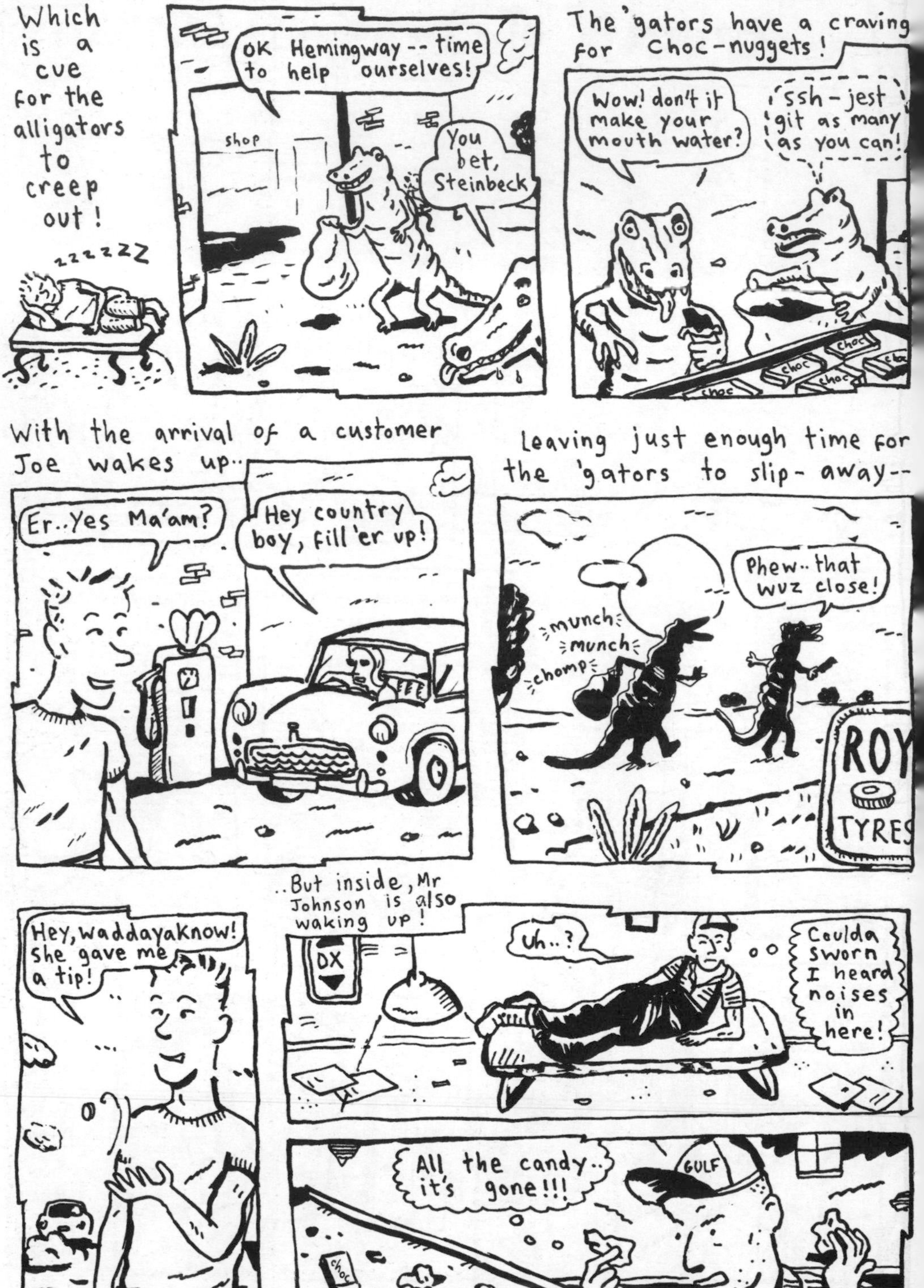
Which is a cue for the alligators to creep out!
zzzzzZ
OK Hemingway -- time to help ourselves!
shop
You bet, Steinbeck
The 'gators have a craving for Choc-nuggets!
Wow! don't it make your mouth water?
ssh - jest git as many as you can!
choc
With the arrival of a customer Joe wakes up..
Er..Yes Ma'am?
Hey country boy, fill 'er up!
Leaving just enough time for the 'gators to slip-away--
munch
munch
chomp
Phew.. that wuz close!
ROY
TYRES
Hey, waddayaknow! she gave me a tip!
..But inside, Mr Johnson is also waking up!
DX
Uh..?
Coulda sworn I heard noises in here!
All the candy.. it's gone!!!
GULF
choc

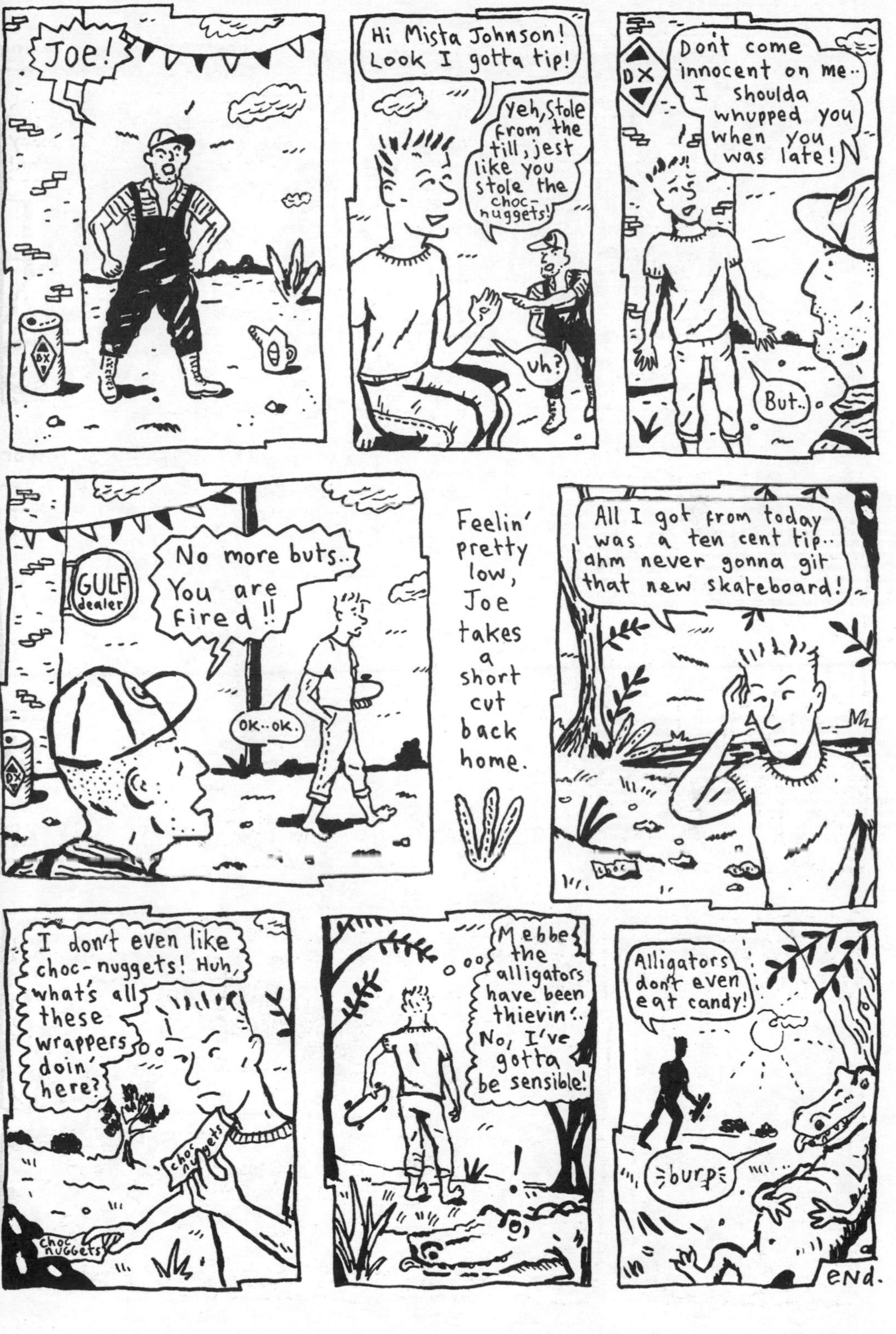
Joe!
Hi Mista Johnson! Look I gotta tip!
Yeh, Stole from the till, jest like you stole the choc-nuggets!
uh?
Don't come innocent on me.. I shoulda whupped you when you was late!
But..
DX
GULF dealer
No more buts.. You are fired!!
OK..OK.
Feelin' pretty low, Joe takes a short cut back home.
All I got from today was a ten cent tip.. ahm never gonna git that new skateboard!
choc
I don't even like choc-nuggets! Huh, what's all these wrappers doin' here?
choc nuggets
choc nuggets
Mebbe the alligators have been thievin'.. No, I've gotta be sensible!
!
Alligators don't even eat candy!
burp
END.

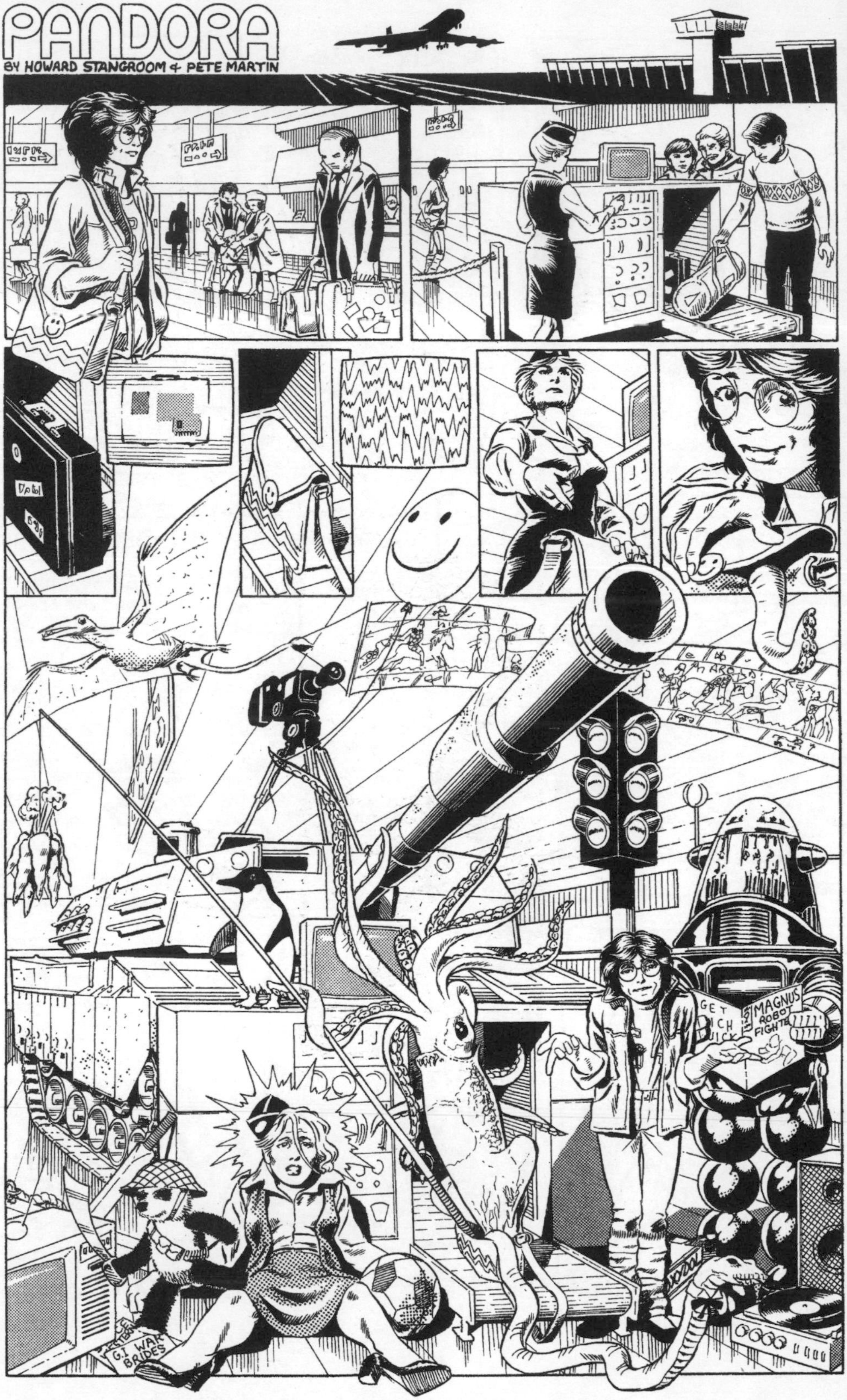
PANDORA
BY HOWARD STANGROOM & PETE MARTIN
GET RICH QUICK
MAGNUS ROBOT FIGHTER
GI WAR BRIDES

the GOATHLAND diary comic

There's as much DEATH on the MOORS as LIFE...
AH!

JAN 1997 - MAR 1998

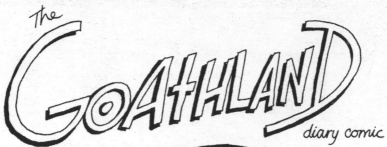

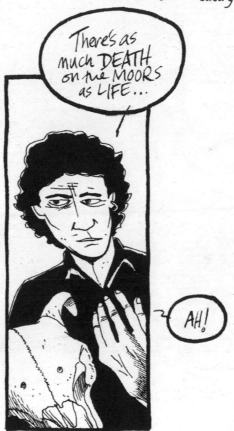

John Welding

GOATHLAND
Self-published, 1997–98

Up until 1996 Welding had been living in a council flat
in Bletchley (Buckinghamshire), working as a graphic
designer by day, drawing fantasy and horror comic
strips by night. He felt ready for a bit of adventure. On
the promise of a cottage to live in and some freelance
illustration work, with partner Helen he moved to a
remote location in North Yorkshire – a mile from the tiny
village of Goathland, twelve miles in turn from the small
east coast town of Whitby [cf. *Dracula*].

Existence on a farm took some adjusting to – surrounded
by bleak brown moorland, which for one solitary month
of the year would explode into stunning purple heather.
Animal carcasses littered the ground, adder snakes slid
through the bracken; life and death in close proximity.

"Jim Cameron started sending me his work (diary comics
with titles such as *Disillusion*, *Confused* and *Transition*) ...
a big influence ... the intimacy of the mundane. Letters
to family and friends turned into a monthly diary comic.
I had found my voice ... the raw honesty and naivety of
discovering something as strange and alien as living in
that cottage on the outskirts of Goathland." – JW

www.johnwelding.blogspot.com

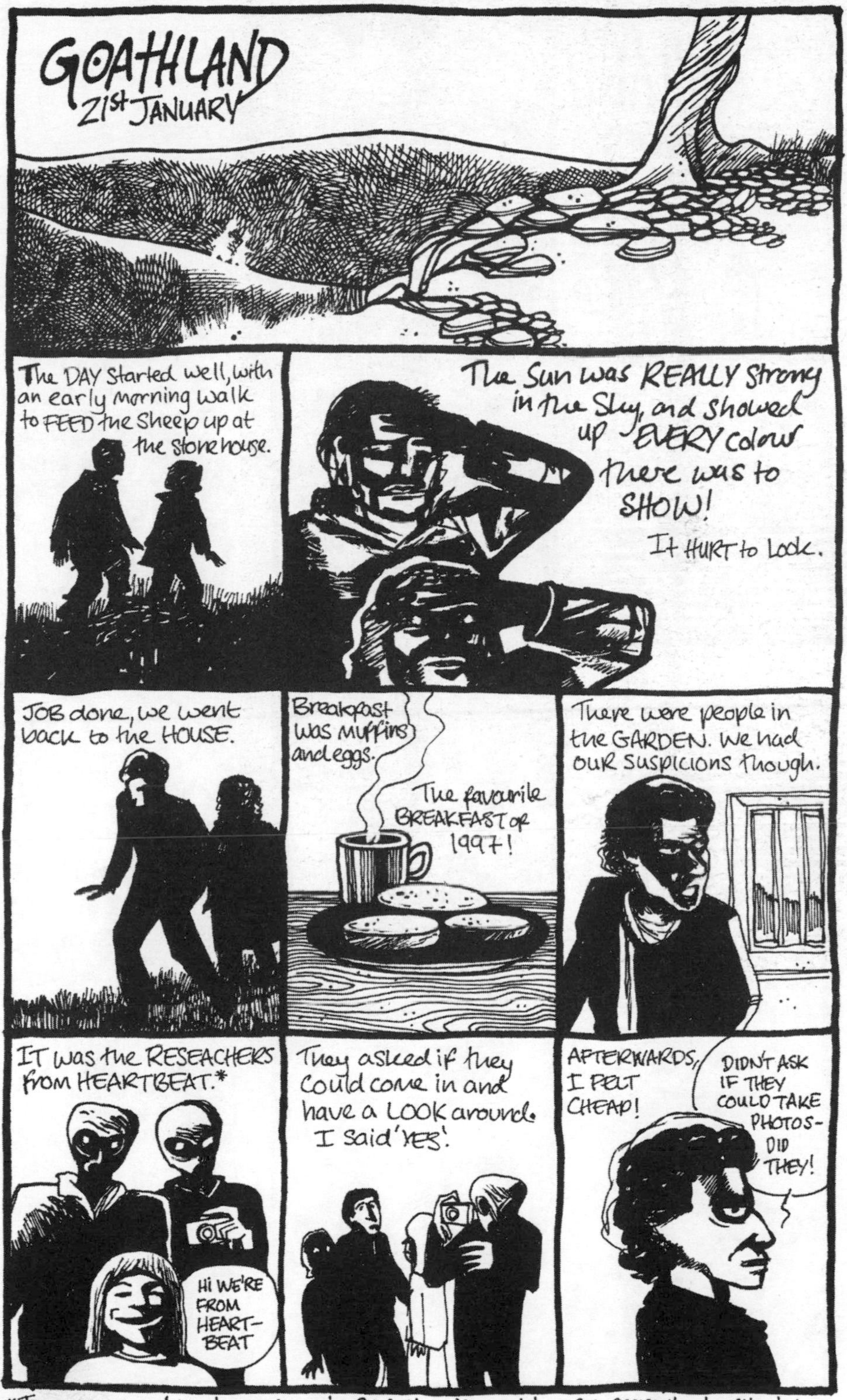
GOATHLAND
21st JANUARY
The DAY started well, with an early morning walk to FEED the sheep up at the stone house.
The Sun was REALLY strong in the Sky, and showed up EVERY colour there was to SHOW!
It HURT to Look.
JOB done, we went back to the HOUSE.
Breakfast was muffins and eggs.
The favourite BREAKFAST OF 1997!
There were people in the GARDEN. We had our suspicions though.
IT was the RESEACHERS from HEARTBEAT.*
HI WE'RE FROM HEART-BEAT
They asked if they could come in and have a LOOK around. I said 'YES'.
AFTERWARDS, I FELT CHEAP!
DIDN'T ASK IF THEY COULD TAKE PHOTOS - DID THEY!

*They go around various places in GOATHLAND, Looking for property to film in!

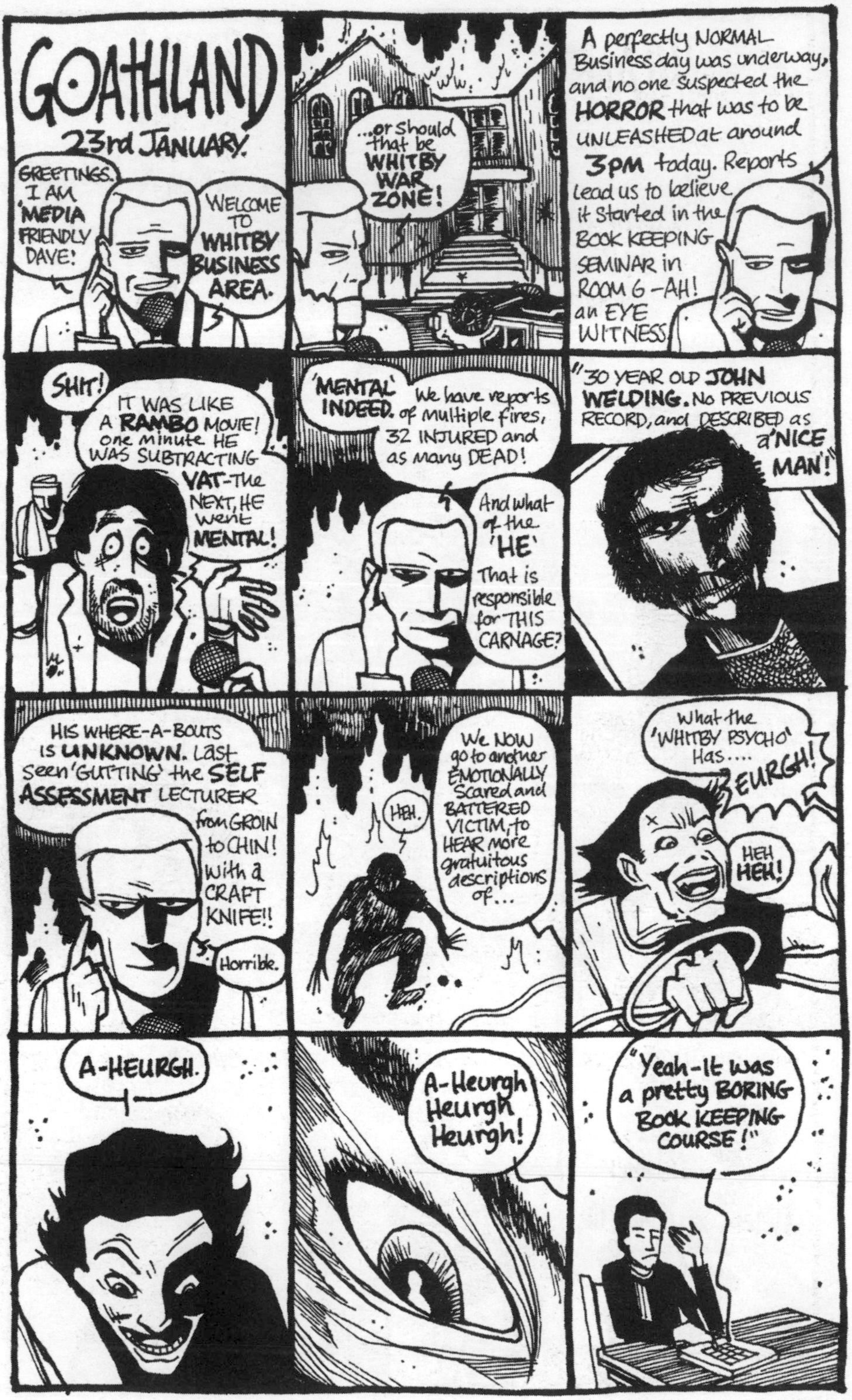
GOATHLAND
23rd JANUARY.
GREETINGS. I AM 'MEDIA FRIENDLY DAVE'!
WELCOME TO WHITBY BUSINESS AREA.
...or should that be WHITBY WAR ZONE!
A perfectly NORMAL Business day was underway, and no one suspected the HORROR that was to be UNLEASHED at around 3PM today. Reports lead us to believe it started in the BOOK KEEPING SEMINAR in ROOM 6 -AH! an EYE WITNESS.
SHIT!
IT WAS LIKE A RAMBO MOVIE! one minute HE WAS SUBTRACTING VAT-the NEXT, HE went MENTAL!
'MENTAL' INDEED. We have reports of multiple fires, 32 INJURED and as many DEAD!
And what of the 'HE' That is responsible for THIS CARNAGE?
"30 YEAR OLD JOHN WELDING. No PREVIOUS RECORD, and DESCRIBED as a 'NICE MAN'!"
HIS WHERE-A-BOUTS IS UNKNOWN. Last seen 'GUTTING' the SELF ASSESSMENT LECTURER from GROIN to CHIN! with a CRAFT KNIFE!!
Horrible.
HEH.
We NOW go to another EMOTIONALLY Scared and BATTERED VICTIM, to HEAR more gratuitous descriptions of...
What the 'WHITBY PSYCHO' Has....
EURGH!
HEH HEH!
A-HEURGH.
A-Heurgh Heurgh Heurgh!
"Yeah-It was a pretty BORING BOOK KEEPING COURSE!"

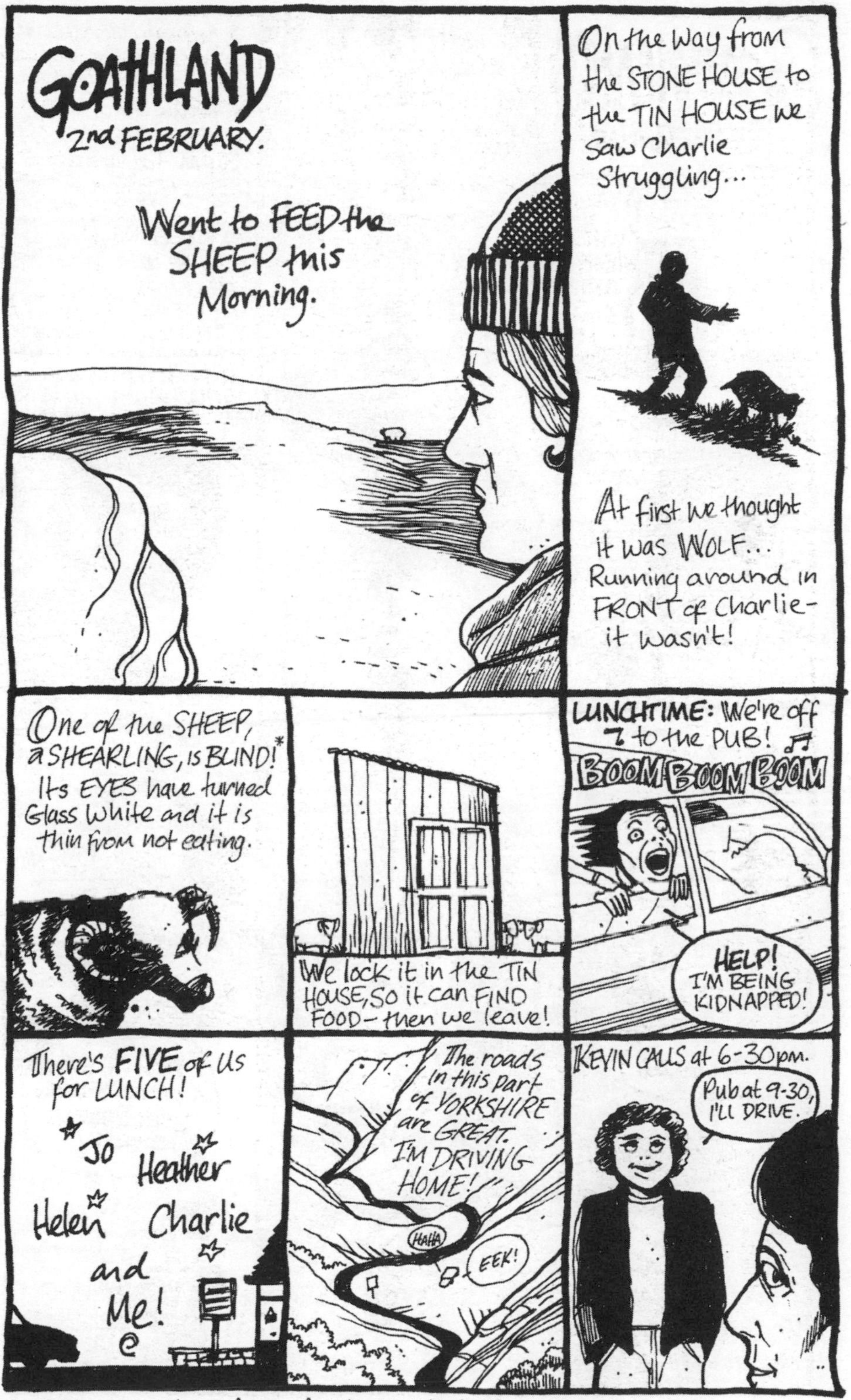
GOATHLAND
2nd FEBRUARY.
Went to FEED the SHEEP this Morning.
On the way from the STONE HOUSE to the TIN HOUSE we Saw Charlie Struggling...
At first we thought it was WOLF... Running around in FRONT of Charlie - it wasn't!
One of the SHEEP, a SHEARLING, is BLIND!* Its EYES have turned Glass White and it is thin from not eating.
We lock it in the TIN HOUSE, so it can FIND FOOD - then we leave!
LUNCHTIME: We're off to the PUB!
BOOM BOOM BOOM
HELP! I'M BEING KIDNAPPED!
There's FIVE of Us for LUNCH!
Jo
Heather
Helen
Charlie
and Me!
The roads in this part of YORKSHIRE are GREAT. I'M DRIVING HOME!
HAHA
EEK!
KEVIN CALLS at 6-30pm.
Pub at 9-30, I'LL DRIVE.
* TURNED out to be a form of SNOWBLINDNESS

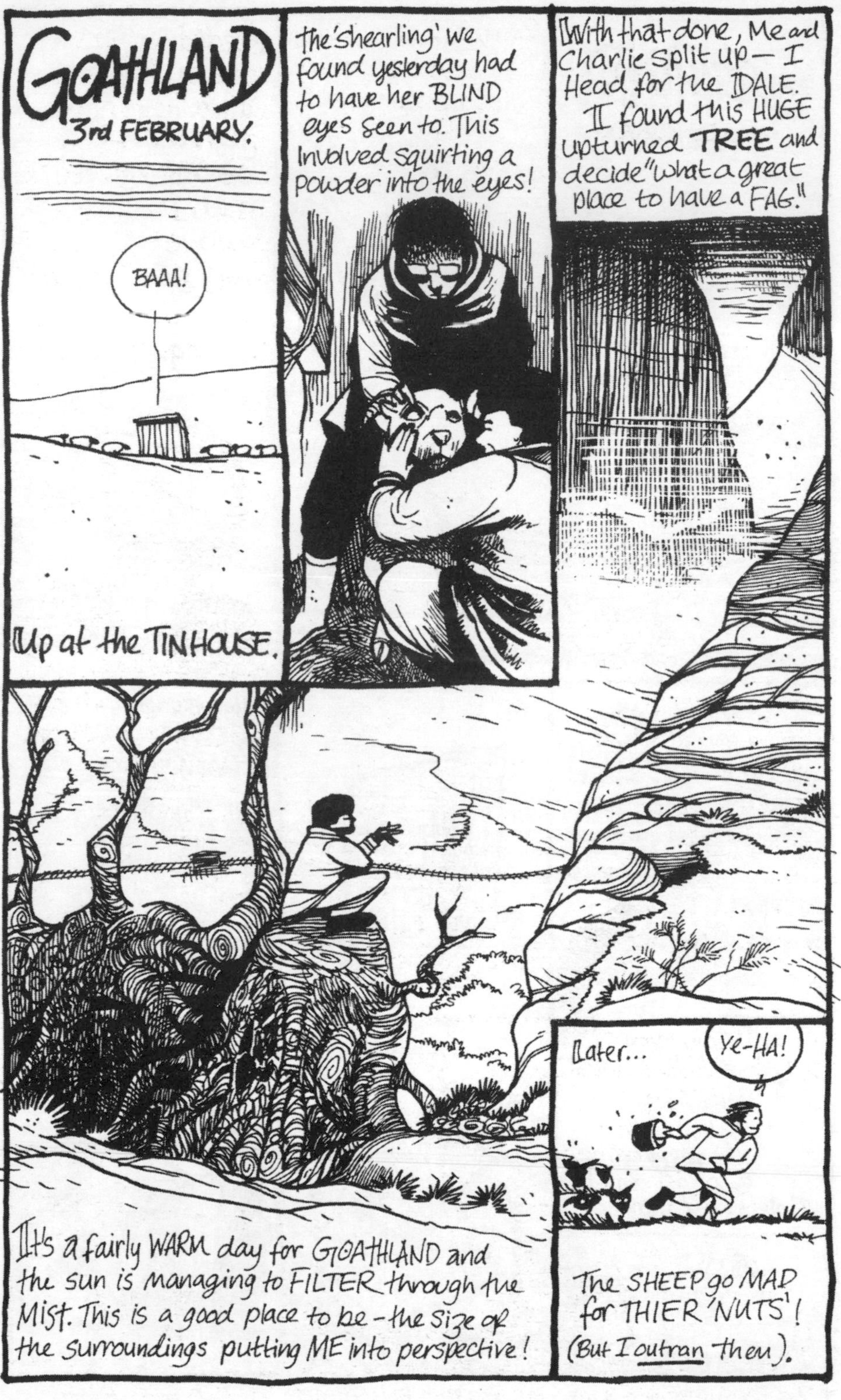
GOATHLAND
3rd FEBRUARY.
BAAA!
Up at the TINHOUSE.
the 'shearling' we found yesterday had to have her BLIND eyes seen to. This involved squirting a powder into the eyes!
With that done, Me and Charlie split up — I Head for the DALE.
I found this HUGE upturned TREE and decide "what a great place to have a FAG."
It's a fairly WARM day for GOATHLAND and the sun is managing to FILTER through the Mist. This is a good place to be - the size of the surroundings putting ME into perspective!
Later...
Ye-HA!
The SHEEP go MAD for THIER 'NUTS'!
(But I outran them).

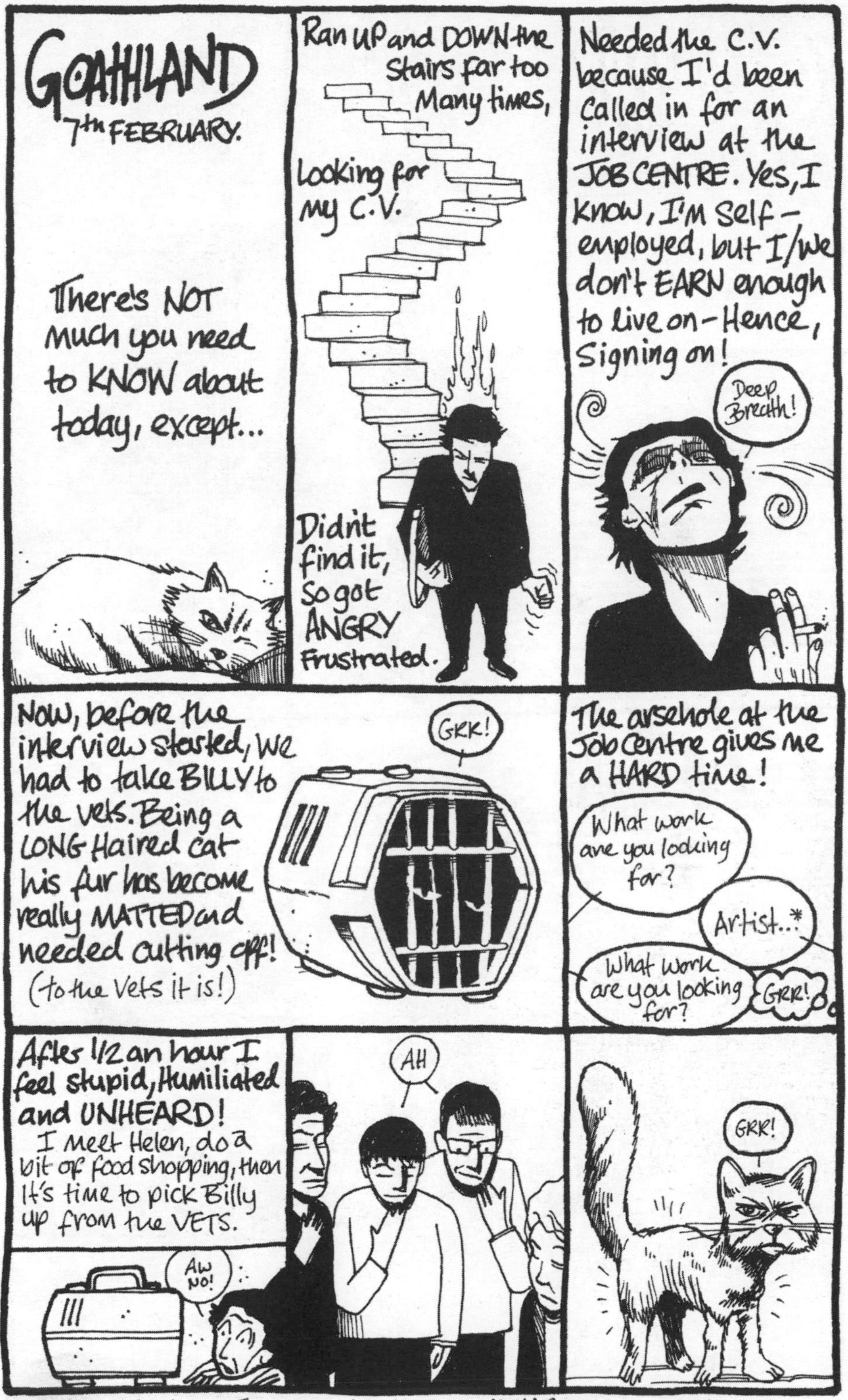
GOATHLAND
7th FEBRUARY.
There's NOT much you need to KNOW about today, except...
Ran UP and DOWN the Stairs far too Many times,
Looking for my C.V.
Didn't find it, So got ANGRY Frustrated.
Needed the C.V. because I'd been Called in for an interview at the JOB CENTRE. Yes, I KNOW, I'M Self-employed, but I/we don't EARN enough to live on - Hence, Signing on!
Deep Breath!
Now, before the interview started, we had to take BILLY to the vets. Being a LONG Haired cat his fur has become really MATTED and needed cutting off!
(to the Vets it is!)
GRK!
The arsehole at the Job Centre gives me a HARD time!
What work are you looking for?
Artist...*
What work are you looking for?
GRR!
After 1/2 an hour I feel stupid, Humiliated and UNHEARD!
I meet Helen, do a bit of food shopping, then it's time to pick Billy up from the VETS.
AH
AW NO!
GRR!
*I've heard that the Job Centre doesn't recognise 'ARTIST' as a profession. The nearest they can get to a description is 'Graphic designer' - HENCE I'm now recorded as a Graphic designer looking for graphic design work!

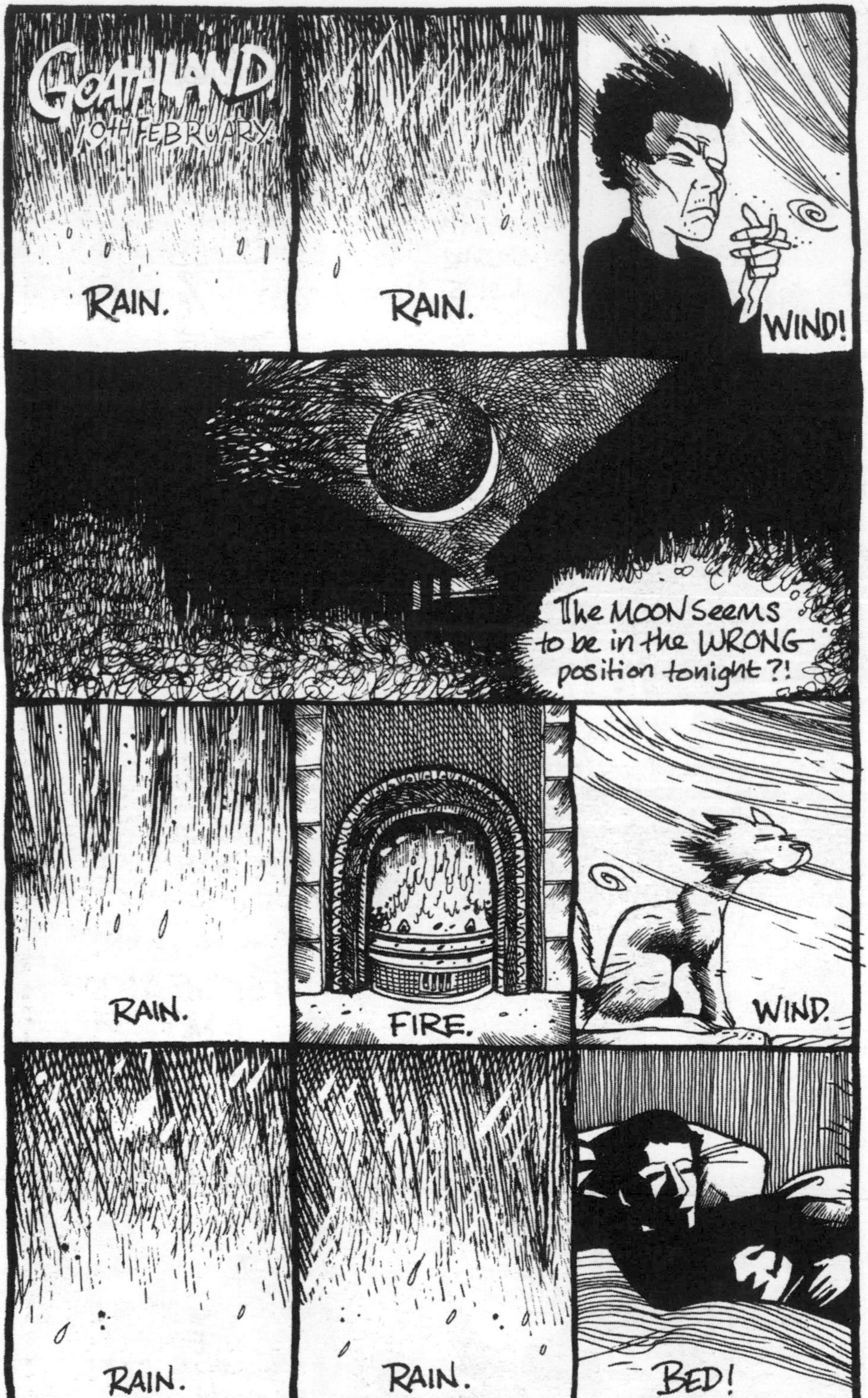
GOATHLAND
10th FEBRUARY
RAIN.
RAIN.
WIND!
The MOON seems to be in the WRONG position tonight?!
RAIN.
FIRE.
WIND.
RAIN.
RAIN.
BED!

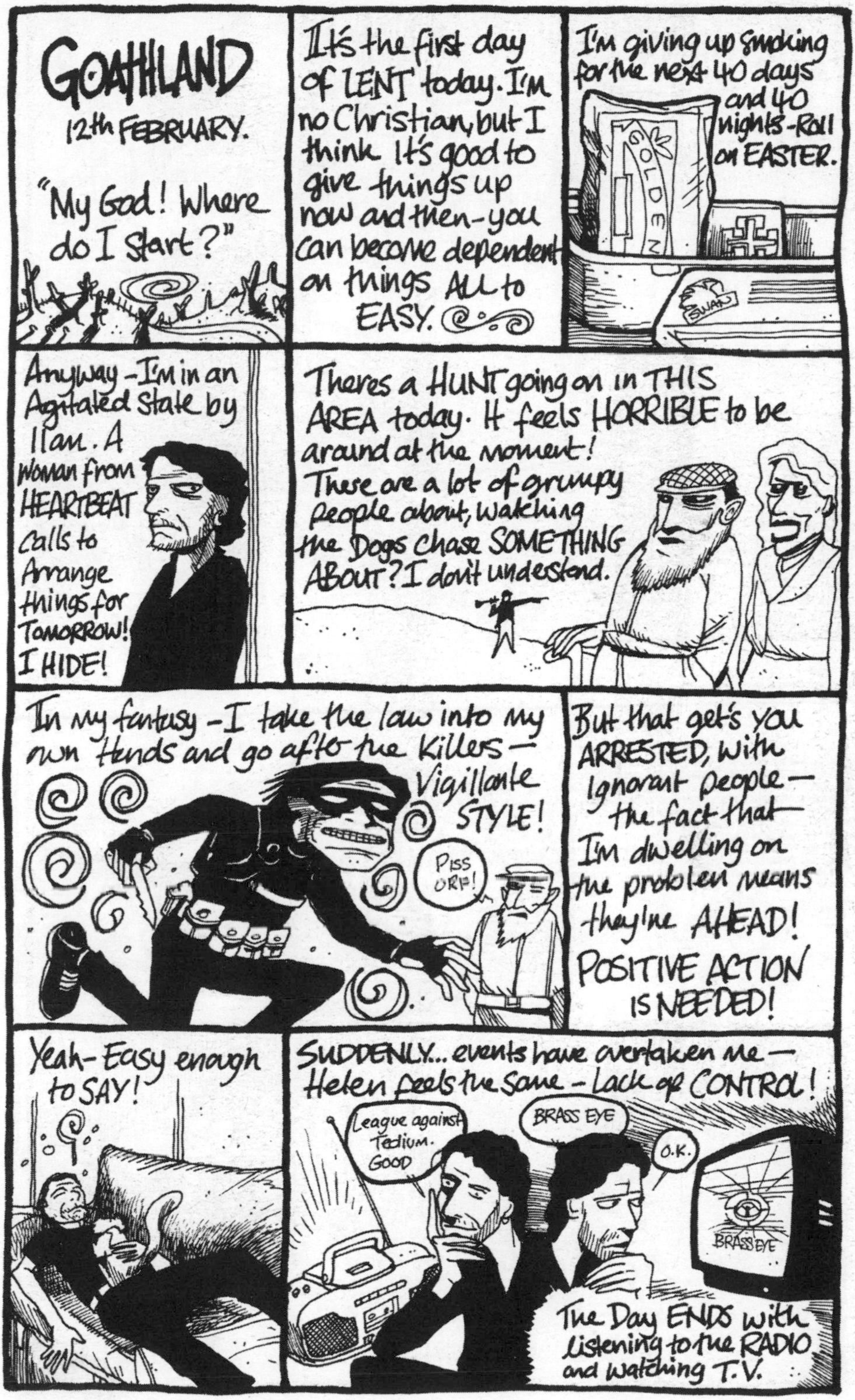
GOATHLAND
12th FEBRUARY.
"My God! Where do I start?"
It's the first day of LENT today. I'm no Christian, but I think it's good to give things up now and then - you can become dependent on things ALL to EASY.
I'm giving up smoking for the next 40 days and 40 nights - Roll on EASTER.
GOLDEN
SWAN
Anyway - I'm in an Agitated State by 11am. A woman from HEARTBEAT calls to Arrange things for TOMORROW! I HIDE!
Theres a HUNT going on in THIS AREA today. It feels HORRIBLE to be around at the moment! There are a lot of grumpy people about, watching the Dogs chase SOMETHING ABOUT? I don't understand.
In my fantasy - I take the law into my own Hands and go after the Killers - Vigillante STYLE!
PISS ORF!
But that get's you ARRESTED, with Ignorant people - the fact that I'm dwelling on the problem means they're AHEAD! POSITIVE ACTION IS NEEDED!
Yeah - Easy enough to SAY!
SUDDENLY... events have overtaken me - Helen feels the same - Lack of CONTROL!
League against Tedium. Good
BRASS EYE
O.K.
BRASS EYE
The Day ENDS with listening to the RADIO and watching T.V.

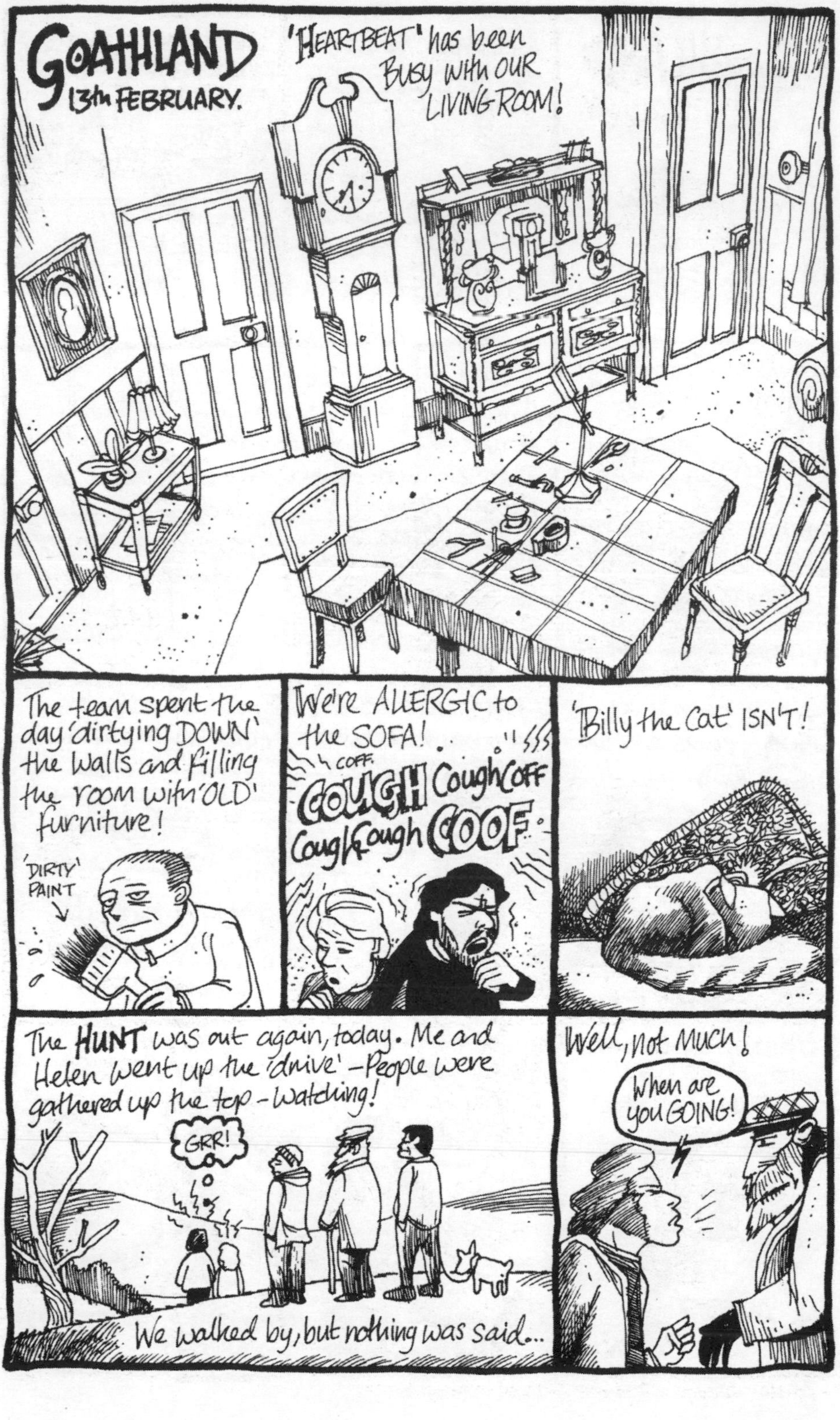
GOATHLAND
13th FEBRUARY.
'HEARTBEAT' has been Busy with OUR LIVING ROOM!
The team spent the day 'dirtying DOWN' the Walls and filling the room with 'OLD' furniture!
'DIRTY' PAINT
We're ALLERGIC to the SOFA!
COFF
COUGH Cough COFF
Cough Cough COOF
'Billy the Cat' ISN'T!
The HUNT was out again, today. Me and Helen went up the 'drive' - People were gathered up the top - Watching!
GRR!
We walked by, but nothing was said...
Well, not Much!
When are you GOING!

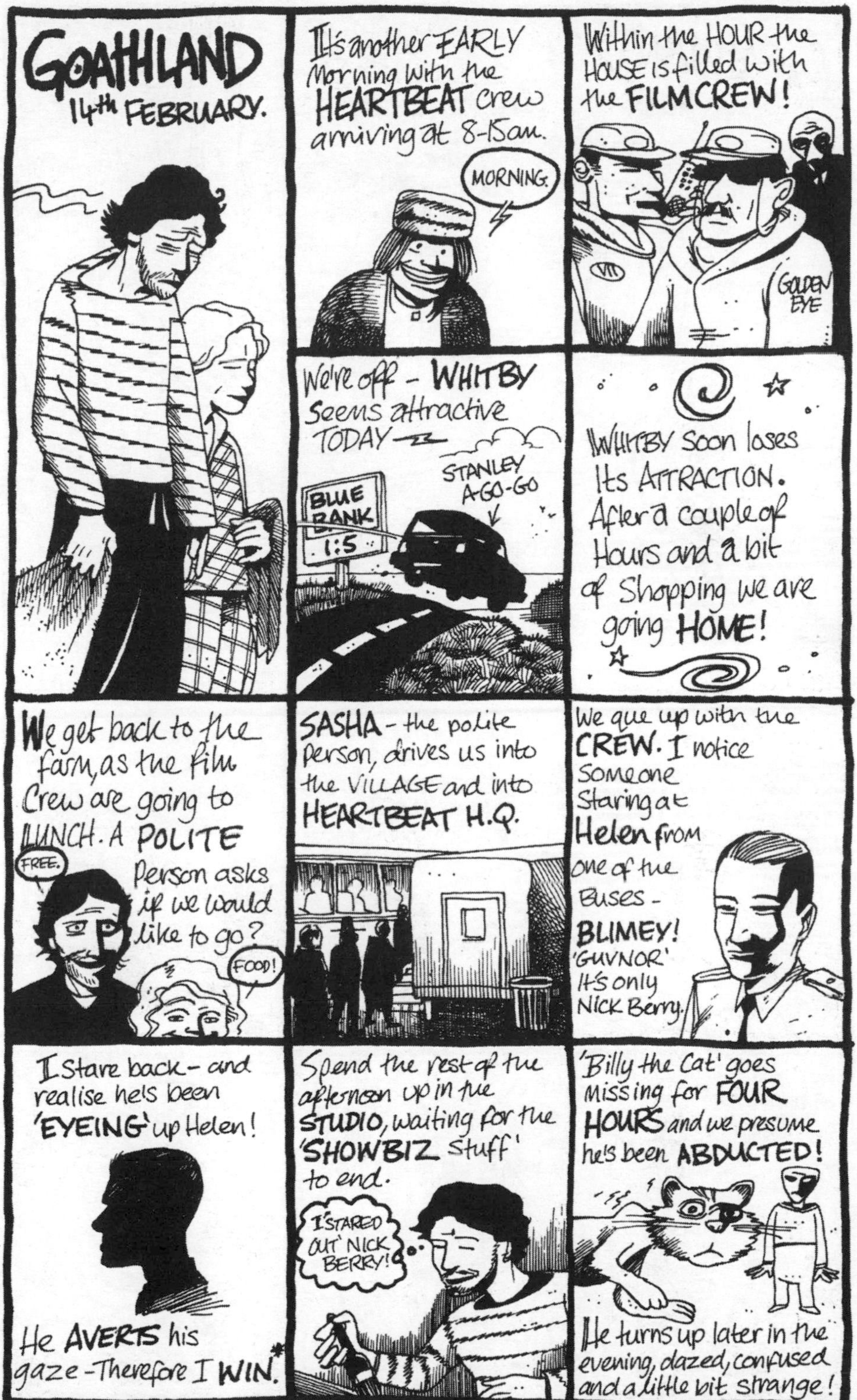
GOATHLAND
14th FEBRUARY.
It's another EARLY Morning with the HEARTBEAT crew arriving at 8-15am.
MORNING.
Within the HOUR the HOUSE is filled with the FILMCREW!
VII
GOLDEN EYE
We're off - WHITBY Seems attractive TODAY
STANLEY A-GO-GO
BLUE BANK
1:5
WHITBY soon loses its ATTRACTION. After a couple of Hours and a bit of Shopping we are going HOME!
We get back to the farm, as the film Crew are going to LUNCH. A POLITE Person asks if we would like to go?
FREE.
FOOD!
SASHA - the polite person, drives us into the VILLAGE and into HEARTBEAT H.Q.
We que up with the CREW. I notice Someone Staring at Helen from one of the Buses - BLIMEY! 'GUVNOR' It's only Nick Berry.
I Stare back - and realise he's been 'EYEING' up Helen!
He AVERTS his gaze - Therefore I WIN.*
Spend the rest of the afternoon up in the STUDIO, waiting for the 'SHOWBIZ stuff' to end.
I STARED OUT NICK BERRY!
'Billy the Cat' goes Missing for FOUR HOURS and we presume he's been ABDUCTED!
He turns up later in the evening, dazed, confused and a little bit strange!

* AW NO! - 'League Against Tedium' catchphrases!!

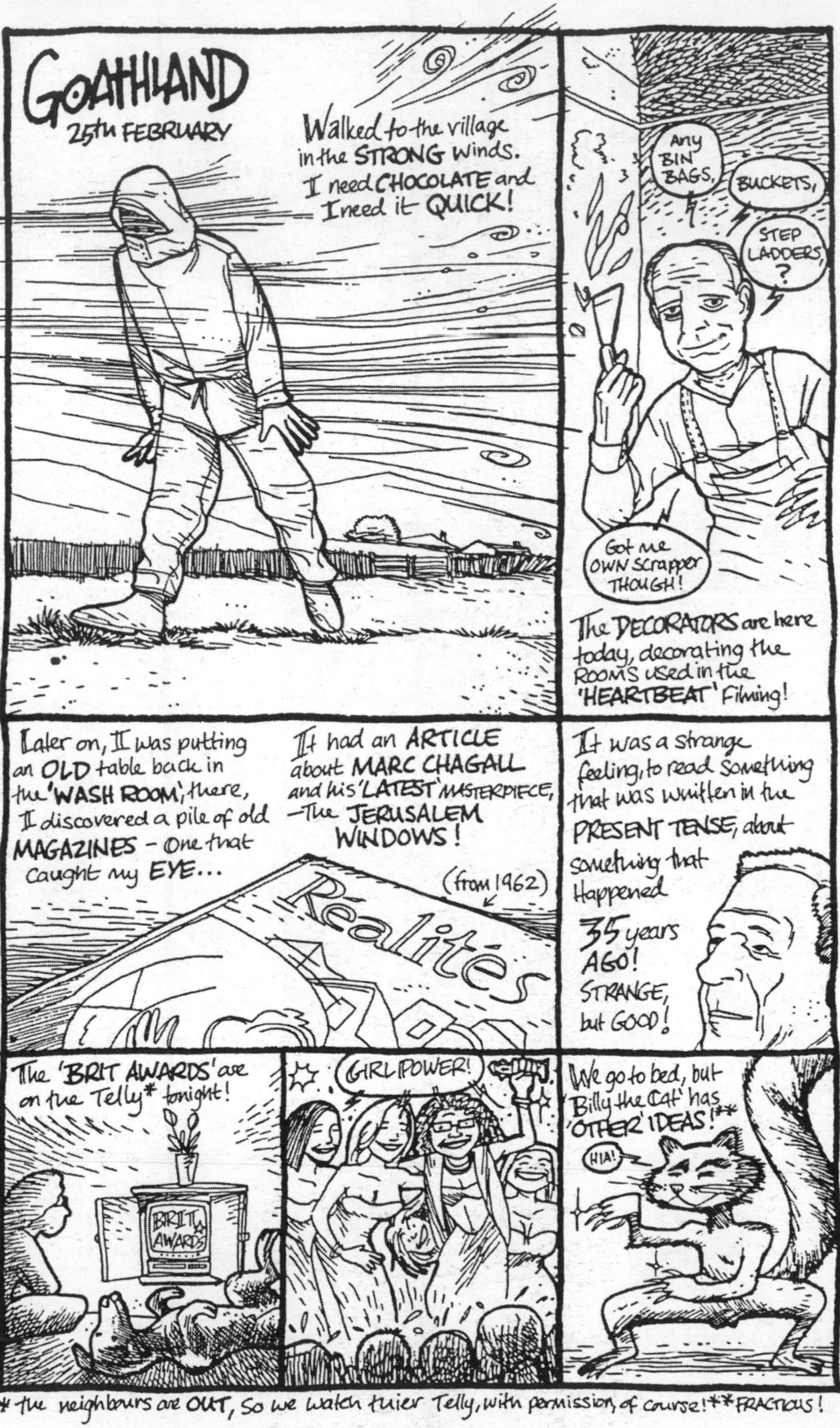
GOATHLAND
25th FEBRUARY
Walked to the village in the STRONG winds. I need CHOCOLATE and I need it QUICK!
Any BIN BAGS,
BUCKETS,
STEP LADDERS, ?
Got me OWN Scrapper THOUGH!
The DECORATORS are here today, decorating the ROOMS used in the 'HEARTBEAT' Filming!
Later on, I was putting an OLD table back in the 'WASH ROOM'; there, I discovered a pile of old MAGAZINES - One that caught my EYE...
It had an ARTICLE about MARC CHAGALL and his 'LATEST' MASTERPIECE, -The JERUSALEM WINDOWS!
(from 1962)
Realités
It was a strange feeling, to read something that was written in the PRESENT TENSE, about something that Happened 35 years AGO! STRANGE, but GOOD!
The 'BRIT AWARDS' are on the Telly* tonight!
BRIT AWARDS
GIRL POWER!
We go to bed, but 'Billy the Cat' has 'OTHER' IDEAS!**
HIA!

* the neighbours are OUT, so we watch their Telly, with permission, of course! ** FRACTIOUS!

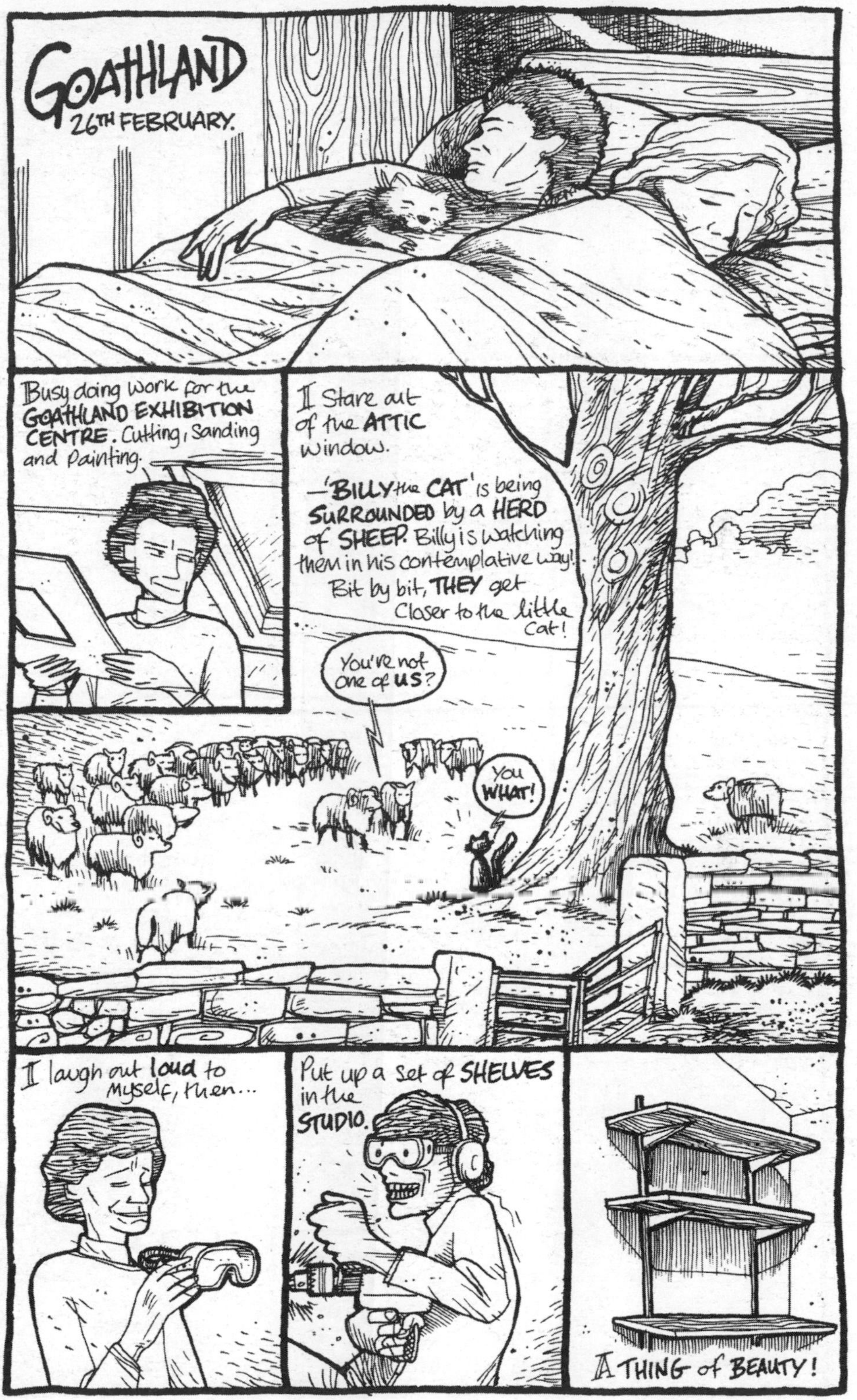
GOATHLAND
26TH FEBRUARY.
Busy doing work for the GOATHLAND EXHIBITION CENTRE. Cutting, Sanding and Painting.
I Stare out of the ATTIC window.
—'BILLY the CAT' is being SURROUNDED by a HERD of SHEEP. Billy is watching them in his contemplative way!
Bit by bit, THEY get Closer to the little Cat!
You're not one of US?
You WHAT!
I laugh out loud to myself, then...
Put up a set of SHELVES in the STUDIO.
A THING of BEAUTY!

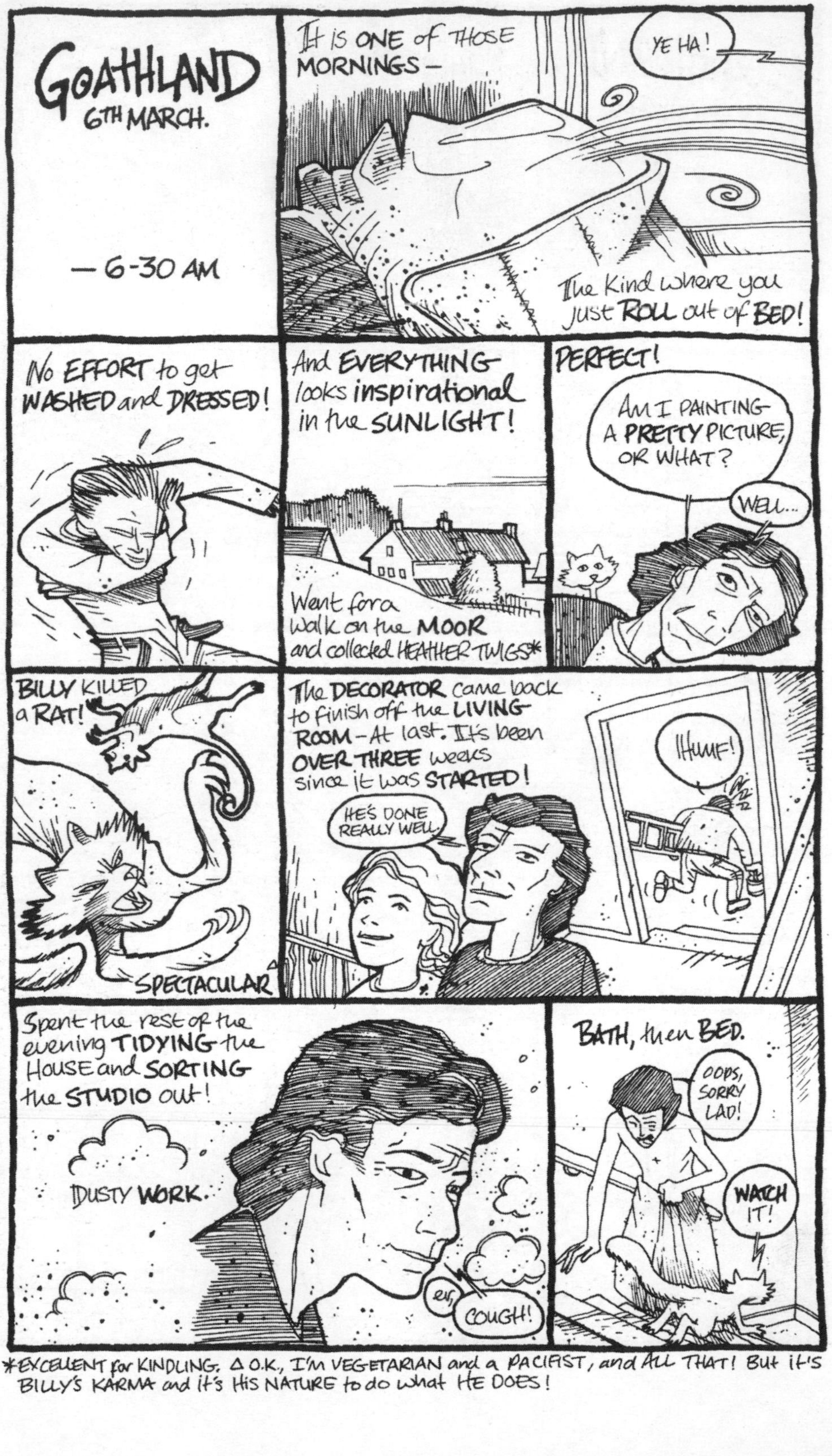
GOATHLAND
6TH MARCH.
— 6-30 AM
IT is ONE of THOSE MORNINGS –
YE HA!
The Kind where you just ROLL out of BED!
No EFFORT to get WASHED and DRESSED!
And EVERYTHING looks inspirational in the SUNLIGHT!
Went for a walk on the MOOR and collected HEATHER TWIGS*
PERFECT!
AM I PAINTING A PRETTY PICTURE, OR WHAT?
WELL...
BILLY KILLED a RAT!
SPECTACULAR△
The DECORATOR came back to finish off the LIVING ROOM – At last. It's been OVER THREE weeks since it was STARTED!
HUMF!
HE'S DONE REALLY WELL.
Spent the rest of the evening TIDYING the HOUSE and SORTING the STUDIO out!
DUSTY WORK.
er,
COUGH!
BATH, then BED.
OOPS, SORRY LAD!
WATCH IT!

*EXCELLENT for KINDLING. △ O.K., I'M VEGETARIAN and a PACIFIST, and ALL THAT! But it's BILLY'S KARMA and it's HIS NATURE to do what HE DOES!

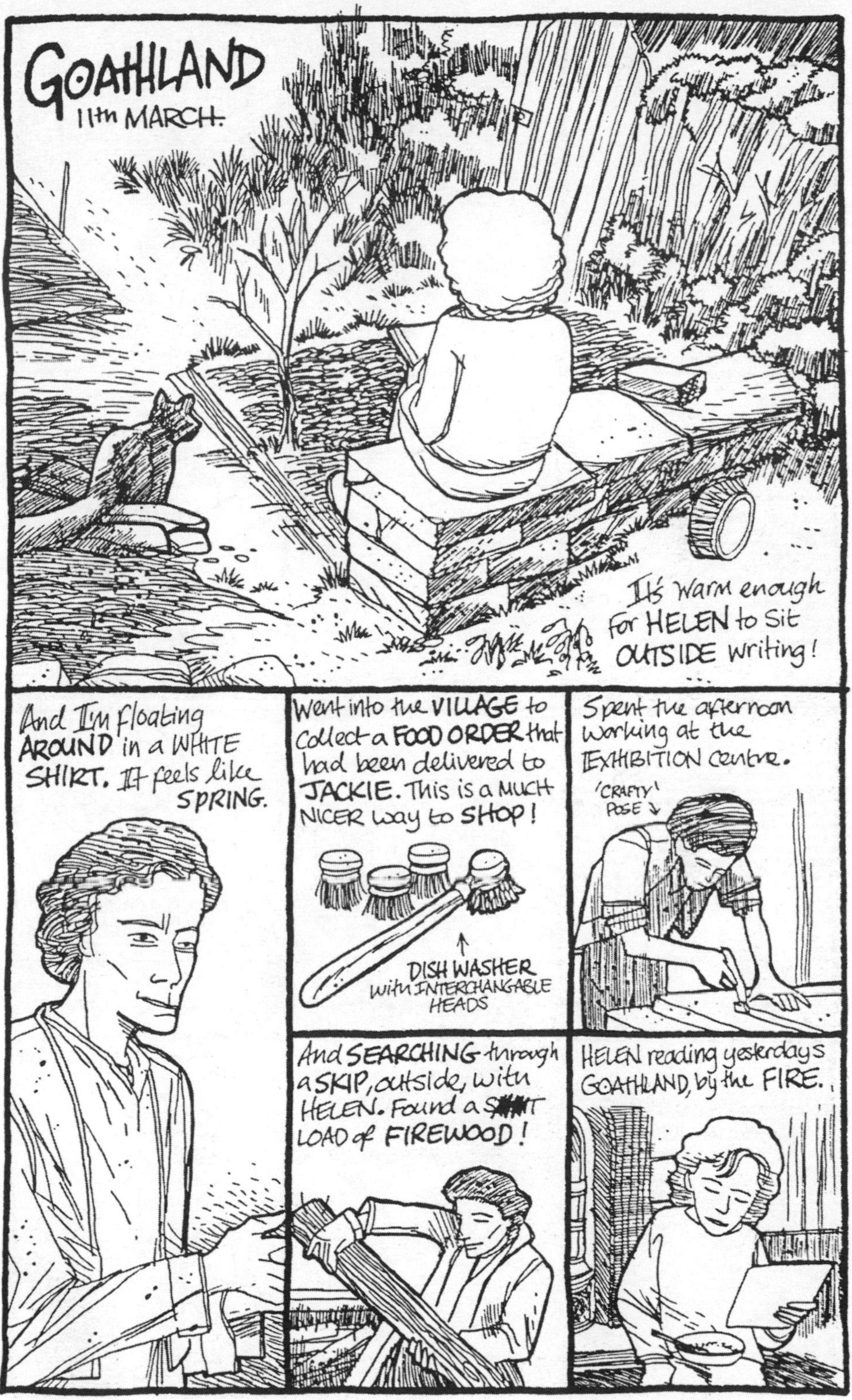
GOATHLAND
11th MARCH.
It's warm enough for HELEN to sit OUTSIDE writing!
And I'm floating AROUND in a WHITE SHIRT. It feels like SPRING.
Went into the VILLAGE to collect a FOOD ORDER that had been delivered to JACKIE. This is a MUCH NICER way to SHOP!
DISH WASHER with INTERCHANGABLE HEADS
Spent the afternoon working at the EXHIBITION centre.
'CRAFTY' POSE
And SEARCHING through a SKIP, outside, with HELEN. Found a S[redacted]T LOAD of FIREWOOD!
HELEN reading yesterdays GOATHLAND, by the FIRE.

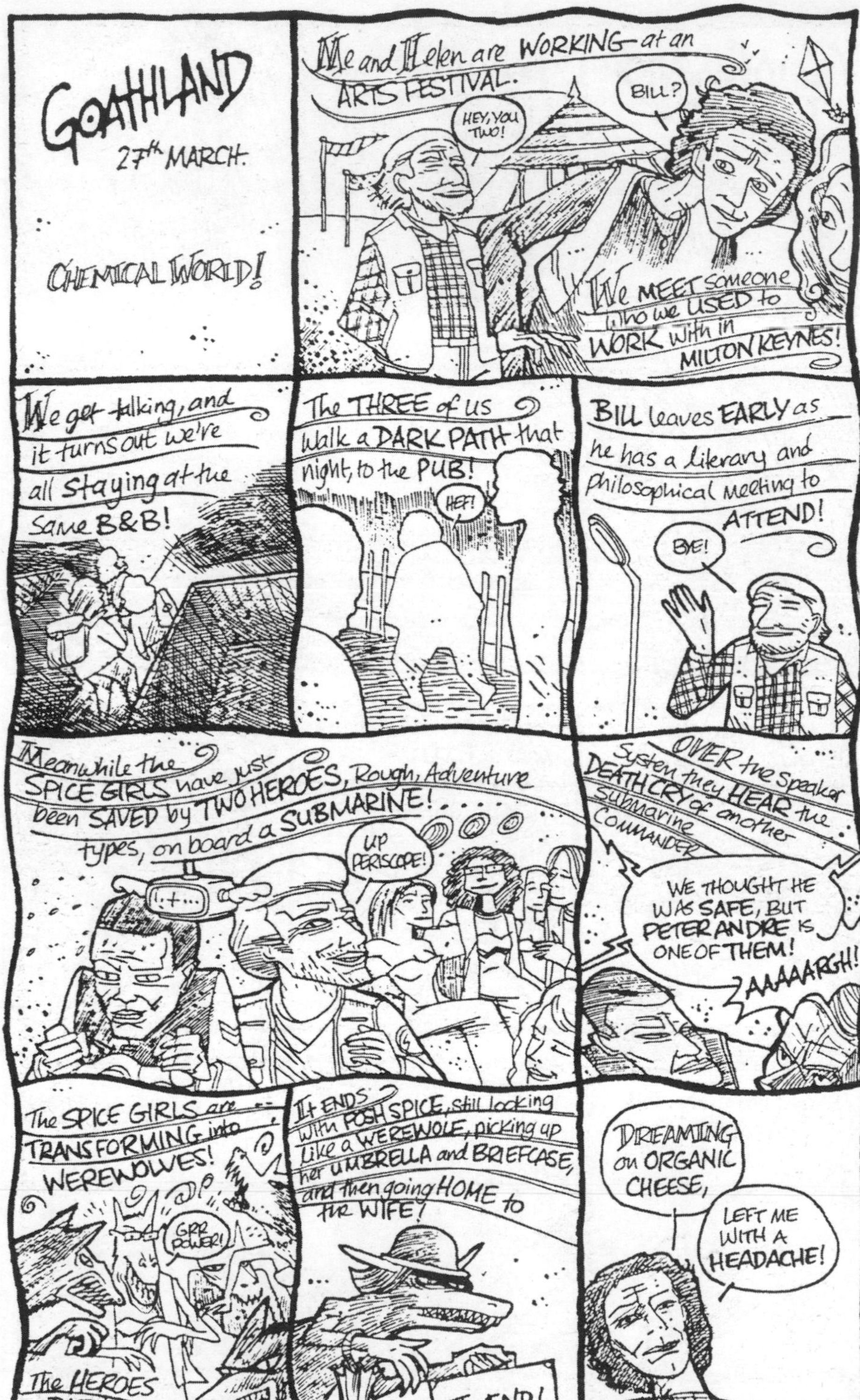

GOATHLAND
27th MARCH.
CHEMICAL WORLD!
Me and Helen are WORKING at an ARTS FESTIVAL.
HEY, YOU TWO!
BILL?
We MEET someone who we USED to WORK with in MILTON KEYNES!
We get talking, and it turns out we're all staying at the same B&B!
The THREE of us walk a DARK PATH that night, to the PUB!
HEF!
BILL leaves EARLY as he has a literary and philosophical meeting to ATTEND!
BYE!
Meanwhile the SPICE GIRLS have just been SAVED by TWO HEROES, Rough, Adventure types, on board a SUBMARINE!
UP PERISCOPE!
OVER the speaker system they HEAR the DEATH CRY of another submarine commander
WE THOUGHT HE WAS SAFE, BUT PETER ANDRE IS ONE OF THEM!
AAAAARGH!
The SPICE GIRLS are TRANSFORMING into WEREWOLVES!
GRR POWER!
The HEROES DIE!
It ENDS with POSH SPICE, still looking like a WEREWOLF, picking up her UMBRELLA and BRIEFCASE, and then going HOME to the WIFE!
The END!
DREAMING on ORGANIC CHEESE,
LEFT ME WITH A HEADACHE!

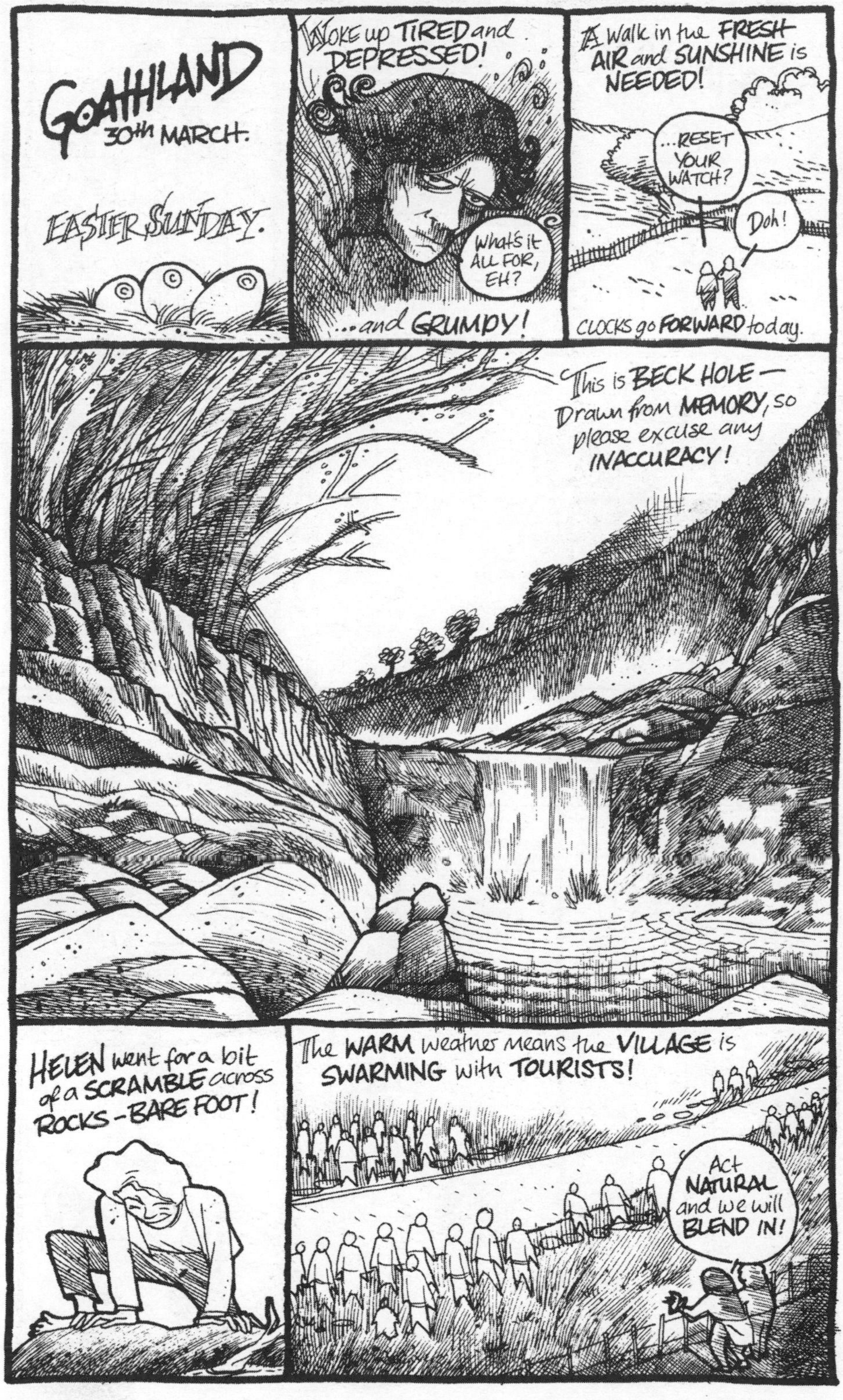
GOATHLAND
30th MARCH.
EASTER SUNDAY.
Woke up TIRED and DEPRESSED!
What's it ALL FOR, EH?
...and GRUMPY!
A walk in the FRESH AIR and SUNSHINE is NEEDED!
...RESET YOUR WATCH?
Doh!
CLOCKS go FORWARD today.
This is BECK HOLE — Drawn from MEMORY, so please excuse any INACCURACY!
HELEN went for a bit of a SCRAMBLE across ROCKS - BARE FOOT!
The WARM weather means the VILLAGE is SWARMING with TOURISTS!
Act NATURAL and we will BLEND IN!

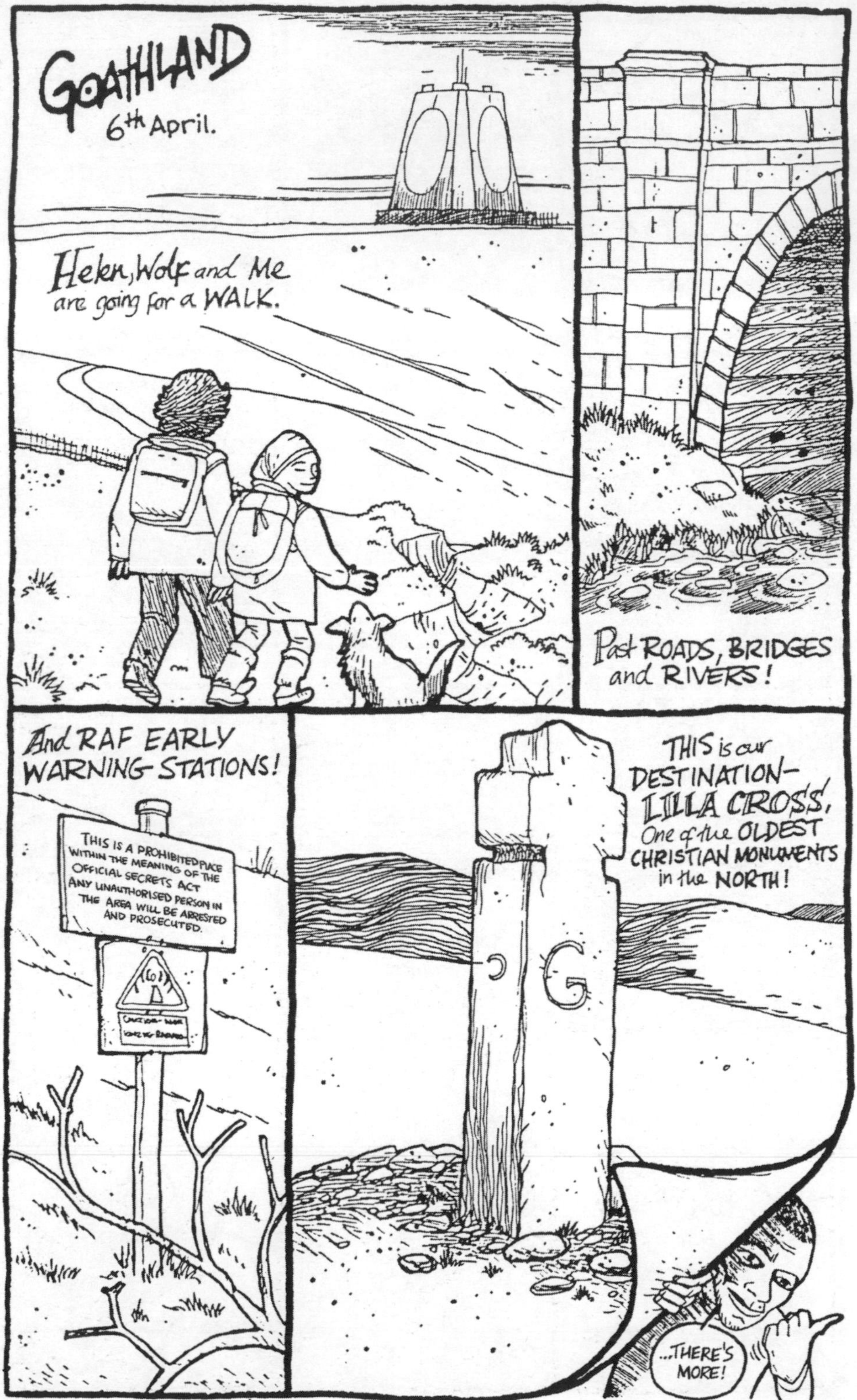
GOATHLAND
6th April.
Helen, Wolf and Me are going for a WALK.
Past ROADS, BRIDGES and RIVERS!
And RAF EARLY WARNING STATIONS!
THIS IS A PROHIBITED PLACE WITHIN THE MEANING OF THE OFFICIAL SECRETS ACT
ANY UNAUTHORISED PERSON IN THE AREA WILL BE ARRESTED AND PROSECUTED.
THIS is our DESTINATION– LILLA CROSS, One of the OLDEST CHRISTIAN MONUMENTS in the NORTH!
...THERE'S MORE!

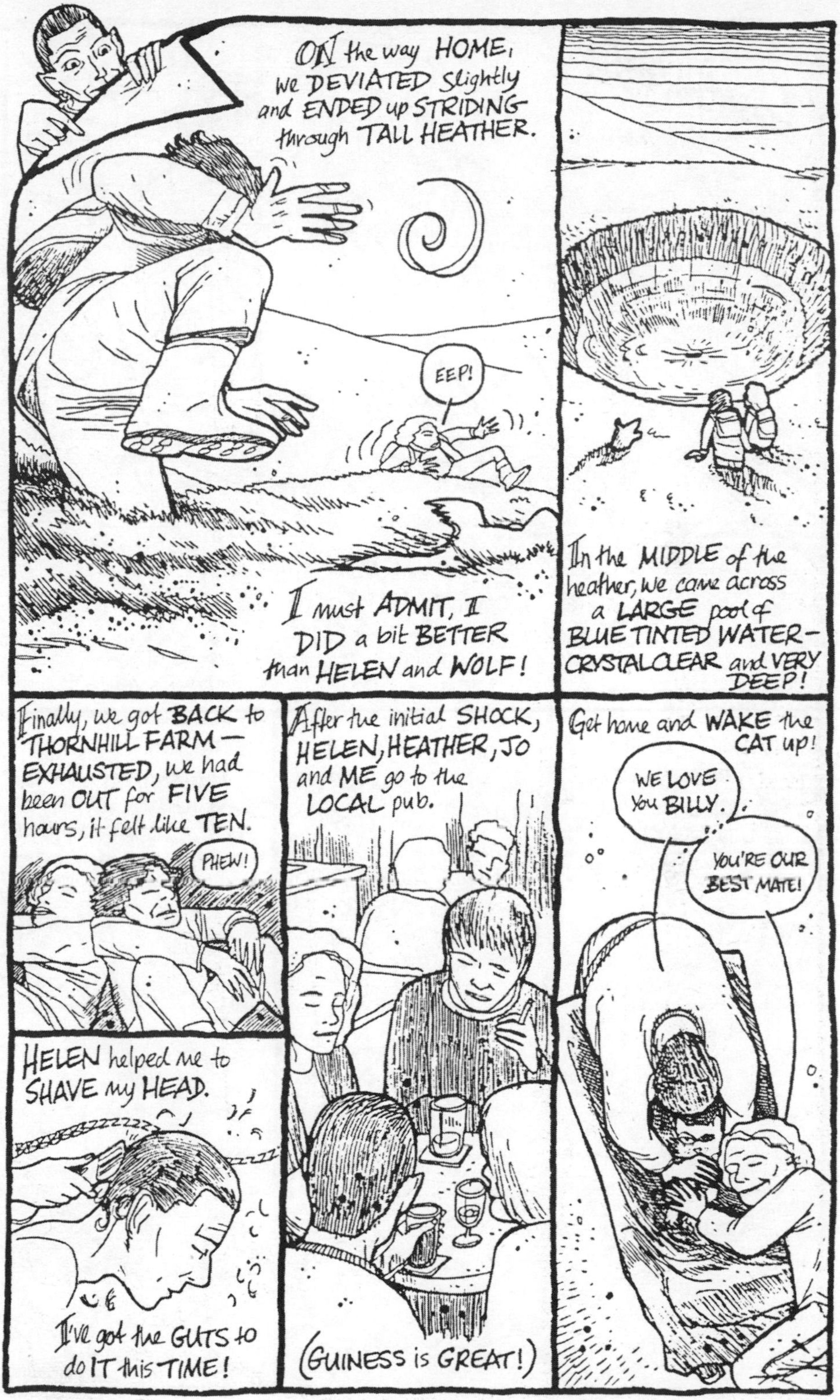
ON the way HOME, we DEVIATED slightly and ENDED up STRIDING through TALL HEATHER.
EEP!
I must ADMIT, I DID a bit BETTER than HELEN and WOLF!
In the MIDDLE of the heather, we came across a LARGE pool of BLUE TINTED WATER - CRYSTAL CLEAR and VERY DEEP!
Finally, we got BACK to THORNHILL FARM - EXHAUSTED, we had been OUT for FIVE hours, it felt like TEN.
PHEW!
HELEN helped me to SHAVE my HEAD.
I've got the GUTS to do IT this TIME!
After the initial SHOCK, HELEN, HEATHER, JO and ME go to the LOCAL pub.
(GUINESS is GREAT!)
Get home and WAKE the CAT up!
WE LOVE You BILLY.
YOU'RE OUR BEST MATE!

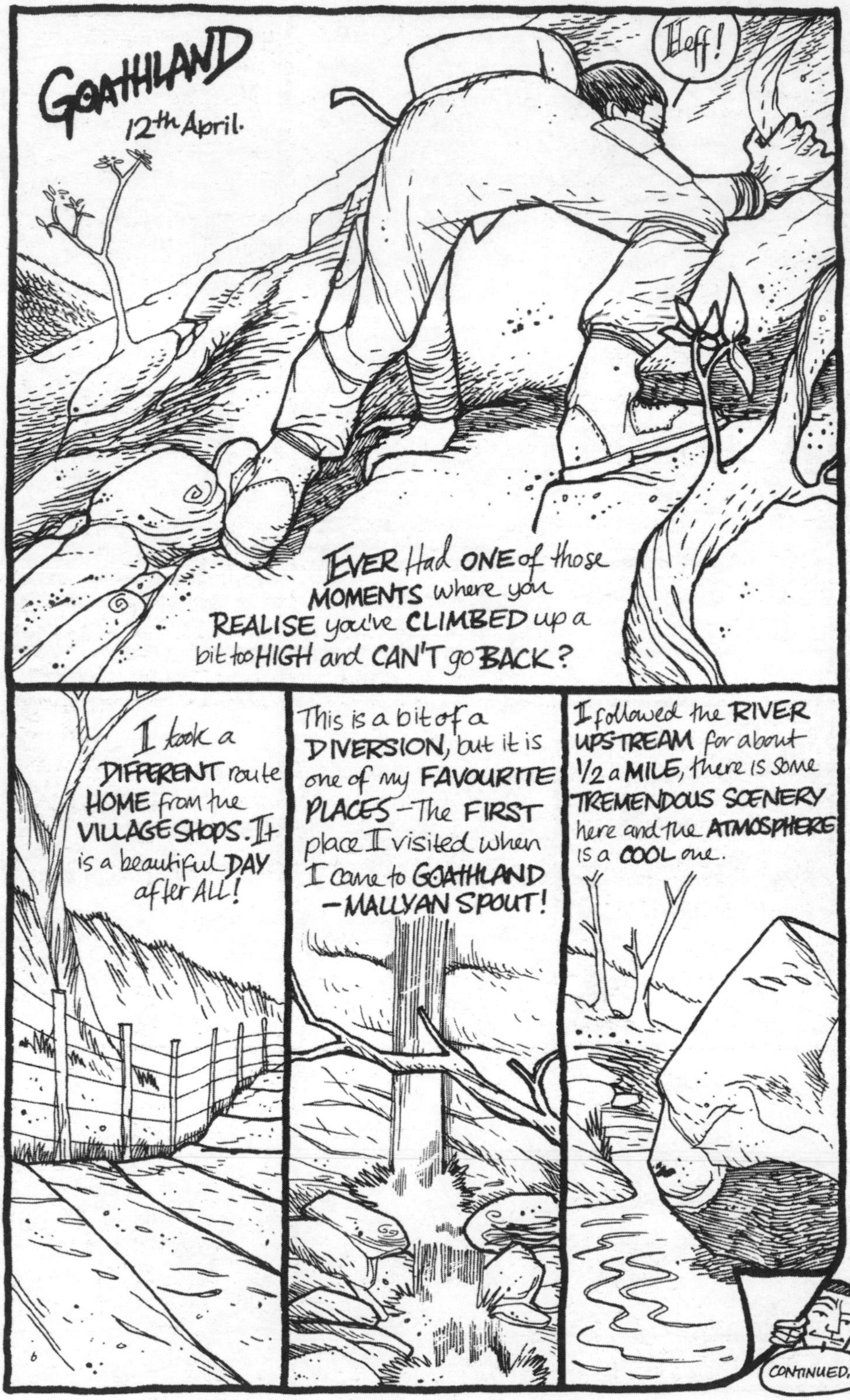

GOATHLAND
12th April.
Heff!
EVER Had ONE of those MOMENTS where you REALISE you've CLIMBED up a bit too HIGH and CAN'T go BACK?
I took a DIFFERENT route HOME from the VILLAGE SHOPS. It is a beautiful DAY after ALL!
This is a bit of a DIVERSION, but it is one of my FAVOURITE PLACES - The FIRST place I visited when I came to GOATHLAND - MALLYAN SPOUT!
I followed the RIVER UPSTREAM for about 1/2 a MILE, there is some TREMENDOUS SCENERY here and the ATMOSPHERE is a COOL one.
CONTINUED...

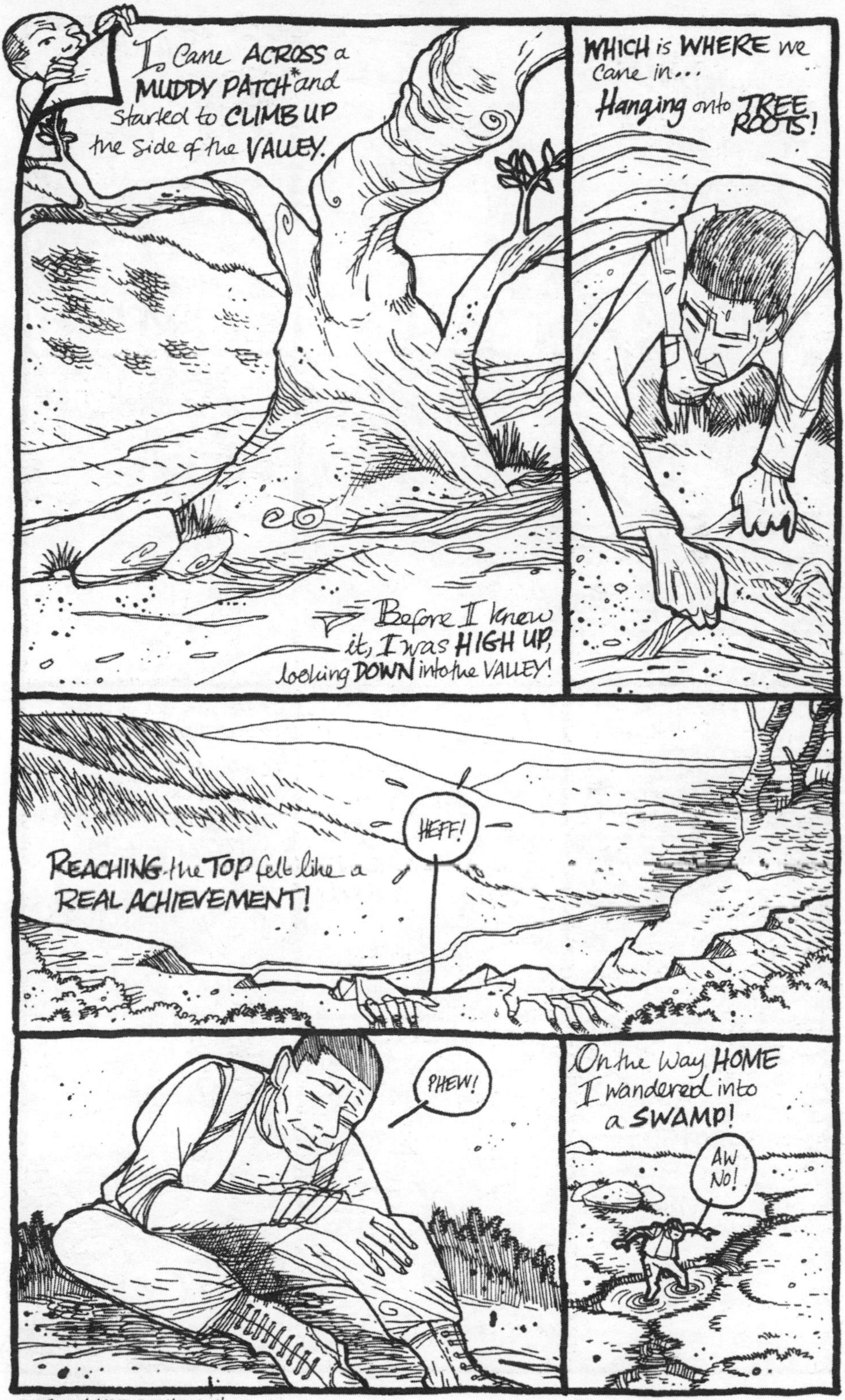
I came ACROSS a MUDDY PATCH* and started to CLIMB UP the side of the VALLEY.
Before I knew it, I was HIGH UP, looking DOWN into the VALLEY!
WHICH is WHERE we came in...
Hanging onto TREE ROOTS!
REACHING the TOP felt like a REAL ACHIEVEMENT!
HEFF!
PHEW!
On the way HOME I wandered into a SWAMP!
AW NO!

* ME and MUD DON'T MIX!

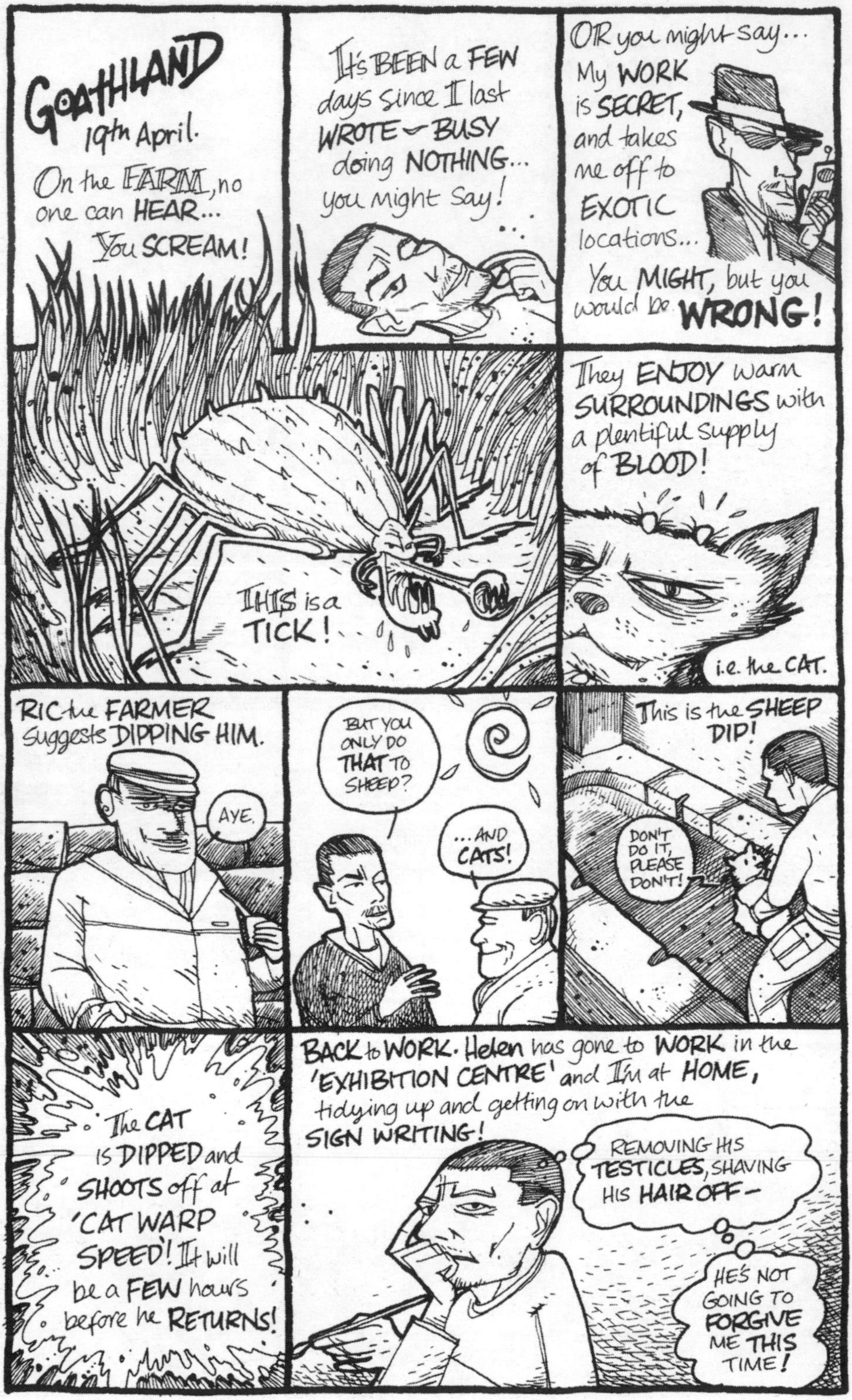
GOATHLAND
19th April.
On the FARM, no one can HEAR... You SCREAM!
It's BEEN a FEW days since I last WROTE — BUSY doing NOTHING... you might say!
OR you might say... My WORK is SECRET, and takes me off to EXOTIC locations...
You MIGHT, but you would be WRONG!
THIS is a TICK!
They ENJOY warm SURROUNDINGS with a plentiful supply of BLOOD!
i.e. the CAT.
RIC the FARMER suggests DIPPING HIM.
AYE.
BUT YOU ONLY DO THAT TO SHEEP?
...AND CATS!
This is the SHEEP DIP!
DON'T DO IT, PLEASE DON'T!
The CAT is DIPPED and SHOOTS off at 'CAT WARP SPEED'! It will be a FEW hours before he RETURNS!
BACK to WORK. Helen has gone to WORK in the 'EXHIBITION CENTRE' and I'm at HOME, tidying up and getting on with the SIGN WRITING!
REMOVING HIS TESTICLES, SHAVING HIS HAIR OFF —
HE'S NOT GOING TO FORGIVE ME THIS TIME!

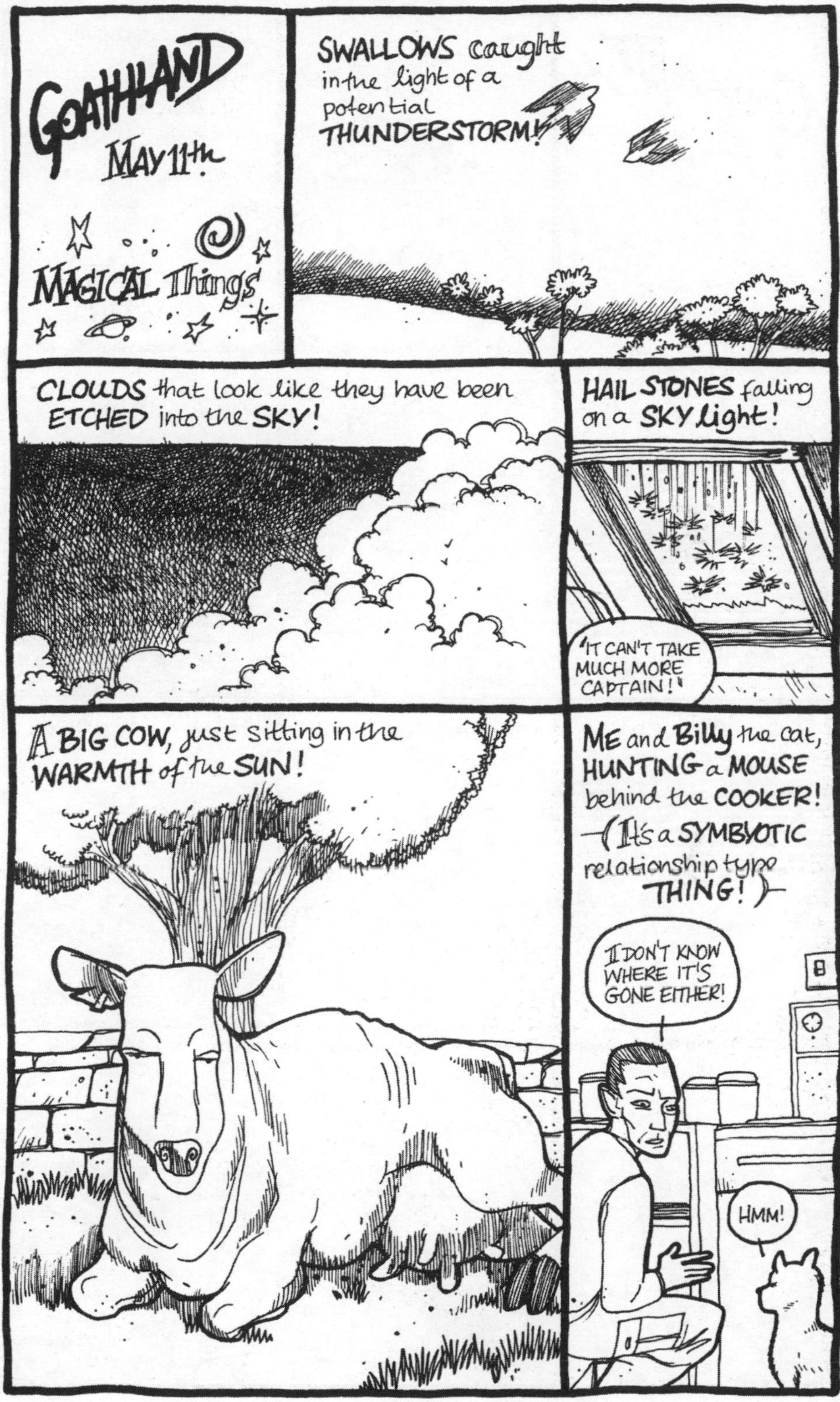
GOATHLAND
MAY 11th
MAGICAL Things
SWALLOWS caught in the light of a potential THUNDERSTORM!
CLOUDS that look like they have been ETCHED into the SKY!
HAIL STONES falling on a SKY light!
"IT CAN'T TAKE MUCH MORE CAPTAIN!"
A BIG COW, just sitting in the WARMTH of the SUN!
ME and Billy the cat, HUNTING a MOUSE behind the COOKER!
(It's a SYMBYOTIC relationship type THING!)
I DON'T KNOW WHERE IT'S GONE EITHER!
HMM!

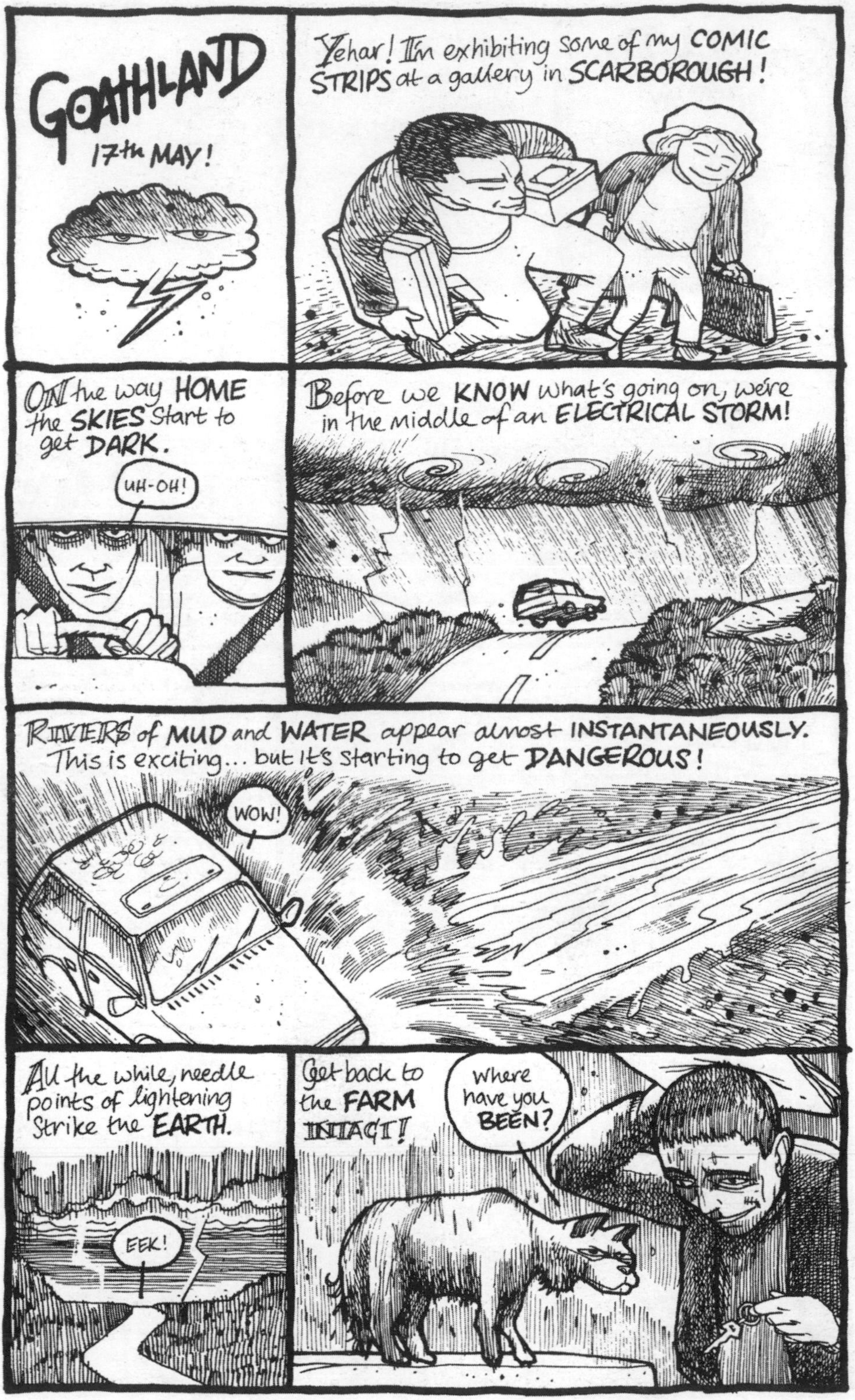
GOATHLAND
17th MAY!
Yehar! I'm exhibiting some of my COMIC STRIPS at a gallery in SCARBOROUGH!
ON the way HOME the SKIES start to get DARK.
UH-OH!
Before we KNOW what's going on, we're in the middle of an ELECTRICAL STORM!
RIVERS of MUD and WATER appear almost INSTANTANEOUSLY. This is exciting... but it's starting to get DANGEROUS!
WOW!
All the while, needle points of lightening strike the EARTH.
EEK!
Get back to the FARM INTACT!
Where have you BEEN?

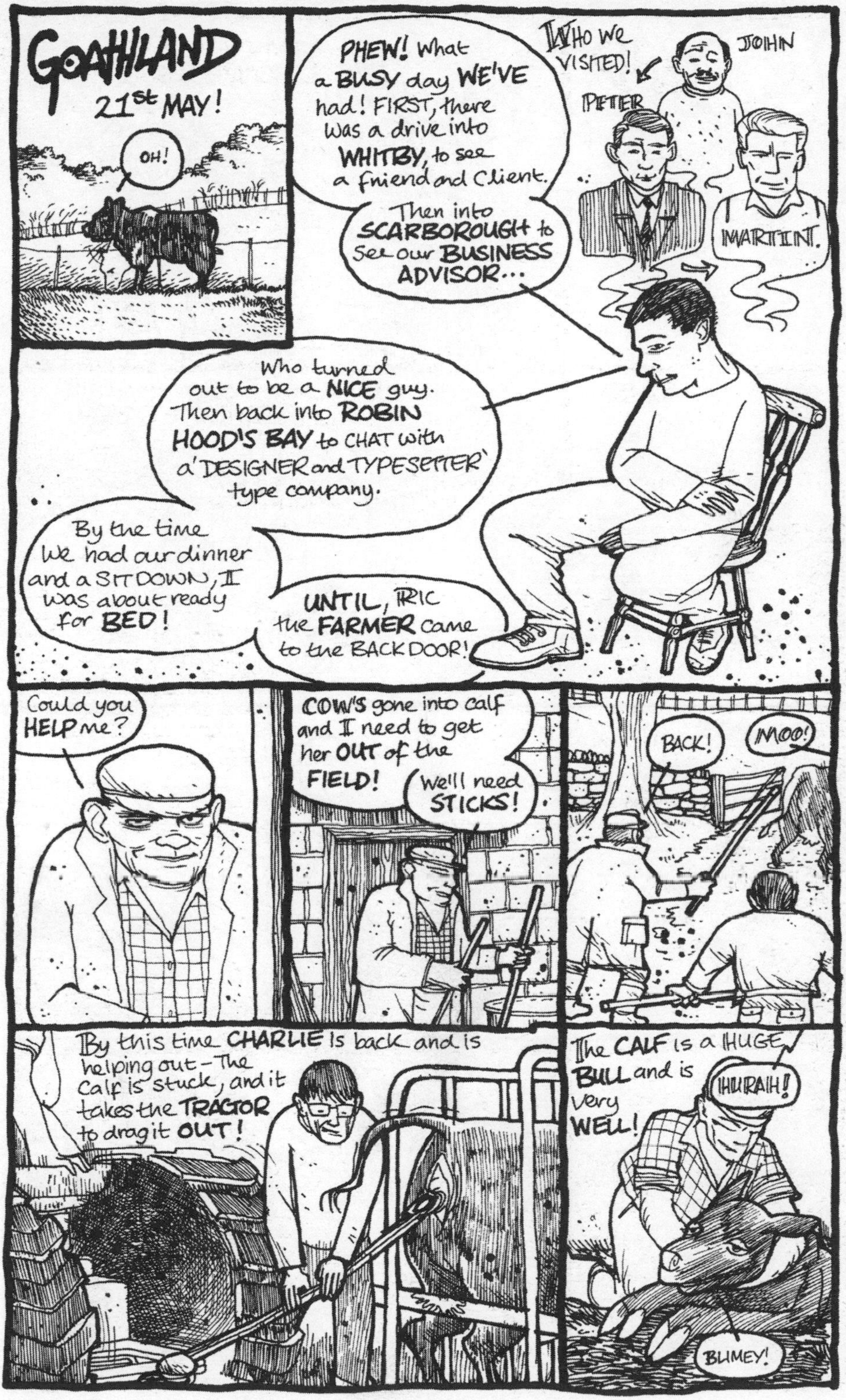
GOATHLAND
21st MAY!
OH!
PHEW! What a BUSY day WE'VE had! FIRST, there was a drive into WHITBY, to see a friend and Client.
Then into SCARBOROUGH to see our BUSINESS ADVISOR...
Who we VISITED!
JOHN
PETER
MARTIN.
Who turned out to be a NICE guy. Then back into ROBIN HOOD'S BAY to CHAT with a 'DESIGNER and TYPESETTER' type company.
By the time we had our dinner and a SIT DOWN, I was about ready for BED!
UNTIL, IRIC the FARMER came to the BACK DOOR!
Could you HELP me?
COW'S gone into calf and I need to get her OUT of the FIELD!
We'll need STICKS!
BACK!
MOO!
By this time CHARLIE is back and is helping out - The calf is stuck, and it takes the TRACTOR to drag it OUT!
The CALF is a HUGE BULL and is very WELL!
HURAH!
BLIMEY!

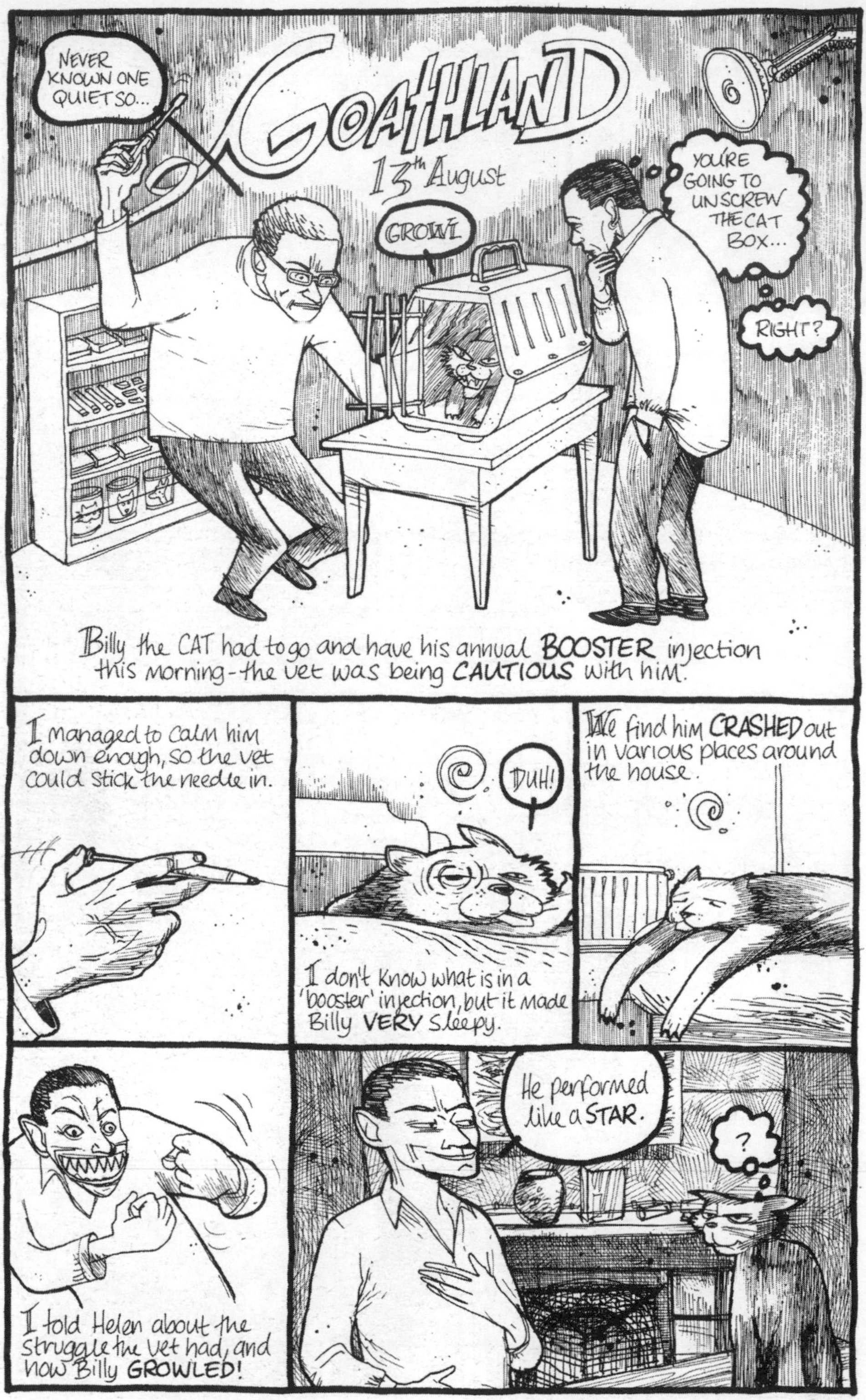
GOATHLAND
13th August
NEVER KNOWN ONE QUIET SO...
GROWL
YOU'RE GOING TO UNSCREW THE CAT BOX...
RIGHT?
Billy the CAT had to go and have his annual BOOSTER injection this morning - the vet was being CAUTIOUS with him.
I managed to calm him down enough, so the vet could stick the needle in.
DUH!
I don't know what is in a 'booster' injection, but it made Billy VERY sleepy.
We find him CRASHED out in various places around the house.
I told Helen about the struggle the vet had, and now Billy GROWLED!
He performed like a STAR.
?

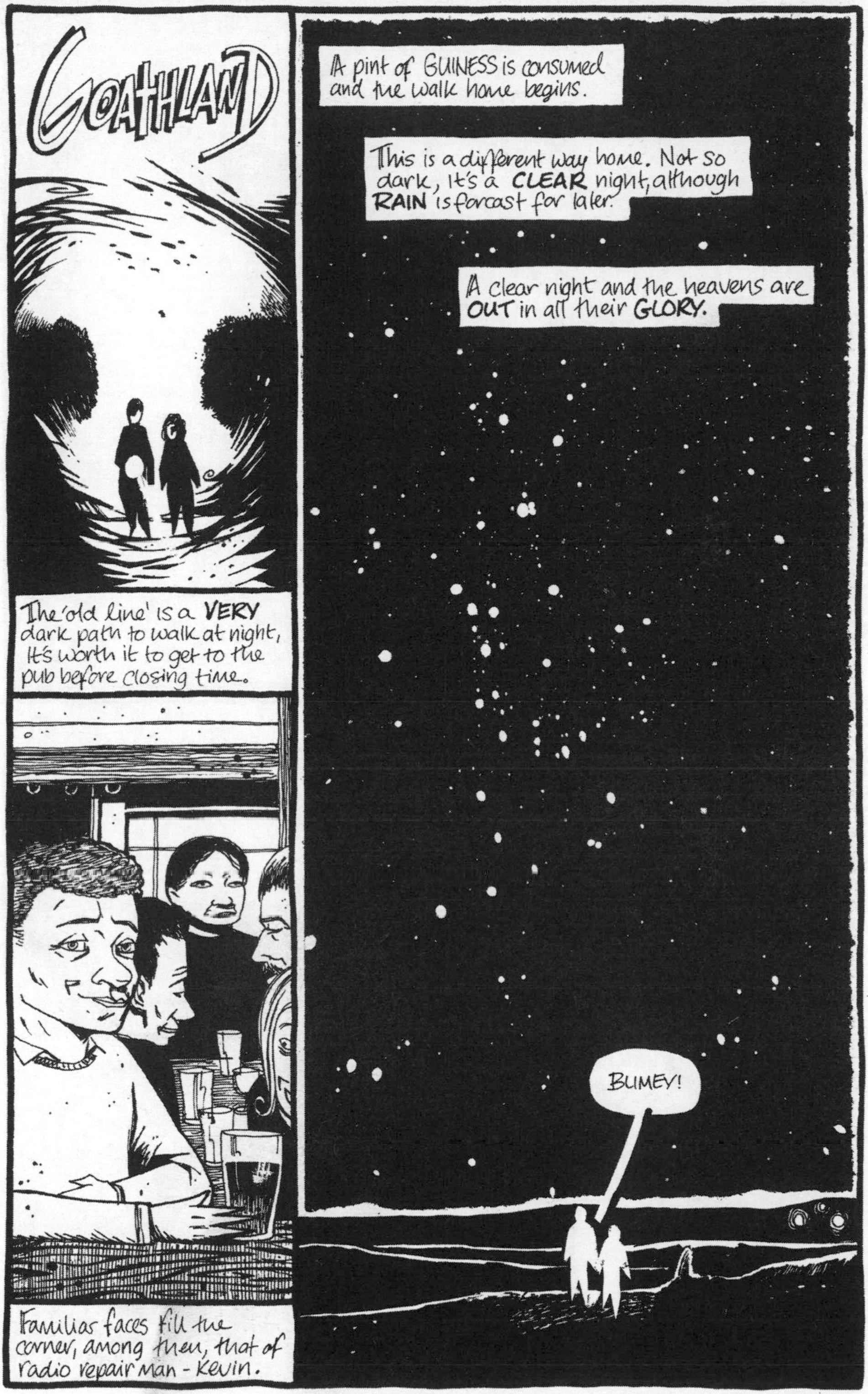
GOATHLAND
The 'old line' is a VERY dark path to walk at night, It's worth it to get to the pub before closing time.
Familiar faces fill the corner, among them, that of radio repair man - Kevin.
A pint of GUINESS is consumed and the walk home begins.
This is a different way home. Not so dark, It's a CLEAR night, although RAIN is forcast for later.
A clear night and the heavens are OUT in all their GLORY.
BLIMEY!

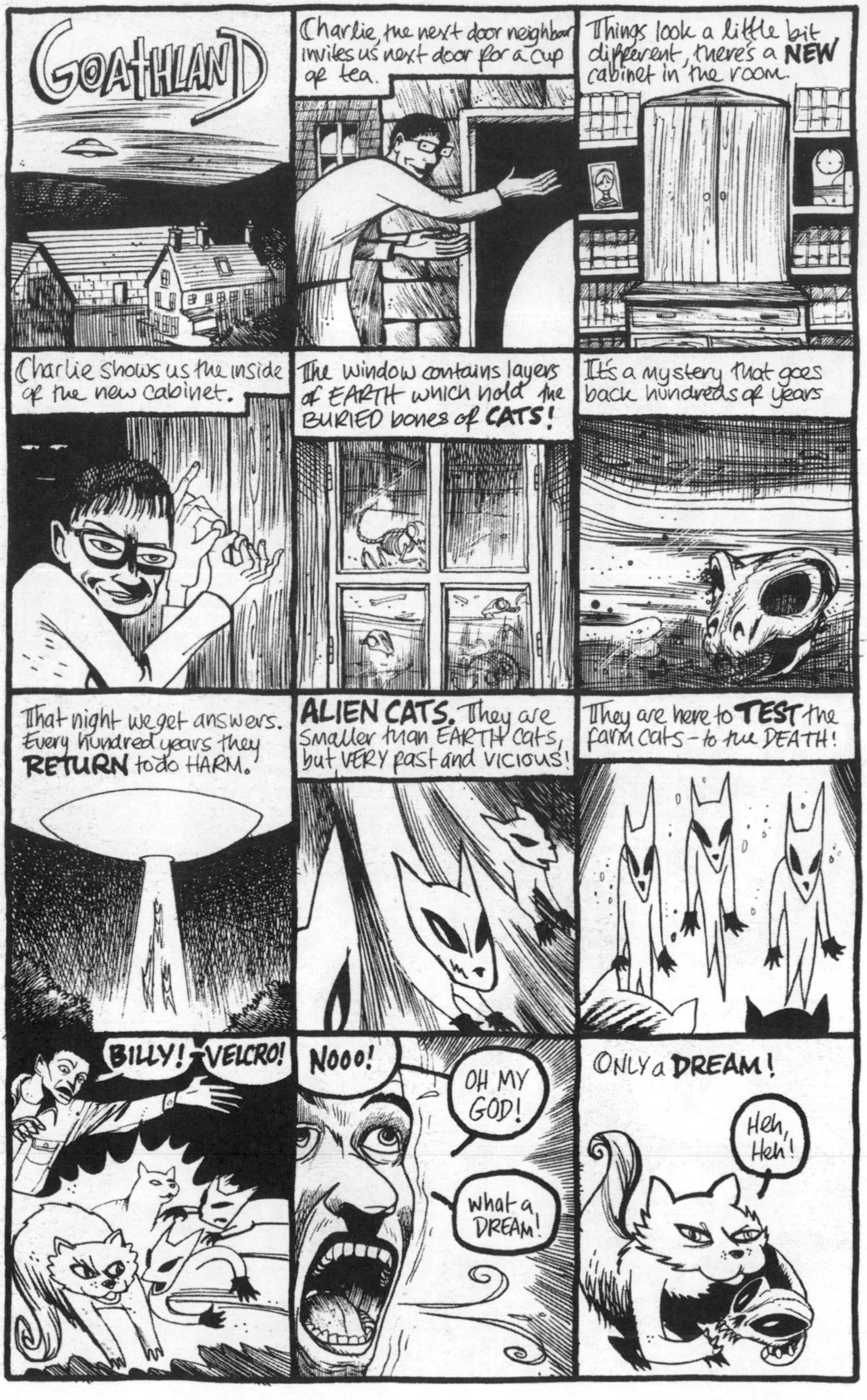

GOATHLAND
Charlie, the next door neighbour invites us next door for a cup of tea.
Things look a little bit different, there's a NEW cabinet in the room.
Charlie shows us the inside of the new cabinet.
The window contains layers of EARTH which hold the BURIED bones of CATS!
It's a mystery that goes back hundreds of years
That night we get answers. Every hundred years they RETURN to do HARM.
ALIEN CATS. They are smaller than EARTH cats, but VERY fast and VICIOUS!
They are here to TEST the farm cats - to the DEATH!
BILLY!
VELCRO!
Nooo!
OH MY GOD!
what a DREAM!
ONLY a DREAM!
Heh, Heh!

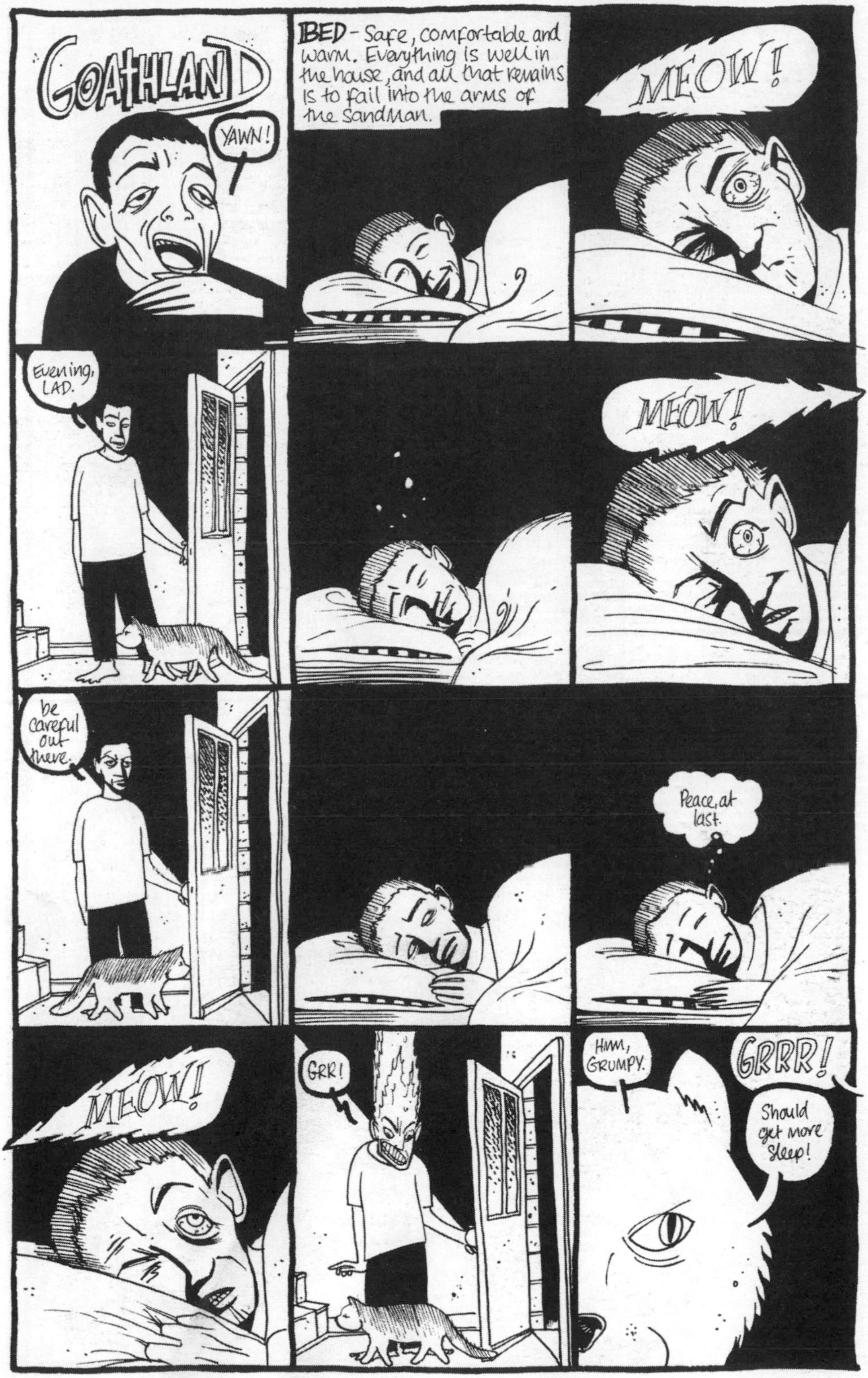

GOATHLAND
YAWN!
BED - Safe, comfortable and warm. Everything is well in the house, and all that remains is to fall into the arms of the sandman.
MEOW!
Evening, LAD.
MEOW!
be careful out there.
Peace, at last.
MEOW!
GRR!
HMM, GRUMPY.
GRRR!
Should get more sleep!

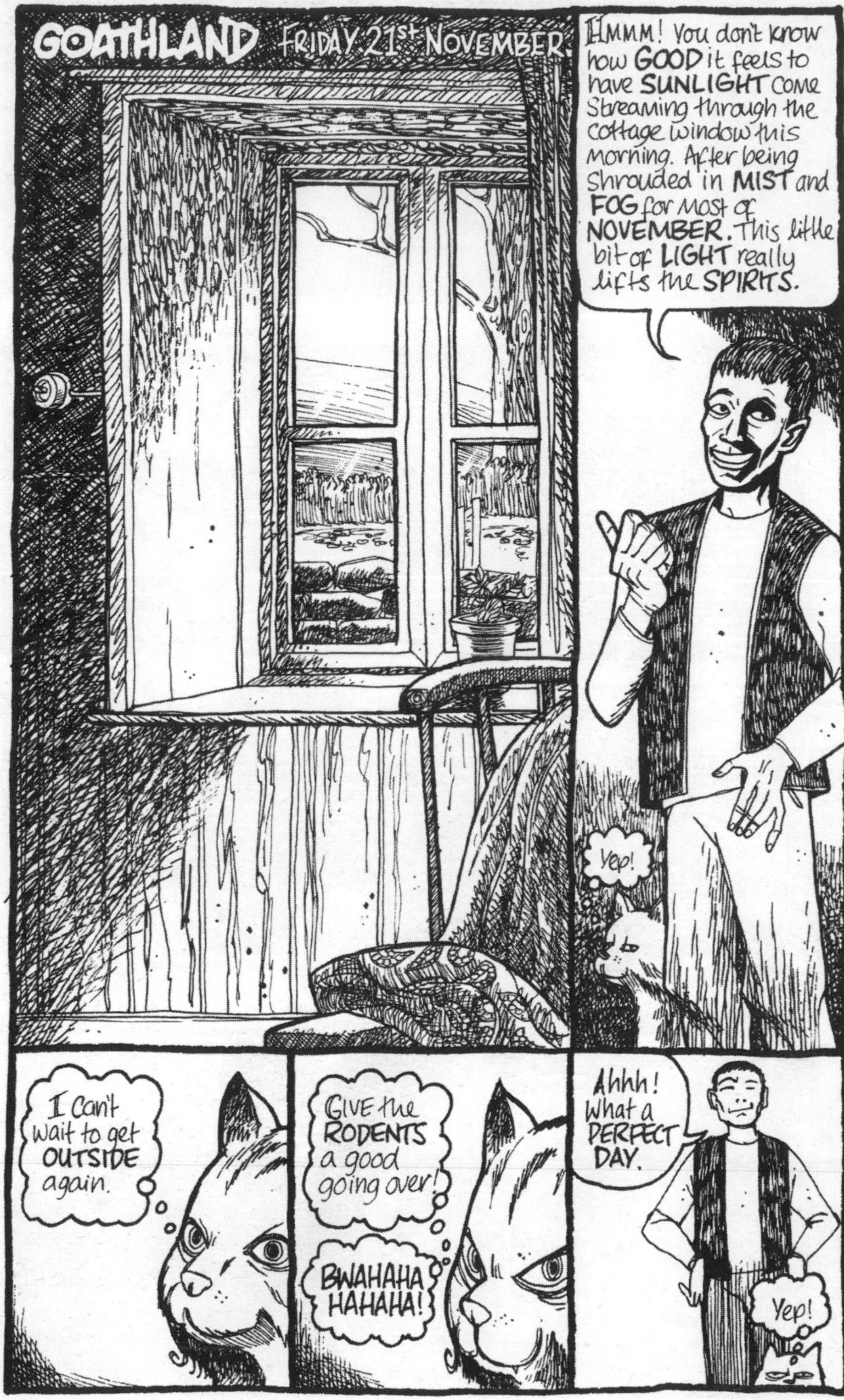
GOATHLAND Friday 21st November
HMMM! You don't know how GOOD it feels to have SUNLIGHT come streaming through the cottage window this morning. After being shrouded in MIST and FOG for most of NOVEMBER. This little bit of LIGHT really lifts the SPIRITS.
Yep!
I can't wait to get OUTSIDE again.
Give the RODENTS a good going over!
BWAHAHA HAHAHA!
Ahhh! What a PERFECT DAY.
Yep!

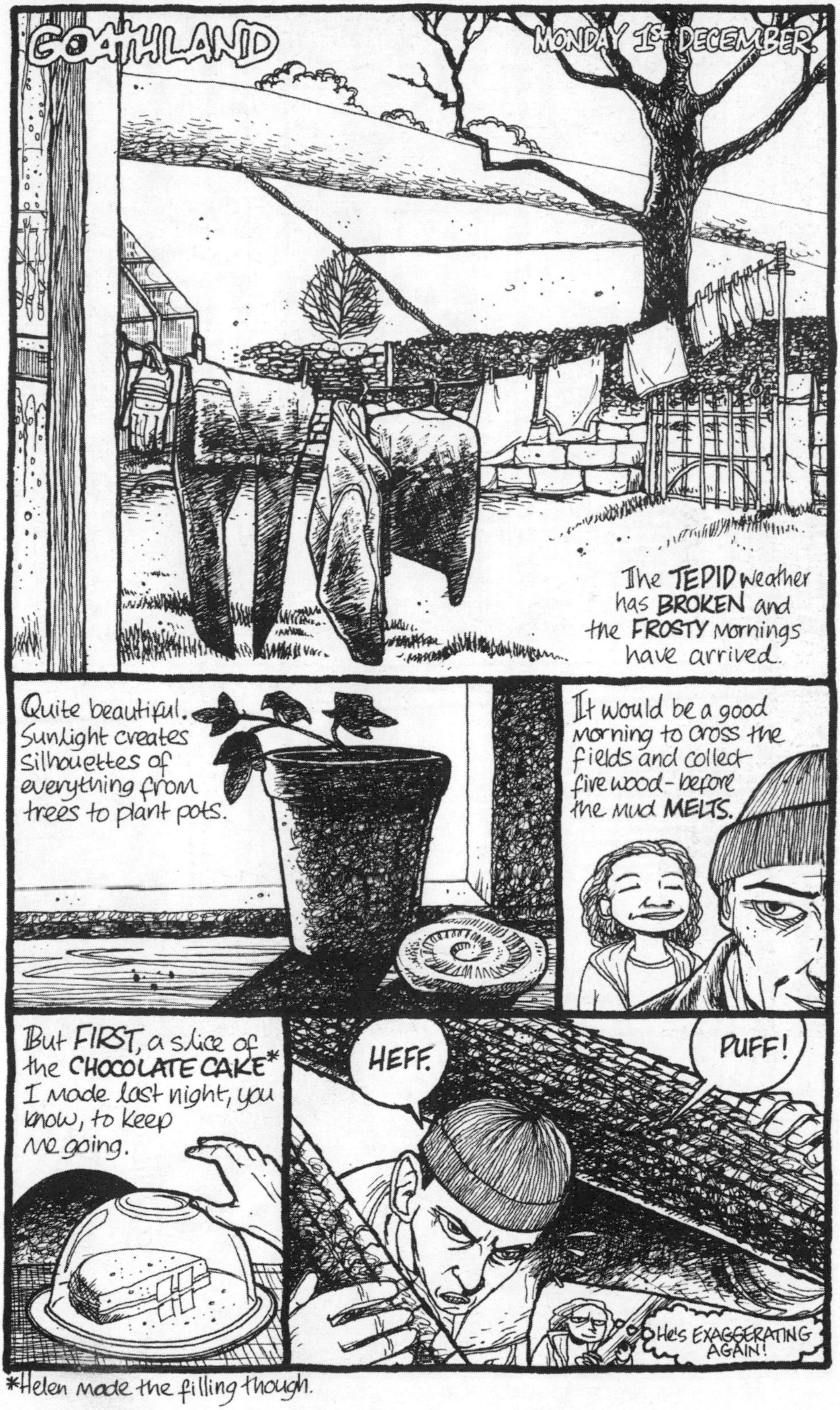
GOATHLAND
MONDAY 1st DECEMBER.
The TEPID weather has BROKEN and the FROSTY mornings have arrived.
Quite beautiful. Sunlight creates silhouettes of everything from trees to plant pots.
It would be a good morning to cross the fields and collect firewood - before the mud MELTS.
But FIRST, a slice of the CHOCOLATE CAKE* I made last night, you know, to keep me going.
HEFF.
PUFF!
He's EXAGGERATING AGAIN!
*Helen made the filling though.

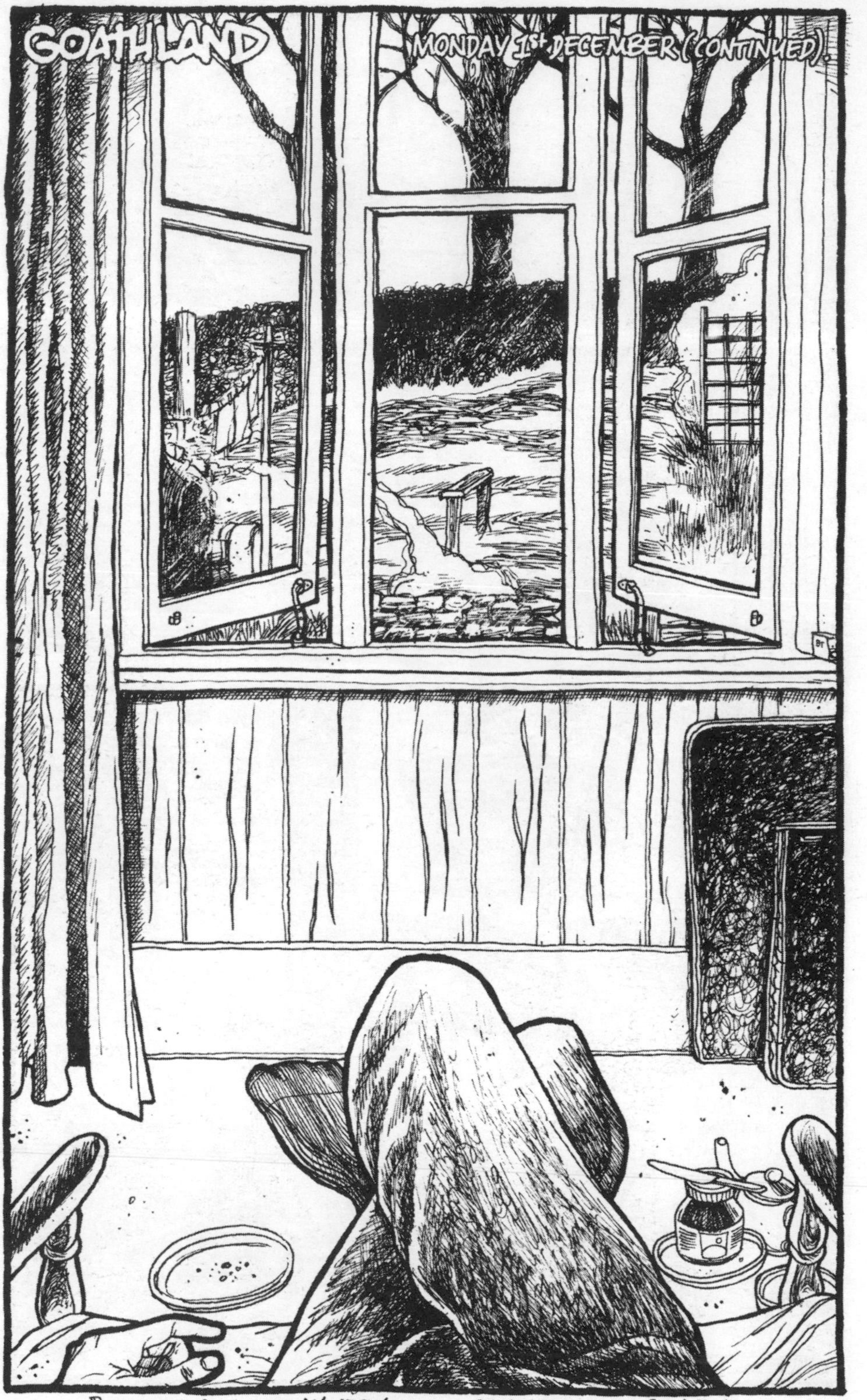
GOATHLAND
MONDAY 1st DECEMBER (CONTINUED).

Breakfast in front of the **WINDOW**, watching **STEAM** rise as the **SUN** finds **FRESH** patches of frost to **HEAT**.

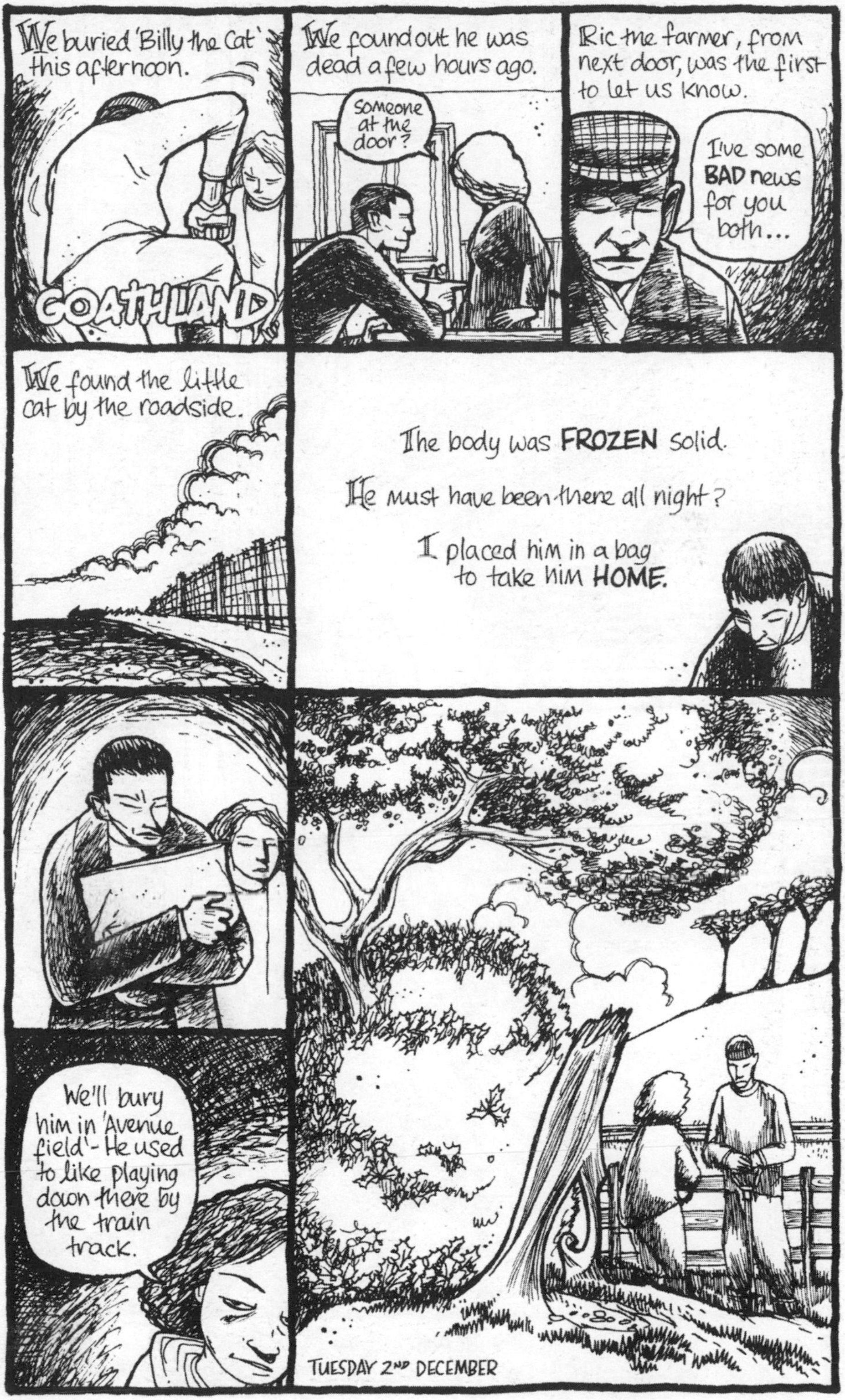
We buried 'Billy the Cat' this afternoon.
COATHLAND
We found out he was dead a few hours ago.
Someone at the door?
Ric the farmer, from next door, was the first to let us know.
I've some BAD news for you both...
We found the little cat by the roadside.
The body was FROZEN solid.
He must have been there all night?
I placed him in a bag to take him HOME.
We'll bury him in 'Avenue field'- He used to like playing down there by the train track.
TUESDAY 2ND DECEMBER

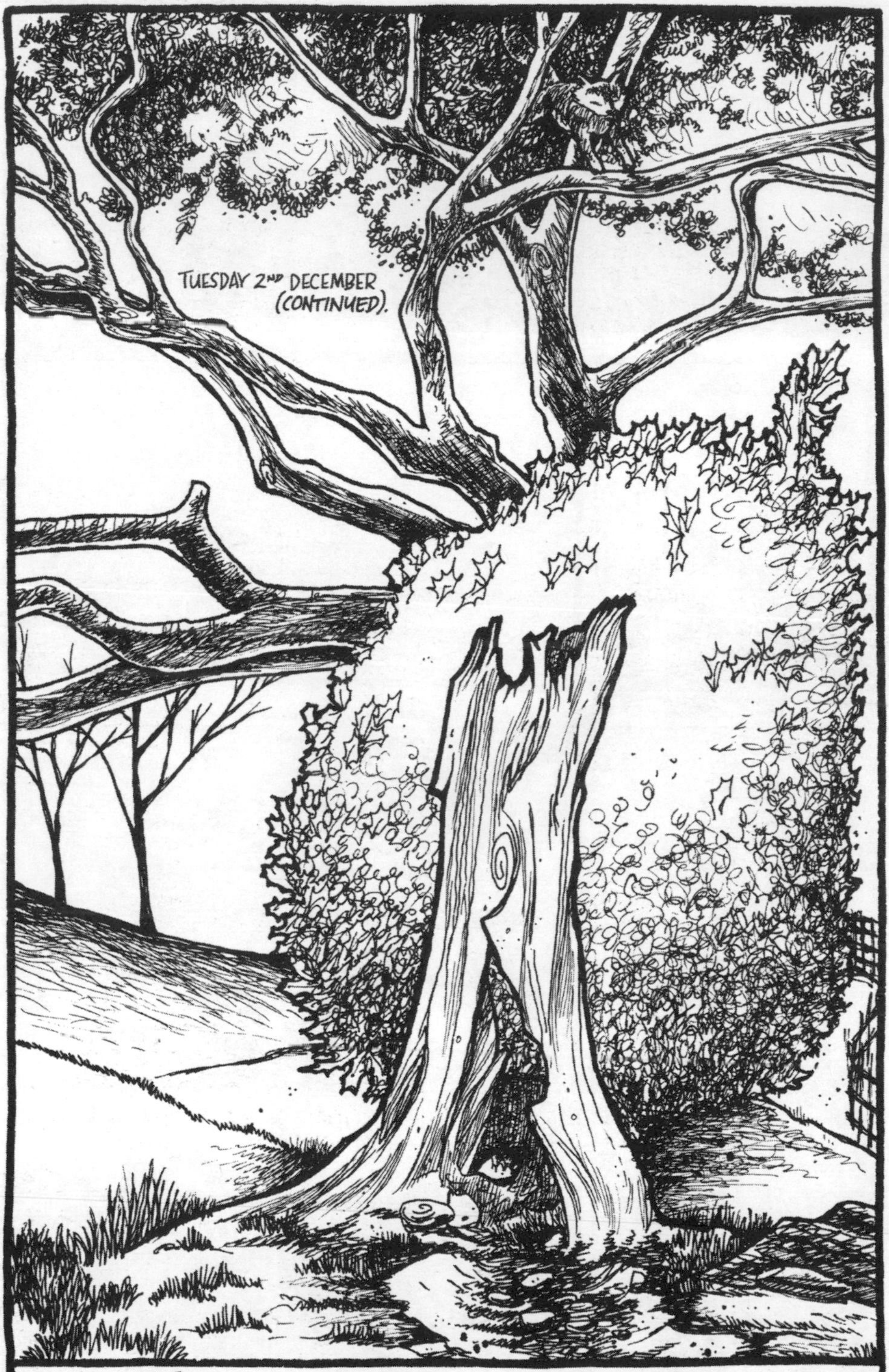
TUESDAY 2ND DECEMBER (CONTINUED).
We all moved to GOATHLAND and the farm TOGETHER.
'Billy the Cat' - Mar 1996 - Dec 1997 — I'm going to miss the grumpy little cat.

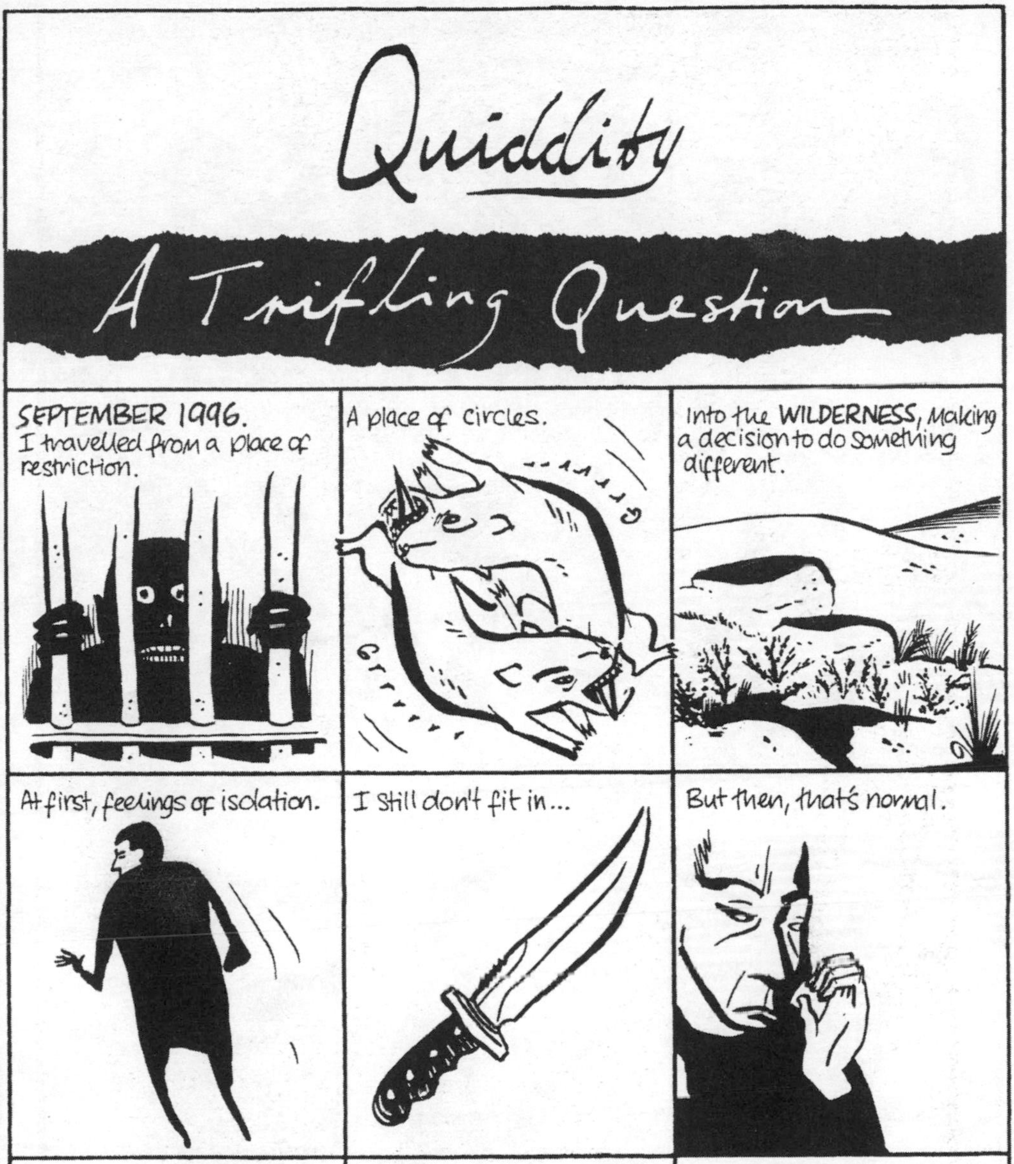
Quiddity
A Trifling Question
SEPTEMBER 1996. I travelled from a place of restriction.
A place of circles.
Into the WILDERNESS, Making a decision to do something different.
At first, feelings of isolation.
I still don't fit in...
But then, that's normal.
My Mother tells me of the time when I was young, I wanted to live somewhere 'oldy worldy'.
At fourteen I plan to RUN away. My savings will go on a quality TENT, stout boots...
And a HUNTING knife.
1

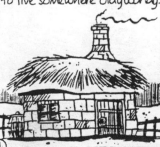

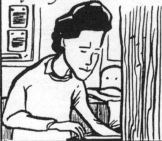

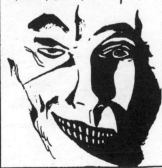

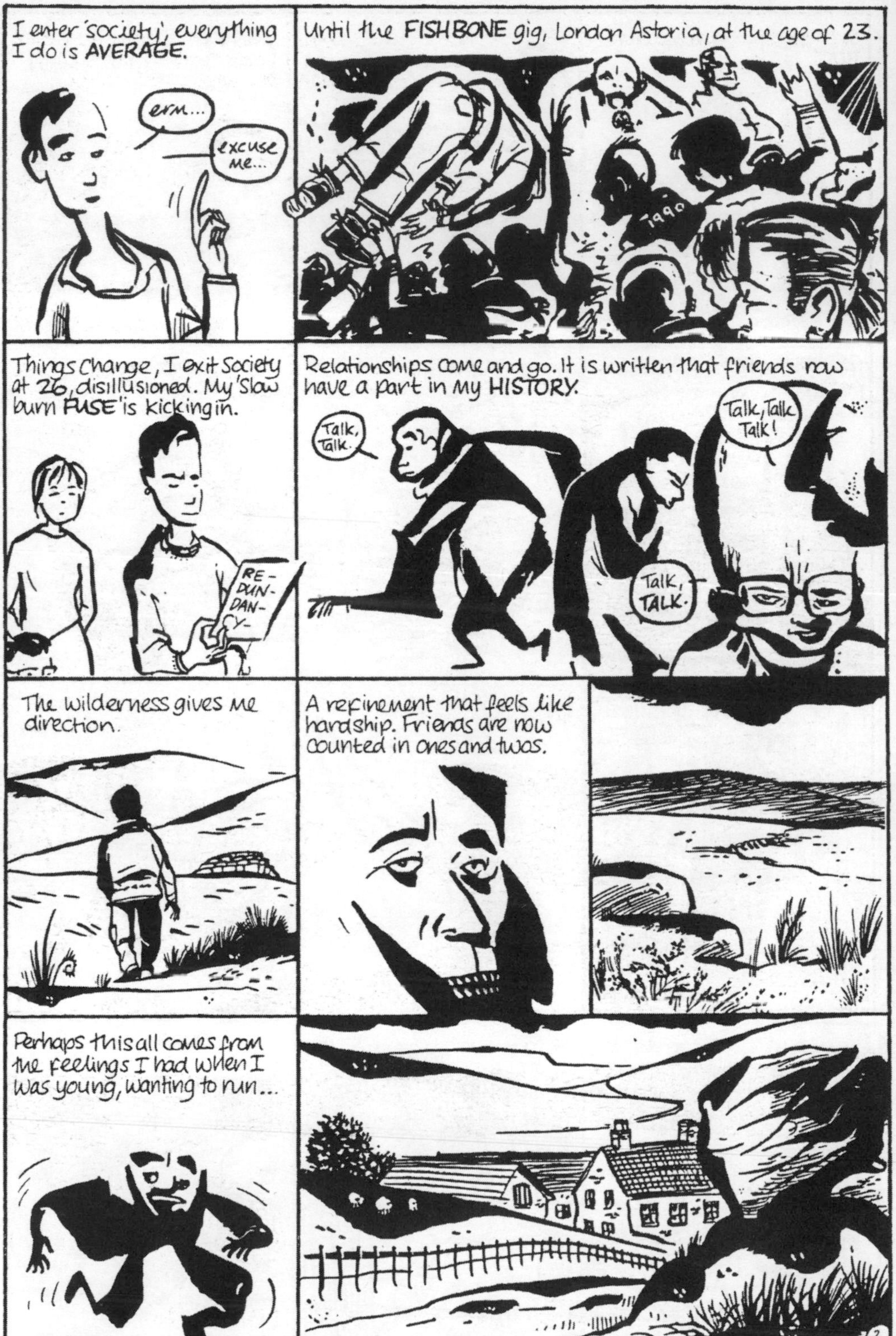

I enter 'society', everything I do is AVERAGE.
erm...
excuse me...
Until the FISHBONE gig, London Astoria, at the age of 23.
1990
Things change, I exit Society at 26, disillusioned. My 'Slow burn FUSE' is kicking in.
RE-DUN-DAN-CY-
Relationships come and go. It is written that friends now have a part in my HISTORY.
Talk, Talk.
Talk, Talk Talk!
Talk, TALK.
The wilderness gives me direction.
A refinement that feels like hardship. Friends are now counted in ones and twos.
Perhaps this all comes from the feelings I had when I was young, wanting to run...

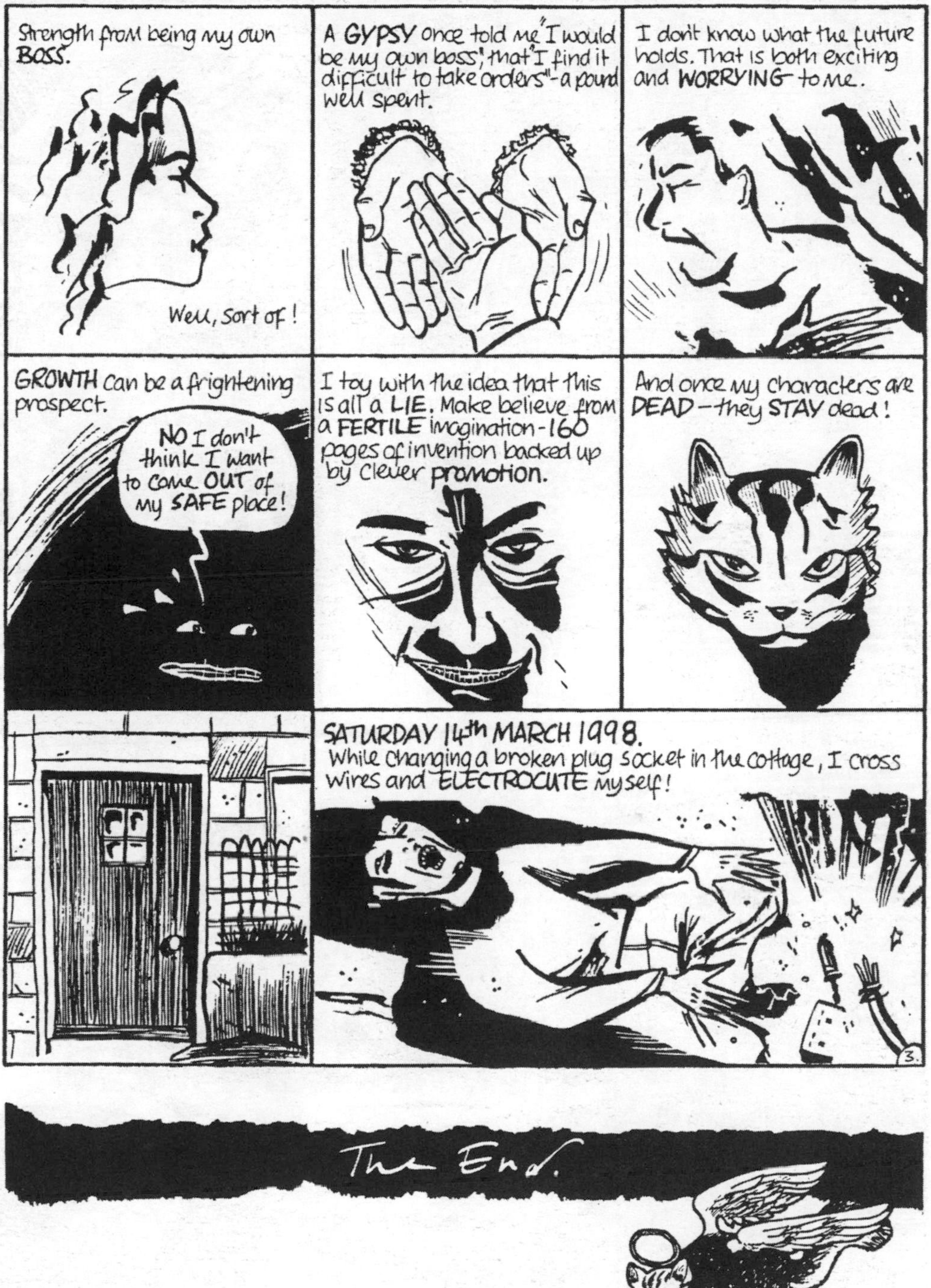
Strength from being my own BOSS.
Well, sort of!
A GYPSY once told me "I would be my own boss", that "I find it difficult to take orders" - a pound well spent.
I don't know what the future holds. That is both exciting and WORRYING to me.
GROWTH can be a frightening prospect.
NO I don't think I want to come OUT of my SAFE place!
I toy with the idea that this is all a LIE. Make believe from a FERTILE imagination - 160 pages of invention backed up by clever promotion.
And once my characters are DEAD - they STAY dead!
SATURDAY 14th MARCH 1998.
While changing a broken plug socket in the cottage, I cross wires and ELECTROCUTE myself!
3.

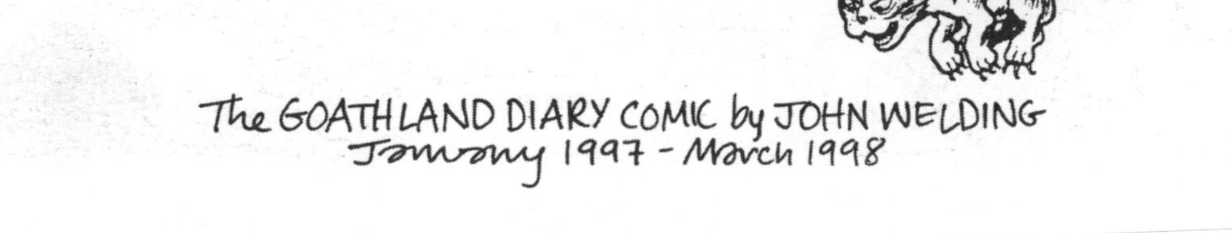
The End.

The GOATHLAND DIARY COMIC by JOHN WELDING
January 1997 - March 1998

PANDORA

ART BY STEVE WHITAKER

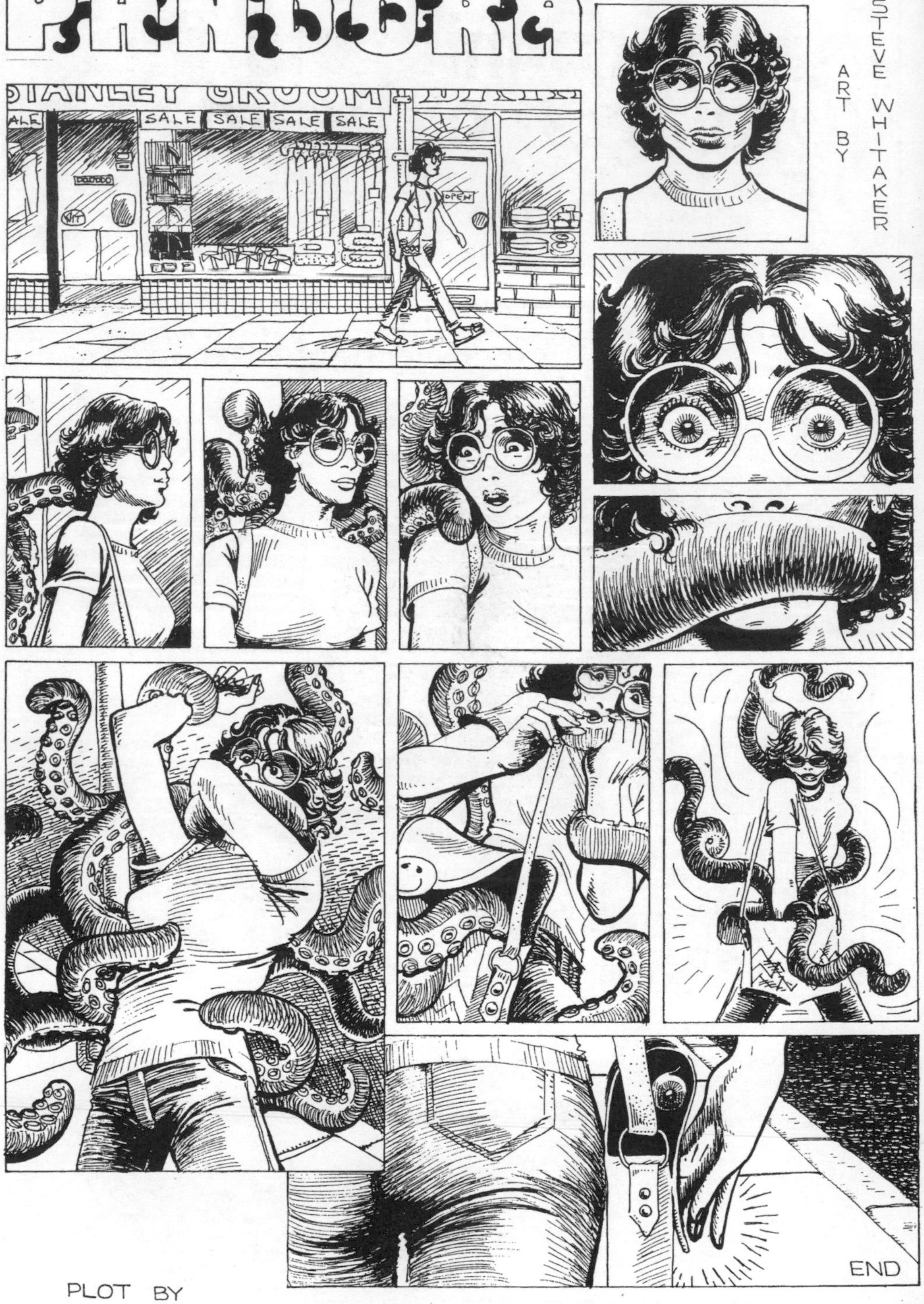
SALE
SALE
SALE
SALE
OPEN
END

PLOT BY
HOWARD STANGROOM

aunt connie and the plague of beards

jonathan edwards

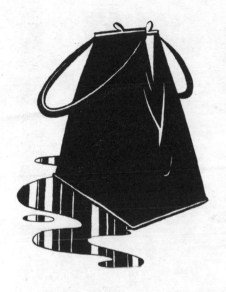

Jonathan Edwards

AUNT CONNIE
AND THE PLAGUE OF BEARDS
Les Cartoonists Dangereux, collection Lilliput, 1999

Welshman Mister Edwards is something of a secret
weapon when it comes to British comics – his strips are
seen in, among others, *Deadline* and *MAD* magazine, and
the music paper *NME*, but also, for more years than we
can count, in the UK's *Guardian* newspaper. (Although, as
he himself admits, he should have drawn a lot more than
he has!)

Aunt Connie was originally published as a mini-comic
by independent UK comics collective "les cartoonists
dangereux" (see if you can imagine anything as
dangerous as a cartoonist) and was available in both
English and French language editions.

"I wanted to cross Damon Runyon with *An American
Werewolf in London*, and find an excuse to use my
Berenice Abbott book as reference. Since then I've
worked as an illustrator and character designer (with my
partner Louise AKA Felt Mistress), exhibited in galleries
all over the world, including LA, Berlin and Osaka.
And I continue to draw comics when I can." – JE

www.jonathan-e.com

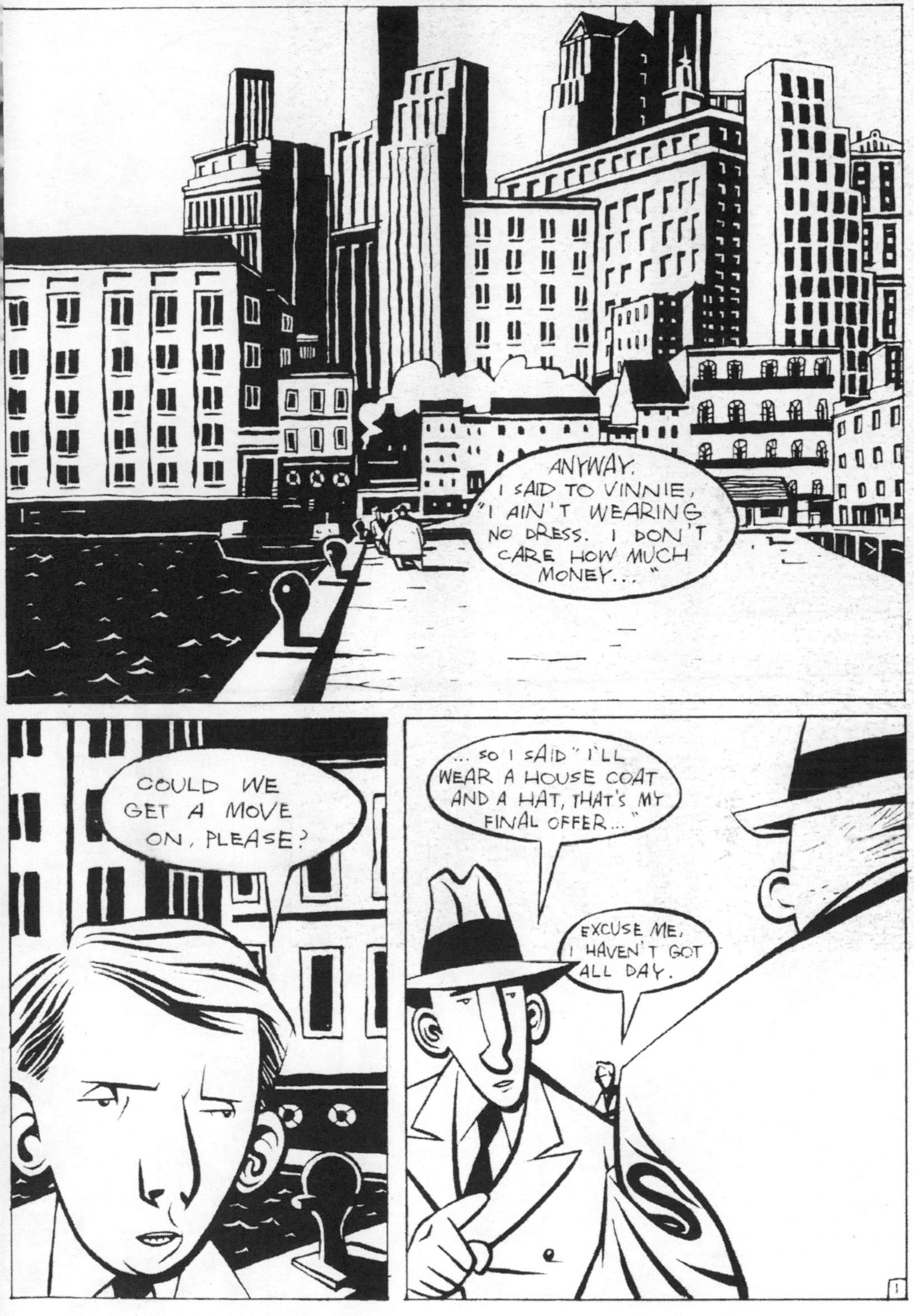
ANYWAY. I SAID TO VINNIE, "I AIN'T WEARING NO DRESS. I DON'T CARE HOW MUCH MONEY..."
COULD WE GET A MOVE ON, PLEASE?
...SO I SAID "I'LL WEAR A HOUSE COAT AND A HAT, THAT'S MY FINAL OFFER..."
EXCUSE ME, I HAVEN'T GOT ALL DAY.

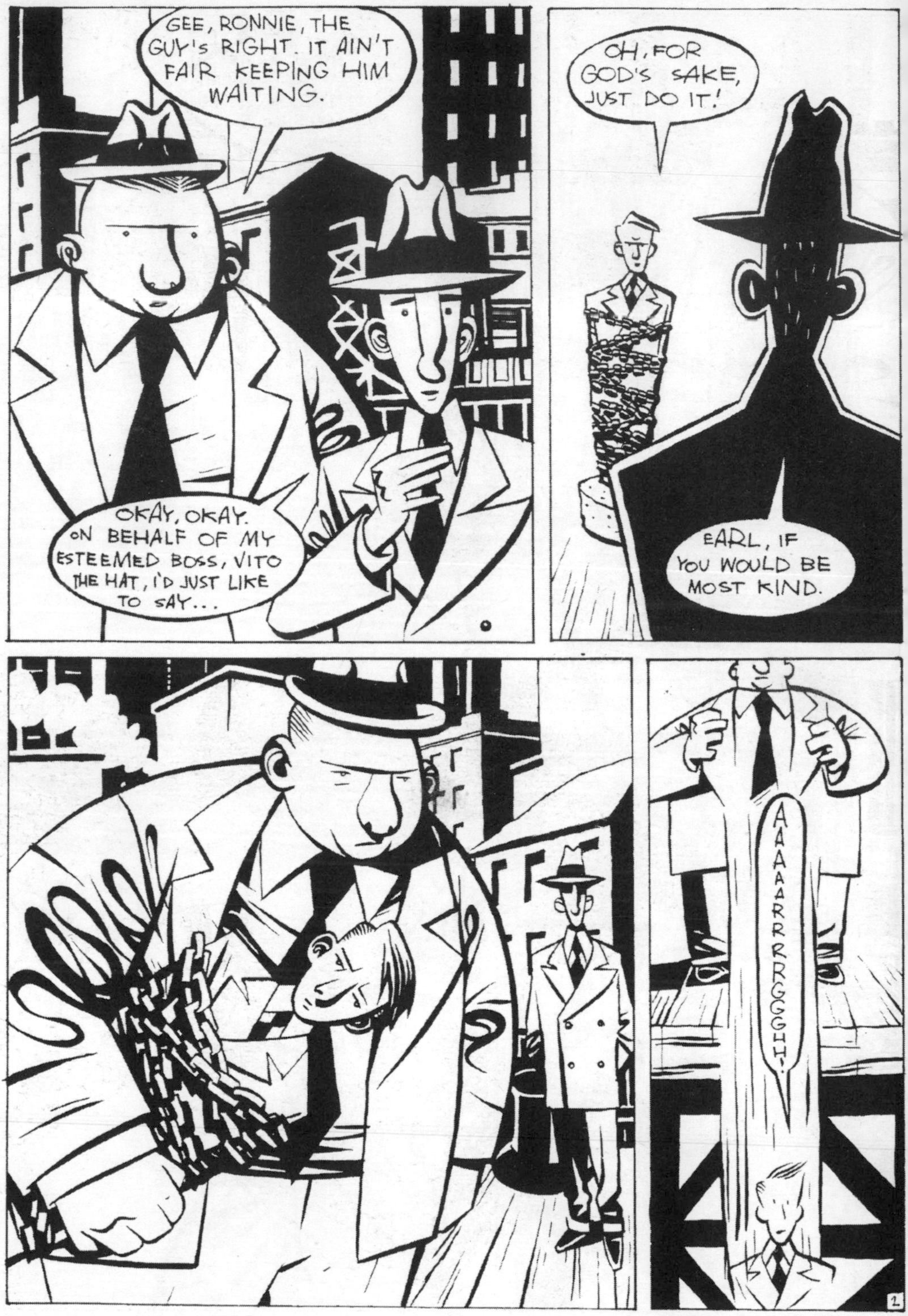
GEE, RONNIE, THE GUY'S RIGHT. IT AIN'T FAIR KEEPING HIM WAITING.
OKAY, OKAY. ON BEHALF OF MY ESTEEMED BOSS, VITO THE HAT, I'D JUST LIKE TO SAY...
OH, FOR GOD'S SAKE, JUST DO IT!
EARL, IF YOU WOULD BE MOST KIND.
AAAAARRRRGGGH!
2

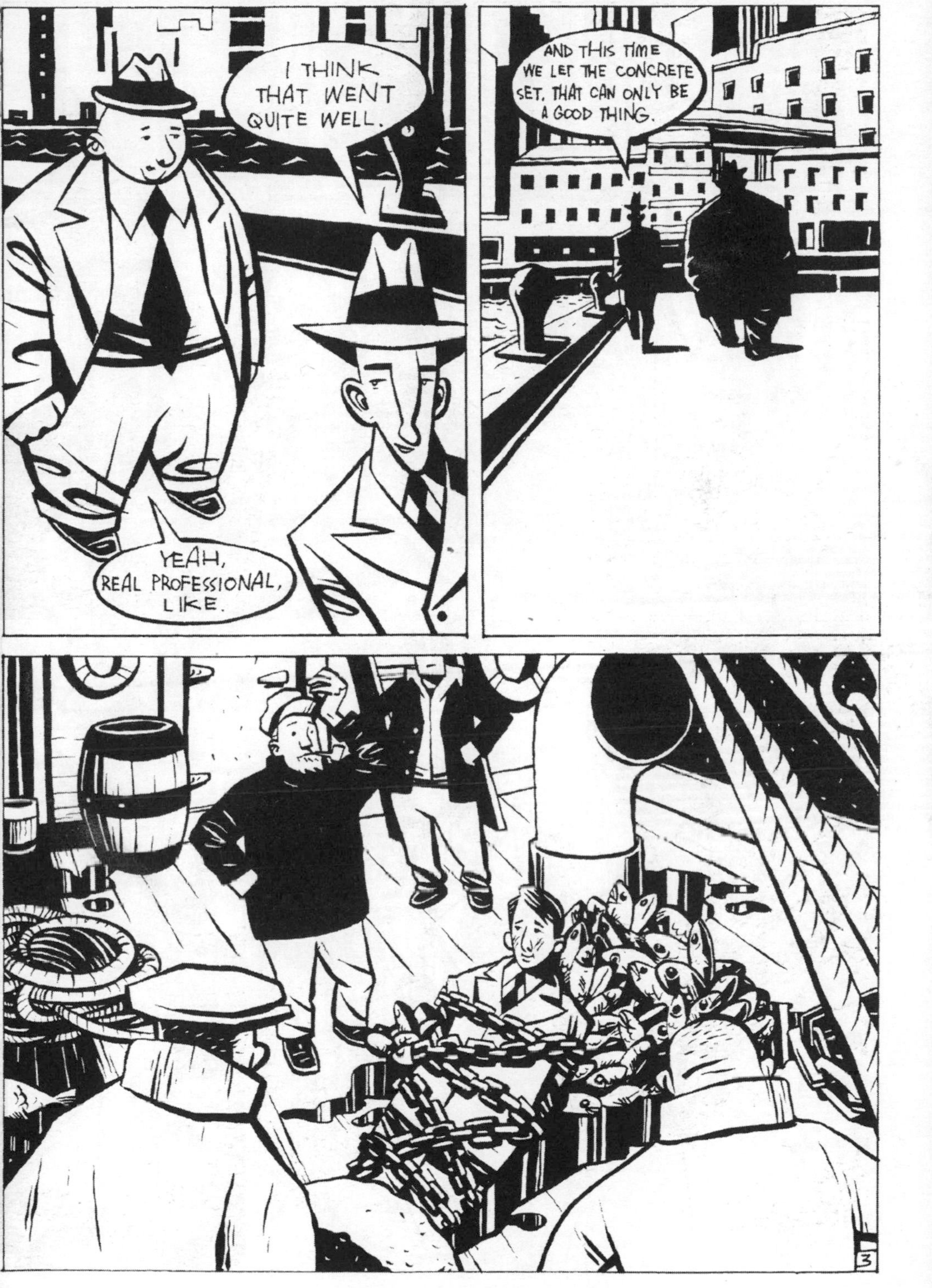
I THINK THAT WENT QUITE WELL.
YEAH, REAL PROFESSIONAL, LIKE.
AND THIS TIME WE LET THE CONCRETE SET. THAT CAN ONLY BE A GOOD THING.
3

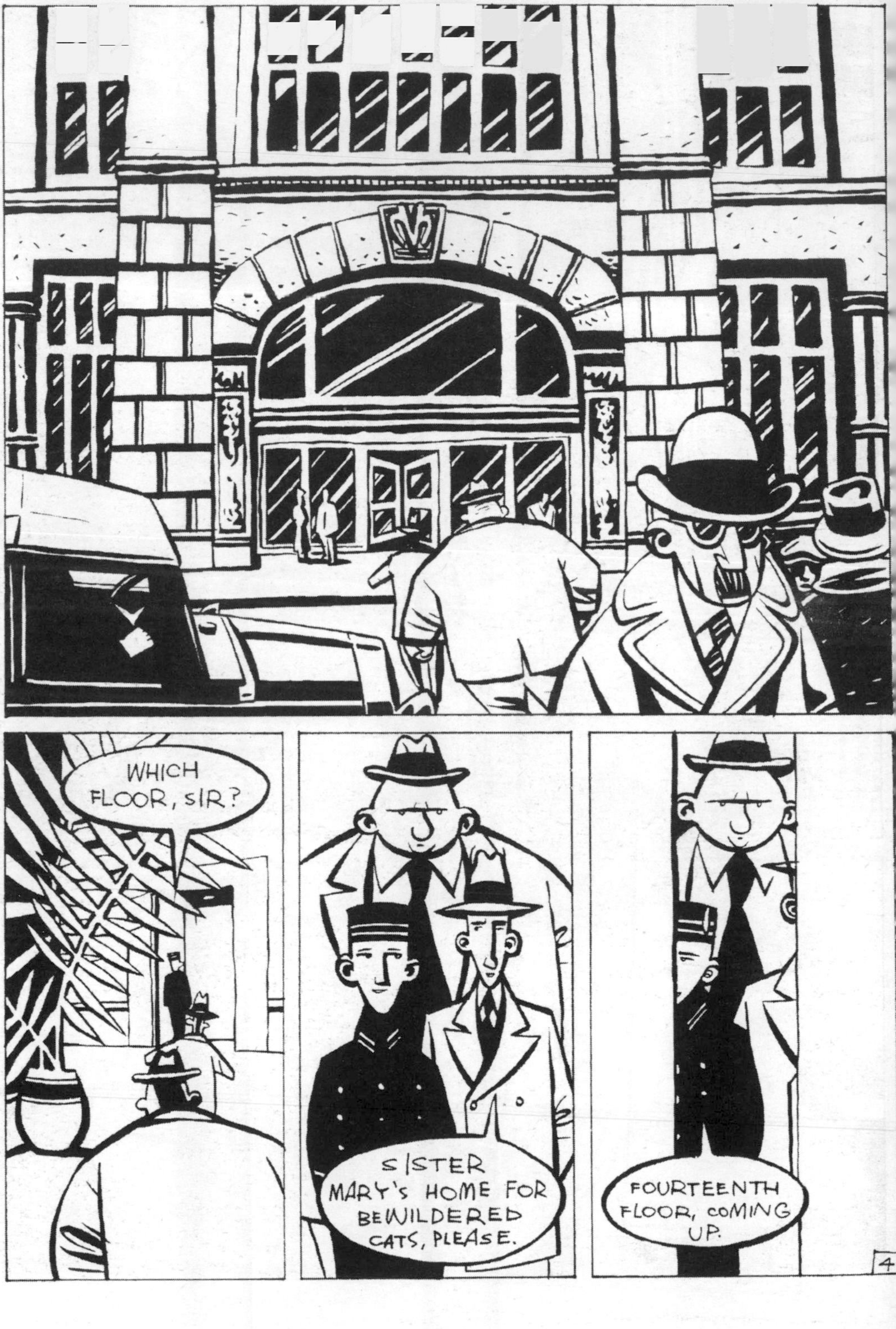
WHICH FLOOR, SIR?
SISTER MARY's HOME FOR BEWILDERED CATS, PLEASE.
FOURTEENTH FLOOR, COMING UP.

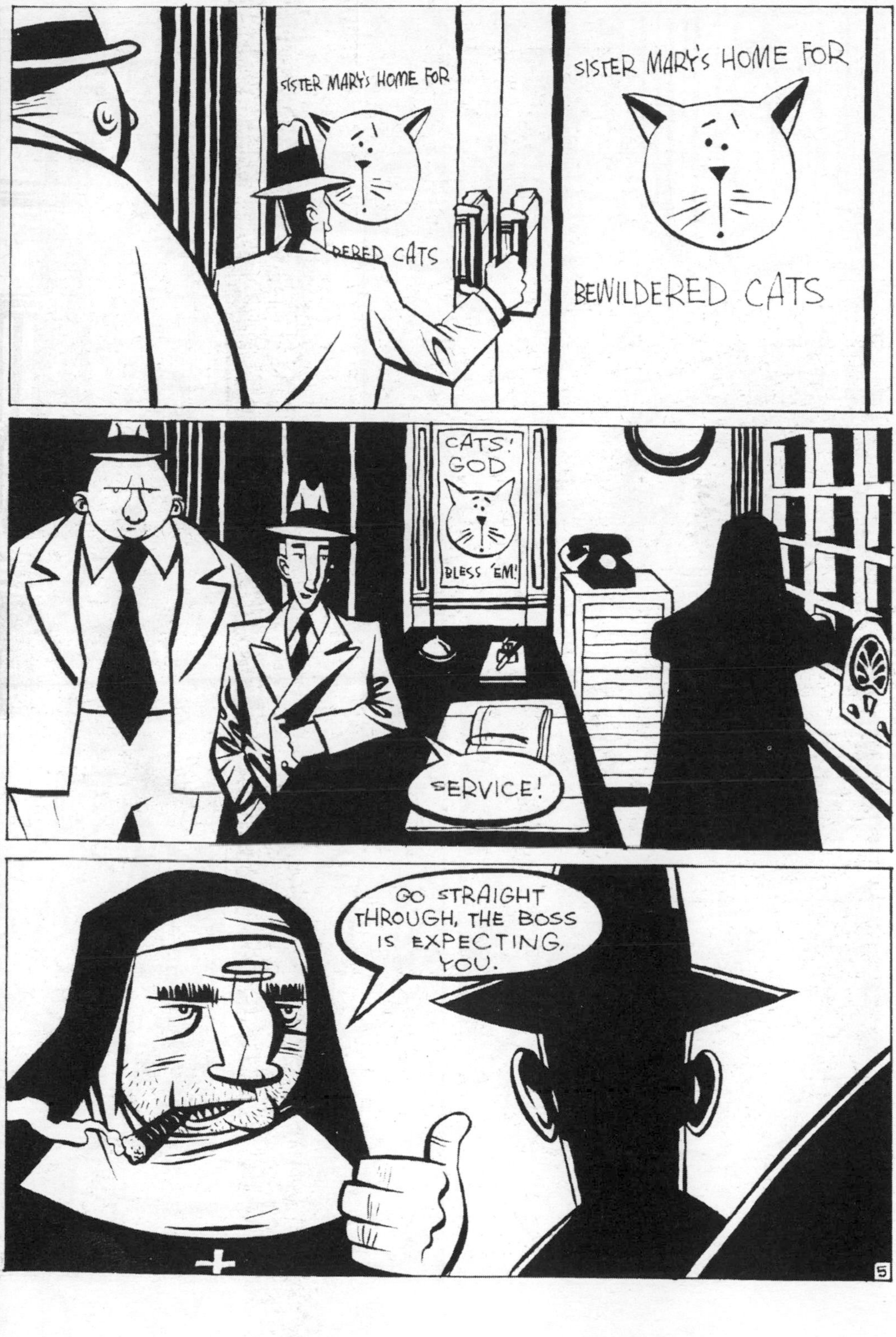
SISTER MARY's HOME FOR
DERED CATS
SISTER MARY's HOME FOR
BEWILDERED CATS
CATS! GOD BLESS 'EM!
SERVICE!
GO STRAIGHT THROUGH, THE BOSS IS EXPECTING YOU.

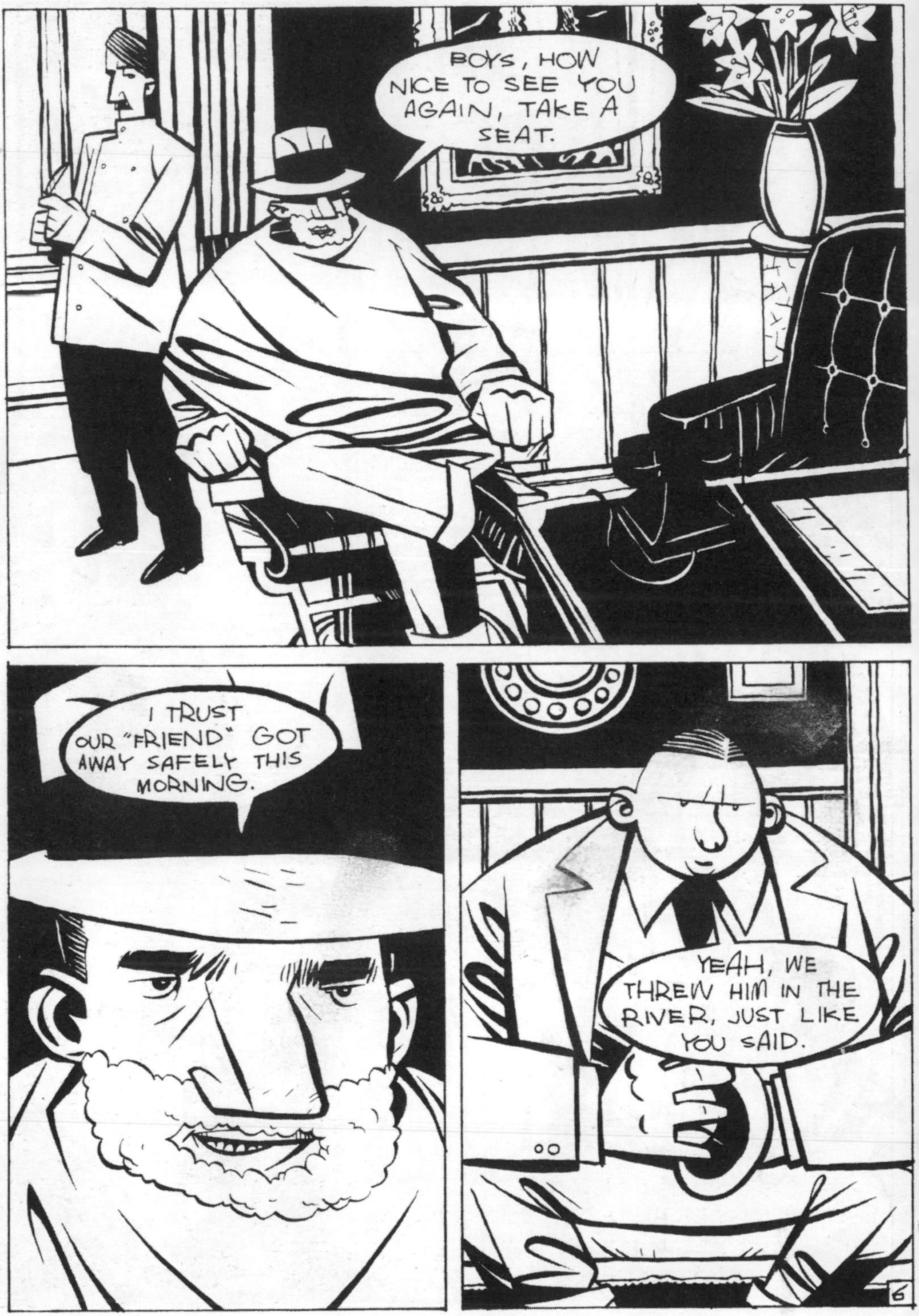
BOYS, HOW NICE TO SEE YOU AGAIN, TAKE A SEAT.
I TRUST OUR "FRIEND" GOT AWAY SAFELY THIS MORNING.
YEAH, WE THREW HIM IN THE RIVER, JUST LIKE YOU SAID.
6

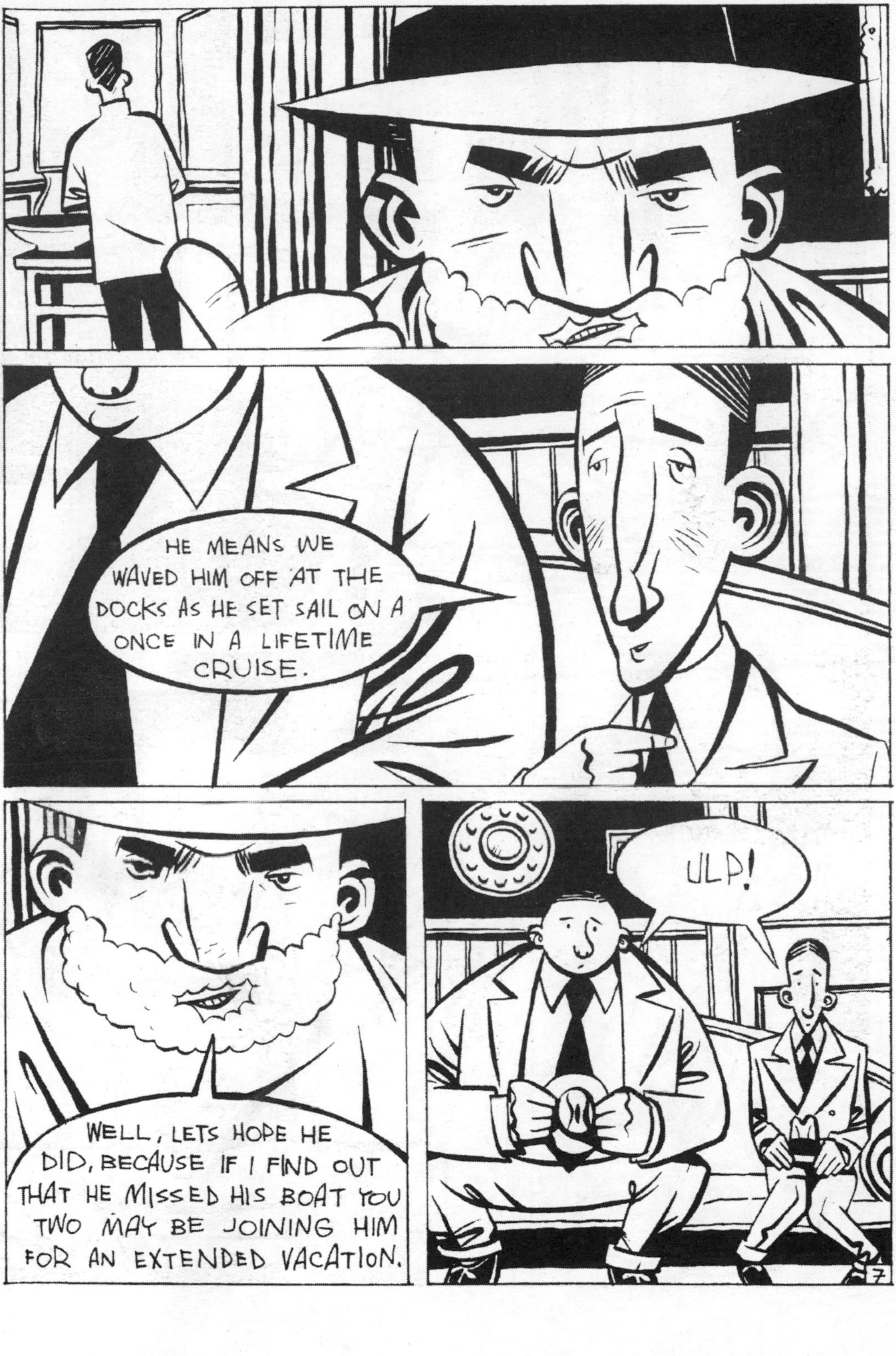
HE MEANS WE WAVED HIM OFF AT THE DOCKS AS HE SET SAIL ON A ONCE IN A LIFETIME CRUISE.
WELL, LETS HOPE HE DID, BECAUSE IF I FIND OUT THAT HE MISSED HIS BOAT YOU TWO MAY BE JOINING HIM FOR AN EXTENDED VACATION.
ULP!
7

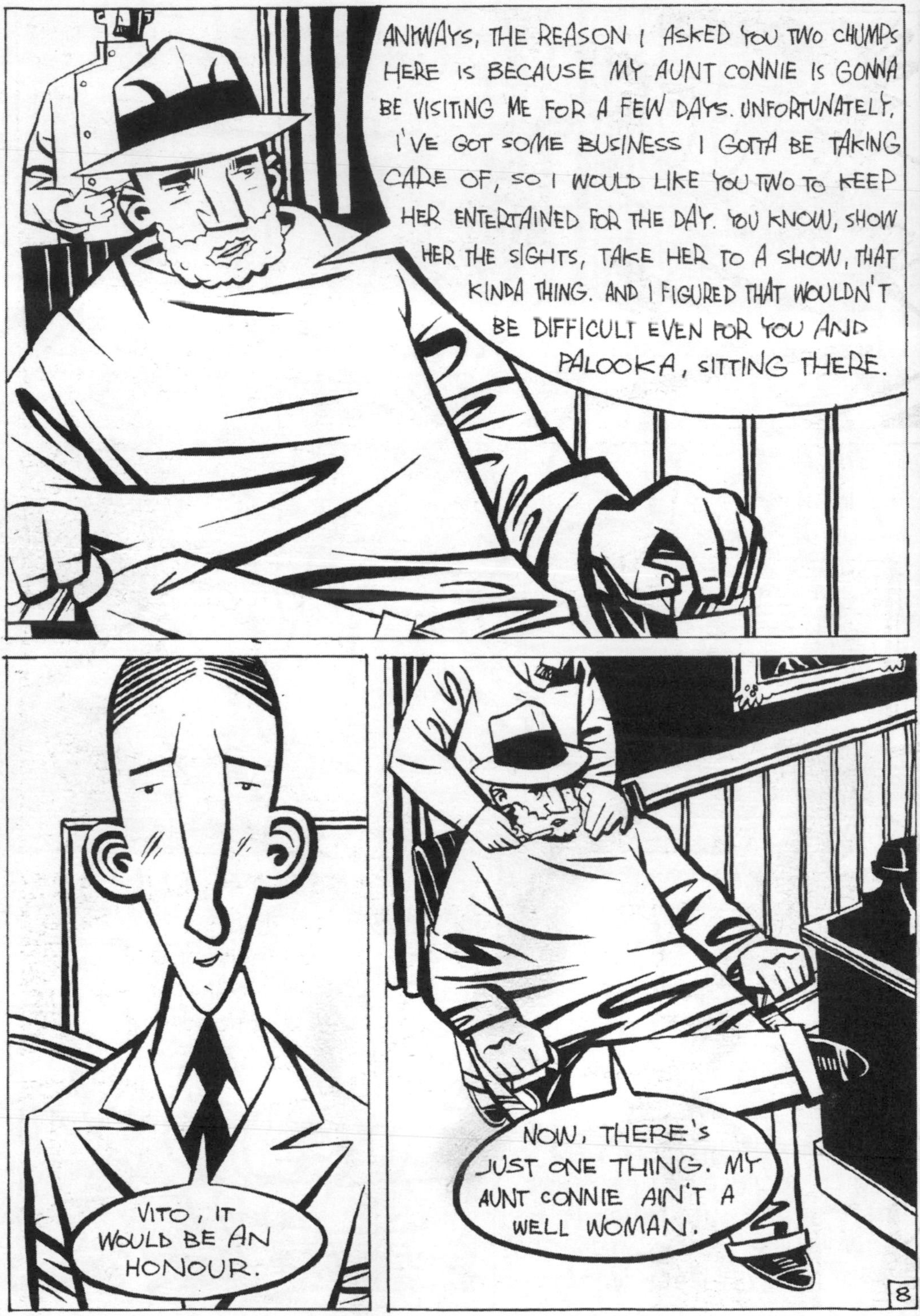
ANYWAYS, THE REASON I ASKED YOU TWO CHUMPS HERE IS BECAUSE MY AUNT CONNIE IS GONNA BE VISITING ME FOR A FEW DAYS. UNFORTUNATELY, I'VE GOT SOME BUSINESS I GOTTA BE TAKING CARE OF, SO I WOULD LIKE YOU TWO TO KEEP HER ENTERTAINED FOR THE DAY. YOU KNOW, SHOW HER THE SIGHTS, TAKE HER TO A SHOW, THAT KINDA THING. AND I FIGURED THAT WOULDN'T BE DIFFICULT EVEN FOR YOU AND PALOOKA, SITTING THERE.
VITO, IT WOULD BE AN HONOUR.
NOW, THERE'S JUST ONE THING. MY AUNT CONNIE AIN'T A WELL WOMAN.
8

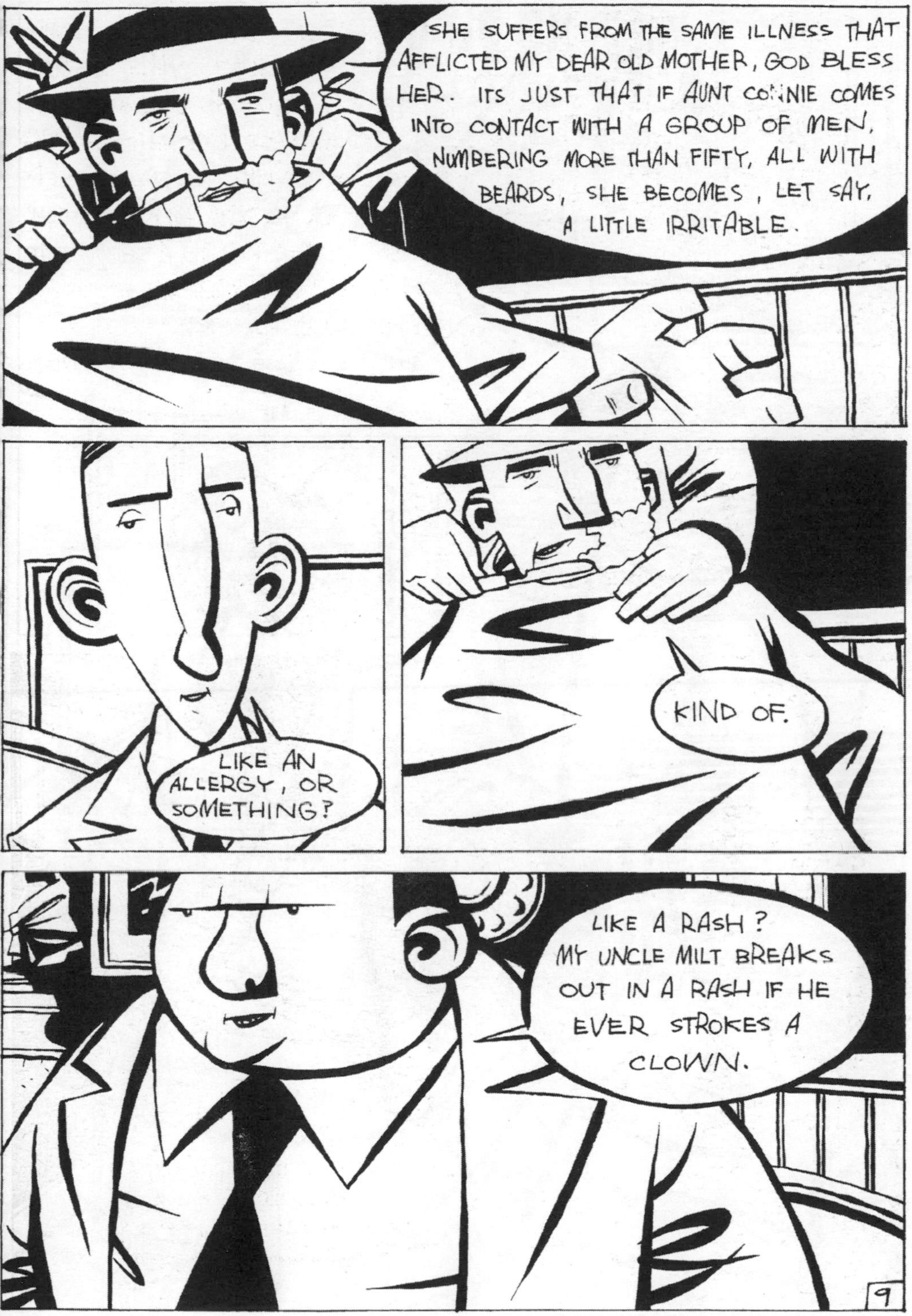
SHE SUFFERS FROM THE SAME ILLNESS THAT AFFLICTED MY DEAR OLD MOTHER, GOD BLESS HER. ITS JUST THAT IF AUNT CONNIE COMES INTO CONTACT WITH A GROUP OF MEN, NUMBERING MORE THAN FIFTY, ALL WITH BEARDS, SHE BECOMES, LET SAY, A LITTLE IRRITABLE.
LIKE AN ALLERGY, OR SOMETHING?
KIND OF.
LIKE A RASH? MY UNCLE MILT BREAKS OUT IN A RASH IF HE EVER STROKES A CLOWN.

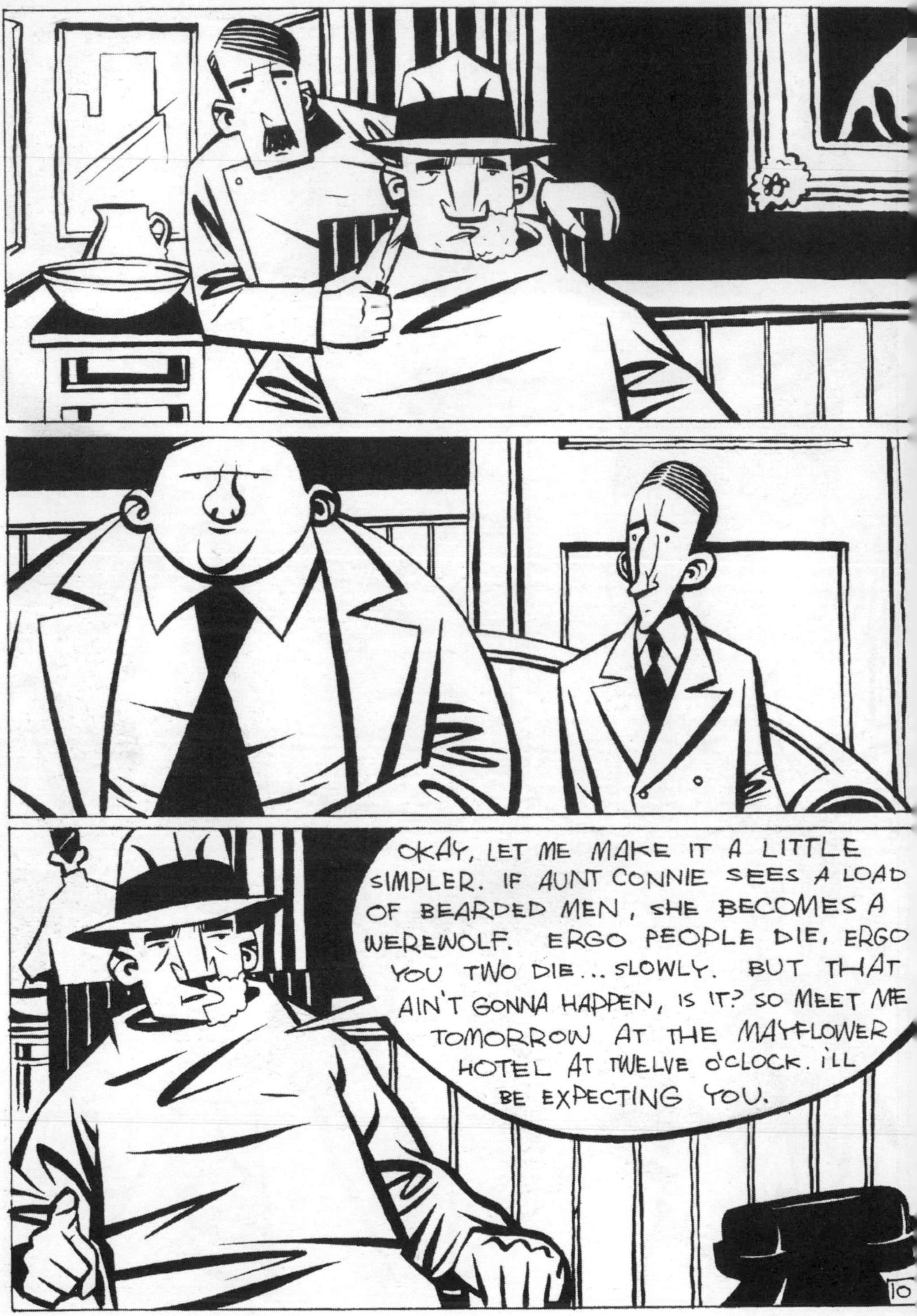
OKAY, LET ME MAKE IT A LITTLE SIMPLER. IF AUNT CONNIE SEES A LOAD OF BEARDED MEN, SHE BECOMES A WEREWOLF. ERGO PEOPLE DIE, ERGO YOU TWO DIE... SLOWLY. BUT THAT AIN'T GONNA HAPPEN, IS IT? SO MEET ME TOMORROW AT THE MAYFLOWER HOTEL AT TWELVE O'CLOCK. I'LL BE EXPECTING YOU.
10

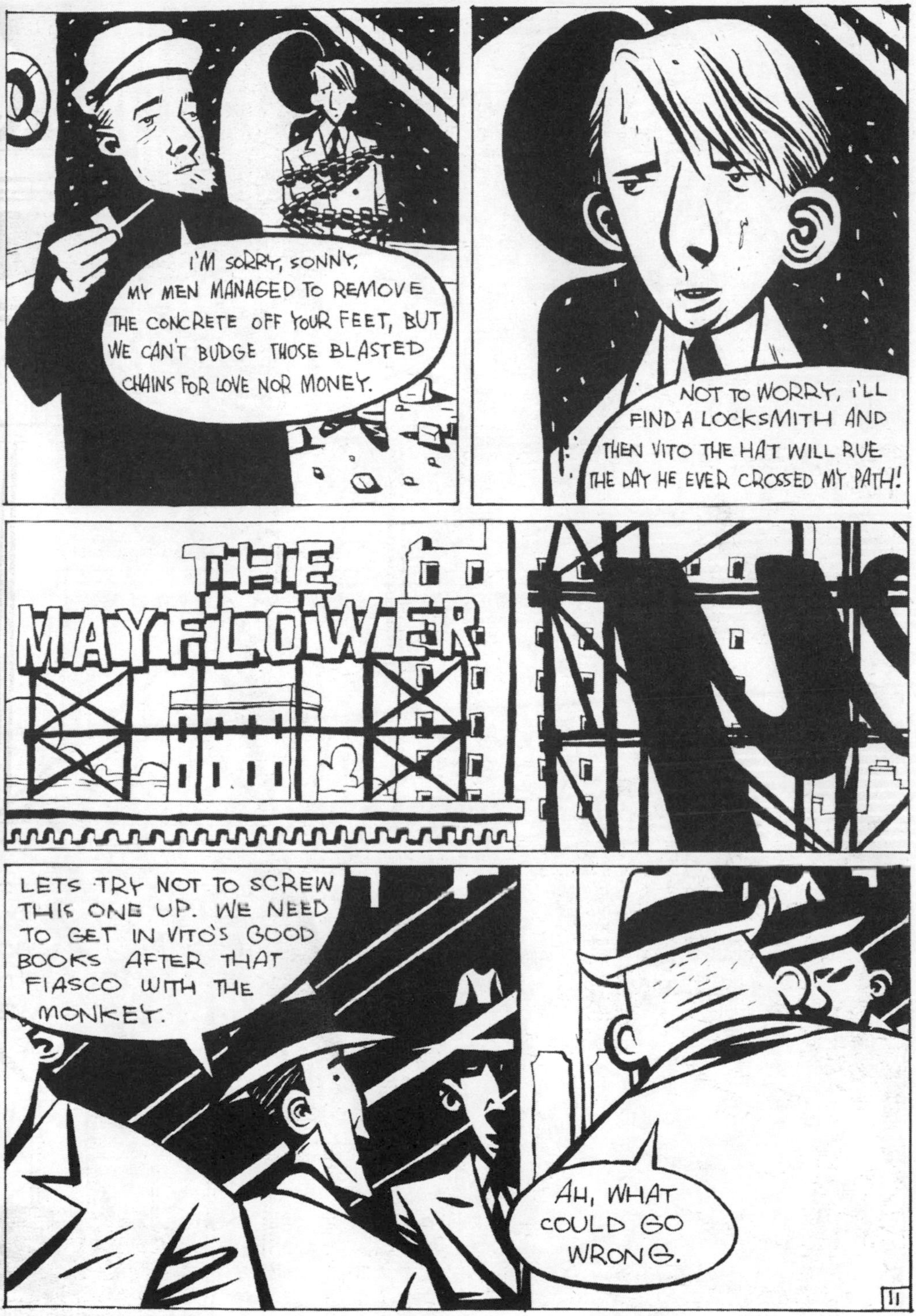

I'M SORRY, SONNY, MY MEN MANAGED TO REMOVE THE CONCRETE OFF YOUR FEET, BUT WE CAN'T BUDGE THOSE BLASTED CHAINS FOR LOVE NOR MONEY.
NOT TO WORRY, I'LL FIND A LOCKSMITH AND THEN VITO THE HAT WILL RUE THE DAY HE EVER CROSSED MY PATH!
THE MAYFLOWER
LETS TRY NOT TO SCREW THIS ONE UP. WE NEED TO GET IN VITO'S GOOD BOOKS AFTER THAT FIASCO WITH THE MONKEY.
AH, WHAT COULD GO WRONG.

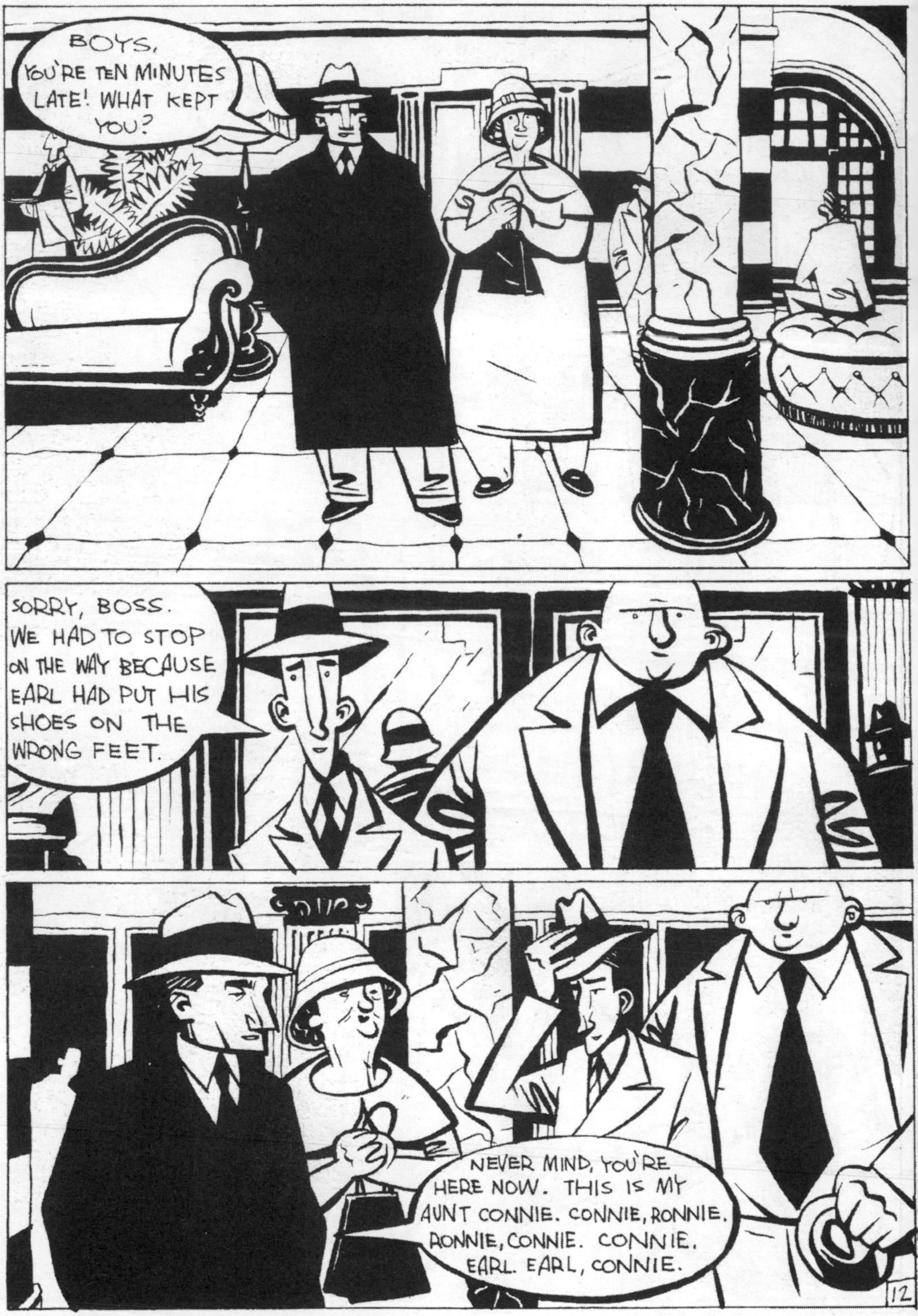
BOYS, YOU'RE TEN MINUTES LATE! WHAT KEPT YOU?
SORRY, BOSS. WE HAD TO STOP ON THE WAY BECAUSE EARL HAD PUT HIS SHOES ON THE WRONG FEET.
NEVER MIND, YOU'RE HERE NOW. THIS IS MY AUNT CONNIE. CONNIE, RONNIE. RONNIE, CONNIE. CONNIE, EARL. EARL, CONNIE.
12

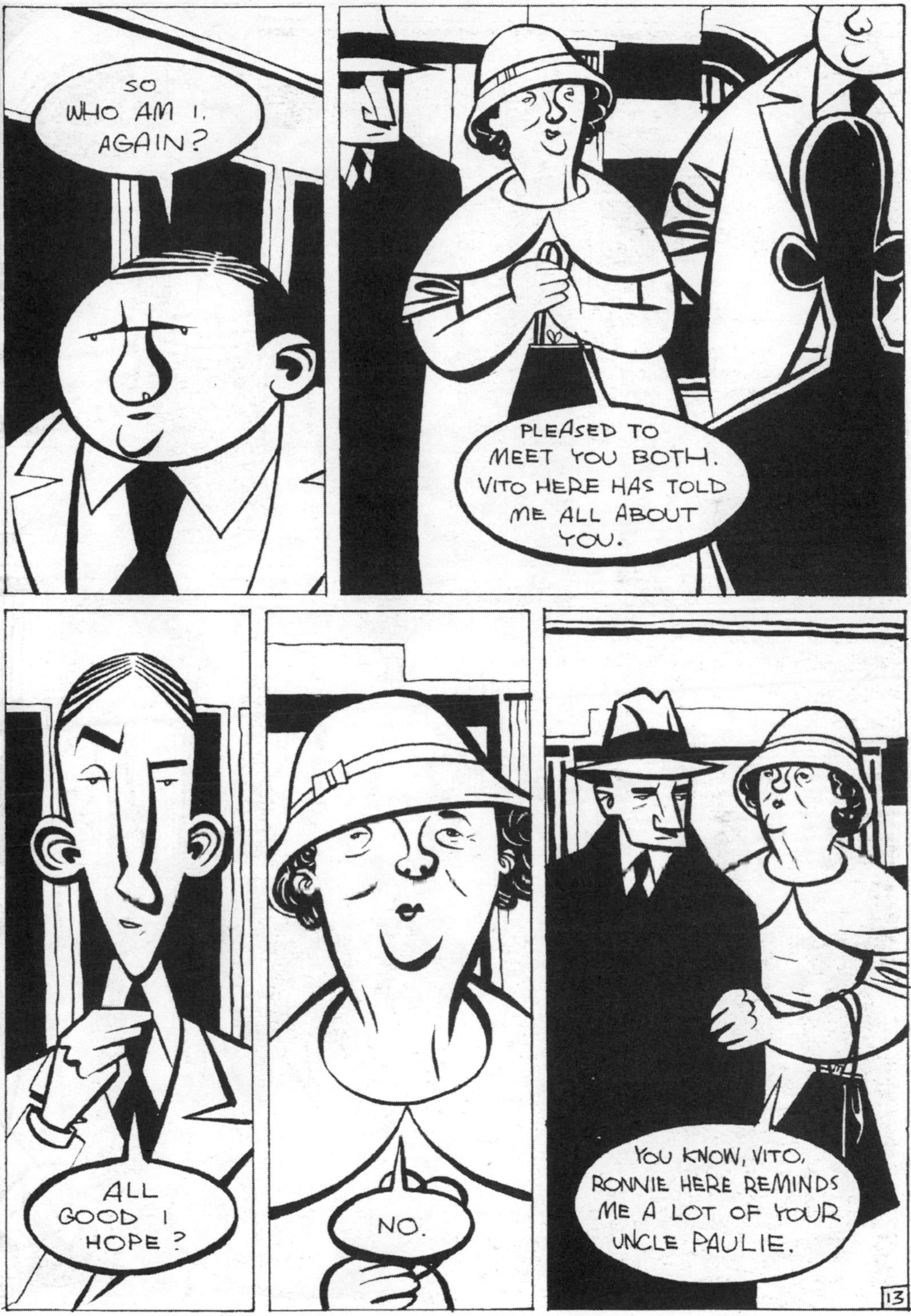
SO WHO AM I, AGAIN?
PLEASED TO MEET YOU BOTH. VITO HERE HAS TOLD ME ALL ABOUT YOU.
ALL GOOD I HOPE?
NO.
YOU KNOW, VITO, RONNIE HERE REMINDS ME A LOT OF YOUR UNCLE PAULIE.
13

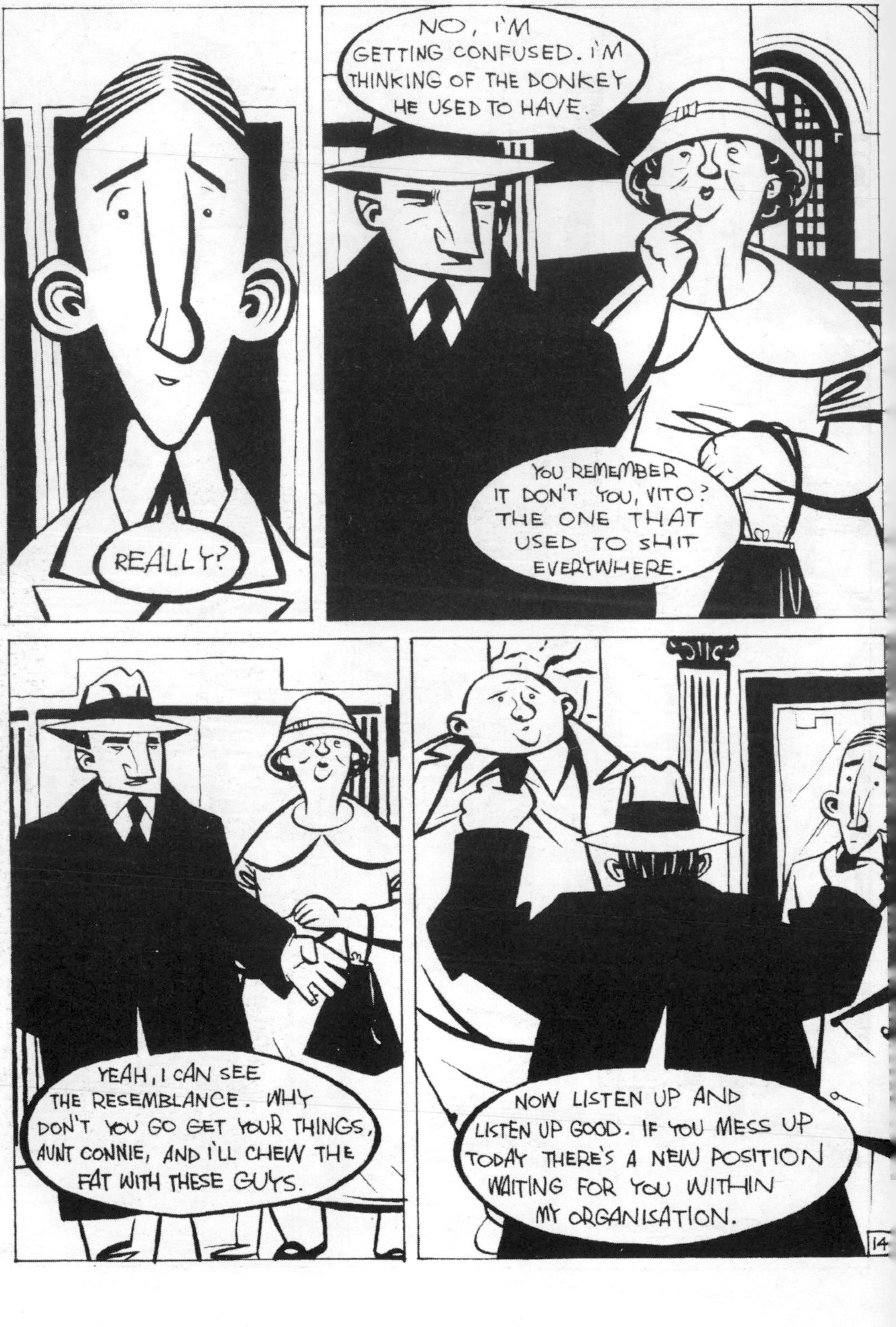
REALLY?
NO, I'M GETTING CONFUSED. I'M THINKING OF THE DONKEY HE USED TO HAVE.
YOU REMEMBER IT DON'T YOU, VITO? THE ONE THAT USED TO SHIT EVERYWHERE.
YEAH, I CAN SEE THE RESEMBLANCE. WHY DON'T YOU GO GET YOUR THINGS, AUNT CONNIE, AND I'LL CHEW THE FAT WITH THESE GUYS.
NOW LISTEN UP AND LISTEN UP GOOD. IF YOU MESS UP TODAY THERE'S A NEW POSITION WAITING FOR YOU WITHIN MY ORGANISATION.
14

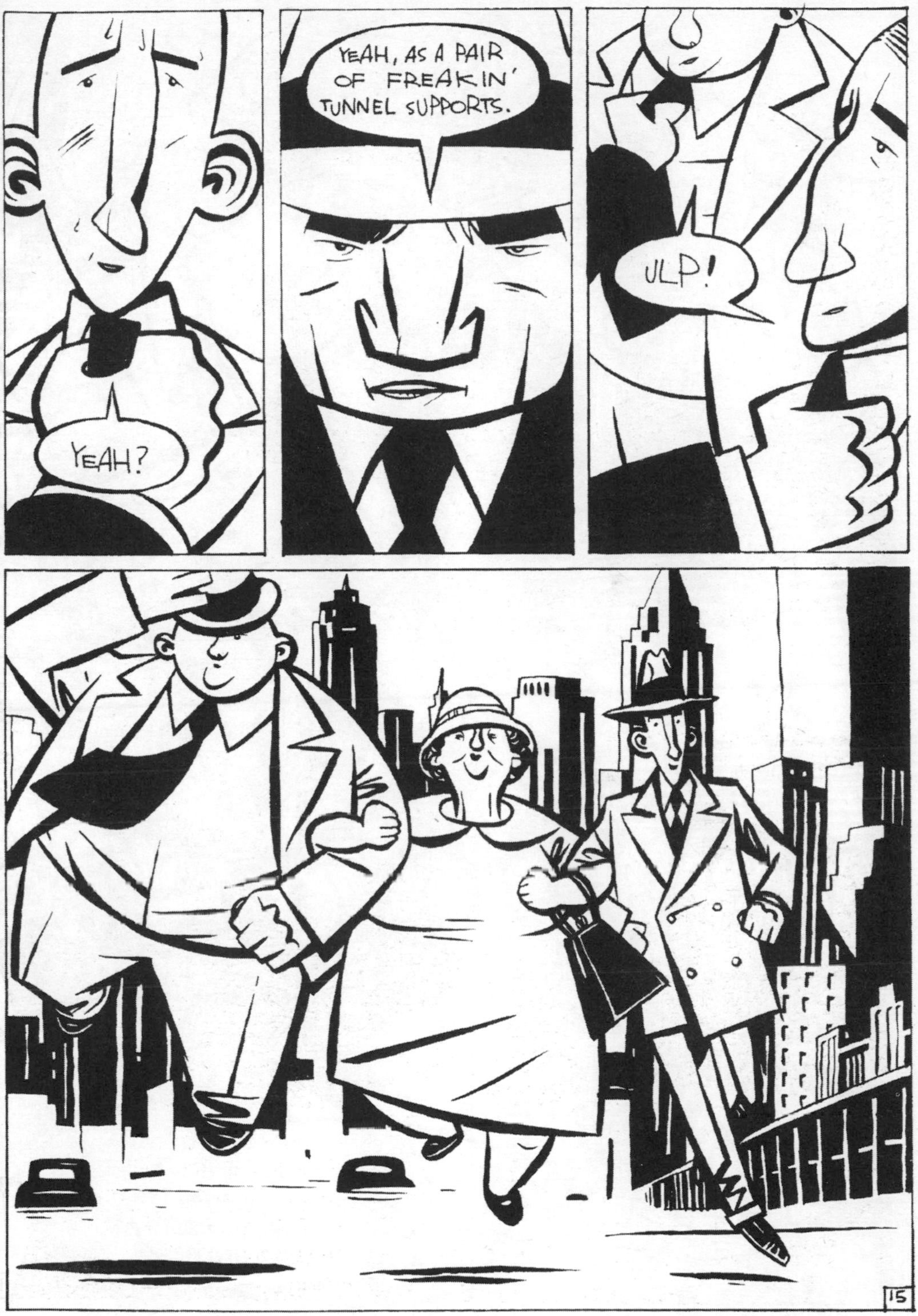
YEAH?
YEAH, AS A PAIR OF FREAKIN' TUNNEL SUPPORTS.
ULP!
15

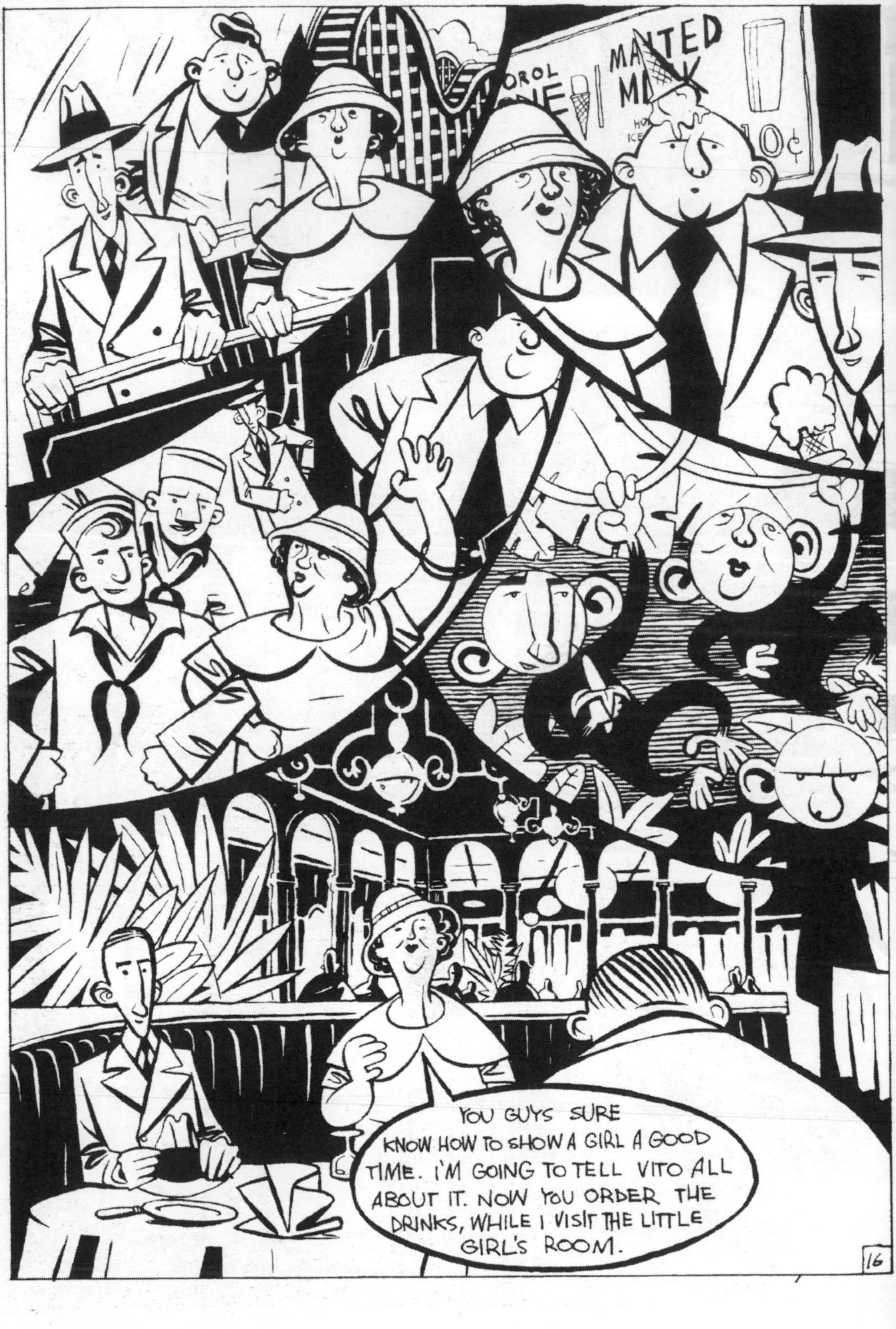
MALTED
10¢
YOU GUYS SURE KNOW HOW TO SHOW A GIRL A GOOD TIME. I'M GOING TO TELL VITO ALL ABOUT IT. NOW YOU ORDER THE DRINKS, WHILE I VISIT THE LITTLE GIRL'S ROOM.

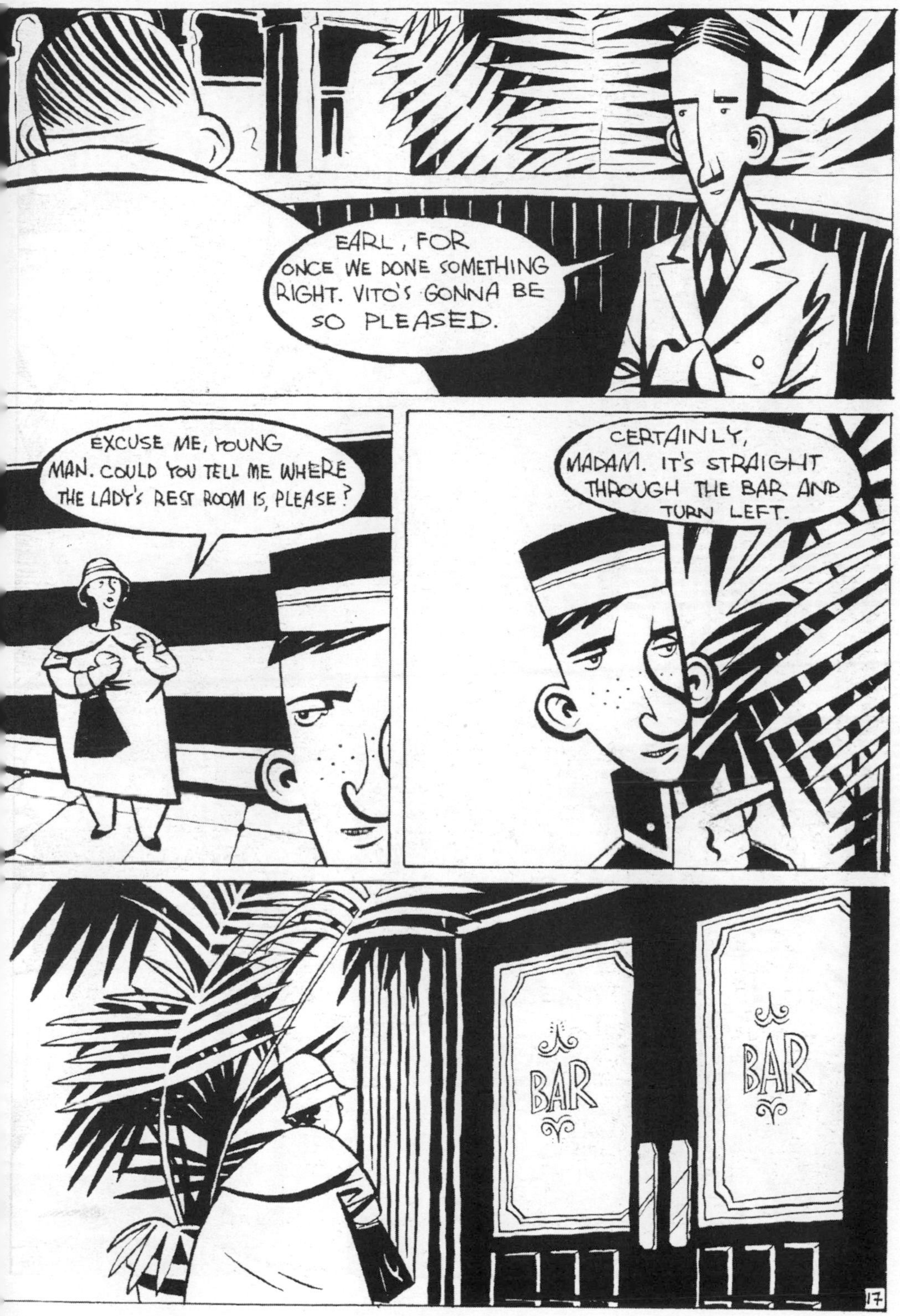
EARL, FOR ONCE WE DONE SOMETHING RIGHT. VITO'S GONNA BE SO PLEASED.
EXCUSE ME, YOUNG MAN. COULD YOU TELL ME WHERE THE LADY'S REST ROOM IS, PLEASE?
CERTAINLY, MADAM. IT'S STRAIGHT THROUGH THE BAR AND TURN LEFT.
BAR
BAR

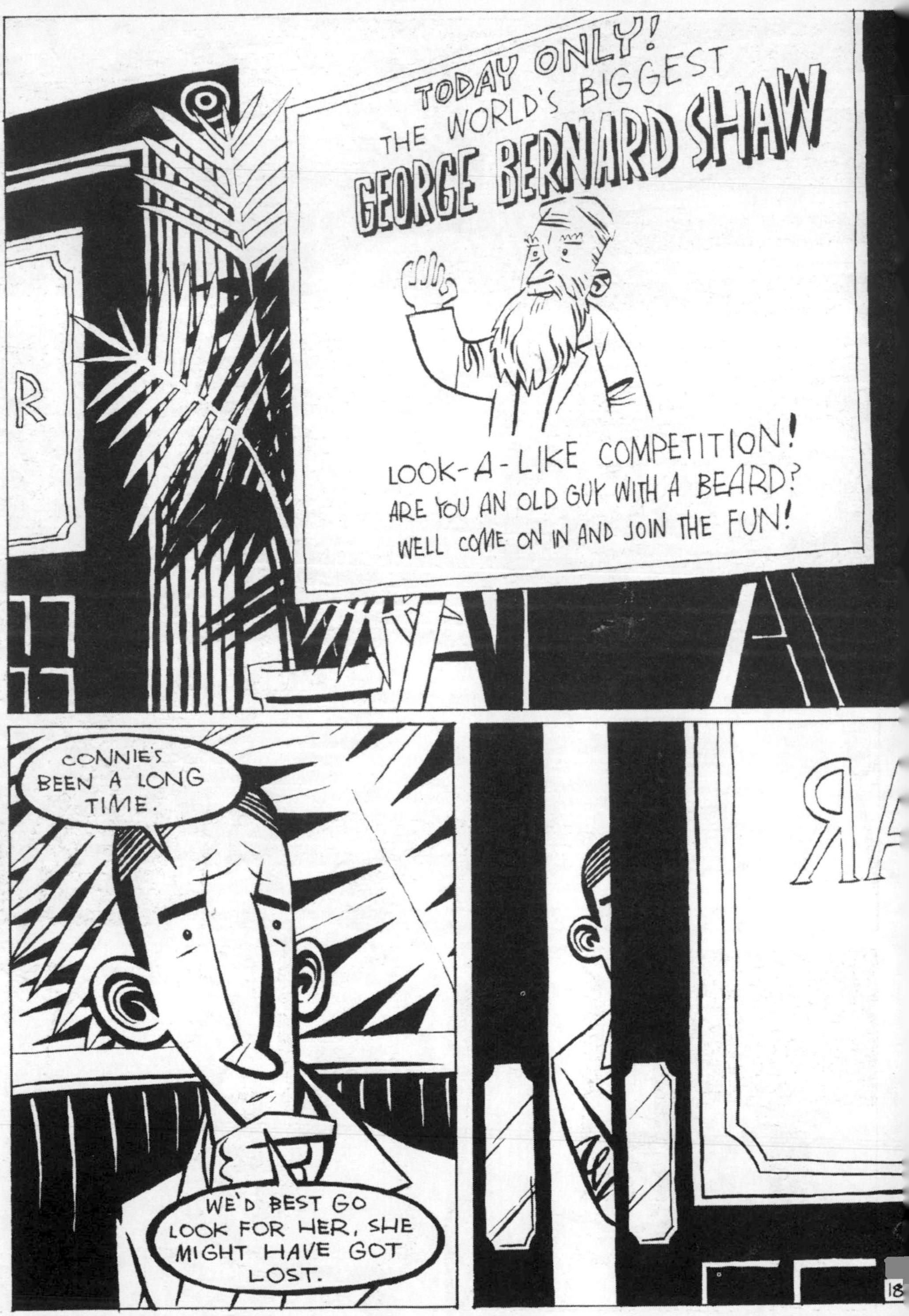
TODAY ONLY!
THE WORLD'S BIGGEST
GEORGE BERNARD SHAW
LOOK-A-LIKE COMPETITION!
ARE YOU AN OLD GUY WITH A BEARD?
WELL COME ON IN AND JOIN THE FUN!
CONNIE'S BEEN A LONG TIME.
WE'D BEST GO LOOK FOR HER, SHE MIGHT HAVE GOT LOST.

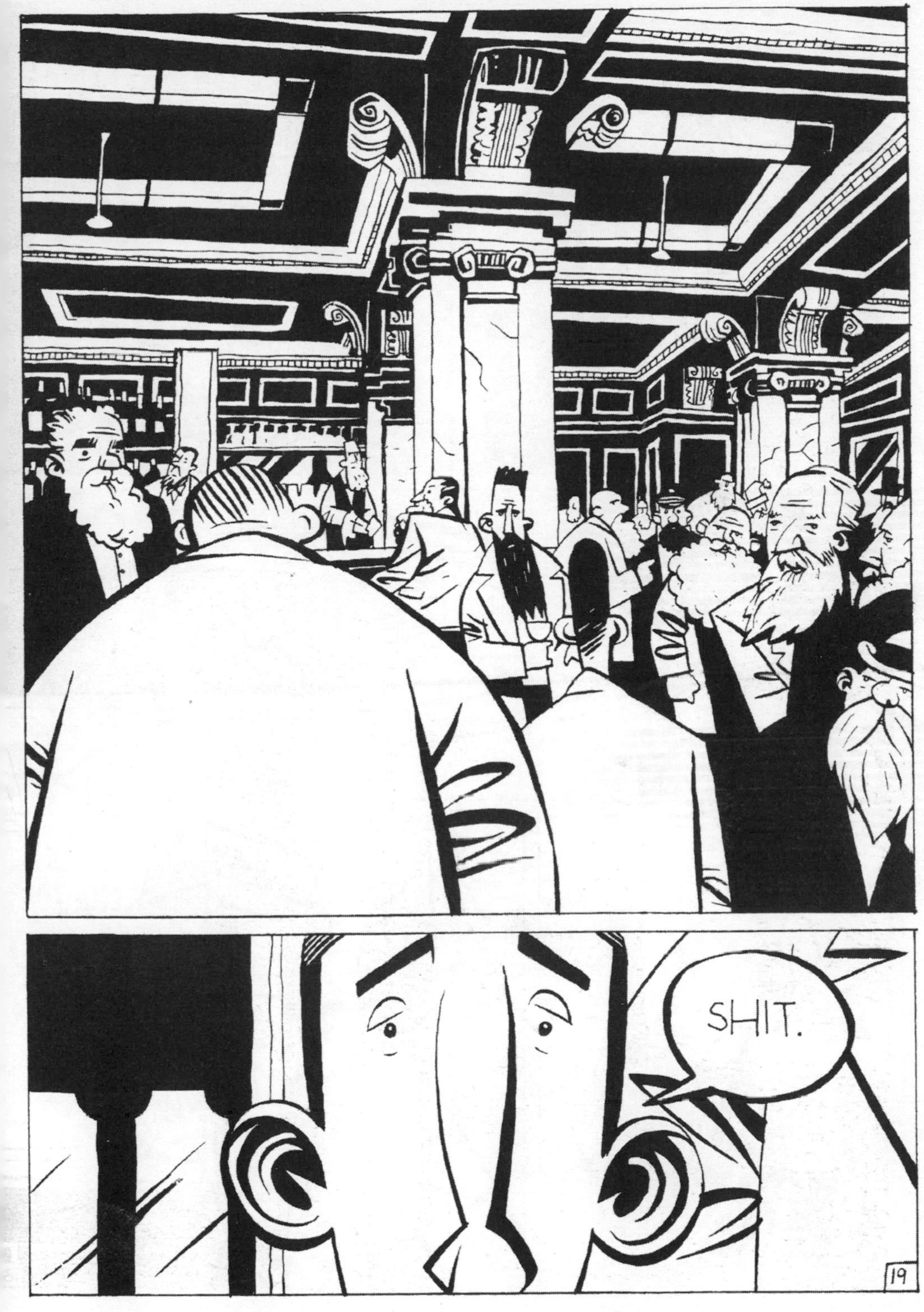
SHIT.

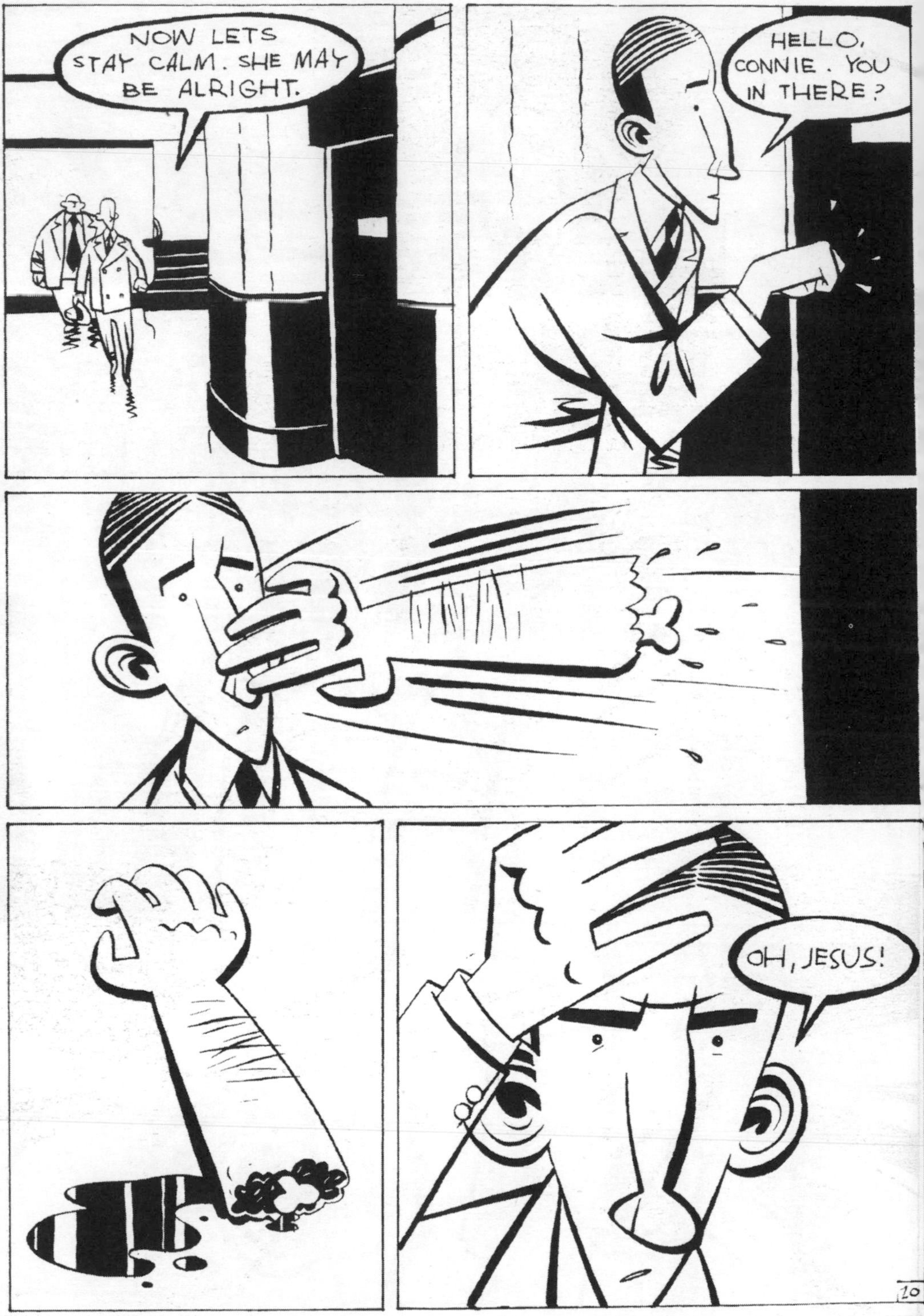
NOW LETS STAY CALM. SHE MAY BE ALRIGHT.
HELLO, CONNIE. YOU IN THERE?
OH, JESUS!
20

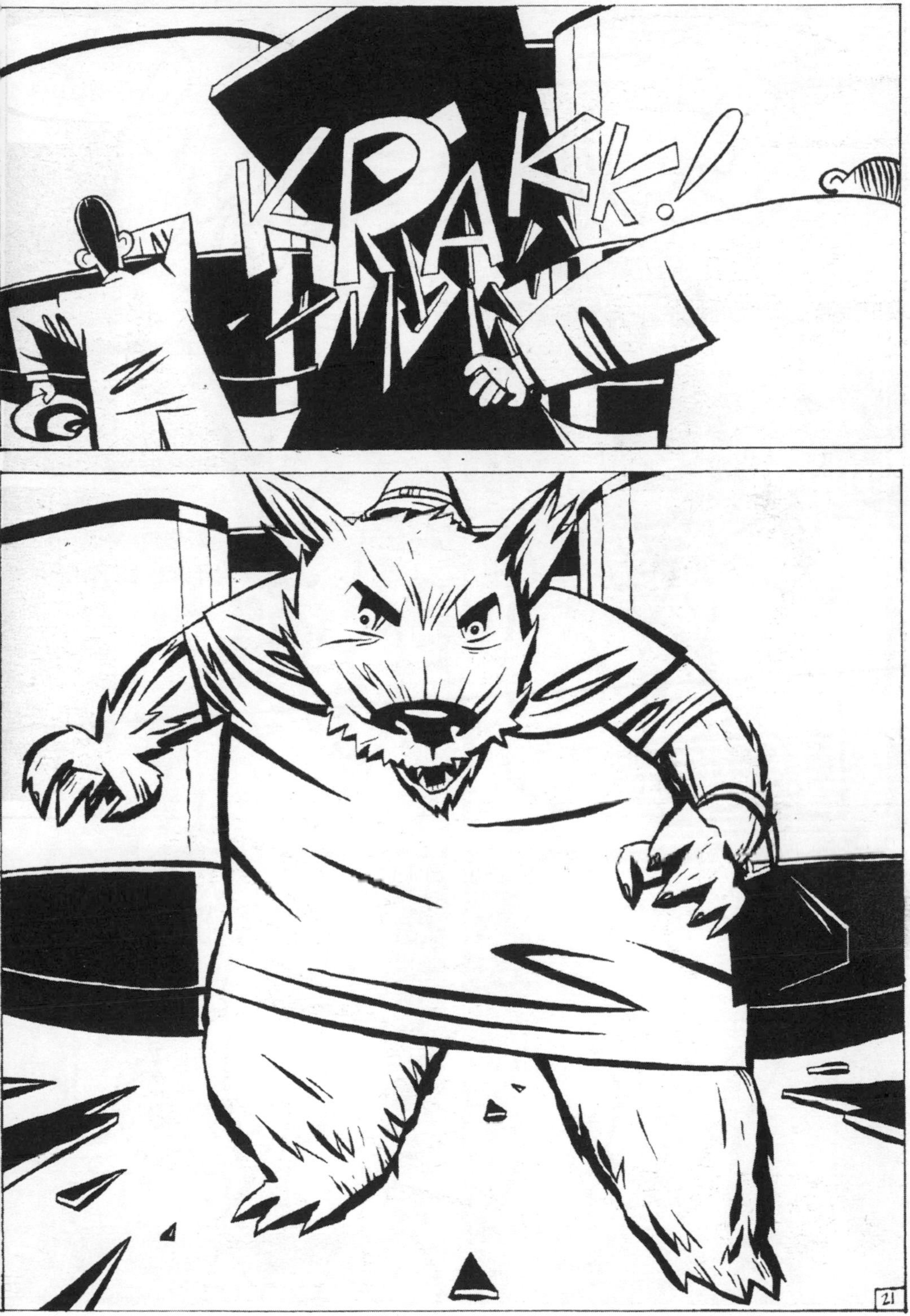
KRAKK!

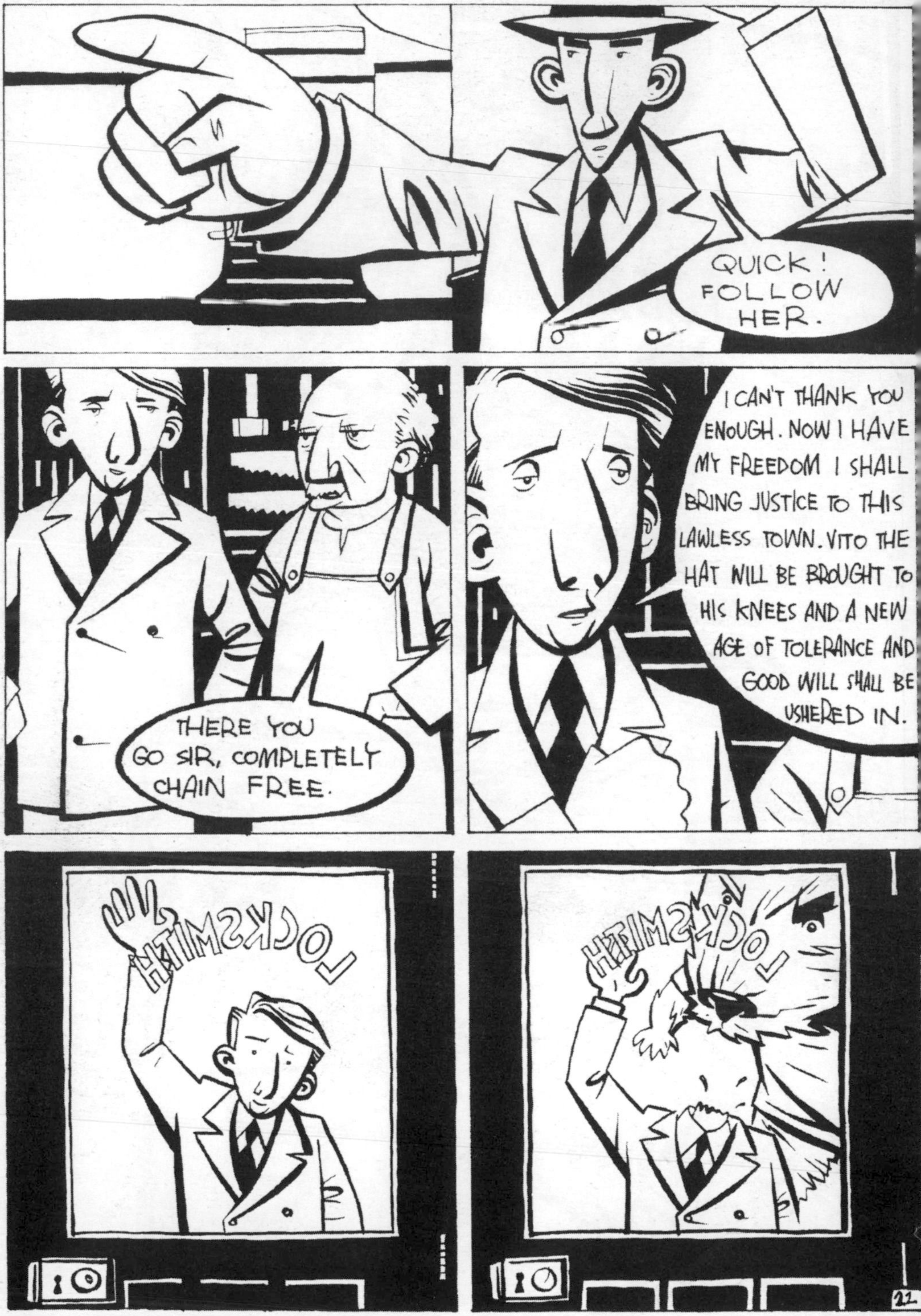
QUICK! FOLLOW HER.
THERE YOU GO SIR, COMPLETELY CHAIN FREE.
I CAN'T THANK YOU ENOUGH. NOW I HAVE MY FREEDOM I SHALL BRING JUSTICE TO THIS LAWLESS TOWN. VITO THE HAT WILL BE BROUGHT TO HIS KNEES AND A NEW AGE OF TOLERANCE AND GOOD WILL SHALL BE USHERED IN.
LOCKSMITH
LOCKSMITH

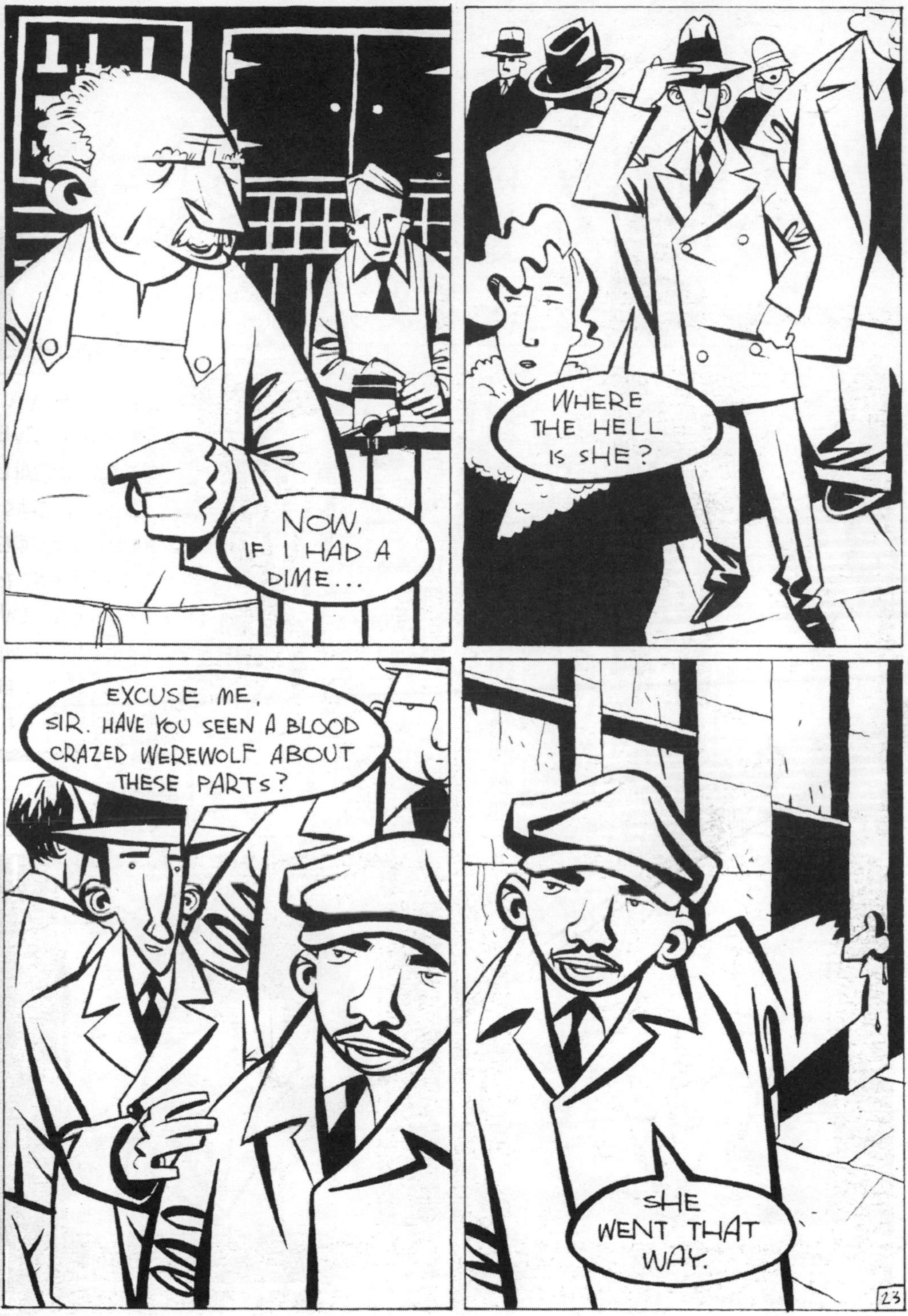
NOW, IF I HAD A DIME...
WHERE THE HELL IS SHE?
EXCUSE ME, SIR. HAVE YOU SEEN A BLOOD CRAZED WEREWOLF ABOUT THESE PARTS?
SHE WENT THAT WAY.
23

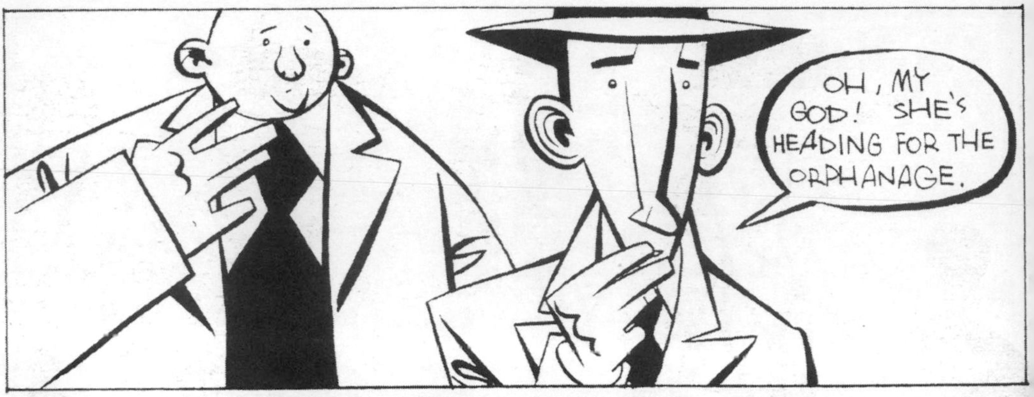
OH, MY GOD! SHE'S HEADING FOR THE ORPHANAGE.

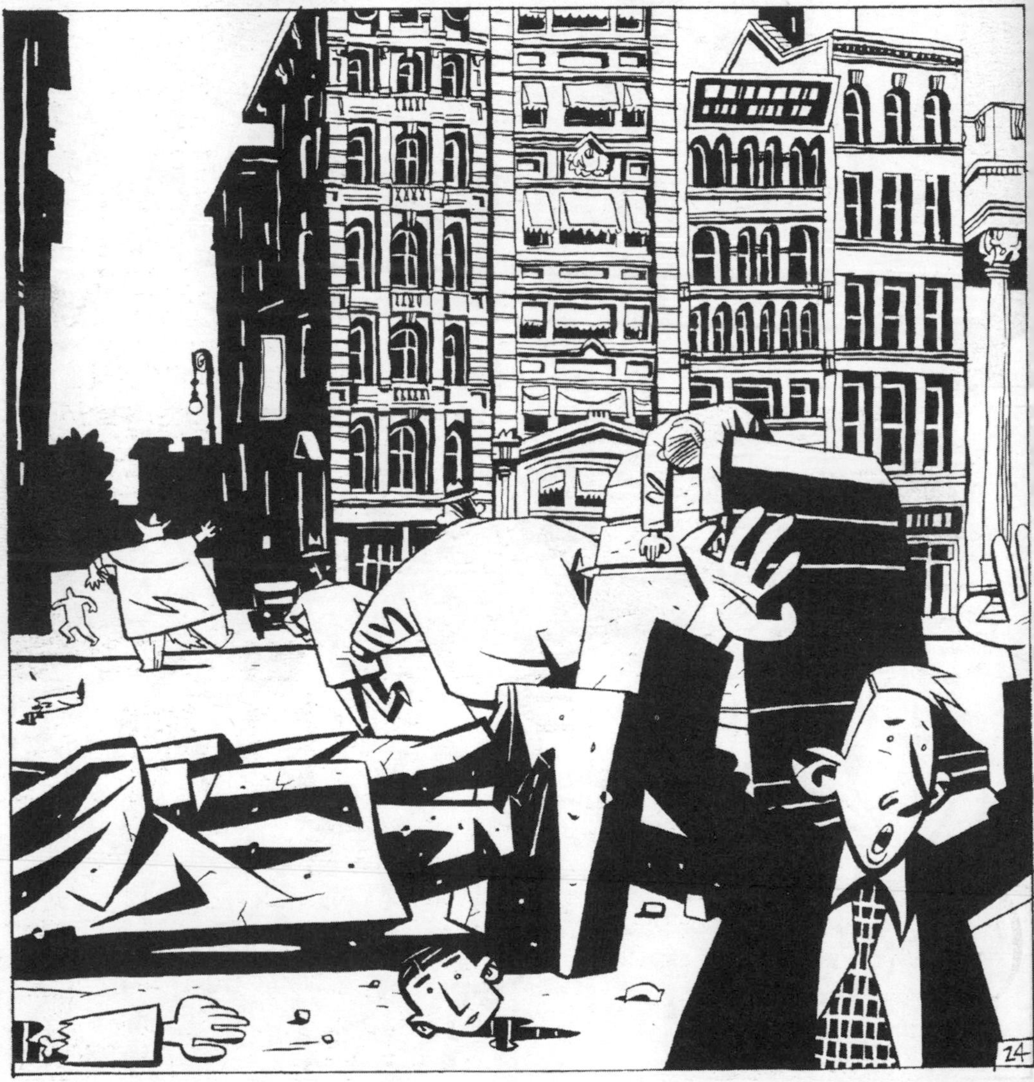

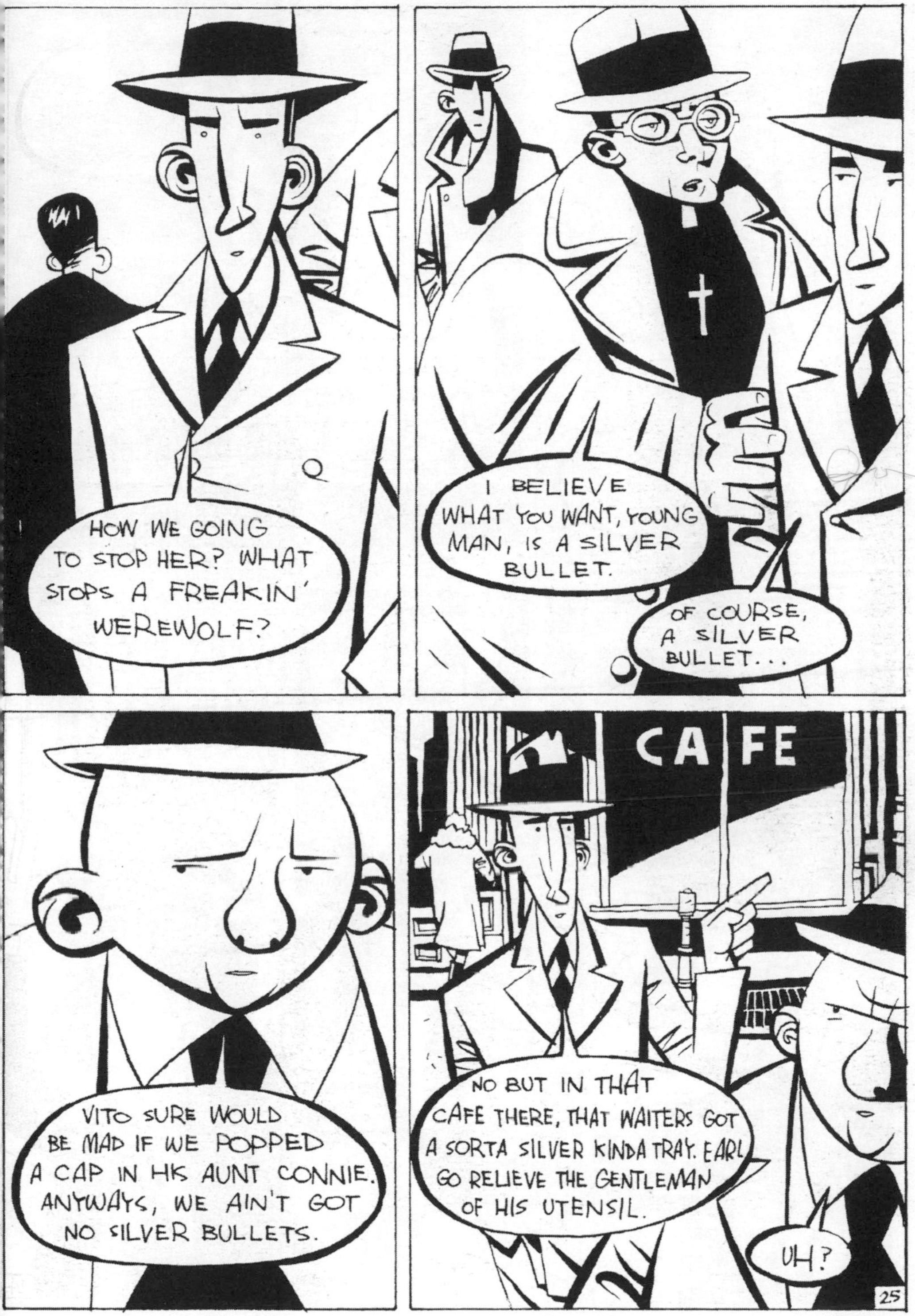
HOW WE GOING TO STOP HER? WHAT STOPS A FREAKIN' WEREWOLF?
I BELIEVE WHAT YOU WANT, YOUNG MAN, IS A SILVER BULLET.
OF COURSE, A SILVER BULLET...
VITO SURE WOULD BE MAD IF WE POPPED A CAP IN HIS AUNT CONNIE. ANYWAYS, WE AIN'T GOT NO SILVER BULLETS.
CAFE
NO BUT IN THAT CAFE THERE, THAT WAITERS GOT A SORTA SILVER KINDA TRAY. EARL GO RELIEVE THE GENTLEMAN OF HIS UTENSIL.
UH?

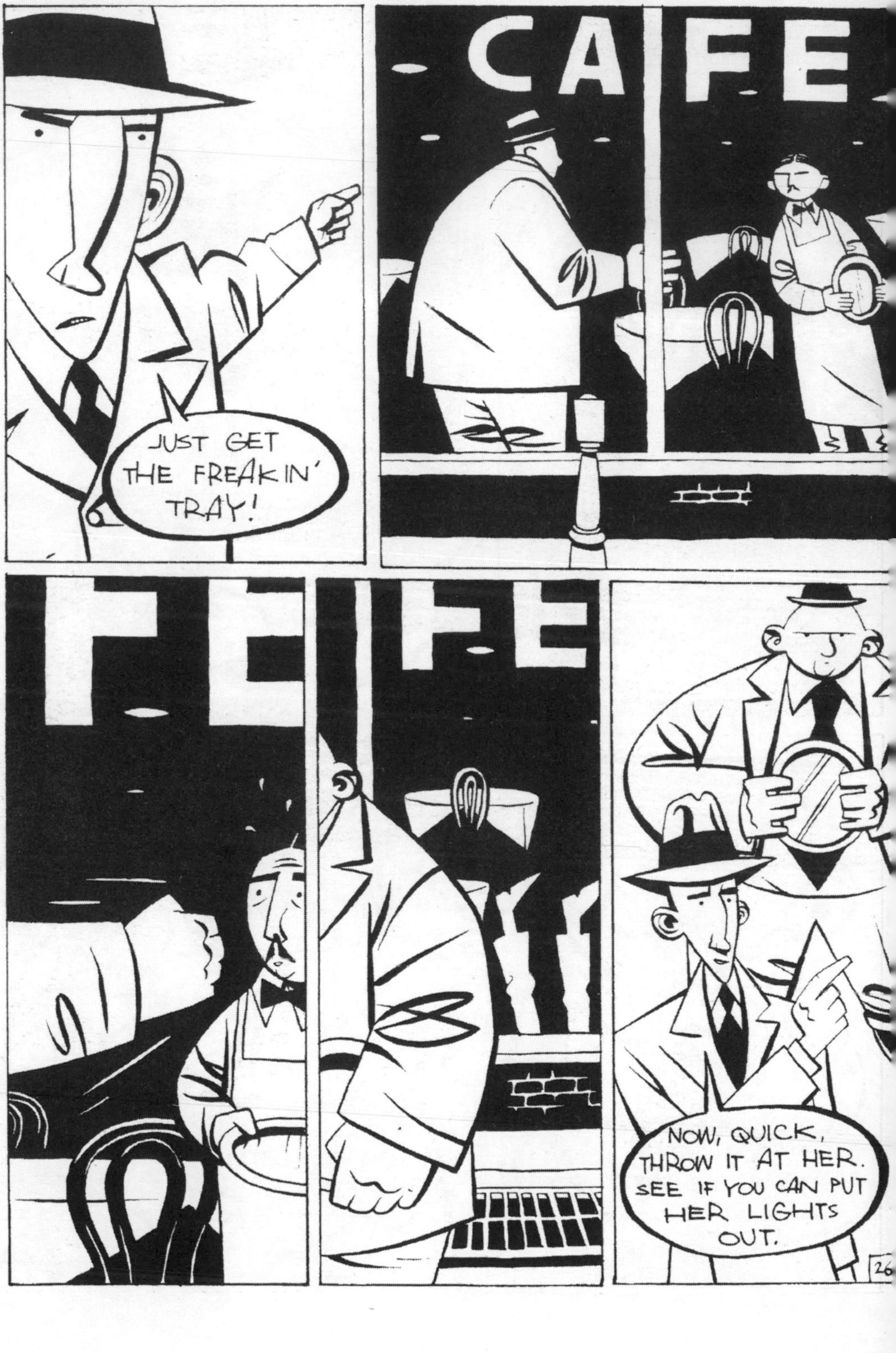
JUST GET THE FREAKIN' TRAY!
CAFE
FE
FE
NOW, QUICK, THROW IT AT HER. SEE IF YOU CAN PUT HER LIGHTS OUT.
26

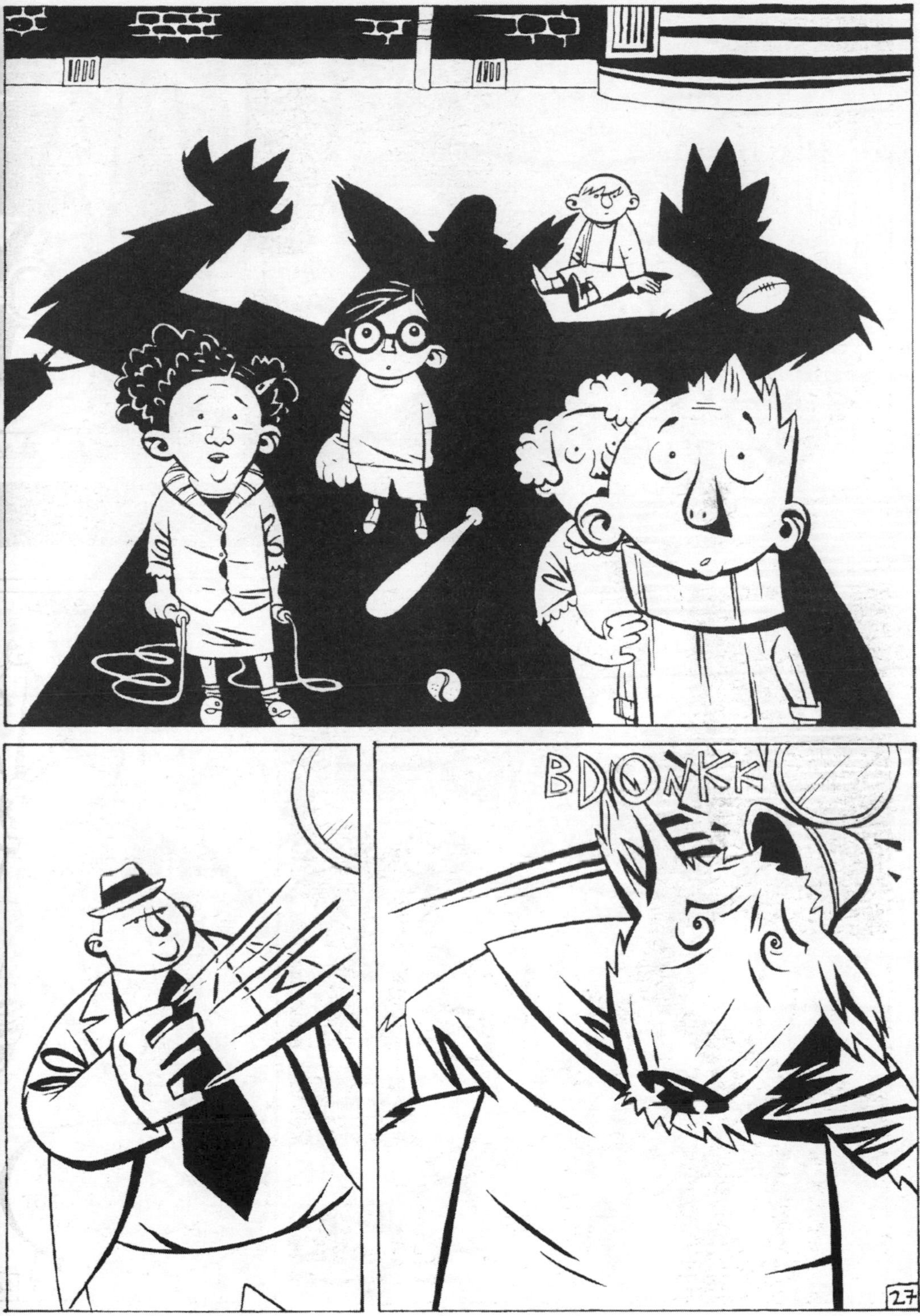
BDONKK

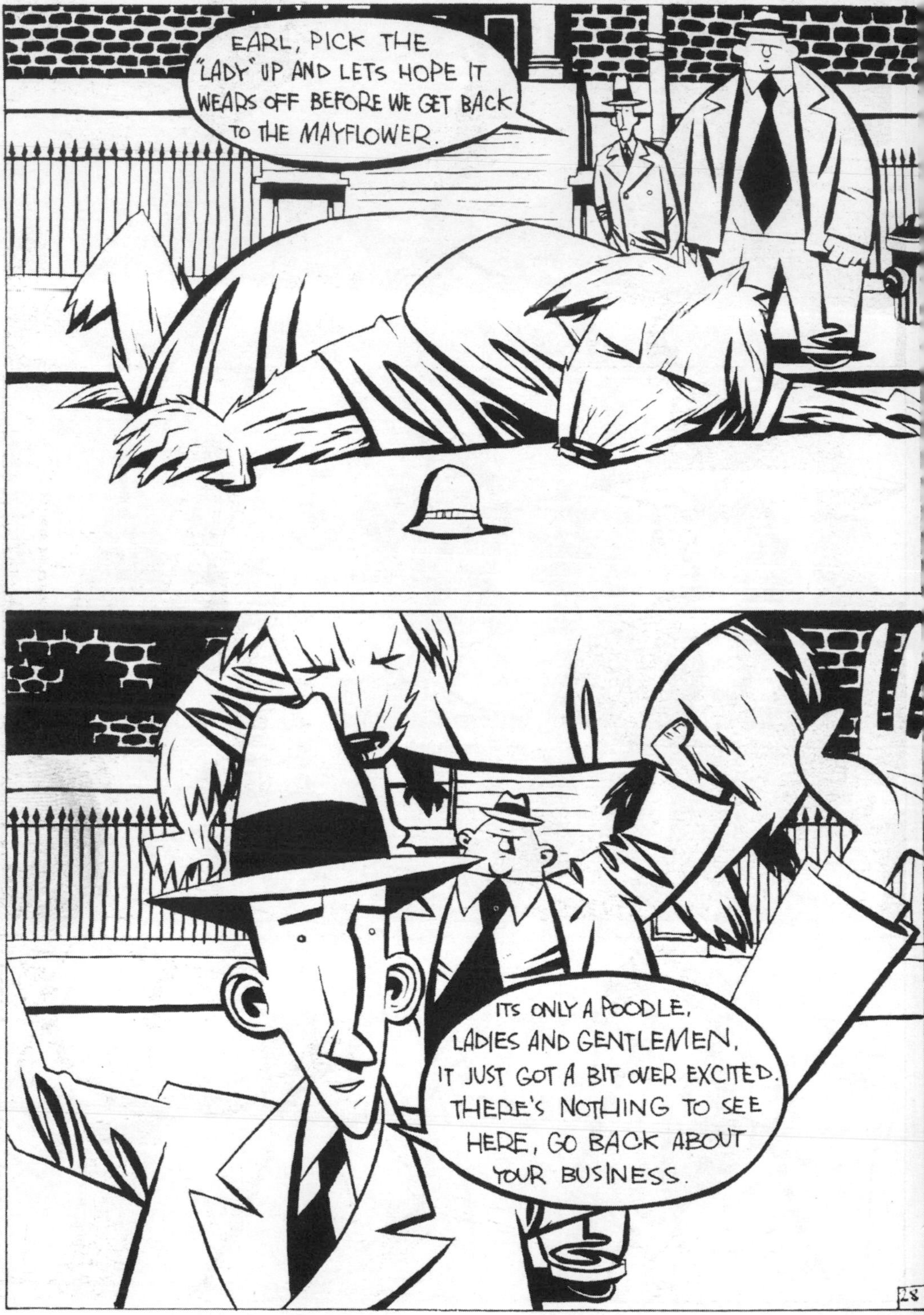
EARL, PICK THE "LADY" UP AND LETS HOPE IT WEARS OFF BEFORE WE GET BACK TO THE MAYFLOWER.
ITS ONLY A POODLE, LADIES AND GENTLEMEN. IT JUST GOT A BIT OVER EXCITED. THERE'S NOTHING TO SEE HERE, GO BACK ABOUT YOUR BUSINESS.

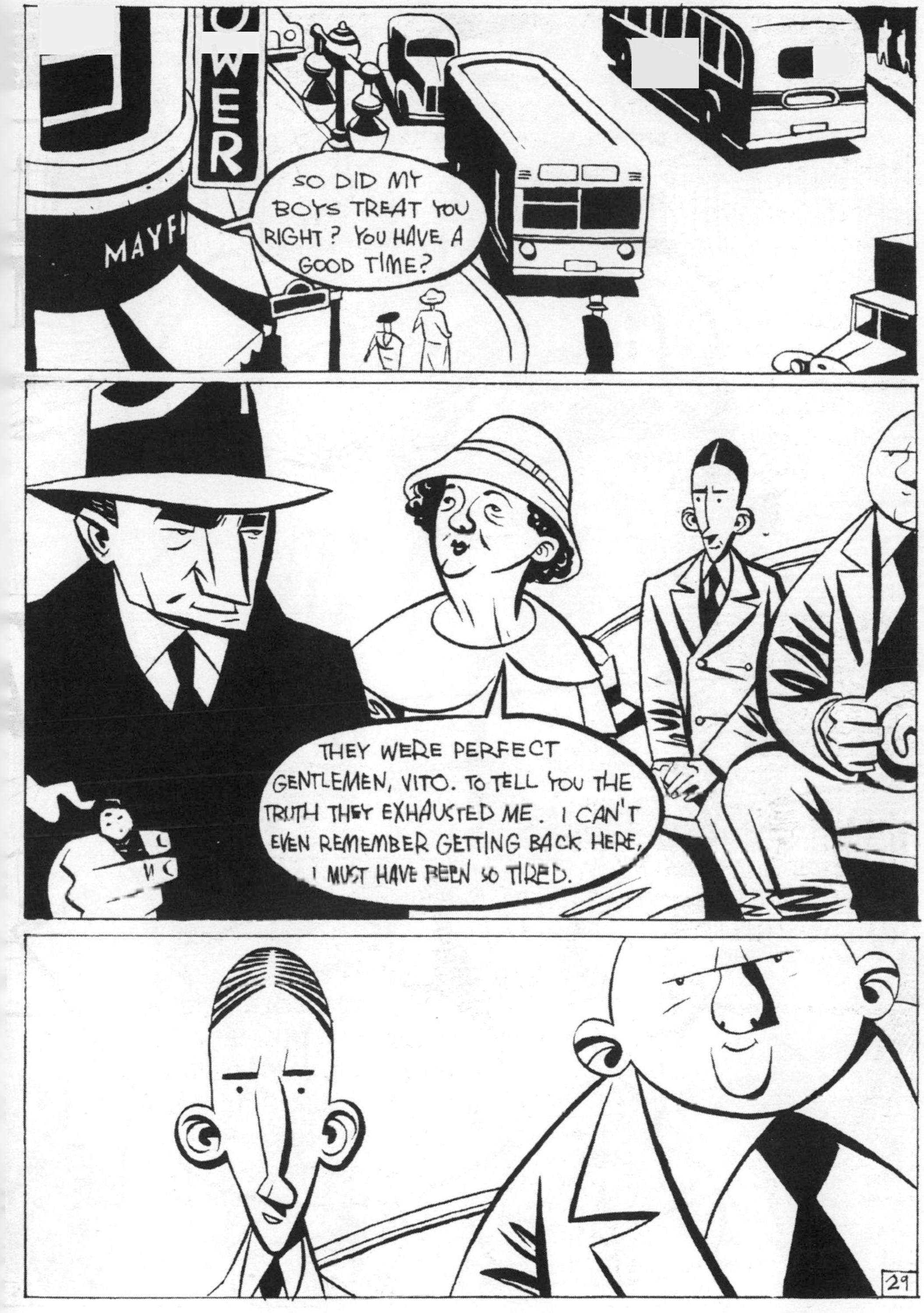
SO DID MY BOYS TREAT YOU RIGHT? YOU HAVE A GOOD TIME?
THEY WERE PERFECT GENTLEMEN, VITO. TO TELL YOU THE TRUTH THEY EXHAUSTED ME. I CAN'T EVEN REMEMBER GETTING BACK HERE, I MUST HAVE BEEN SO TIRED.

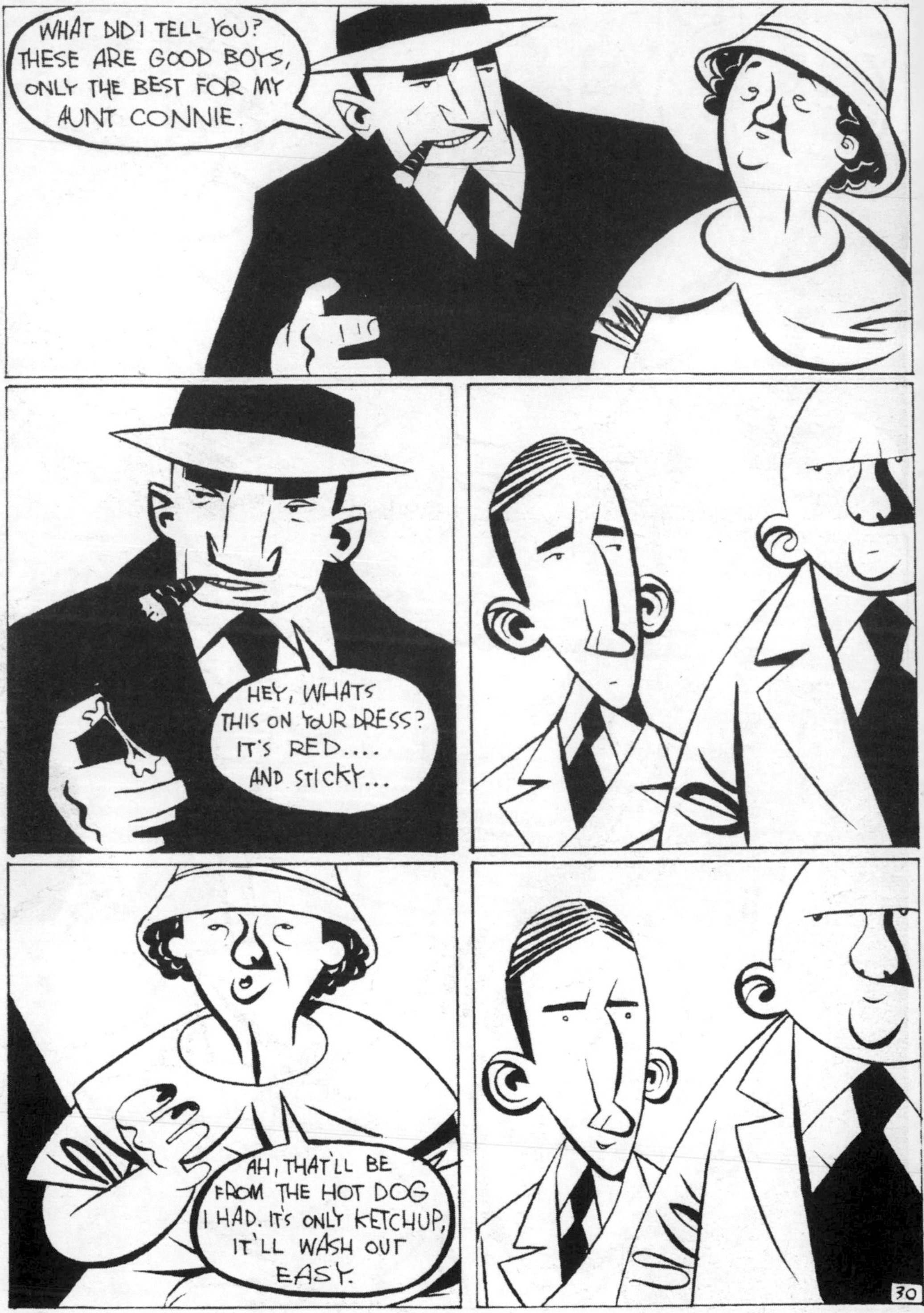
WHAT DID I TELL YOU? THESE ARE GOOD BOYS, ONLY THE BEST FOR MY AUNT CONNIE.
HEY, WHATS THIS ON YOUR DRESS? IT'S RED.... AND STICKY...
AH, THAT'LL BE FROM THE HOT DOG I HAD. IT'S ONLY KETCHUP, IT'LL WASH OUT EASY.

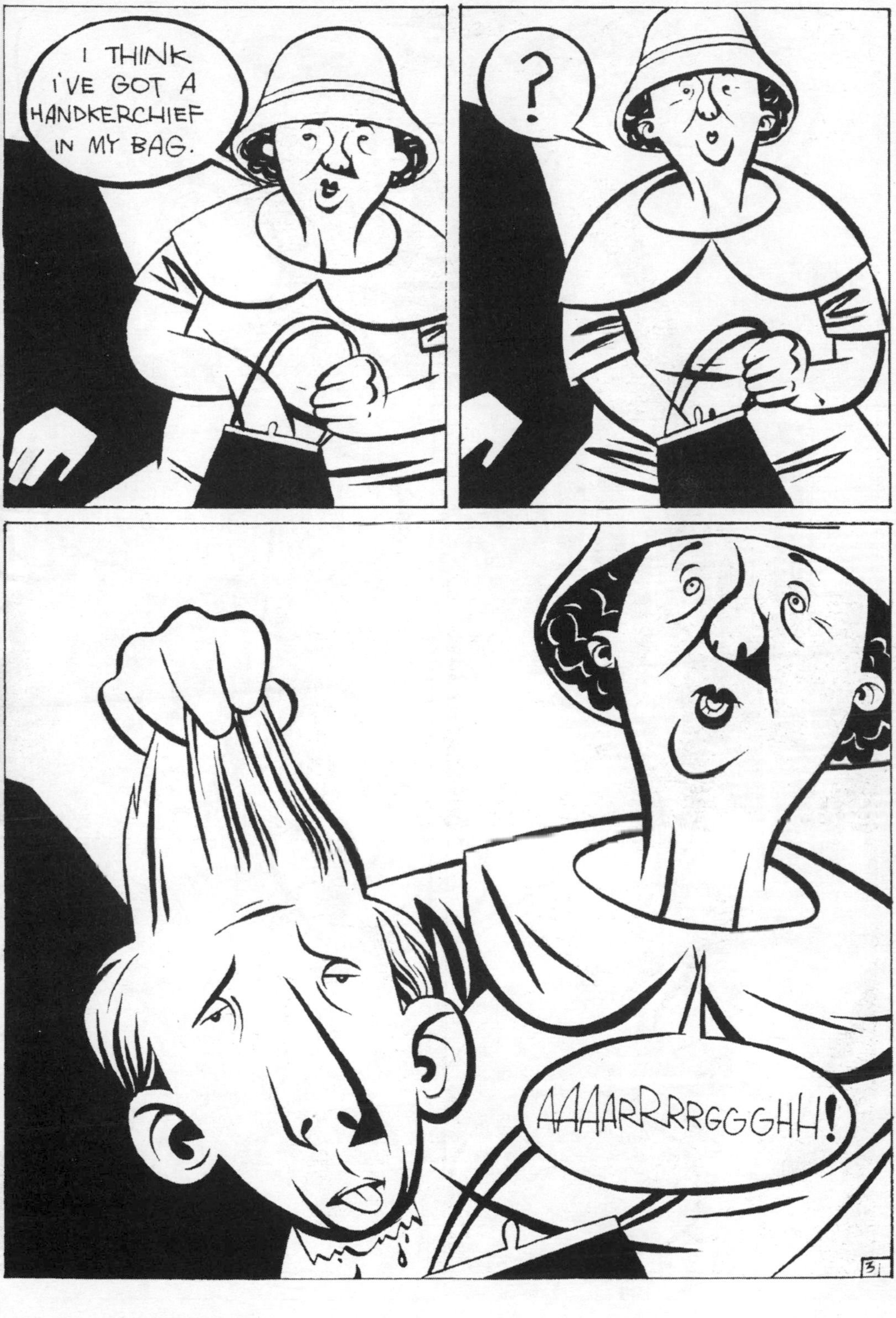
I THINK I'VE GOT A HANDKERCHIEF IN MY BAG.
?
AAAARRRRGGGHH!

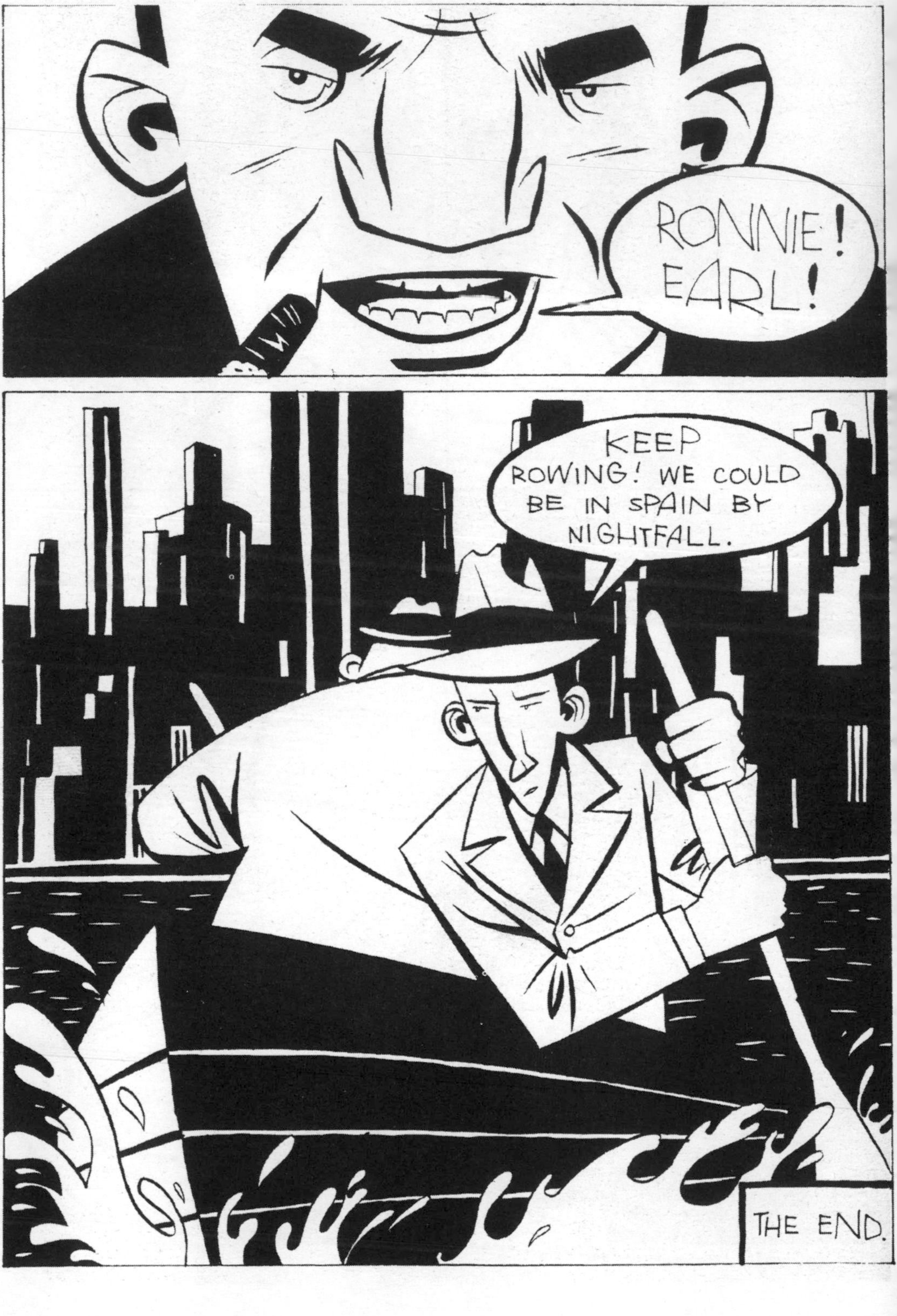
RONNIE! EARL!
KEEP ROWING! WE COULD BE IN SPAIN BY NIGHTFALL.
THE END.

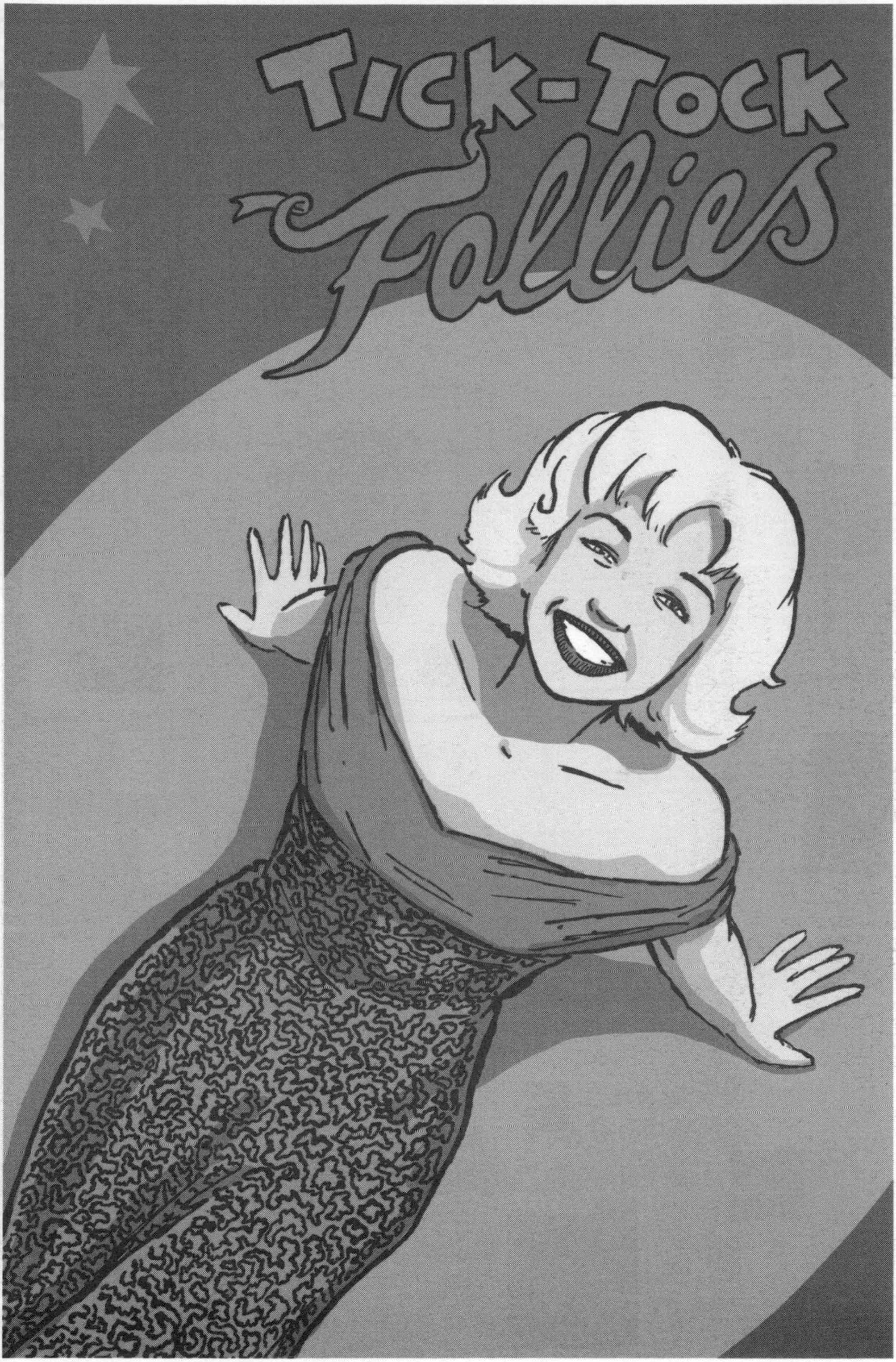
TICK-TOCK
Follies

Chris Butler (words) and **Chris Hogg** (pictures)

TICK-TOCK FOLLIES
Slave Labor Graphics, 1996

Butler & Hogg's near symbiotic partnership began with five self-published numbers of *Tales of Skittle-Sharpers & Thimble-Riggers*. A small Arts Council grant funded light-hearted one-shot *Comico* (whence *Murphy the Lizard* appears) before Slave Labor published their next three-issue miniseries, *Killer Fly*.

First issues get around double the order numbers from retailers as any subsequent issue, so next SLG wanted a new #1. Cue *Tick-Tock Follies*, a "slice of unusual life". Initially planned as a longer story, the travails of a nostalgic dance troupe touring East Anglia proved less than commercial dynamite. So they co-created *Monster!* #1 ... about a vampire.

Following two anthology volumes of *Monkey Punk*, real life began to bang on their respective doors. Butler went to teach English abroad whilst computer game graphics won Hogg. Now back in the UK and writing comics again, Butler is about to return to square one with his Volcano Comics imprint.

"No one has ever commented on this story's odd ending. I have to tip the reader's hand and say, it's not quite what it seems." – CB

tochrisbutler@hotmail.co.uk

Tick-Tock Follies.

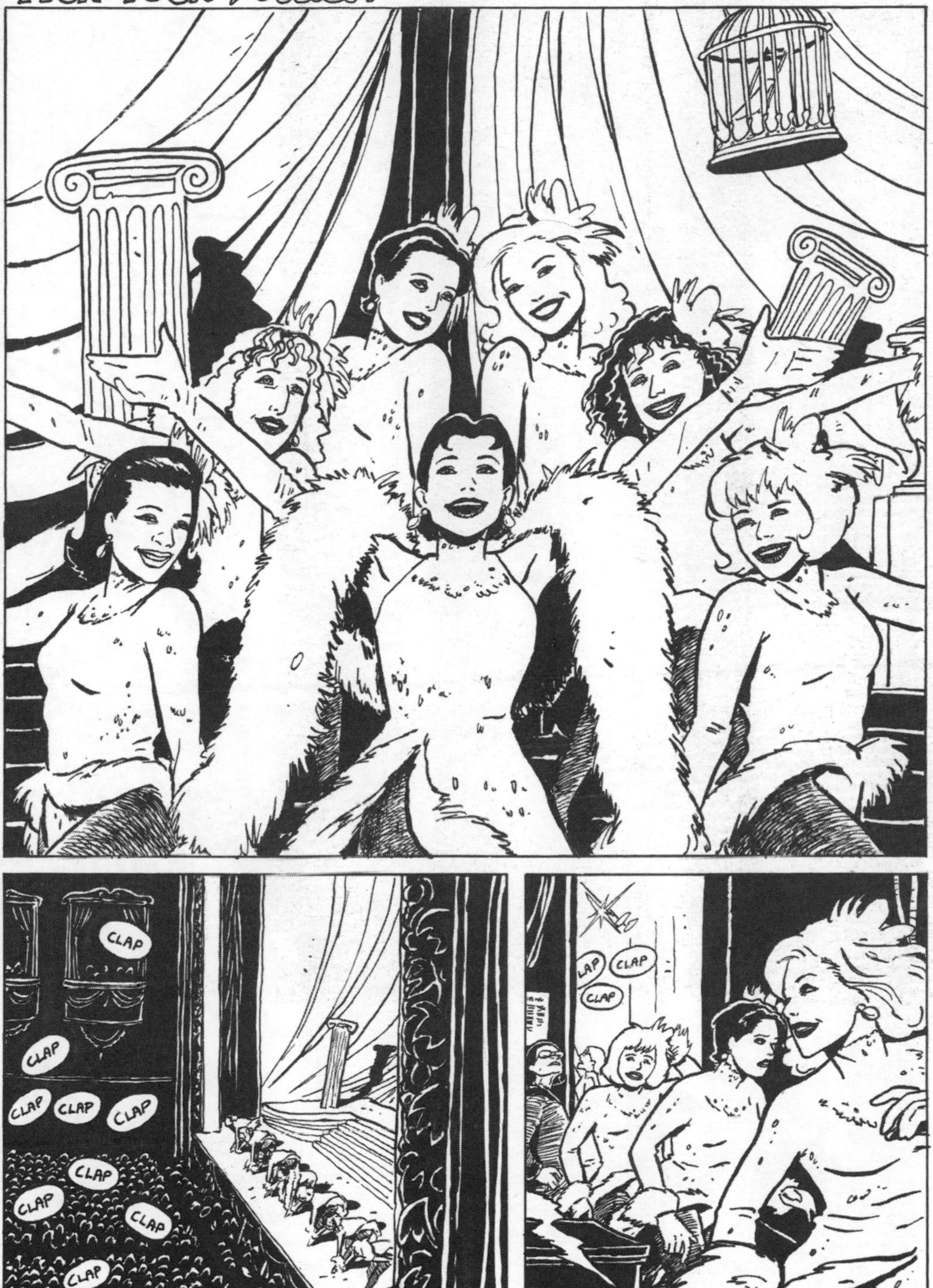

CLAP
CLAP
CLAP
CLAP
CLAP
CLAP
CLAP
CLAP
CLAP
CLAP
CLAP

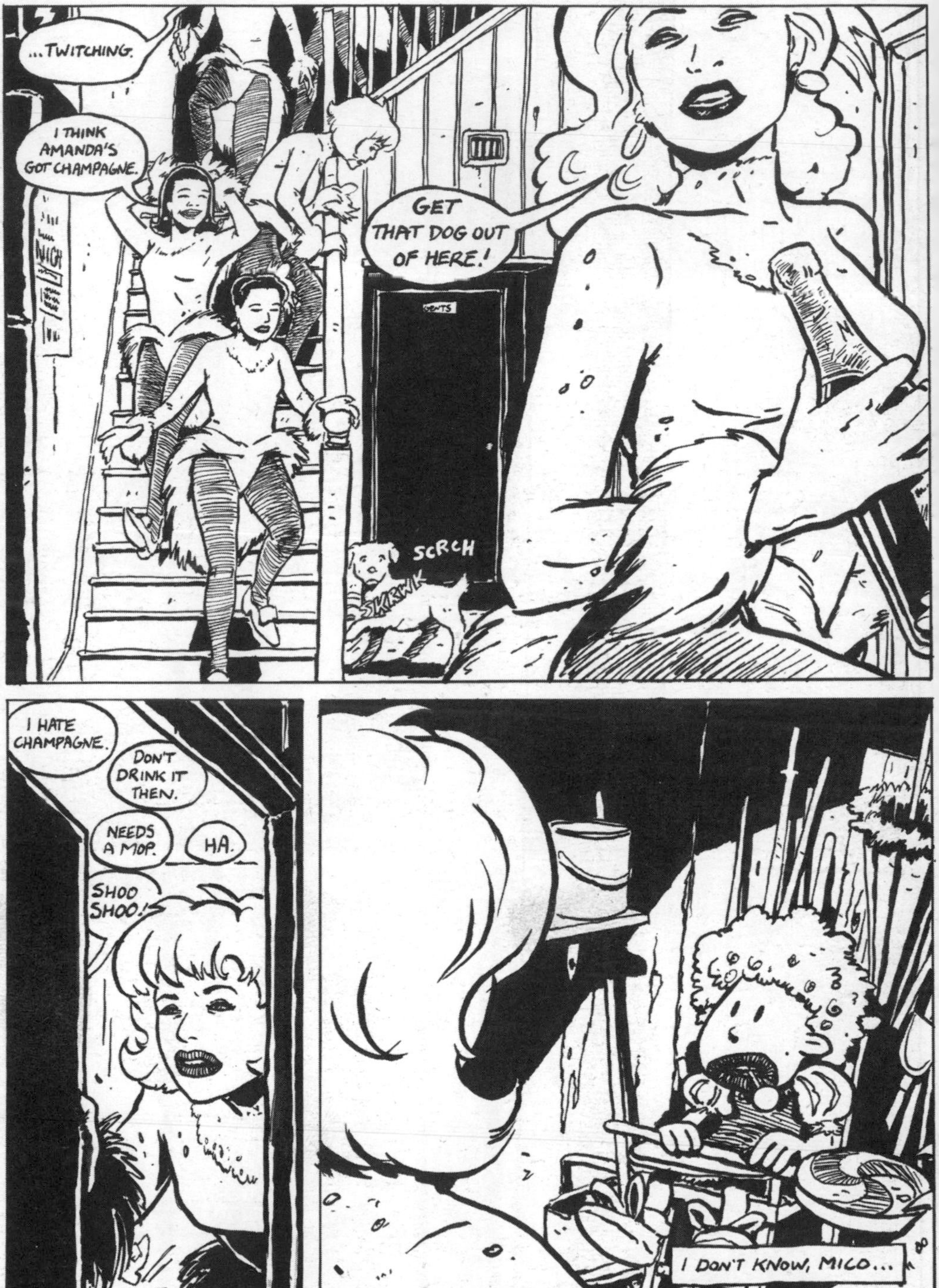
...TWITCHING.
I THINK AMANDA'S GOT CHAMPAGNE.
GET THAT DOG OUT OF HERE!
GENTS
SCRCH
SKRWK
I HATE CHAMPAGNE.
DON'T DRINK IT THEN.
NEEDS A MOP.
HA.
SHOO SHOO!
I DON'T KNOW, MICO...

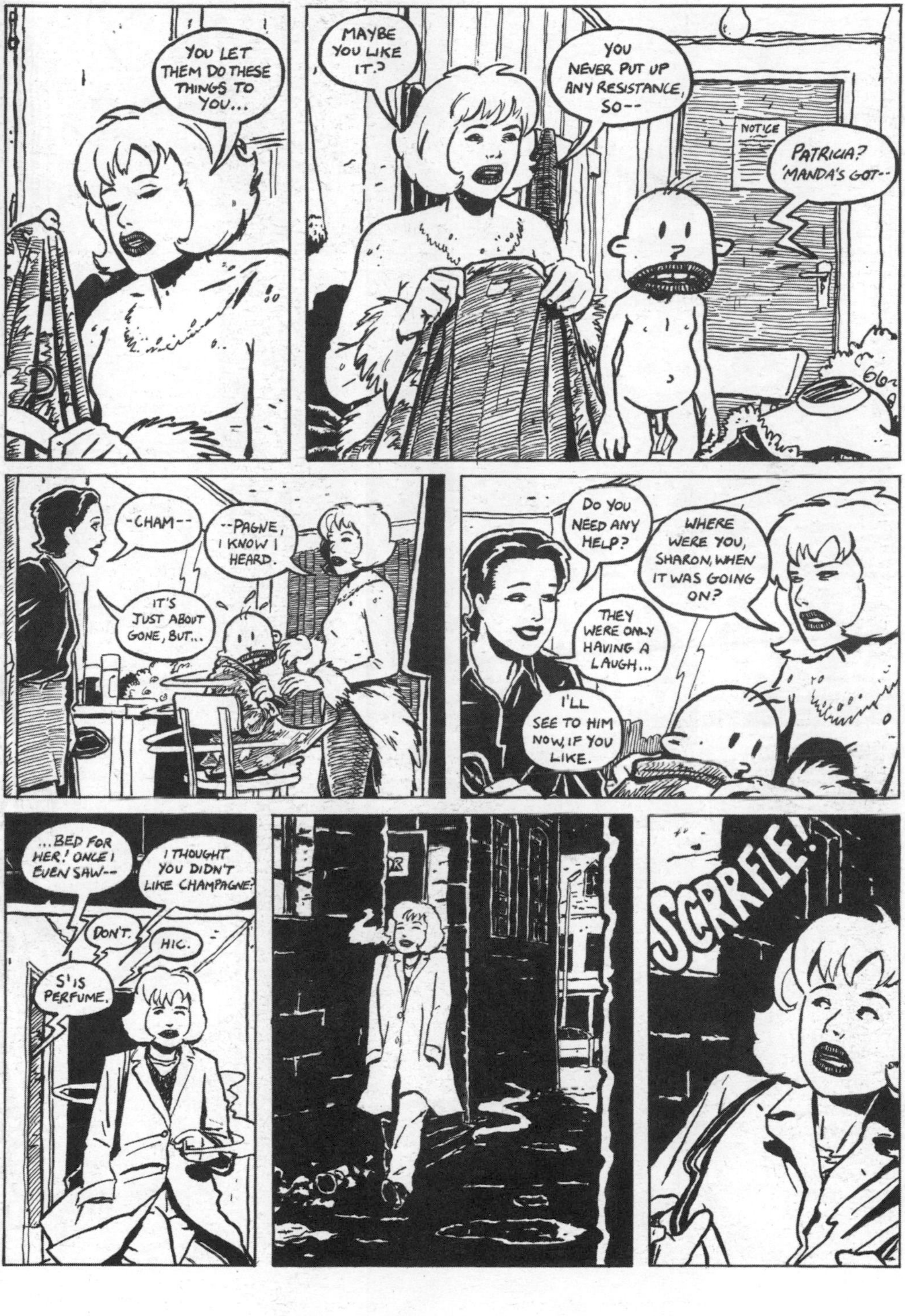
YOU LET THEM DO THESE THINGS TO YOU...
MAYBE YOU LIKE IT?
YOU NEVER PUT UP ANY RESISTANCE, SO--
NOTICE
PATRICIA? 'MANDA'S GOT--
-CHAM--
--PAGNE, I KNOW I HEARD.
IT'S JUST ABOUT GONE, BUT...
DO YOU NEED ANY HELP?
WHERE WERE YOU, SHARON, WHEN IT WAS GOING ON?
THEY WERE ONLY HAVING A LAUGH...
I'LL SEE TO HIM NOW, IF YOU LIKE.
...BED FOR HER! ONCE I EVEN SAW--
I THOUGHT YOU DIDN'T LIKE CHAMPAGNE?
DON'T.
HIC.
S'IS PERFUME.
SCRRFLE!

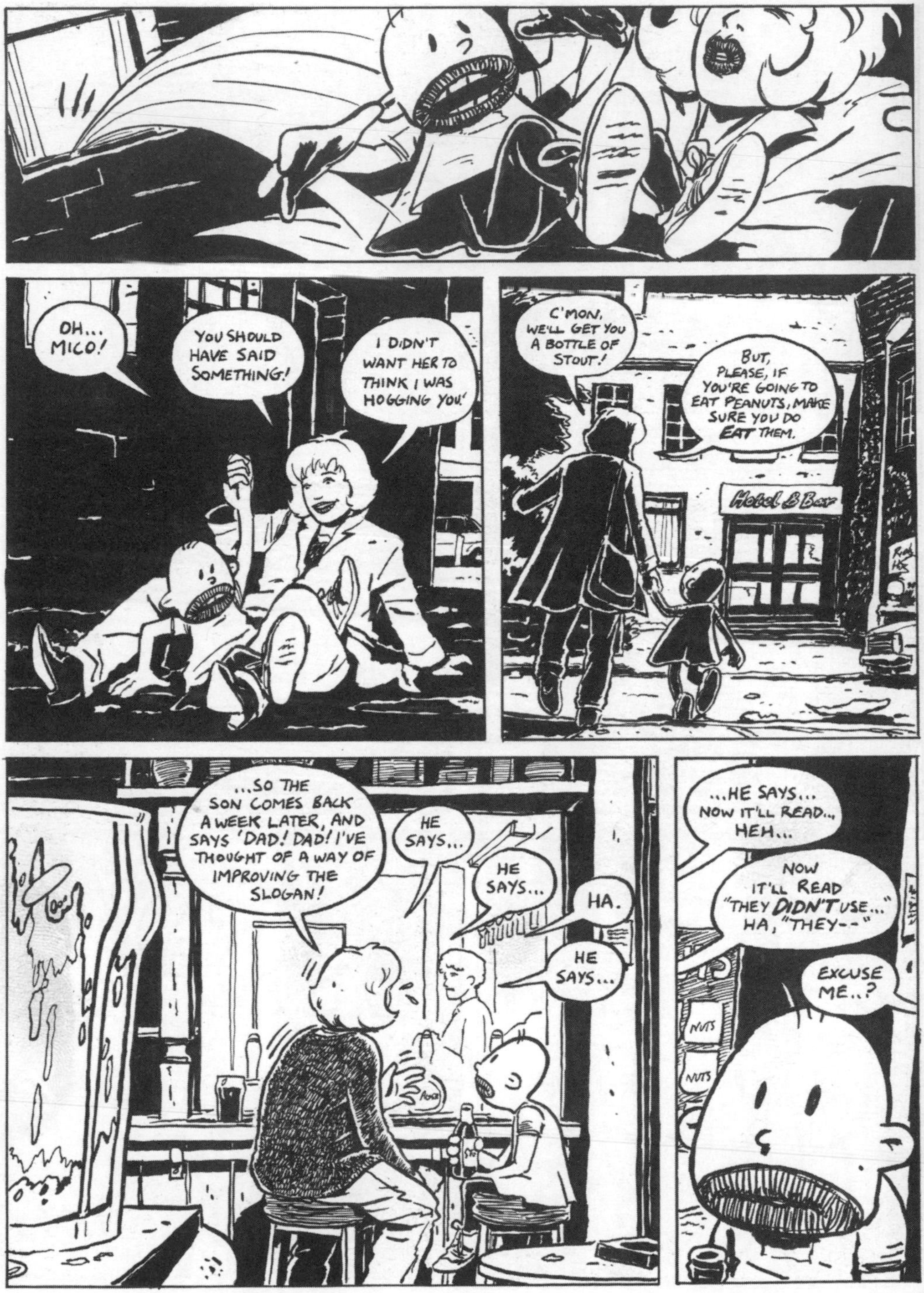
OH... MICO!
YOU SHOULD HAVE SAID SOMETHING!
I DIDN'T WANT HER TO THINK I WAS HOGGING YOU!
C'MON. WE'LL GET YOU A BOTTLE OF STOUT!
BUT, PLEASE, IF YOU'RE GOING TO EAT PEANUTS, MAKE SURE YOU DO EAT THEM.
Hotel & Bar
...SO THE SON COMES BACK A WEEK LATER, AND SAYS 'DAD! DAD! I'VE THOUGHT OF A WAY OF IMPROVING THE SLOGAN!
HE SAYS...
HE SAYS...
HA.
HE SAYS...
...HE SAYS... NOW IT'LL READ... HEH...
NOW IT'LL READ "THEY DIDN'T USE..." HA, "THEY--"
EXCUSE ME..?
NUTS
NUTS

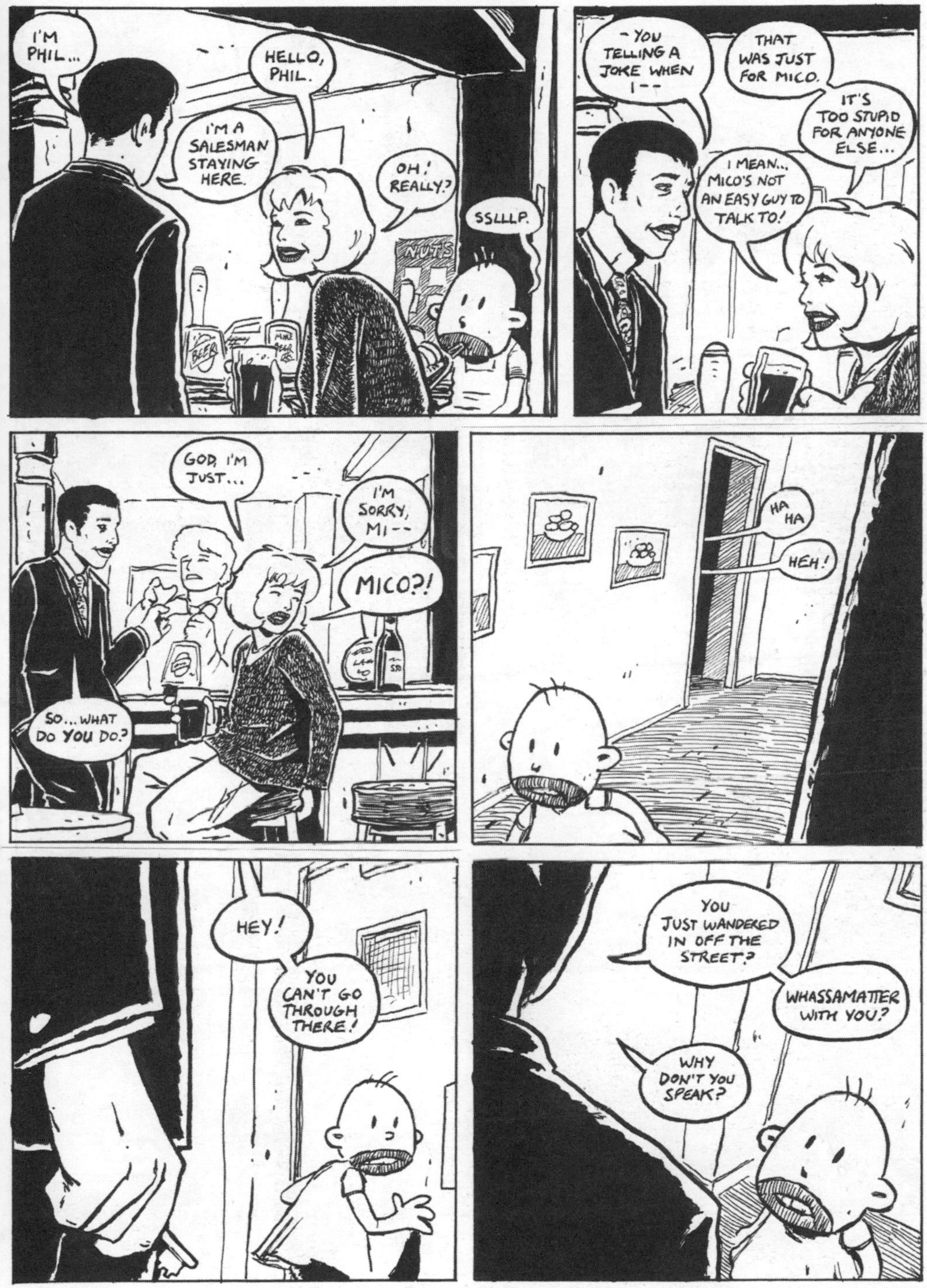
I'M PHIL...
HELLO, PHIL.
I'M A SALESMAN STAYING HERE.
OH! REALLY?
SSLLLP.
BEER
NUTS
-YOU TELLING A JOKE WHEN I--
THAT WAS JUST FOR MICO.
IT'S TOO STUPID FOR ANYONE ELSE...
I MEAN... MICO'S NOT AN EASY GUY TO TALK TO!
GOD, I'M JUST...
I'M SORRY, MI--
MICO?!
SO... WHAT DO YOU DO?
HA HA
HEH!
HEY!
YOU CAN'T GO THROUGH THERE!
YOU JUST WANDERED IN OFF THE STREET?
WHASSAMATTER WITH YOU?
WHY DON'T YOU SPEAK?

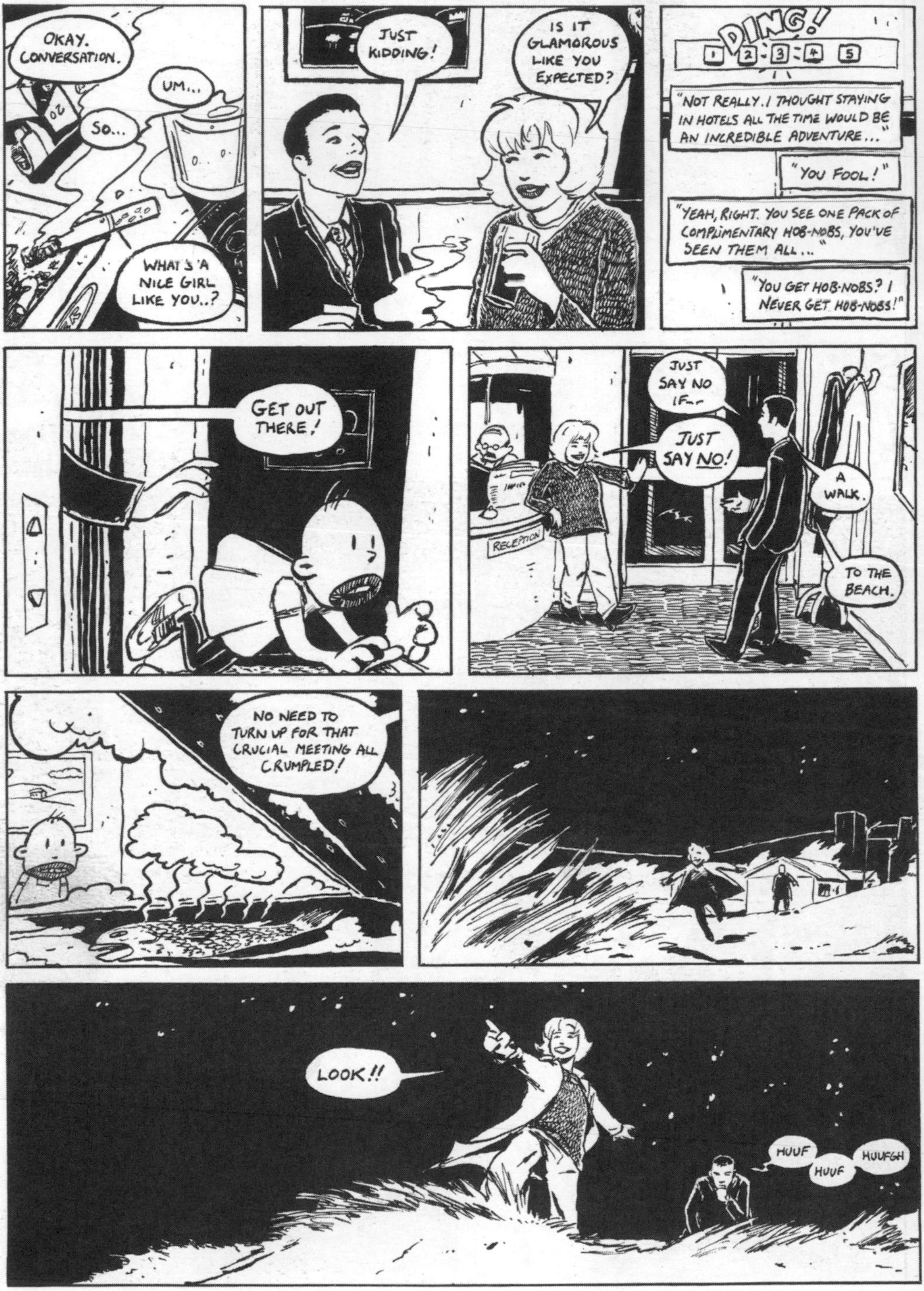

OKAY. CONVERSATION.
UM...
SO...
WHAT'S 'A NICE GIRL LIKE YOU..?
JUST KIDDING!
IS IT GLAMOROUS LIKE YOU EXPECTED?
DING!
1 2 3 4 5
"NOT REALLY. I THOUGHT STAYING IN HOTELS ALL THE TIME WOULD BE AN INCREDIBLE ADVENTURE..."
"YOU FOOL!"
"YEAH, RIGHT. YOU SEE ONE PACK OF COMPLIMENTARY HOB-NOBS, YOU'VE SEEN THEM ALL..."
"YOU GET HOB-NOBS? I NEVER GET HOB-NOBS!"
GET OUT THERE!
JUST SAY NO IF--
JUST SAY NO!
RECEPTION
A WALK.
TO THE BEACH.
NO NEED TO TURN UP FOR THAT CRUCIAL MEETING ALL CRUMPLED!
LOOK!!
HUUF
HUUF
HUUFGH

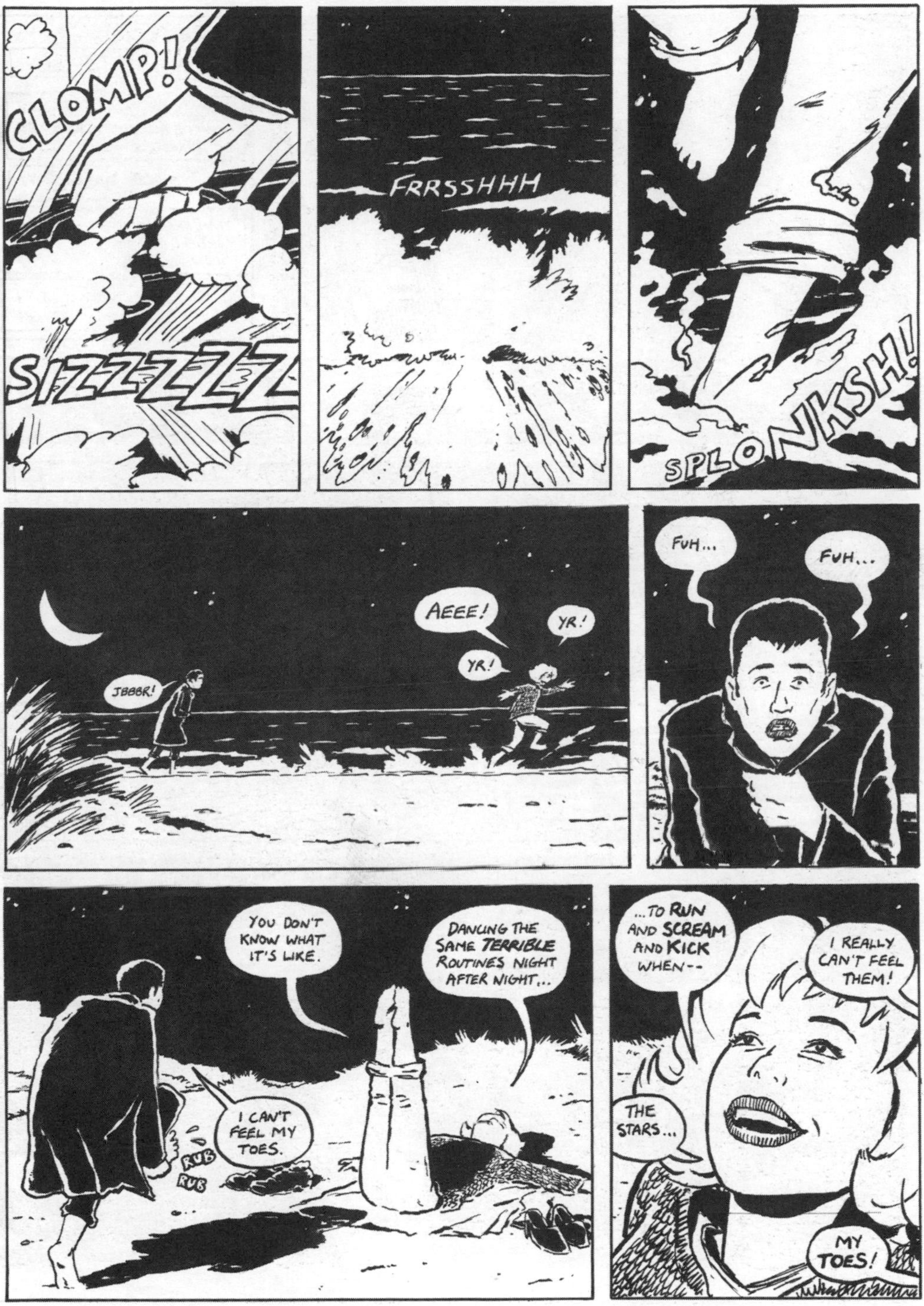
CLOMP!
SIZZZZZZ
FRRSSHHH
SPLONKSH!
JBBBR!
AEEE!
YR!
YR!
FUH...
FUH...
YOU DON'T KNOW WHAT IT'S LIKE.
DANCING THE SAME TERRIBLE ROUTINES NIGHT AFTER NIGHT...
I CAN'T FEEL MY TOES.
RUB
RUB
...TO RUN AND SCREAM AND KICK WHEN--
I REALLY CAN'T FEEL THEM!
THE STARS...
MY TOES!

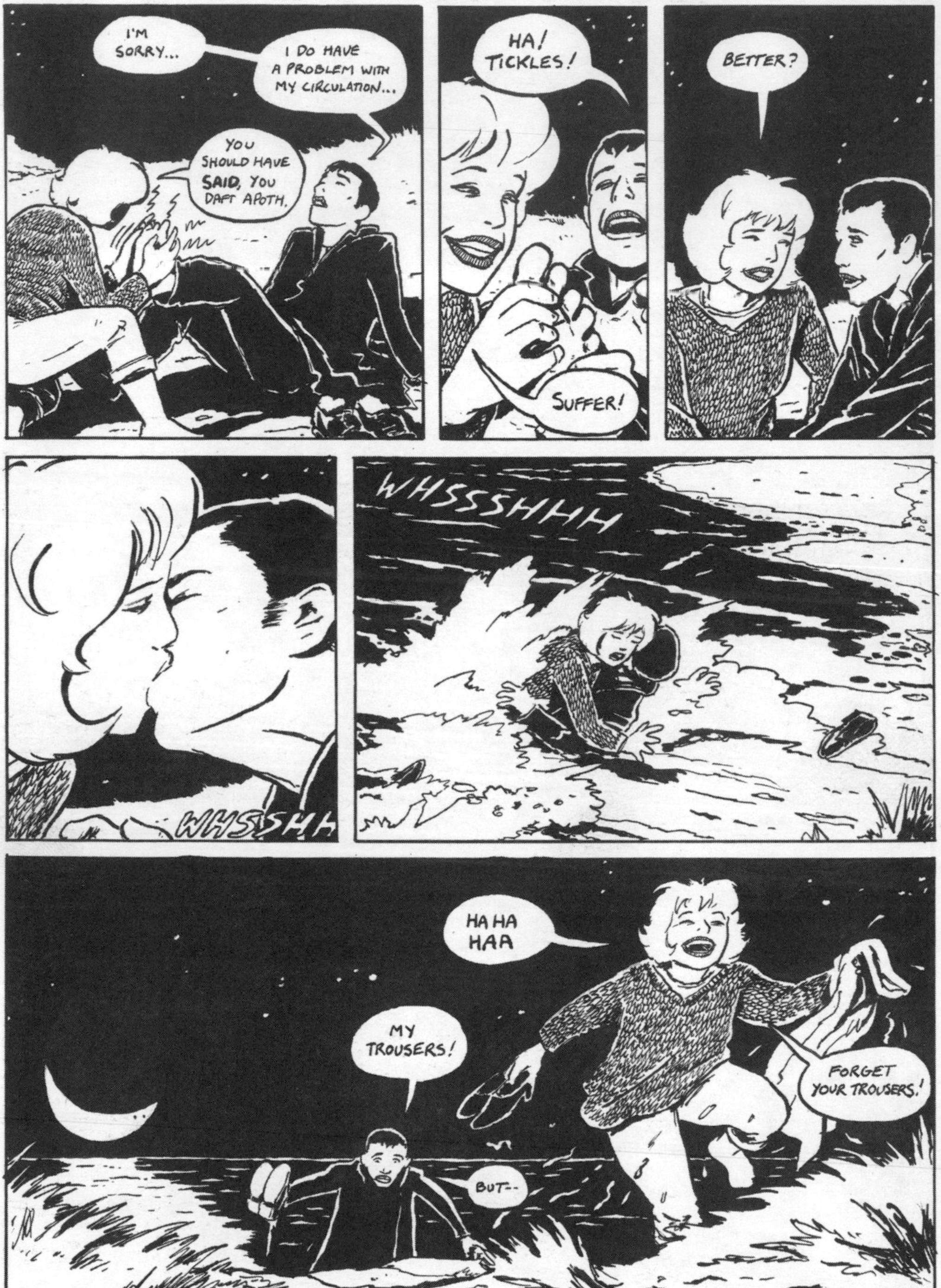
I'M SORRY...
I DO HAVE A PROBLEM WITH MY CIRCULATION...
YOU SHOULD HAVE SAID, YOU DAFT APOTH.
HA! TICKLES!
SUFFER!
BETTER?
WHSSSHH
WHSSSHHH
HA HA HAA
MY TROUSERS!
FORGET YOUR TROUSERS!
BUT--

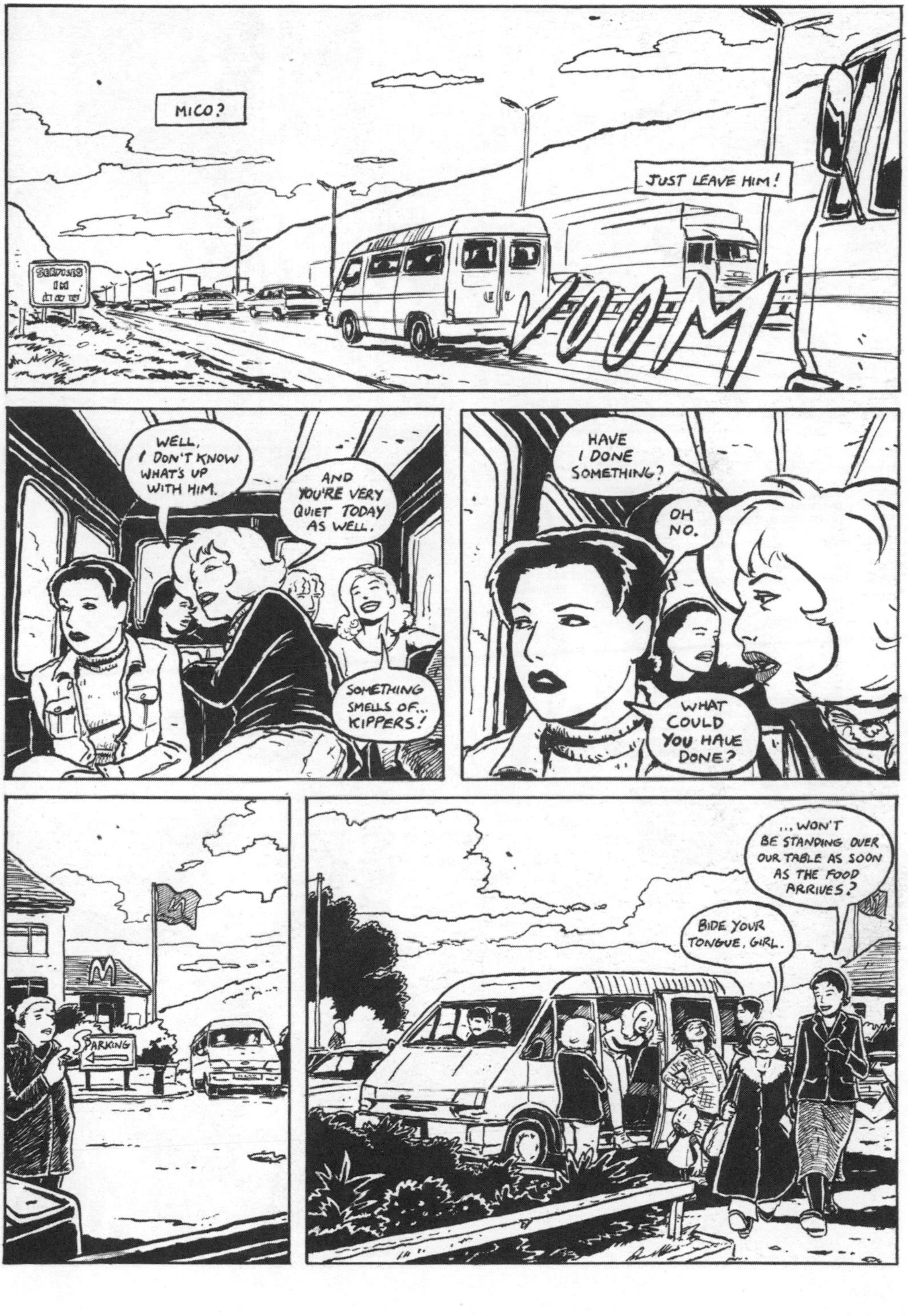
MICO?
JUST LEAVE HIM!
VOOM
WELL, I DON'T KNOW WHAT'S UP WITH HIM.
AND YOU'RE VERY QUIET TODAY AS WELL.
SOMETHING SMELLS OF... KIPPERS!
HAVE I DONE SOMETHING?
OH NO.
WHAT COULD YOU HAVE DONE?
PARKING
...WON'T BE STANDING OVER OUR TABLE AS SOON AS THE FOOD ARRIVES?
BIDE YOUR TONGUE, GIRL.

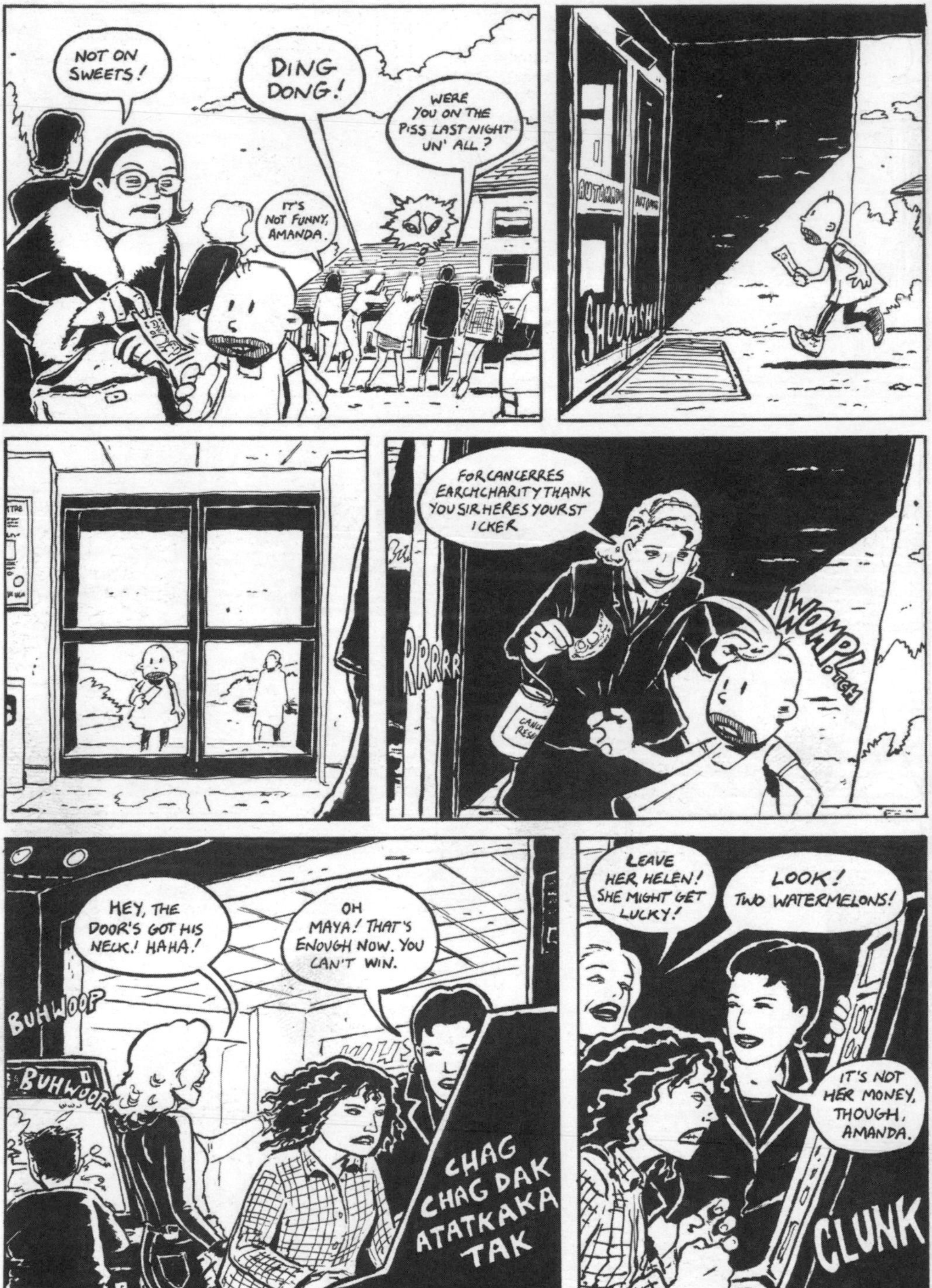
NOT ON SWEETS!
DING DONG!
WERE YOU ON THE PISS LAST NIGHT UN' ALL?
IT'S NOT FUNNY, AMANDA.
SHOOMSH
FOR CANCERRES EARCHCHARITYTHANK YOUSIRHERESYOURST ICKER
RRRRR
WOMPL
HEY, THE DOOR'S GOT HIS NECK! HAHA!
OH MAYA! THAT'S ENOUGH NOW. YOU CAN'T WIN.
BUHWOOP
BUHWOOP
CHAG CHAG DAK ATATKAKA TAK
LEAVE HER, HELEN! SHE MIGHT GET LUCKY!
LOOK! TWO WATERMELONS!
IT'S NOT HER MONEY, THOUGH, AMANDA.
CLUNK

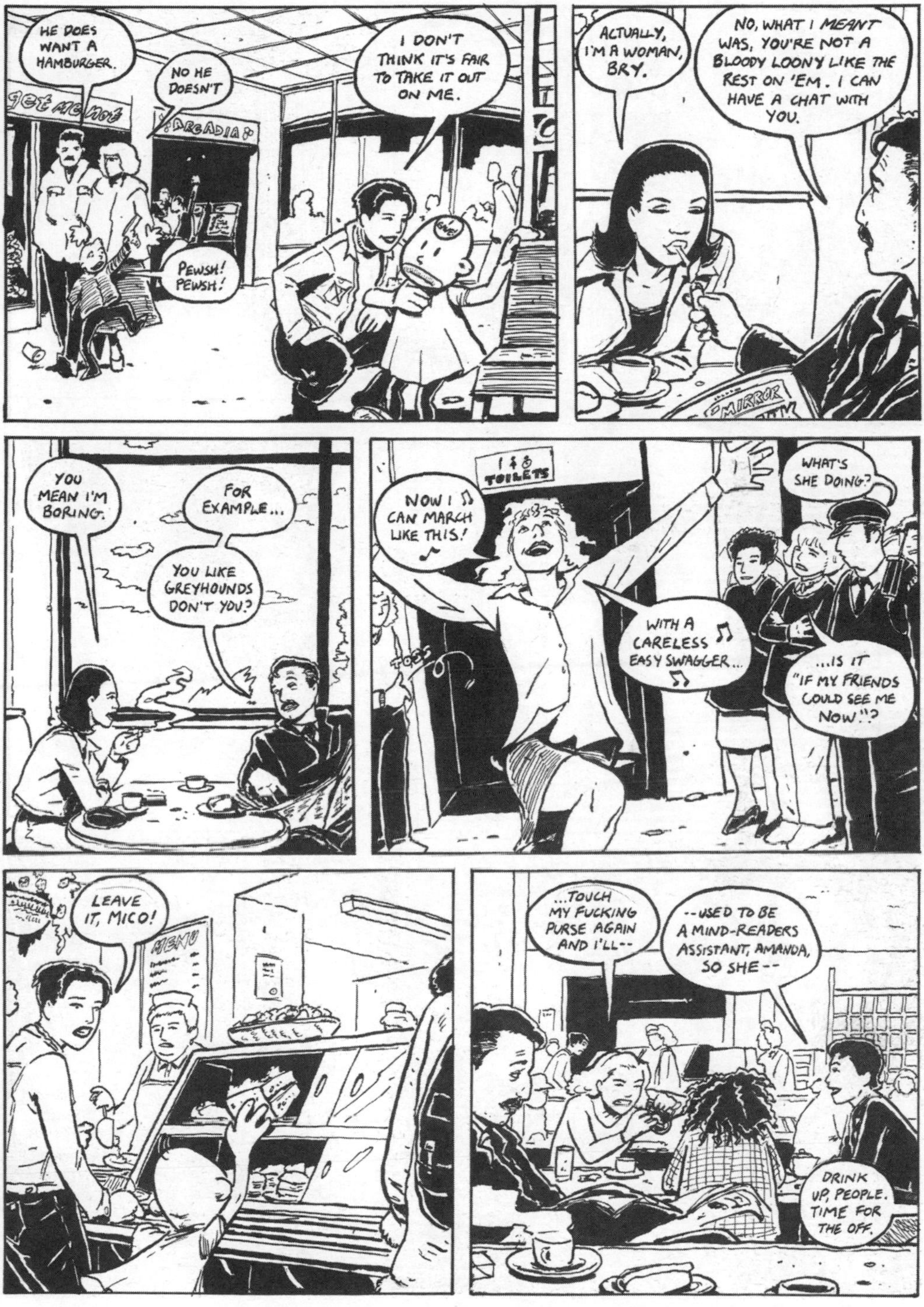
HE DOES WANT A HAMBURGER.
NO HE DOESN'T
I DON'T THINK IT'S FAIR TO TAKE IT OUT ON ME.
PEWSH! PEWSH!
ACTUALLY, I'M A WOMAN, BRY.
NO, WHAT I MEANT WAS, YOU'RE NOT A BLOODY LOONY LIKE THE REST ON 'EM. I CAN HAVE A CHAT WITH YOU.
MIRROR
YOU MEAN I'M BORING.
FOR EXAMPLE...
YOU LIKE GREYHOUNDS DON'T YOU?
TOILETS
NOW I CAN MARCH LIKE THIS!
WHAT'S SHE DOING?
WITH A CARELESS EASY SWAGGER...
...IS IT "IF MY FRIENDS COULD SEE ME NOW"?
LEAVE IT, MICO!
MENU
...TOUCH MY FUCKING PURSE AGAIN AND I'LL--
--USED TO BE A MIND-READERS ASSISTANT, AMANDA, SO SHE--
DRINK UP, PEOPLE. TIME FOR THE OFF.

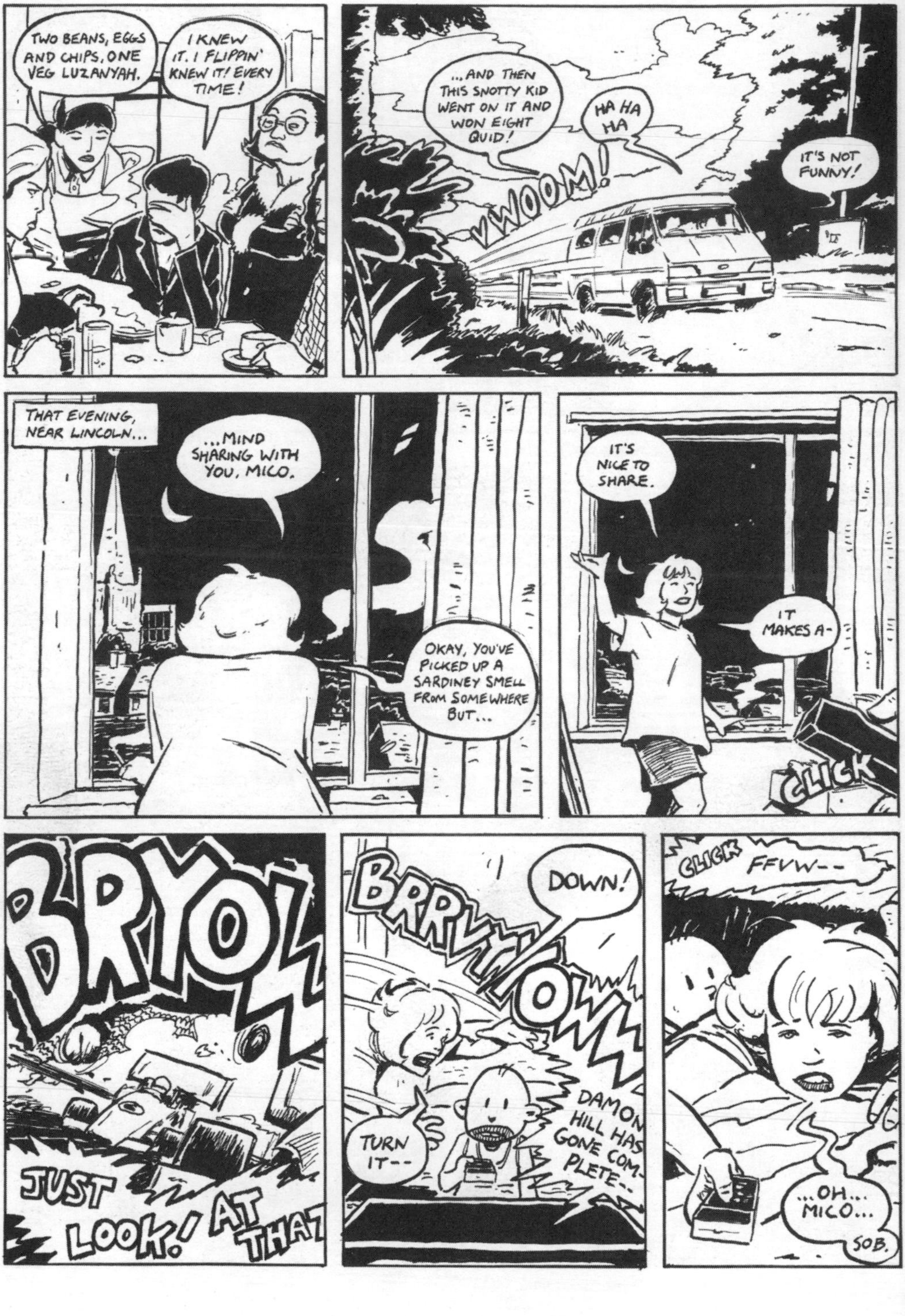
TWO BEANS, EGGS AND CHIPS, ONE VEG LUZANYAH.
I KNEW IT. I FLIPPIN' KNEW IT! EVERY TIME!
...AND THEN THIS SNOTTY KID WENT ON IT AND WON EIGHT QUID!
HA HA HA
VWOOM!
IT'S NOT FUNNY!
THAT EVENING, NEAR LINCOLN...
...MIND SHARING WITH YOU, MICO.
OKAY, YOU'VE PICKED UP A SARDINEY SMELL FROM SOMEWHERE BUT...
IT'S NICE TO SHARE.
IT MAKES A-
CLICK
BRYOL
JUST LOOK! AT THAT
BRRVVOW
DOWN!
TURN IT--
DAMON HILL HAS GONE COM-PLETE--
CLICK
FFVW--
...OH... MICO...
SOB.

LATER.

RIGHT...

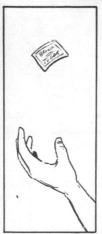

BAT

ONE TO ME! WEE-HEE!

THERE WAS A BLOKE HERE ASKING FOR YOU.

MM...

IF I EAT ANY MORE, ONE OF MY BUTTONS'LL POP ON STAGE AND TAKE OUT A PUNTER'S EYE!

STUDENTS ARE THE WORST.

THEY WON'T BE LOOKING AT YOUR SEAMS... THEY'LL BE SHOUTING "GET YOUR TITS OUT FOR THE LADS!"

OH STOP EXAGGERATING. THEY'RE PROBABLY MORE INTO MARX THAN YOUR CROTCH!

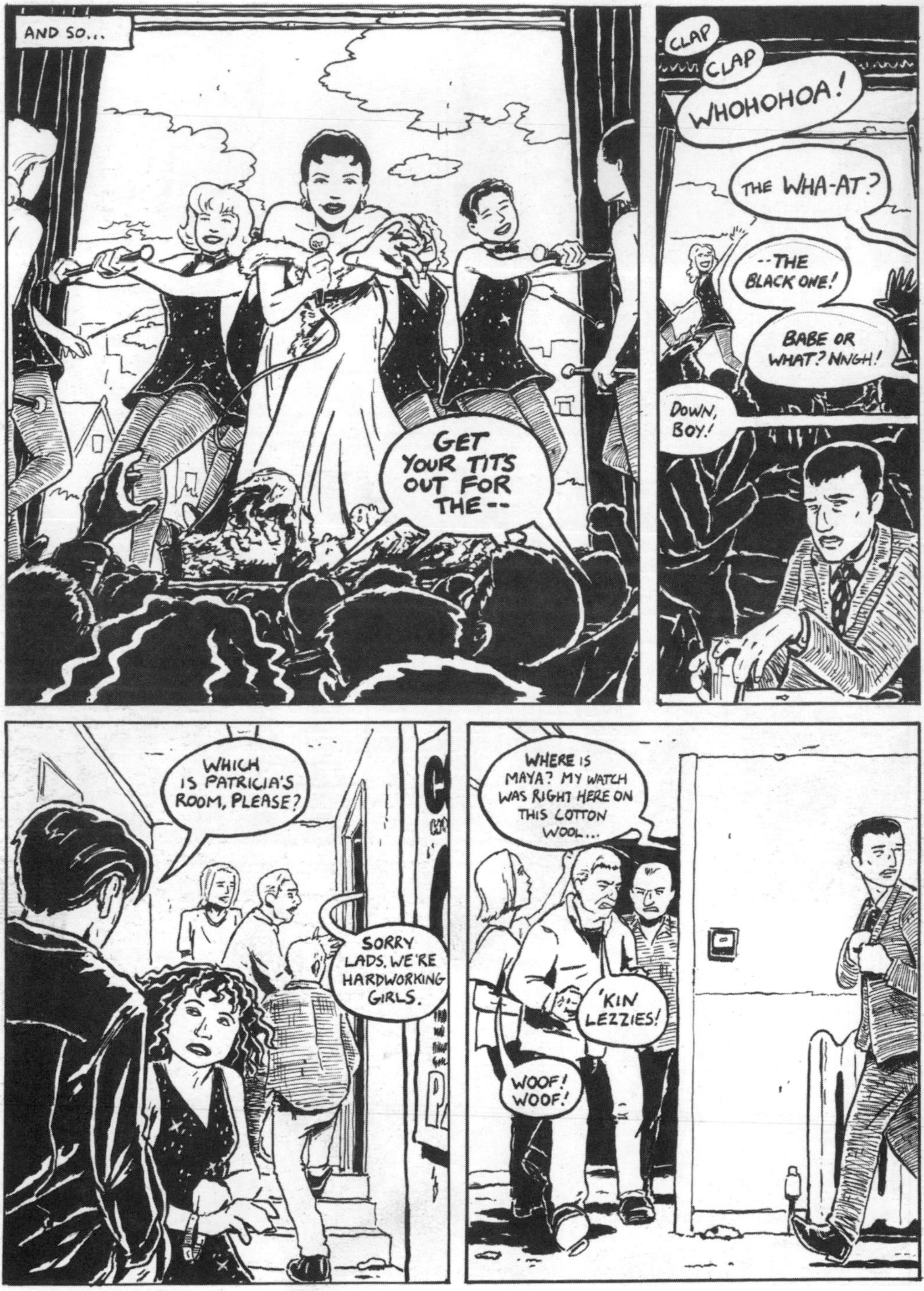
AND SO...
GET YOUR TITS OUT FOR THE--
CLAP
CLAP
WHOHOHOA!
THE WHA-AT?
--THE BLACK ONE!
BABE OR WHAT? NNGH!
DOWN, BOY!
WHICH IS PATRICIA'S ROOM, PLEASE?
SORRY LADS. WE'RE HARDWORKING GIRLS.
WHERE IS MAYA? MY WATCH WAS RIGHT HERE ON THIS COTTON WOOL...
'KIN LEZZIES!
WOOF! WOOF!

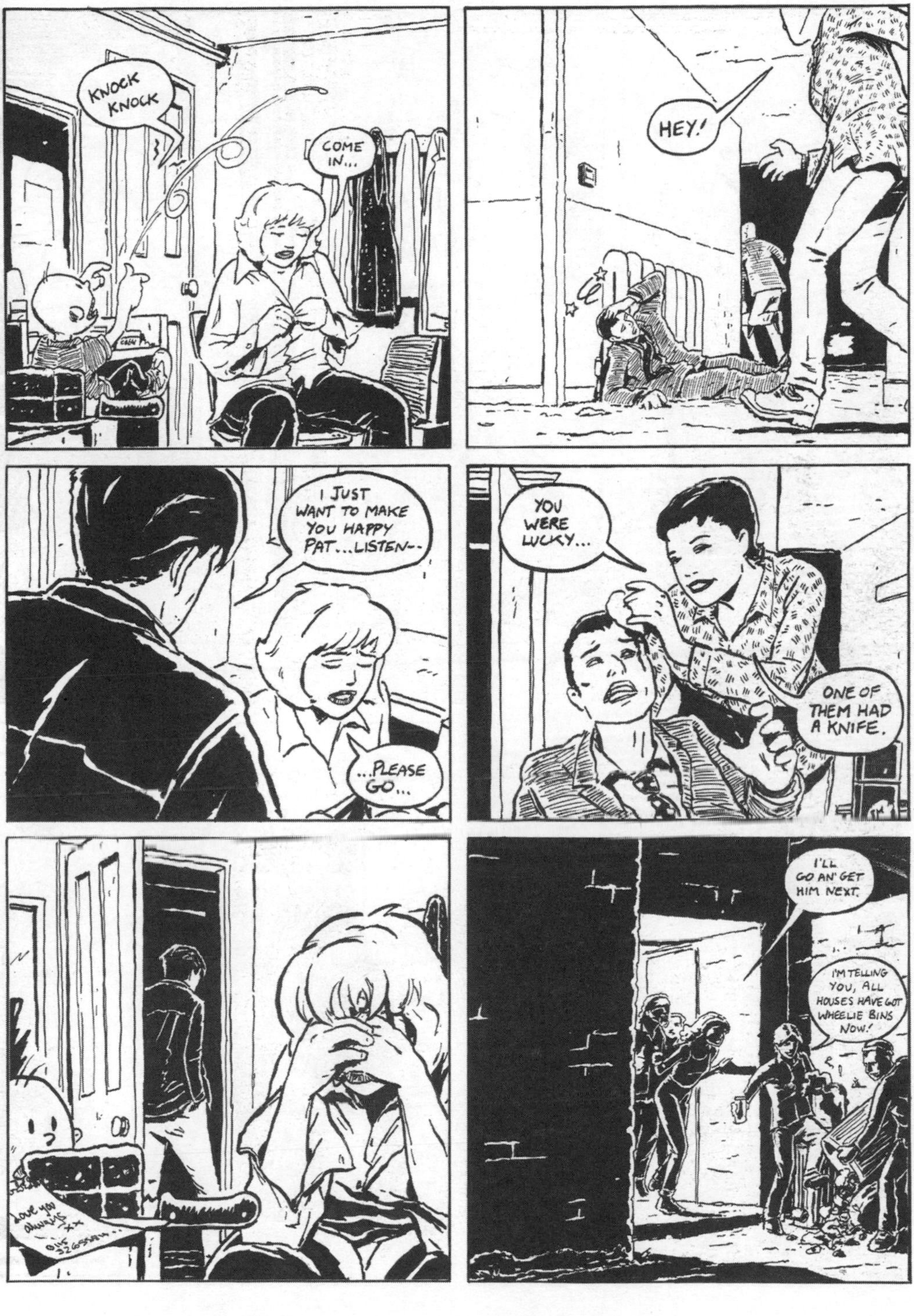
KNOCK KNOCK
COME IN...
HEY!
I JUST WANT TO MAKE YOU HAPPY PAT...LISTEN--
...PLEASE GO...
YOU WERE LUCKY...
ONE OF THEM HAD A KNIFE.
Love you always xx
I'LL GO AN' GET HIM NEXT.
I'M TELLING YOU, ALL HOUSES HAVE GOT WHEELIE BINS NOW!

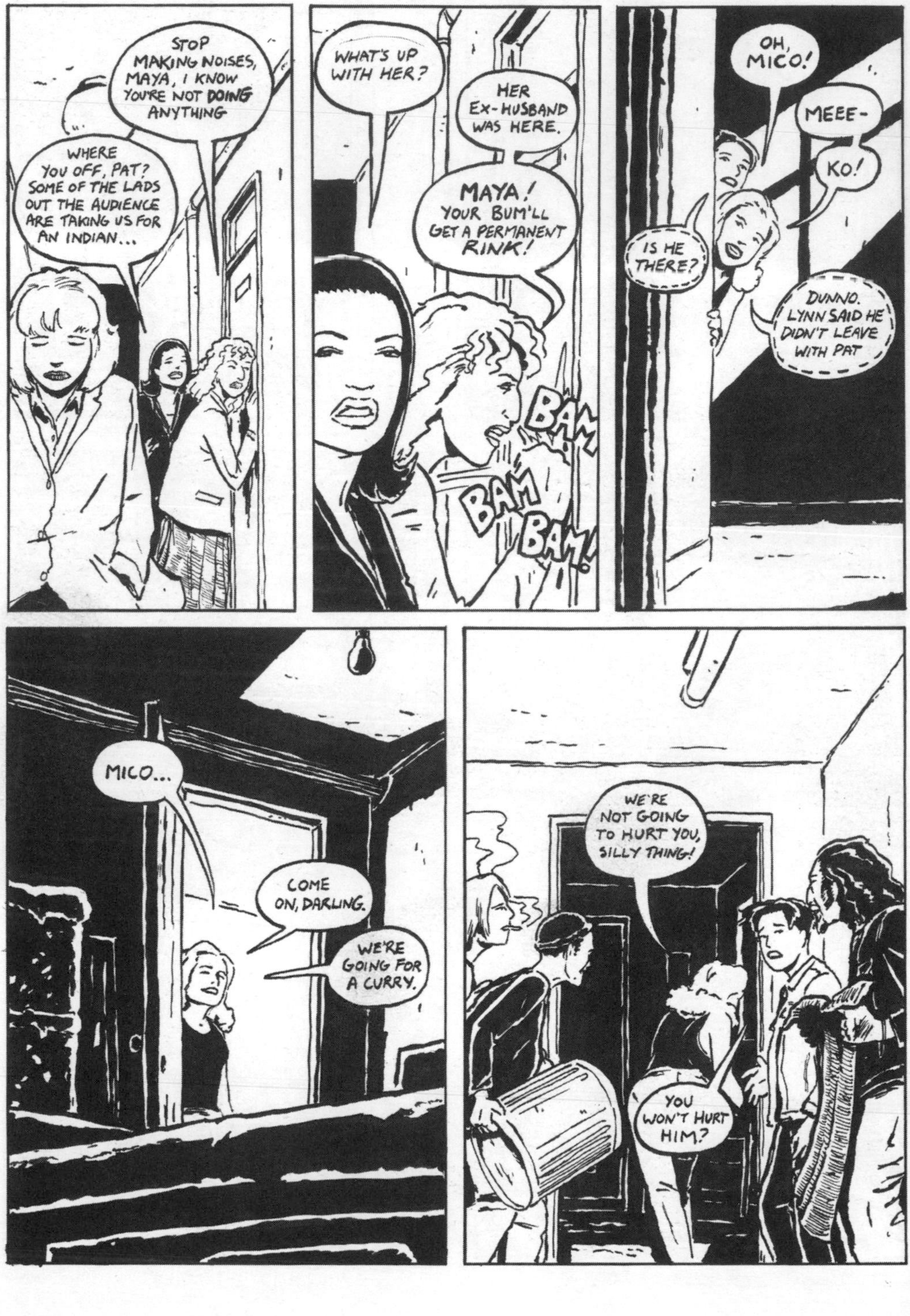
STOP MAKING NOISES, MAYA, I KNOW YOU'RE NOT DOING ANYTHING
WHERE YOU OFF, PAT? SOME OF THE LADS OUT THE AUDIENCE ARE TAKING US FOR AN INDIAN...
WHAT'S UP WITH HER?
HER EX-HUSBAND WAS HERE.
MAYA! YOUR BUM'LL GET A PERMANENT RINK!
BAM
BAM BAM
BAM!
OH, MICO!
MEEE-
KO!
IS HE THERE?
DUNNO. LYNN SAID HE DIDN'T LEAVE WITH PAT
MICO...
COME ON, DARLING.
WE'RE GOING FOR A CURRY.
WE'RE NOT GOING TO HURT YOU, SILLY THING!
YOU WON'T HURT HIM?

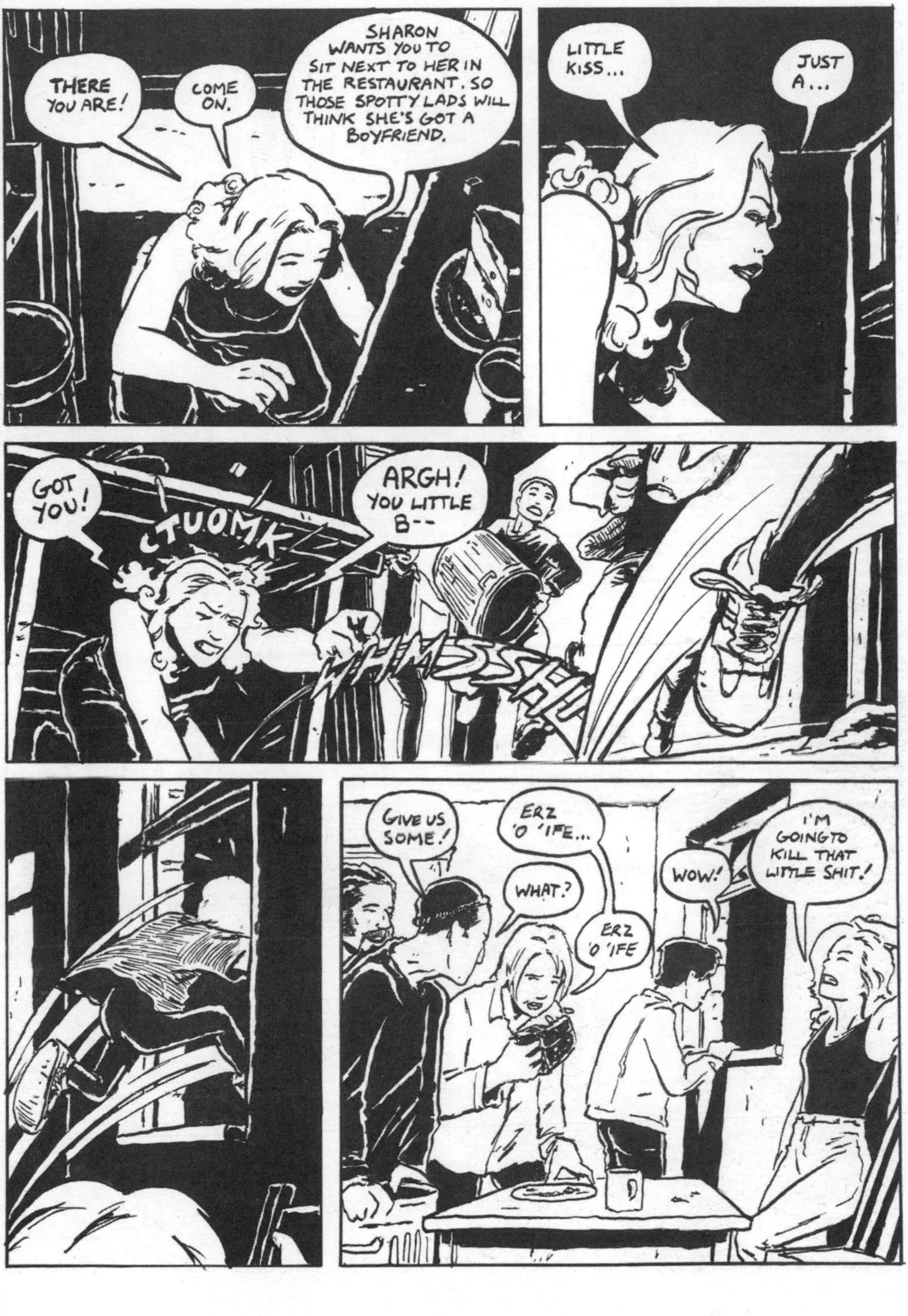
THERE YOU ARE!
COME ON.
SHARON WANTS YOU TO SIT NEXT TO HER IN THE RESTAURANT. SO THOSE SPOTTY LADS WILL THINK SHE'S GOT A BOYFRIEND.
LITTLE KISS...
JUST A...
GOT YOU!
CTUOMK
ARGH! YOU LITTLE B--
GIVE US SOME!
ERZ 'O 'IFE...
WHAT?
ERZ 'O 'IFE
WOW!
I'M GOING TO KILL THAT LITTLE SHIT!

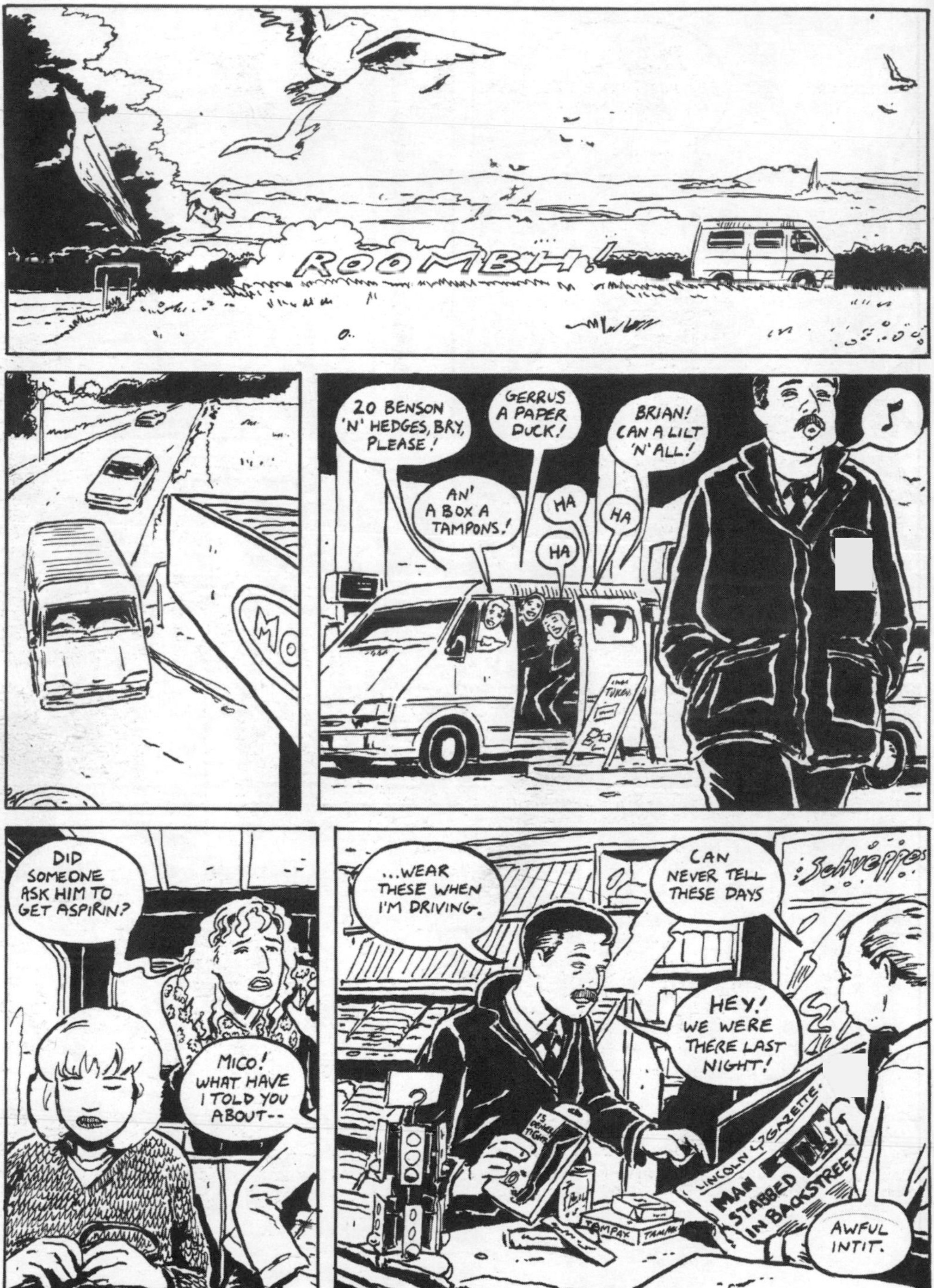
ROOMBH!
MO
20 BENSON 'N' HEDGES, BRY, PLEASE!
GERRUS A PAPER DUCK!
BRIAN! CAN A LILT 'N' ALL!
AN' A BOX A TAMPONS!
HA
HA
HA
DID SOMEONE ASK HIM TO GET ASPIRIN?
MICO! WHAT HAVE I TOLD YOU ABOUT--
...WEAR THESE WHEN I'M DRIVING.
CAN NEVER TELL THESE DAYS
Schweppes
HEY! WE WERE THERE LAST NIGHT!
LINCOLN GAZETTE
MAN STABBED IN BACKSTREET
TAMPAX
AWFUL INTIT.

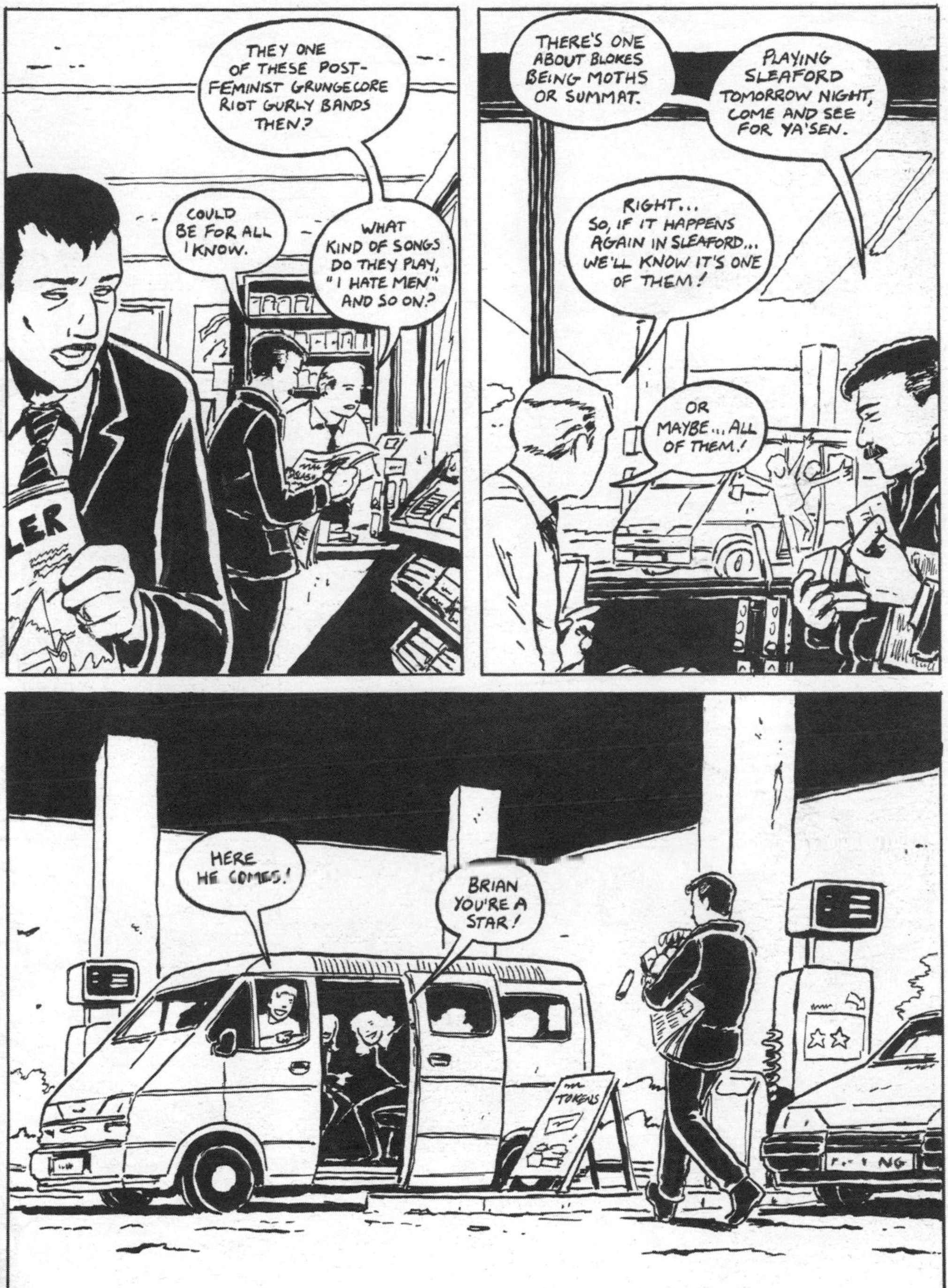
THEY ONE OF THESE POST-FEMINIST GRUNGECORE RIOT GURLY BANDS THEN?
COULD BE FOR ALL I KNOW.
WHAT KIND OF SONGS DO THEY PLAY, "I HATE MEN" AND SO ON?
THERE'S ONE ABOUT BLOKES BEING MOTHS OR SUMMAT.
PLAYING SLEAFORD TOMORROW NIGHT, COME AND SEE FOR YA'SEN.
RIGHT... SO, IF IT HAPPENS AGAIN IN SLEAFORD... WE'LL KNOW IT'S ONE OF THEM!
OR MAYBE... ALL OF THEM!
HERE HE COMES!
BRIAN YOU'RE A STAR!
TOKENS

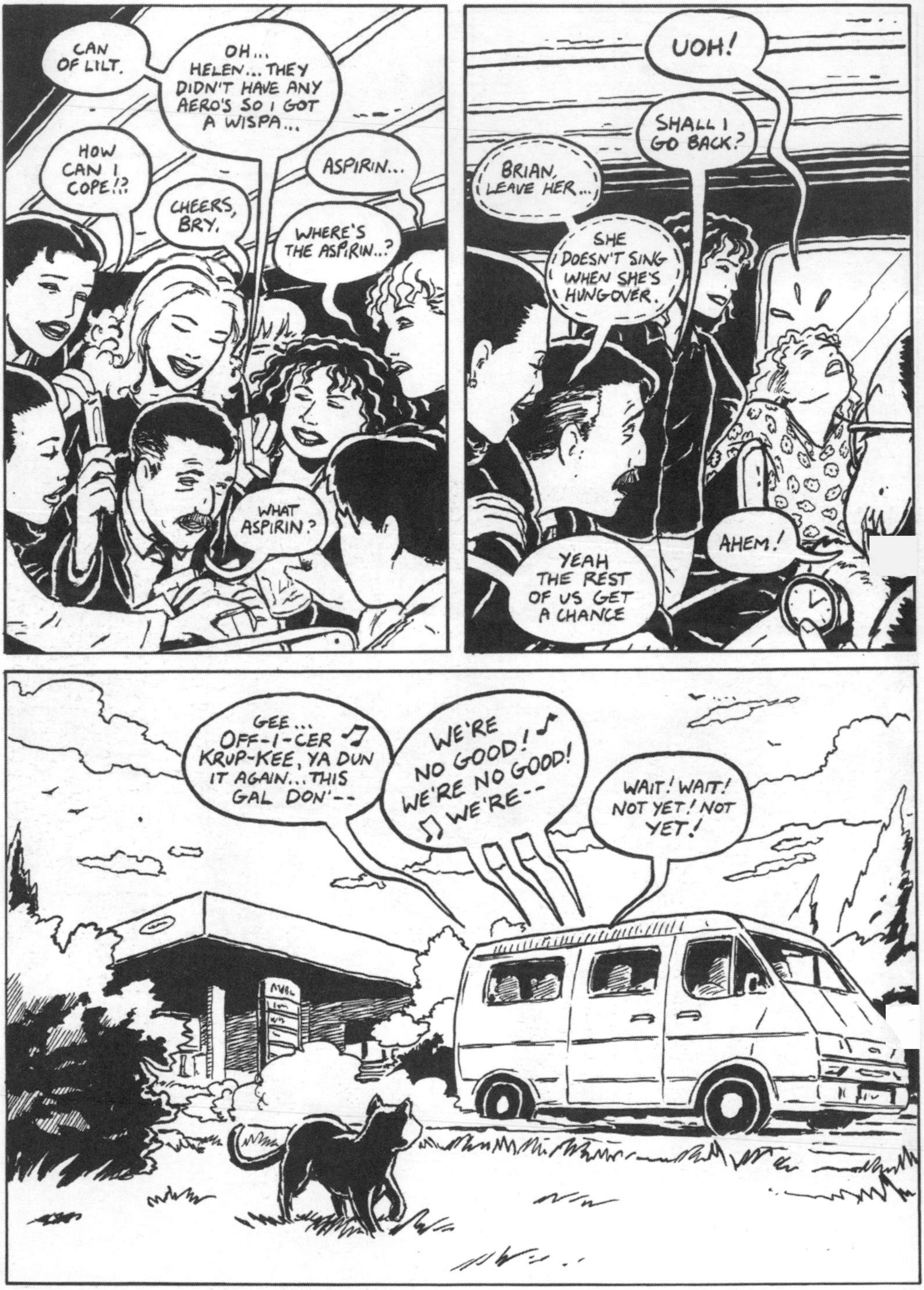
CAN OF LILT.
OH... HELEN... THEY DIDN'T HAVE ANY AERO'S SO I GOT A WISPA...
HOW CAN I COPE!?
CHEERS, BRY.
ASPIRIN...
WHERE'S THE ASPIRIN..?
WHAT ASPIRIN?
UOH!
SHALL I GO BACK?
BRIAN, LEAVE HER...
SHE DOESN'T SING WHEN SHE'S HUNGOVER.
YEAH THE REST OF US GET A CHANCE
AHEM!
GEE... OFF-I-CER KRUP-KEE, YA DUN IT AGAIN... THIS GAL DON'--
WE'RE NO GOOD! WE'RE NO GOOD! WE'RE--
WAIT! WAIT! NOT YET! NOT YET!

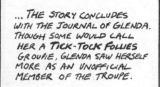

...THE STORY CONCLUDES WITH THE JOURNAL OF GLENDA. THOUGH SOME WOULD CALL HER A *TICK-TOCK FOLLIES* GROUPIE, GLENDA SAW HERSELF MORE AS AN UNOFFICIAL MEMBER OF THE TROUPE.

GLENDA.

ONCE UPON A TIME THERE WERE SEVEN DANCERS CALLED THE *TICK-TOCK FOLLIES*...

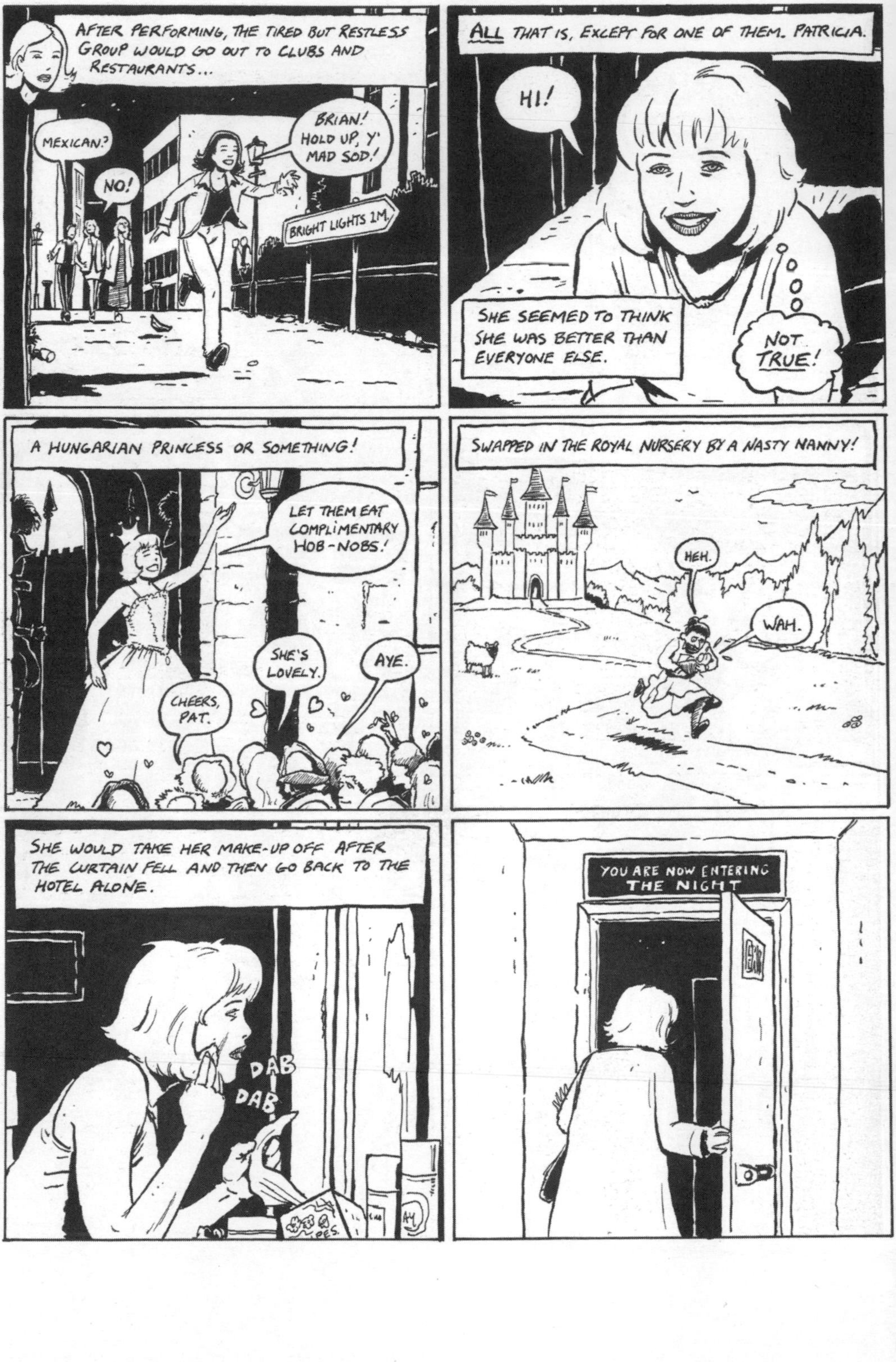
AFTER PERFORMING, THE TIRED BUT RESTLESS GROUP WOULD GO OUT TO CLUBS AND RESTAURANTS...
MEXICAN?
NO!
BRIAN! HOLD UP, Y' MAD SOD!
BRIGHT LIGHTS 1M.
ALL THAT IS, EXCEPT FOR ONE OF THEM. PATRICIA.
HI!
SHE SEEMED TO THINK SHE WAS BETTER THAN EVERYONE ELSE.
NOT TRUE!
A HUNGARIAN PRINCESS OR SOMETHING!
LET THEM EAT COMPLIMENTARY HOB-NOBS!
SHE'S LOVELY.
AYE.
CHEERS, PAT.
SWAPPED IN THE ROYAL NURSERY BY A NASTY NANNY!
HEH.
WAH.
SHE WOULD TAKE HER MAKE-UP OFF AFTER THE CURTAIN FELL AND THEN GO BACK TO THE HOTEL ALONE.
DAB
DAB
YOU ARE NOW ENTERING THE NIGHT

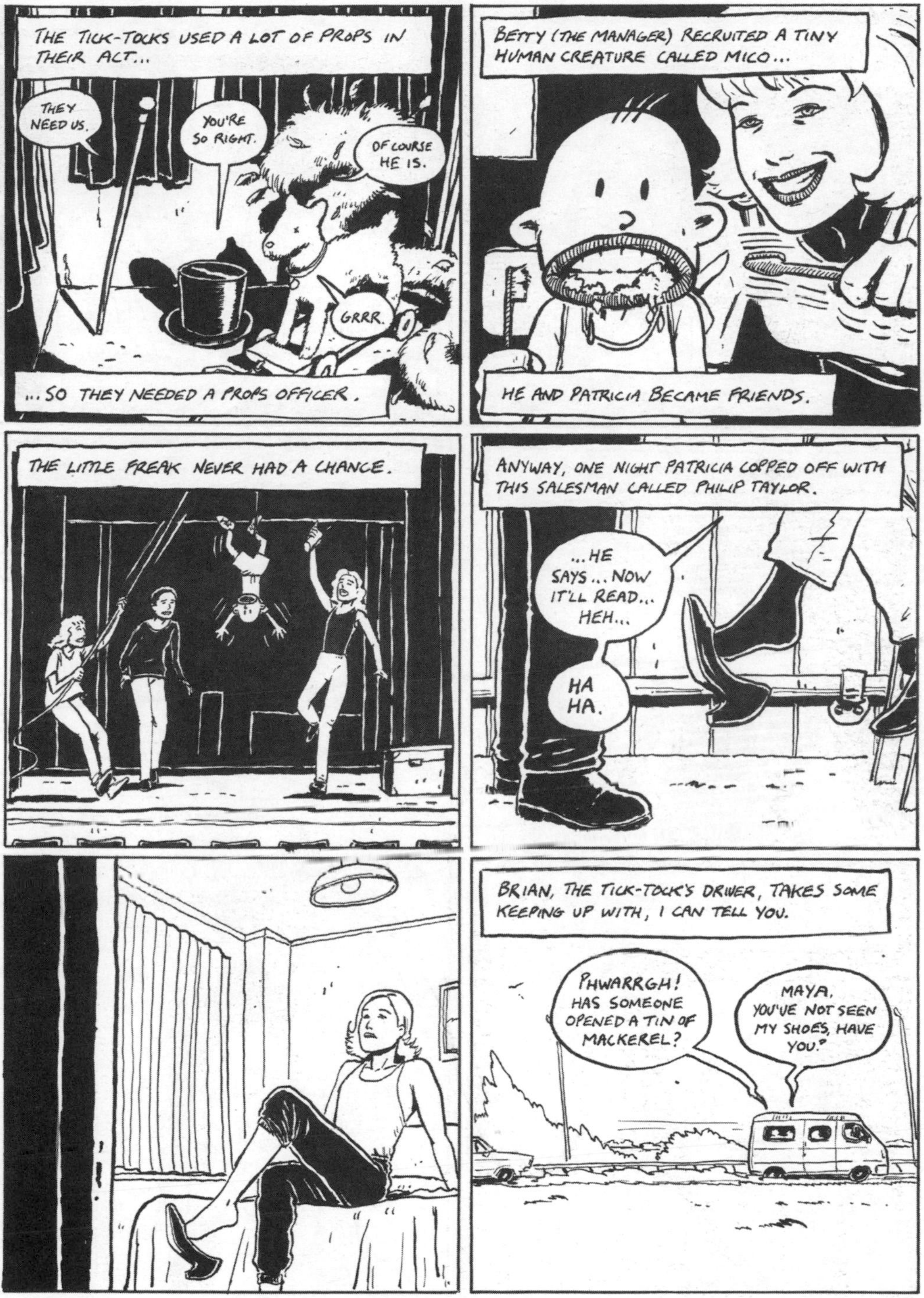
THE TICK-TOCKS USED A LOT OF PROPS IN THEIR ACT...
THEY NEED US.
YOU'RE SO RIGHT.
OF COURSE HE IS.
GRRR.
...SO THEY NEEDED A PROPS OFFICER.
BETTY (THE MANAGER) RECRUITED A TINY HUMAN CREATURE CALLED MICO...
HE AND PATRICIA BECAME FRIENDS.
THE LITTLE FREAK NEVER HAD A CHANCE.
ANYWAY, ONE NIGHT PATRICIA COPPED OFF WITH THIS SALESMAN CALLED PHILIP TAYLOR.
...HE SAYS... NOW IT'LL READ... HEH...
HA HA.
BRIAN, THE TICK-TOCK'S DRIVER, TAKES SOME KEEPING UP WITH, I CAN TELL YOU.
PHWARRGH! HAS SOMEONE OPENED A TIN OF MACKEREL?
MAYA, YOU'VE NOT SEEN MY SHOES, HAVE YOU?

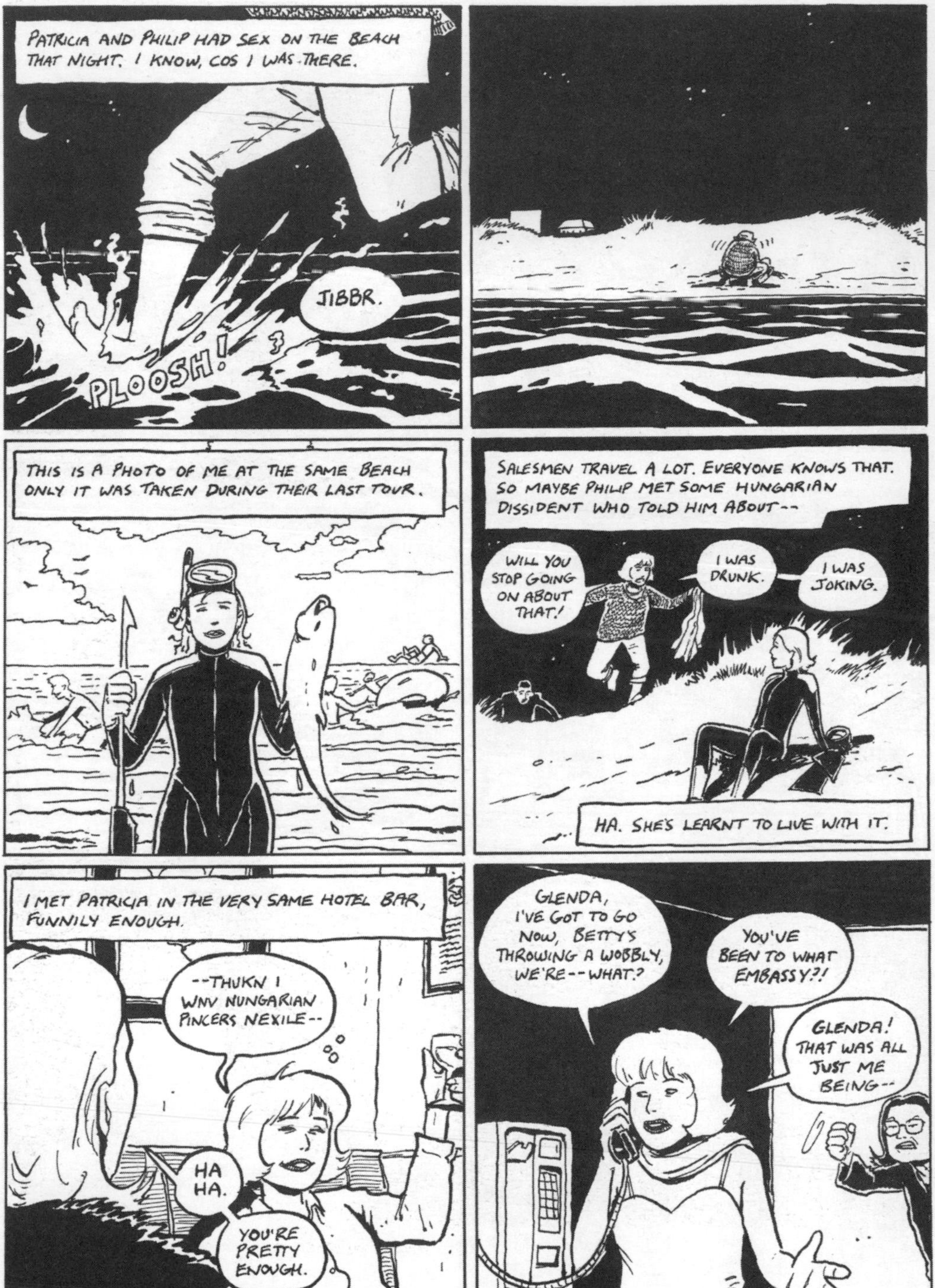
PATRICIA AND PHILIP HAD SEX ON THE BEACH THAT NIGHT. I KNOW, COS I WAS THERE.
JIBBR.
PLOOSH!
THIS IS A PHOTO OF ME AT THE SAME BEACH ONLY IT WAS TAKEN DURING THEIR LAST TOUR.
SALESMEN TRAVEL A LOT. EVERYONE KNOWS THAT. SO MAYBE PHILIP MET SOME HUNGARIAN DISSIDENT WHO TOLD HIM ABOUT--
WILL YOU STOP GOING ON ABOUT THAT!
I WAS DRUNK.
I WAS JOKING.
HA. SHE'S LEARNT TO LIVE WITH IT.
I MET PATRICIA IN THE VERY SAME HOTEL BAR, FUNNILY ENOUGH.
--THUKN I WNV NUNGARIAN PINCERS NEXILE--
HA HA.
YOU'RE PRETTY ENOUGH.
GLENDA, I'VE GOT TO GO NOW, BETTY'S THROWING A WOBBLY, WE'RE--WHAT?
YOU'VE BEEN TO WHAT EMBASSY?!
GLENDA! THAT WAS ALL JUST ME BEING--

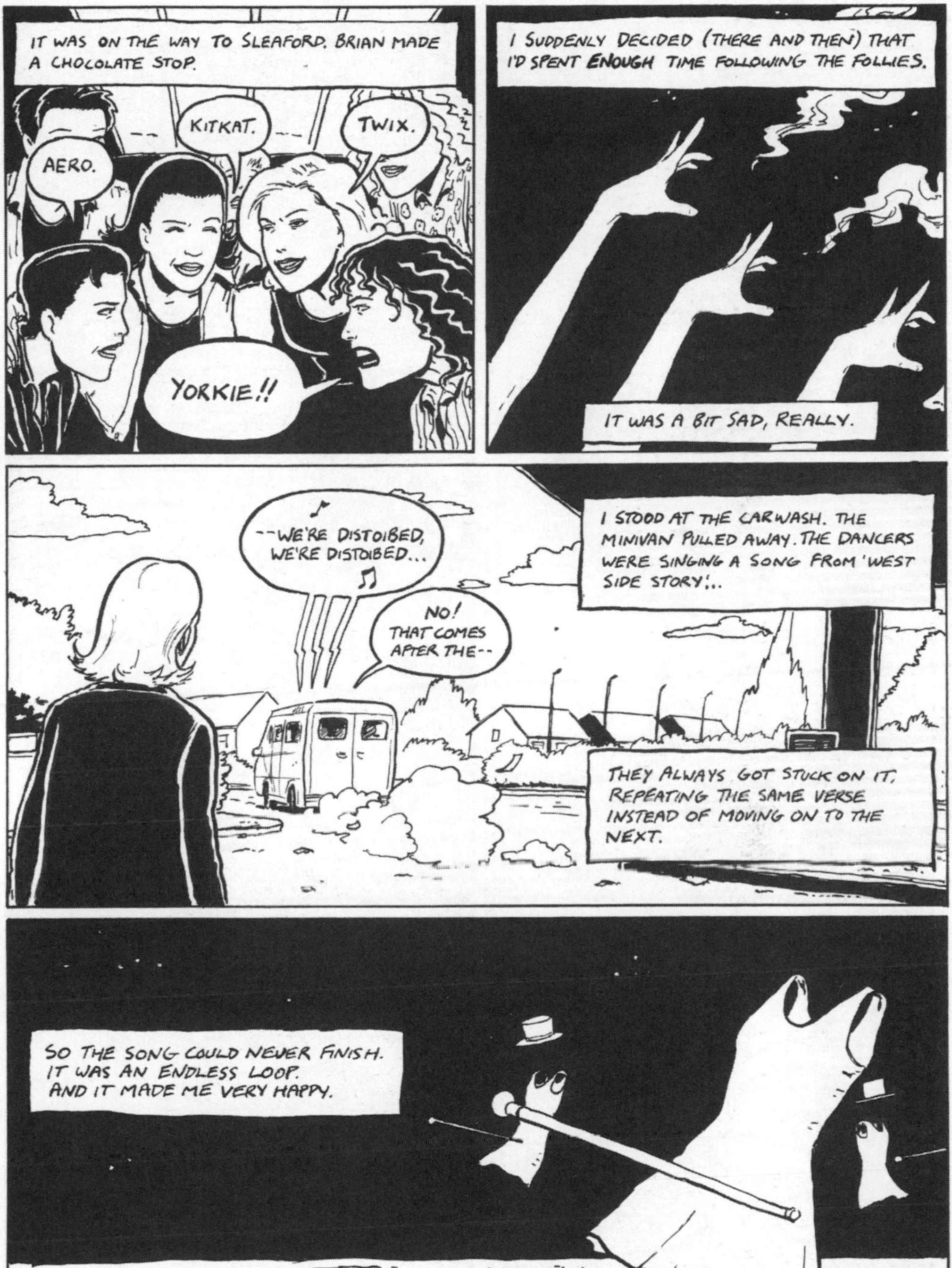

IT WAS ON THE WAY TO SLEAFORD. BRIAN MADE A CHOCOLATE STOP.
AERO.
KITKAT.
TWIX.
YORKIE!!
I SUDDENLY DECIDED (THERE AND THEN) THAT I'D SPENT ENOUGH TIME FOLLOWING THE FOLLIES.
IT WAS A BIT SAD, REALLY.
I STOOD AT THE CARWASH. THE MINIVAN PULLED AWAY. THE DANCERS WERE SINGING A SONG FROM 'WEST SIDE STORY'...
--WE'RE DISTOIBED, WE'RE DISTOIBED...
NO! THAT COMES AFTER THE--
THEY ALWAYS GOT STUCK ON IT, REPEATING THE SAME VERSE INSTEAD OF MOVING ON TO THE NEXT.
SO THE SONG COULD NEVER FINISH. IT WAS AN ENDLESS LOOP. AND IT MADE ME VERY HAPPY.

END.

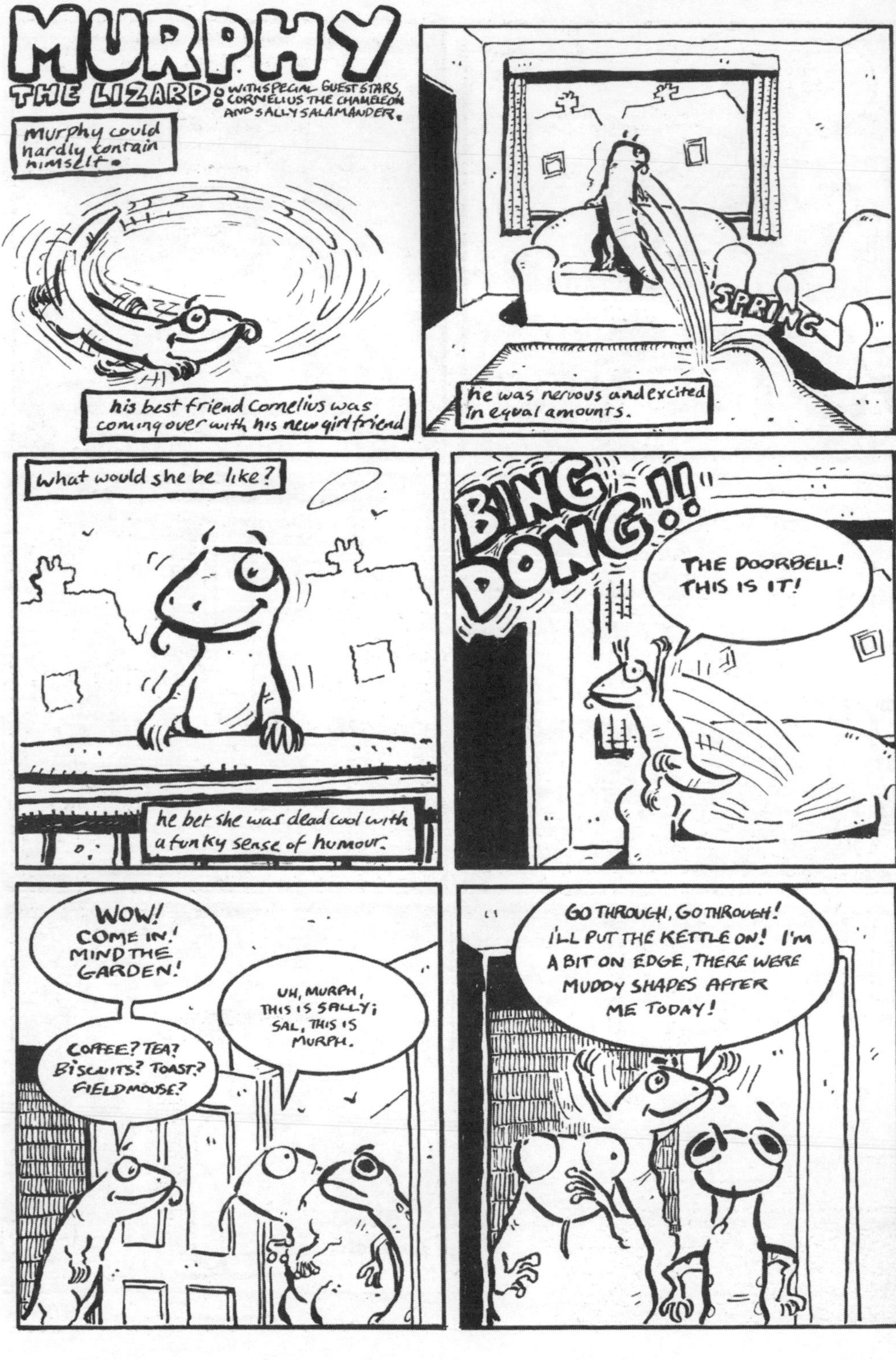
MURPHY THE LIZARD:
WITH SPECIAL GUEST STARS, CORNELIUS THE CHAMELEON AND SALLY SALAMANDER.
murphy could hardly contain himself.
his best friend Cornelius was coming over with his new girl friend
SPRING
he was nervous and excited in equal amounts.
what would she be like?
he bet she was dead cool with a funky sense of humour.
BING DONG!!
THE DOORBELL! THIS IS IT!
WOW! COME IN! MIND THE GARDEN!
COFFEE? TEA? BISCUITS? TOAST? FIELDMOUSE?
UH, MURPH, THIS IS SALLY; SAL, THIS IS MURPH.
GO THROUGH, GO THROUGH! I'LL PUT THE KETTLE ON! I'M A BIT ON EDGE, THERE WERE MUDDY SHADES AFTER ME TODAY!

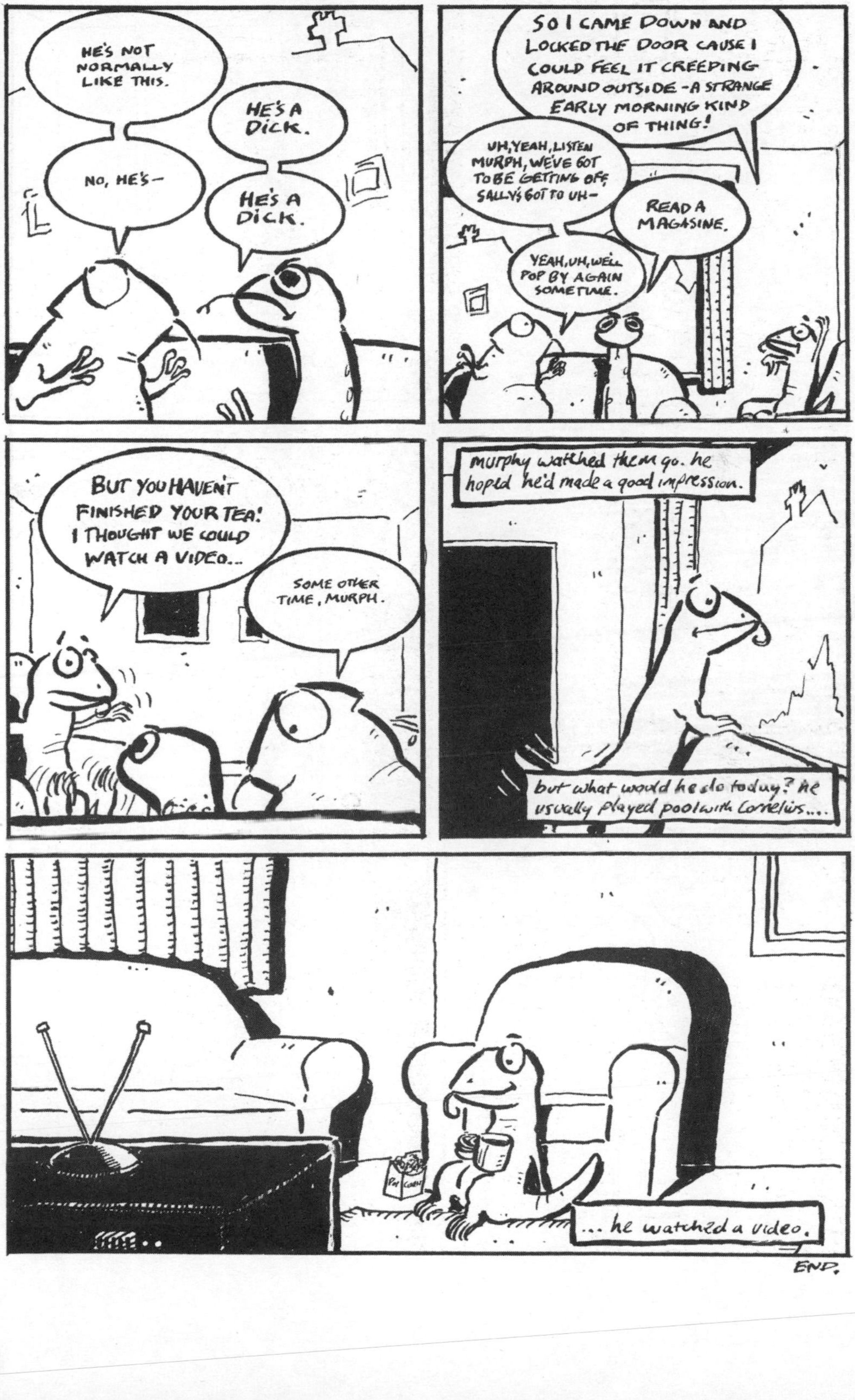
HE'S NOT NORMALLY LIKE THIS.
HE'S A DICK.
NO, HE'S—
HE'S A DICK.
SO I CAME DOWN AND LOCKED THE DOOR CAUSE I COULD FEEL IT CREEPING AROUND OUTSIDE - A STRANGE EARLY MORNING KIND OF THING!
UH, YEAH, LISTEN MURPH, WE'VE GOT TO BE GETTING OFF, SALLY'S GOT TO UH—
READ A MAGASINE.
YEAH, UH, WELL POP BY AGAIN SOMETIME.
BUT YOU HAVEN'T FINISHED YOUR TEA! I THOUGHT WE COULD WATCH A VIDEO...
SOME OTHER TIME, MURPH.
murphy watched them go. he hoped he'd made a good impression.
but what would he do today? he usually played pool with Cornelius....
... he watched a video.
END.

Oscar Zarate, with Susan Catherine

WALKING WITH MELANIE KLEIN
Zero Zero #24, Fantagraphics, 1998

A student of Breccia alongside compatriot José Muñoz, Argentinean comics maestro Oscar Zarate has been a collaborator of Alan Moore, Richard Appignanesi, the comedian Alexei Sayle, and Carlos Sampayo.

"*Walking with Melanie Klein* is the outcome of a cluster of events. One was meeting Susan Catherine (please get in touch with me, wherever you are). Second was the launch of the fantastic bimonthly magazine *Zero Zero*. Around that time I was working on a picture book about Melanie Klein's writings, as part of a series called 'Introducing'.

"Last October SelfMadeHero published my first solo graphic novel, *The Park*. Right now, I'm working on another concerning Sigmund Freud's first clinical case of hysteria. I'm also gradually developing my next solo work, a story about three friends ..." – OZ

Melanie Klein was one of the founding figures of psychoanalysis. Exploring how early mental processes built up a person's inner emotional world, she posited that, every day, adults should take the time to visit with their childhood selves.

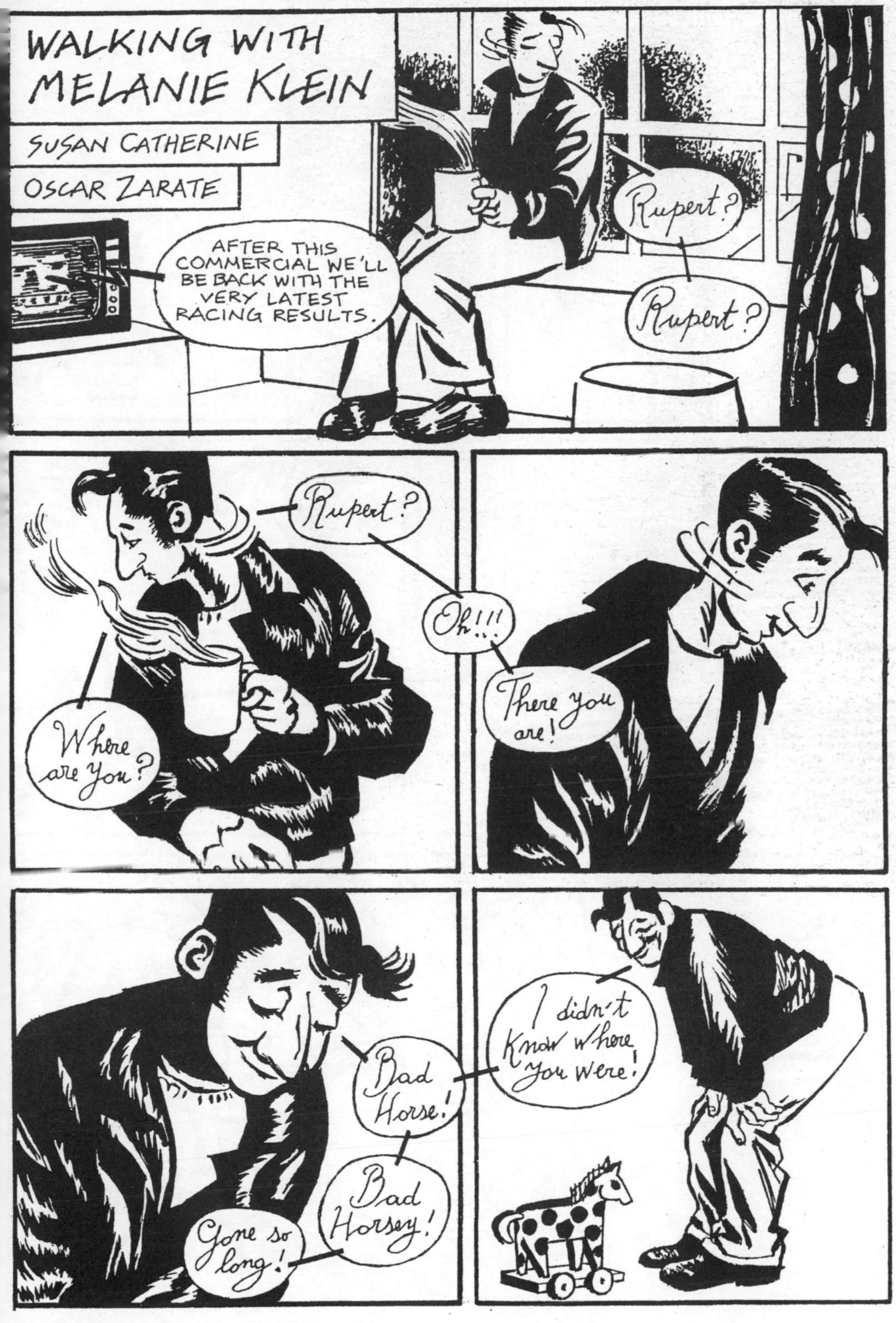
WALKING WITH MELANIE KLEIN
SUSAN CATHERINE
OSCAR ZARATE
AFTER THIS COMMERCIAL WE'LL BE BACK WITH THE VERY LATEST RACING RESULTS.
Rupert?
Rupert?
Rupert?
Where are you?
Oh!!!
There you are!
Bad Horse!
Bad Horsey!
Gone so long!
I didn't know where you were!

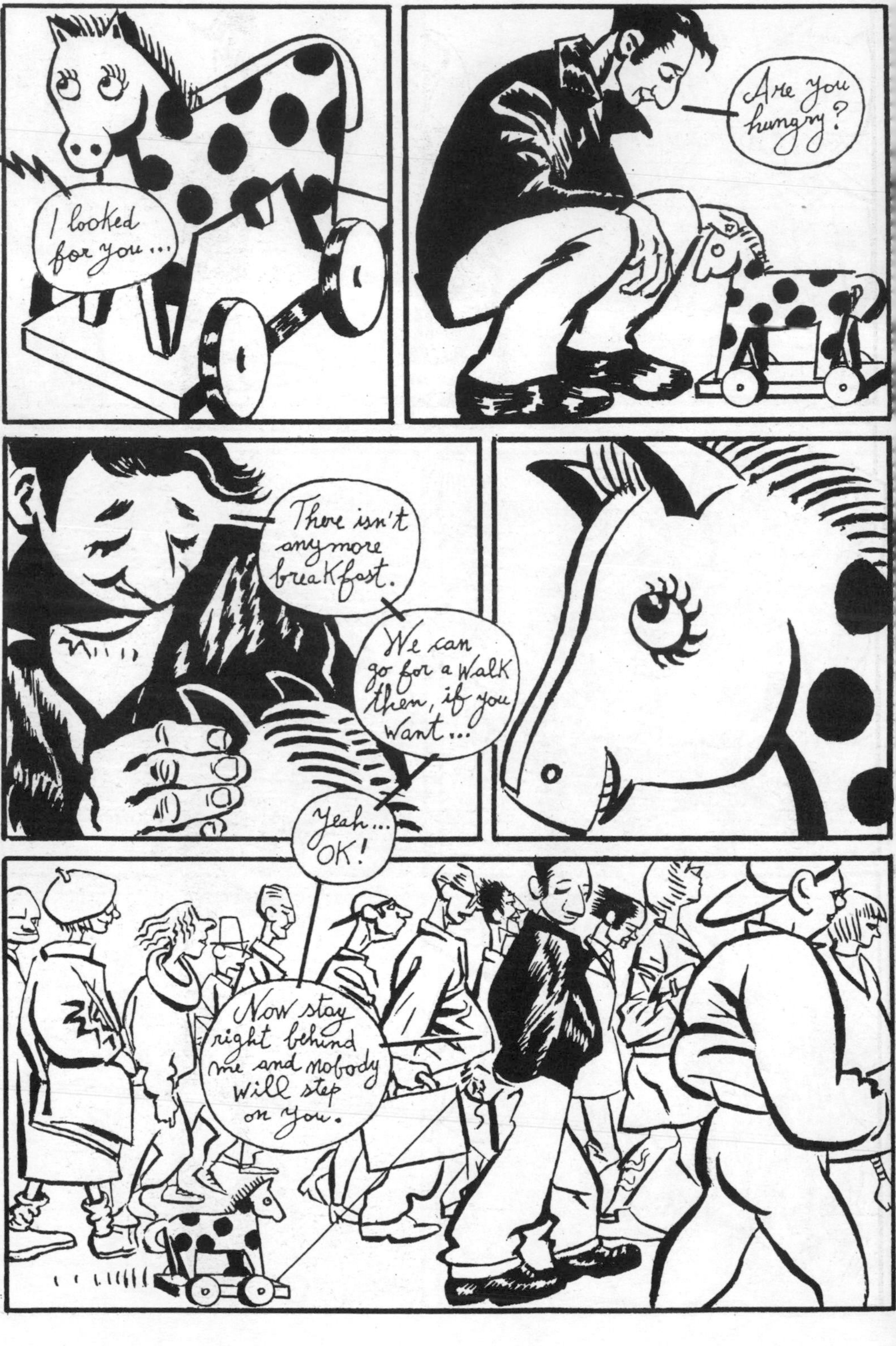
I looked for you...
Are you hungry?
There isn't any more breakfast.
We can go for a walk then, if you want...
Yeah... OK!
Now stay right behind me and nobody will step on you.

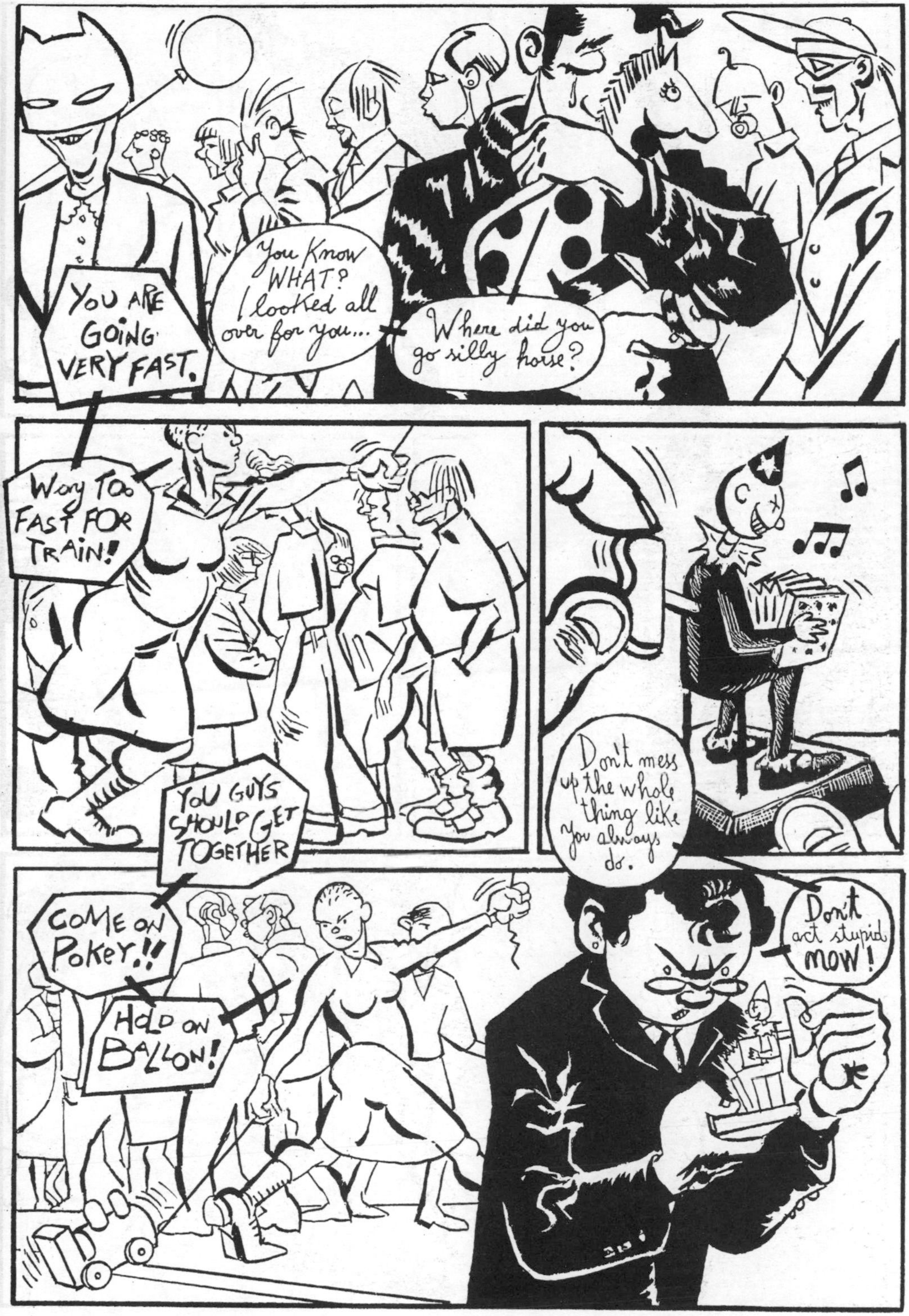
YOU ARE GOING VERY FAST.
You Know WHAT? I looked all over for you...
Where did you go silly horse?
Way TOO FAST FOR TRAIN!
Don't mess up the whole thing like you always do.
YOU GUYS SHOULD GET TOGETHER
COME ON POKEY!!
HOLD ON BALLON!
Don't act stupid NOW!

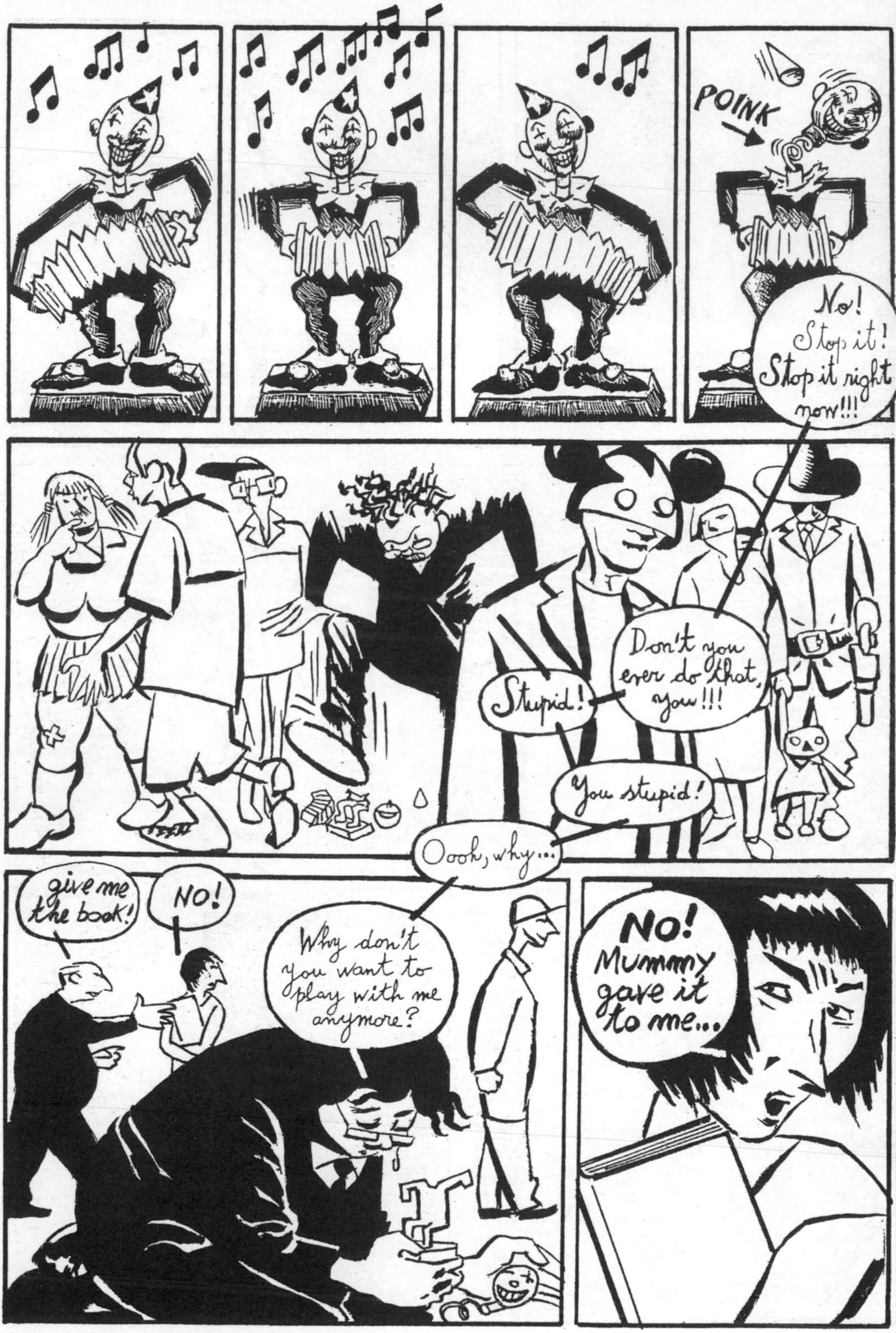
POINK
No! Stop it! Stop it right now!!!
Don't you ever do that, you!!!
Stupid!
You stupid!
Oooh, why...
give me the book!
NO!
Why don't you want to play with me anymore?
NO! Mummy gave it to me...

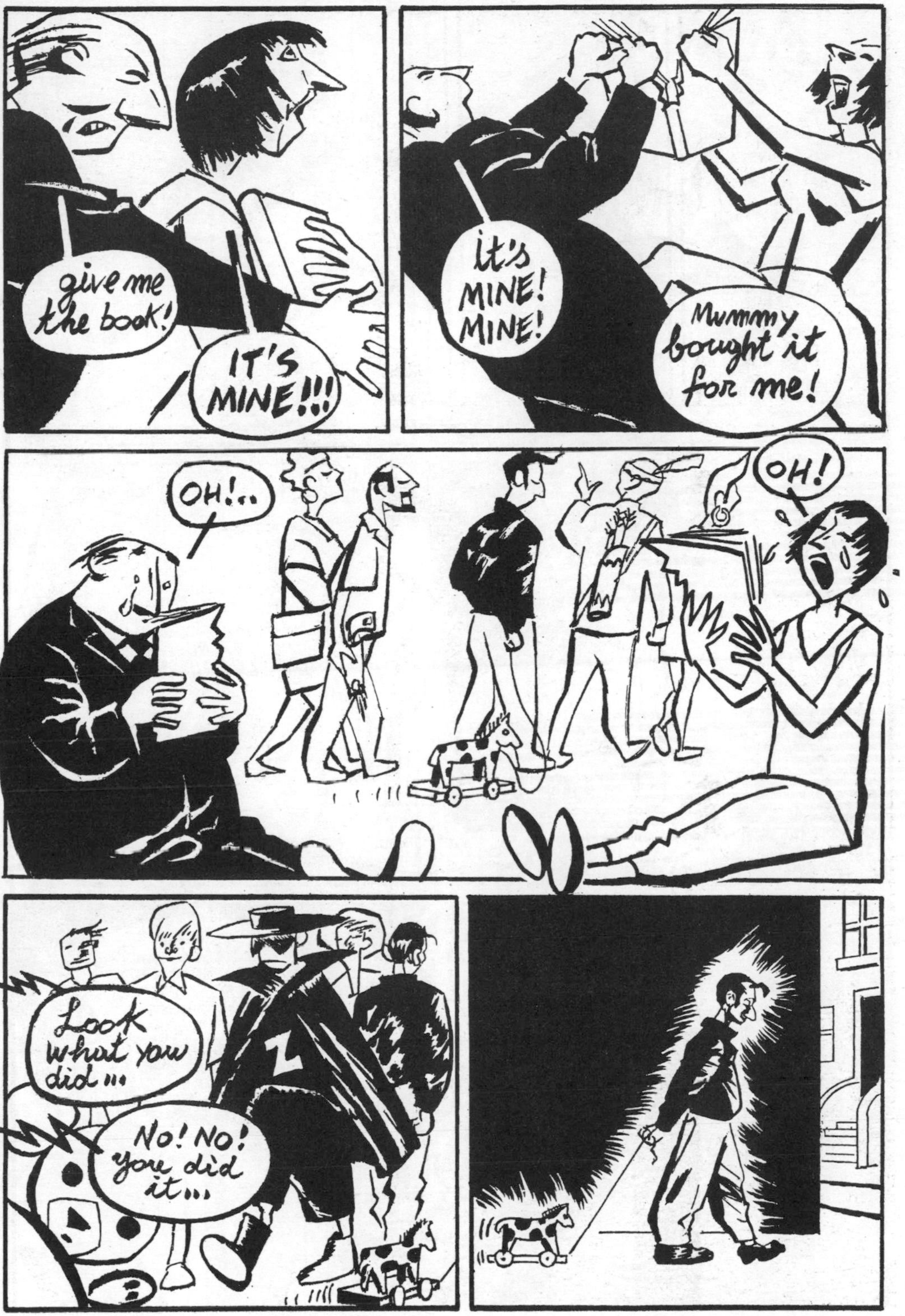
give me the book!
IT'S MINE!!!
it's MINE! MINE!
Mummy bought it for me!
OH!..
OH!
Look what you did...
No! No! you did it...

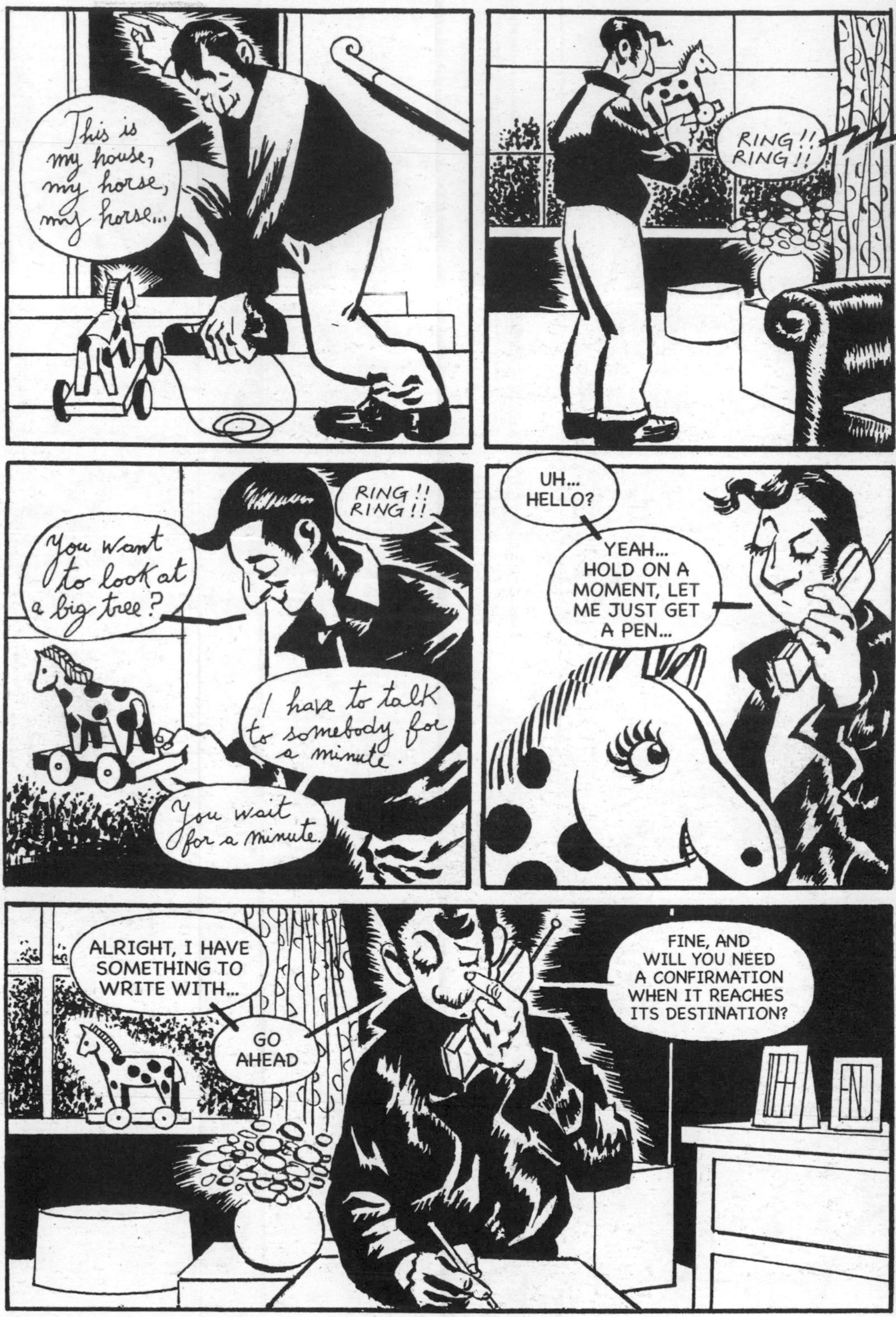

This is my house, my horse, my horse...
RING!! RING!!
RING!! RING!!
You want to look at a big tree?
I have to talk to somebody for a minute.
You wait for a minute.
UH... HELLO?
YEAH... HOLD ON A MOMENT, LET ME JUST GET A PEN...
ALRIGHT, I HAVE SOMETHING TO WRITE WITH...
GO AHEAD
FINE, AND WILL YOU NEED A CONFIRMATION WHEN IT REACHES ITS DESTINATION?

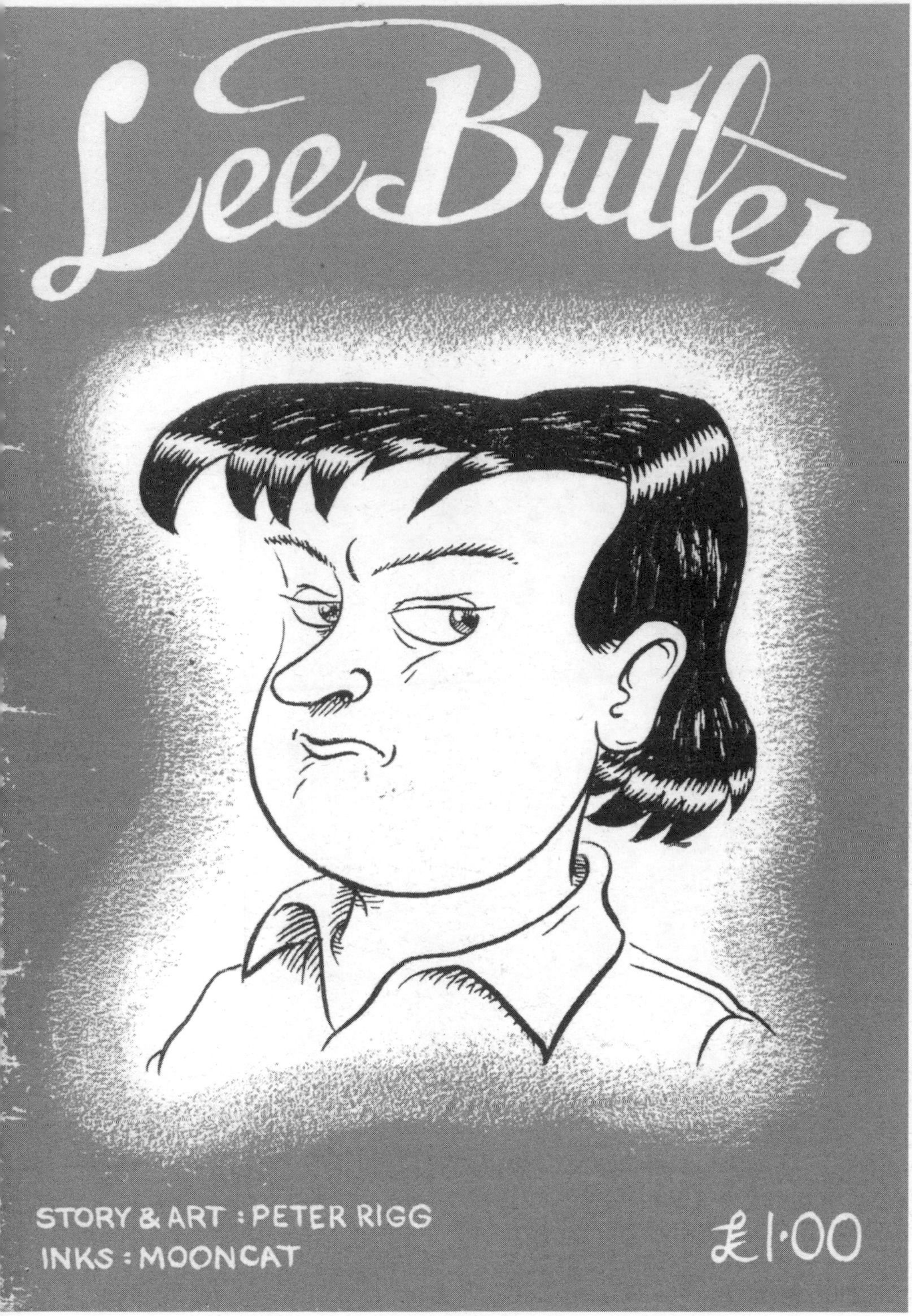
Lee Butler
STORY & ART : PETER RIGG
INKS : MOONCAT
£1·00

Peter Rigg (story/pencils), with
Paul "Mooncat" Schroeder (inks)

LEE & JENNY BUTLER
Self-published in two issues, 1993–94

"The inspiration for Lee Butler was my interest in
psychology, which was growing apace at the time
I wrote it. It is, I suppose, largely a psychological
strip. This interest led me subsequently to train as
a psychotherapist, which is my job now. I have been
working for the last seven years in private practice at a
psychotherapy centre in Manchester.

"I still write and draw cartoons. In fact I'm just about to
publish a collection of the cartoon strip I produce for the
journal *Socialist Standard*, which, published continuously
since 1904, predates the Labour Party. The strip is called
Free Lunch because the *Standard* advocates a moneyless
society." – PR

"I really can't remember how it all started – [comix
review organ] *ZUM!* will have been responsible for
introducing me to Peter's stuff and I could see so much
life in it. We corresponded for some time, and Peter was
gracious enough to share Lee Butler with me. I had a lot
of faith in it, I wanted a good standard of presentation.
I'm sure I got a chance through Andy Roberts to use a
risograph at some point. The print run will have been
small, but I think there were a couple of reprints from my
efforts (selling Sale Or Return to comics shops and other
distributors). Now I do a job not related to art, and draw –
I enjoy drawing." – PS

www.freelunchcartoons.com
www.comix.org.uk/mooncat

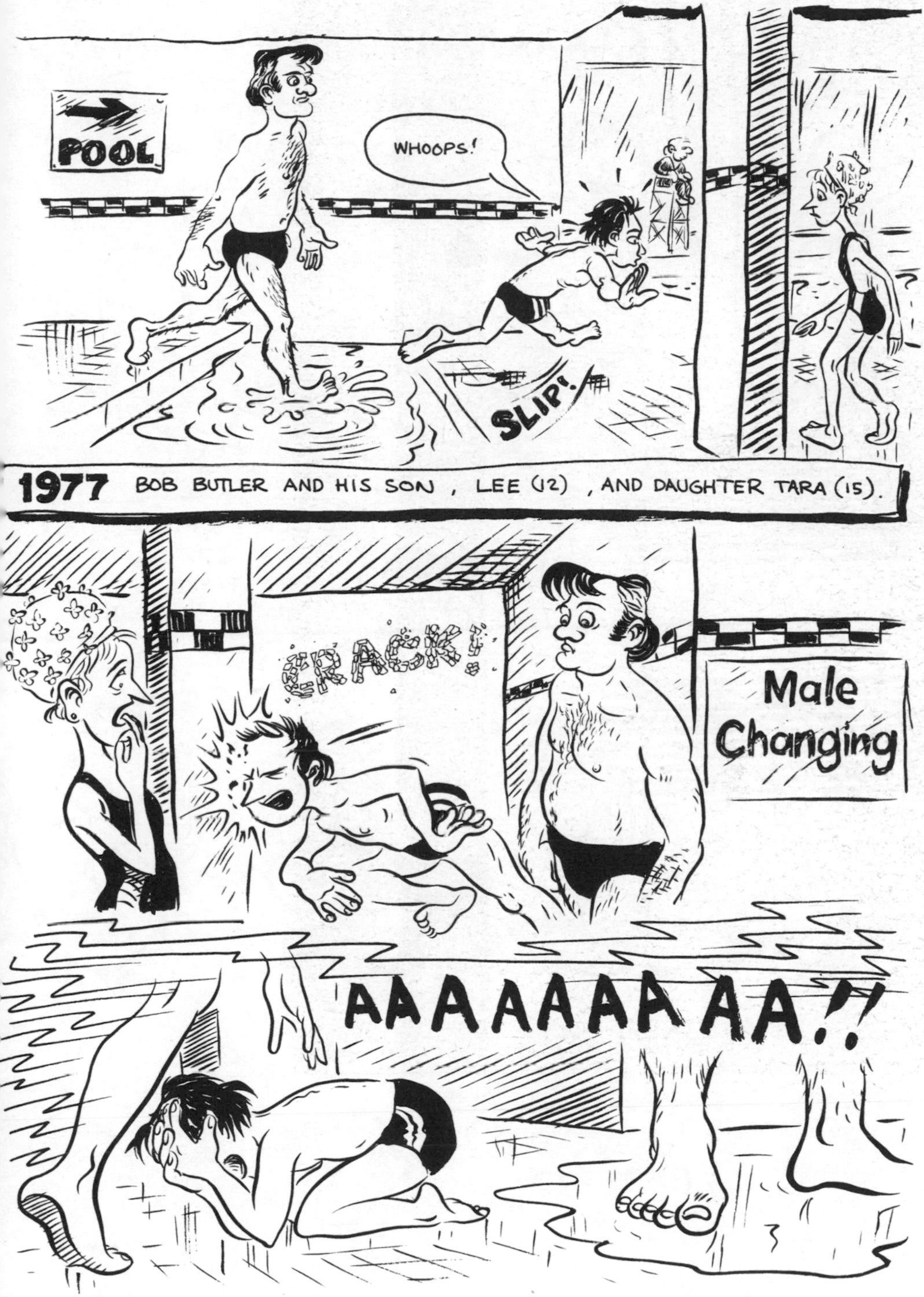
POOL
WHOOPS!
SLIP!
1977 BOB BUTLER AND HIS SON, LEE (12), AND DAUGHTER TARA (15).
CRACK!
Male Changing
AAAAAAA AA!!

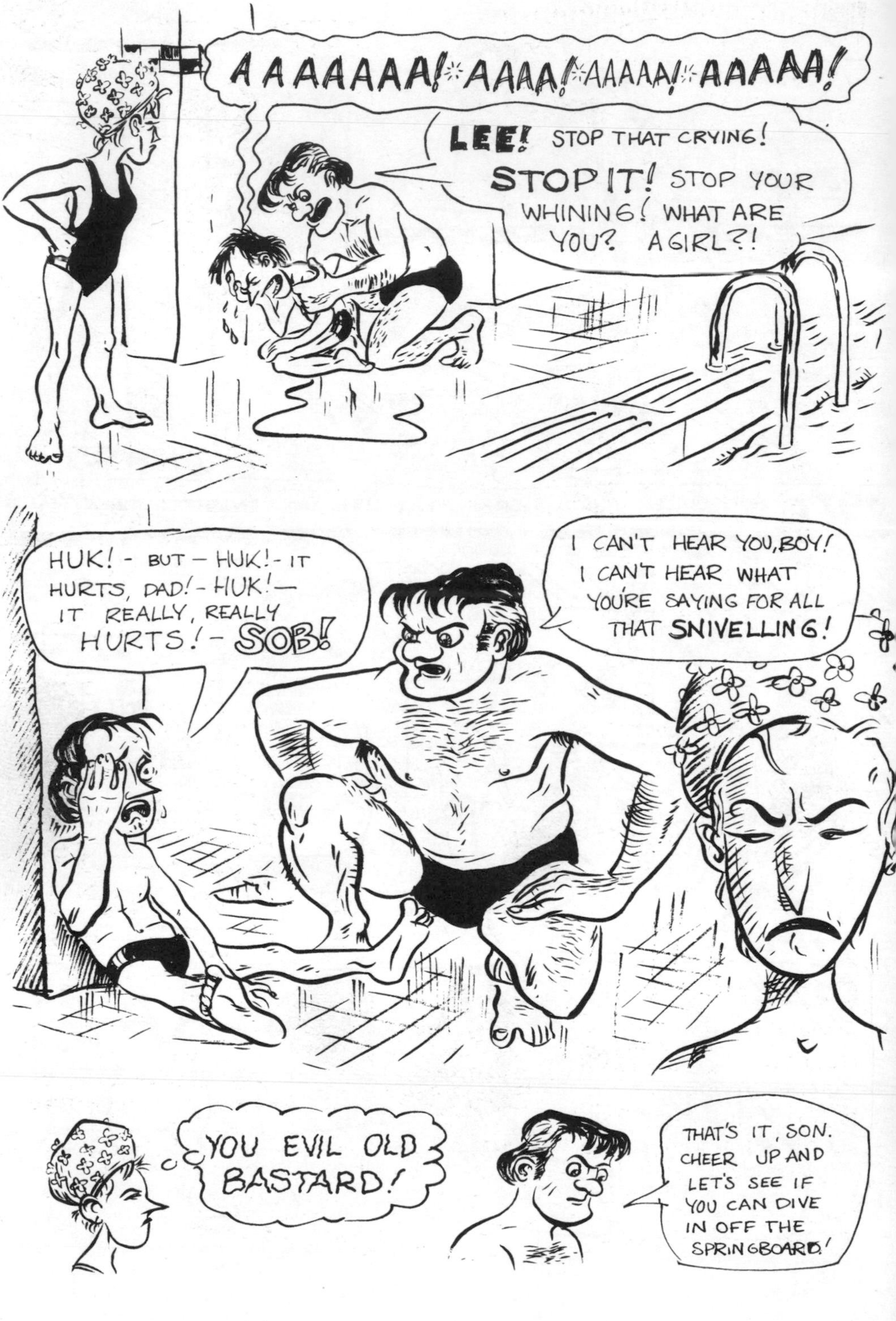
AAAAAAA! AAAA! AAAAA! AAAAA!
LEE! STOP THAT CRYING! STOP IT! STOP YOUR WHINING! WHAT ARE YOU? A GIRL?!
HUK! - BUT - HUK! - IT HURTS, DAD! - HUK! - IT REALLY, REALLY HURTS! - SOB!
I CAN'T HEAR YOU, BOY! I CAN'T HEAR WHAT YOU'RE SAYING FOR ALL THAT SNIVELLING!
YOU EVIL OLD BASTARD!
THAT'S IT, SON. CHEER UP AND LET'S SEE IF YOU CAN DIVE IN OFF THE SPRINGBOARD!

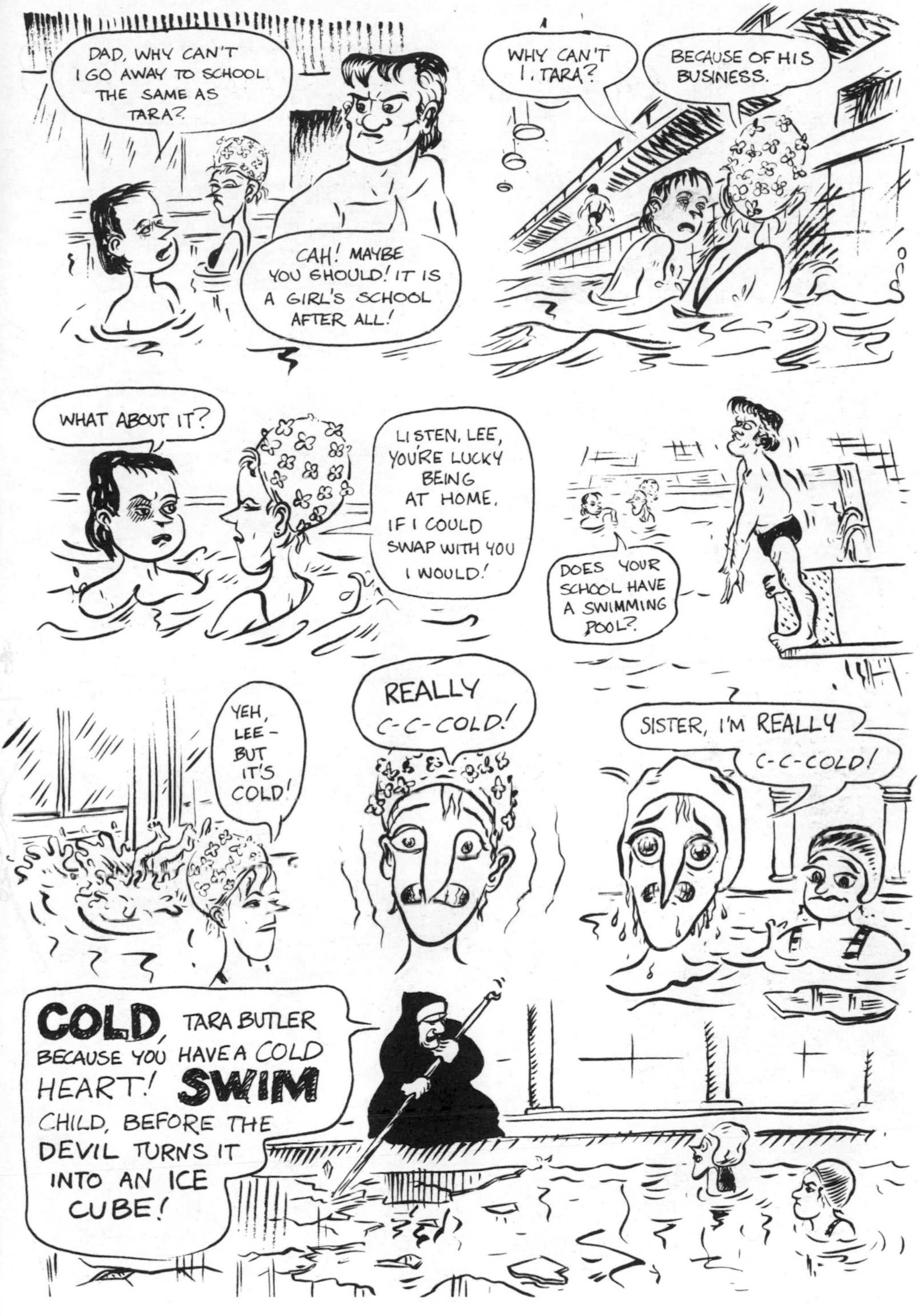
DAD, WHY CAN'T I GO AWAY TO SCHOOL THE SAME AS TARA?
CAH! MAYBE YOU SHOULD! IT IS A GIRL'S SCHOOL AFTER ALL!
WHY CAN'T I, TARA?
BECAUSE OF HIS BUSINESS.
WHAT ABOUT IT?
LISTEN, LEE, YOU'RE LUCKY BEING AT HOME. IF I COULD SWAP WITH YOU I WOULD!
DOES YOUR SCHOOL HAVE A SWIMMING POOL?
YEH, LEE- BUT IT'S COLD!
REALLY C-C-COLD!
SISTER, I'M REALLY C-C-COLD!
COLD, TARA BUTLER BECAUSE YOU HAVE A COLD HEART! SWIM CHILD, BEFORE THE DEVIL TURNS IT INTO AN ICE CUBE!

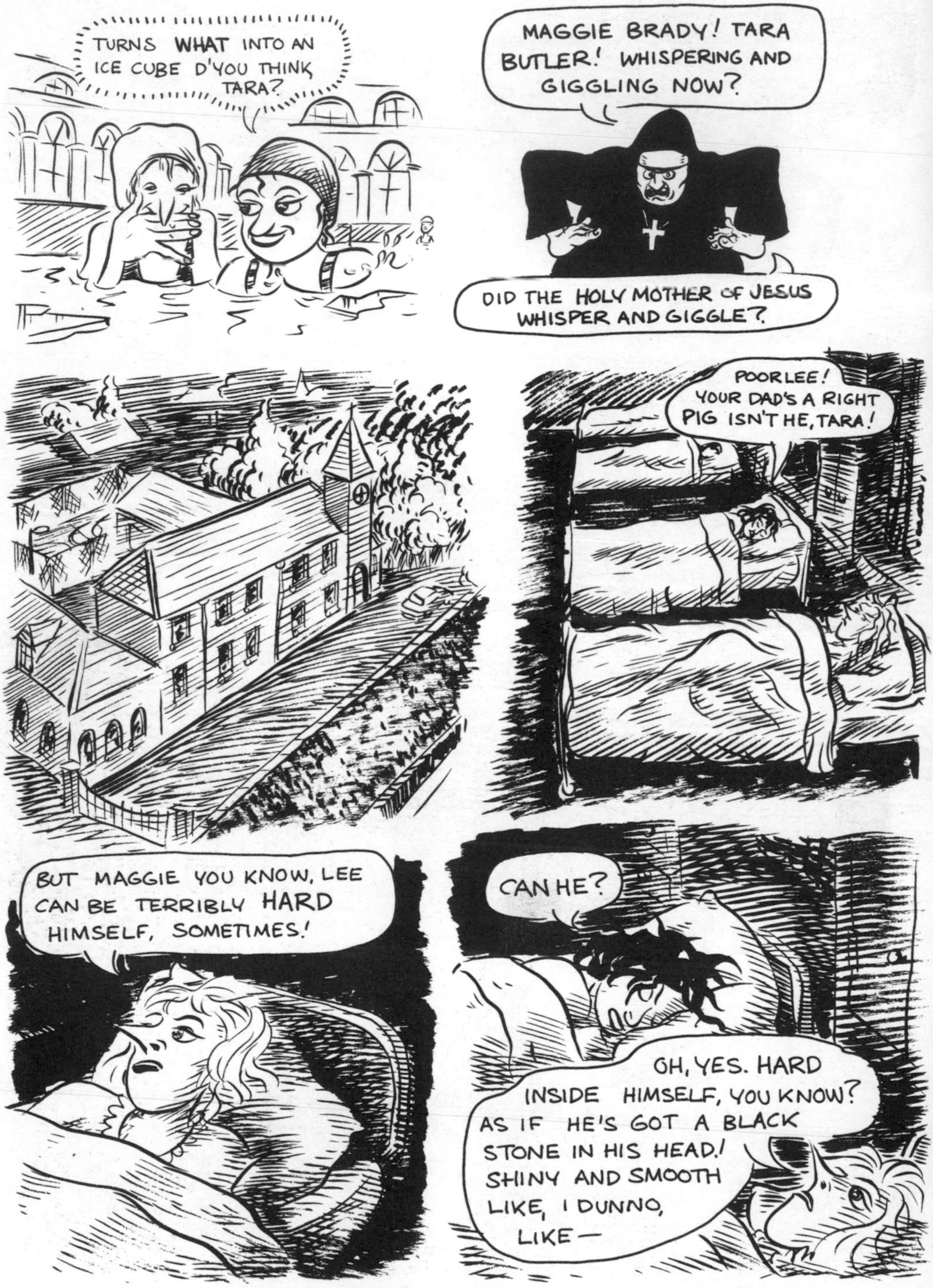
TURNS WHAT INTO AN ICE CUBE D'YOU THINK TARA?
MAGGIE BRADY! TARA BUTLER! WHISPERING AND GIGGLING NOW?
DID THE HOLY MOTHER OF JESUS WHISPER AND GIGGLE?
POOR LEE! YOUR DAD'S A RIGHT PIG ISN'T HE, TARA!
BUT MAGGIE YOU KNOW, LEE CAN BE TERRIBLY HARD HIMSELF, SOMETIMES!
CAN HE?
OH, YES. HARD INSIDE HIMSELF, YOU KNOW? AS IF HE'S GOT A BLACK STONE IN HIS HEAD! SHINY AND SMOOTH LIKE, I DUNNO, LIKE—

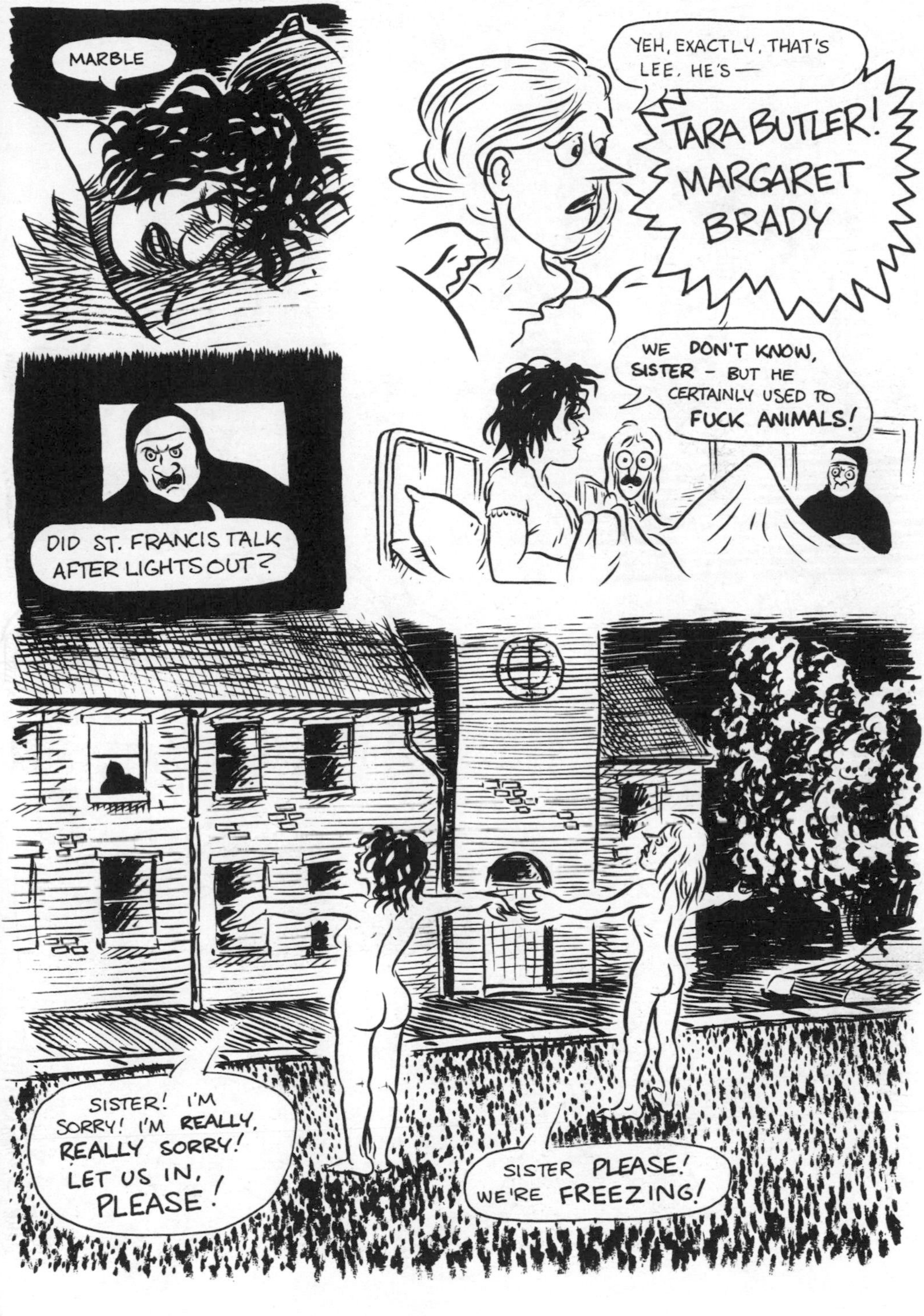
MARBLE
YEH, EXACTLY, THAT'S LEE, HE'S—
TARA BUTLER! MARGARET BRADY
DID ST. FRANCIS TALK AFTER LIGHTS OUT?
WE DON'T KNOW, SISTER - BUT HE CERTAINLY USED TO FUCK ANIMALS!
SISTER! I'M SORRY! I'M REALLY, REALLY SORRY! LET US IN, PLEASE!
SISTER PLEASE! WE'RE FREEZING!

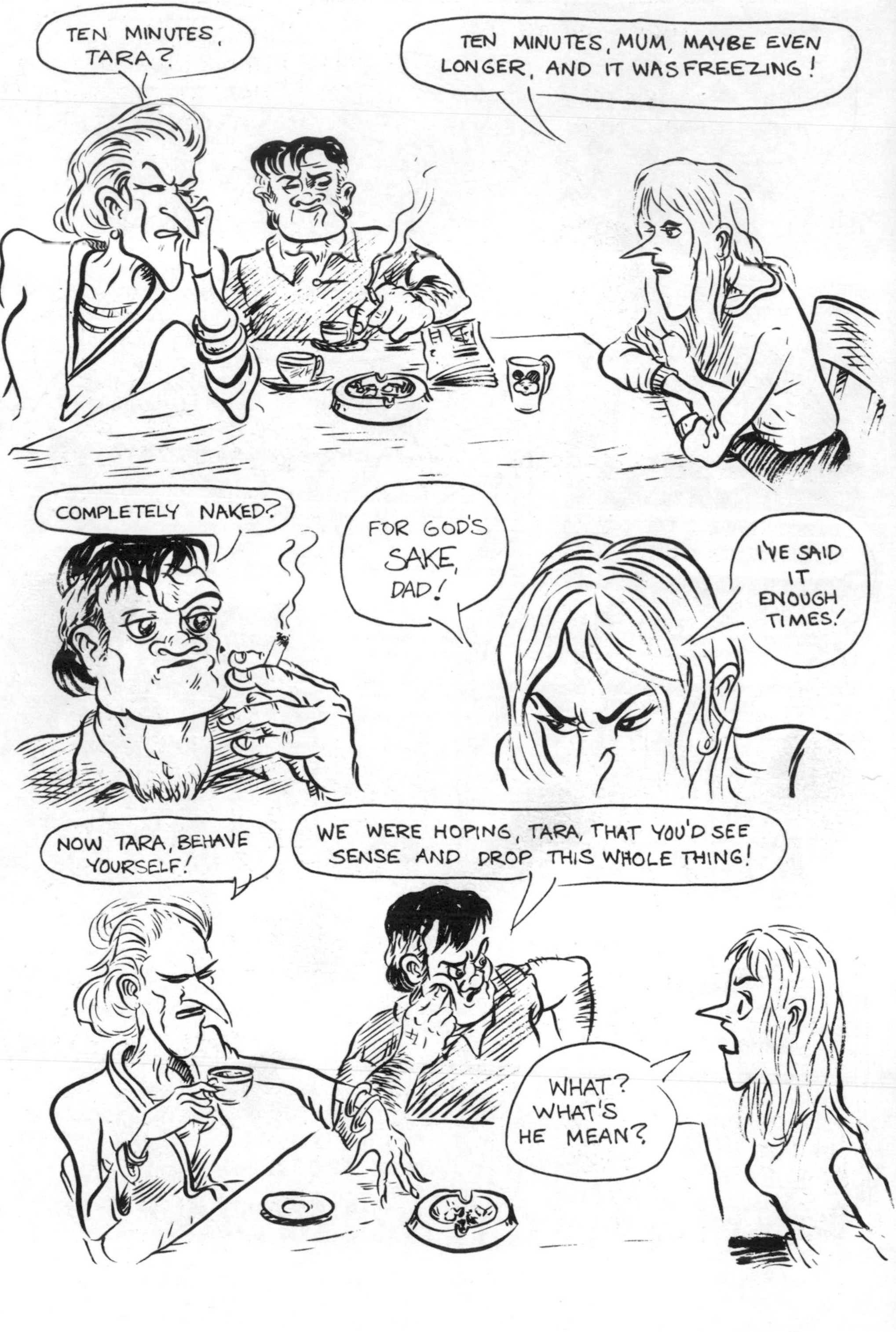
TEN MINUTES, TARA?
TEN MINUTES, MUM, MAYBE EVEN LONGER, AND IT WAS FREEZING!
COMPLETELY NAKED?
FOR GOD'S SAKE, DAD!
I'VE SAID IT ENOUGH TIMES!
NOW TARA, BEHAVE YOURSELF!
WE WERE HOPING, TARA, THAT YOU'D SEE SENSE AND DROP THIS WHOLE THING!
WHAT? WHAT'S HE MEAN?

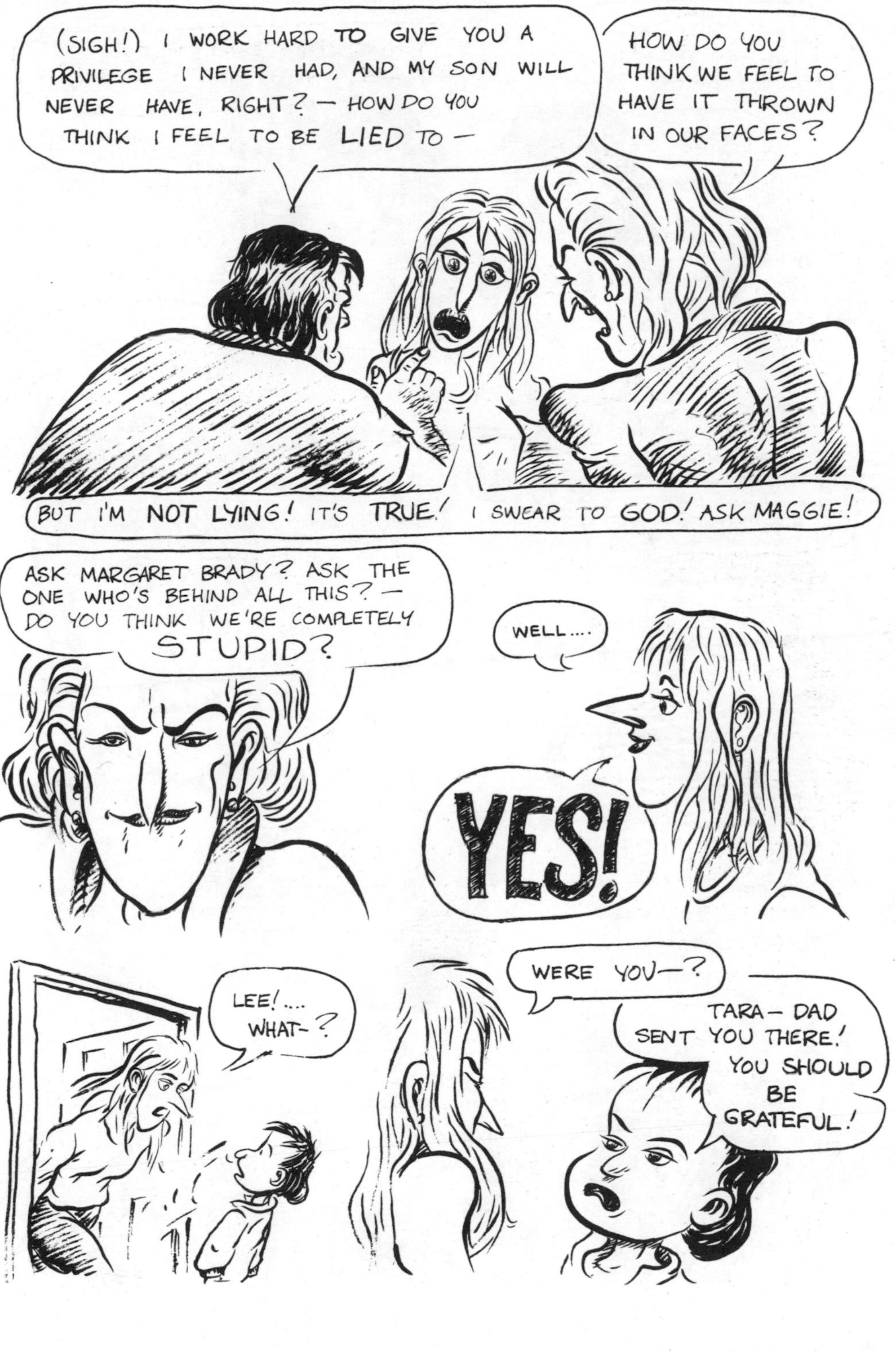
(SIGH!) I WORK HARD TO GIVE YOU A PRIVILEGE I NEVER HAD, AND MY SON WILL NEVER HAVE, RIGHT? — HOW DO YOU THINK I FEEL TO BE LIED TO —
HOW DO YOU THINK WE FEEL TO HAVE IT THROWN IN OUR FACES?
BUT I'M NOT LYING! IT'S TRUE! I SWEAR TO GOD! ASK MAGGIE!
ASK MARGARET BRADY? ASK THE ONE WHO'S BEHIND ALL THIS? — DO YOU THINK WE'RE COMPLETELY STUPID?
WELL....
YES!
LEE!.... WHAT-?
WERE YOU—?
TARA— DAD SENT YOU THERE! YOU SHOULD BE GRATEFUL!

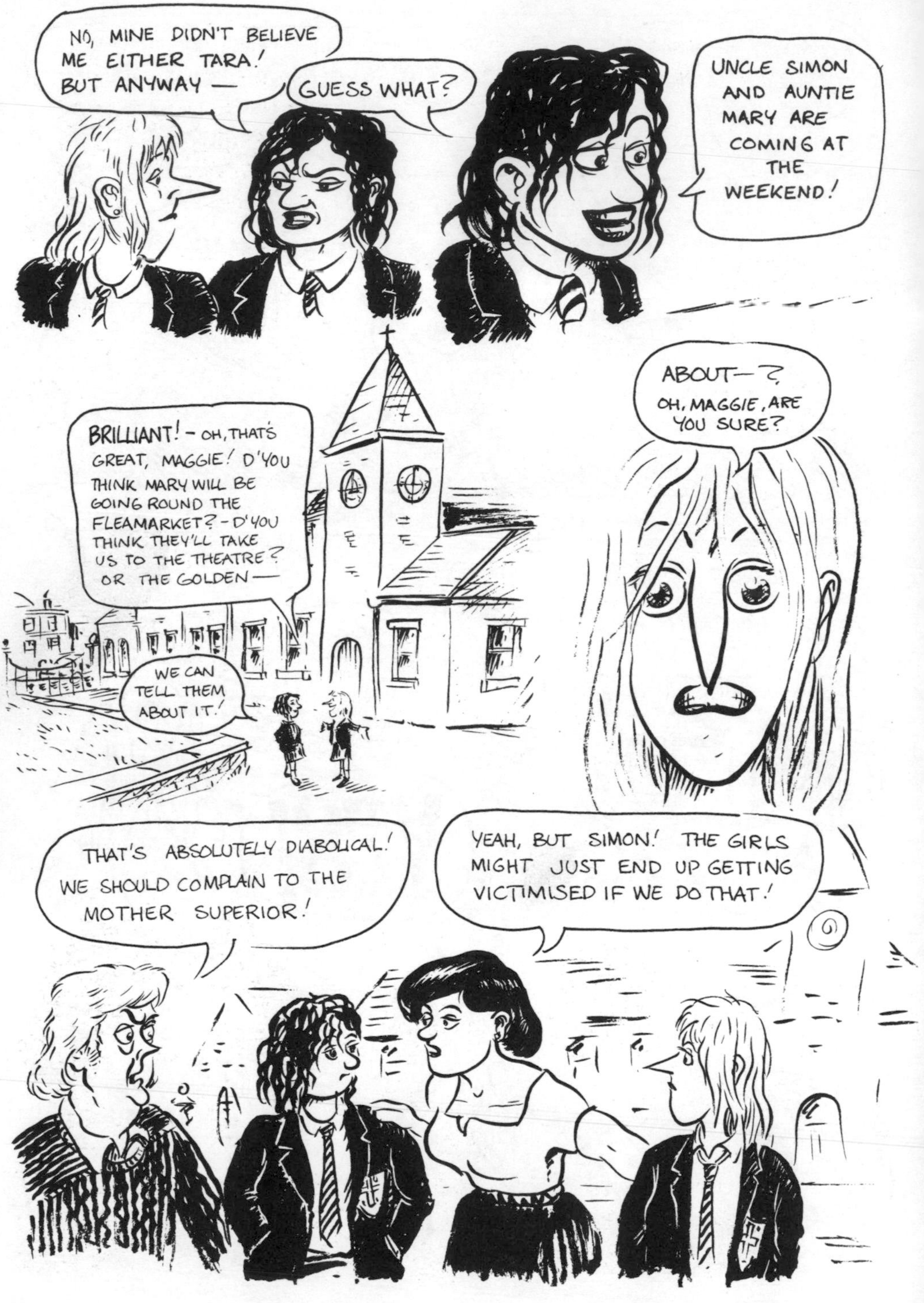
NO, MINE DIDN'T BELIEVE ME EITHER TARA! BUT ANYWAY —
GUESS WHAT?
UNCLE SIMON AND AUNTIE MARY ARE COMING AT THE WEEKEND!
BRILLIANT! – OH, THAT'S GREAT, MAGGIE! D'YOU THINK MARY WILL BE GOING ROUND THE FLEAMARKET? – D'YOU THINK THEY'LL TAKE US TO THE THEATRE? OR THE GOLDEN —
WE CAN TELL THEM ABOUT IT!
ABOUT—? OH, MAGGIE, ARE YOU SURE?
THAT'S ABSOLUTELY DIABOLICAL! WE SHOULD COMPLAIN TO THE MOTHER SUPERIOR!
YEAH, BUT SIMON! THE GIRLS MIGHT JUST END UP GETTING VICTIMISED IF WE DO THAT!

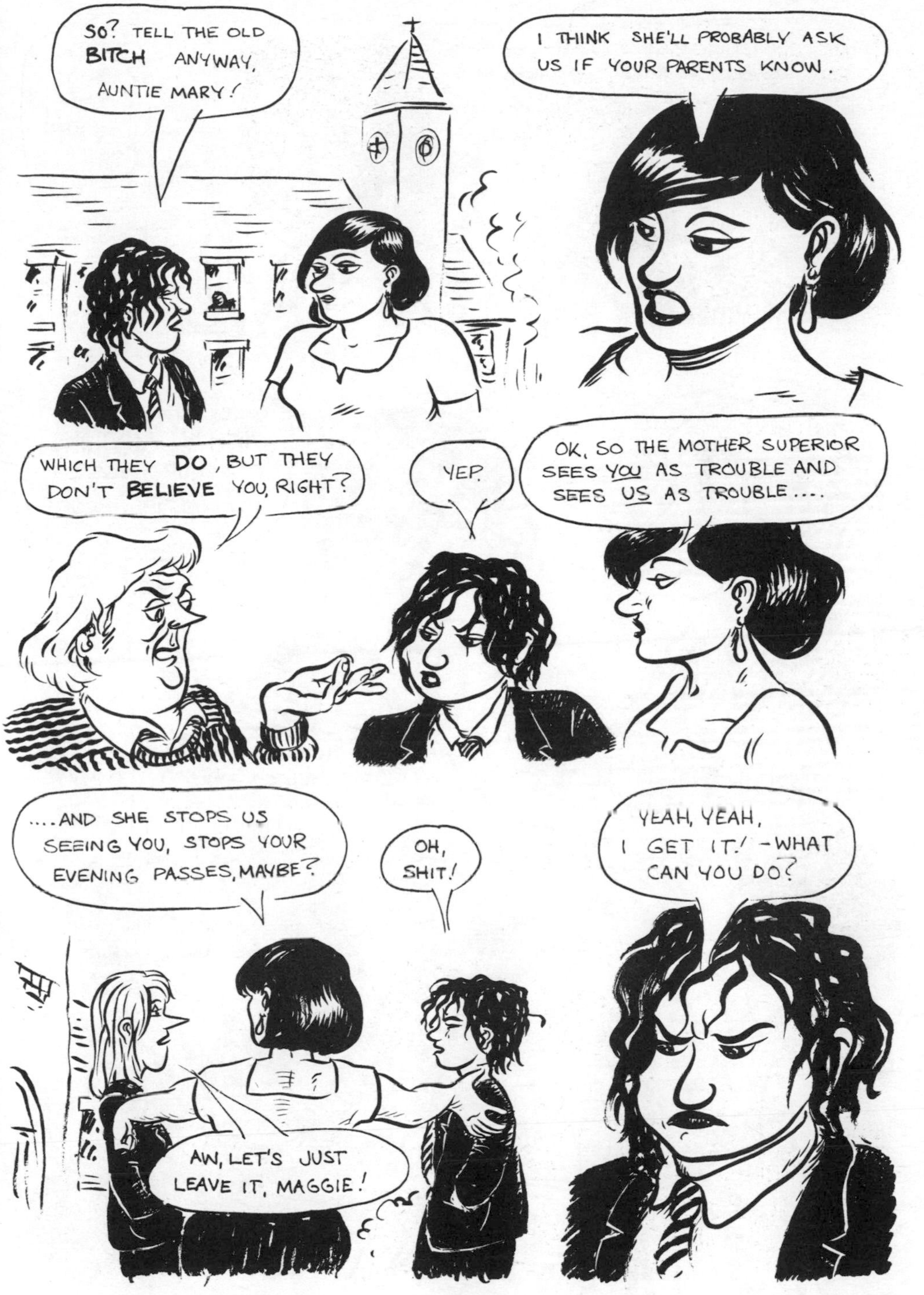
SO? TELL THE OLD BITCH ANYWAY, AUNTIE MARY!
I THINK SHE'LL PROBABLY ASK US IF YOUR PARENTS KNOW.
WHICH THEY DO, BUT THEY DON'T BELIEVE YOU, RIGHT?
YEP.
OK, SO THE MOTHER SUPERIOR SEES YOU AS TROUBLE AND SEES US AS TROUBLE....
....AND SHE STOPS US SEEING YOU, STOPS YOUR EVENING PASSES, MAYBE?
OH, SHIT!
AW, LET'S JUST LEAVE IT, MAGGIE!
YEAH, YEAH, I GET IT! -WHAT CAN YOU DO?

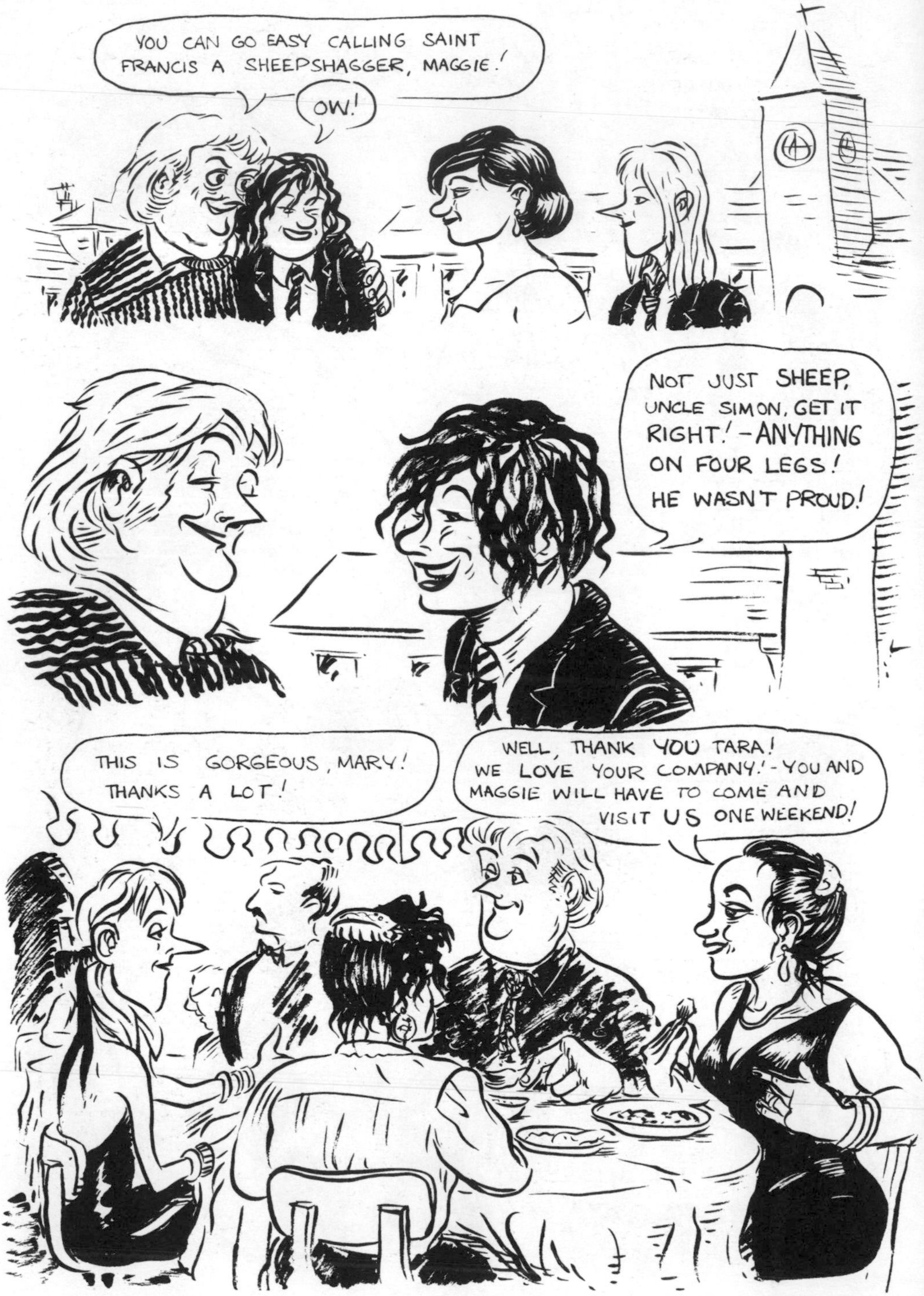
YOU CAN GO EASY CALLING SAINT FRANCIS A SHEEPSHAGGER, MAGGIE!
OW!
NOT JUST SHEEP, UNCLE SIMON, GET IT RIGHT! - ANYTHING ON FOUR LEGS! HE WASN'T PROUD!
THIS IS GORGEOUS, MARY! THANKS A LOT!
WELL, THANK YOU TARA! WE LOVE YOUR COMPANY! - YOU AND MAGGIE WILL HAVE TO COME AND VISIT US ONE WEEKEND!

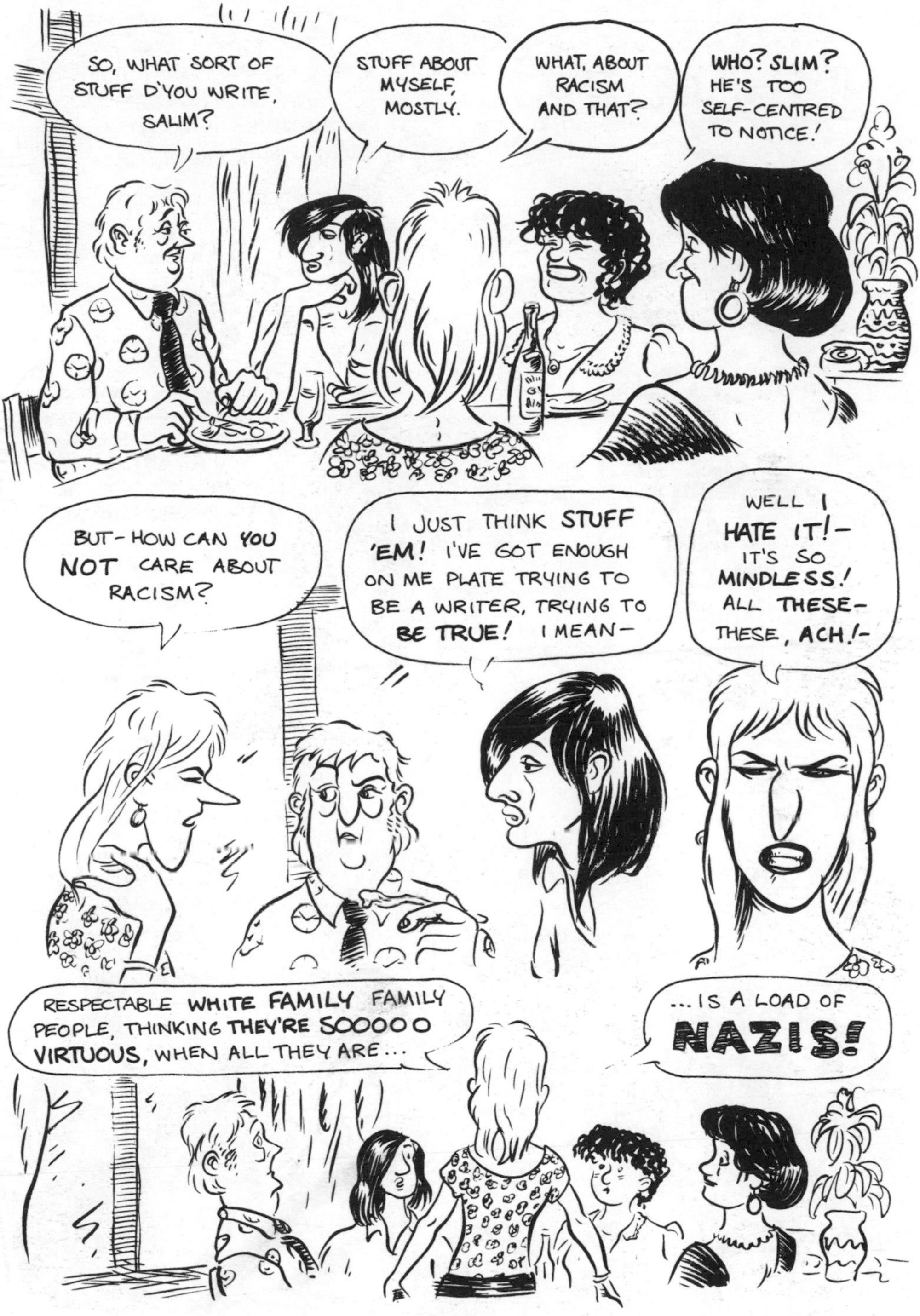
SO, WHAT SORT OF STUFF D'YOU WRITE, SALIM?
STUFF ABOUT MYSELF, MOSTLY.
WHAT, ABOUT RACISM AND THAT?
WHO? SLIM? HE'S TOO SELF-CENTRED TO NOTICE!
BUT- HOW CAN YOU NOT CARE ABOUT RACISM?
I JUST THINK STUFF 'EM! I'VE GOT ENOUGH ON ME PLATE TRYING TO BE A WRITER, TRYING TO BE TRUE! I MEAN-
WELL I HATE IT!- IT'S SO MINDLESS! ALL THESE- THESE, ACH!-
RESPECTABLE WHITE FAMILY FAMILY PEOPLE, THINKING THEY'RE SOOOOO VIRTUOUS, WHEN ALL THEY ARE...
...IS A LOAD OF NAZIS!

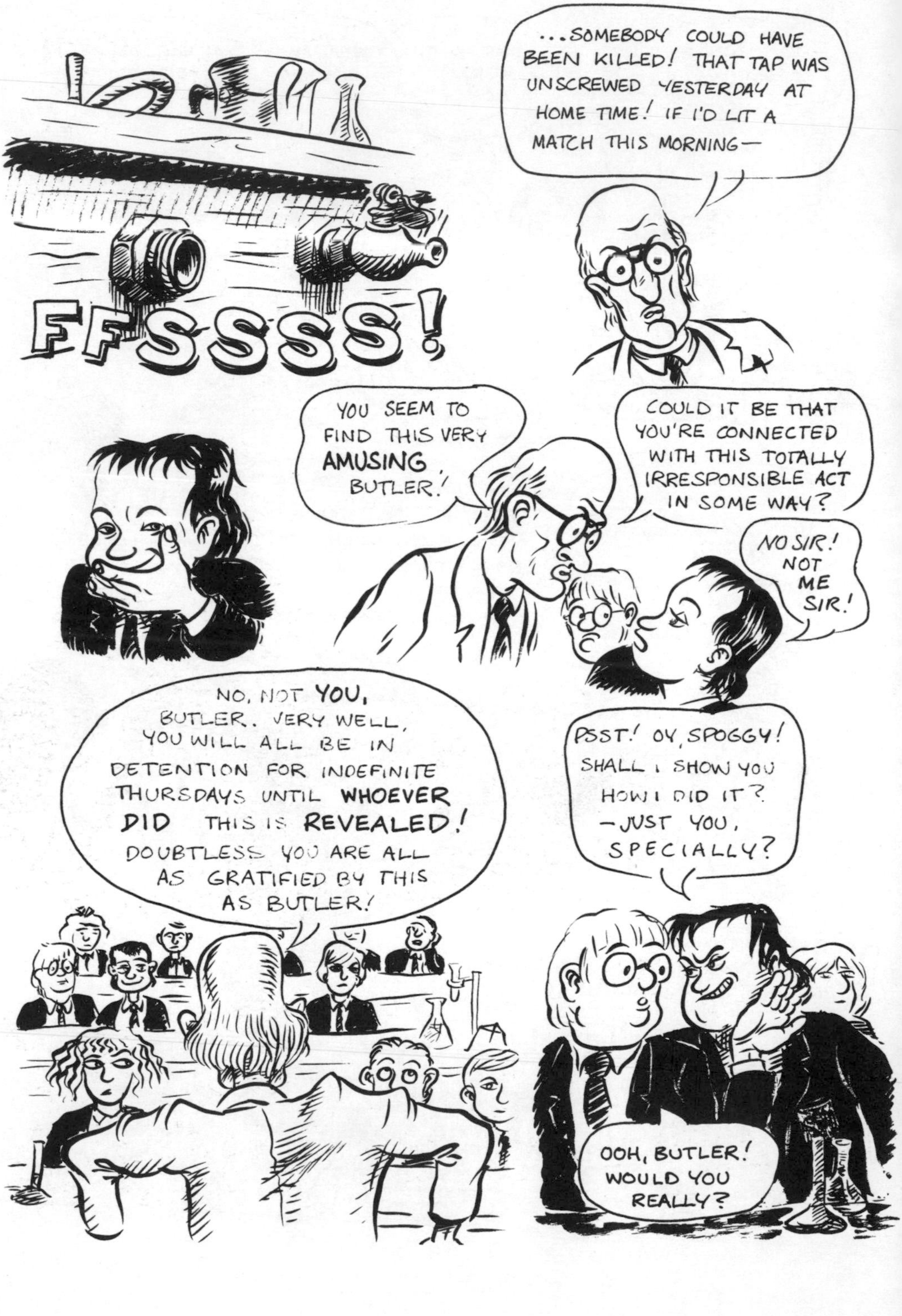
FFSSSS!
...SOMEBODY COULD HAVE BEEN KILLED! THAT TAP WAS UNSCREWED YESTERDAY AT HOME TIME! IF I'D LIT A MATCH THIS MORNING—
YOU SEEM TO FIND THIS VERY AMUSING BUTLER!
COULD IT BE THAT YOU'RE CONNECTED WITH THIS TOTALLY IRRESPONSIBLE ACT IN SOME WAY?
NO SIR! NOT ME SIR!
NO, NOT YOU, BUTLER. VERY WELL, YOU WILL ALL BE IN DETENTION FOR INDEFINITE THURSDAYS UNTIL WHOEVER DID THIS IS REVEALED! DOUBTLESS YOU ARE ALL AS GRATIFIED BY THIS AS BUTLER!
PSST! OY, SPOGGY! SHALL I SHOW YOU HOW I DID IT? —JUST YOU, SPECIALLY?
OOH, BUTLER! WOULD YOU REALLY?

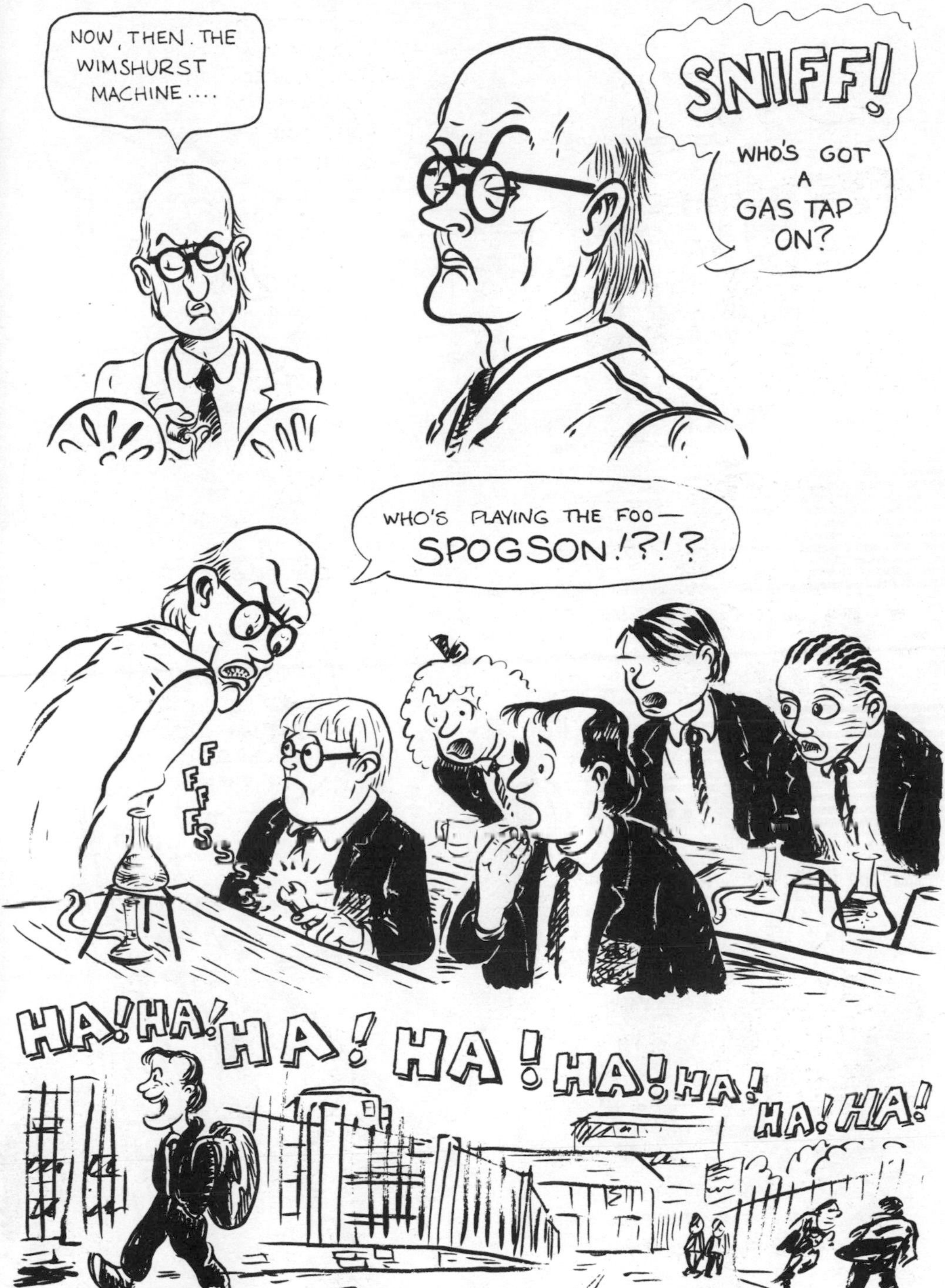
NOW, THEN. THE WIMSHURST MACHINE....
SNIFF!
WHO'S GOT A GAS TAP ON?
WHO'S PLAYING THE FOO— SPOGSON!?!?
FFFFS
HA! HA! HA! HA! HA! HA! HA! HA!

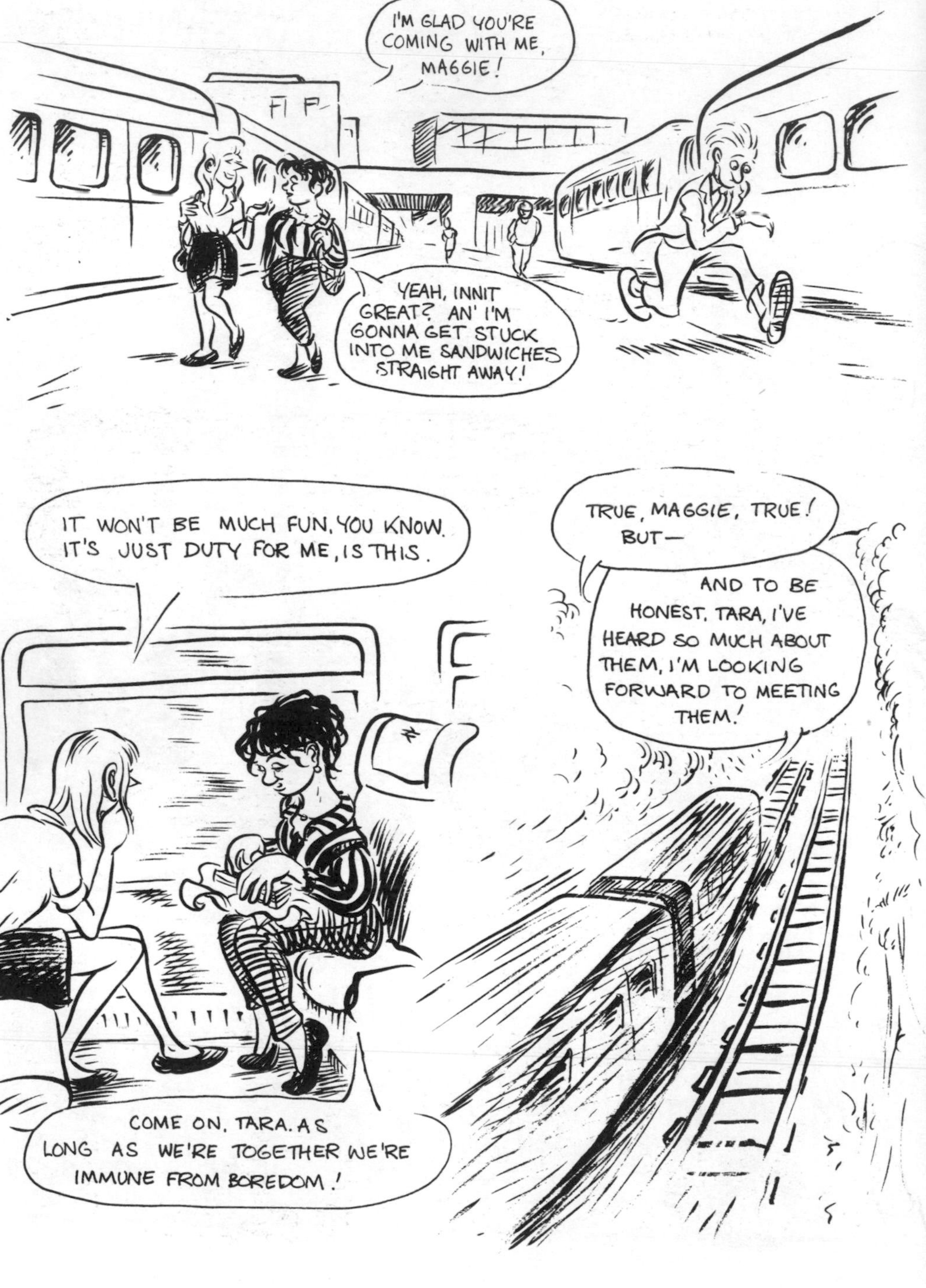
I'M GLAD YOU'RE COMING WITH ME, MAGGIE!
YEAH, INNIT GREAT? AN' I'M GONNA GET STUCK INTO ME SANDWICHES STRAIGHT AWAY!
IT WON'T BE MUCH FUN, YOU KNOW. IT'S JUST DUTY FOR ME, IS THIS.
COME ON, TARA. AS LONG AS WE'RE TOGETHER WE'RE IMMUNE FROM BOREDOM!
TRUE, MAGGIE, TRUE! BUT—
AND TO BE HONEST, TARA, I'VE HEARD SO MUCH ABOUT THEM, I'M LOOKING FORWARD TO MEETING THEM!

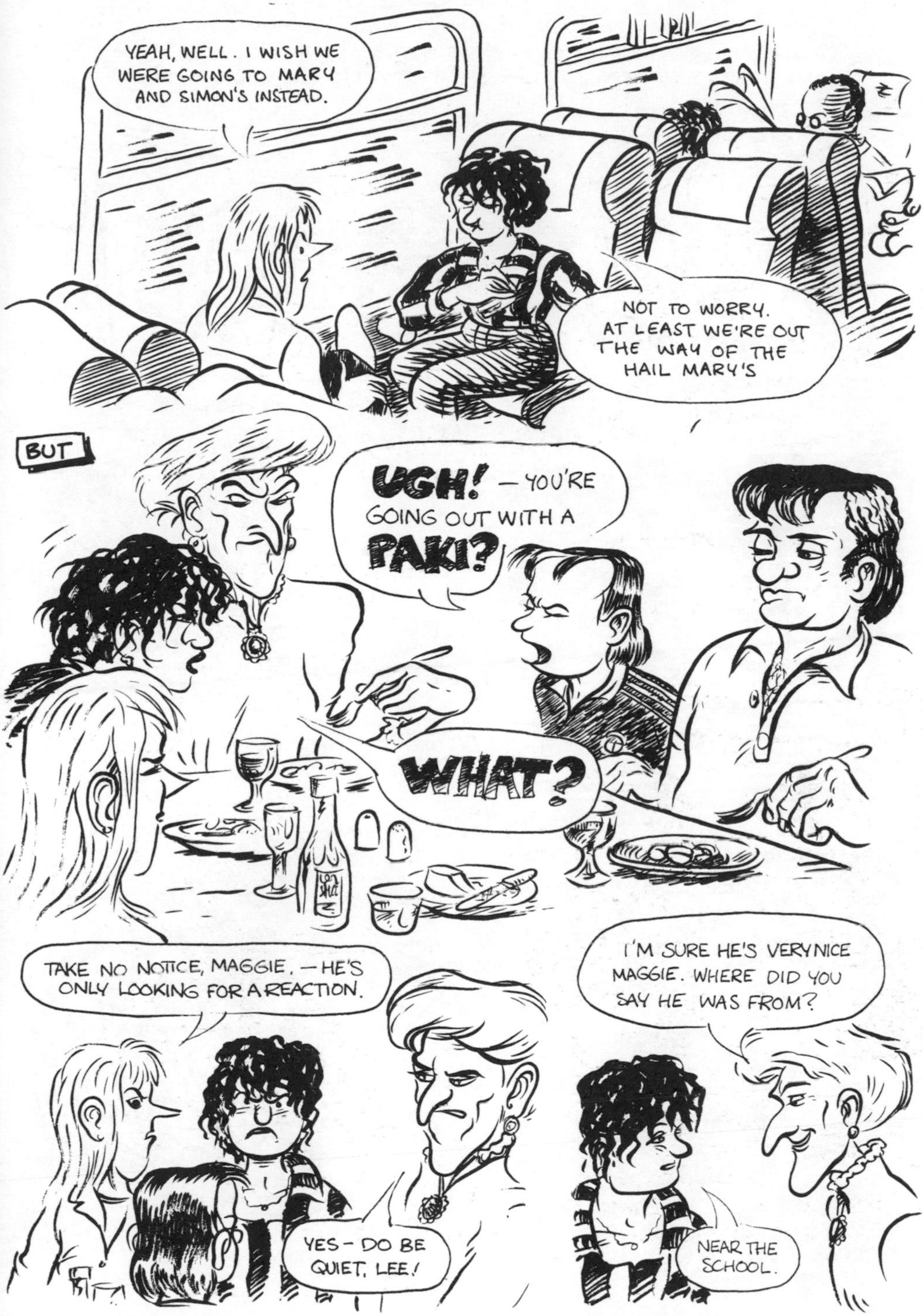
YEAH, WELL. I WISH WE WERE GOING TO MARY AND SIMON'S INSTEAD.
NOT TO WORRY. AT LEAST WE'RE OUT THE WAY OF THE HAIL MARY'S
BUT
UGH! — YOU'RE GOING OUT WITH A PAKI?
WHAT?
TAKE NO NOTICE, MAGGIE. — HE'S ONLY LOOKING FOR A REACTION.
YES — DO BE QUIET, LEE!
I'M SURE HE'S VERY NICE MAGGIE. WHERE DID YOU SAY HE WAS FROM?
NEAR THE SCHOOL.

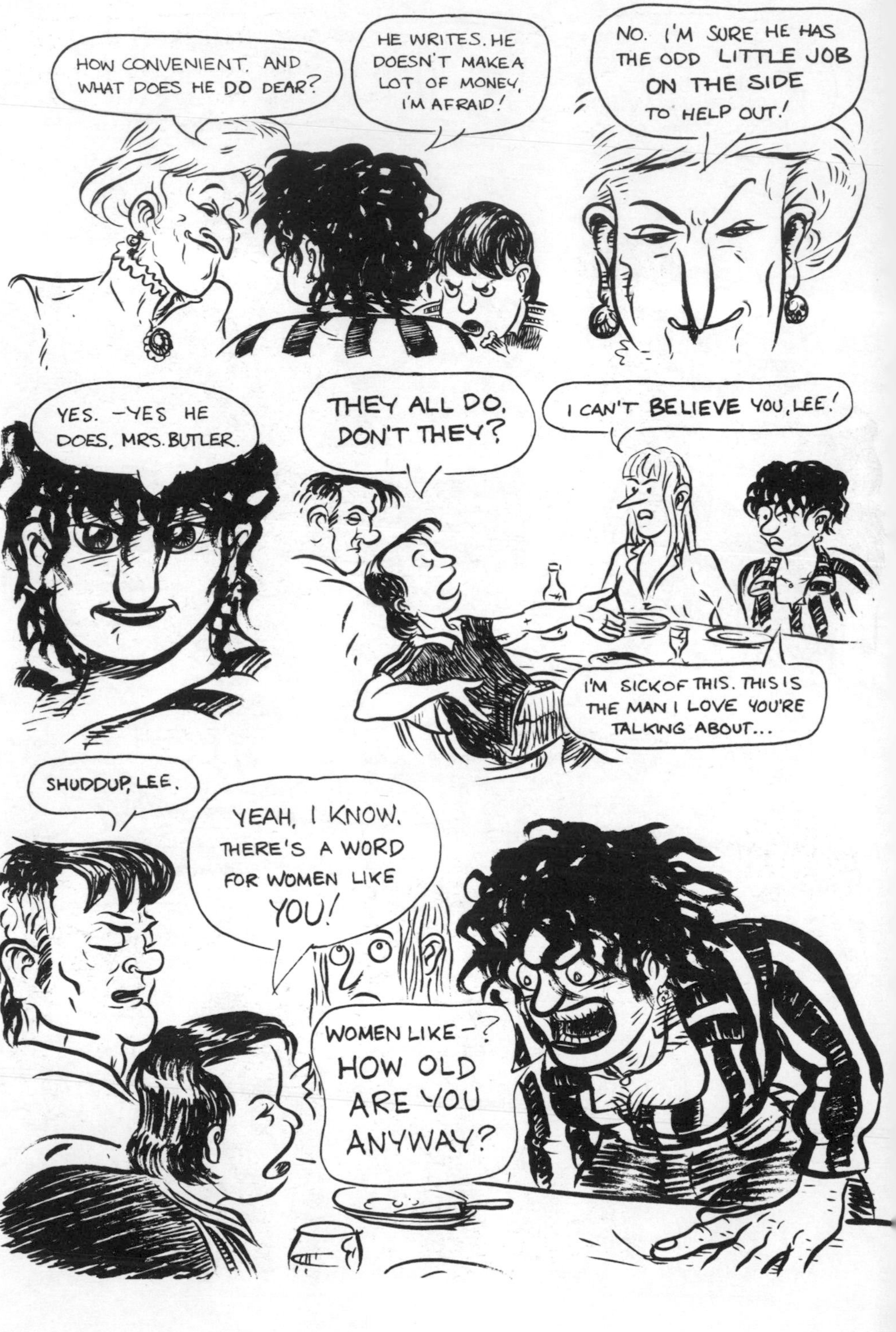
HOW CONVENIENT. AND WHAT DOES HE DO DEAR?
HE WRITES. HE DOESN'T MAKE A LOT OF MONEY, I'M AFRAID!
NO. I'M SURE HE HAS THE ODD LITTLE JOB ON THE SIDE TO HELP OUT!
YES. —YES HE DOES, MRS. BUTLER.
THEY ALL DO, DON'T THEY?
I CAN'T BELIEVE YOU, LEE!
I'M SICK OF THIS. THIS IS THE MAN I LOVE YOU'RE TALKING ABOUT...
SHUDDUP, LEE.
YEAH, I KNOW. THERE'S A WORD FOR WOMEN LIKE YOU!
WOMEN LIKE—? HOW OLD ARE YOU ANYWAY?

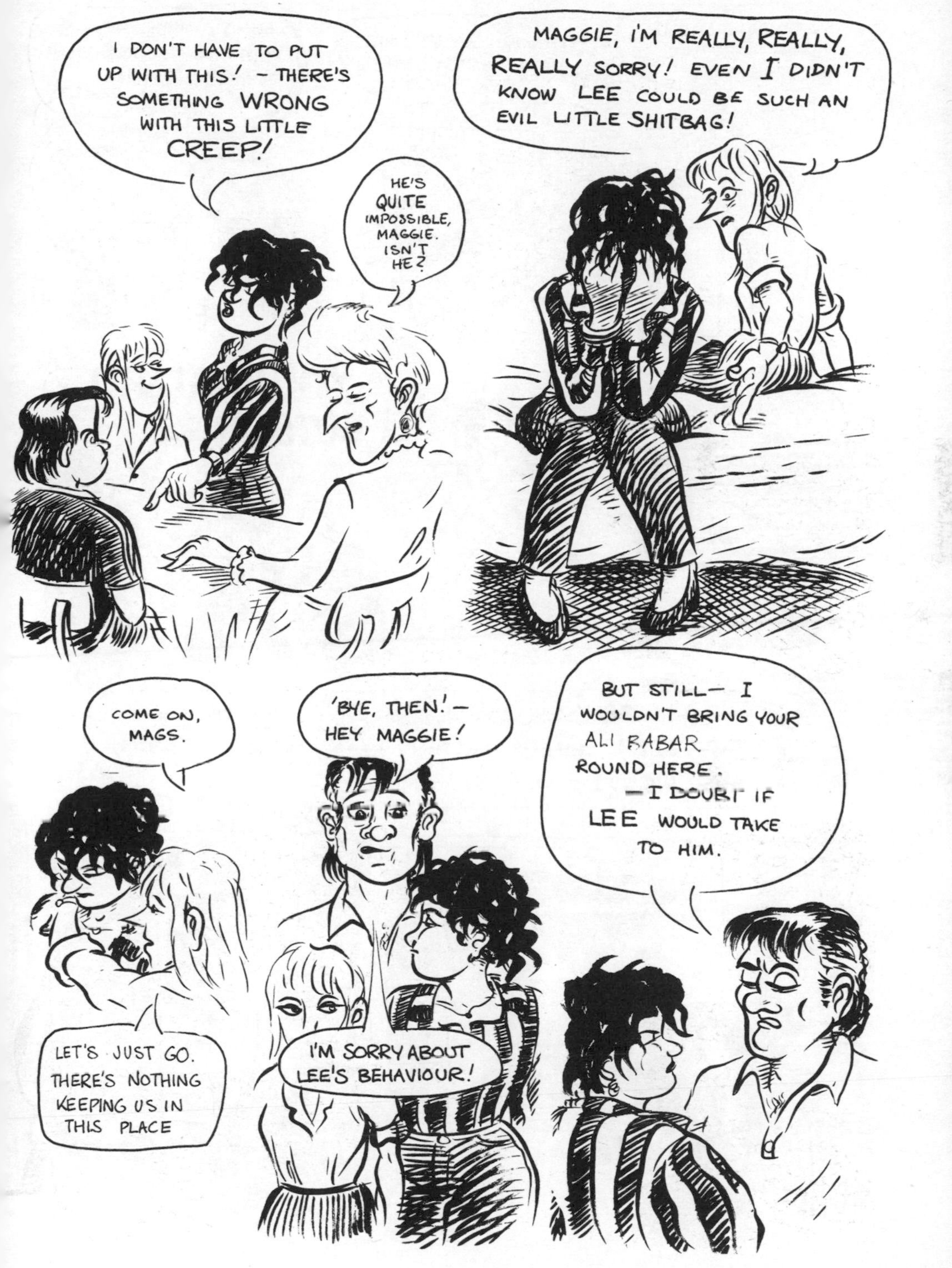

I DON'T HAVE TO PUT UP WITH THIS! – THERE'S SOMETHING WRONG WITH THIS LITTLE CREEP!
HE'S QUITE IMPOSSIBLE, MAGGIE. ISN'T HE?
MAGGIE, I'M REALLY, REALLY, REALLY SORRY! EVEN I DIDN'T KNOW LEE COULD BE SUCH AN EVIL LITTLE SHITBAG!
COME ON, MAGS.
LET'S JUST GO. THERE'S NOTHING KEEPING US IN THIS PLACE
'BYE, THEN! – HEY MAGGIE!
I'M SORRY ABOUT LEE'S BEHAVIOUR!
BUT STILL – I WOULDN'T BRING YOUR ALI BABAR ROUND HERE.
– I DOUBT IF LEE WOULD TAKE TO HIM.

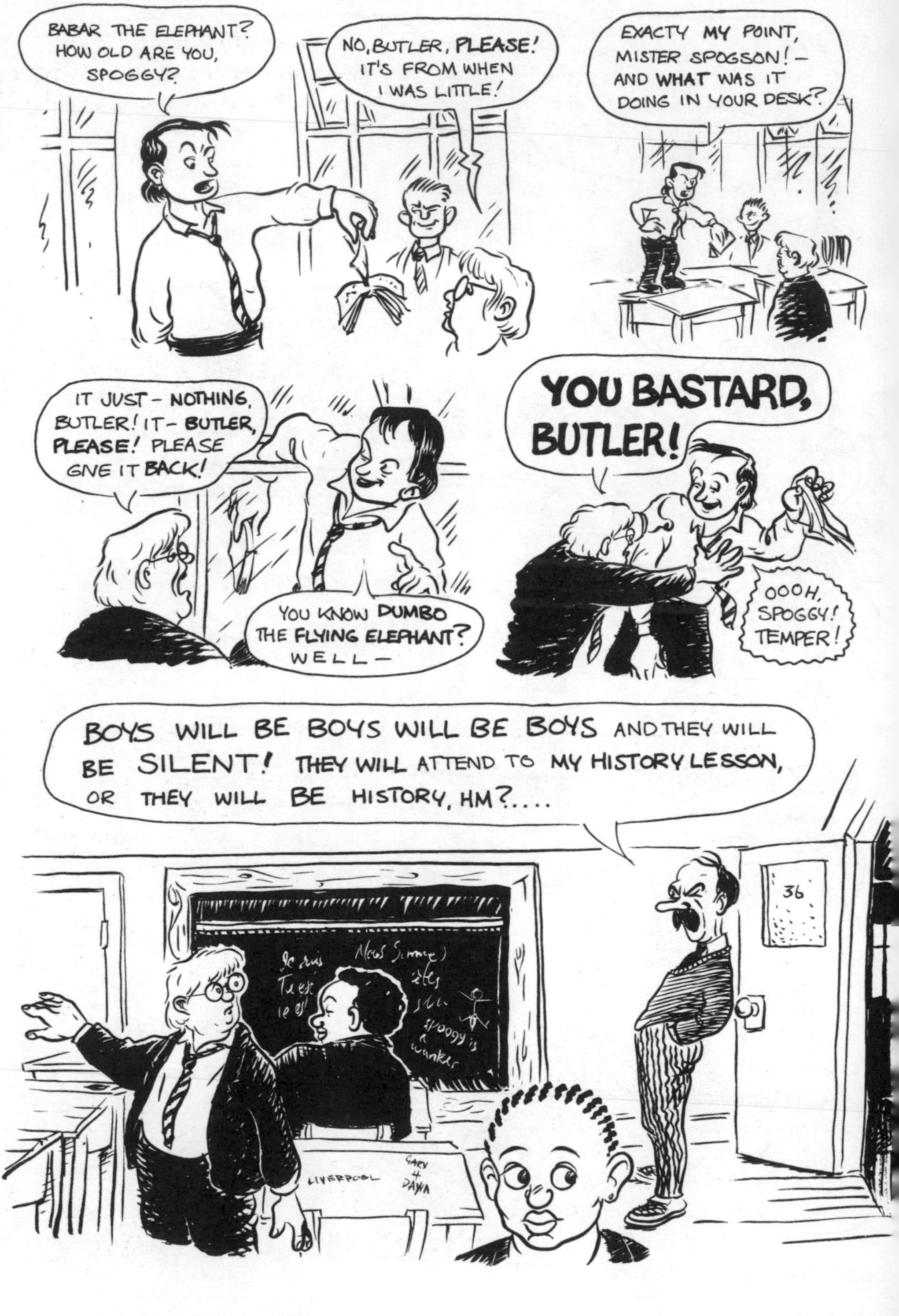
BABAR THE ELEPHANT? HOW OLD ARE YOU, SPOGGY?
NO, BUTLER, PLEASE! IT'S FROM WHEN I WAS LITTLE!
EXACTY MY POINT, MISTER SPOGSON! – AND WHAT WAS IT DOING IN YOUR DESK?
IT JUST – NOTHING, BUTLER! IT – BUTLER, PLEASE! PLEASE GIVE IT BACK!
YOU KNOW DUMBO THE FLYING ELEPHANT? WELL –
YOU BASTARD, BUTLER!
OOOH, SPOGGY! TEMPER!
BOYS WILL BE BOYS WILL BE BOYS AND THEY WILL BE SILENT! THEY WILL ATTEND TO MY HISTORY LESSON, OR THEY WILL BE HISTORY, HM?....
36
spoggy is a wanker
LIVERPOOL
GARY + DAWN

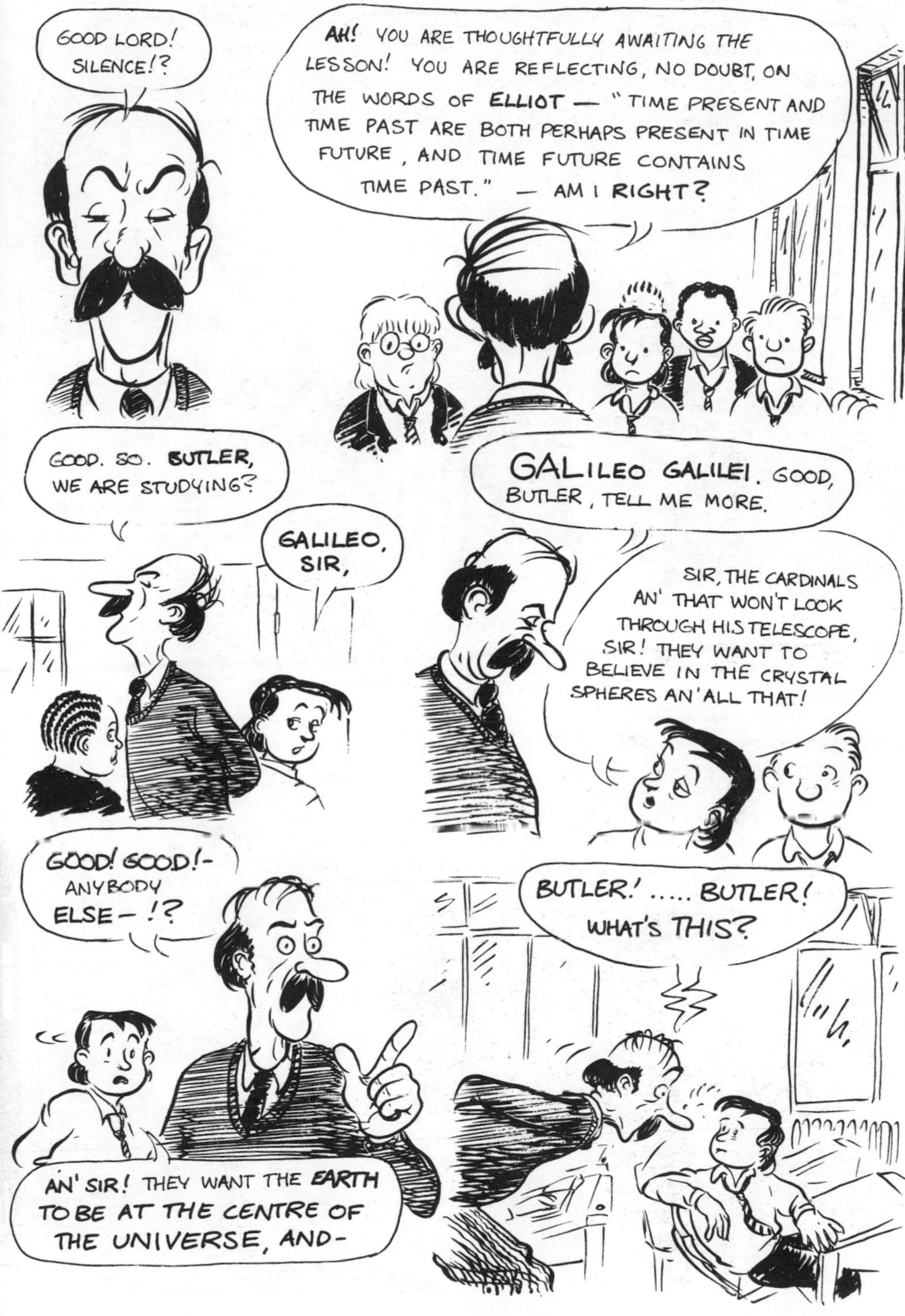
GOOD LORD! SILENCE!?
AH! YOU ARE THOUGHTFULLY AWAITING THE LESSON! YOU ARE REFLECTING, NO DOUBT, ON THE WORDS OF ELLIOT — "TIME PRESENT AND TIME PAST ARE BOTH PERHAPS PRESENT IN TIME FUTURE, AND TIME FUTURE CONTAINS TIME PAST." — AM I RIGHT?
GOOD. SO. BUTLER, WE ARE STUDYING?
GALILEO, SIR,
GALILEO GALILEI. GOOD, BUTLER, TELL ME MORE.
SIR, THE CARDINALS AN' THAT WON'T LOOK THROUGH HIS TELESCOPE, SIR! THEY WANT TO BELIEVE IN THE CRYSTAL SPHERES AN' ALL THAT!
GOOD! GOOD! - ANYBODY ELSE - !?
AN' SIR! THEY WANT THE EARTH TO BE AT THE CENTRE OF THE UNIVERSE, AND-
BUTLER! ..... BUTLER! WHAT'S THIS?

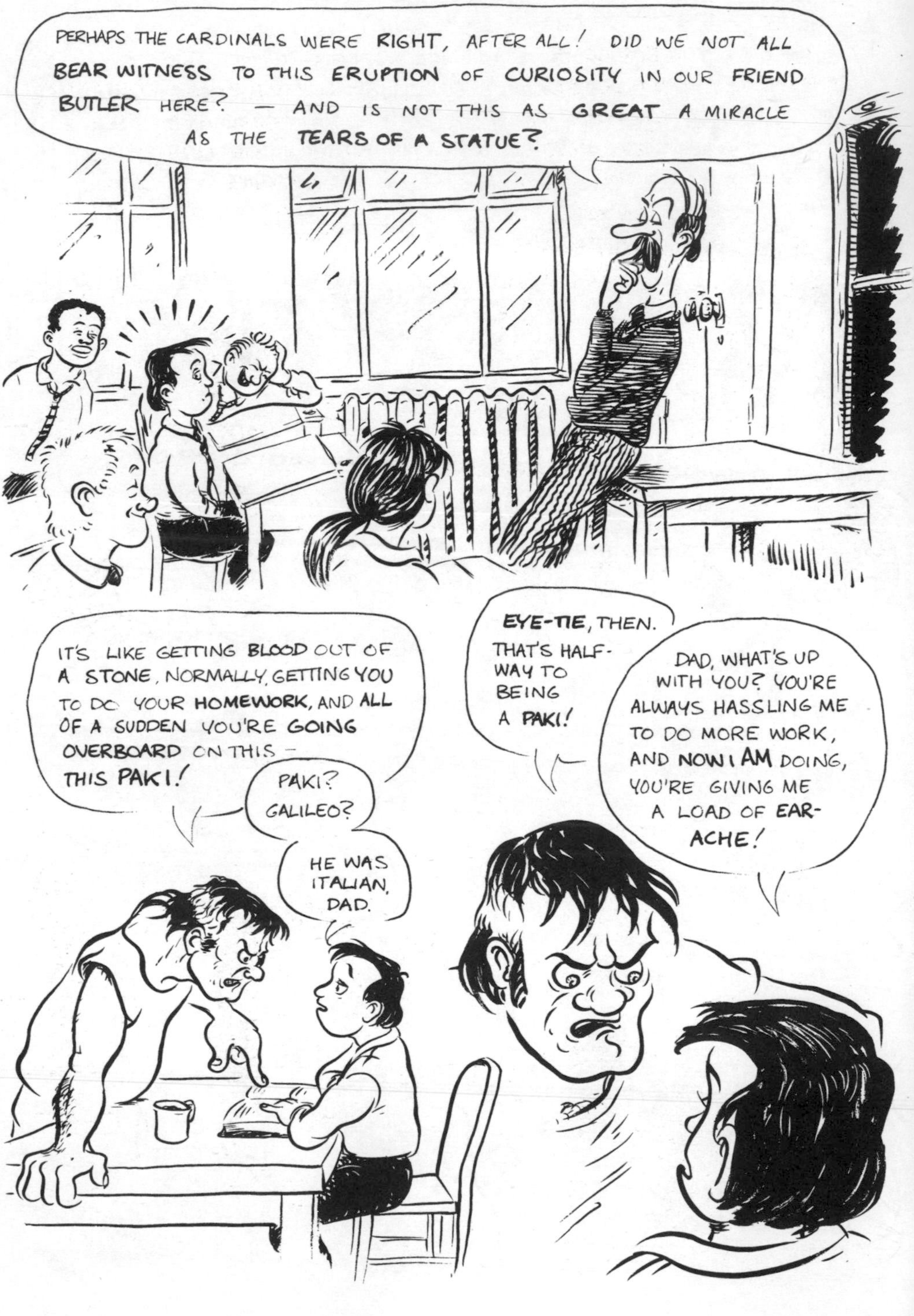
PERHAPS THE CARDINALS WERE RIGHT, AFTER ALL! DID WE NOT ALL BEAR WITNESS TO THIS ERUPTION OF CURIOSITY IN OUR FRIEND BUTLER HERE? — AND IS NOT THIS AS GREAT A MIRACLE AS THE TEARS OF A STATUE?
IT'S LIKE GETTING BLOOD OUT OF A STONE, NORMALLY, GETTING YOU TO DO YOUR HOMEWORK, AND ALL OF A SUDDEN YOU'RE GOING OVERBOARD ON THIS — THIS PAKI!
PAKI? GALILEO?
HE WAS ITALIAN, DAD.
EYE-TIE, THEN. THAT'S HALF-WAY TO BEING A PAKI!
DAD, WHAT'S UP WITH YOU? YOU'RE ALWAYS HASSLING ME TO DO MORE WORK, AND NOW I AM DOING, YOU'RE GIVING ME A LOAD OF EAR-ACHE!

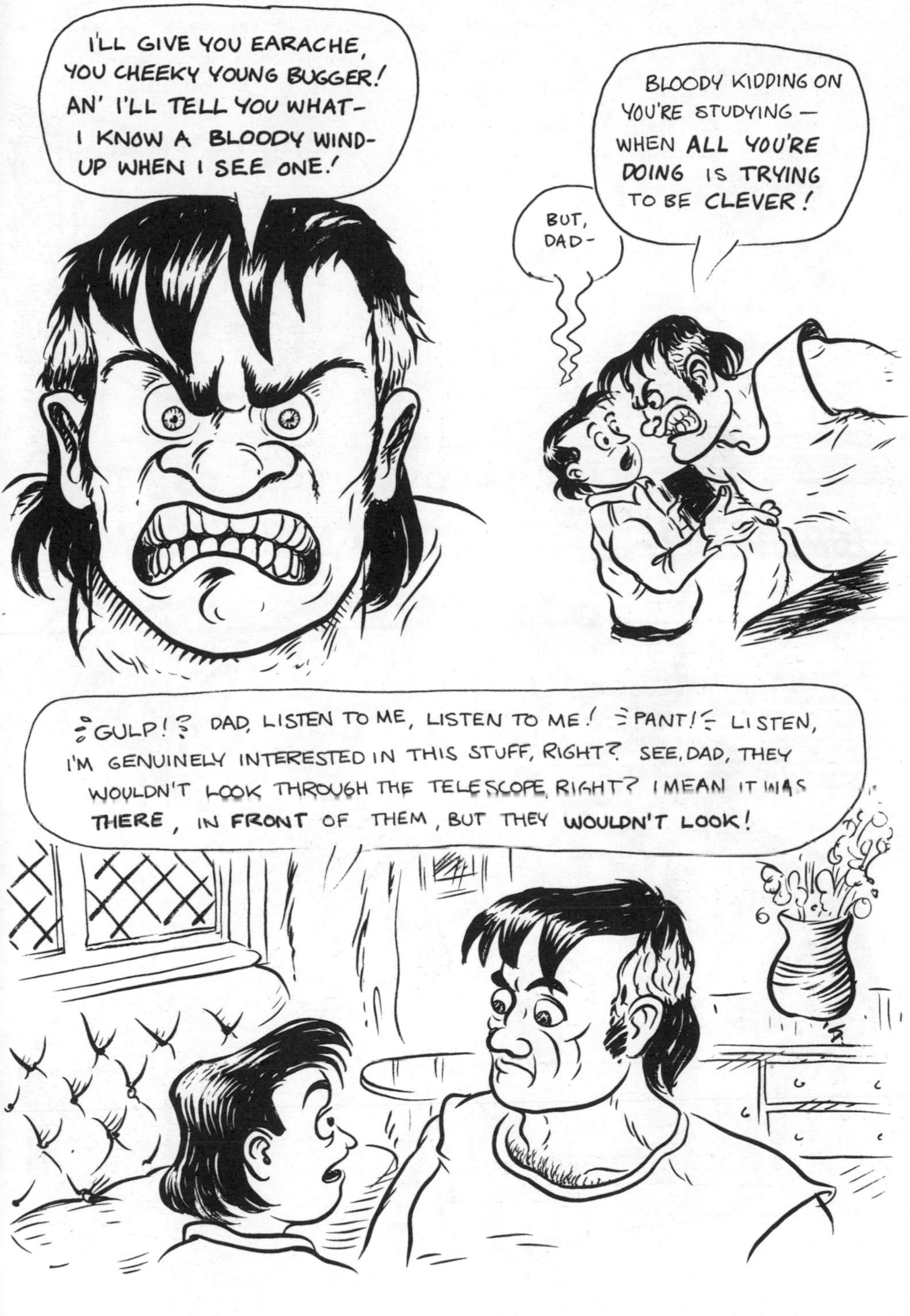
I'LL GIVE YOU EARACHE, YOU CHEEKY YOUNG BUGGER! AN' I'LL TELL YOU WHAT- I KNOW A BLOODY WIND-UP WHEN I SEE ONE!
BUT, DAD-
BLOODY KIDDING ON YOU'RE STUDYING — WHEN ALL YOU'RE DOING IS TRYING TO BE CLEVER!
GULP! DAD, LISTEN TO ME, LISTEN TO ME! PANT! LISTEN, I'M GENUINELY INTERESTED IN THIS STUFF, RIGHT? SEE, DAD, THEY WOULDN'T LOOK THROUGH THE TELESCOPE, RIGHT? I MEAN IT WAS THERE, IN FRONT OF THEM, BUT THEY WOULDN'T LOOK!

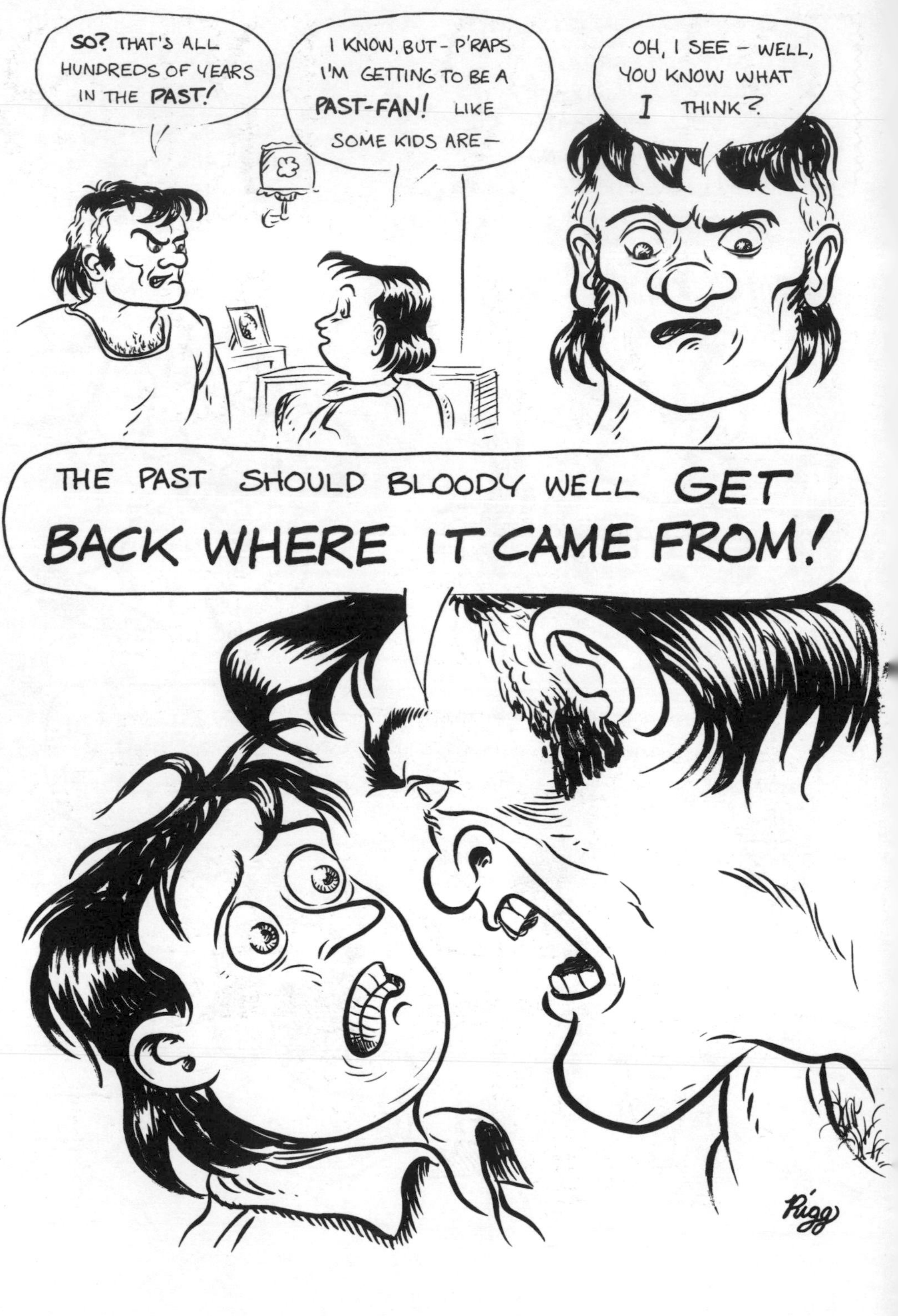
SO? THAT'S ALL HUNDREDS OF YEARS IN THE PAST!
I KNOW, BUT - P'RAPS I'M GETTING TO BE A PAST-FAN! LIKE SOME KIDS ARE—
OH, I SEE - WELL, YOU KNOW WHAT I THINK?
THE PAST SHOULD BLOODY WELL GET BACK WHERE IT CAME FROM!
Rigg

PLAYING WAR

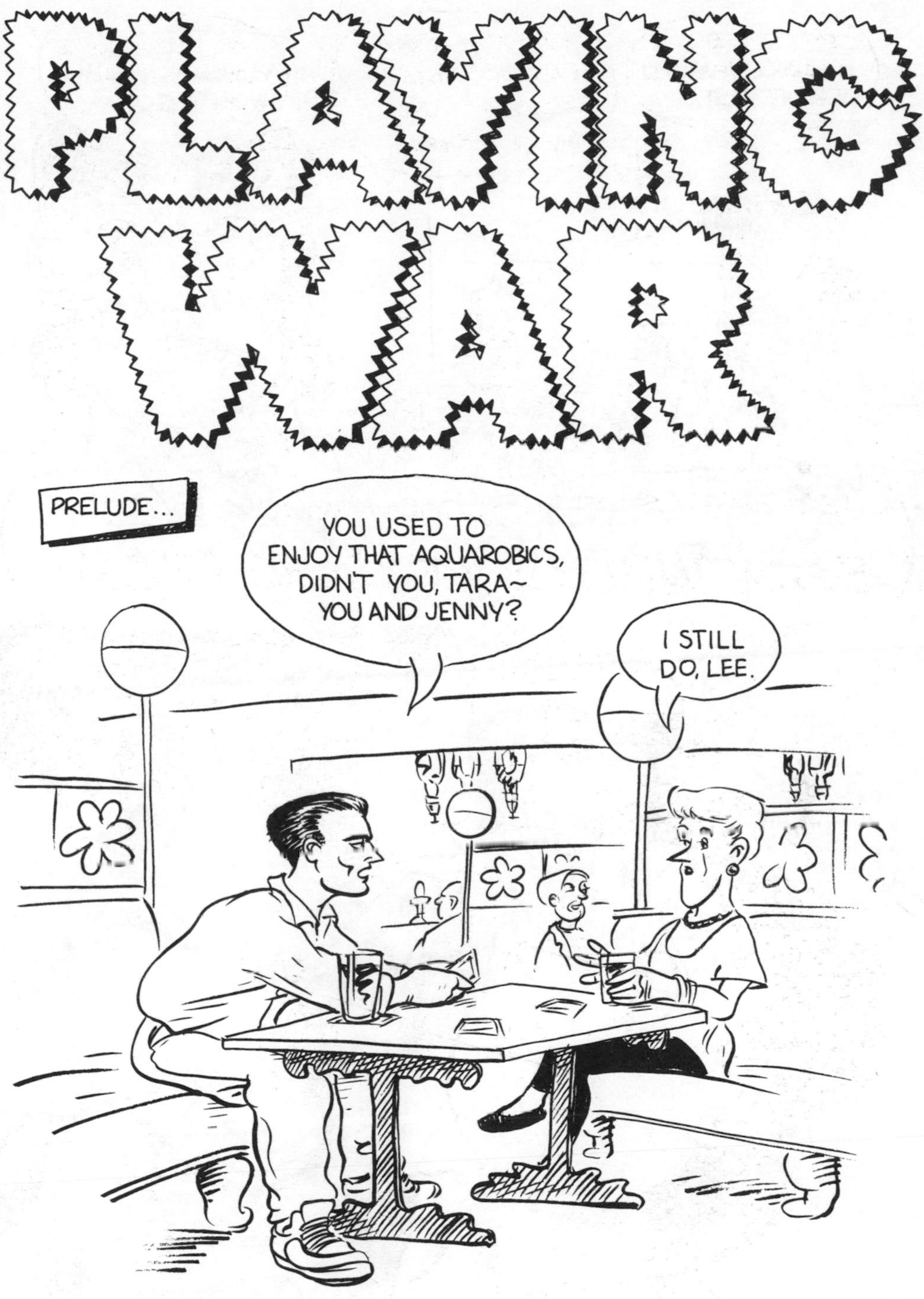
PRELUDE...
YOU USED TO ENJOY THAT AQUAROBICS, DIDN'T YOU, TARA~ YOU AND JENNY?
I STILL DO, LEE.

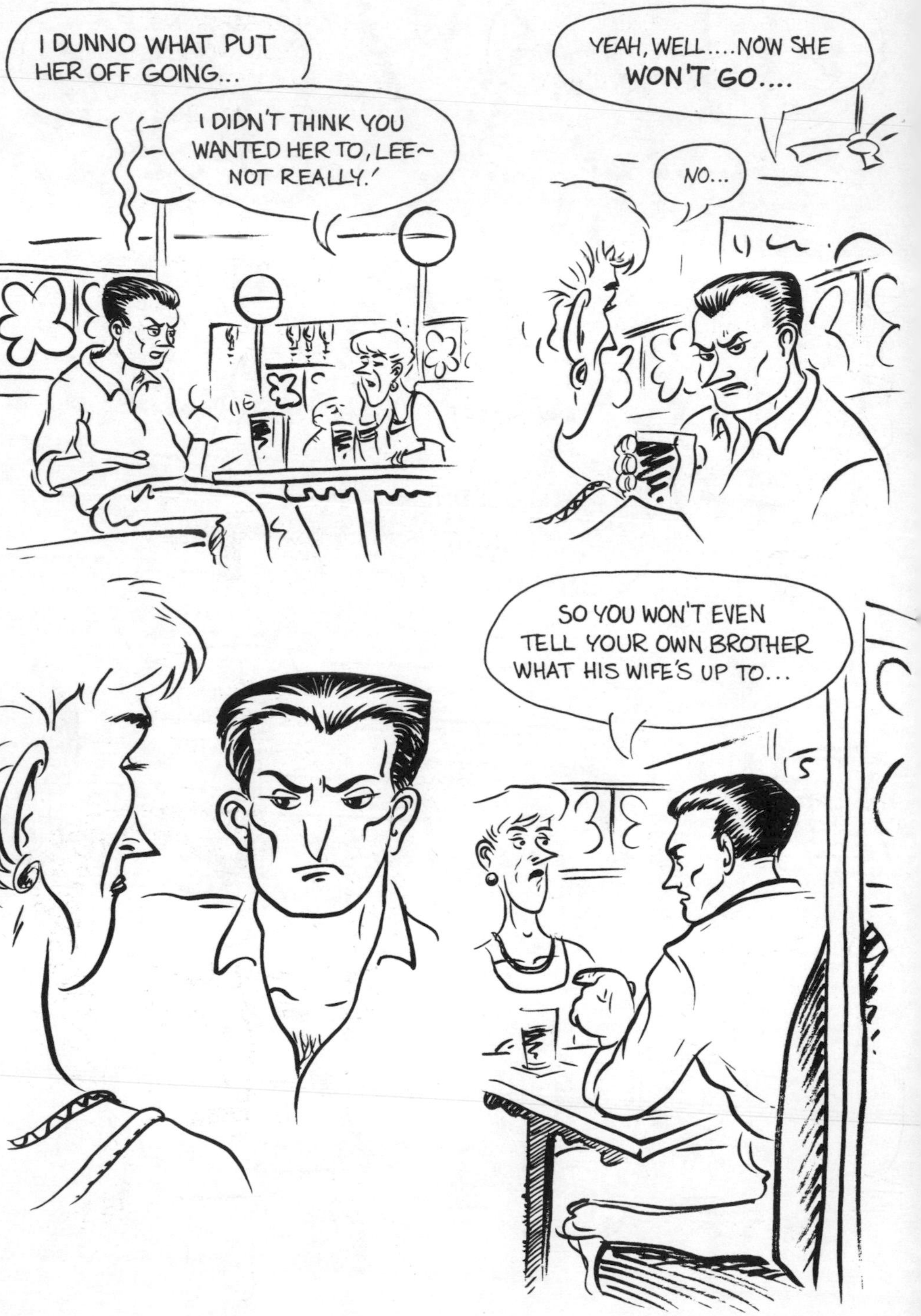
I DUNNO WHAT PUT HER OFF GOING...
I DIDN'T THINK YOU WANTED HER TO, LEE~ NOT REALLY.'
YEAH, WELL....NOW SHE WON'T GO....
NO...
SO YOU WON'T EVEN TELL YOUR OWN BROTHER WHAT HIS WIFE'S UP TO...

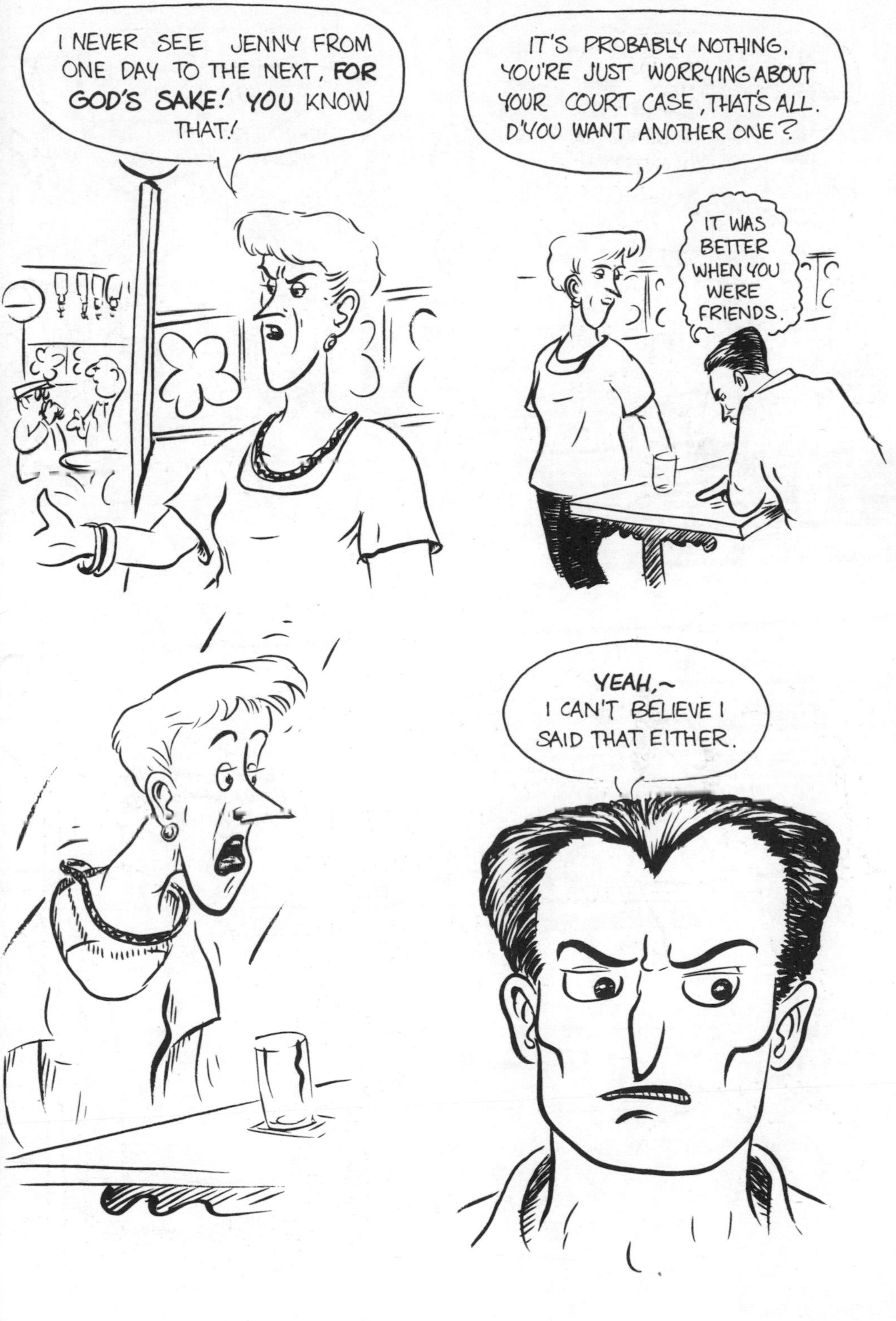
I NEVER SEE JENNY FROM ONE DAY TO THE NEXT, FOR GOD'S SAKE! YOU KNOW THAT!
IT'S PROBABLY NOTHING. YOU'RE JUST WORRYING ABOUT YOUR COURT CASE, THAT'S ALL. D'YOU WANT ANOTHER ONE?
IT WAS BETTER WHEN YOU WERE FRIENDS.
YEAH,~ I CAN'T BELIEVE I SAID THAT EITHER.

1994

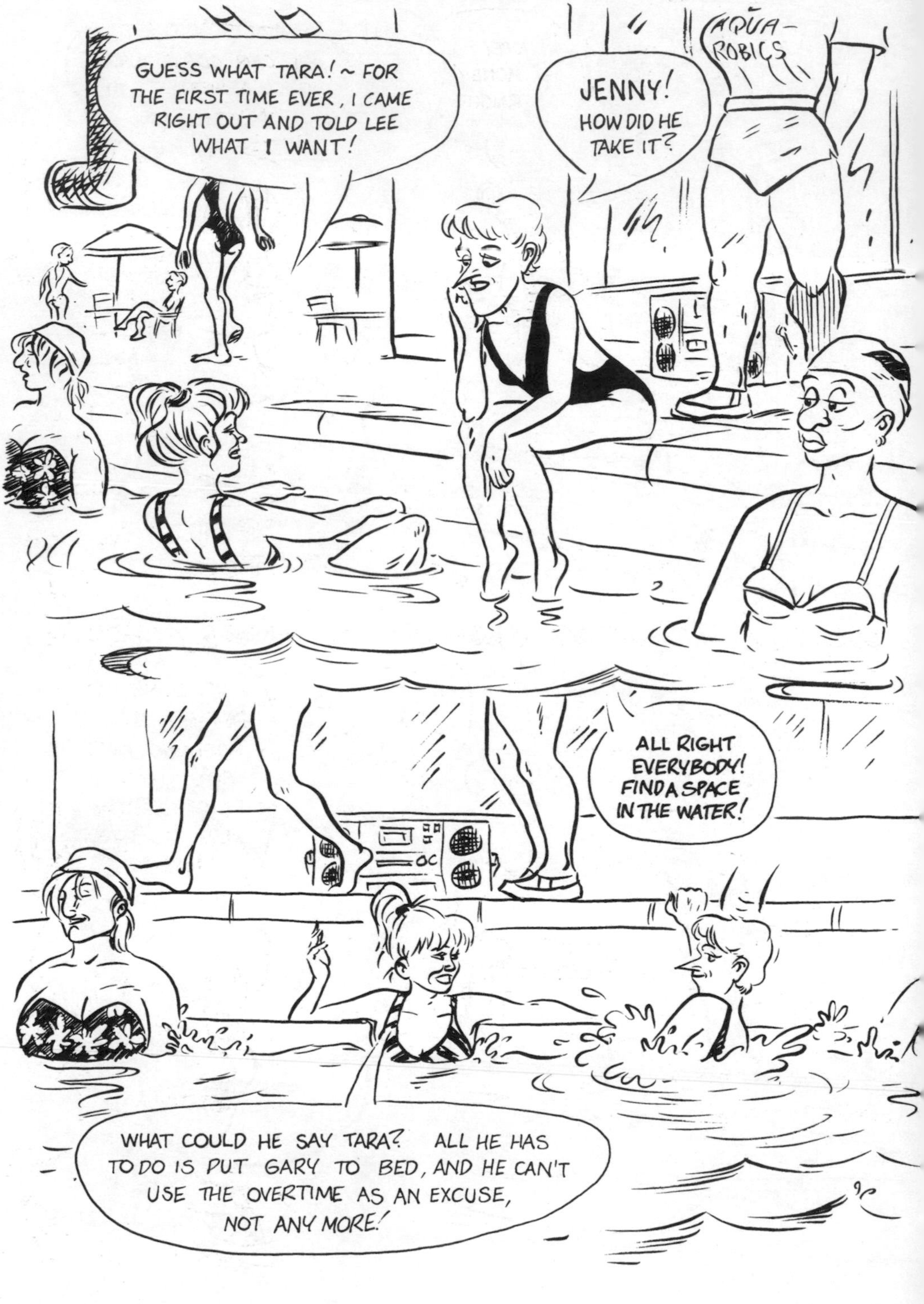

AQUA-ROBICS
GUESS WHAT TARA! ~ FOR THE FIRST TIME EVER, I CAME RIGHT OUT AND TOLD LEE WHAT I WANT!
JENNY! HOW DID HE TAKE IT?
ALL RIGHT EVERYBODY! FIND A SPACE IN THE WATER!
WHAT COULD HE SAY TARA? ALL HE HAS TO DO IS PUT GARY TO BED, AND HE CAN'T USE THE OVERTIME AS AN EXCUSE, NOT ANY MORE!

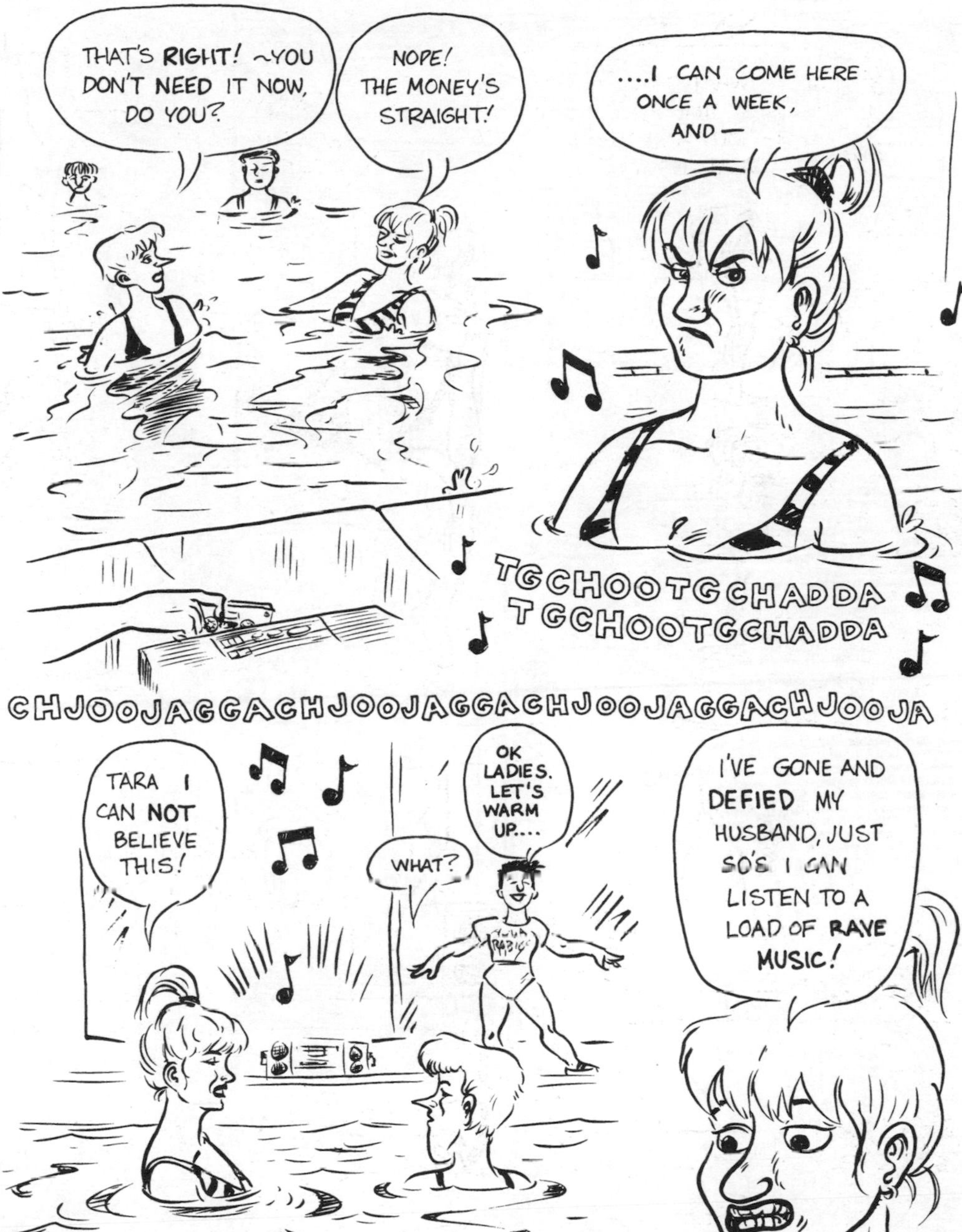
THAT'S RIGHT! ~YOU DON'T NEED IT NOW, DO YOU?
NOPE! THE MONEY'S STRAIGHT!
....I CAN COME HERE ONCE A WEEK, AND—
TGCHOOTGCHADDA TGCHOOTGCHADDA
CHJOOJAGGACHJOOJAGGACHJOOJAGGACHJOOJA
TARA I CAN NOT BELIEVE THIS!
WHAT?
OK LADIES. LET'S WARM UP....
I'VE GONE AND DEFIED MY HUSBAND, JUST SO'S I CAN LISTEN TO A LOAD OF RAVE MUSIC!

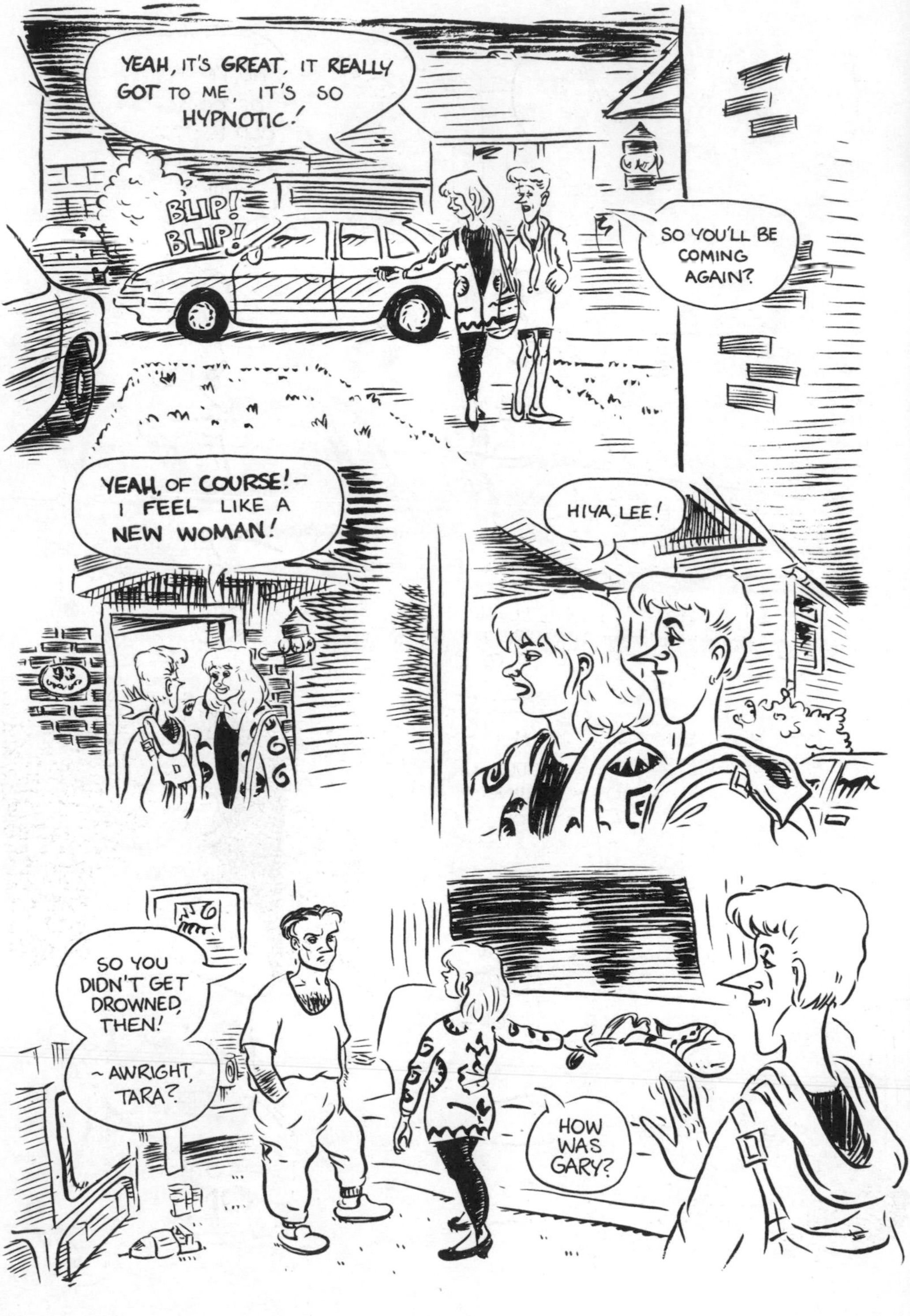
YEAH, IT'S GREAT, IT REALLY GOT TO ME, IT'S SO HYPNOTIC!
BLIP! BLIP!
SO YOU'LL BE COMING AGAIN?
YEAH, OF COURSE! — I FEEL LIKE A NEW WOMAN!
HIYA, LEE!
SO YOU DIDN'T GET DROWNED, THEN!
~ AWRIGHT, TARA?
HOW WAS GARY?

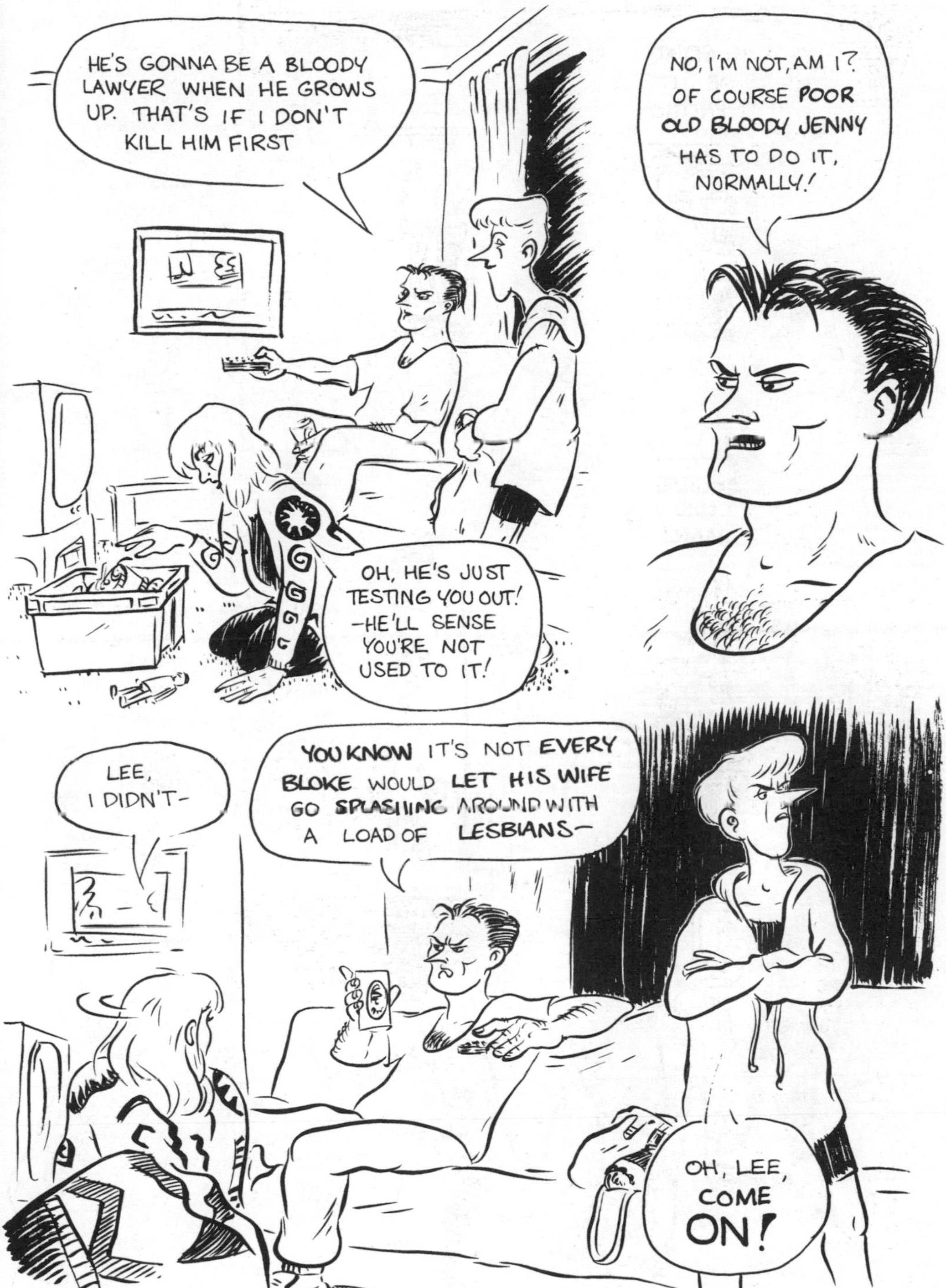
HE'S GONNA BE A BLOODY LAWYER WHEN HE GROWS UP. THAT'S IF I DON'T KILL HIM FIRST
OH, HE'S JUST TESTING YOU OUT! -HE'LL SENSE YOU'RE NOT USED TO IT!
NO, I'M NOT, AM I? OF COURSE POOR OLD BLOODY JENNY HAS TO DO IT, NORMALLY!
LEE, I DIDN'T-
YOU KNOW IT'S NOT EVERY BLOKE WOULD LET HIS WIFE GO SPLASHING AROUND WITH A LOAD OF LESBIANS-
OH, LEE, COME ON!

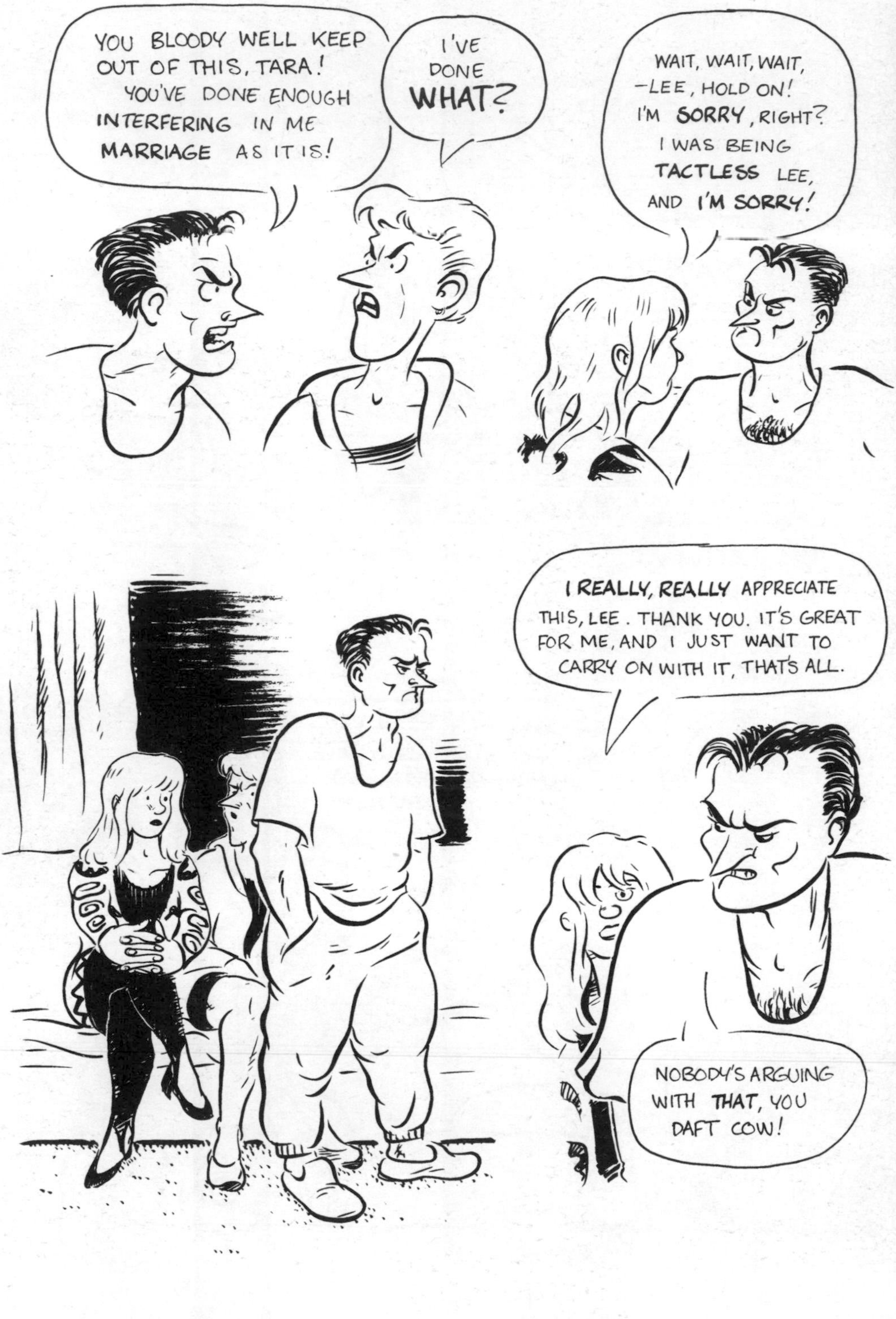
YOU BLOODY WELL KEEP OUT OF THIS, TARA! YOU'VE DONE ENOUGH **INTERFERING** IN ME **MARRIAGE** AS IT IS!
I'VE DONE **WHAT?**
WAIT, WAIT, WAIT, —LEE, HOLD ON! I'M **SORRY**, RIGHT? I WAS BEING **TACTLESS** LEE, AND **I'M SORRY!**
I REALLY, REALLY APPRECIATE THIS, LEE. THANK YOU. IT'S GREAT FOR ME, AND I JUST WANT TO CARRY ON WITH IT, THAT'S ALL.
NOBODY'S ARGUING WITH **THAT**, YOU DAFT COW!

ACT

I

PRE-WAR

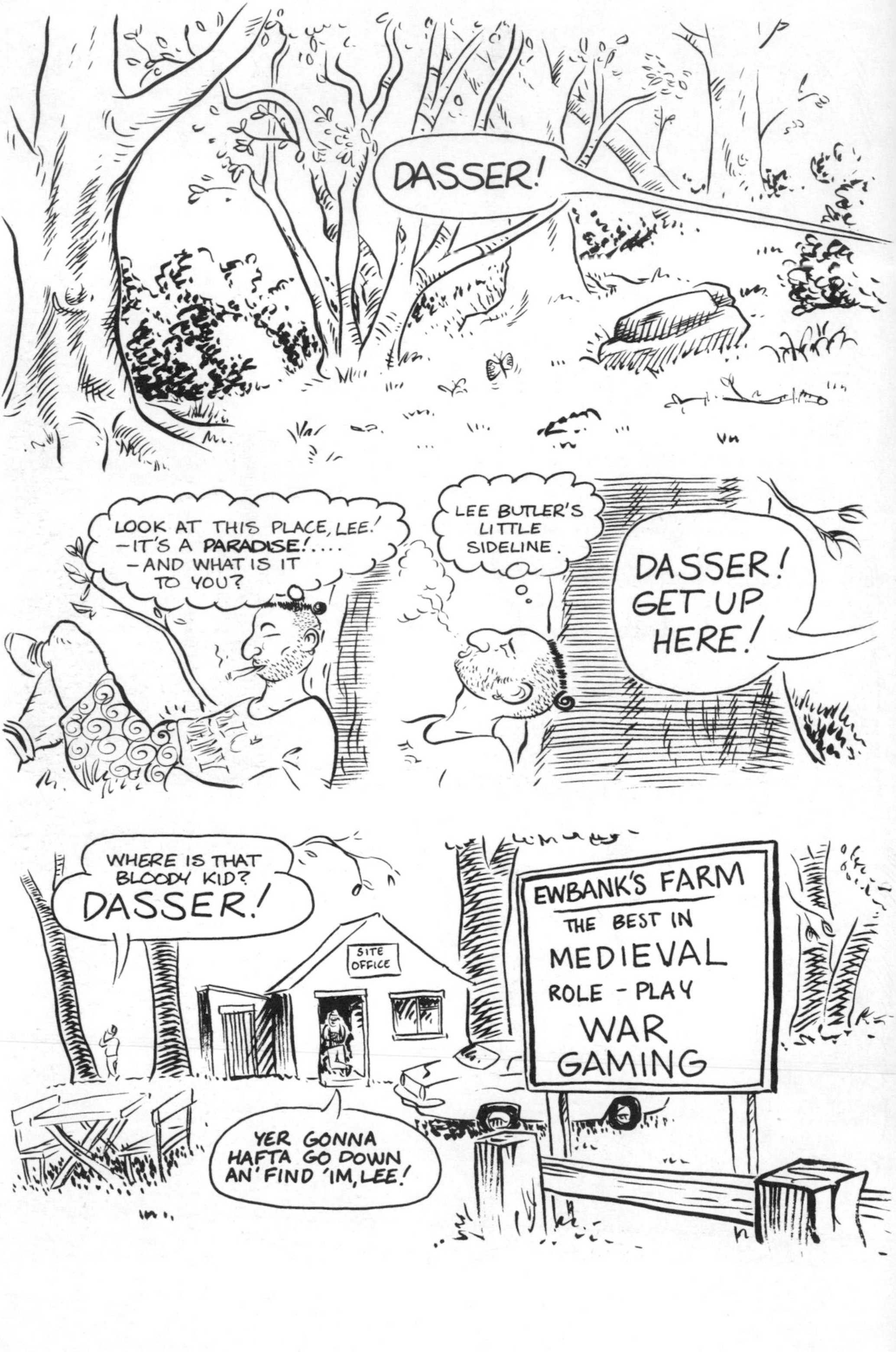
DASSER!
LOOK AT THIS PLACE, LEE! -IT'S A PARADISE!.... -AND WHAT IS IT TO YOU?
LEE BUTLER'S LITTLE SIDELINE.
DASSER! GET UP HERE!
WHERE IS THAT BLOODY KID? DASSER!
SITE OFFICE
EWBANK'S FARM
THE BEST IN
MEDIEVAL
ROLE - PLAY
WAR
GAMING
YER GONNA HAFTA GO DOWN AN' FIND 'IM, LEE!

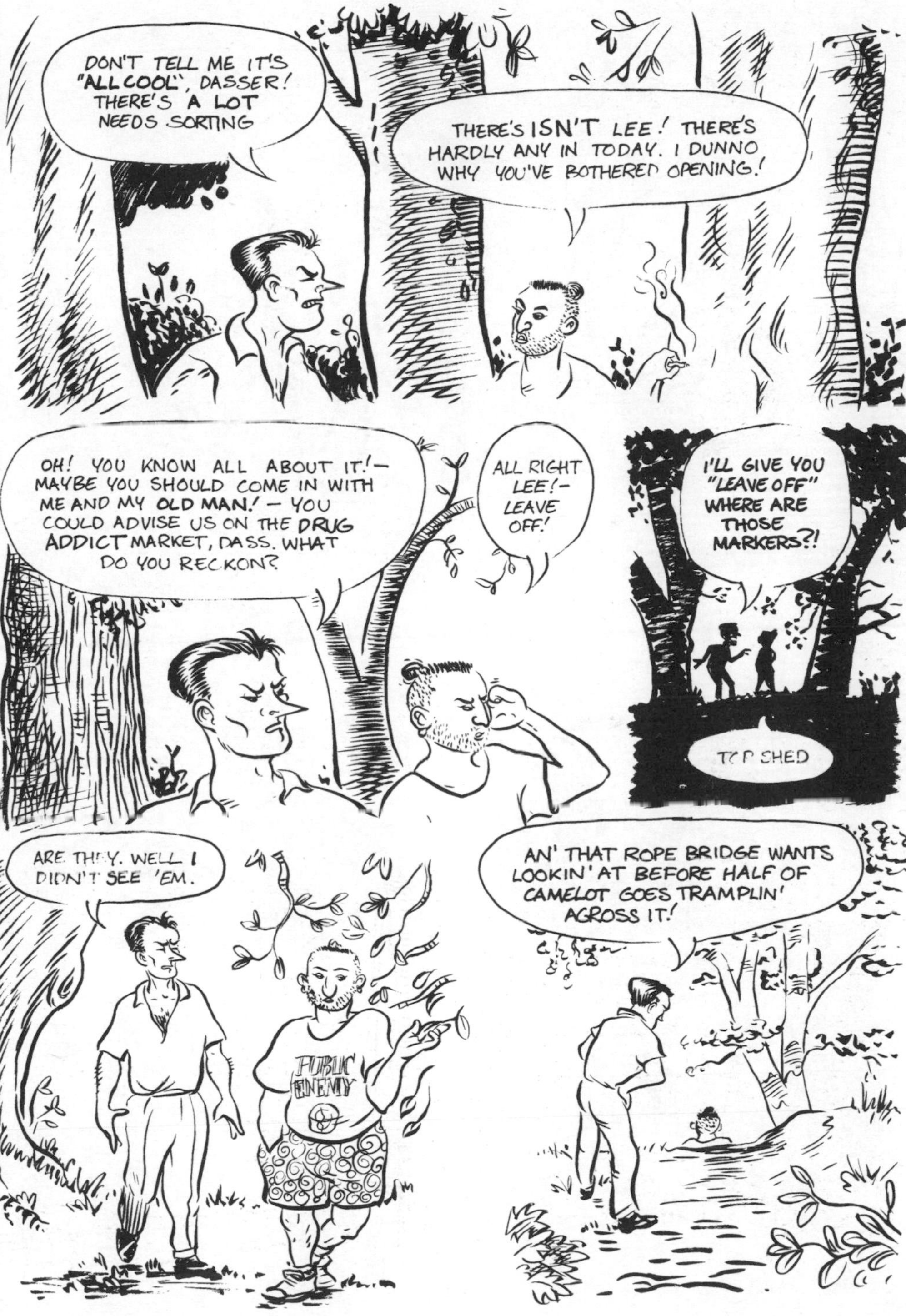

DON'T TELL ME IT'S "ALL COOL", DASSER! THERE'S A LOT NEEDS SORTING
THERE'S ISN'T LEE! THERE'S HARDLY ANY IN TODAY. I DUNNO WHY YOU'VE BOTHERED OPENING!
OH! YOU KNOW ALL ABOUT IT!— MAYBE YOU SHOULD COME IN WITH ME AND MY OLD MAN! — YOU COULD ADVISE US ON THE DRUG ADDICT MARKET, DASS. WHAT DO YOU RECKON?
ALL RIGHT LEE!— LEAVE OFF!
I'LL GIVE YOU "LEAVE OFF" WHERE ARE THOSE MARKERS?!
TOP SHED
ARE THEY. WELL I DIDN'T SEE 'EM.
PUBLIC ENEMY
AN' THAT ROPE BRIDGE WANTS LOOKIN' AT BEFORE HALF OF CAMELOT GOES TRAMPLIN' AGROSS IT!

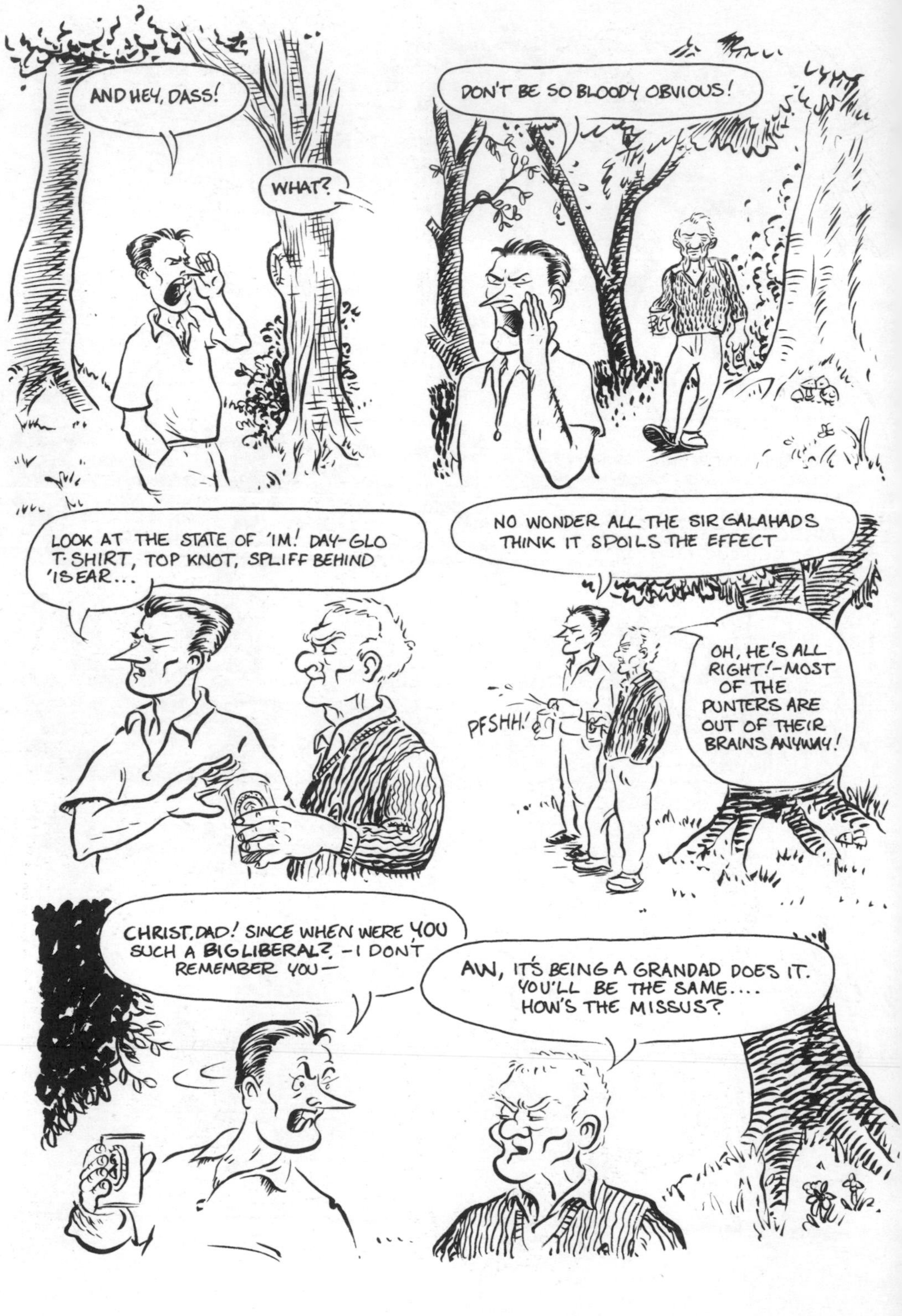
AND HEY, DASS!
WHAT?
DON'T BE SO BLOODY OBVIOUS!
LOOK AT THE STATE OF 'IM! DAY-GLO T-SHIRT, TOP KNOT, SPLIFF BEHIND 'IS EAR...
NO WONDER ALL THE SIR GALAHADS THINK IT SPOILS THE EFFECT
OH, HE'S ALL RIGHT!—MOST OF THE PUNTERS ARE OUT OF THEIR BRAINS ANYWAY!
PFSHH!
CHRIST, DAD! SINCE WHEN WERE YOU SUCH A BIG LIBERAL? —I DON'T REMEMBER YOU—
AW, IT'S BEING A GRANDAD DOES IT. YOU'LL BE THE SAME.... HOW'S THE MISSUS?
....

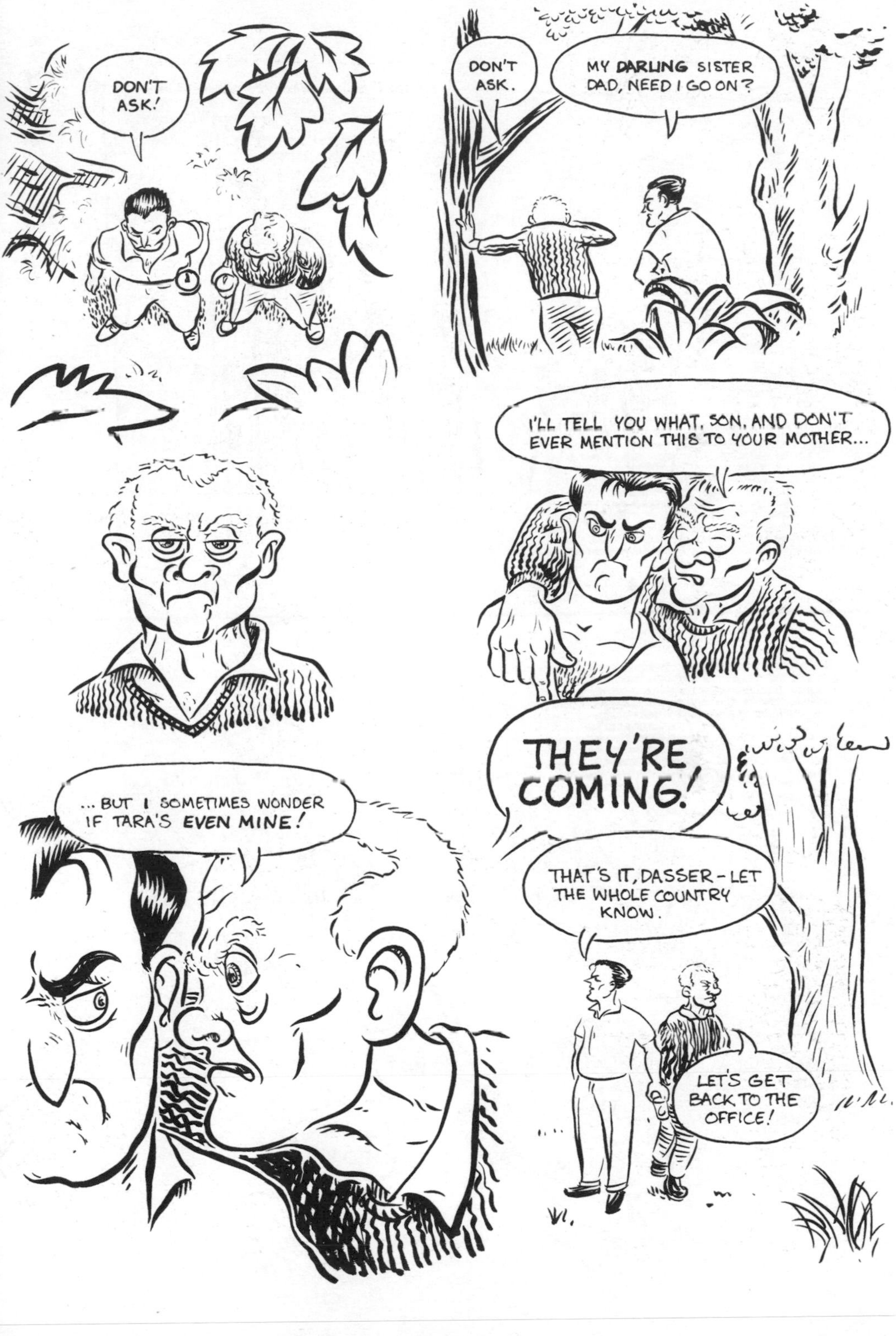
DON'T ASK!
DON'T ASK.
MY DARLING SISTER DAD, NEED I GO ON?
I'LL TELL YOU WHAT, SON, AND DON'T EVER MENTION THIS TO YOUR MOTHER...
... BUT I SOMETIMES WONDER IF TARA'S EVEN MINE!
THEY'RE COMING!
THAT'S IT, DASSER - LET THE WHOLE COUNTRY KNOW.
LET'S GET BACK TO THE OFFICE!

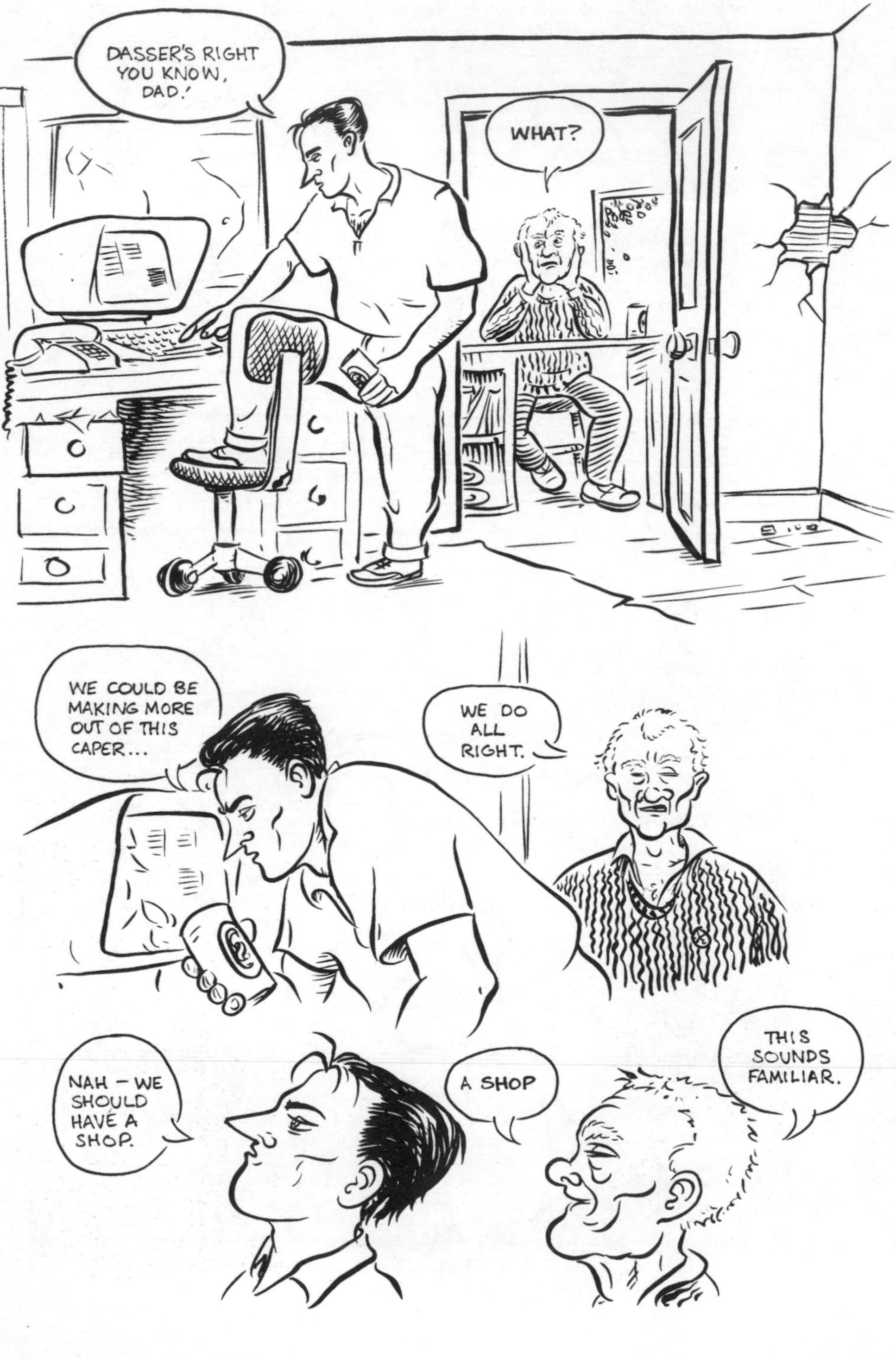
DASSER'S RIGHT YOU KNOW, DAD!
WHAT?
WE COULD BE MAKING MORE OUT OF THIS CAPER...
WE DO ALL RIGHT.
NAH - WE SHOULD HAVE A SHOP.
A SHOP
THIS SOUNDS FAMILIAR.

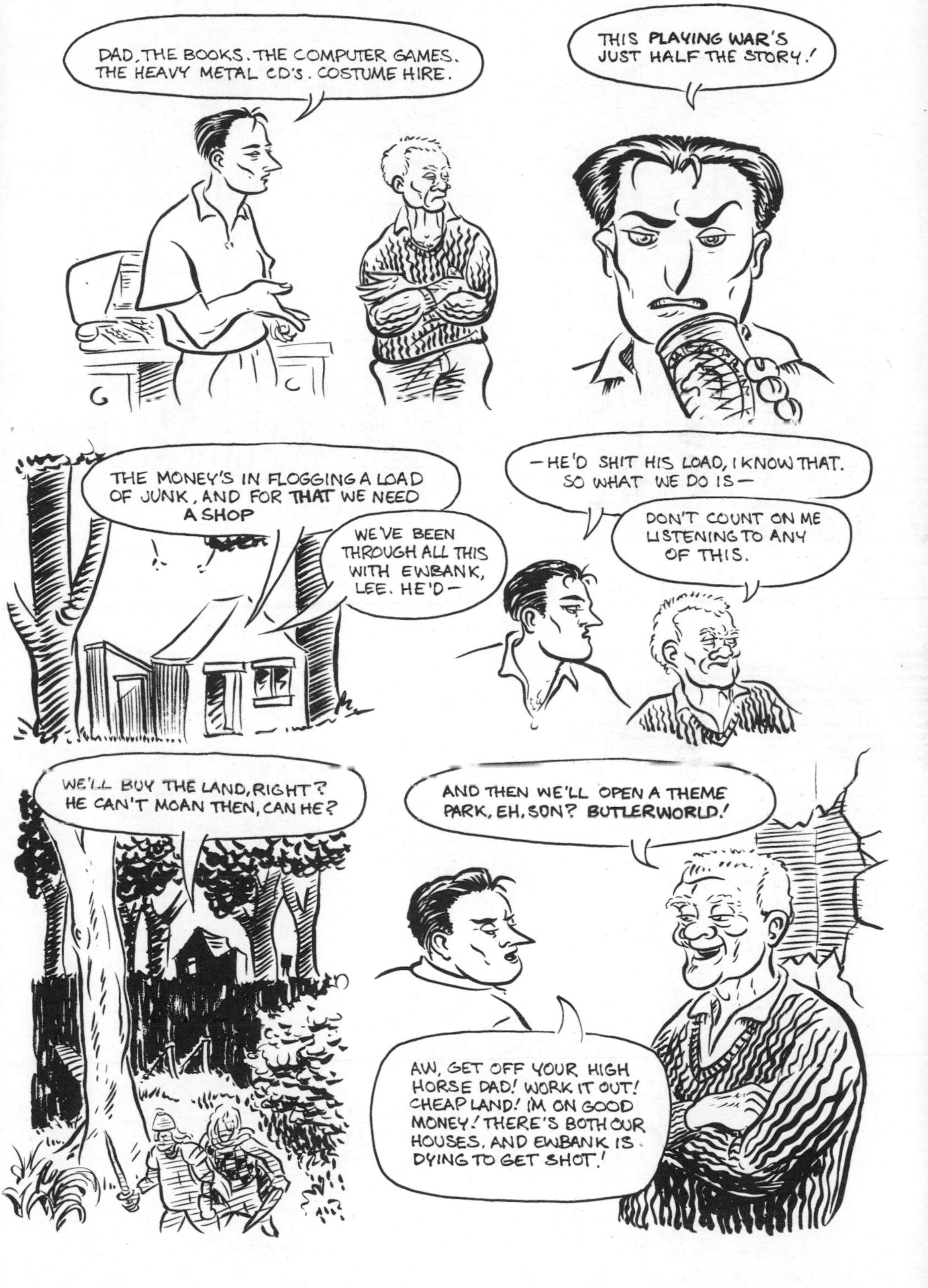
DAD, THE BOOKS. THE COMPUTER GAMES. THE HEAVY METAL CD'S. COSTUME HIRE.
THIS PLAYING WAR'S JUST HALF THE STORY!
THE MONEY'S IN FLOGGING A LOAD OF JUNK, AND FOR THAT WE NEED A SHOP
WE'VE BEEN THROUGH ALL THIS WITH EWBANK, LEE. HE'D–
–HE'D SHIT HIS LOAD, I KNOW THAT. SO WHAT WE DO IS–
DON'T COUNT ON ME LISTENING TO ANY OF THIS.
WE'LL BUY THE LAND, RIGHT? HE CAN'T MOAN THEN, CAN HE?
AND THEN WE'LL OPEN A THEME PARK, EH, SON? BUTLERWORLD!
AW, GET OFF YOUR HIGH HORSE DAD! WORK IT OUT! CHEAP LAND! I'M ON GOOD MONEY! THERE'S BOTH OUR HOUSES. AND EWBANK IS DYING TO GET SHOT!

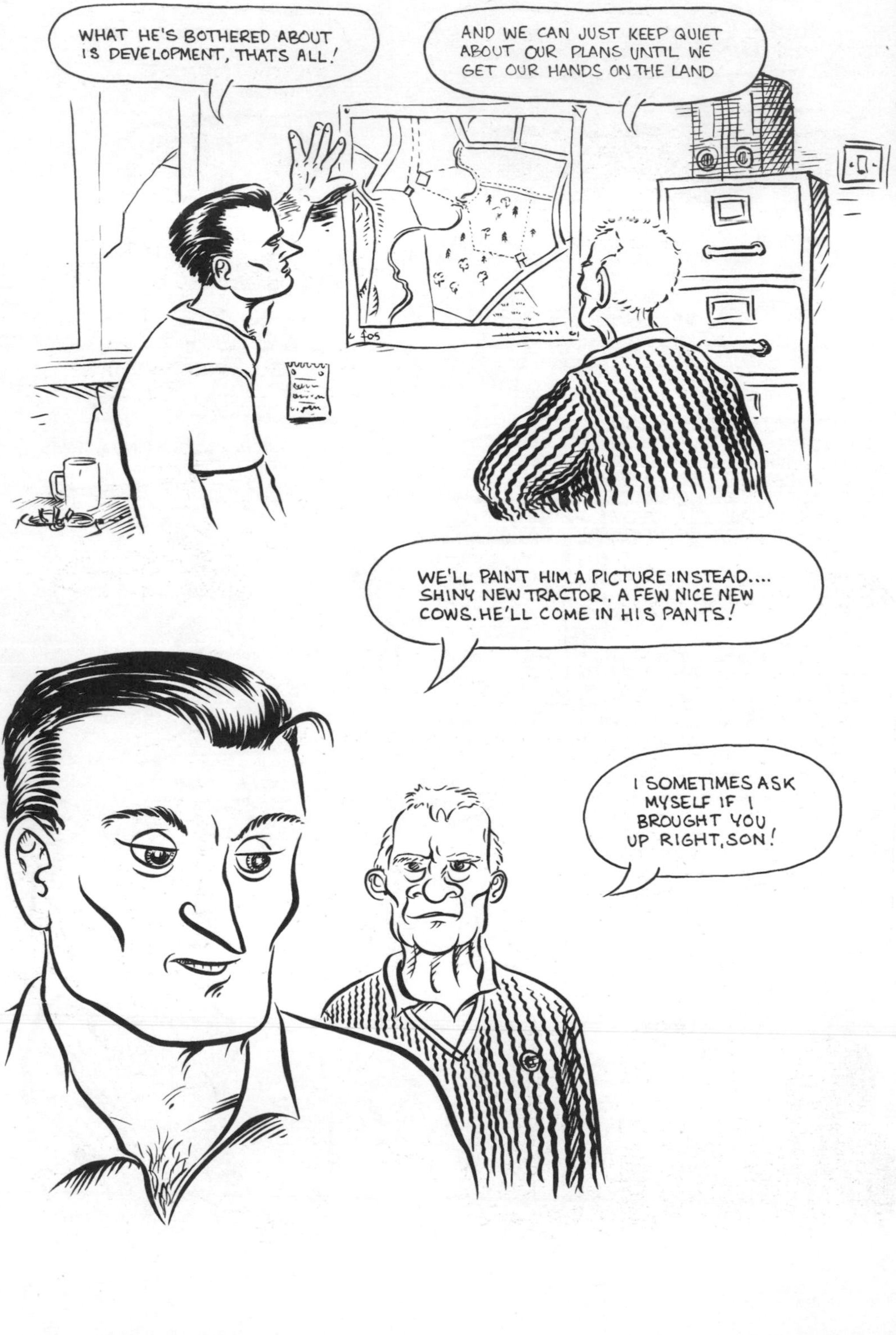
WHAT HE'S BOTHERED ABOUT IS DEVELOPMENT, THATS ALL!
AND WE CAN JUST KEEP QUIET ABOUT OUR PLANS UNTIL WE GET OUR HANDS ON THE LAND
WE'LL PAINT HIM A PICTURE INSTEAD.... SHINY NEW TRACTOR, A FEW NICE NEW COWS. HE'LL COME IN HIS PANTS!
I SOMETIMES ASK MYSELF IF I BROUGHT YOU UP RIGHT, SON!

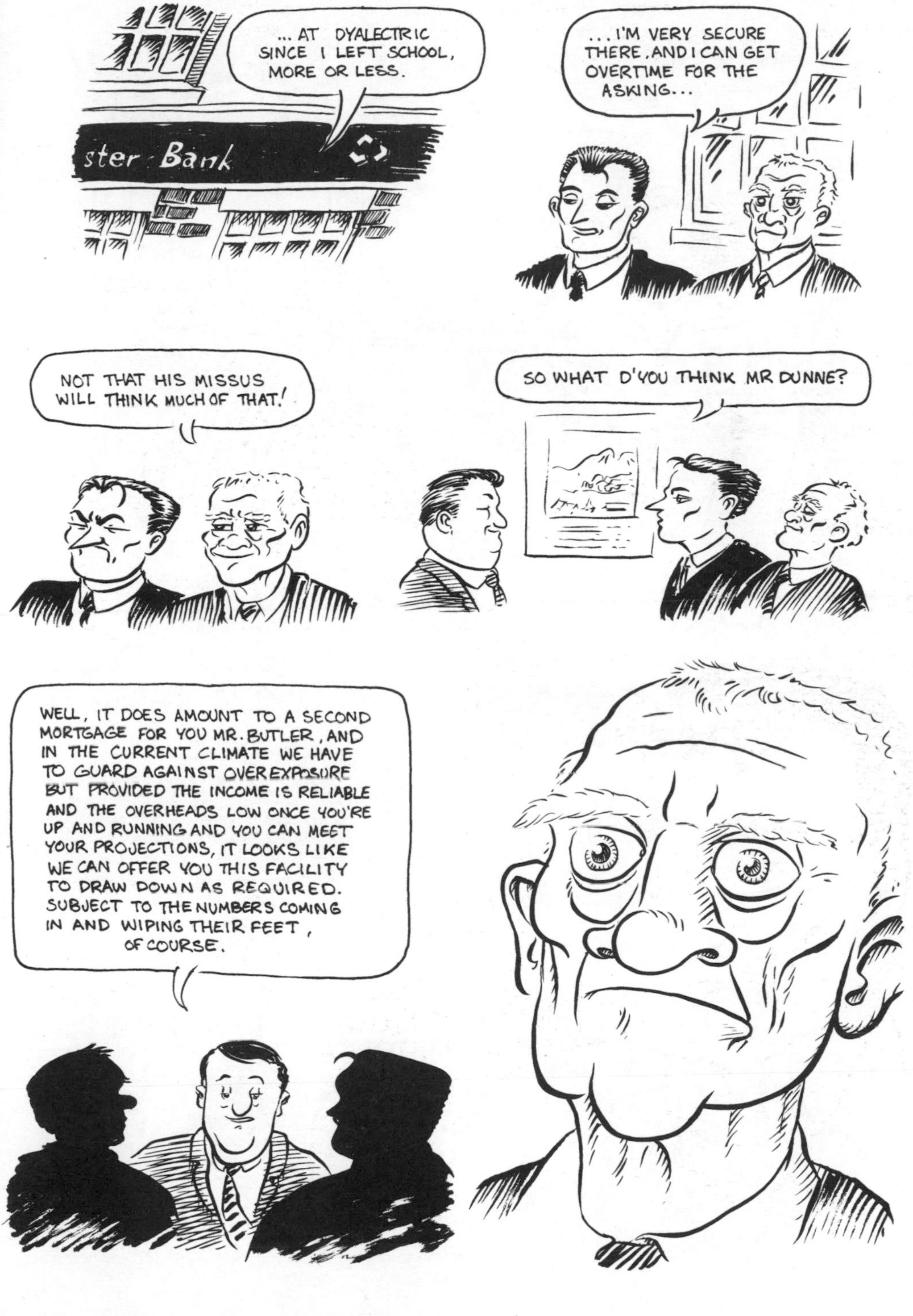
...AT DYALECTRIC SINCE I LEFT SCHOOL, MORE OR LESS.
ster Bank
...I'M VERY SECURE THERE, AND I CAN GET OVERTIME FOR THE ASKING...
NOT THAT HIS MISSUS WILL THINK MUCH OF THAT!
SO WHAT D'YOU THINK MR DUNNE?
WELL, IT DOES AMOUNT TO A SECOND MORTGAGE FOR YOU MR. BUTLER, AND IN THE CURRENT CLIMATE WE HAVE TO GUARD AGAINST OVEREXPOSURE BUT PROVIDED THE INCOME IS RELIABLE AND THE OVERHEADS LOW ONCE YOU'RE UP AND RUNNING AND YOU CAN MEET YOUR PROJECTIONS, IT LOOKS LIKE WE CAN OFFER YOU THIS FACILITY TO DRAW DOWN AS REQUIRED. SUBJECT TO THE NUMBERS COMING IN AND WIPING THEIR FEET, OF COURSE.

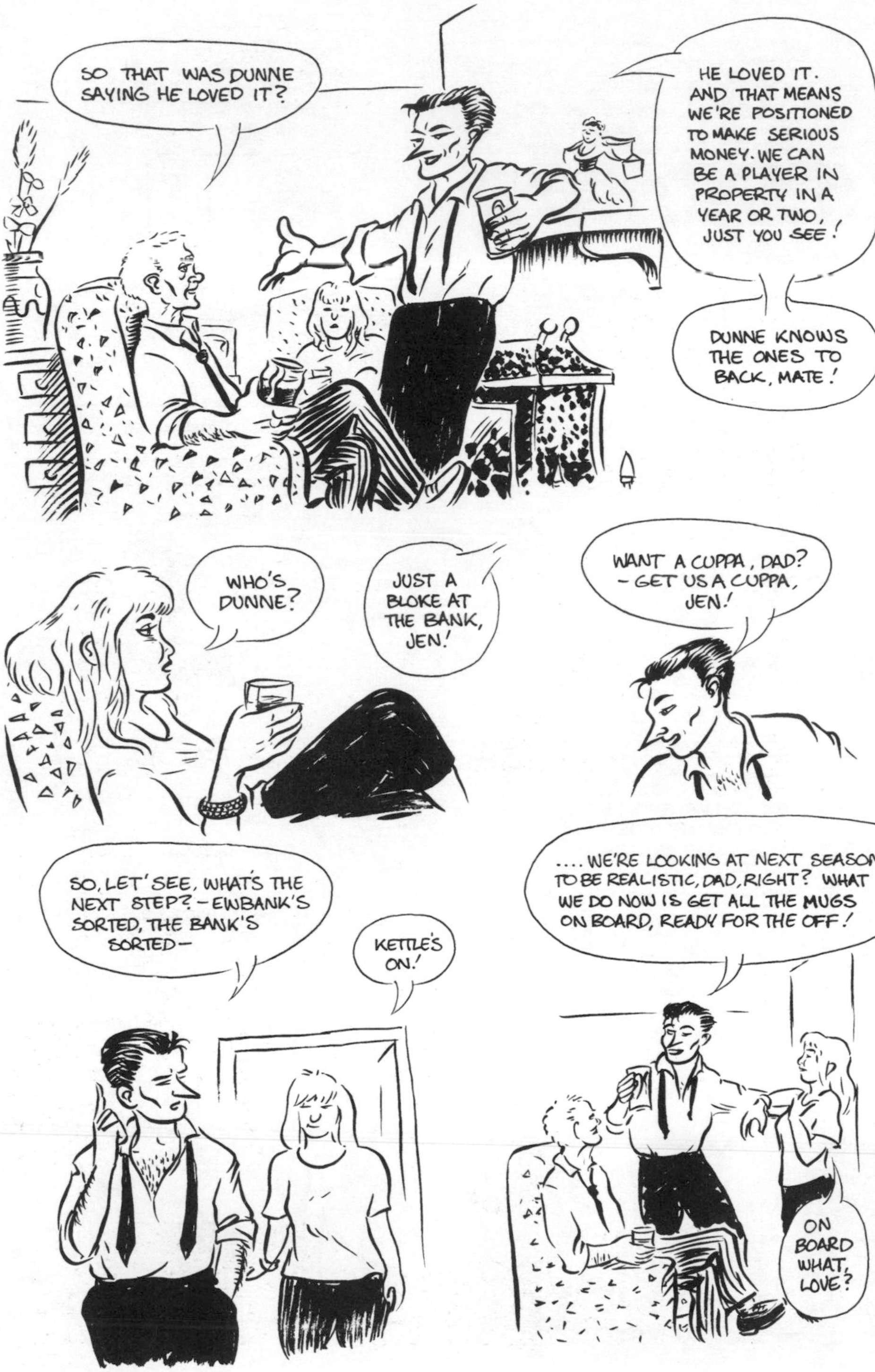
SO THAT WAS DUNNE SAYING HE LOVED IT?
HE LOVED IT. AND THAT MEANS WE'RE POSITIONED TO MAKE SERIOUS MONEY. WE CAN BE A PLAYER IN PROPERTY IN A YEAR OR TWO, JUST YOU SEE!
DUNNE KNOWS THE ONES TO BACK, MATE!
WHO'S DUNNE?
JUST A BLOKE AT THE BANK, JEN!
WANT A CUPPA, DAD? - GET US A CUPPA, JEN!
SO, LET' SEE, WHAT'S THE NEXT STEP? - EWBANK'S SORTED, THE BANK'S SORTED -
KETTLE'S ON!
.... WE'RE LOOKING AT NEXT SEASON, TO BE REALISTIC, DAD, RIGHT? WHAT WE DO NOW IS GET ALL THE MUGS ON BOARD, READY FOR THE OFF!
ON BOARD WHAT, LOVE?

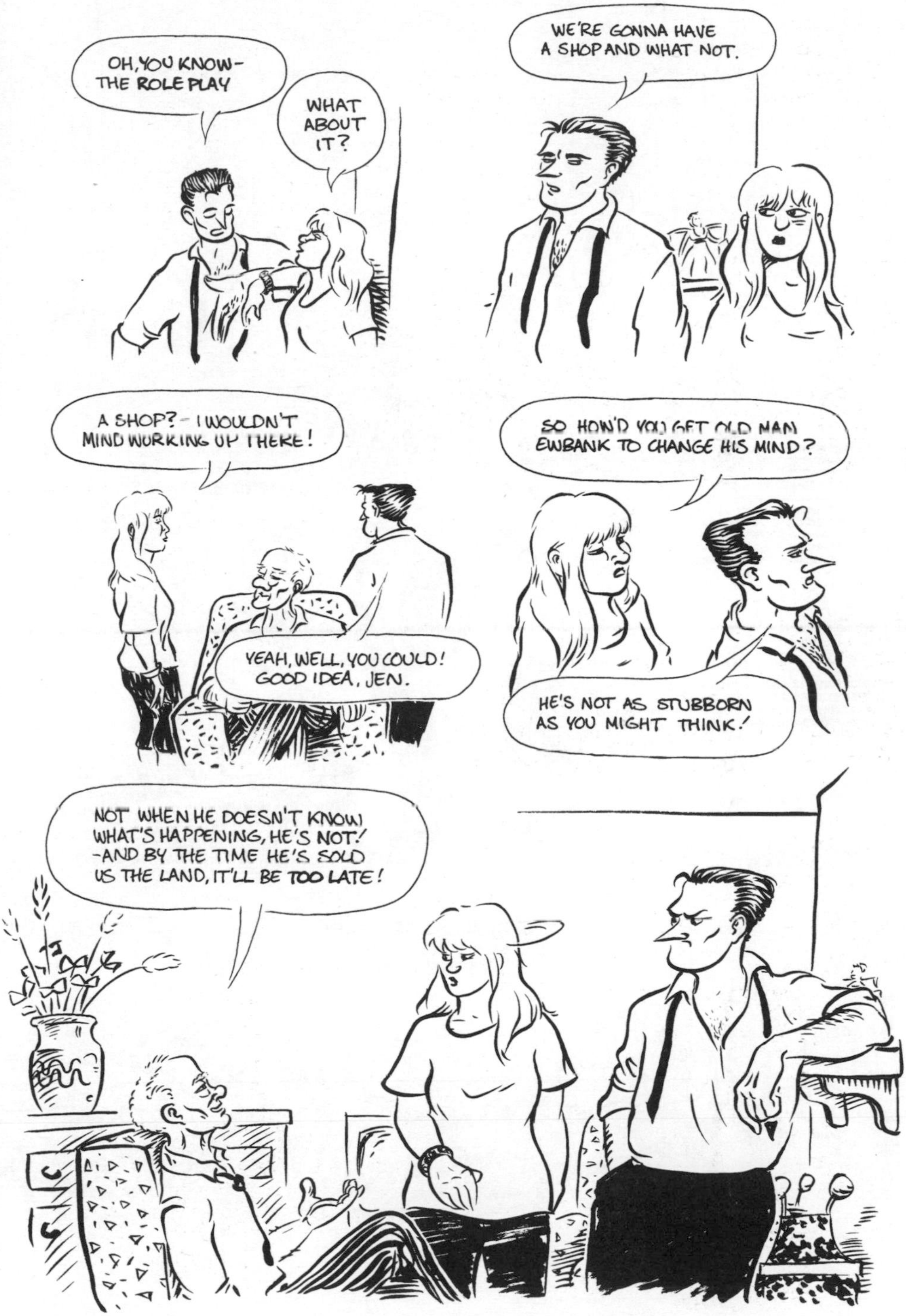
OH, YOU KNOW- THE ROLE PLAY
WHAT ABOUT IT?
WE'RE GONNA HAVE A SHOP AND WHAT NOT.
A SHOP? - I WOULDN'T MIND WORKING UP THERE!
YEAH, WELL, YOU COULD! GOOD IDEA, JEN.
SO HOW'D YOU GET OLD MAN EWBANK TO CHANGE HIS MIND?
HE'S NOT AS STUBBORN AS YOU MIGHT THINK!
NOT WHEN HE DOESN'T KNOW WHAT'S HAPPENING, HE'S NOT! -AND BY THE TIME HE'S SOLD US THE LAND, IT'LL BE TOO LATE!

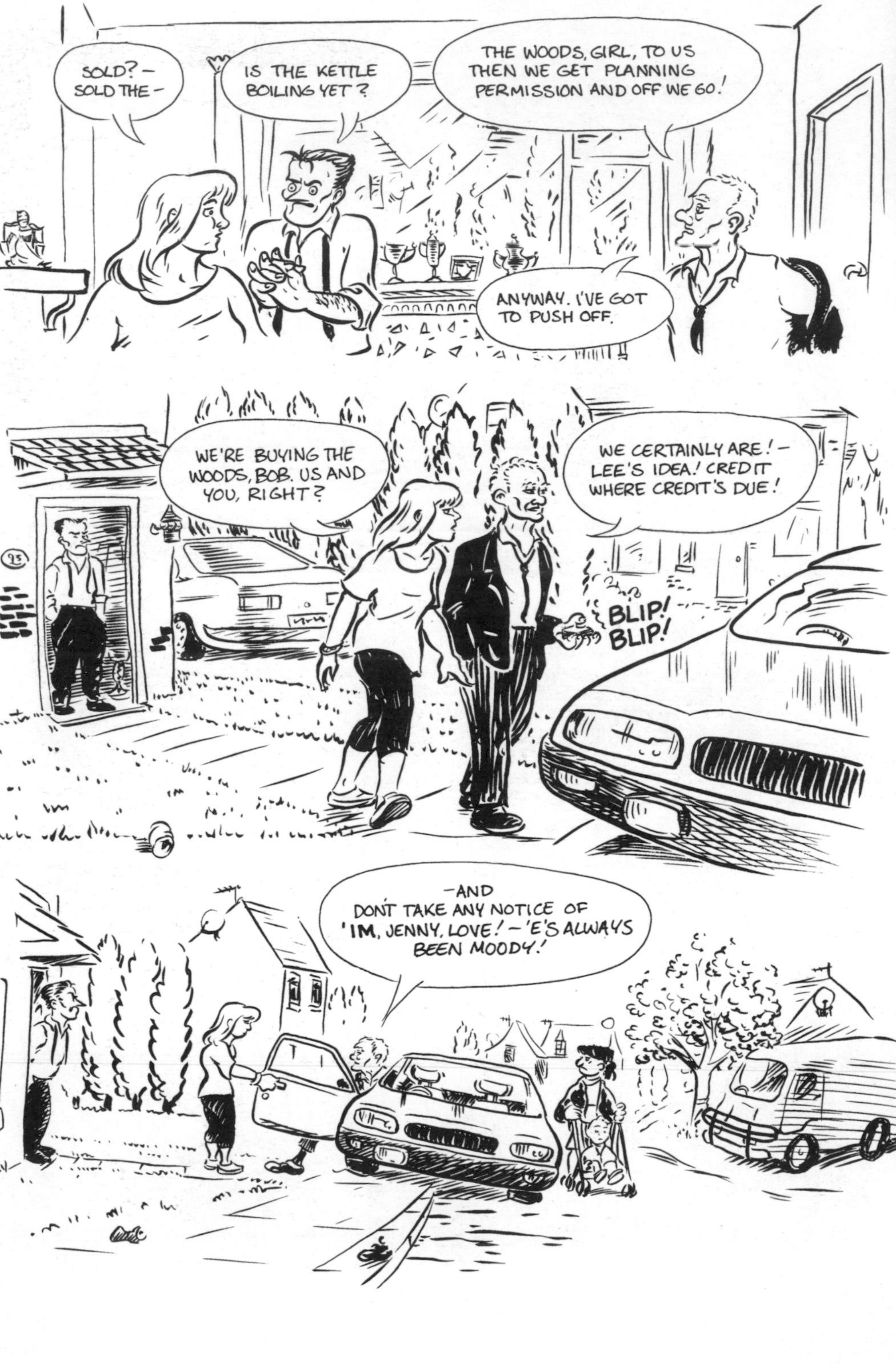

SOLD? — SOLD THE —
IS THE KETTLE BOILING YET?
THE WOODS, GIRL, TO US THEN WE GET PLANNING PERMISSION AND OFF WE GO!
ANYWAY. I'VE GOT TO PUSH OFF.
WE'RE BUYING THE WOODS, BOB. US AND YOU, RIGHT?
WE CERTAINLY ARE! — LEE'S IDEA! CREDIT WHERE CREDIT'S DUE!
BLIP! BLIP!
—AND DON'T TAKE ANY NOTICE OF 'IM, JENNY, LOVE! — 'E'S ALWAYS BEEN MOODY!

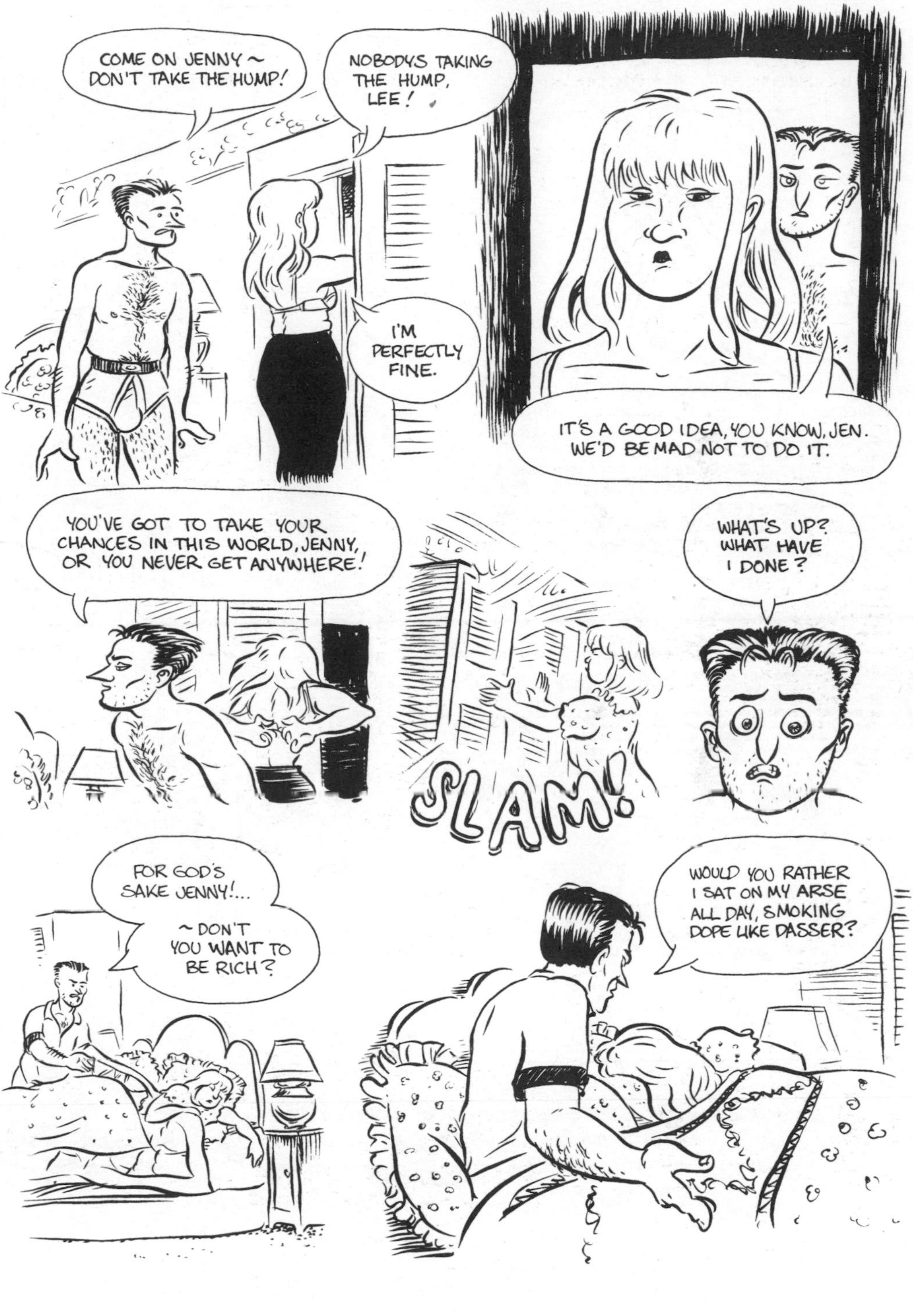
COME ON JENNY ~ DON'T TAKE THE HUMP!
NOBODY'S TAKING THE HUMP, LEE!
I'M PERFECTLY FINE.
IT'S A GOOD IDEA, YOU KNOW, JEN. WE'D BE MAD NOT TO DO IT.
YOU'VE GOT TO TAKE YOUR CHANCES IN THIS WORLD, JENNY, OR YOU NEVER GET ANYWHERE!
SLAM!
WHAT'S UP? WHAT HAVE I DONE?
FOR GOD'S SAKE JENNY!...
~ DON'T YOU WANT TO BE RICH?
WOULD YOU RATHER I SAT ON MY ARSE ALL DAY, SMOKING DOPE LIKE DASSER?

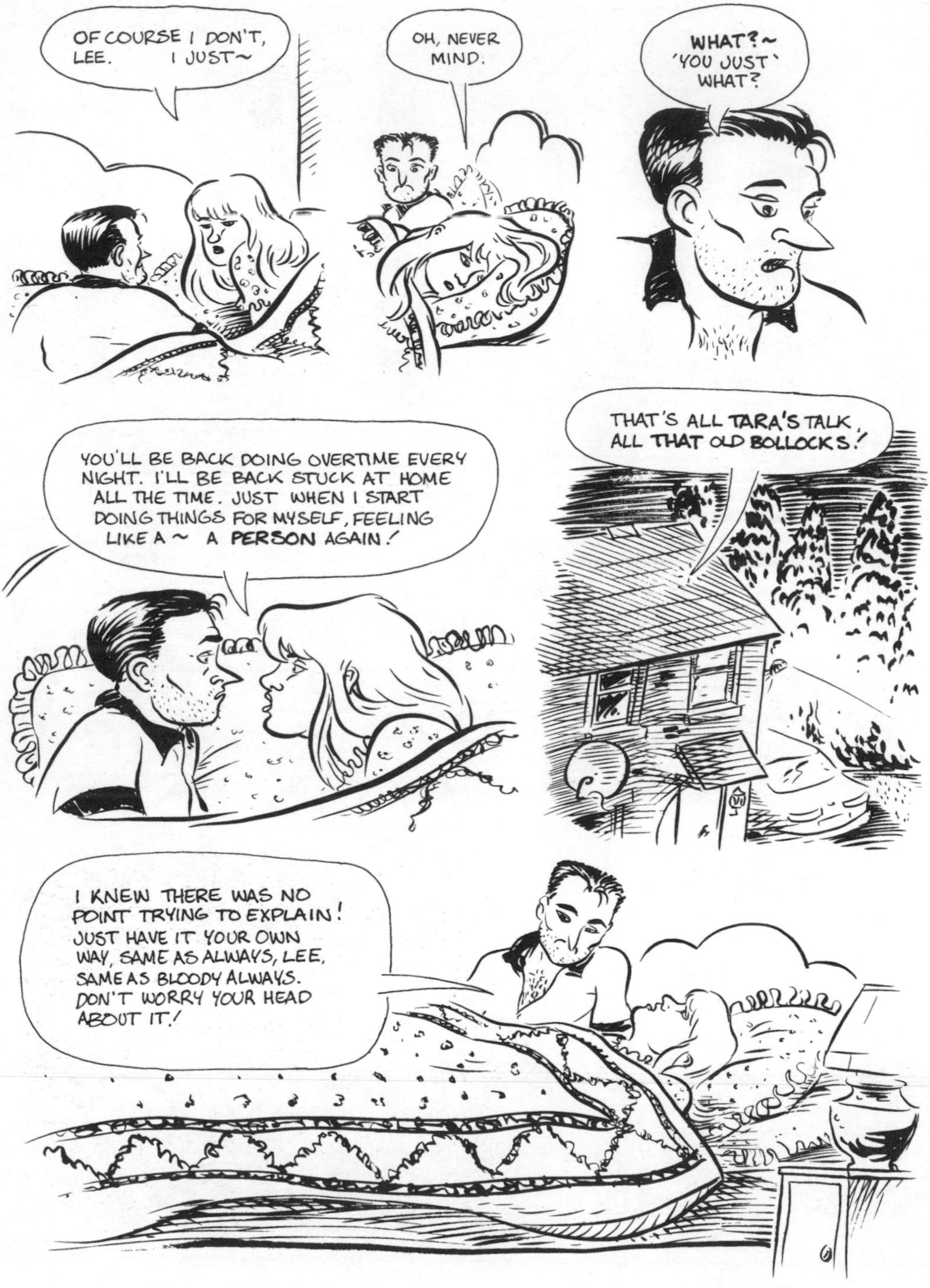
OF COURSE I DON'T, LEE. I JUST~
OH, NEVER MIND.
WHAT?~ 'YOU JUST' WHAT?
YOU'LL BE BACK DOING OVERTIME EVERY NIGHT. I'LL BE BACK STUCK AT HOME ALL THE TIME. JUST WHEN I START DOING THINGS FOR MYSELF, FEELING LIKE A ~ A PERSON AGAIN!
THAT'S ALL TARA'S TALK, ALL THAT OLD BOLLOCKS!
I KNEW THERE WAS NO POINT TRYING TO EXPLAIN! JUST HAVE IT YOUR OWN WAY, SAME AS ALWAYS, LEE, SAME AS BLOODY ALWAYS. DON'T WORRY YOUR HEAD ABOUT IT!

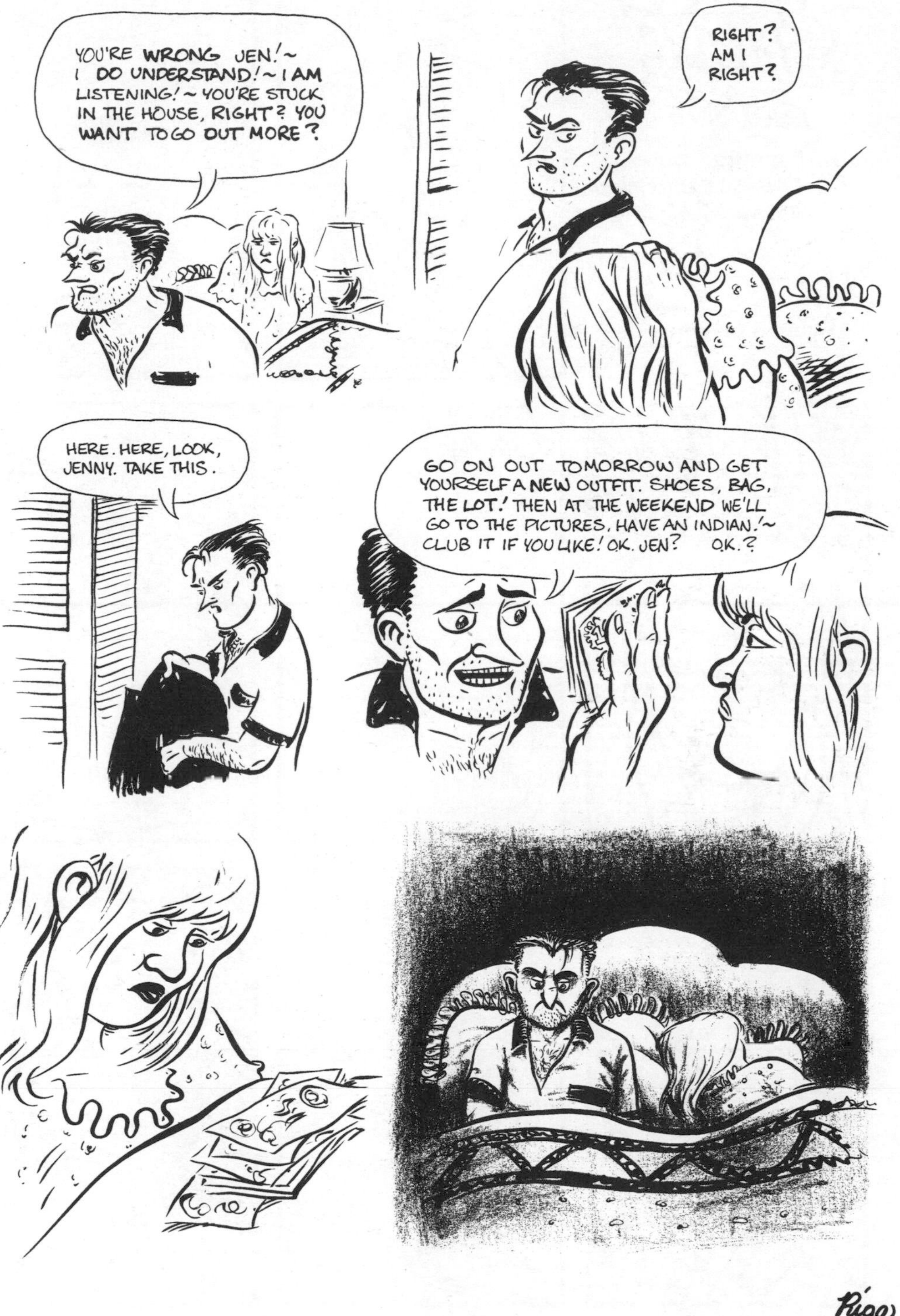
YOU'RE WRONG JEN!~ I DO UNDERSTAND!~ I AM LISTENING!~ YOU'RE STUCK IN THE HOUSE, RIGHT? YOU WANT TO GO OUT MORE?
RIGHT? AM I RIGHT?
HERE. HERE, LOOK, JENNY. TAKE THIS.
GO ON OUT TOMORROW AND GET YOURSELF A NEW OUTFIT. SHOES, BAG, THE LOT! THEN AT THE WEEKEND WE'LL GO TO THE PICTURES, HAVE AN INDIAN!~ CLUB IT IF YOU LIKE! OK. JEN? OK.?
Rigg

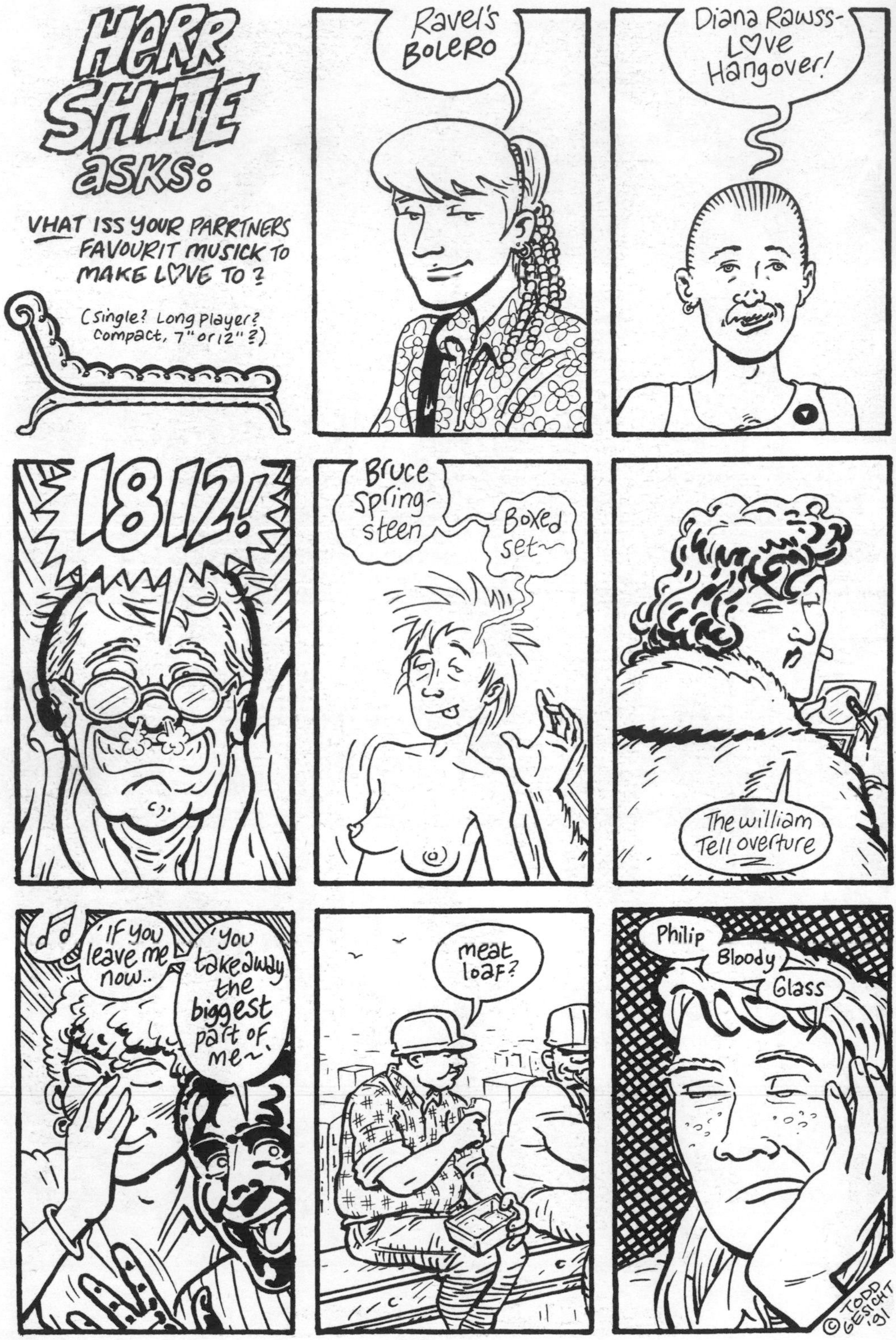
HERR SHITE asks:
VHAT ISS YOUR PARRTNERS FAVOURIT MUSICK TO MAKE LOVE TO?
(single? Long player? compact, 7" or 12"?)
Ravel's BOLERO
Diana Rawss- Love Hangover!
1812!
Bruce Spring-steen
Boxed set~
The william Tell overture
'If you leave me now..
'You take away the biggest part of me~'
meat loaf?
Philip
Bloody
Glass
© TODD GESICHT '91

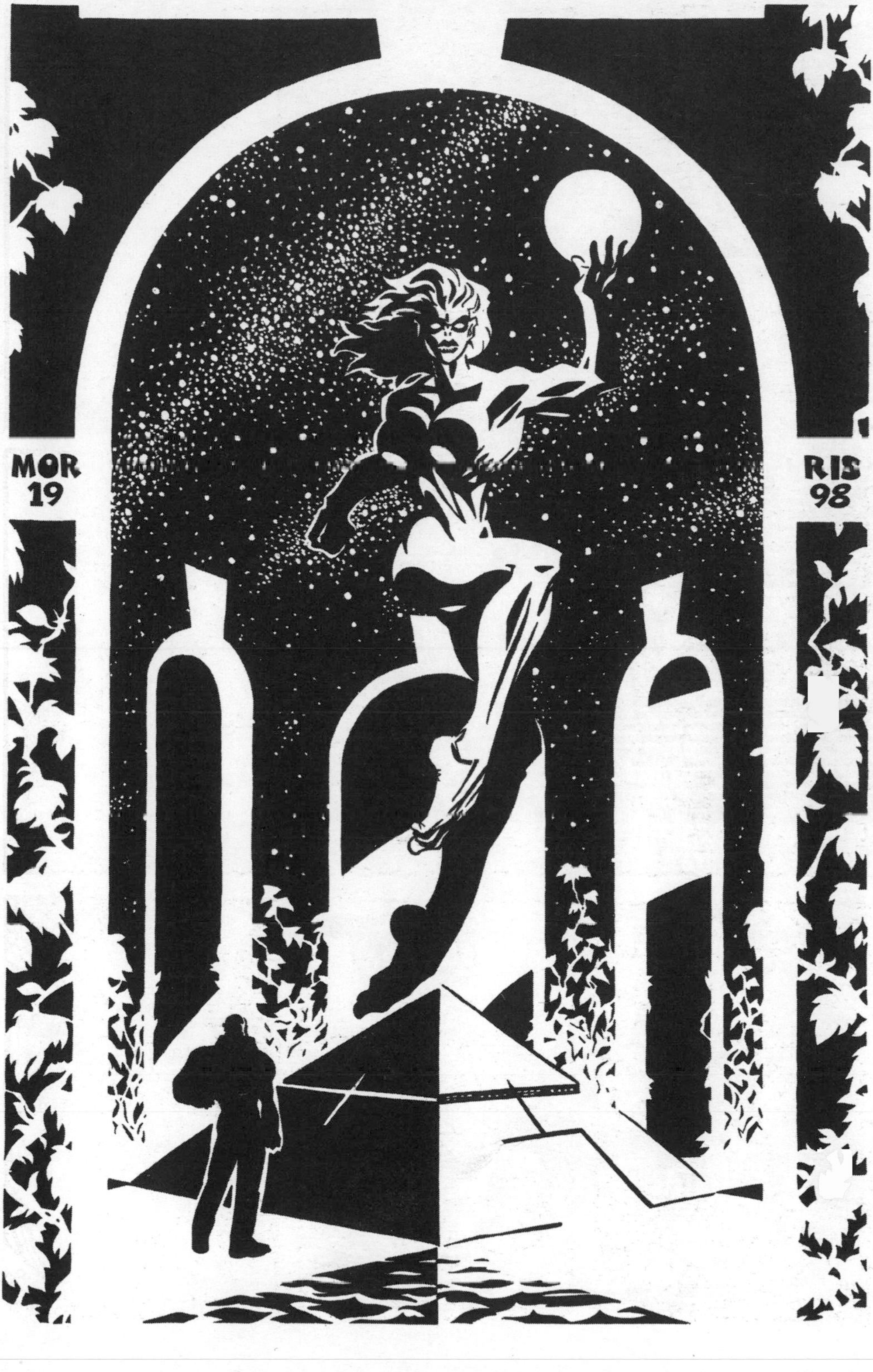
MOR
19
RIS
98

Dom Morris

SADIST
Self-published (in a tiny print run), 1998

The *Sadist* strip evolved from doodles in school notepads, via fanzine *Lobster Telephone* to national circulation in *Deadline* magazine (home of Jamie Hewlett's *Tank Girl*). The misadventures of a cold-blooded media mogul and his strangely inhuman minder in a near-future UK, it collapses pop culture, kung fu, sci-fi, cars, guns, gore and weirdness into a single bastard hard core. Famously, a Princess Diana-type character died after a high-speed car chase, several years before her real-life counterpart. Of the minor celebs parodied in this episode, Rod Hull then plunged to his death whilst fixing the roof, and East 17's Brian Harvey somehow managed to run himself over in his own car.

"Perhaps a break in publication was for the best in light of this chilling 'medusa touch'. These days I'm a video artist and animator, but the *Sadist* characters are alive and well in my head and evolving all the time. Harry will return!" – DM

www.harrysadist.com

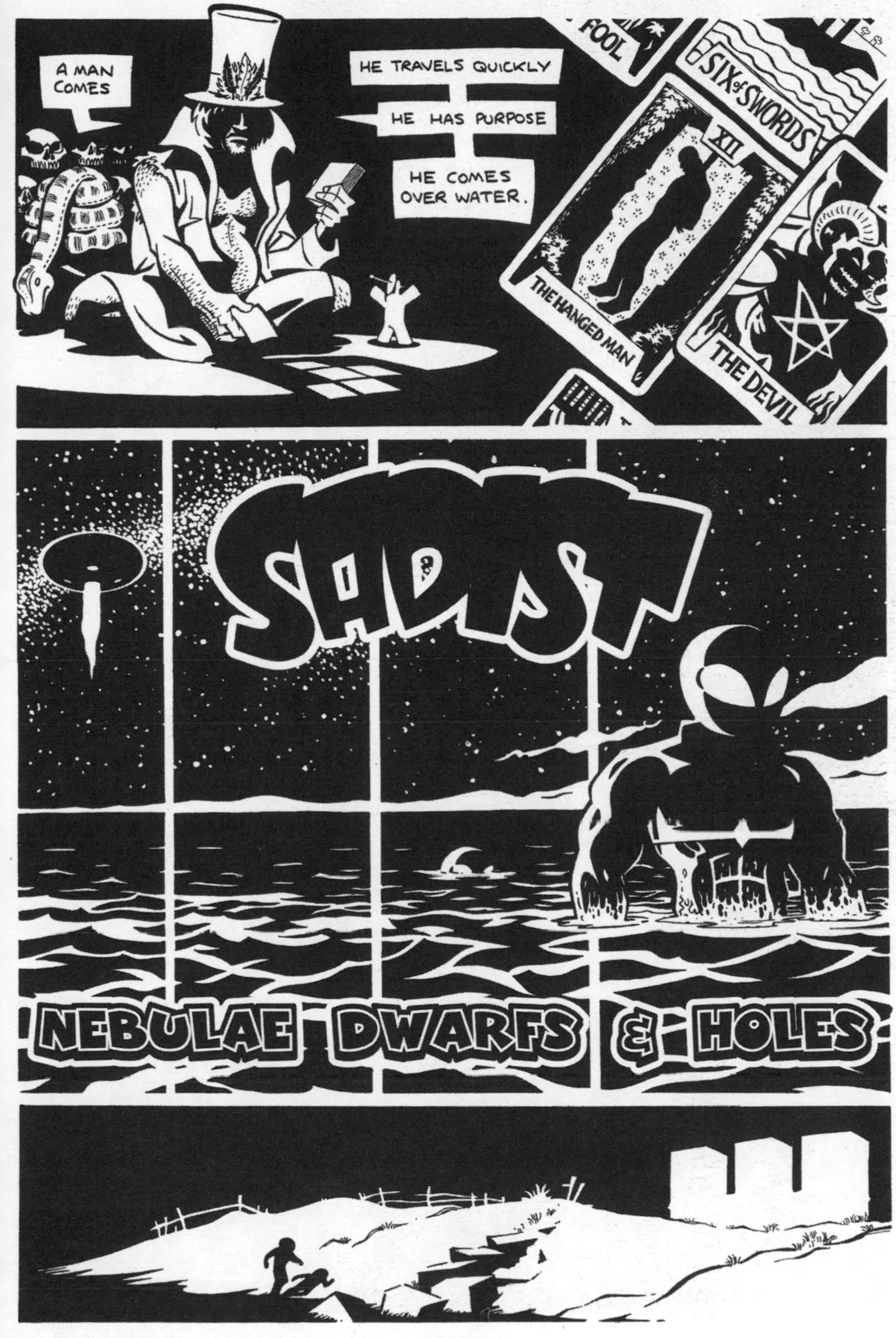
A MAN COMES
HE TRAVELS QUICKLY
HE HAS PURPOSE
HE COMES OVER WATER.
FOOL
SIX of SWORDS
XII
THE HANGED MAN
THE DEVIL
SADIST
NEBULAE DWARFS & HOLES

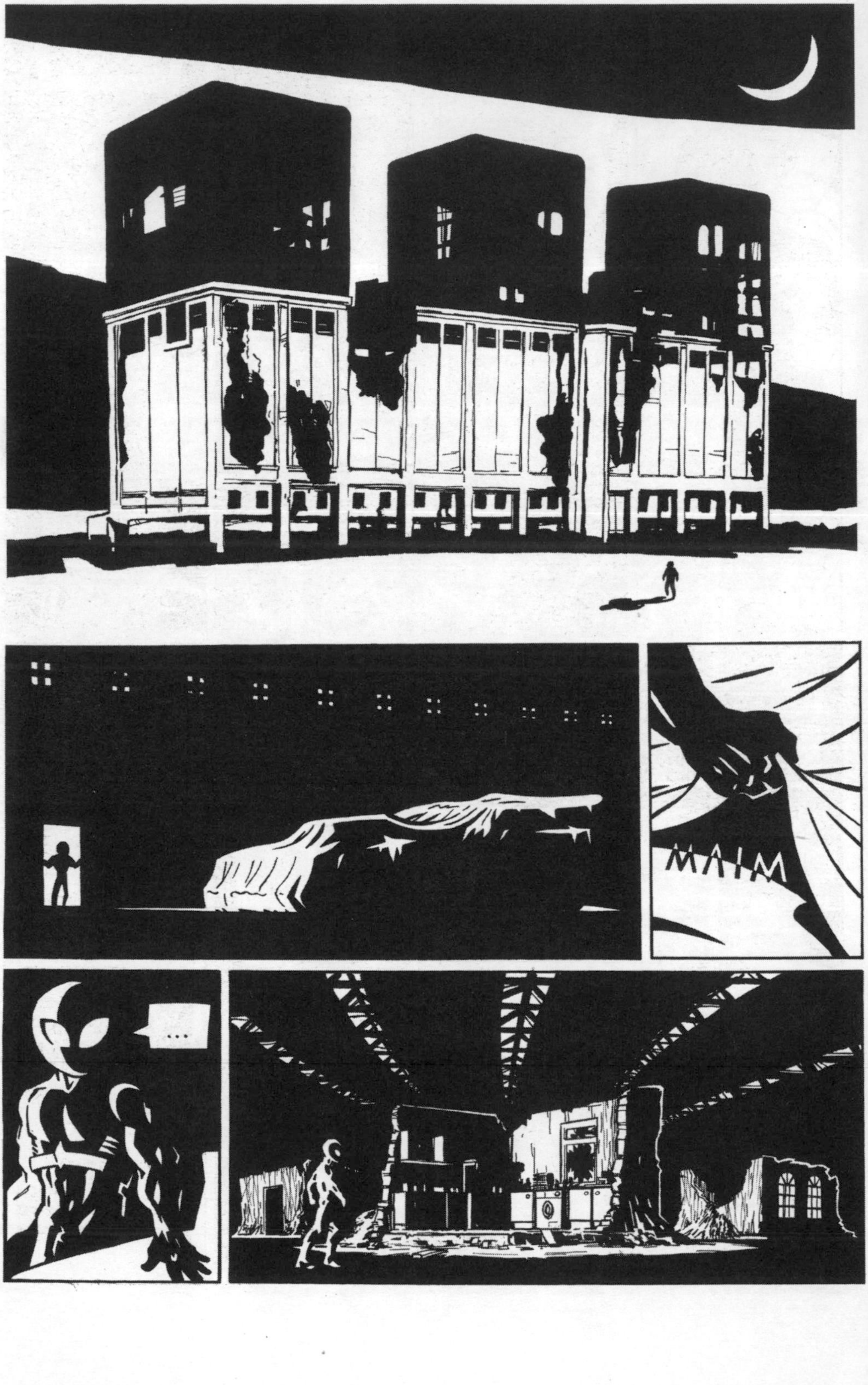
MAIM
...

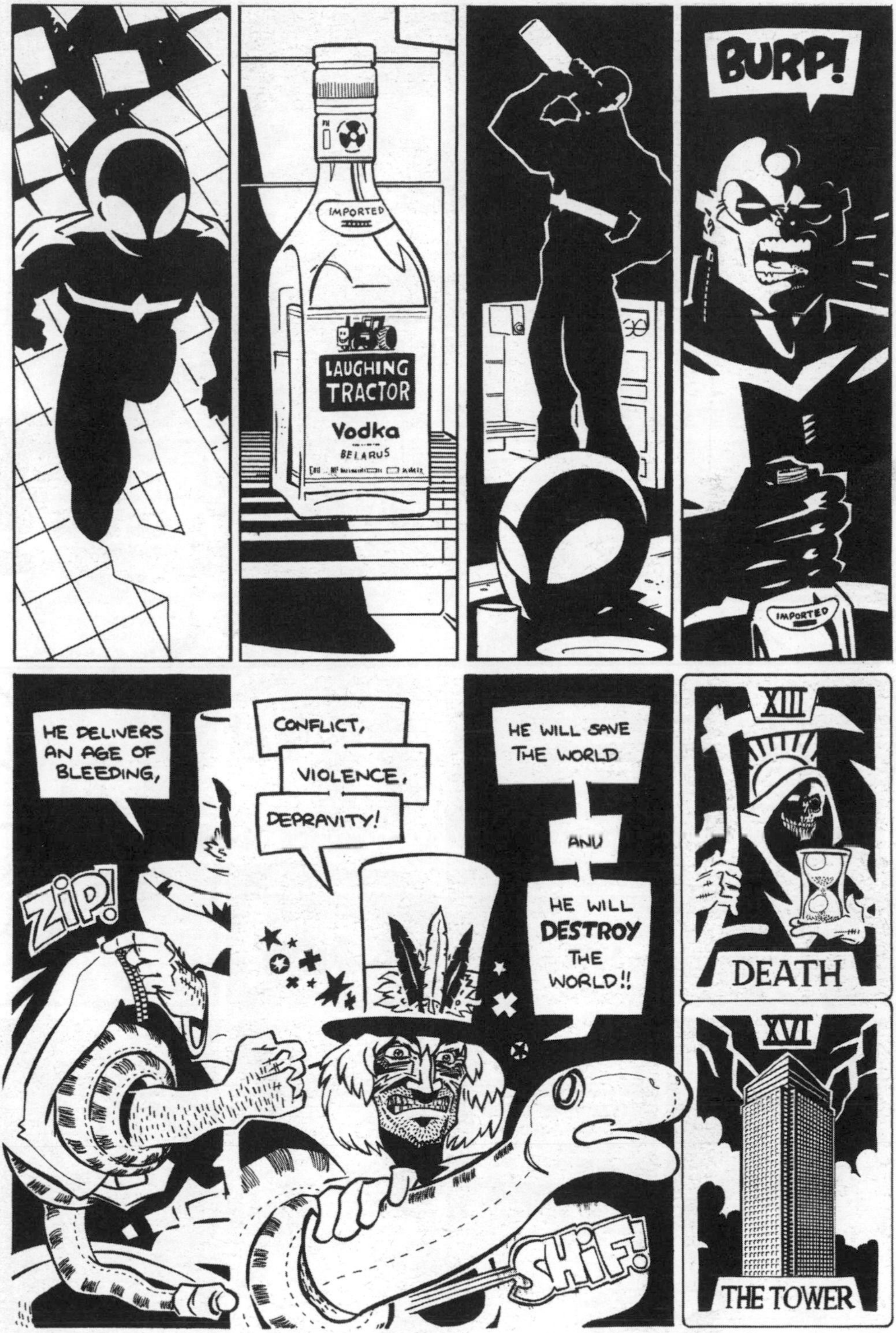
IMPORTED
LAUGHING TRACTOR
Vodka
BELARUS
BURP!
IMPORTED
HE DELIVERS AN AGE OF BLEEDING,
ZIP!
CONFLICT,
VIOLENCE,
DEPRAVITY!
HE WILL SAVE THE WORLD
AND
HE WILL DESTROY THE WORLD!!
SHIF!
XIII
DEATH
XVI
THE TOWER

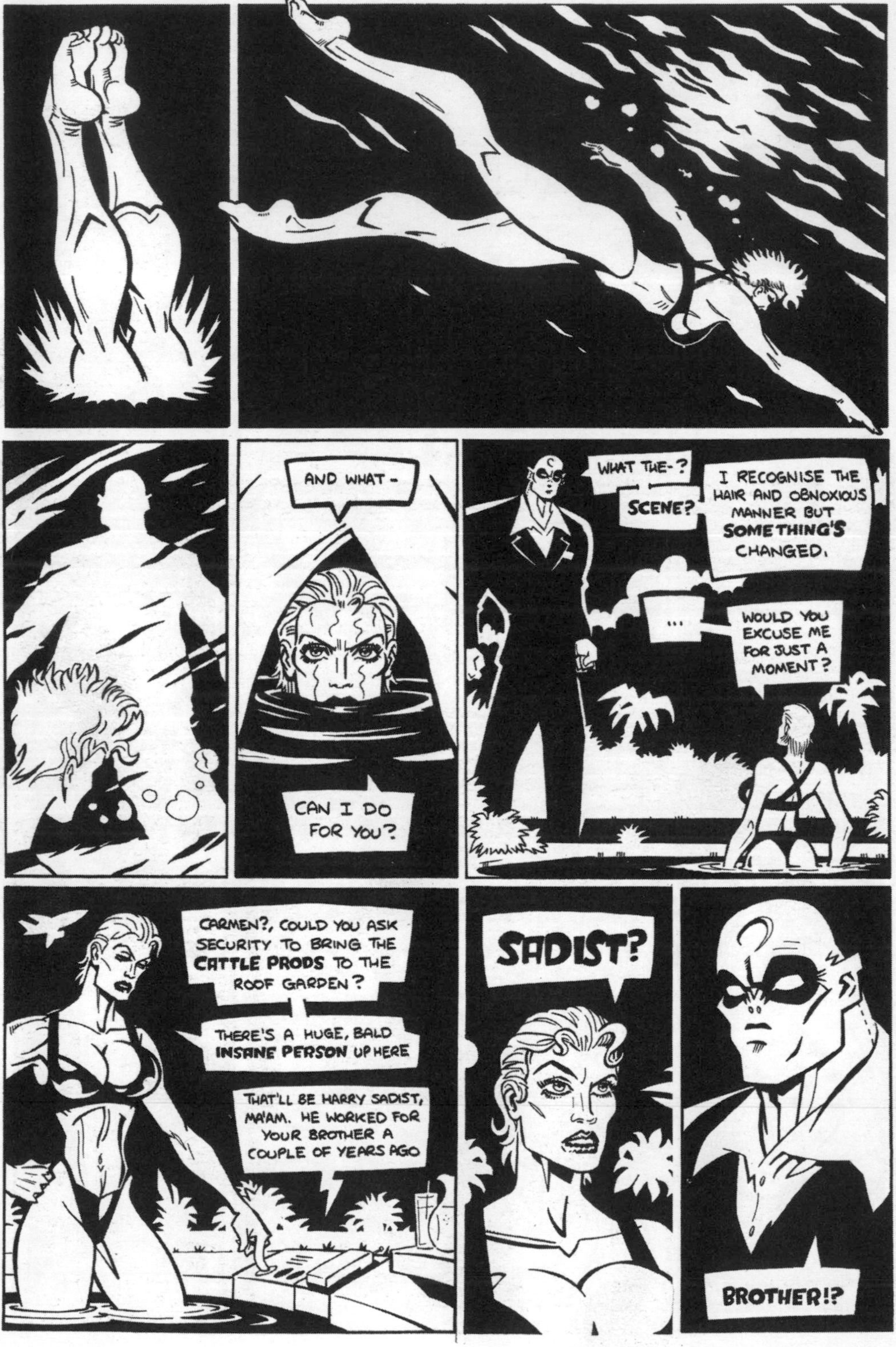

AND WHAT-
CAN I DO FOR YOU?
WHAT THE-?
SCENE?
I RECOGNISE THE HAIR AND OBNOXIOUS MANNER BUT SOMETHING'S CHANGED.
...
WOULD YOU EXCUSE ME FOR JUST A MOMENT?
CARMEN?, COULD YOU ASK SECURITY TO BRING THE CATTLE PRODS TO THE ROOF GARDEN?
THERE'S A HUGE, BALD INSANE PERSON UP HERE
THAT'LL BE HARRY SADIST, MA'AM. HE WORKED FOR YOUR BROTHER A COUPLE OF YEARS AGO
SADIST?
BROTHER!?

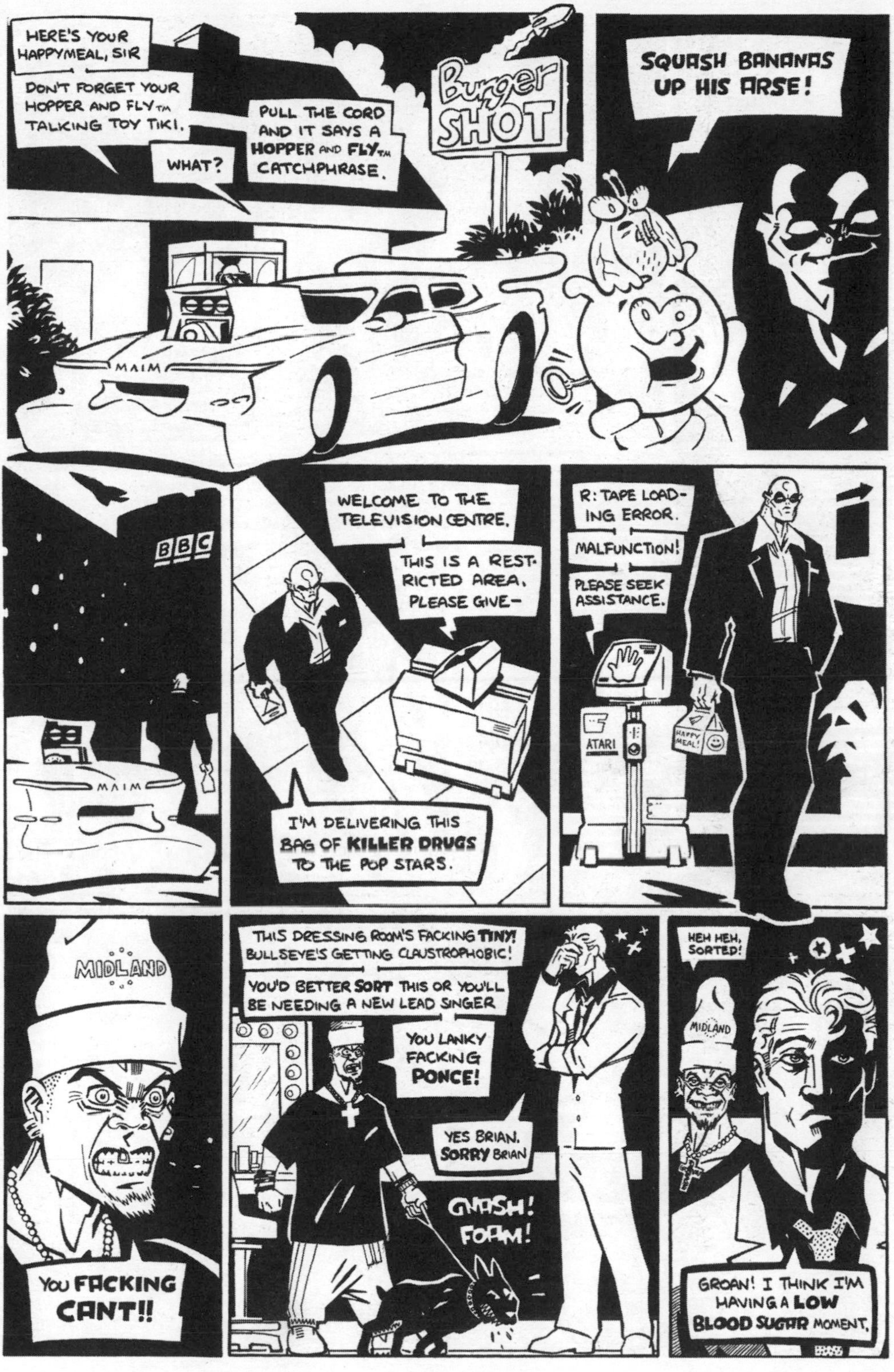
HERE'S YOUR HAPPYMEAL, SIR
DON'T FORGET YOUR HOPPER AND FLY™ TALKING TOY TIKI.
WHAT?
PULL THE CORD AND IT SAYS A HOPPER AND FLY™ CATCHPHRASE.
Burger SHOT
MAIM
SQUASH BANANAS UP HIS ARSE!
BBC
MAIM
WELCOME TO THE TELEVISION CENTRE.
THIS IS A RESTRICTED AREA. PLEASE GIVE-
I'M DELIVERING THIS BAG OF KILLER DRUGS TO THE POP STARS.
R: TAPE LOADING ERROR.
MALFUNCTION!
PLEASE SEEK ASSISTANCE.
ATARI
HAPPY MEAL!
MIDLAND
You FACKING CANT!!
THIS DRESSING ROOM'S FACKING TINY! BULLSEYE'S GETTING CLAUSTROPHOBIC!
YOU'D BETTER SORT THIS OR YOU'LL BE NEEDING A NEW LEAD SINGER
YOU LANKY FACKING PONCE!
YES BRIAN. SORRY BRIAN
GNASH! FOAM!
HEH HEH, SORTED!
MIDLAND
GROAN! I THINK I'M HAVING A LOW BLOOD SUGAR MOMENT.

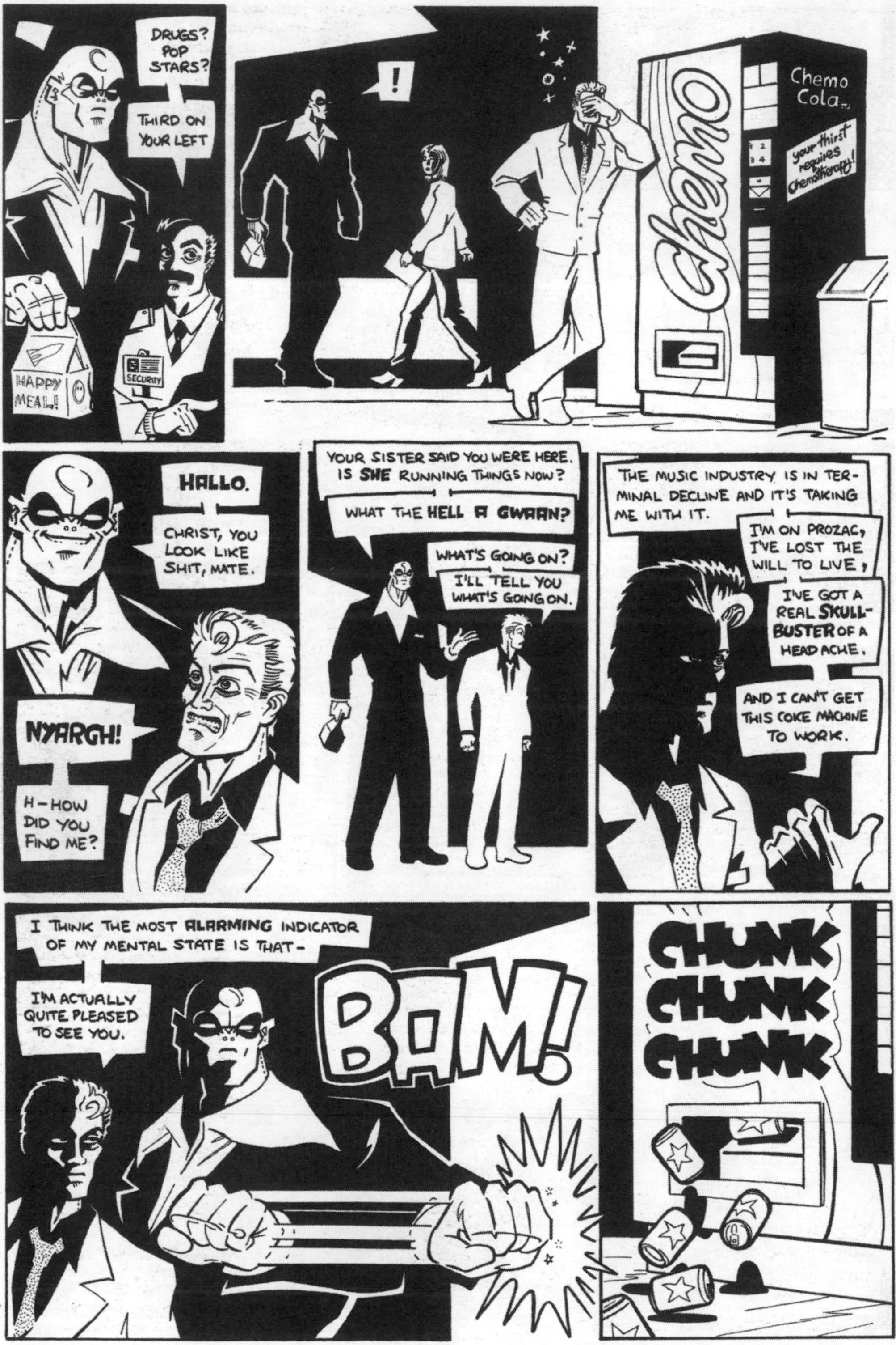
DRUGS? POP STARS?
THIRD ON YOUR LEFT
HAPPY MEAL!
SECURITY
!
Chemo
Chemo Cola
your thirst requires Chemotherapy!
HALLO.
CHRIST, YOU LOOK LIKE SHIT, MATE.
NYARGH!
H-HOW DID YOU FIND ME?
YOUR SISTER SAID YOU WERE HERE. IS SHE RUNNING THINGS NOW?
WHAT THE HELL A GWAAN?
WHAT'S GOING ON?
I'LL TELL YOU WHAT'S GOING ON.
THE MUSIC INDUSTRY IS IN TERMINAL DECLINE AND IT'S TAKING ME WITH IT.
I'M ON PROZAC, I'VE LOST THE WILL TO LIVE,
I'VE GOT A REAL SKULL-BUSTER OF A HEADACHE.
AND I CAN'T GET THIS COKE MACHINE TO WORK.
I THINK THE MOST ALARMING INDICATOR OF MY MENTAL STATE IS THAT-
I'M ACTUALLY QUITE PLEASED TO SEE YOU.
BAM!
CHUNK
CHUNK
CHUNK

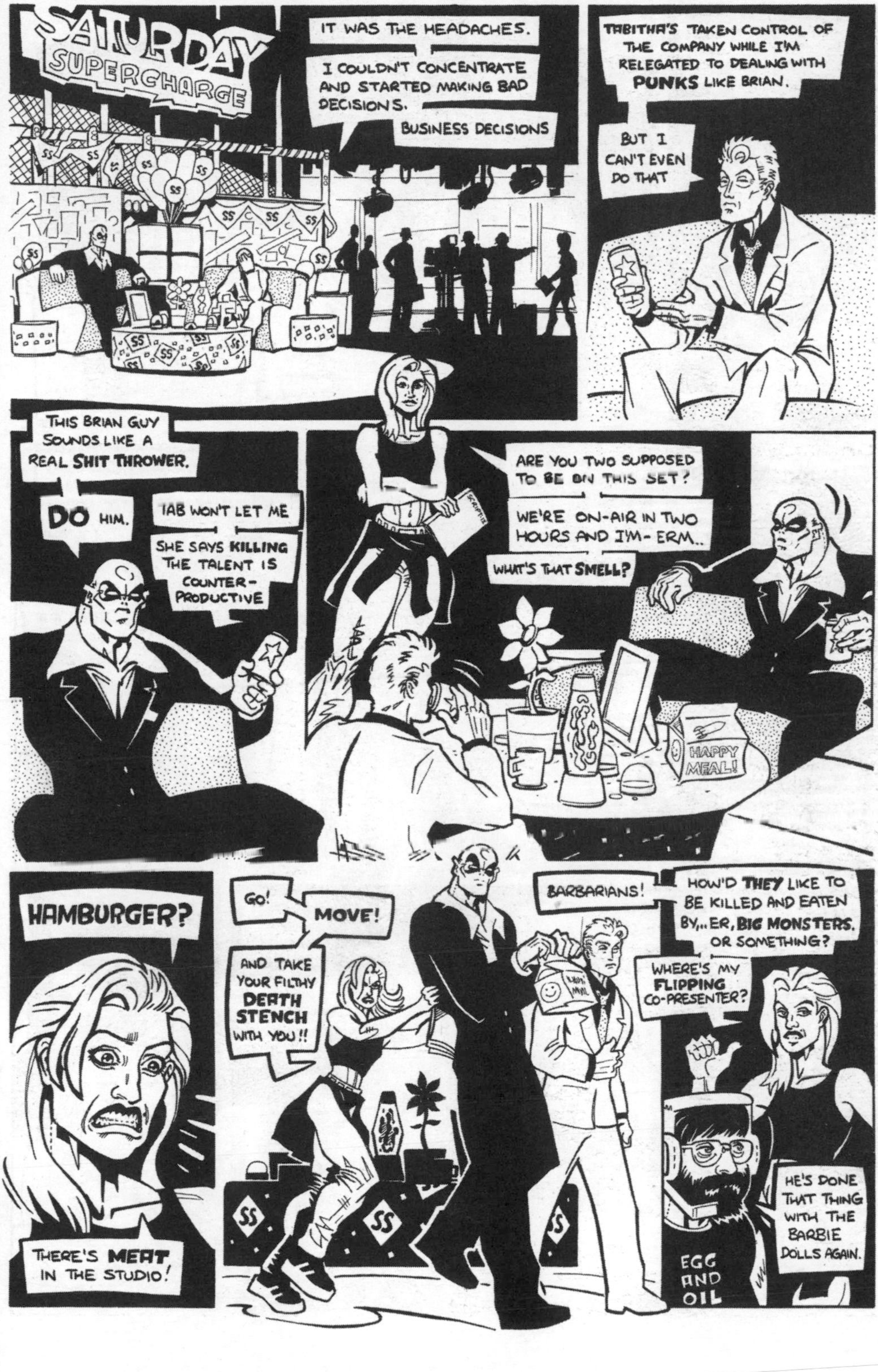
SATURDAY SUPERCHARGE
IT WAS THE HEADACHES.
I COULDN'T CONCENTRATE AND STARTED MAKING BAD DECISIONS.
BUSINESS DECISIONS
TABITHA'S TAKEN CONTROL OF THE COMPANY WHILE I'M RELEGATED TO DEALING WITH PUNKS LIKE BRIAN.
BUT I CAN'T EVEN DO THAT
THIS BRIAN GUY SOUNDS LIKE A REAL SHIT THROWER.
DO HIM.
TAB WON'T LET ME
SHE SAYS KILLING THE TALENT IS COUNTER-PRODUCTIVE
ARE YOU TWO SUPPOSED TO BE ON THIS SET?
WE'RE ON-AIR IN TWO HOURS AND I'M - ERM..
WHAT'S THAT SMELL?
HAPPY MEAL!
HAMBURGER?
THERE'S MEAT IN THE STUDIO!
GO!
MOVE!
AND TAKE YOUR FILTHY DEATH STENCH WITH YOU!!
BARBARIANS!
HOW'D THEY LIKE TO BE KILLED AND EATEN BY... ER, BIG MONSTERS. OR SOMETHING?
WHERE'S MY FLIPPING CO-PRESENTER?
HE'S DONE THAT THING WITH THE BARBIE DOLLS AGAIN.
EGG AND OIL

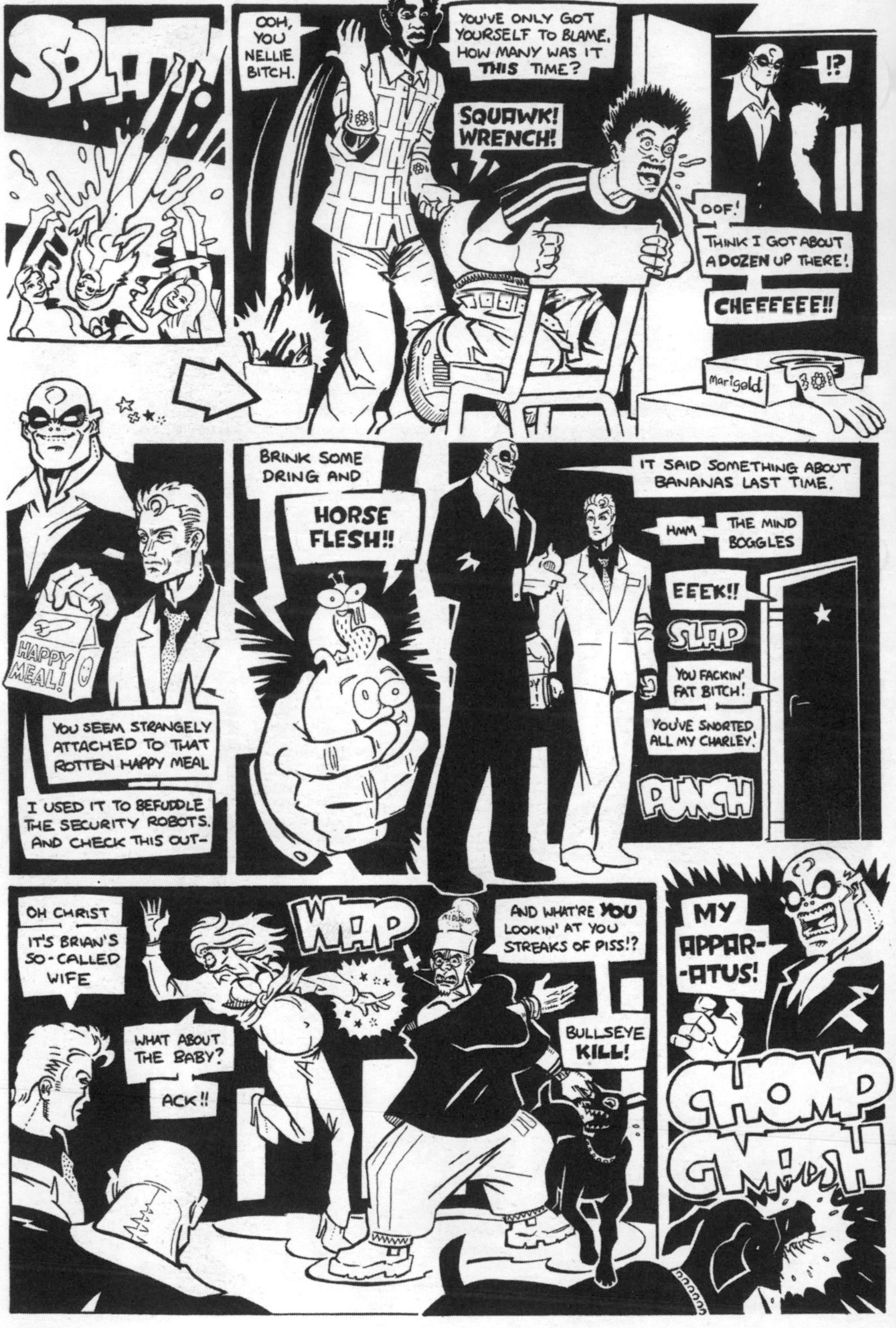
SPLAT!
OOH, YOU NELLIE BITCH.
YOU'VE ONLY GOT YOURSELF TO BLAME. HOW MANY WAS IT THIS TIME?
SQUAWK! WRENCH!
!?
OOF!
THINK I GOT ABOUT A DOZEN UP THERE!
CHEEEEEE!!
marigold
YOU SEEM STRANGELY ATTACHED TO THAT ROTTEN HAPPY MEAL
HAPPY MEAL!
I USED IT TO BEFUDDLE THE SECURITY ROBOTS. AND CHECK THIS OUT-
BRINK SOME DRING AND
HORSE FLESH!!
IT SAID SOMETHING ABOUT BANANAS LAST TIME.
HMM
THE MIND BOGGLES
EEEK!!
SLAP
YOU FACKIN' FAT BITCH!
YOU'VE SNORTED ALL MY CHARLEY!
PUNCH
OH CHRIST
IT'S BRIAN'S SO-CALLED WIFE
WHAT ABOUT THE BABY?
ACK!!
WAP
AND WHAT'RE YOU LOOKIN' AT YOU STREAKS OF PISS!?
BULLSEYE KILL!
MY APPAR- -ATUS!
CHOMP
GNASH

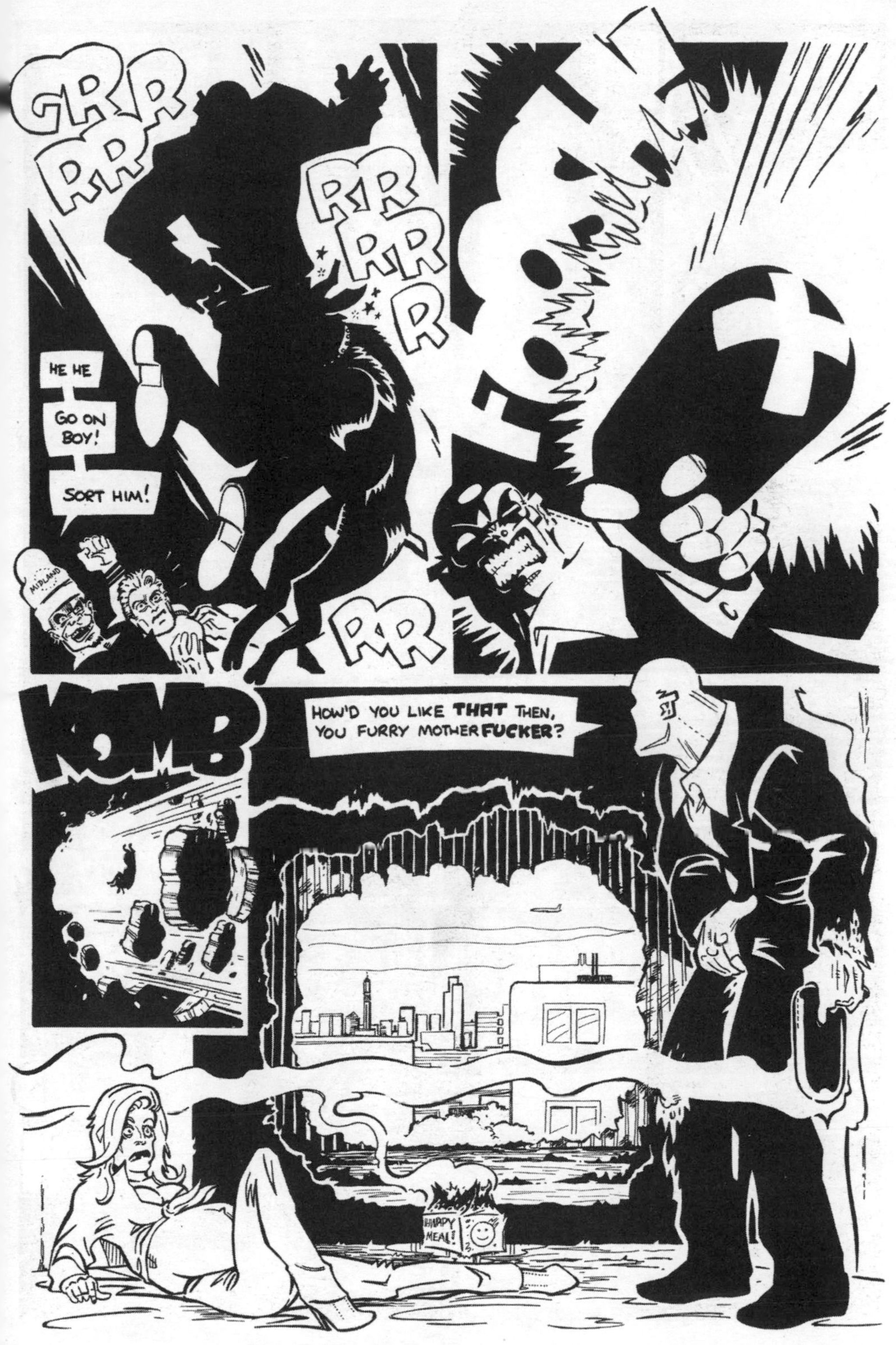

GRR
RR
RR
RR
R
HE HE
GO ON BOY!
SORT HIM!
MIDLAND
RR
KOMB
HOW'D YOU LIKE THAT THEN, YOU FURRY MOTHER FUCKER?
HAPPY MEAL!

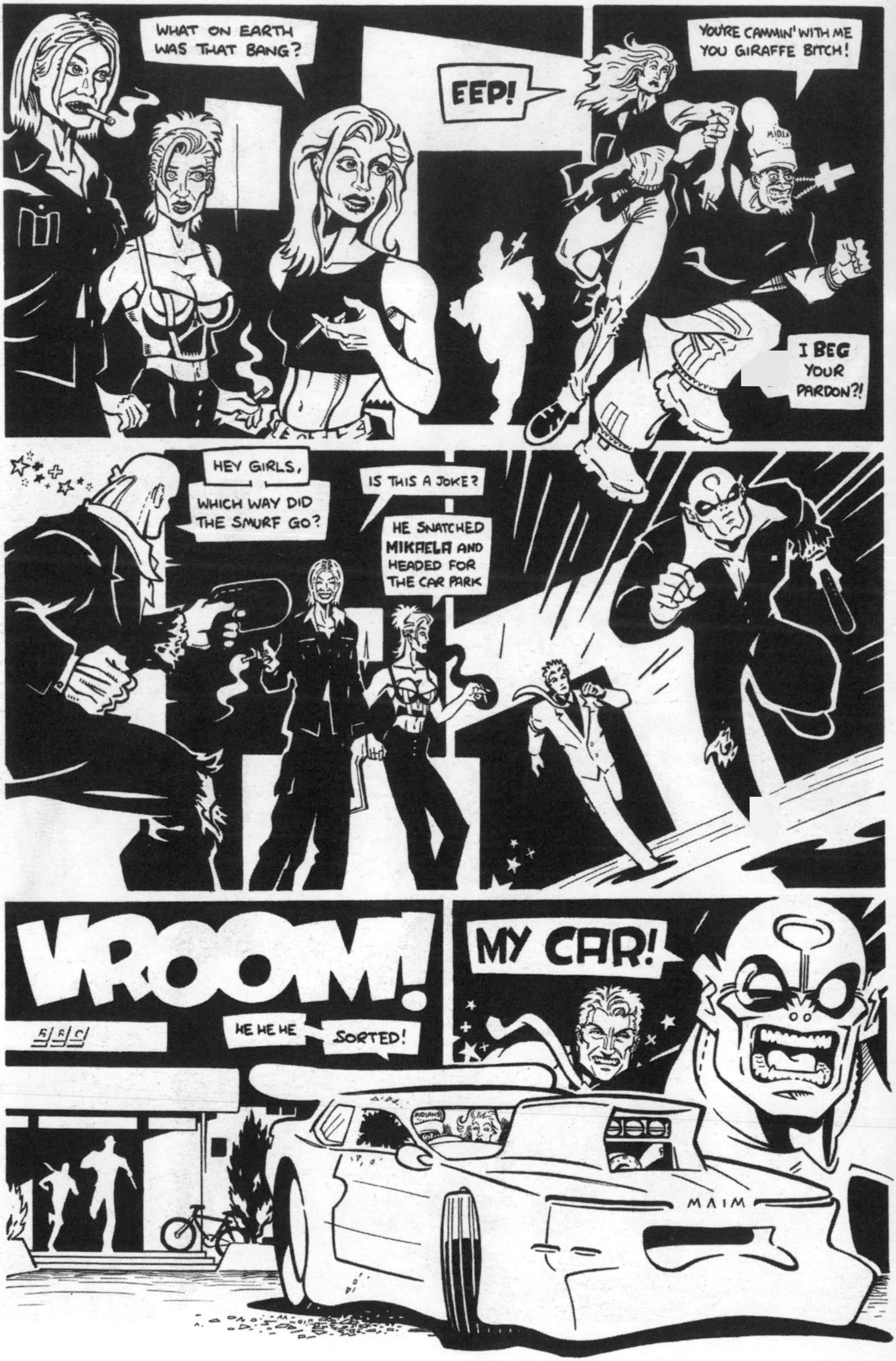
WHAT ON EARTH WAS THAT BANG?
EEP!
YOU'RE CAMMIN' WITH ME YOU GIRAFFE BITCH!
I BEG YOUR PARDON?!
HEY GIRLS,
WHICH WAY DID THE SMURF GO?
IS THIS A JOKE?
HE SNATCHED MIKAELA AND HEADED FOR THE CAR PARK
VROOM!
HE HE HE
SORTED!
MY CAR!
MAIM

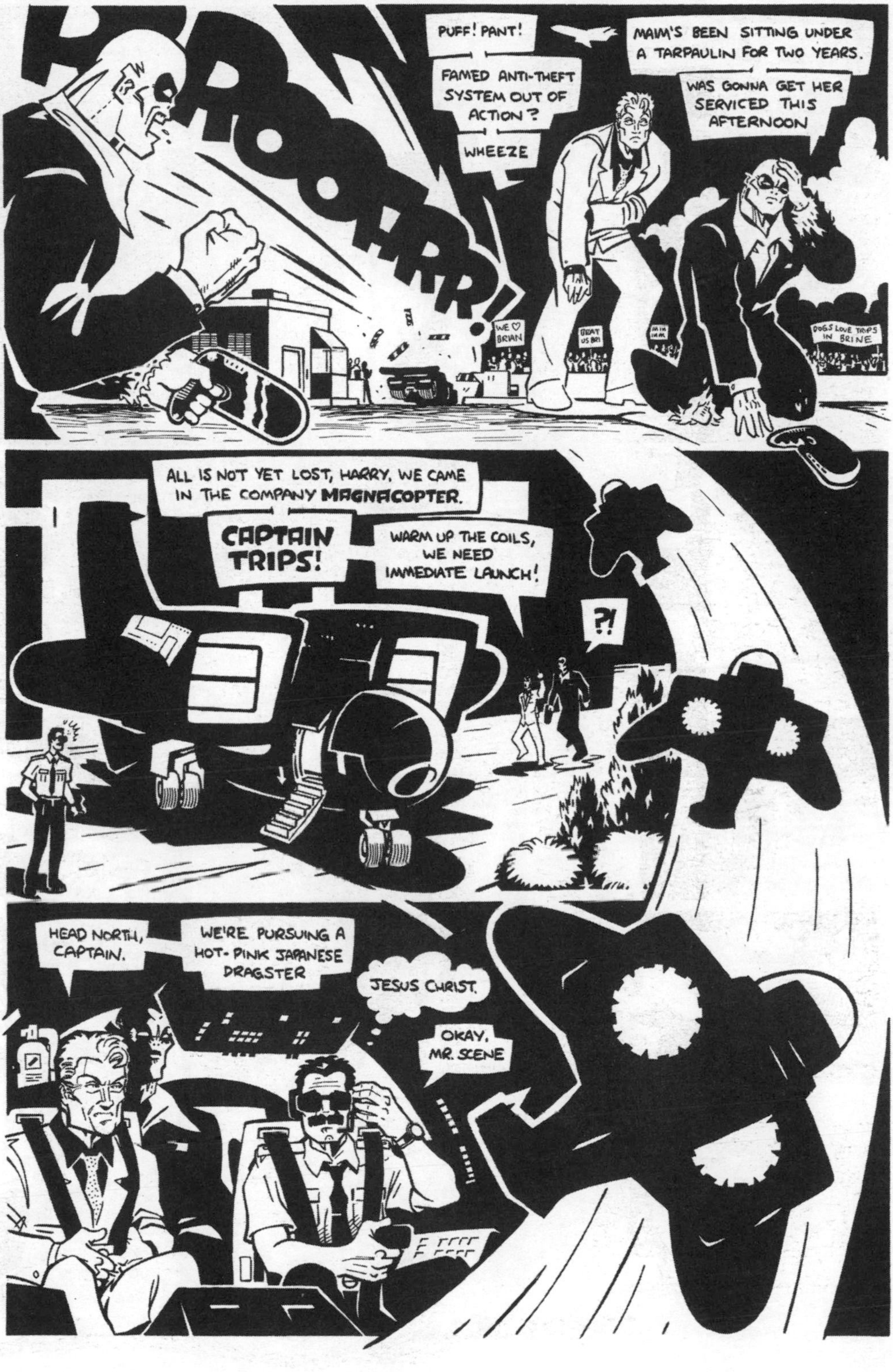
VROOOHRRR!
PUFF! PANT!
FAMED ANTI-THEFT SYSTEM OUT OF ACTION?
WHEEZE
MAIM'S BEEN SITTING UNDER A TARPAULIN FOR TWO YEARS.
WAS GONNA GET HER SERVICED THIS AFTERNOON
WE ♡ BRIAN
DOGS LOVE TRIPS IN BRINE
ALL IS NOT YET LOST, HARRY. WE CAME IN THE COMPANY MAGNICOPTER.
CAPTAIN TRIPS!
WARM UP THE COILS, WE NEED IMMEDIATE LAUNCH!
?!
HEAD NORTH, CAPTAIN.
WE'RE PURSUING A HOT-PINK JAPANESE DRAGSTER
JESUS CHRIST.
OKAY, MR. SCENE

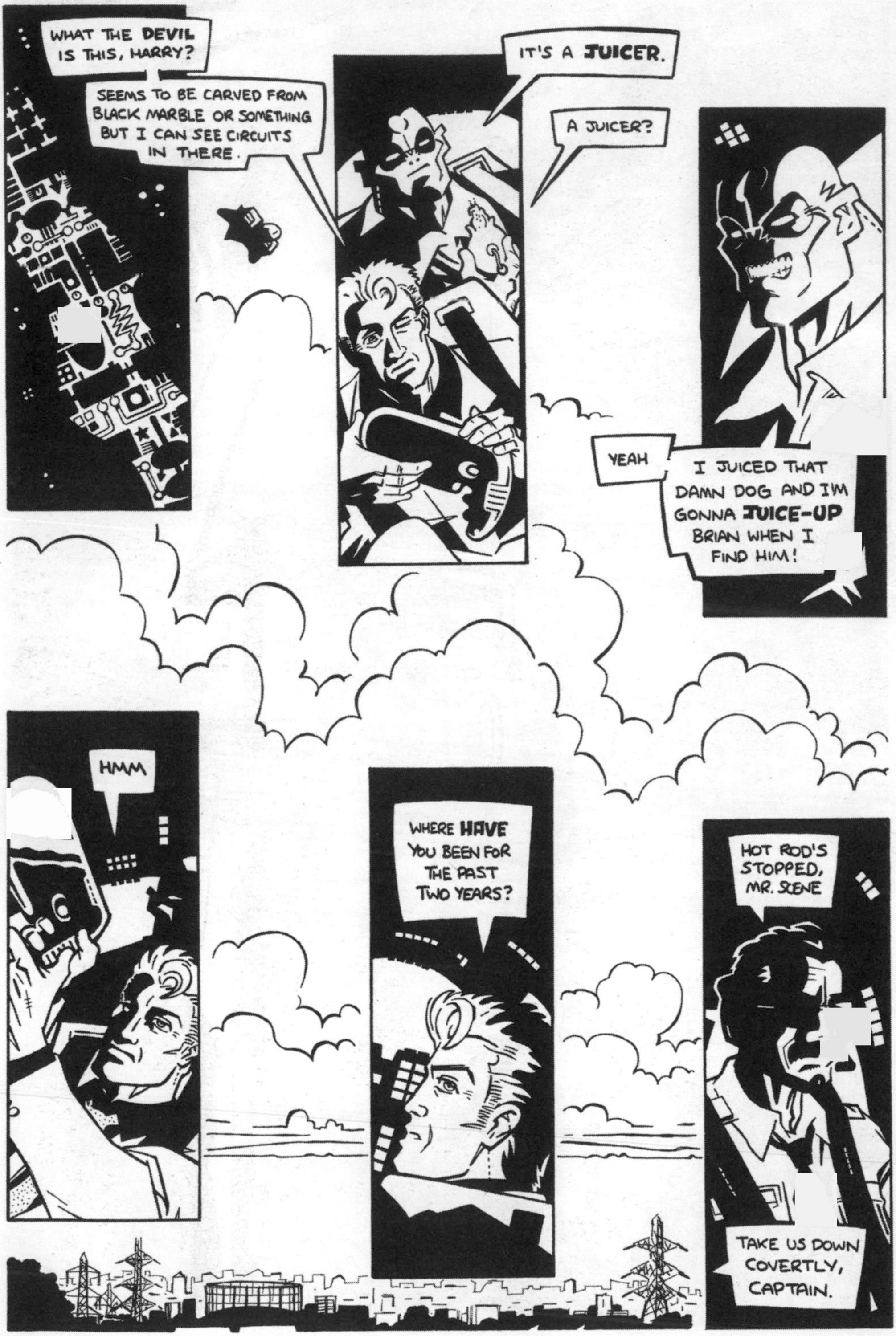
WHAT THE DEVIL IS THIS, HARRY?
SEEMS TO BE CARVED FROM BLACK MARBLE OR SOMETHING BUT I CAN SEE CIRCUITS IN THERE.
IT'S A JUICER.
A JUICER?
YEAH
I JUICED THAT DAMN DOG AND I'M GONNA JUICE-UP BRIAN WHEN I FIND HIM!
HMM
WHERE HAVE YOU BEEN FOR THE PAST TWO YEARS?
HOT ROD'S STOPPED, MR. SCENE
TAKE US DOWN COVERTLY, CAPTAIN.

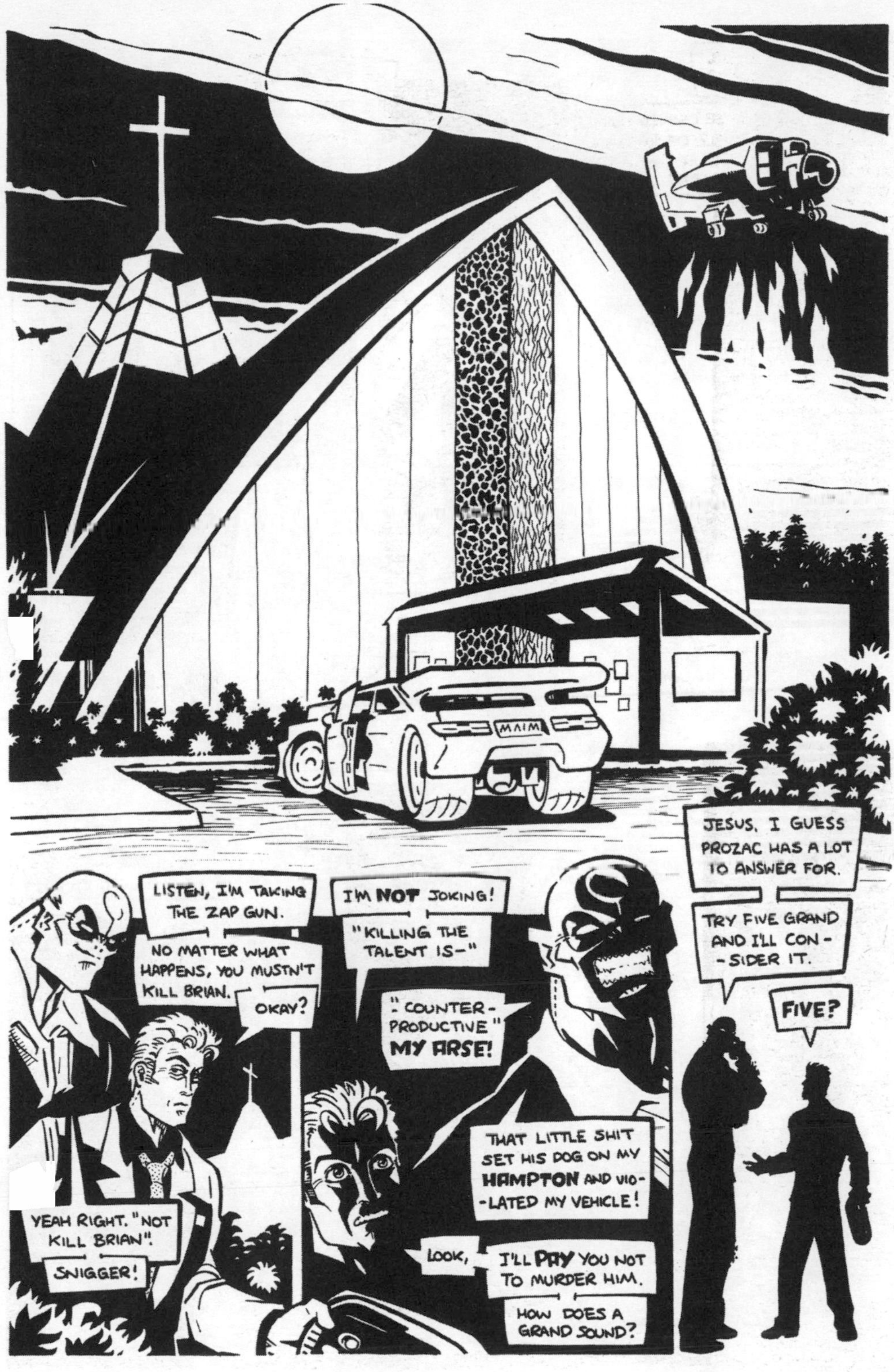
MAIM
LISTEN, I'M TAKING THE ZAP GUN.
NO MATTER WHAT HAPPENS, YOU MUSTN'T KILL BRIAN.
OKAY?
YEAH RIGHT. "NOT KILL BRIAN".
SNIGGER!
I'M NOT JOKING!
"KILLING THE TALENT IS–"
"– COUNTER-PRODUCTIVE" MY ARSE!
THAT LITTLE SHIT SET HIS DOG ON MY HAMPTON AND VIO-LATED MY VEHICLE!
LOOK,
I'LL PAY YOU NOT TO MURDER HIM.
HOW DOES A GRAND SOUND?
JESUS, I GUESS PROZAC HAS A LOT TO ANSWER FOR.
TRY FIVE GRAND AND I'LL CON-SIDER IT.
FIVE?

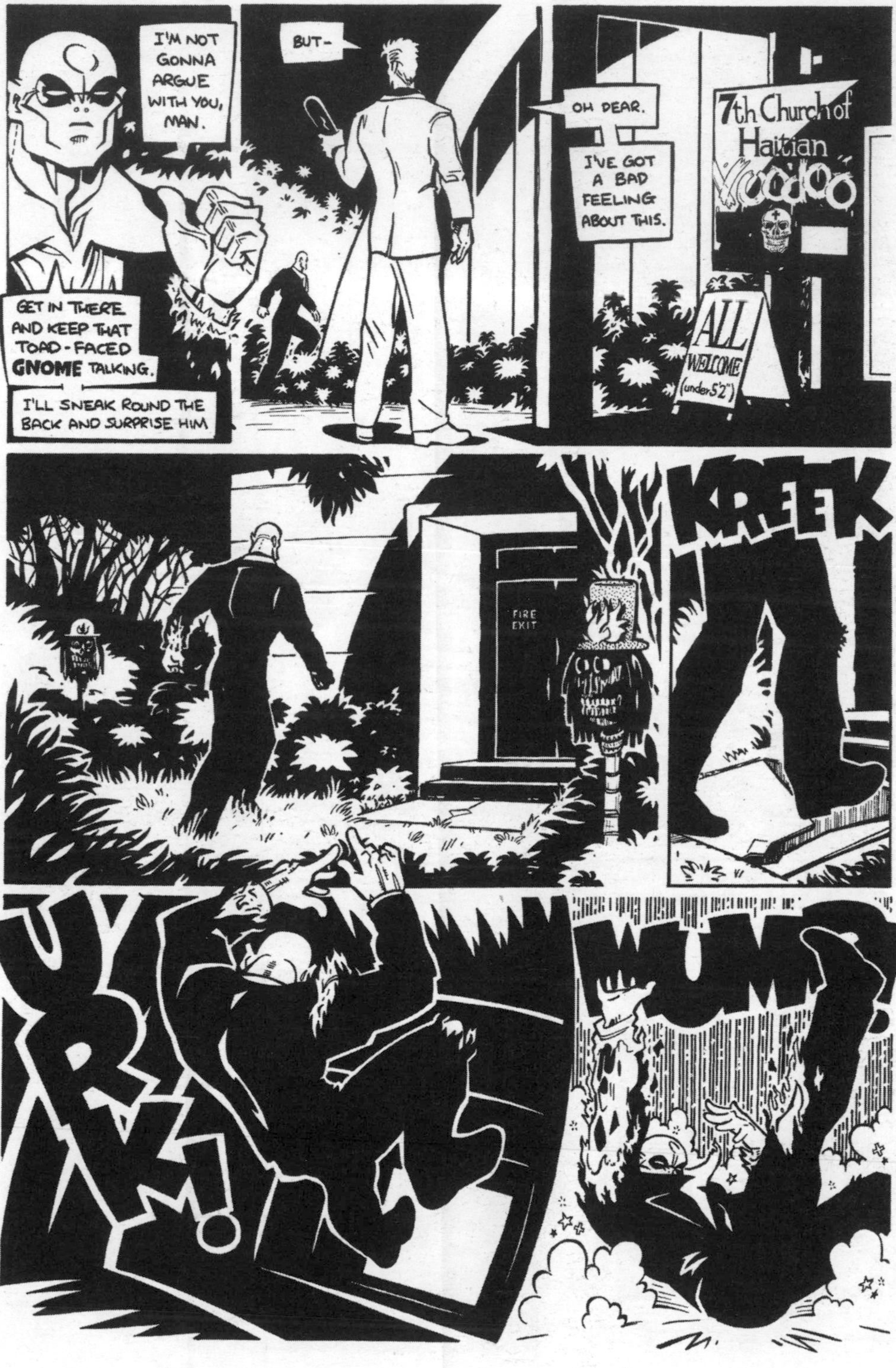
I'M NOT GONNA ARGUE WITH YOU, MAN.
GET IN THERE AND KEEP THAT TOAD-FACED GNOME TALKING.
I'LL SNEAK ROUND THE BACK AND SURPRISE HIM
BUT-
OH DEAR.
I'VE GOT A BAD FEELING ABOUT THIS.
7th Church of Haitian Voodoo
ALL WELCOME (under 5'2")
FIRE EXIT
KREEK
KRAK!
WUMP!

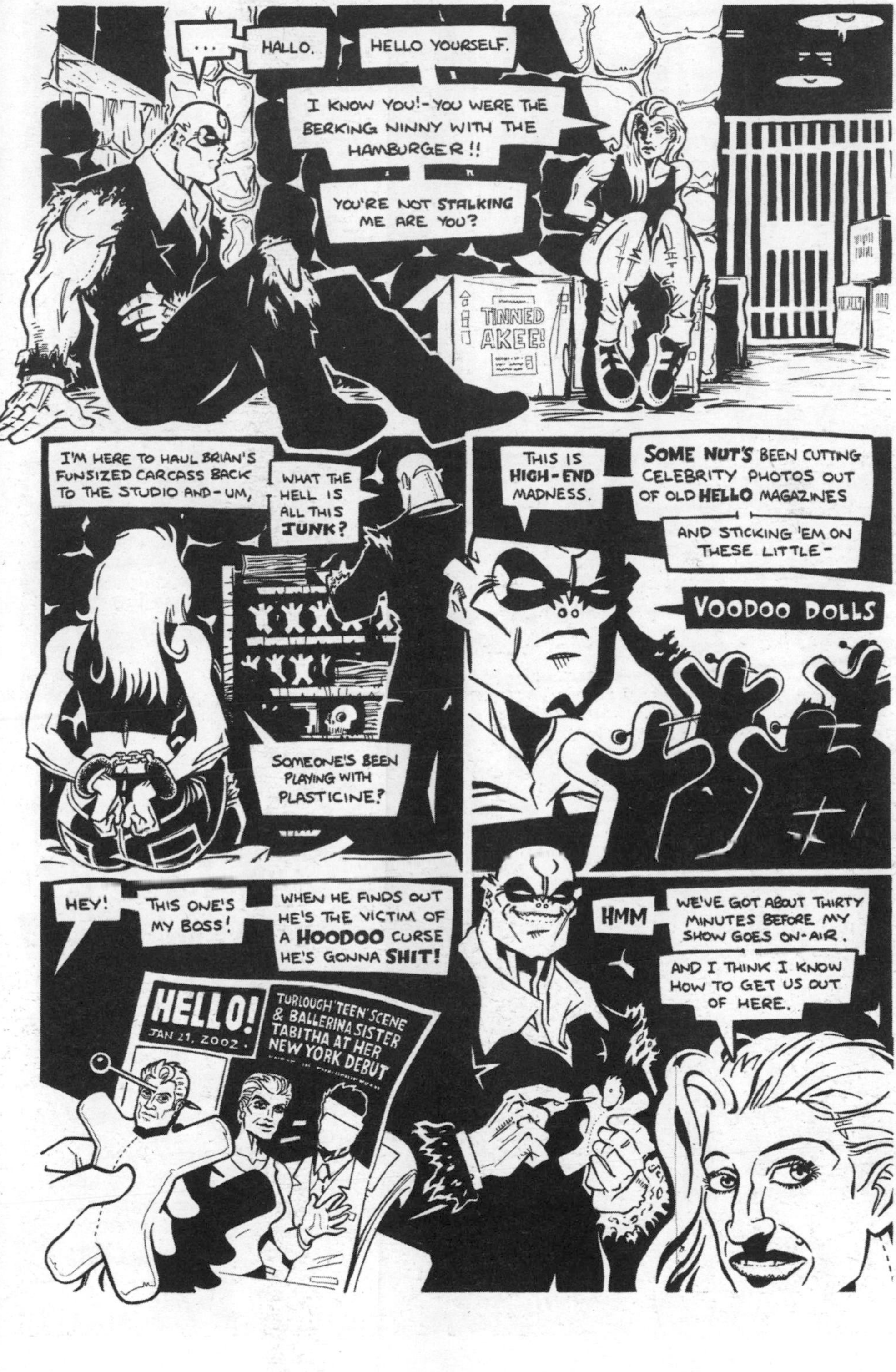
...
HALLO.
HELLO YOURSELF.
I KNOW YOU!- YOU WERE THE BERKING NINNY WITH THE HAMBURGER!!
YOU'RE NOT STALKING ME ARE YOU?
TINNED AKEE!
I'M HERE TO HAUL BRIAN'S FUNSIZED CARCASS BACK TO THE STUDIO AND-UM,
WHAT THE HELL IS ALL THIS JUNK?
SOMEONE'S BEEN PLAYING WITH PLASTICINE?
THIS IS HIGH-END MADNESS.
SOME NUT'S BEEN CUTTING CELEBRITY PHOTOS OUT OF OLD HELLO MAGAZINES
AND STICKING 'EM ON THESE LITTLE-
VOODOO DOLLS
HEY!
THIS ONE'S MY BOSS!
WHEN HE FINDS OUT HE'S THE VICTIM OF A HOODOO CURSE HE'S GONNA SHIT!
HELLO!
JAN 21, 2002.
TURLOUGH 'TEEN' SCENE & BALLERINA SISTER TABITHA AT HER NEW YORK DEBUT
HMM
WE'VE GOT ABOUT THIRTY MINUTES BEFORE MY SHOW GOES ON-AIR.
AND I THINK I KNOW HOW TO GET US OUT OF HERE.

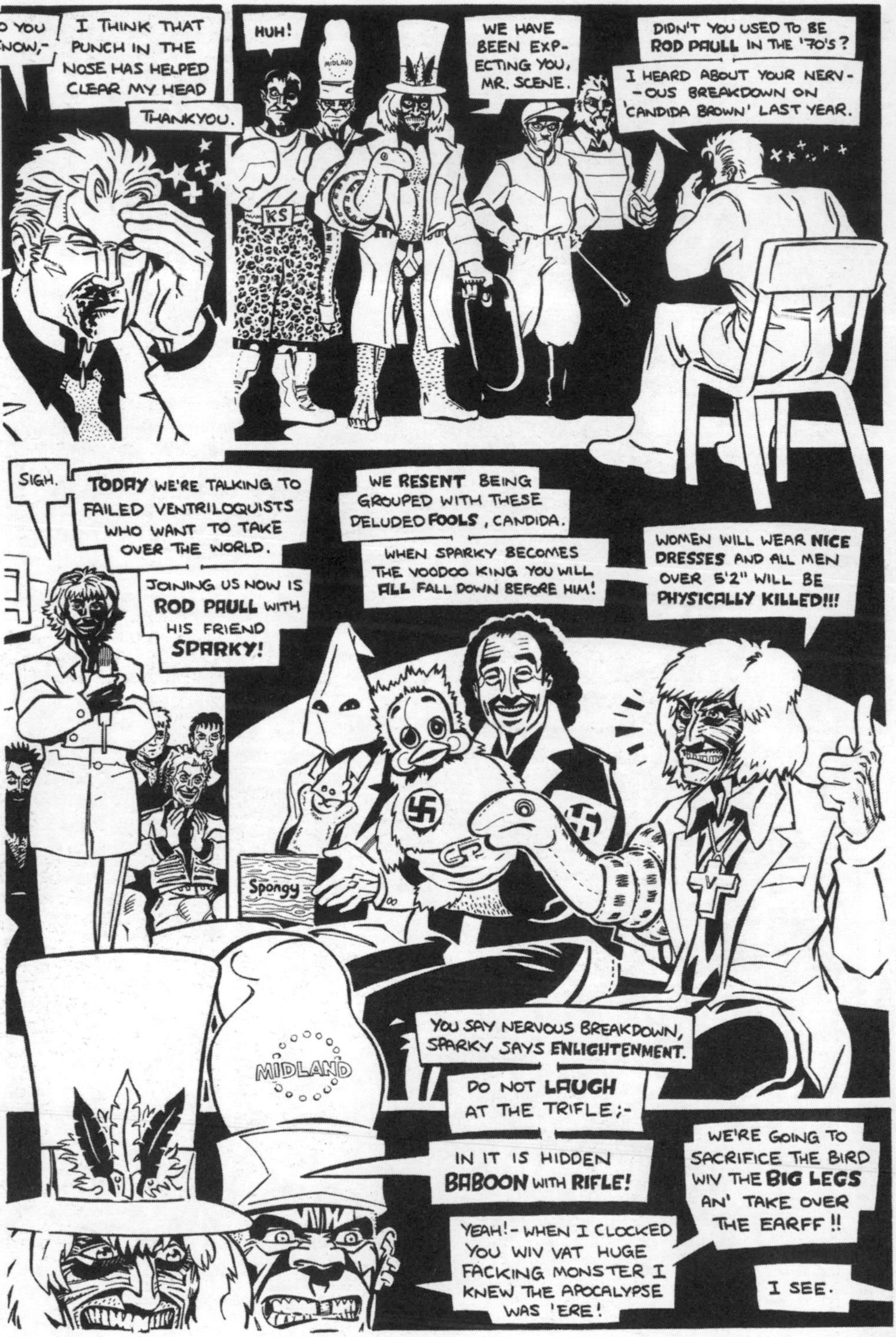

DO YOU KNOW,-
I THINK THAT PUNCH IN THE NOSE HAS HELPED CLEAR MY HEAD
THANKYOU.
HUH!
MIDLAND
KS
WE HAVE BEEN EXP-ECTING YOU, MR. SCENE.
DIDN'T YOU USED TO BE ROD PAULL IN THE '70'S?
I HEARD ABOUT YOUR NERV--OUS BREAKDOWN ON 'CANDIDA BROWN' LAST YEAR.
SIGH.
TODAY WE'RE TALKING TO FAILED VENTRILOQUISTS WHO WANT TO TAKE OVER THE WORLD.
JOINING US NOW IS ROD PAULL WITH HIS FRIEND SPARKY!
WE RESENT BEING GROUPED WITH THESE DELUDED FOOLS, CANDIDA.
WHEN SPARKY BECOMES THE VOODOO KING YOU WILL ALL FALL DOWN BEFORE HIM!
WOMEN WILL WEAR NICE DRESSES AND ALL MEN OVER 5'2" WILL BE PHYSICALLY KILLED!!!
Spongy
MIDLAND
YOU SAY NERVOUS BREAKDOWN, SPARKY SAYS ENLIGHTENMENT.
DO NOT LAUGH AT THE TRIFLE;-
IN IT IS HIDDEN BABOON WITH RIFLE!
WE'RE GOING TO SACRIFICE THE BIRD WIV THE BIG LEGS AN' TAKE OVER THE EARFF!!
YEAH!- WHEN I CLOCKED YOU WIV VAT HUGE FACKING MONSTER I KNEW THE APOCALYPSE WAS 'ERE!
I SEE.

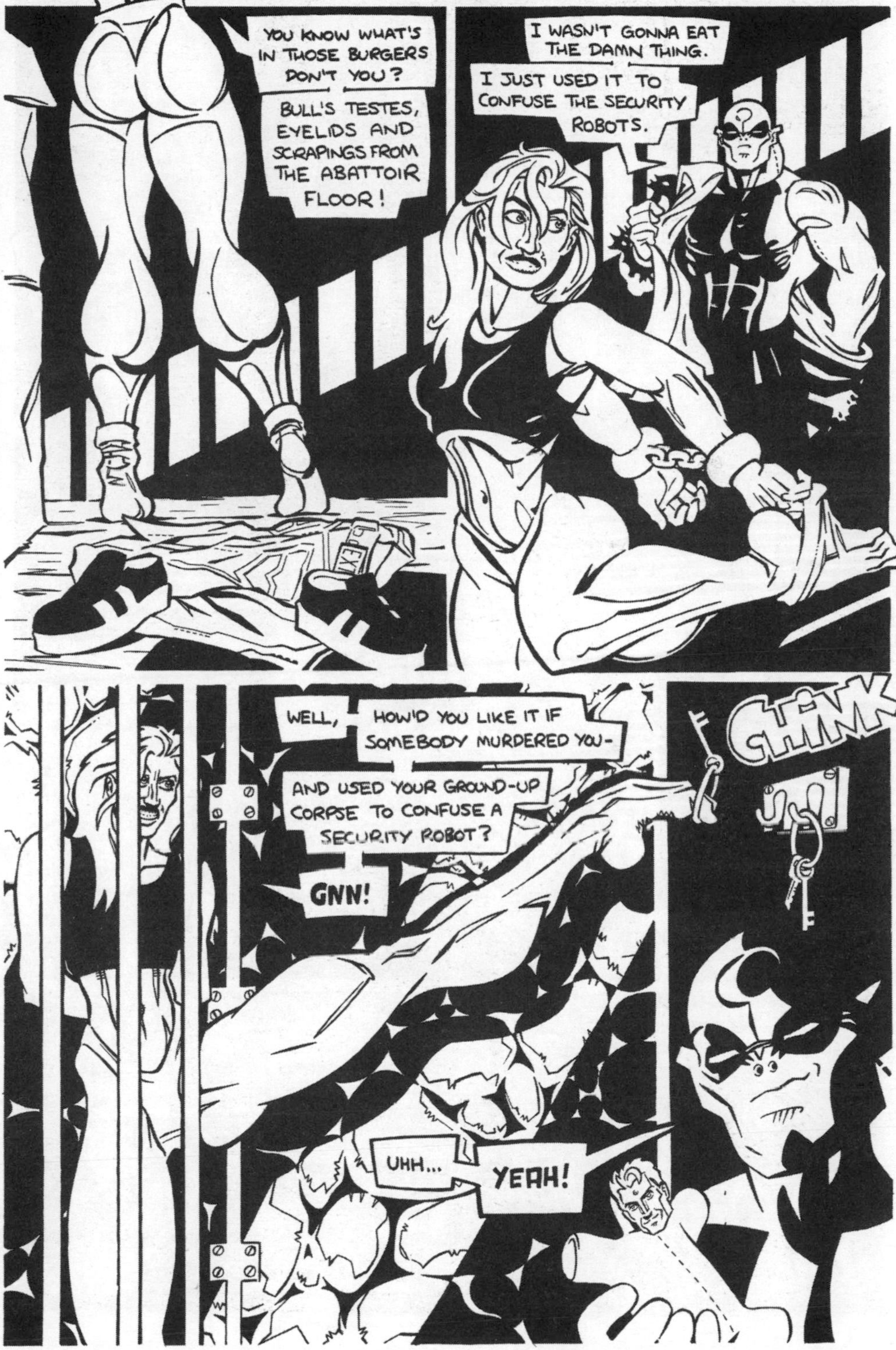

YOU KNOW WHAT'S IN THOSE BURGERS DON'T YOU?
BULL'S TESTES, EYELIDS AND SCRAPINGS FROM THE ABATTOIR FLOOR!
I WASN'T GONNA EAT THE DAMN THING.
I JUST USED IT TO CONFUSE THE SECURITY ROBOTS.
WELL,
HOW'D YOU LIKE IT IF SOMEBODY MURDERED YOU-
AND USED YOUR GROUND-UP CORPSE TO CONFUSE A SECURITY ROBOT?
GNN!
CHINK
UHH...
YEAH!

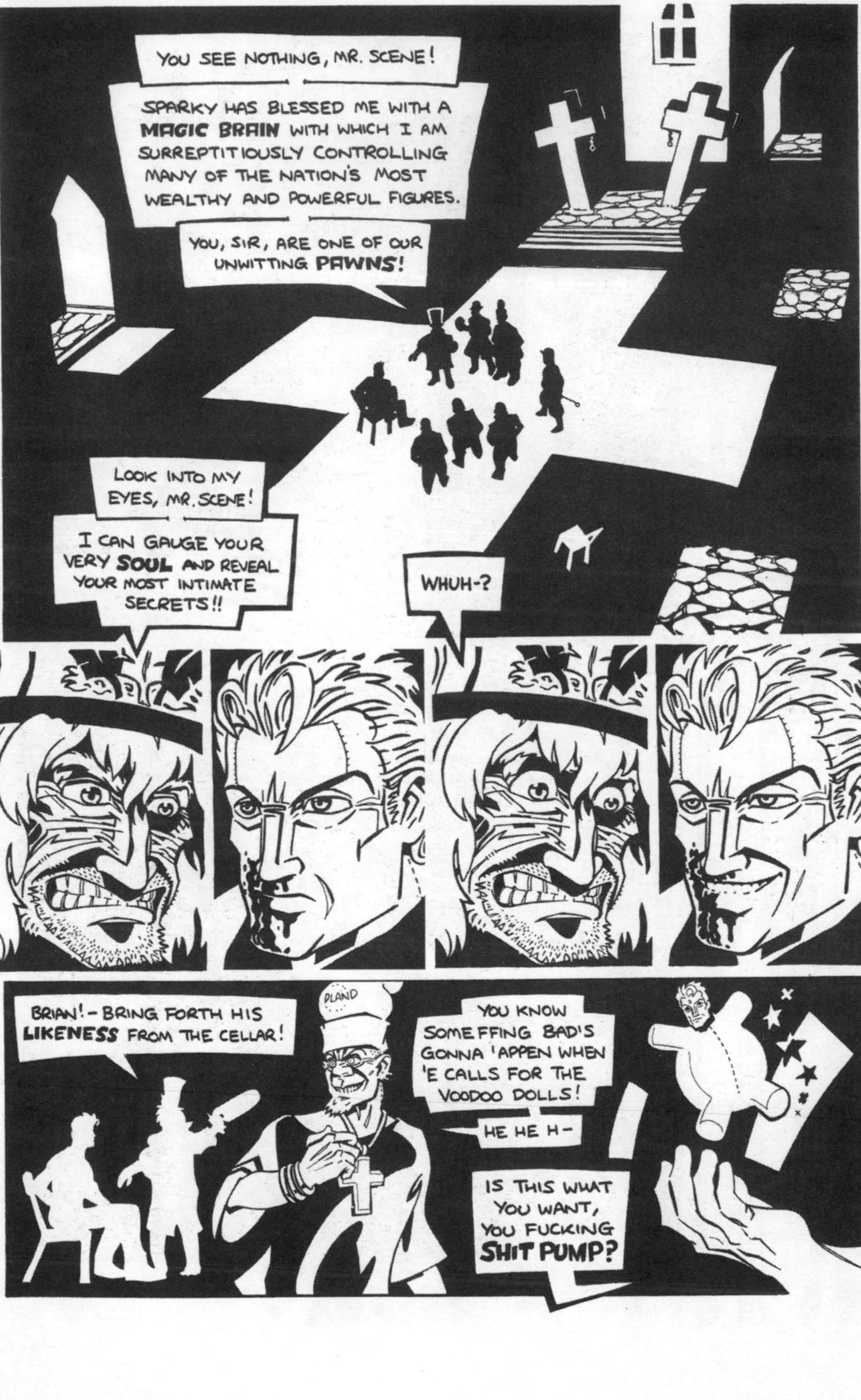
YOU SEE NOTHING, MR. SCENE!
SPARKY HAS BLESSED ME WITH A MAGIC BRAIN WITH WHICH I AM SURREPTITIOUSLY CONTROLLING MANY OF THE NATION'S MOST WEALTHY AND POWERFUL FIGURES.
YOU, SIR, ARE ONE OF OUR UNWITTING PAWNS!
LOOK INTO MY EYES, MR. SCENE!
I CAN GAUGE YOUR VERY SOUL AND REVEAL YOUR MOST INTIMATE SECRETS!!
WHUH-?
BRIAN! - BRING FORTH HIS LIKENESS FROM THE CELLAR!
PLAND
YOU KNOW SOMEFFING BAD'S GONNA 'APPEN WHEN 'E CALLS FOR THE VOODOO DOLLS!
HE HE H-
IS THIS WHAT YOU WANT, YOU FUCKING SHIT PUMP?

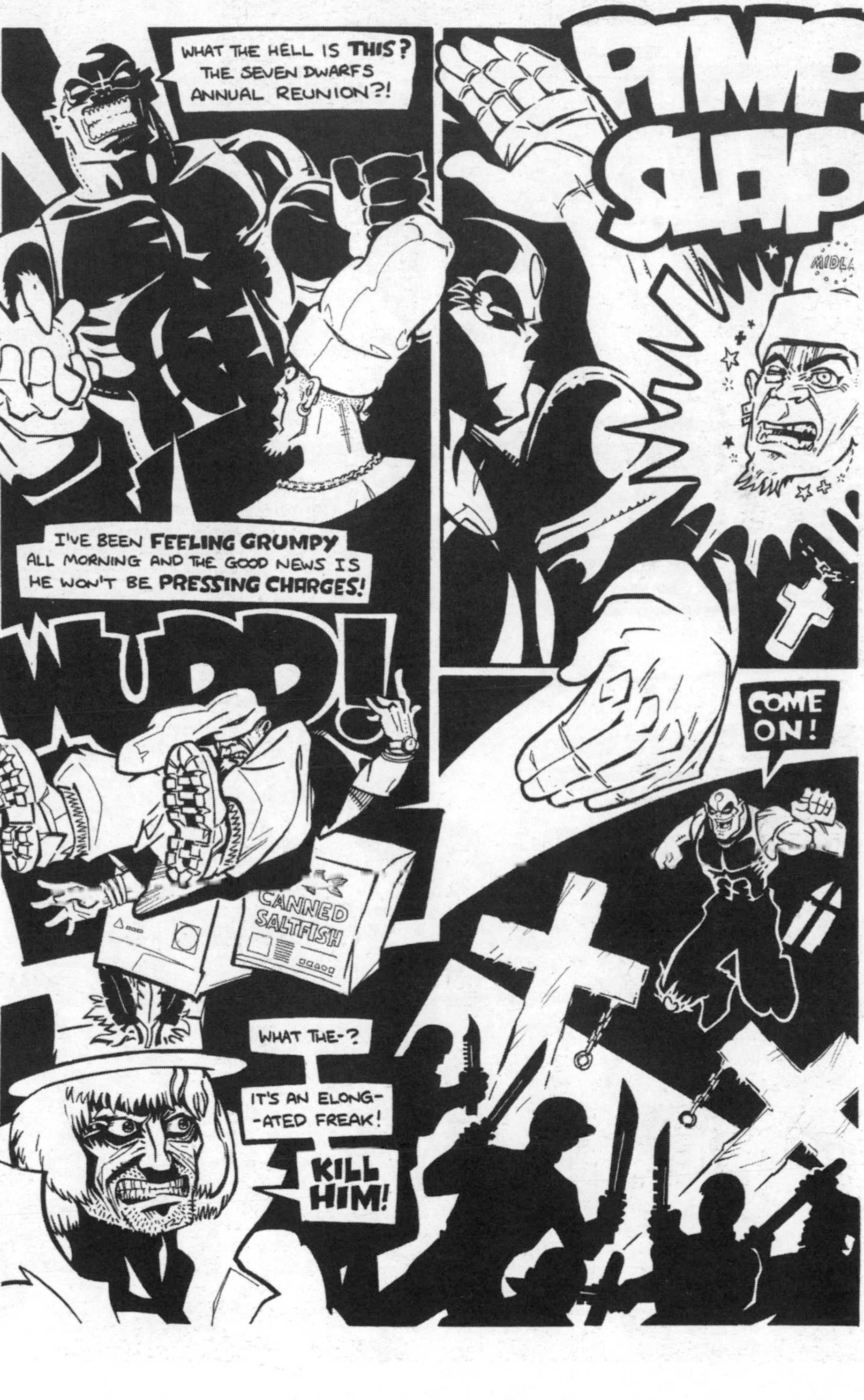
WHAT THE HELL IS THIS? THE SEVEN DWARFS ANNUAL REUNION?!
I'VE BEEN FEELING GRUMPY ALL MORNING AND THE GOOD NEWS IS HE WON'T BE PRESSING CHARGES!
WUDD!
CANNED SALTFISH
PIMP SLAP
COME ON!
WHAT THE-?
IT'S AN ELONG-ATED FREAK!
KILL HIM!

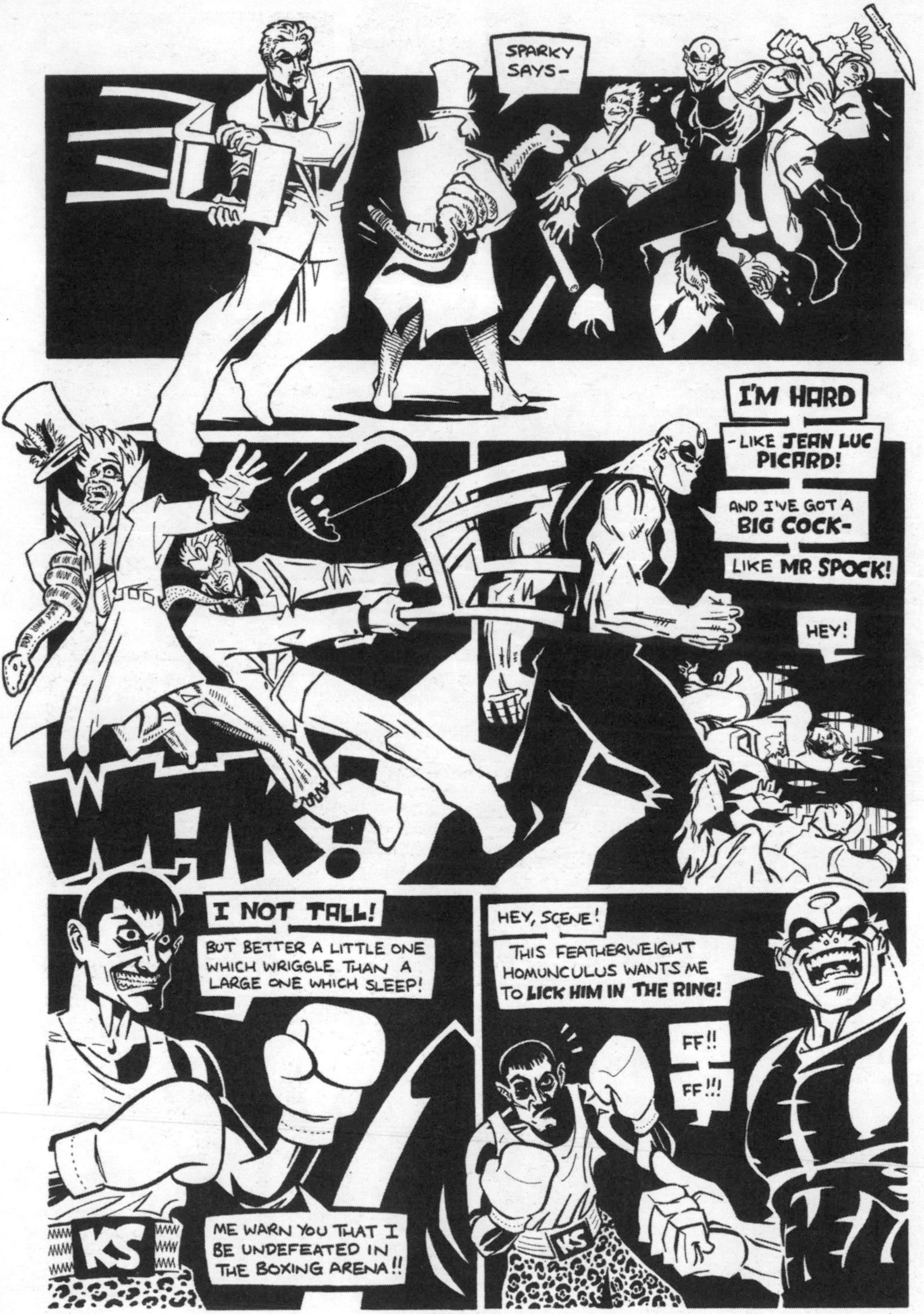
SPARKY SAYS-
I'M HARD
-LIKE JEAN LUC PICARD!
AND I'VE GOT A BIG COCK-
LIKE MR SPOCK!
HEY!
WAK!
I NOT TALL!
BUT BETTER A LITTLE ONE WHICH WRIGGLE THAN A LARGE ONE WHICH SLEEP!
ME WARN YOU THAT I BE UNDEFEATED IN THE BOXING ARENA!!
KS
HEY, SCENE!
THIS FEATHERWEIGHT HOMUNCULUS WANTS ME TO LICK HIM IN THE RING!
FF!!
FF!!!
KS

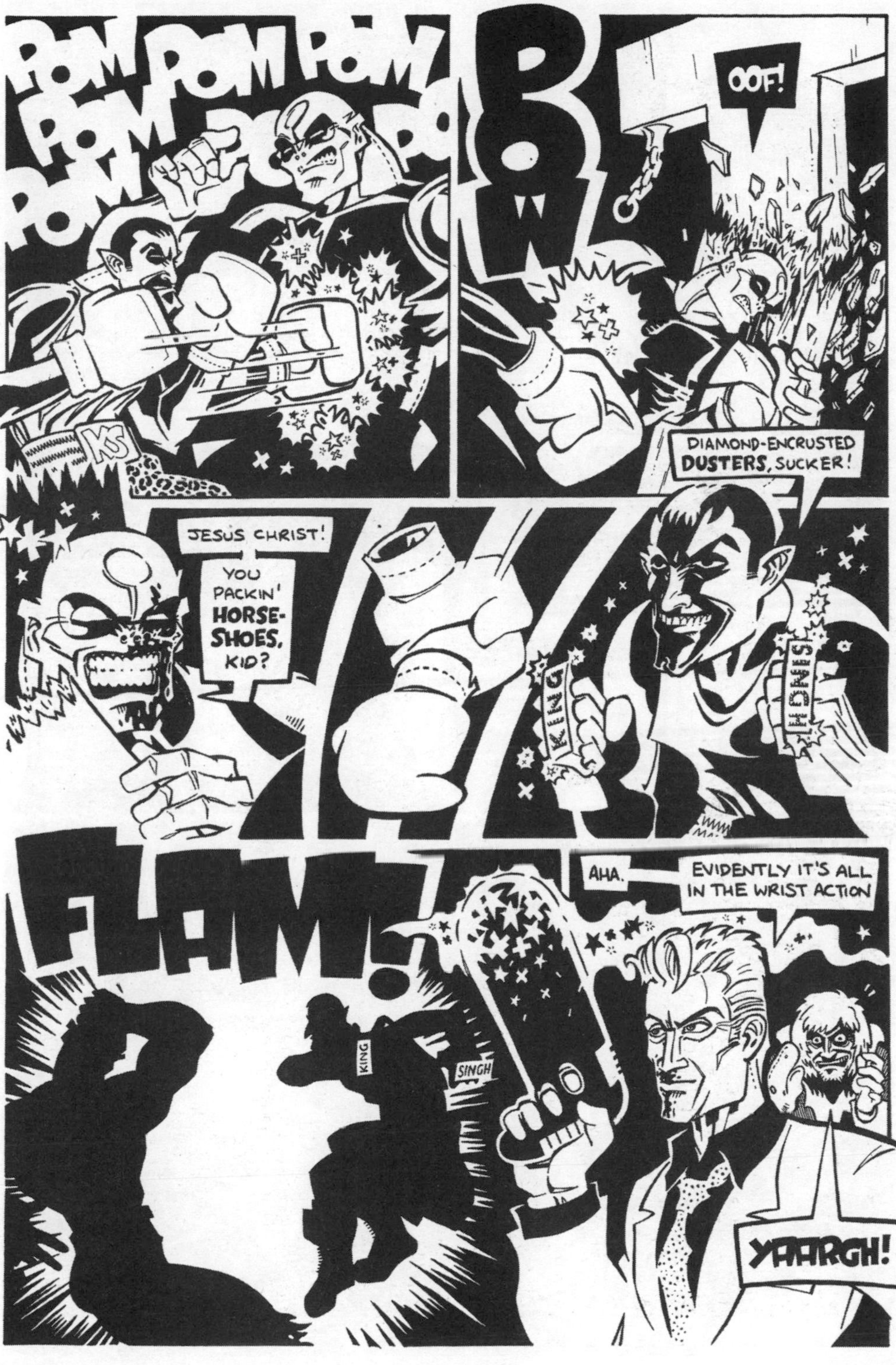
POM POM POM POM
POM POM PO PO
POM POM
KS
BOW
OOF!
DIAMOND-ENCRUSTED DUSTERS, SUCKER!
JESUS CHRIST!
YOU PACKIN' HORSE-SHOES, KID?
KING
SINGH
FLAM!
KING
SINGH
AHA.
EVIDENTLY IT'S ALL IN THE WRIST ACTION
YAARGH!

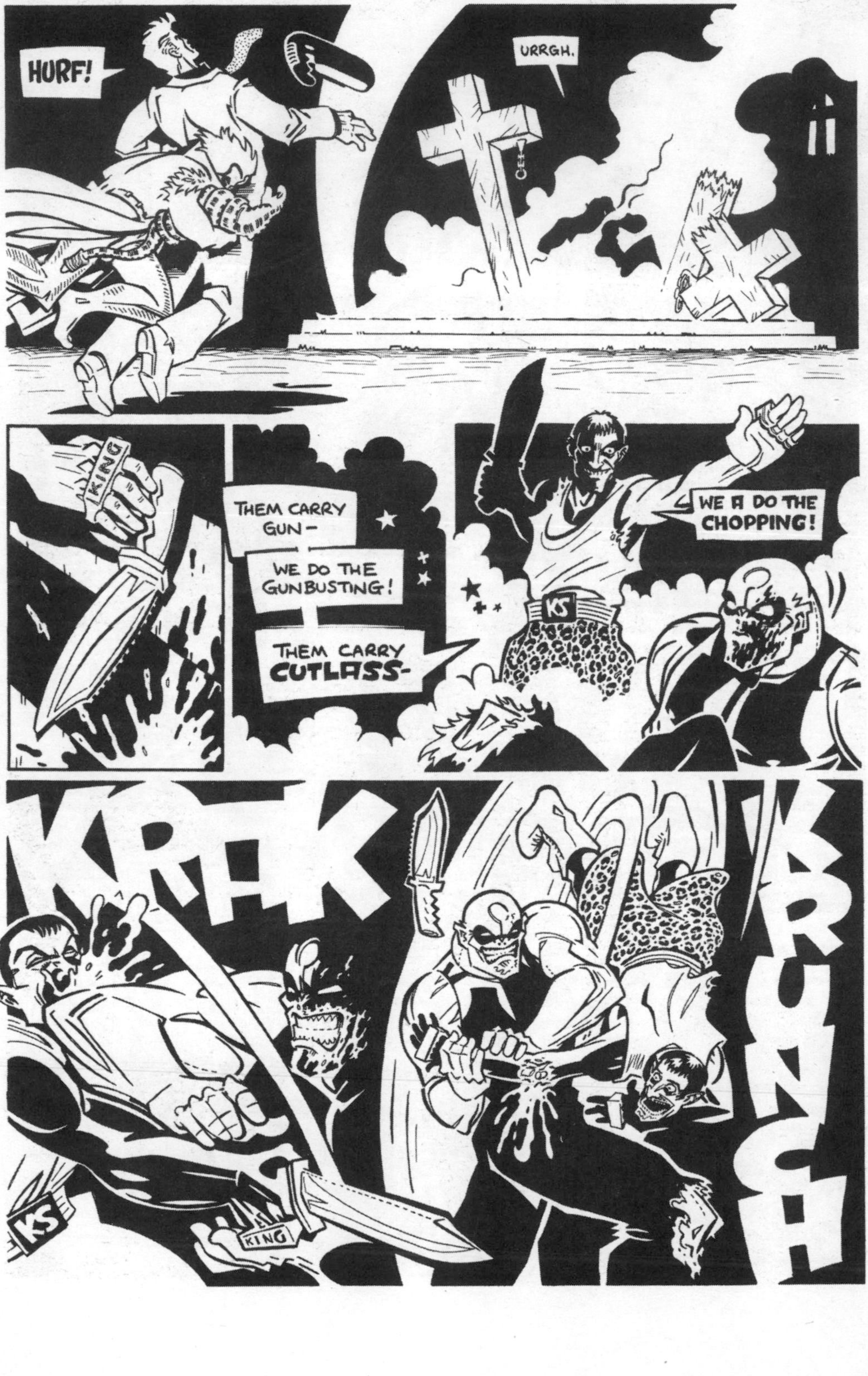

HURF!
URRGH.
KING
THEM CARRY GUN-
WE DO THE GUNBUSTING!
THEM CARRY CUTLASS-
WE A DO THE CHOPPING!
KS
KRAK
KRUNCH
KS
KING

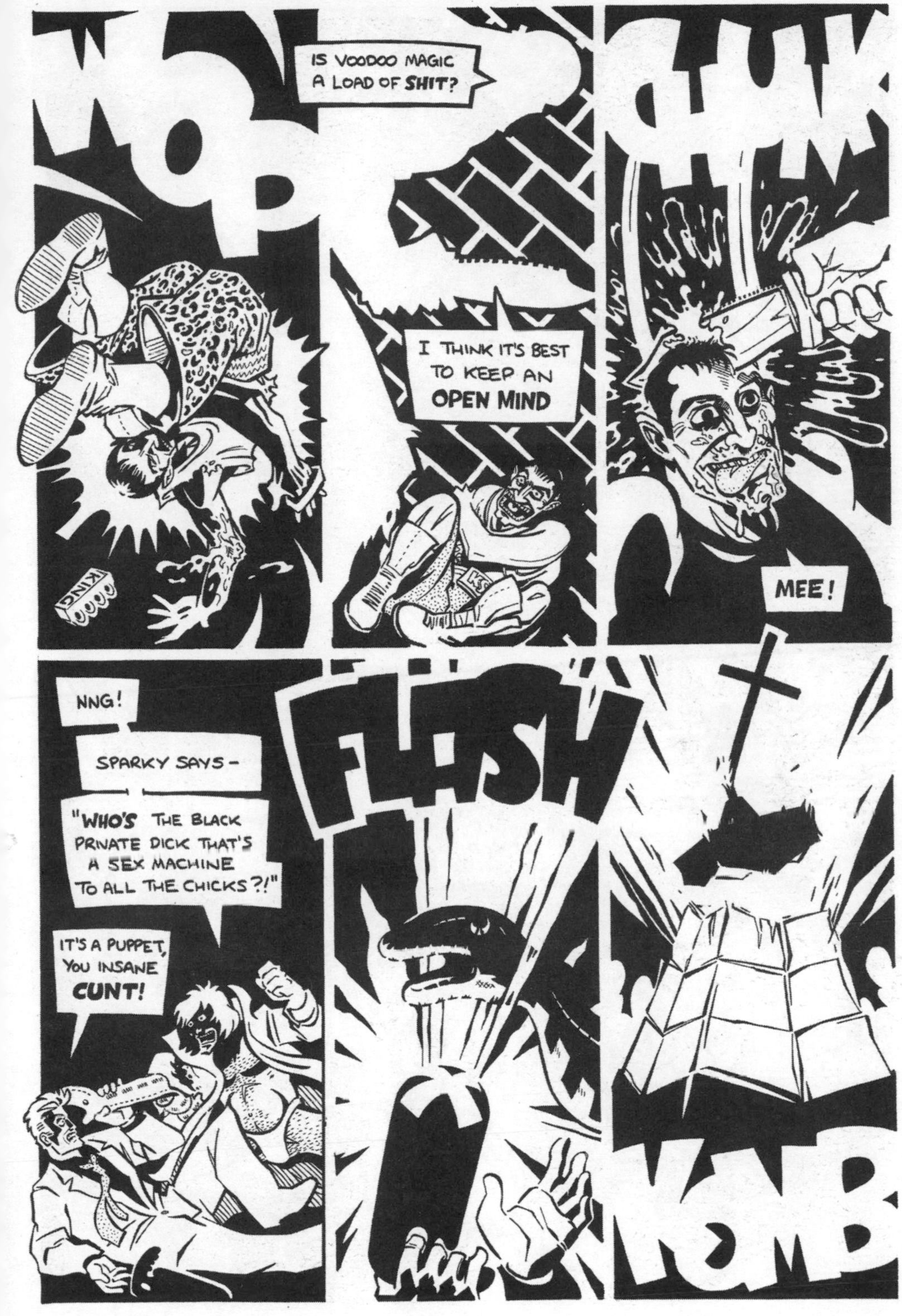

IS VOODOO MAGIC A LOAD OF SHIT?
I THINK IT'S BEST TO KEEP AN OPEN MIND
MEE!
NNG!
SPARKY SAYS -
"WHO'S THE BLACK PRIVATE DICK THAT'S A SEX MACHINE TO ALL THE CHICKS?!"
IT'S A PUPPET, YOU INSANE CUNT!
FLASH

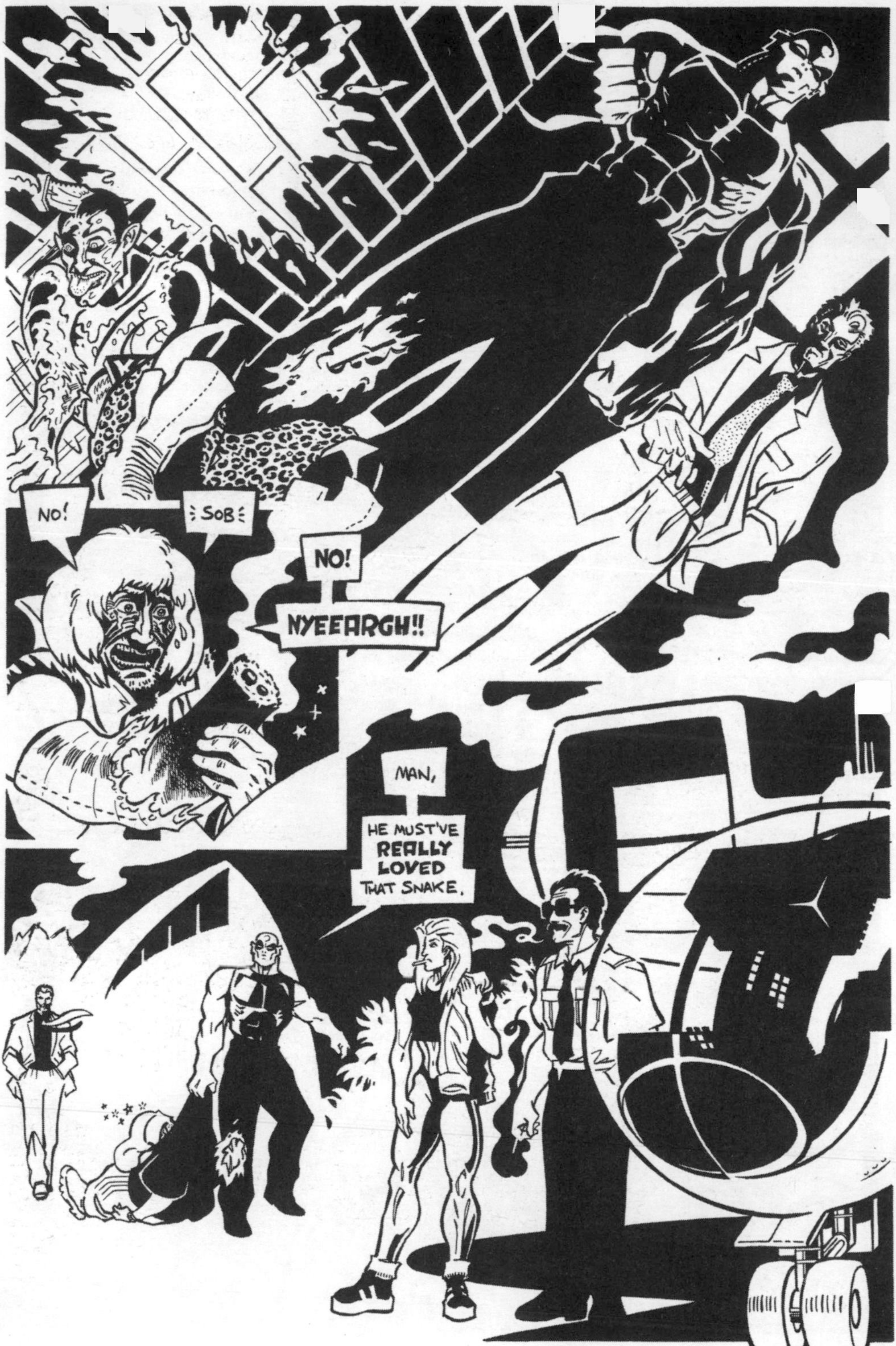
NO!
SOB
NO!
NYEEARGH!!
MAN,
HE MUST'VE REALLY LOVED THAT SNAKE.

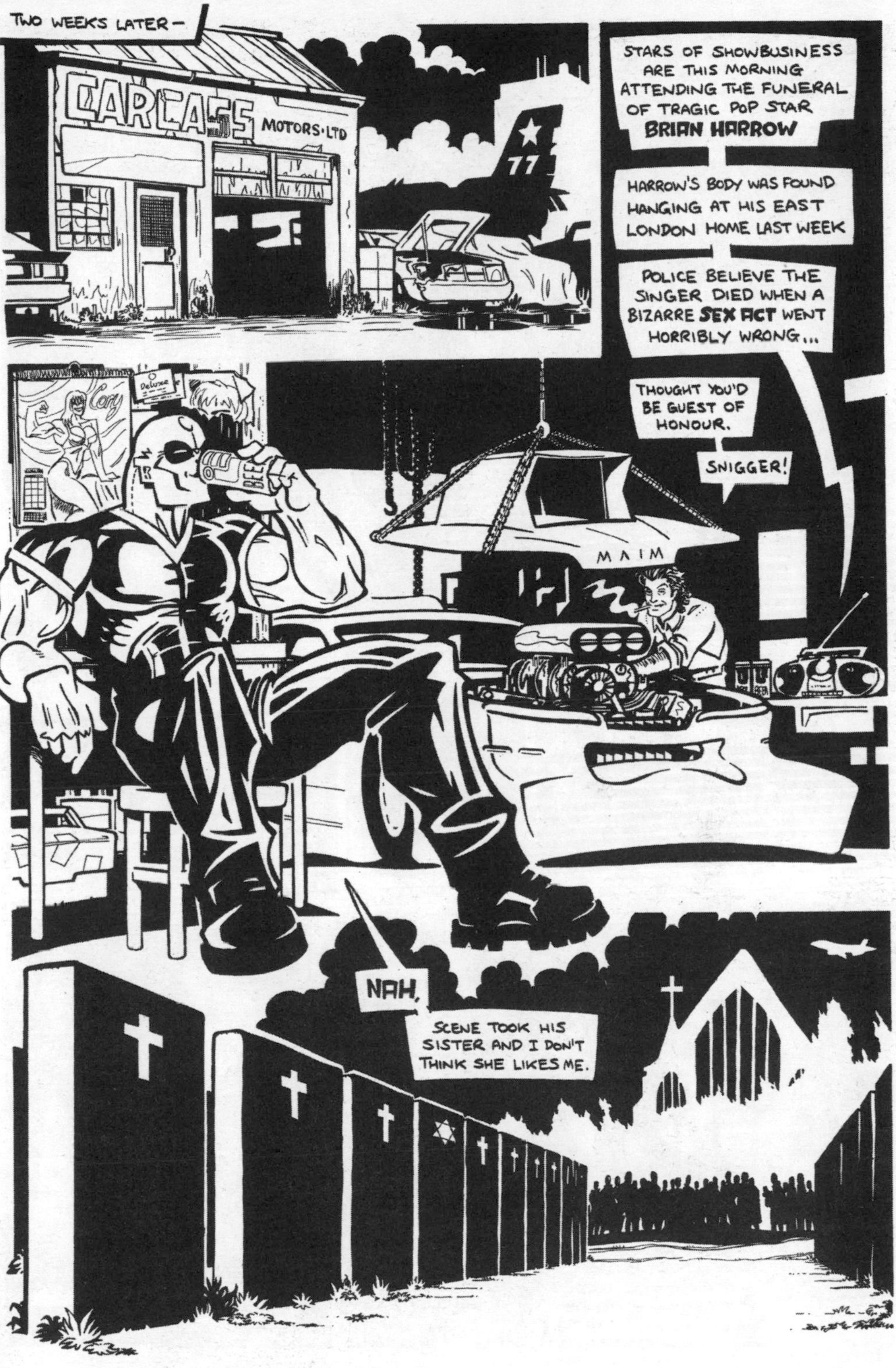
TWO WEEKS LATER—
CARCASS MOTORS·LTD
STARS OF SHOWBUSINESS ARE THIS MORNING ATTENDING THE FUNERAL OF TRAGIC POP STAR BRIAN HARROW
HARROW'S BODY WAS FOUND HANGING AT HIS EAST LONDON HOME LAST WEEK
POLICE BELIEVE THE SINGER DIED WHEN A BIZARRE SEX ACT WENT HORRIBLY WRONG...
THOUGHT YOU'D BE GUEST OF HONOUR.
SNIGGER!
MAIM
NAH,
SCENE TOOK HIS SISTER AND I DON'T THINK SHE LIKES ME.

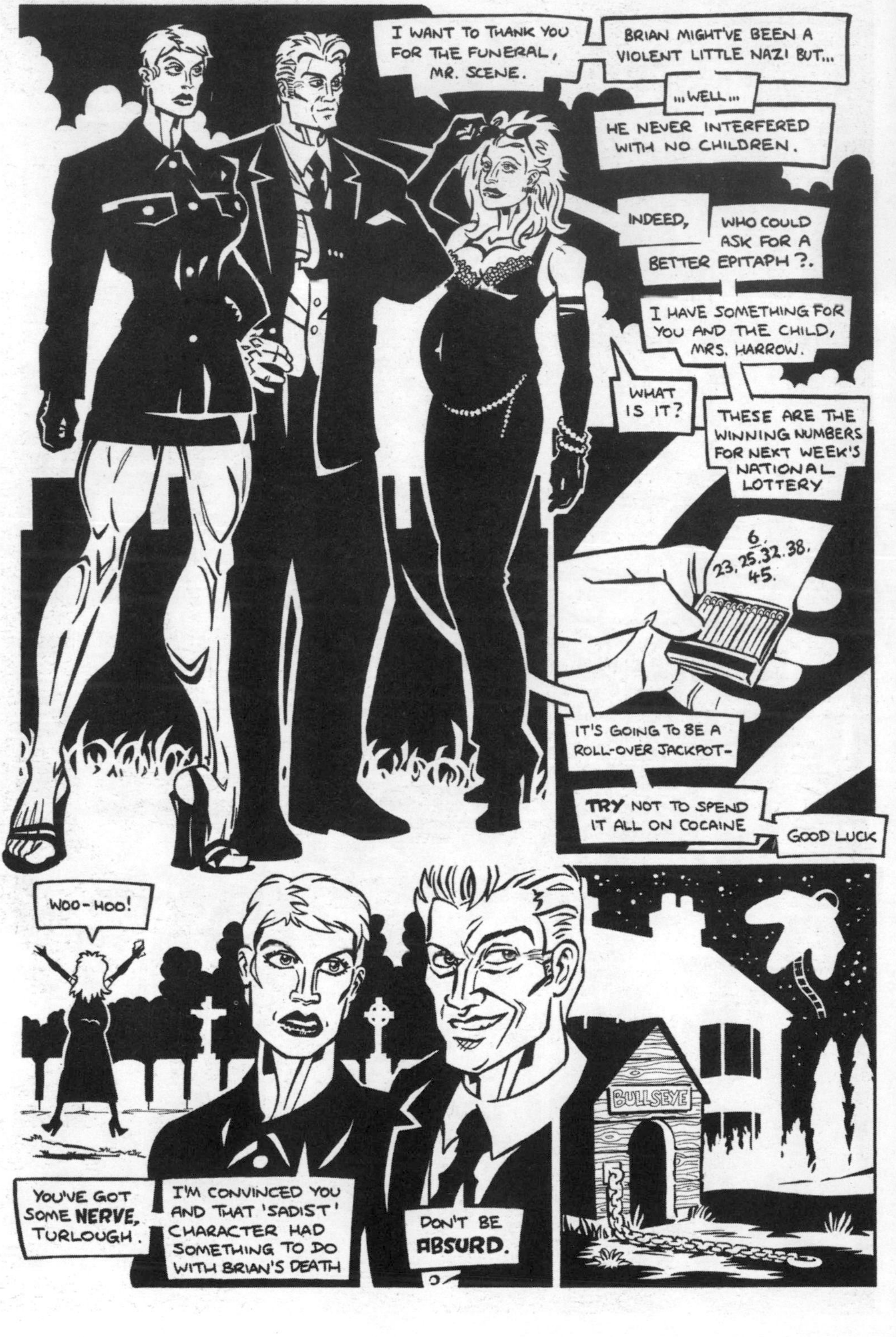
I WANT TO THANK YOU FOR THE FUNERAL, MR. SCENE.
BRIAN MIGHT'VE BEEN A VIOLENT LITTLE NAZI BUT...
...WELL...
HE NEVER INTERFERED WITH NO CHILDREN.
INDEED,
WHO COULD ASK FOR A BETTER EPITAPH ?.
I HAVE SOMETHING FOR YOU AND THE CHILD, MRS. HARROW.
WHAT IS IT?
THESE ARE THE WINNING NUMBERS FOR NEXT WEEK'S NATIONAL LOTTERY
6. 23.25.32.38. 45.
IT'S GOING TO BE A ROLL-OVER JACKPOT-
TRY NOT TO SPEND IT ALL ON COCAINE
GOOD LUCK
WOO-HOO!
YOU'VE GOT SOME NERVE, TURLOUGH.
I'M CONVINCED YOU AND THAT 'SADIST' CHARACTER HAD SOMETHING TO DO WITH BRIAN'S DEATH
DON'T BE ABSURD.
BULLSEYE

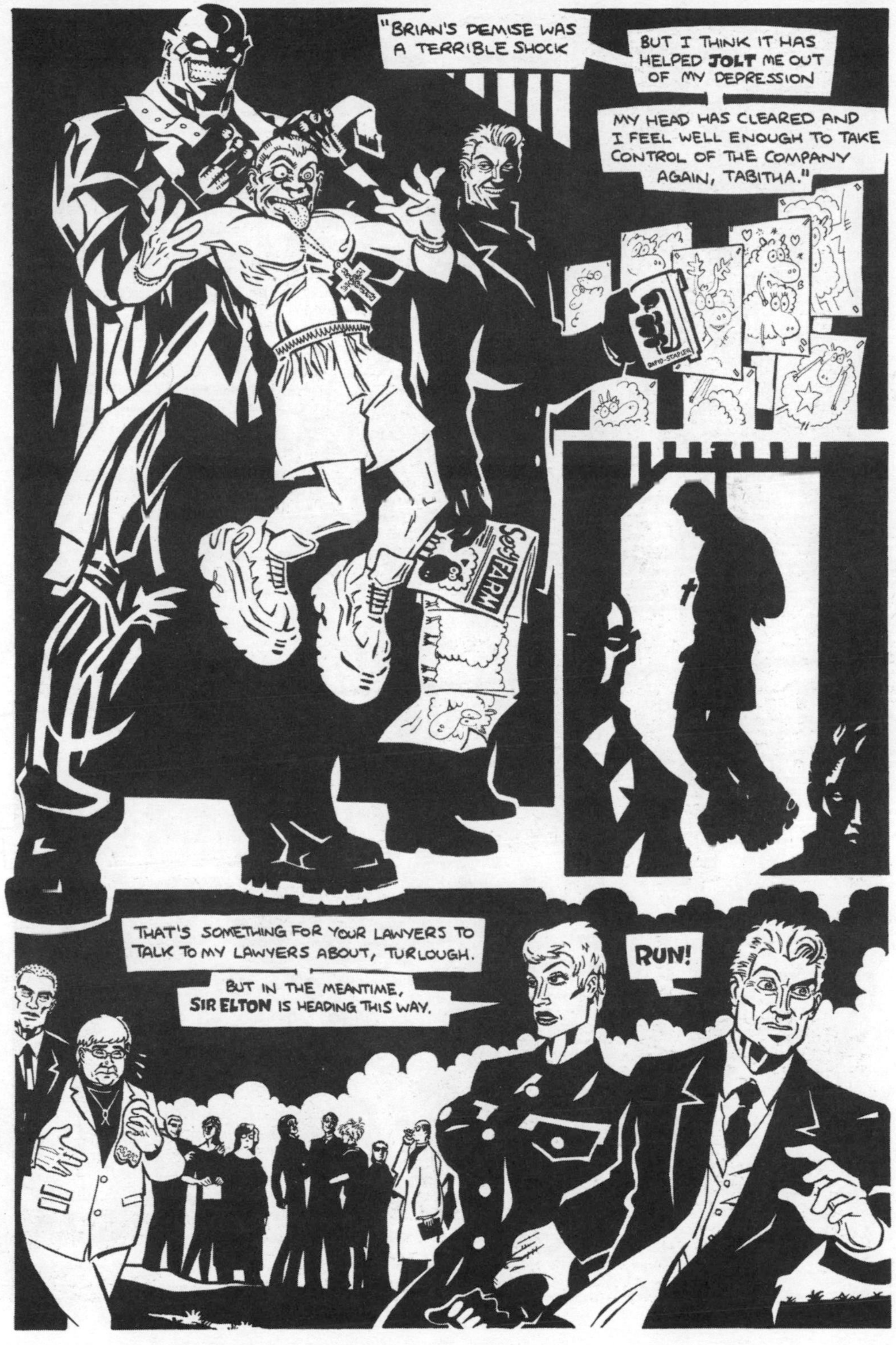
"BRIAN'S DEMISE WAS A TERRIBLE SHOCK
BUT I THINK IT HAS HELPED JOLT ME OUT OF MY DEPRESSION
MY HEAD HAS CLEARED AND I FEEL WELL ENOUGH TO TAKE CONTROL OF THE COMPANY AGAIN, TABITHA."
THAT'S SOMETHING FOR YOUR LAWYERS TO TALK TO MY LAWYERS ABOUT, TURLOUGH.
BUT IN THE MEANTIME, SIR ELTON IS HEADING THIS WAY.
RUN!

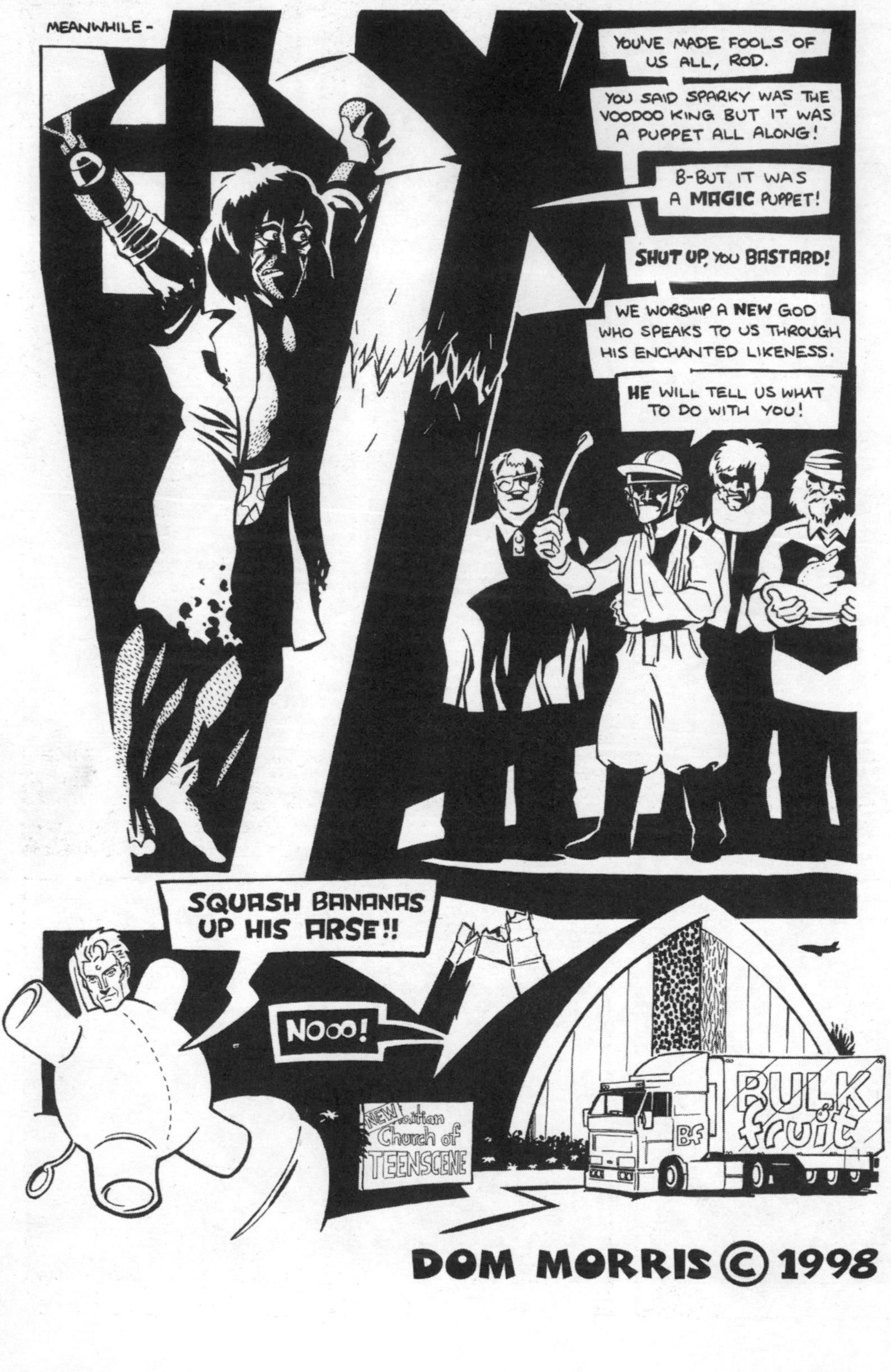
MEANWHILE -
YOU'VE MADE FOOLS OF US ALL, ROD.
YOU SAID SPARKY WAS THE VOODOO KING BUT IT WAS A PUPPET ALL ALONG!
B-BUT IT WAS A **MAGIC** PUPPET!
SHUT UP, YOU **BASTARD!**
WE WORSHIP A **NEW** GOD WHO SPEAKS TO US THROUGH HIS ENCHANTED LIKENESS.
HE WILL TELL US WHAT TO DO WITH YOU!
SQUASH BANANAS UP HIS ARSE!!
NOoo!
NEW
Church of
TEENSCENE
BULK fruit
BF
DOM MORRIS © 1998

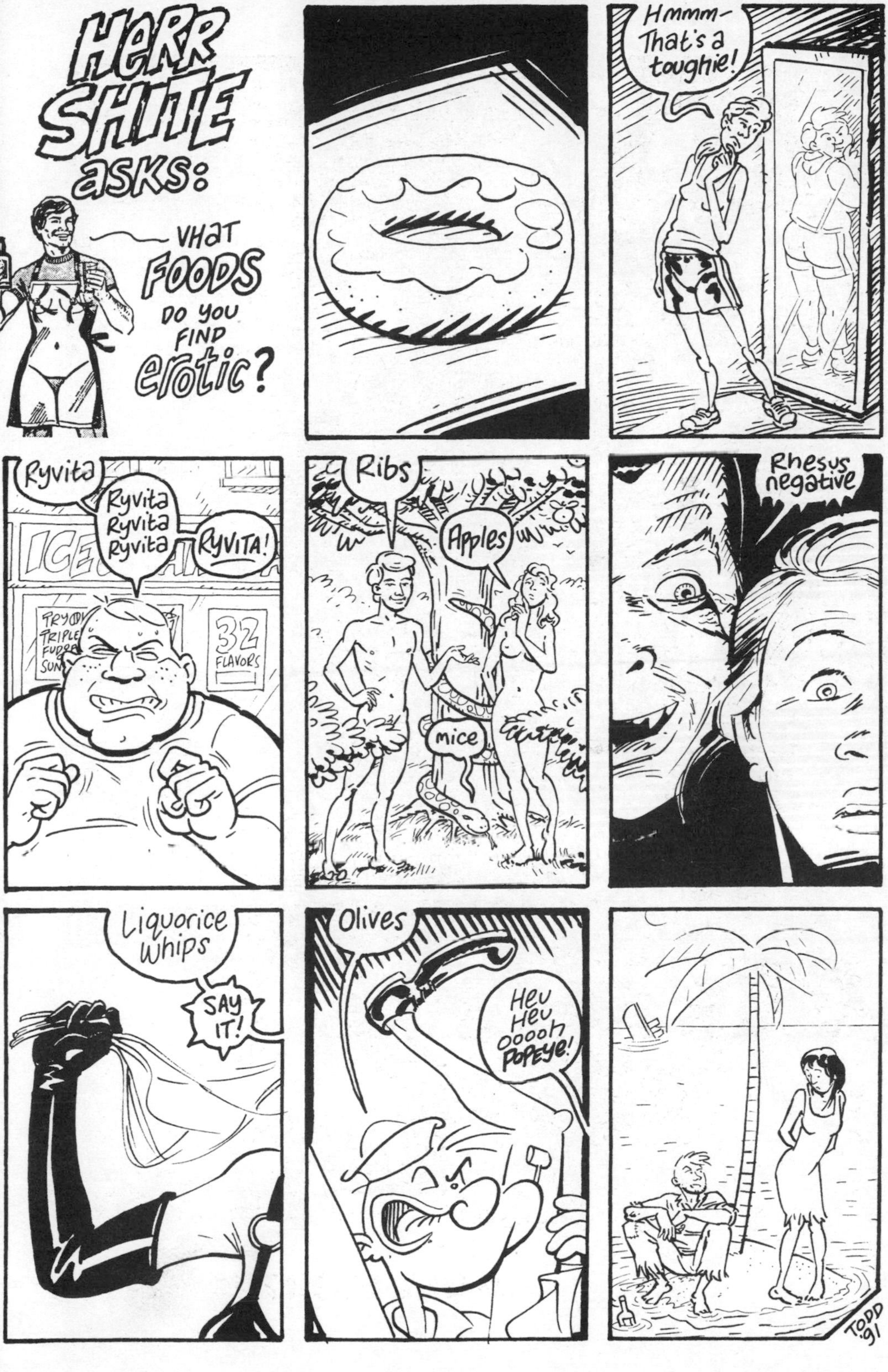

HERR SHITE asks:
VHAT FOODS DO YOU FIND erotic?
Hmmm- That's a toughie!
Ryvita
Ryvita Ryvita Ryvita
RYVITA!
ICE
TRY OUR TRIPLE FUDGE SUN
32 FLAVORS
Ribs
Apples
mice
Rhesus negative
Liquorice Whips
SAY IT!
Olives
Heu Heu Ooooh POPEYE!
TODD '91

Paul O'Connell (with Laurence Elwick)

THE SOUND OF DROWNING
The Sound of Drowning #11, self-published, 2008

In *Happy Daze*, Doris Day is a post-apocalyptic Avon lady, travelling around America's atomic wastelands offering makeovers to survivors (the perfect nuclear family from TV's *Happy Days*). It's a feminist *Mad Max* in the style of a 1950's B-movie. An aborted sequel saw Doris in Las Vegas, upsetting the misogynist rule of a radioactive rat pack.

Charlie Parker "Handyman", illustrated by Lawrence Elwick, ran as a serial for several years in free music newspaper, *The Stool Pigeon*. An alternate-reality Charlie Parker has no skill with musical instruments, although everything he touches still turns to jazz.

"The idea here was to take an iconic scenario and put Charlie into it to see what happened. We're both big fans of old silent comedy. Having our Charlie channeling another, it's very Chaplin-esque. Although the image of a group of construction workers having lunch on a girder high above New York is well known, the final image, of Charlie lying alone on the beam listening to a radio, is also based on a real photograph.

"These days I'm working on stories for younger readers, with artists Lawrence Elwick, Nelson Evergreen and Lord Hurk, doing my best to inject weirdness and darkness back into children's literature!" – POC

www.soundofdrowning.com

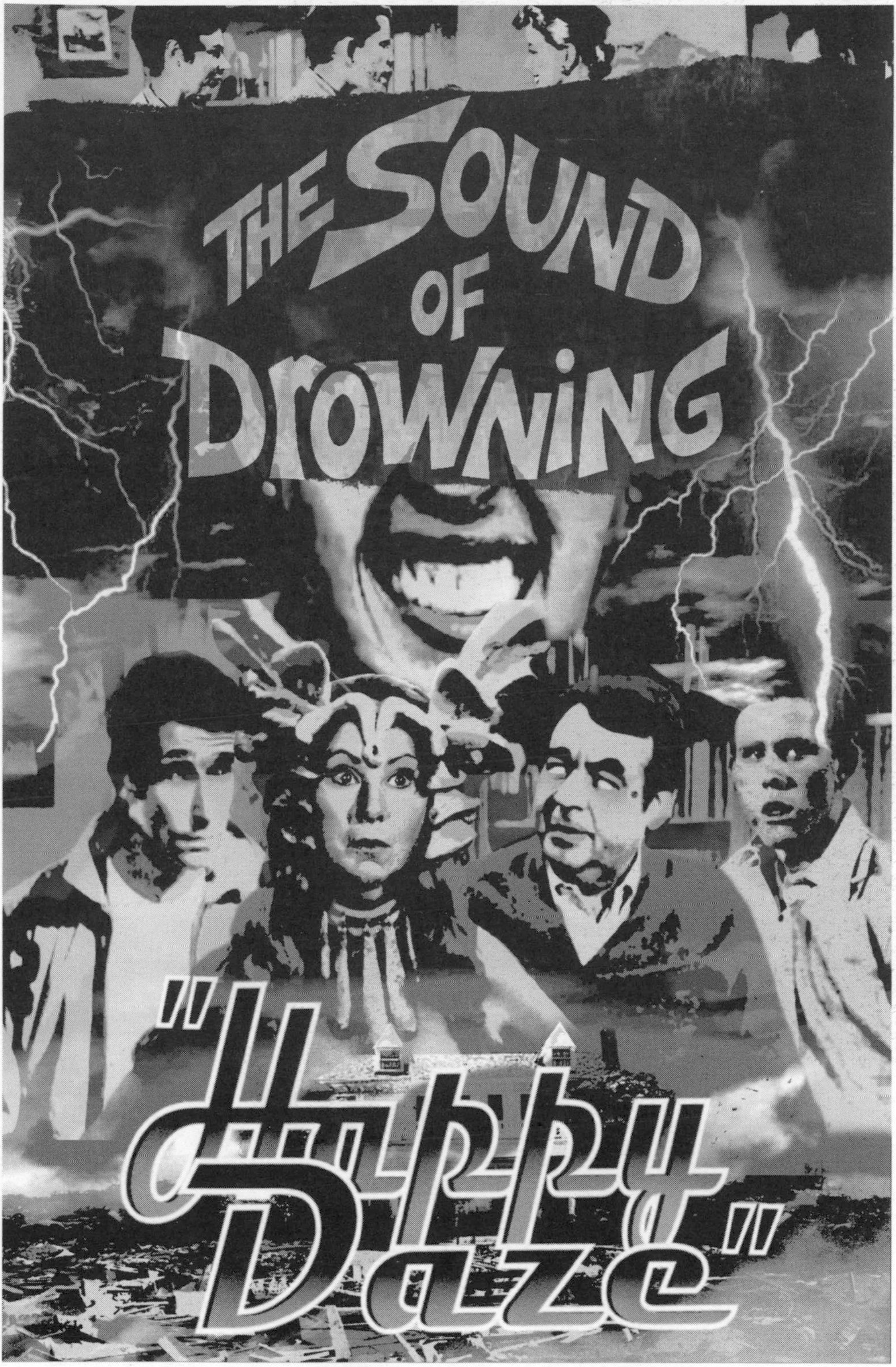
THE SOUND OF DROWNING
"Happy Daze"

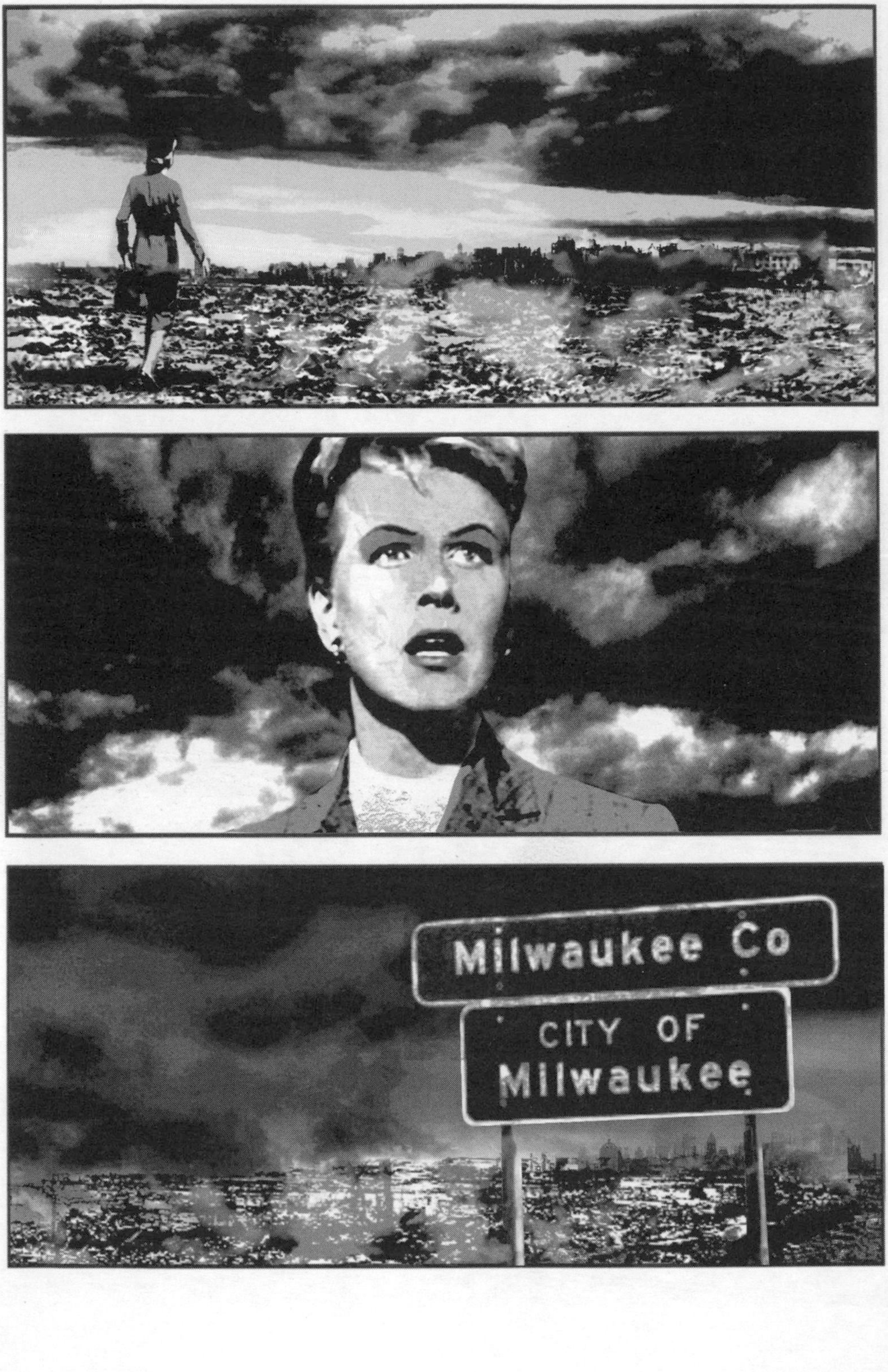
Milwaukee Co
CITY OF
Milwaukee

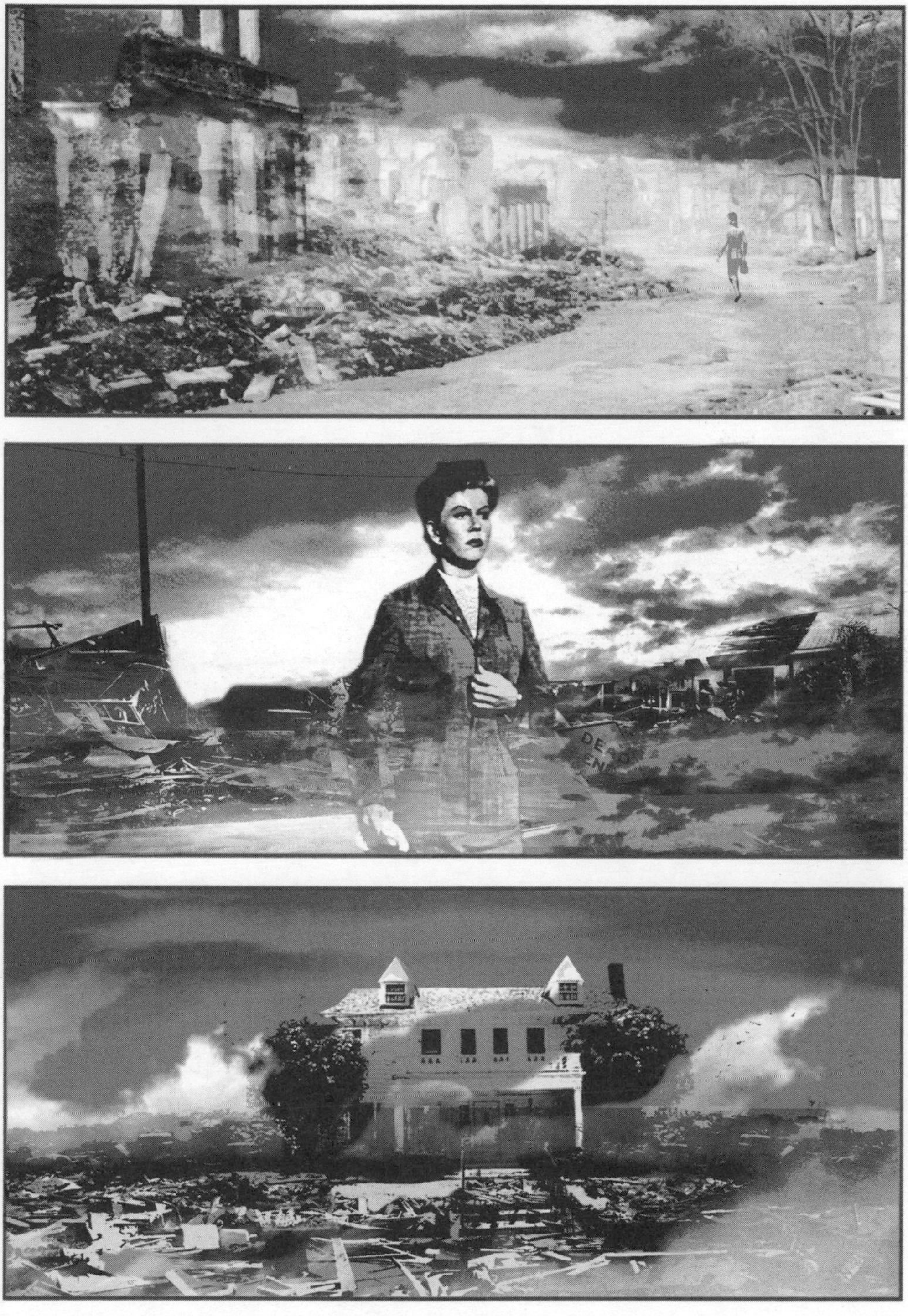

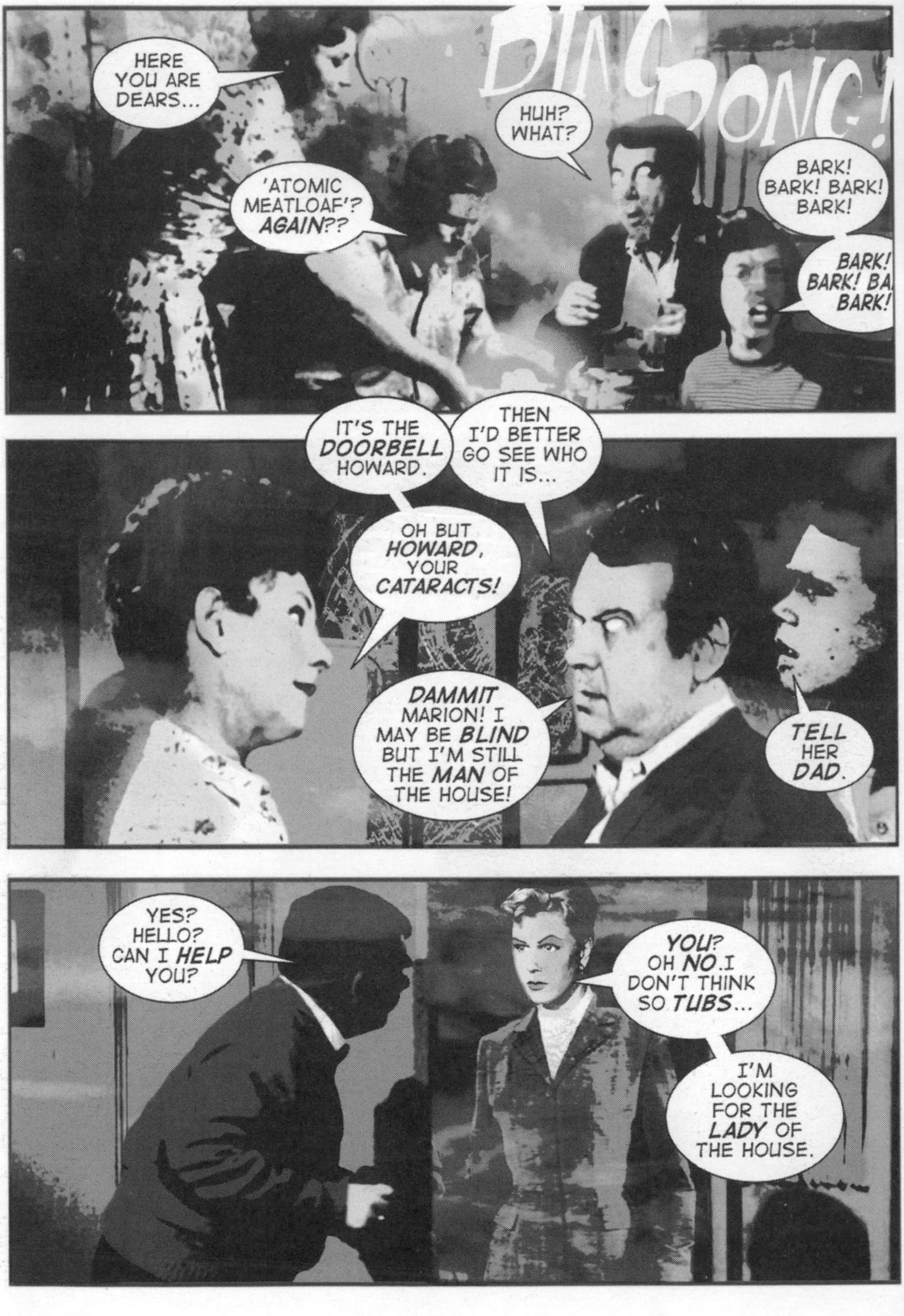

HERE YOU ARE DEARS...
DING DONG!
HUH? WHAT?
BARK! BARK! BARK! BARK!
'ATOMIC MEATLOAF'? AGAIN??
BARK! BARK! BA BARK!
IT'S THE DOORBELL HOWARD.
THEN I'D BETTER GO SEE WHO IT IS...
OH BUT HOWARD, YOUR CATARACTS!
DAMMIT MARION! I MAY BE BLIND BUT I'M STILL THE MAN OF THE HOUSE!
TELL HER DAD.
YES? HELLO? CAN I HELP YOU?
YOU? OH NO. I DON'T THINK SO TUBS...
I'M LOOKING FOR THE LADY OF THE HOUSE.

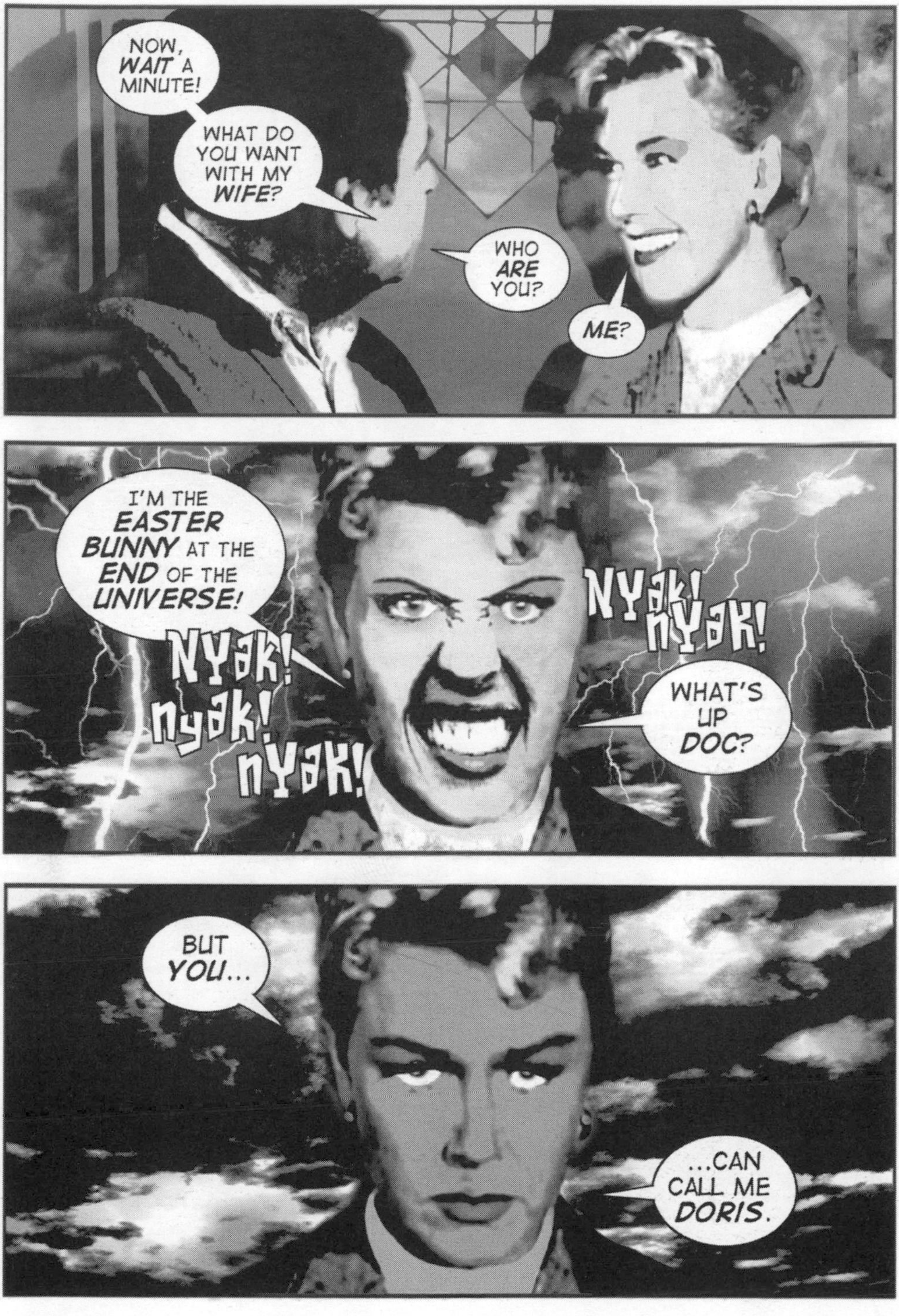
NOW, WAIT A MINUTE!
WHAT DO YOU WANT WITH MY WIFE?
WHO ARE YOU?
ME?
I'M THE EASTER BUNNY AT THE END OF THE UNIVERSE!
NYAK! NYAK! NYAK!
NYAK! NYAK!
WHAT'S UP DOC?
BUT YOU...
...CAN CALL ME DORIS.

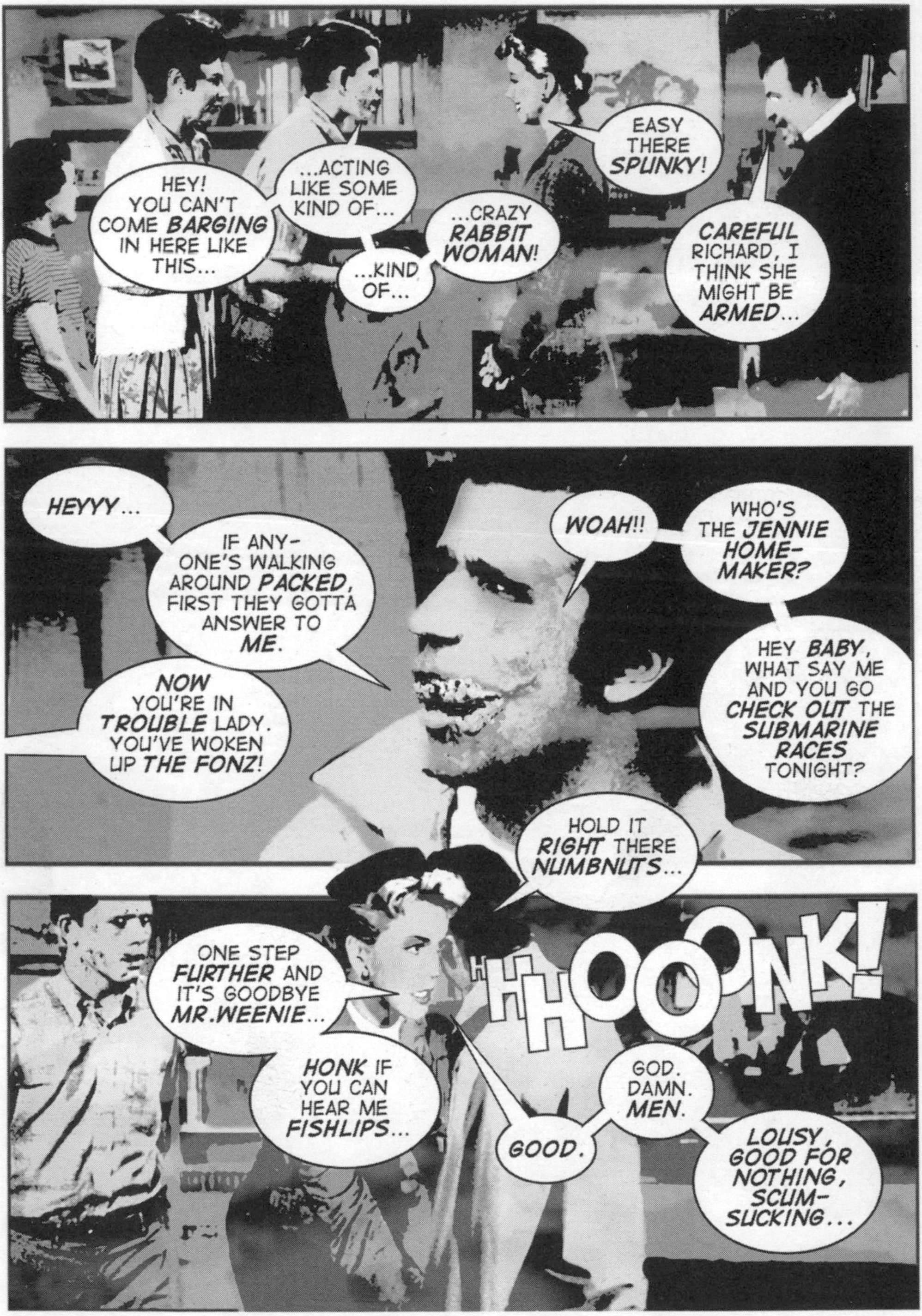

HEY! YOU CAN'T COME BARGING IN HERE LIKE THIS...
...ACTING LIKE SOME KIND OF...
...KIND OF...
...CRAZY RABBIT WOMAN!
EASY THERE SPUNKY!
CAREFUL RICHARD, I THINK SHE MIGHT BE ARMED...
HEYYY...
IF ANYONE'S WALKING AROUND PACKED, FIRST THEY GOTTA ANSWER TO ME.
NOW YOU'RE IN TROUBLE LADY. YOU'VE WOKEN UP THE FONZ!
WOAH!!
WHO'S THE JENNIE HOMEMAKER?
HEY BABY, WHAT SAY ME AND YOU GO CHECK OUT THE SUBMARINE RACES TONIGHT?
HOLD IT RIGHT THERE NUMBNUTS...
ONE STEP FURTHER AND IT'S GOODBYE MR.WEENIE...
HHHOOONK!
HONK IF YOU CAN HEAR ME FISHLIPS...
GOOD.
GOD. DAMN. MEN.
LOUSY, GOOD FOR NOTHING, SCUM-SUCKING...

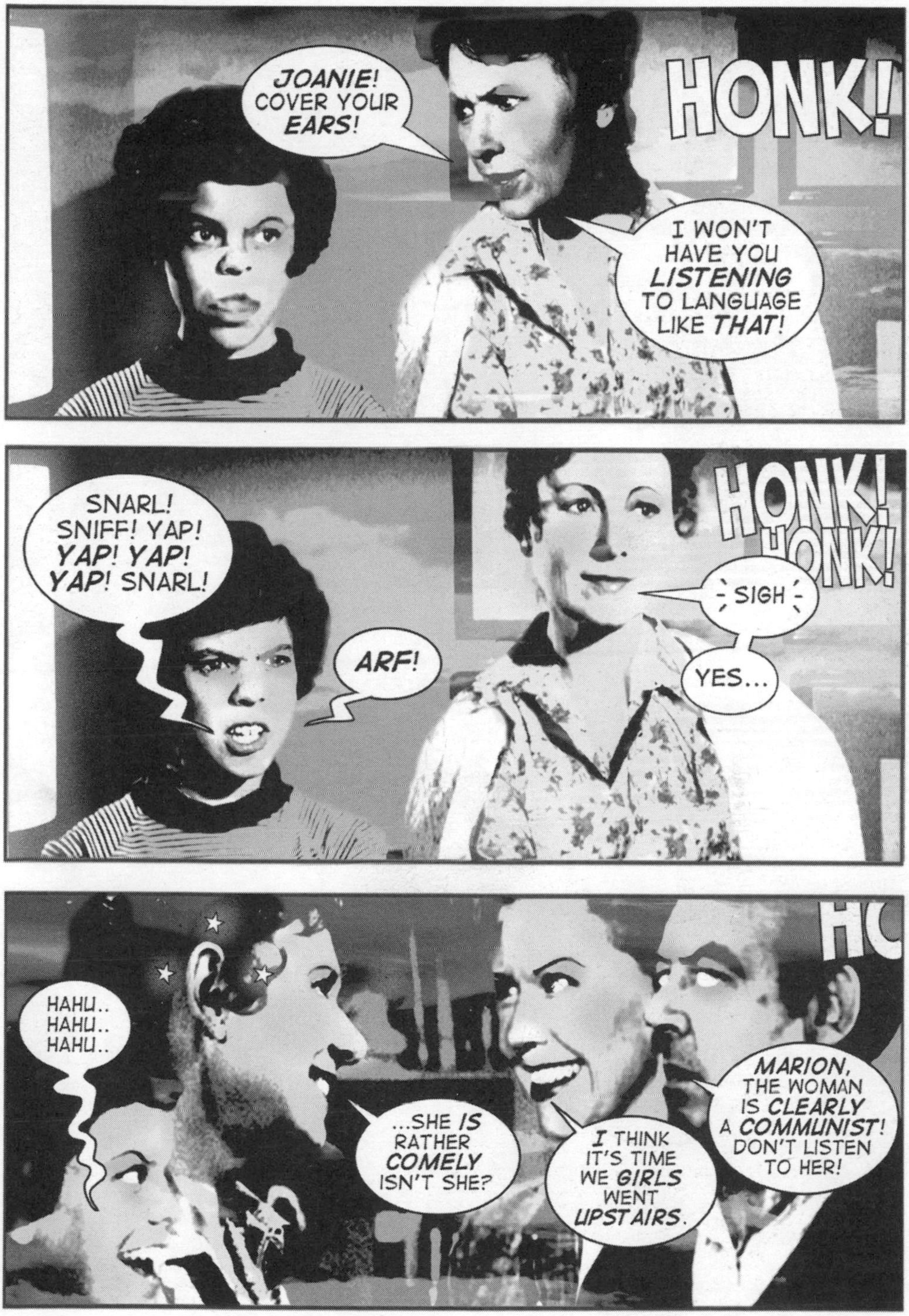
JOANIE! COVER YOUR EARS!
HONK!
I WON'T HAVE YOU LISTENING TO LANGUAGE LIKE THAT!
SNARL! SNIFF! YAP! YAP! YAP! YAP! SNARL!
ARF!
HONK! HONK!
SIGH
YES...
HAHU.. HAHU.. HAHU..
...SHE IS RATHER COMELY ISN'T SHE?
I THINK IT'S TIME WE GIRLS WENT UPSTAIRS.
MARION, THE WOMAN IS CLEARLY A COMMUNIST! DON'T LISTEN TO HER!

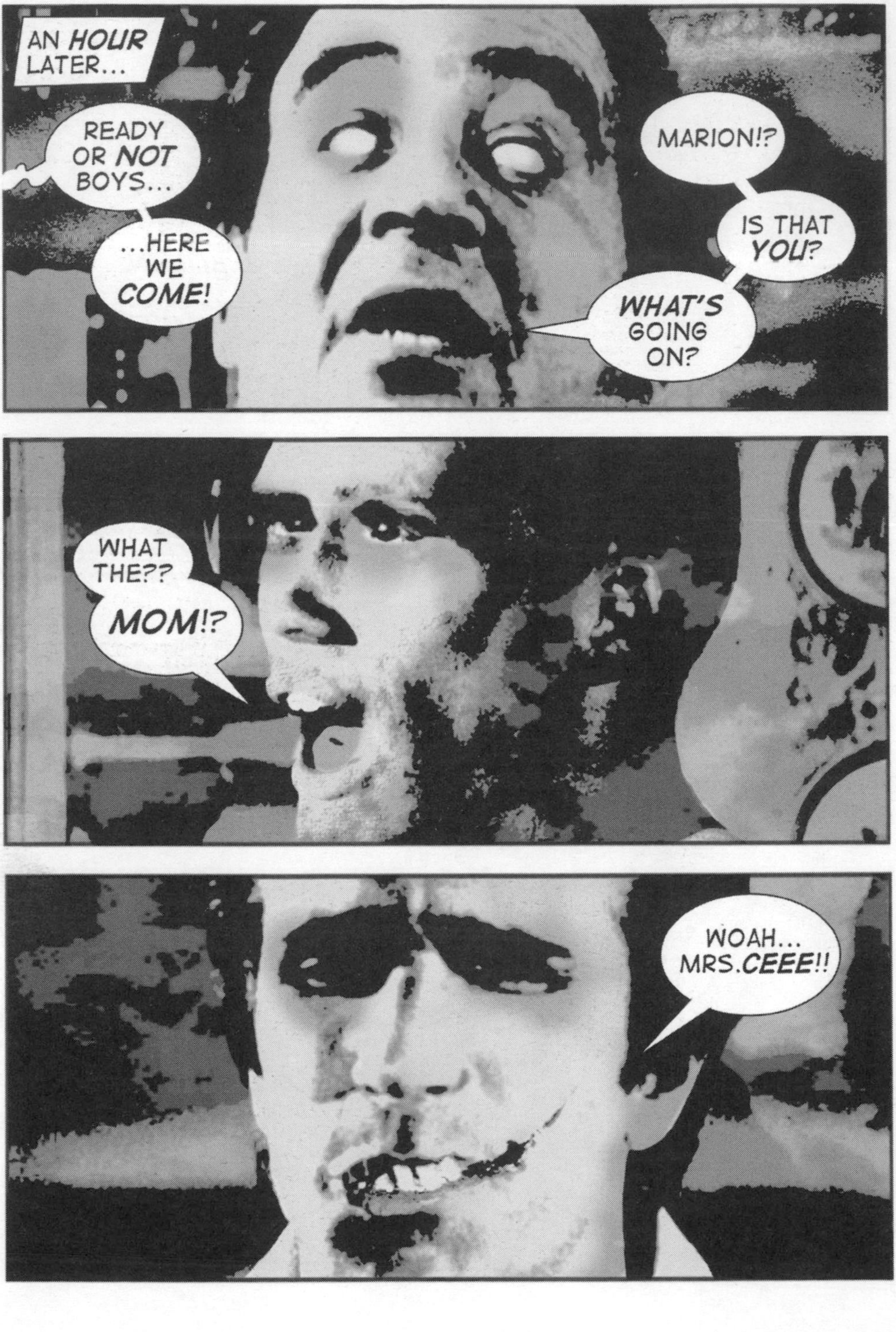
AN HOUR LATER...
READY OR NOT BOYS...
...HERE WE COME!
MARION!?
IS THAT YOU?
WHAT'S GOING ON?
WHAT THE??
MOM!?
WOAH... MRS.CEEE!!

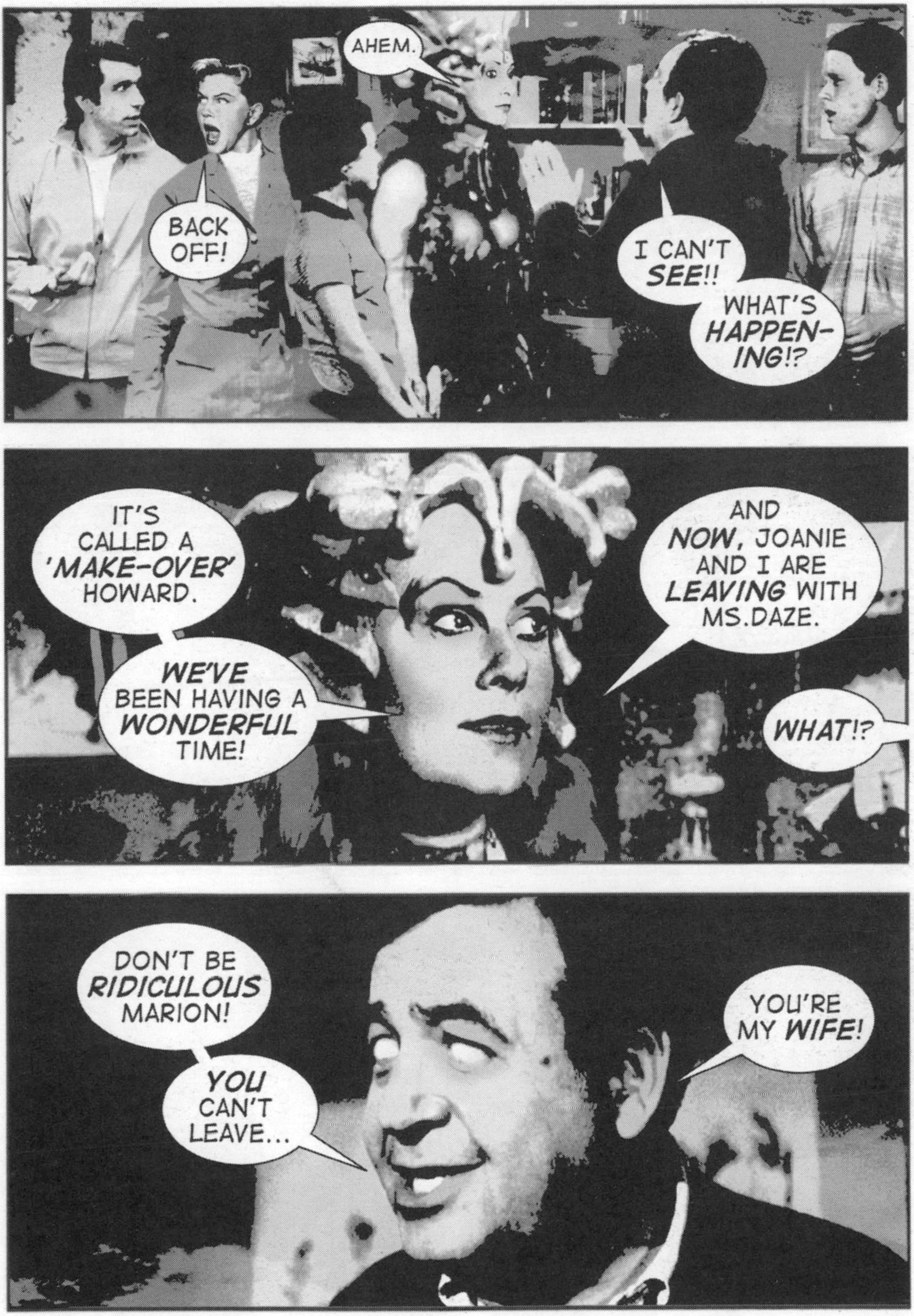
AHEM.
BACK OFF!
I CAN'T SEE!!
WHAT'S HAPPEN-ING!?
IT'S CALLED A 'MAKE-OVER' HOWARD.
WE'VE BEEN HAVING A WONDERFUL TIME!
AND NOW, JOANIE AND I ARE LEAVING WITH MS.DAZE.
WHAT!?
DON'T BE RIDICULOUS MARION!
YOU CAN'T LEAVE...
YOU'RE MY WIFE!

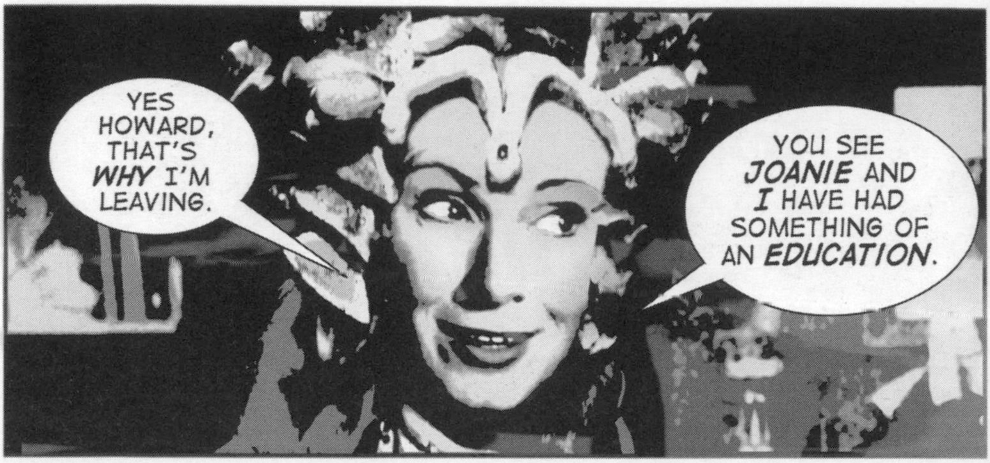
YES HOWARD, THAT'S WHY I'M LEAVING.
YOU SEE JOANIE AND I HAVE HAD SOMETHING OF AN EDUCATION.

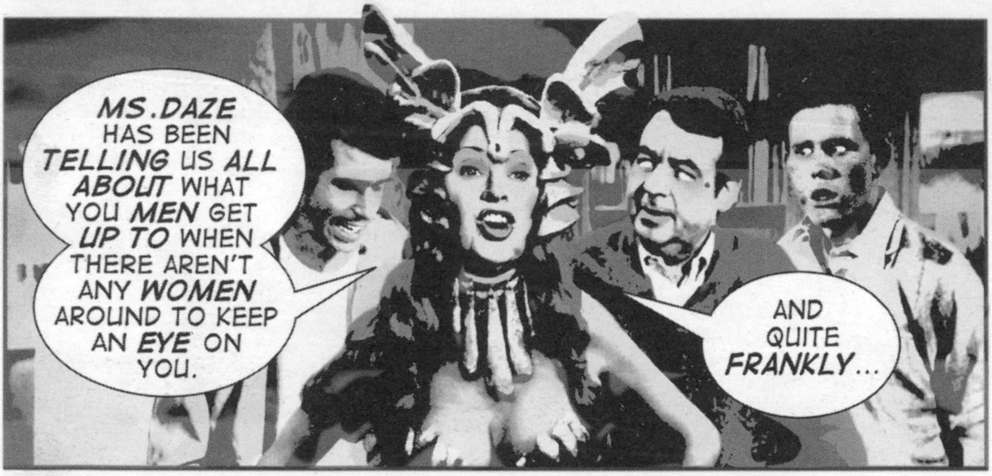
MS.DAZE HAS BEEN TELLING US ALL ABOUT WHAT YOU MEN GET UP TO WHEN THERE AREN'T ANY WOMEN AROUND TO KEEP AN EYE ON YOU.
AND QUITE FRANKLY...

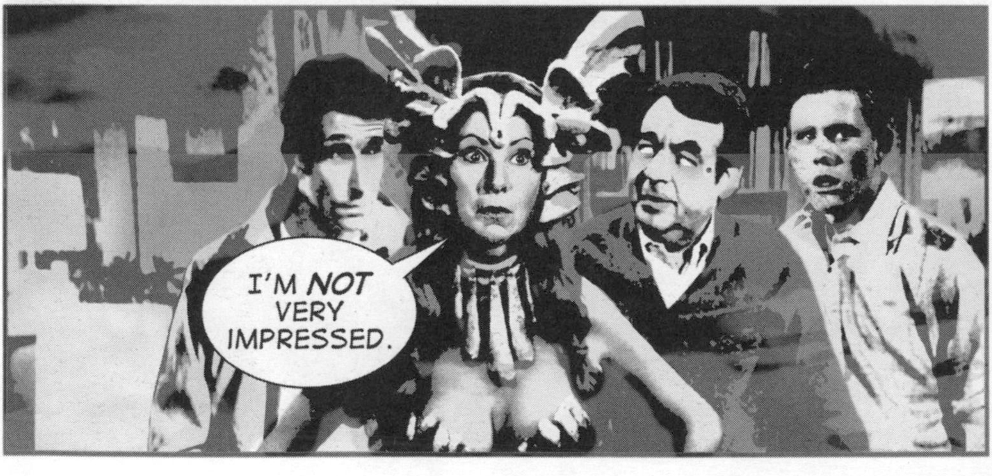
I'M NOT VERY IMPRESSED.

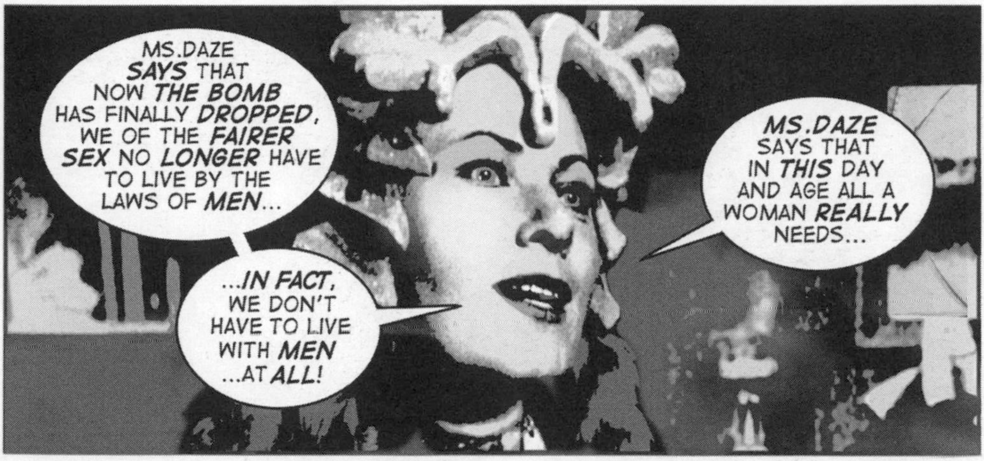
MS.DAZE SAYS THAT NOW THE BOMB HAS FINALLY DROPPED, WE OF THE FAIRER SEX NO LONGER HAVE TO LIVE BY THE LAWS OF MEN...
...IN FACT, WE DON'T HAVE TO LIVE WITH MEN ...AT ALL!
MS.DAZE SAYS THAT IN THIS DAY AND AGE ALL A WOMAN REALLY NEEDS...

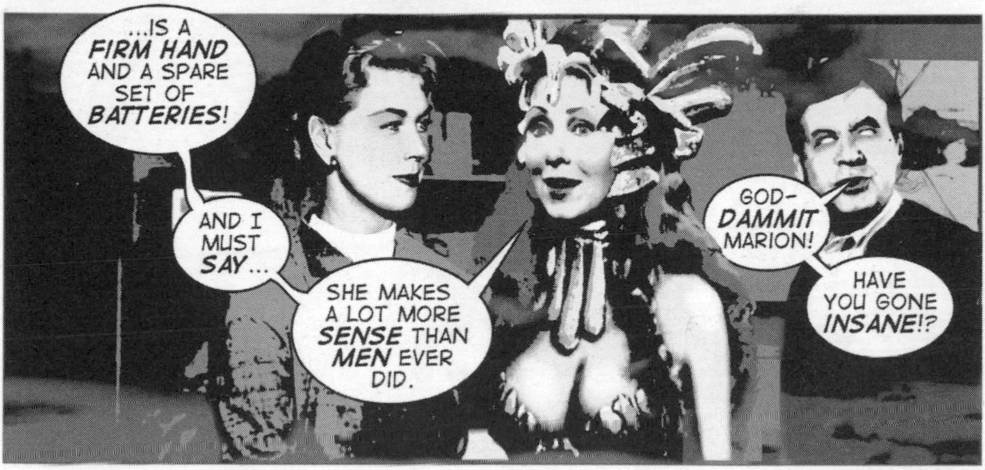
...IS A FIRM HAND AND A SPARE SET OF BATTERIES!
AND I MUST SAY...
SHE MAKES A LOT MORE SENSE THAN MEN EVER DID.
GOD-DAMMIT MARION!
HAVE YOU GONE INSANE!?

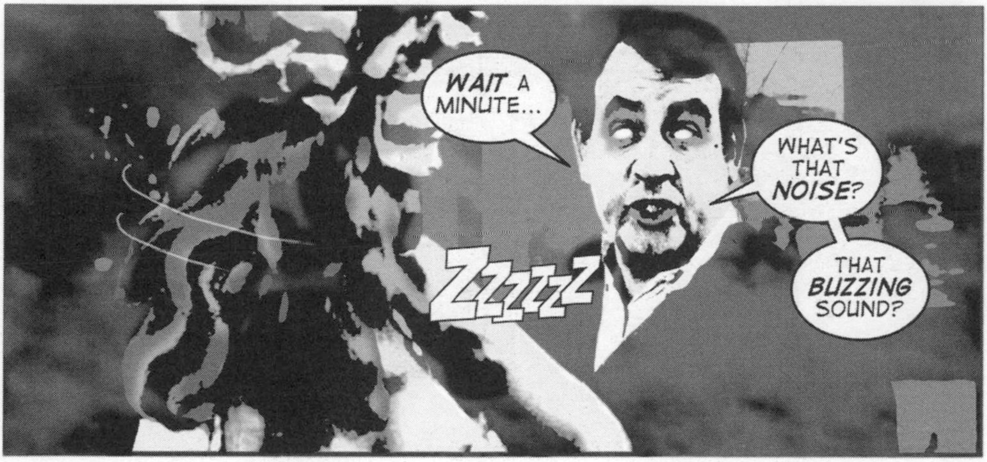
WAIT A MINUTE...
WHAT'S THAT NOISE?
THAT BUZZING SOUND?
ZZZZZZ

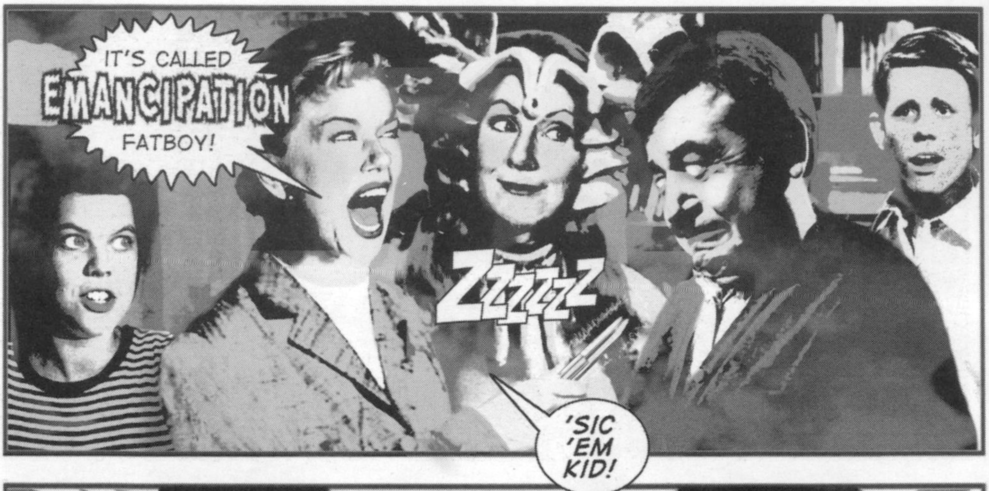
IT'S CALLED EMANCIPATION FATBOY!
ZZZZZZ
'SIC 'EM KID!

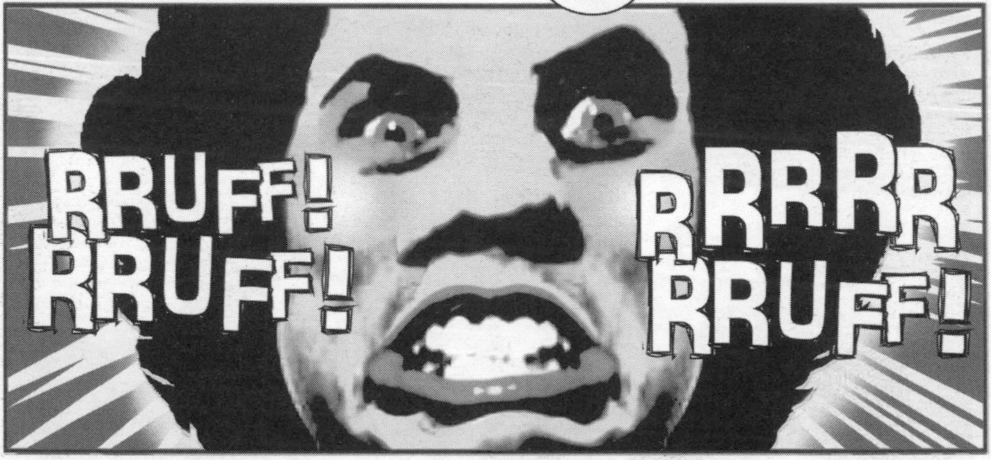
RRUFF! RRUFF!
RRRRR RRUFF!

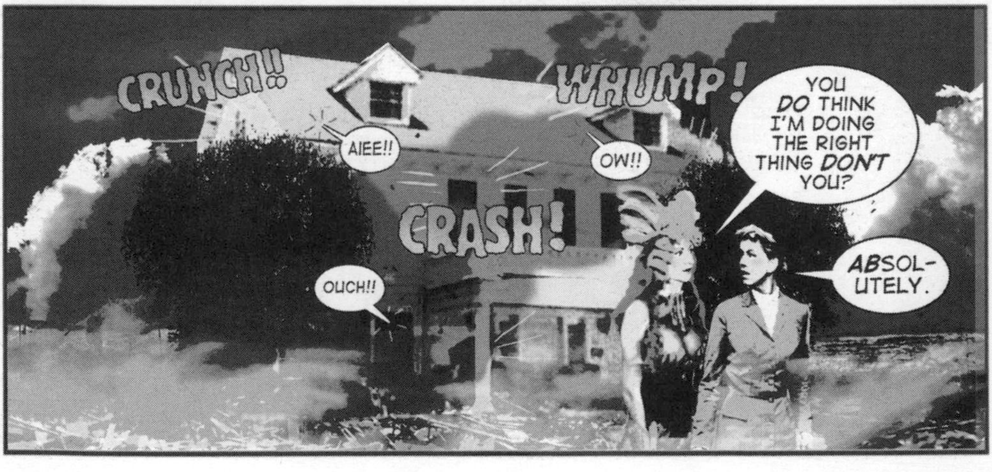
CRUNCH!!
AIEE!!
WHUMP!
OW!!
YOU DO THINK I'M DOING THE RIGHT THING DON'T YOU?
CRASH!
OUCH!!
ABSOL-UTELY.

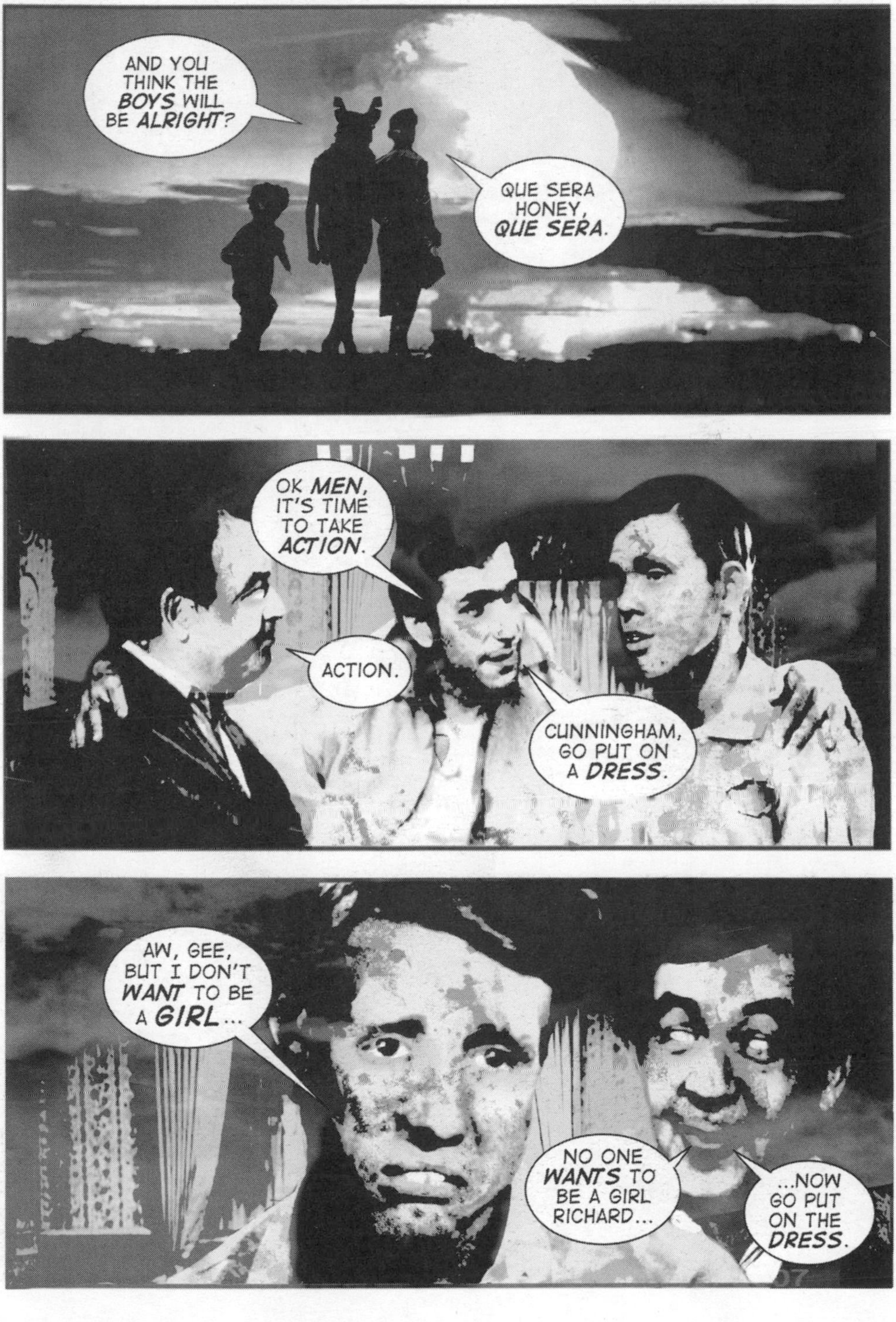
AND YOU THINK THE BOYS WILL BE ALRIGHT?
QUE SERA HONEY, QUE SERA.
OK MEN, IT'S TIME TO TAKE ACTION.
ACTION.
CUNNINGHAM, GO PUT ON A DRESS.
AW, GEE, BUT I DON'T WANT TO BE A GIRL...
NO ONE WANTS TO BE A GIRL RICHARD...
...NOW GO PUT ON THE DRESS.

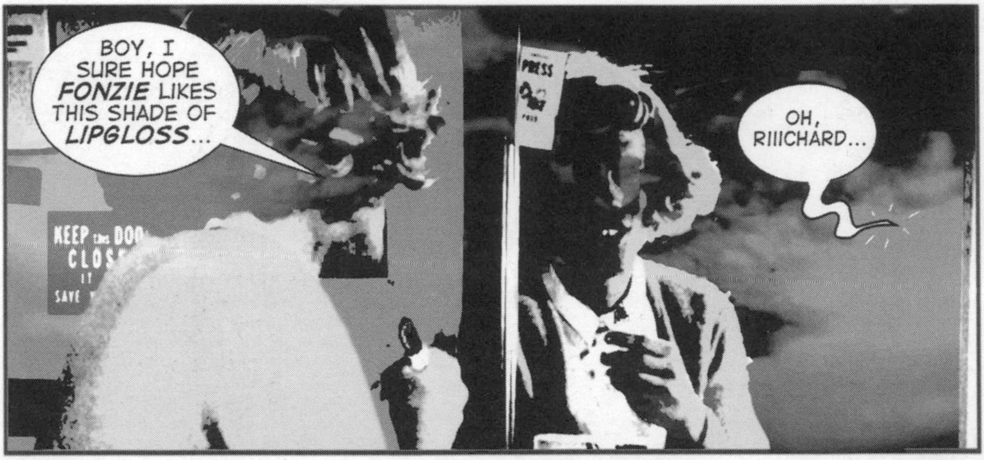
BOY, I SURE HOPE *FONZIE* LIKES THIS SHADE OF *LIPGLOSS*...
OH, RIIICHARD...

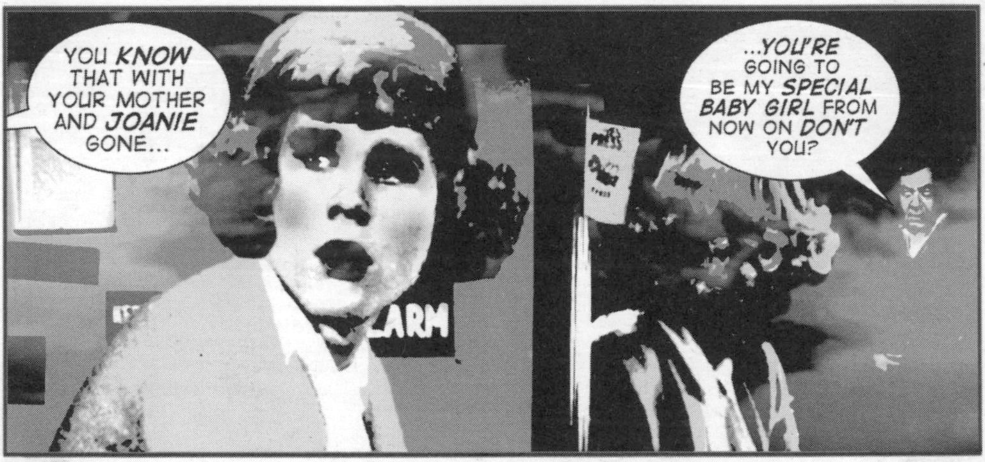
YOU *KNOW* THAT WITH YOUR MOTHER AND *JOANIE* GONE...
...*YOU'RE* GOING TO BE MY *SPECIAL BABY GIRL* FROM NOW ON *DON'T* YOU?

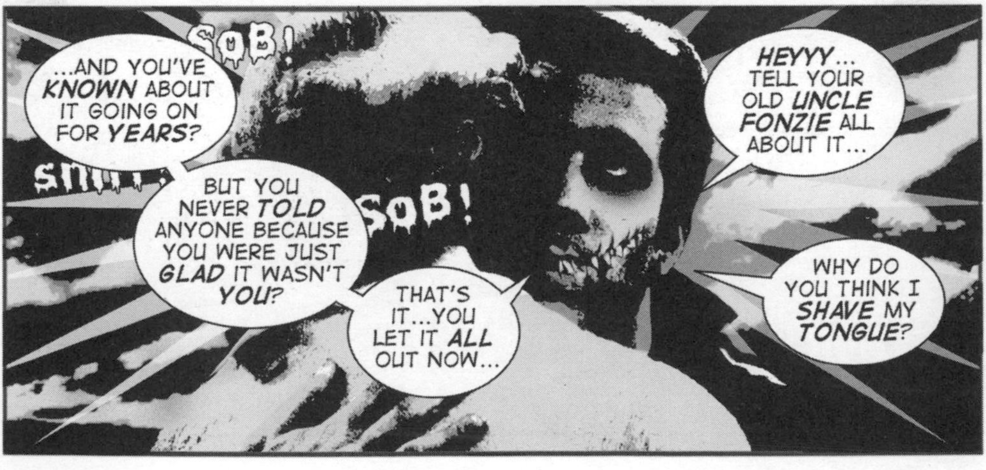
SOB!
...AND YOU'VE *KNOWN* ABOUT IT GOING ON FOR *YEARS*?
BUT YOU NEVER *TOLD* ANYONE BECAUSE YOU WERE JUST *GLAD* IT WASN'T *YOU*?
SOB!
THAT'S IT...YOU LET IT *ALL* OUT NOW...
HEYYY... TELL YOUR OLD *UNCLE FONZIE* ALL ABOUT IT...
WHY DO YOU THINK I *SHAVE* MY *TONGUE*?

Charlie Parker
"HANDYMAN"

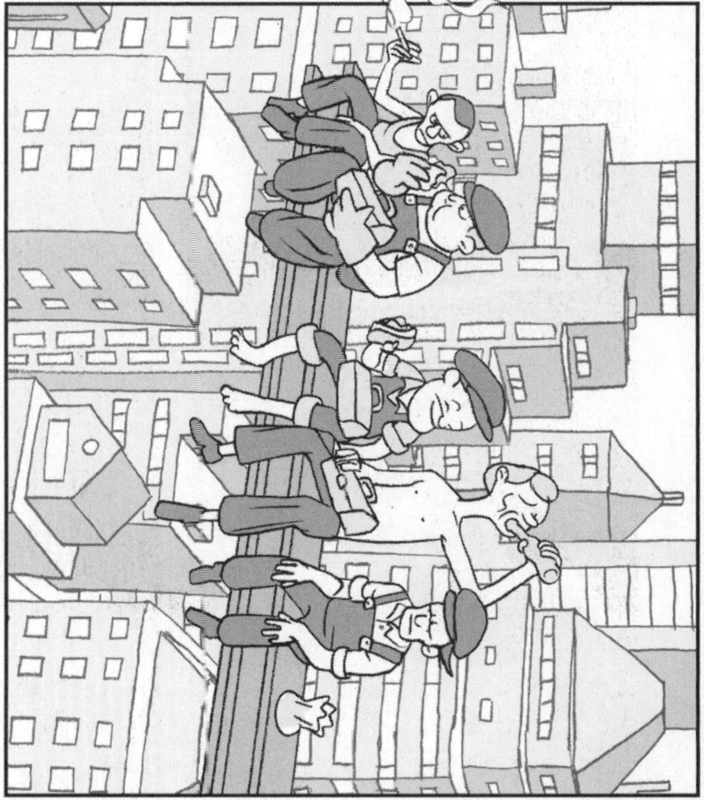

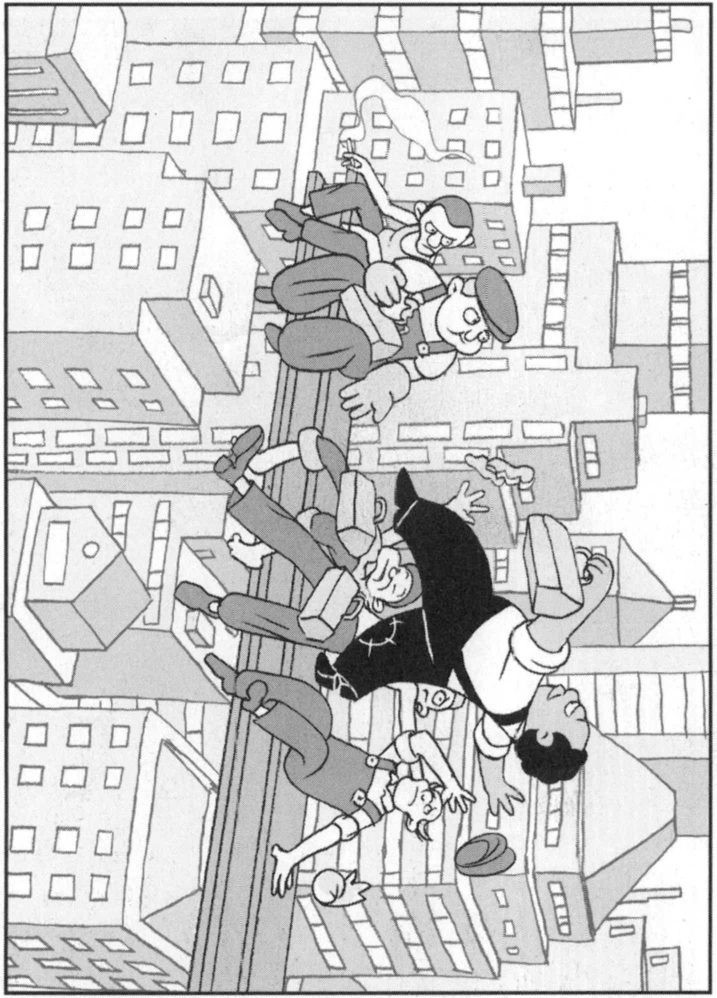

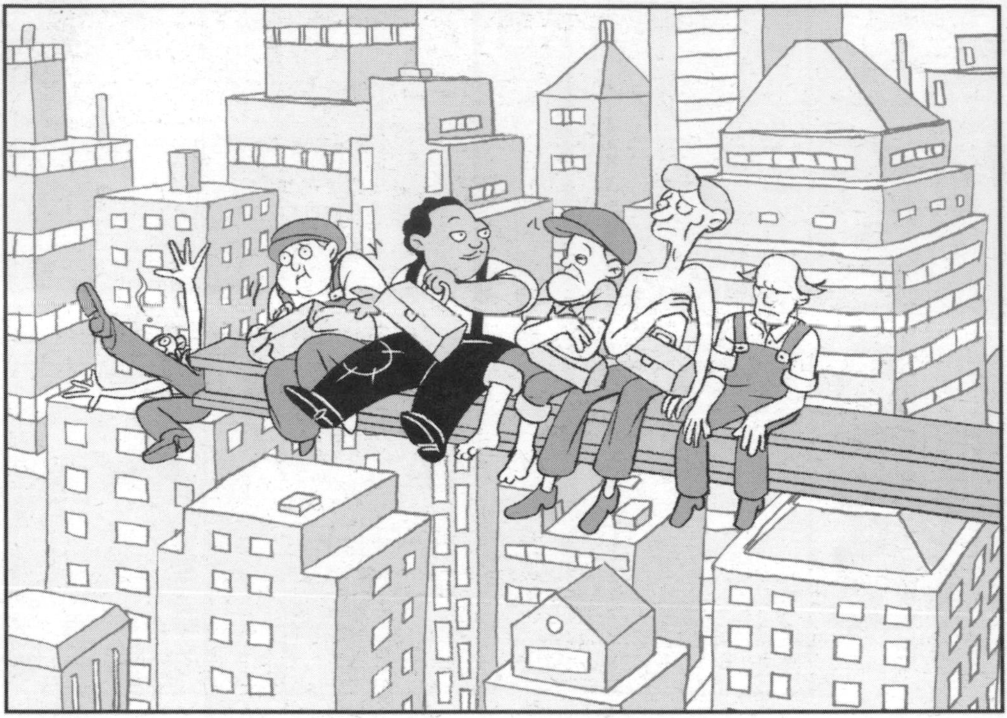

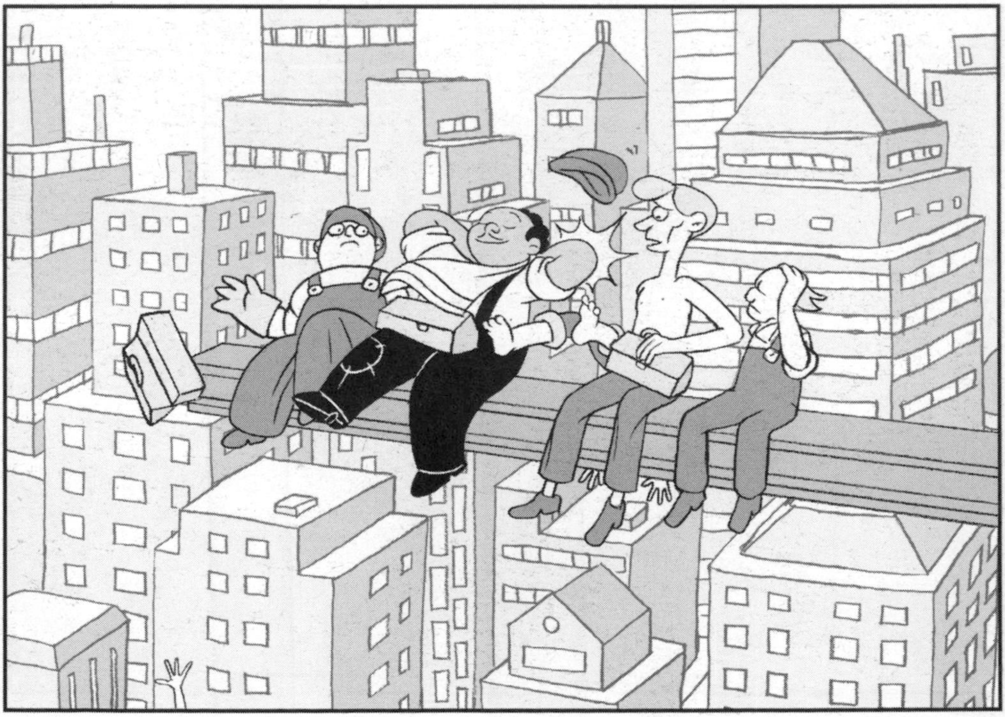

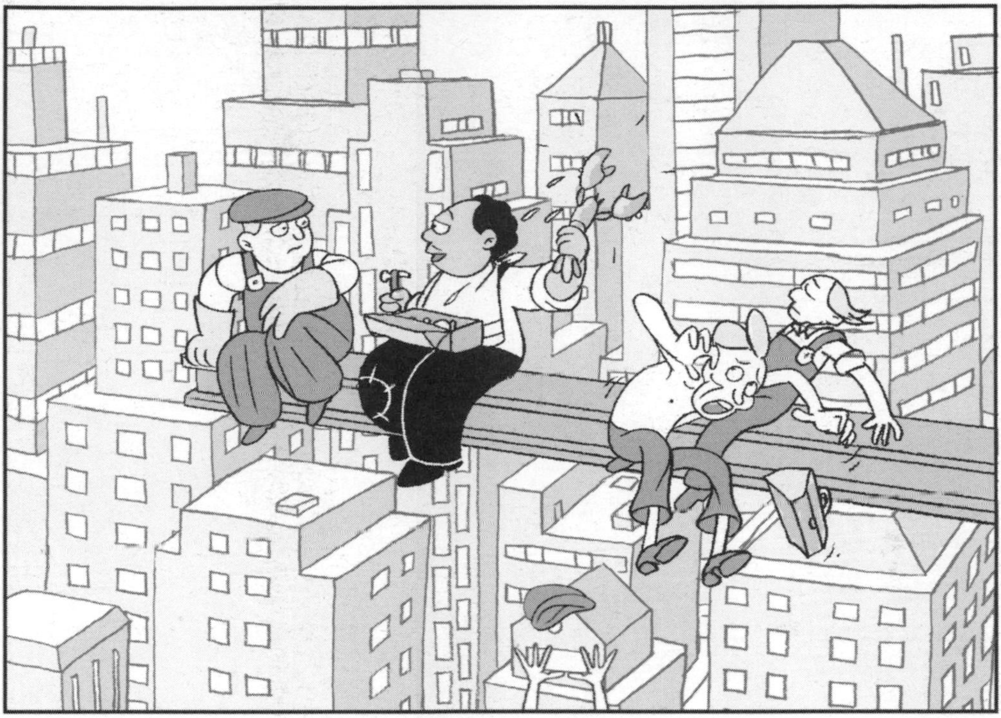

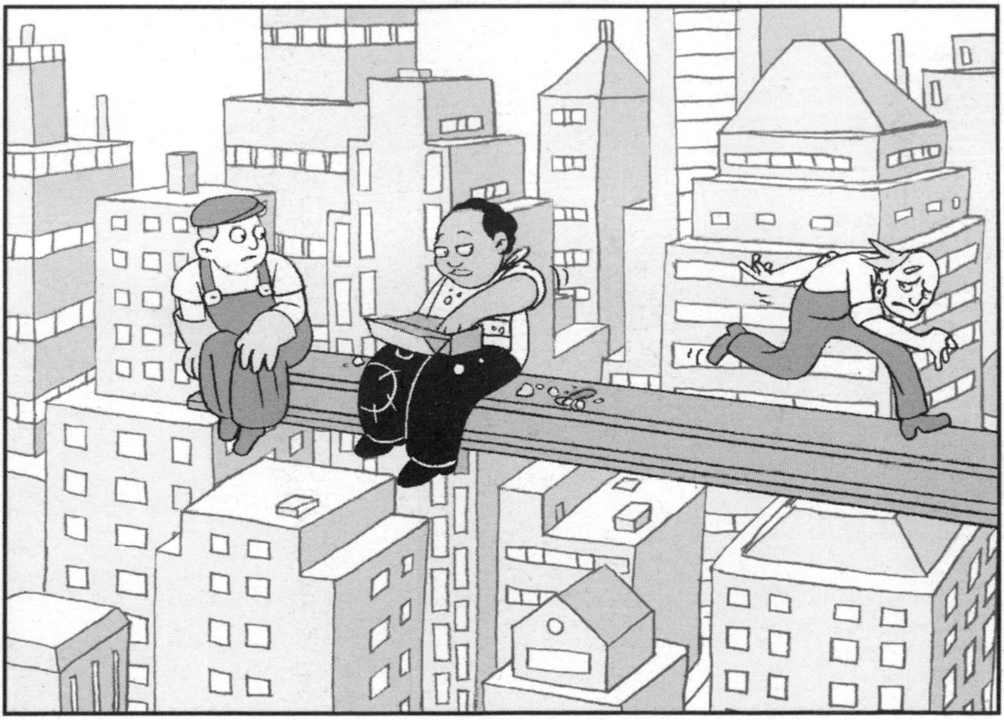

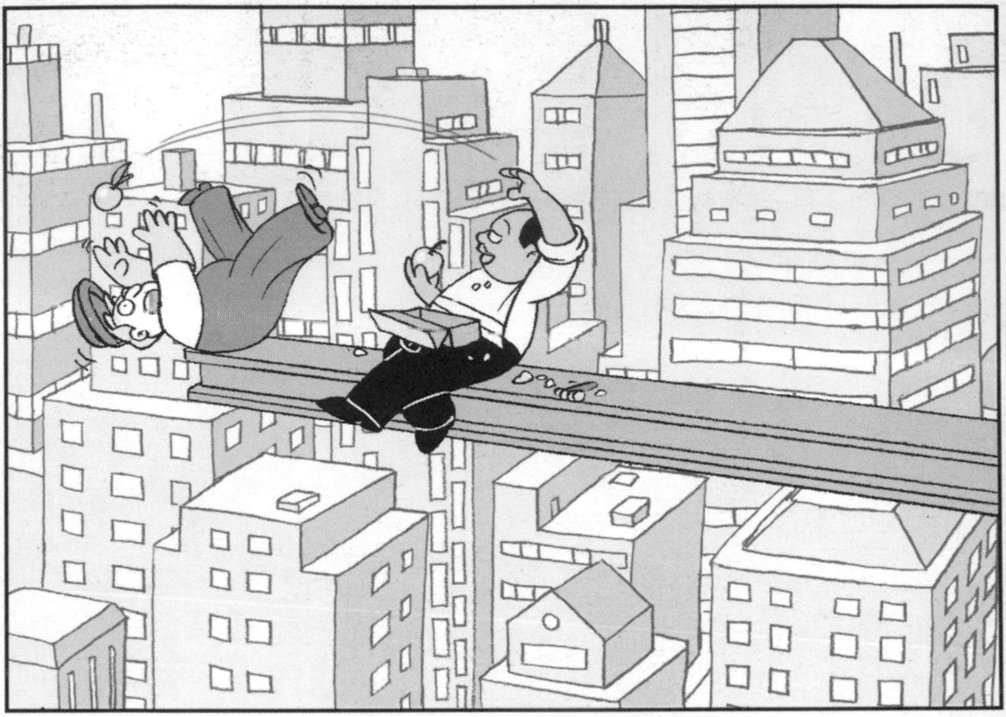

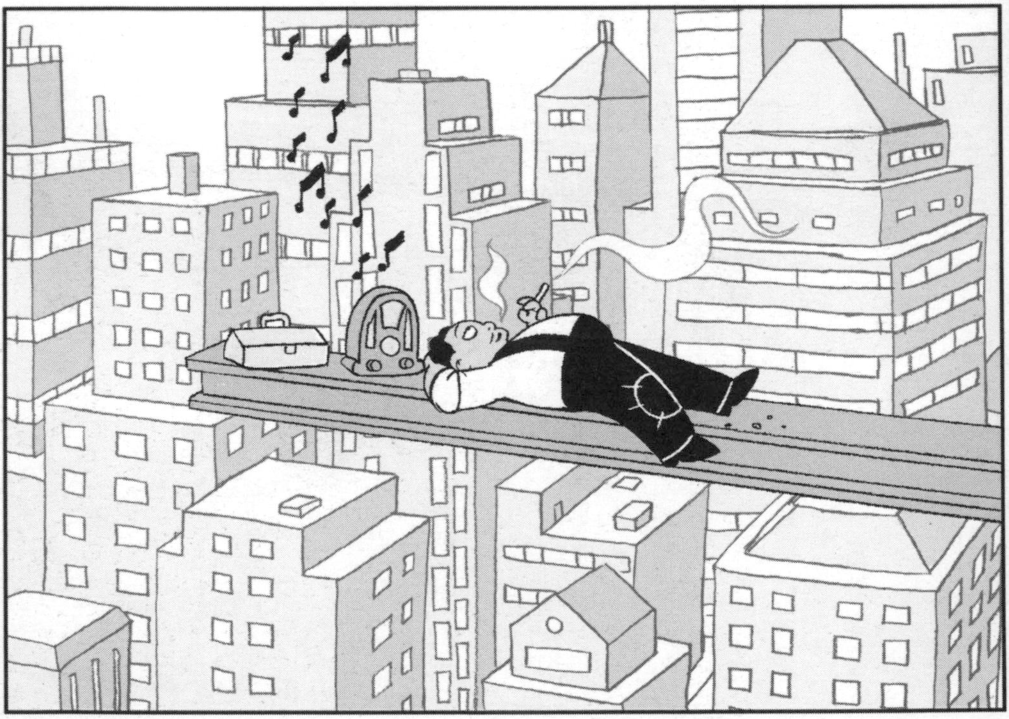

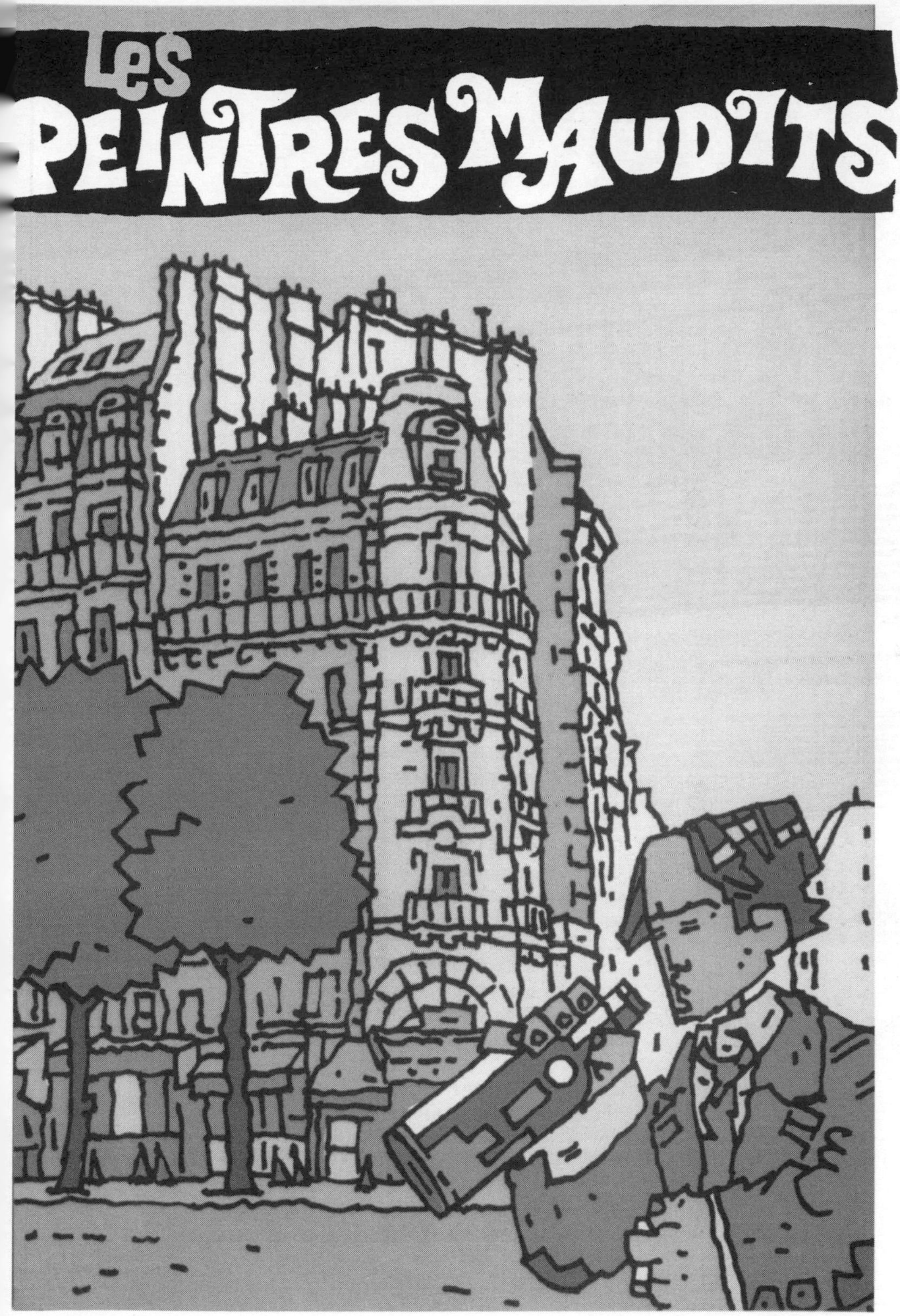
LES PEINTRES MAUDITS

Simon Gane

LES PEINTRES MAUDITS
(*The Cursed Painters*)
Arnie Comix #2, Slab-O-Concrete, 1997

"Not for sale to the rich or right wing, this is a 100 per cent DIY publication. If you think the colour cover equals selling out you can kiss my ass and work my shifts at the Post Office."

So read the short and snappy editorial to Gane's second issue of his *Arnie Comix*, released through Slab-O-Concrete Publications – Peter Pavement's (sorely missed) small-press powerhouse, based in Brighton, UK.

So-called "King of the Punk Comics Aesthetic" (move over Bobby Madness!), for his ornate and borderline obsessive style, Gane has gone on to (relative) fame, if not yet fortune – appearing in Top Shelf's line of *Graphic Classics*: collaborating with writer Andi Watson on SLG's *Paris*, Gavin Burrows for *All Flee!* and Darryl (*Psychiatric Tales*) Cunningham on the graphic novel, *Meet John Dark: Dark Rain, A New Orleans Story*, written by Mat Johnson, and issues of *Northlanders*, for DC/Vertigo and IDW's *Godzilla*. You heard me.

His sketchbooks, to be found on his blog, are a veritable wonder to behold. Go, seek!

www.simongane.blogspot.co.uk

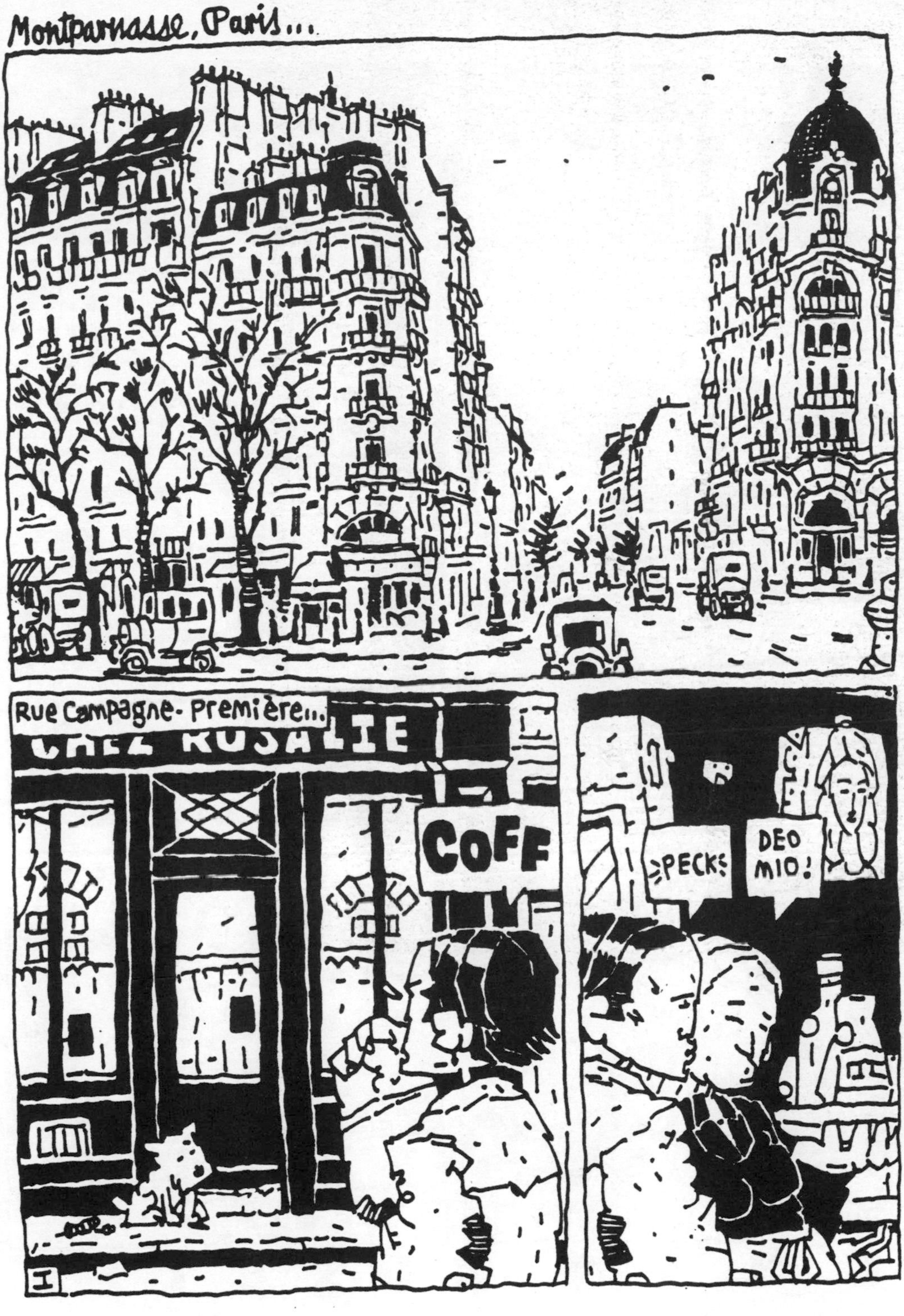
Montparnasse, Paris...
Rue Campagne- Première...
ROSALIE
COFF
PECK
DEO MIO!

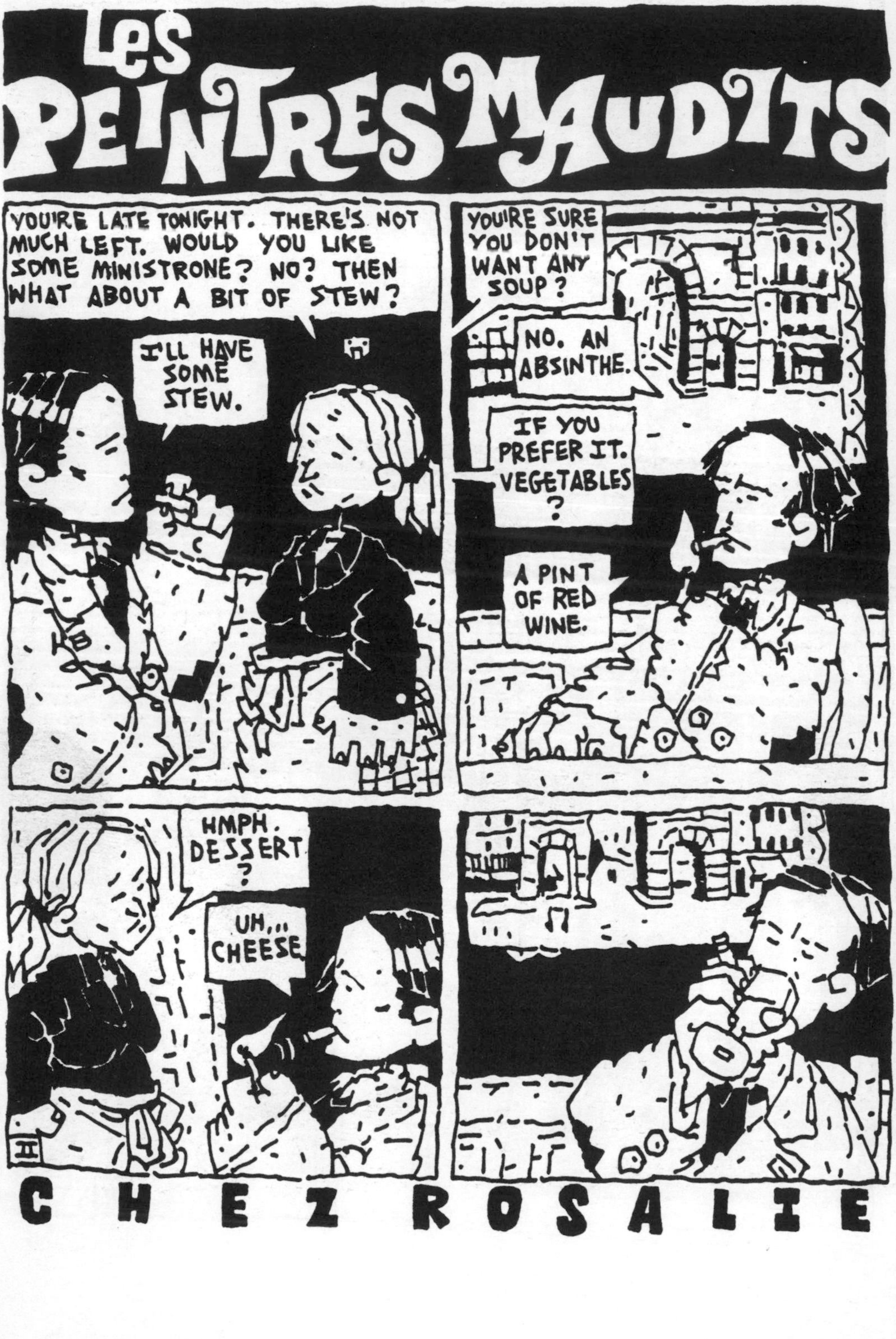
LES PEINTRES MAUDITS
YOU'RE LATE TONIGHT. THERE'S NOT MUCH LEFT. WOULD YOU LIKE SOME MINISTRONE? NO? THEN WHAT ABOUT A BIT OF STEW?
I'LL HAVE SOME STEW.
YOU'RE SURE YOU DON'T WANT ANY SOUP?
NO. AN ABSINTHE.
IF YOU PREFER IT. VEGETABLES?
A PINT OF RED WINE.
HMPH. DESSERT?
UH... CHEESE
CHEZ ROSALIE

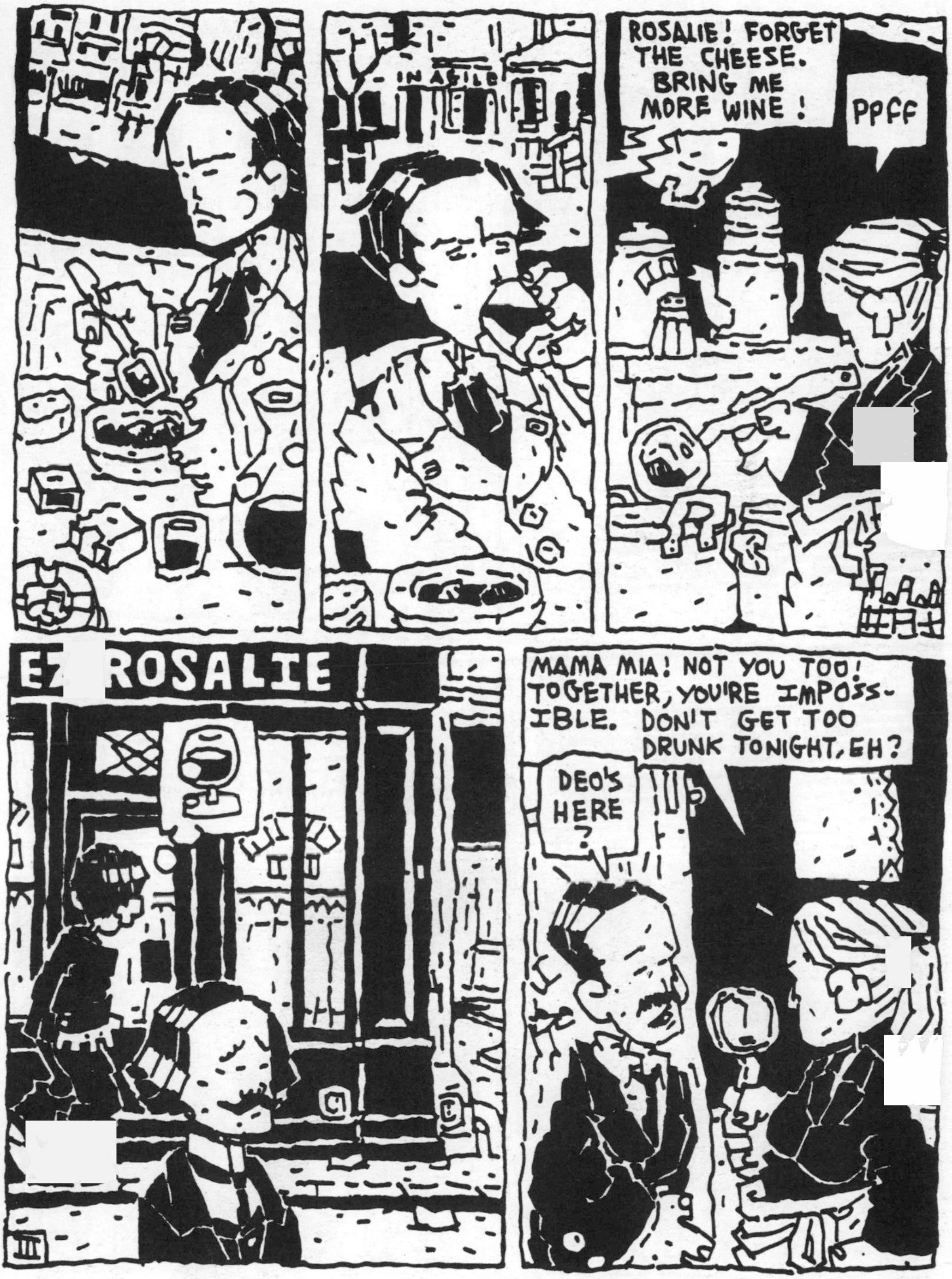
IN AGILE
ROSALIE! FORGET THE CHEESE. BRING ME MORE WINE!
PPFF
EZ ROSALIE
MAMA MIA! NOT YOU TOO! TOGETHER, YOU'RE IMPOSS-IBLE. DON'T GET TOO DRUNK TONIGHT, EH?
DEO'S HERE?

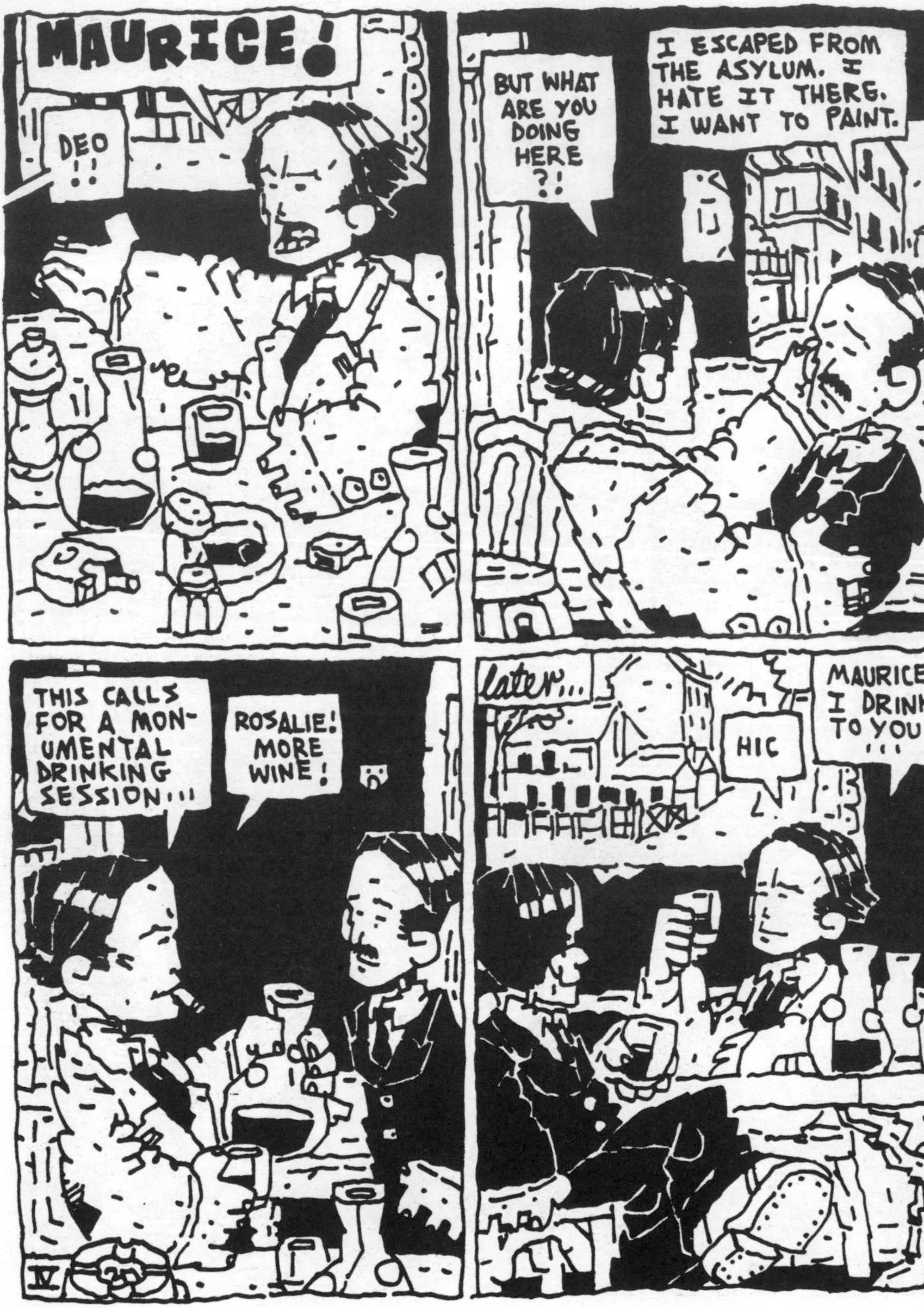
MAURICE!
DEO !!
BUT WHAT ARE YOU DOING HERE ?!
I ESCAPED FROM THE ASYLUM. I HATE IT THERE. I WANT TO PAINT.
THIS CALLS FOR A MON-UMENTAL DRINKING SESSION...
ROSALIE! MORE WINE!
IV
later...
HIC
MAURICE, I DRINK TO YOU ...

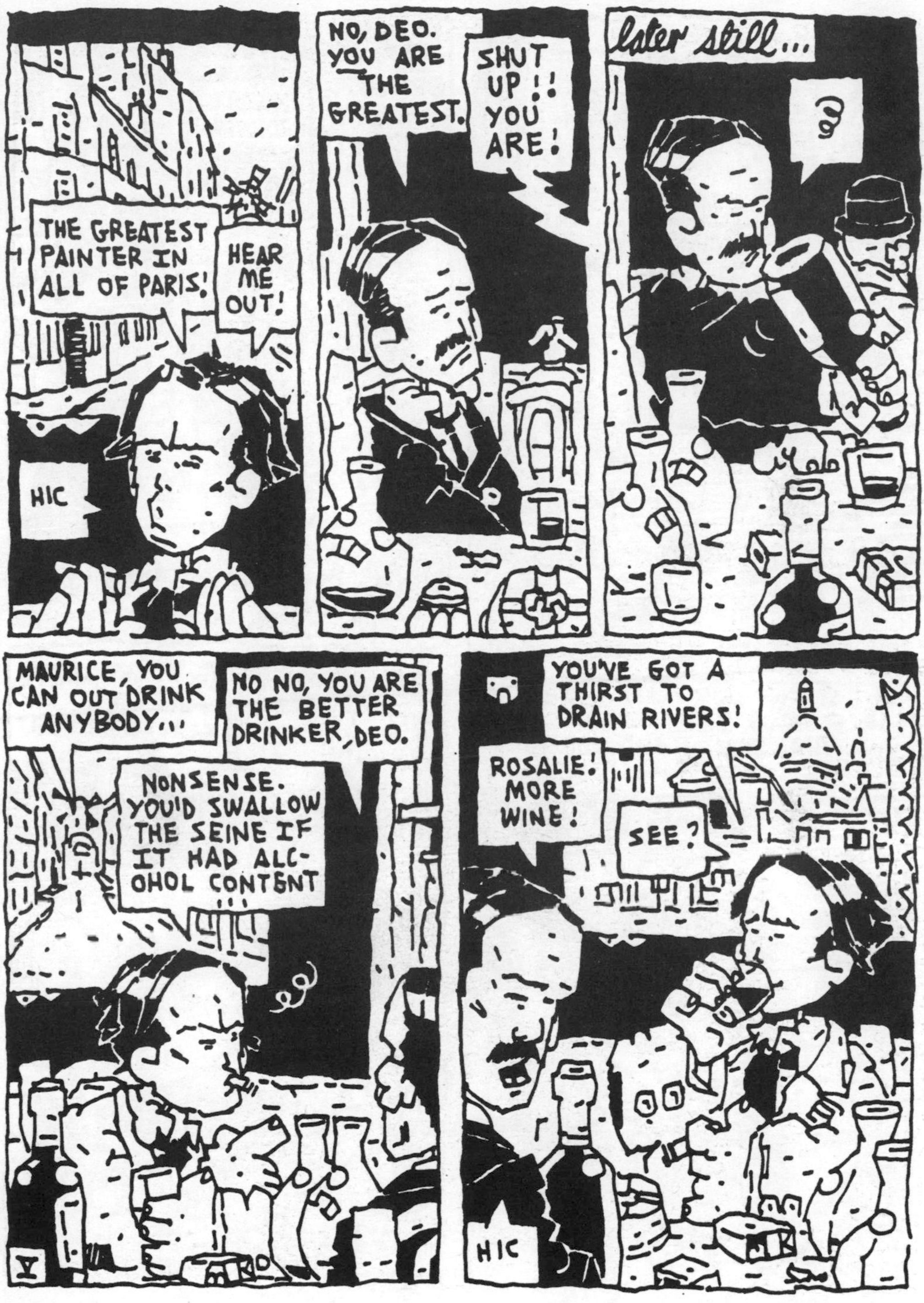
THE GREATEST PAINTER IN ALL OF PARIS!
HEAR ME OUT!
HIC
NO, DEO. YOU ARE THE GREATEST.
SHUT UP!! YOU ARE!
later still...
MAURICE, YOU CAN OUT DRINK ANYBODY...
NO NO, YOU ARE THE BETTER DRINKER, DEO.
NONSENSE. YOU'D SWALLOW THE SEINE IF IT HAD ALCOHOL CONTENT...
YOU'VE GOT A THIRST TO DRAIN RIVERS!
ROSALIE! MORE WINE!
SEE?
HIC

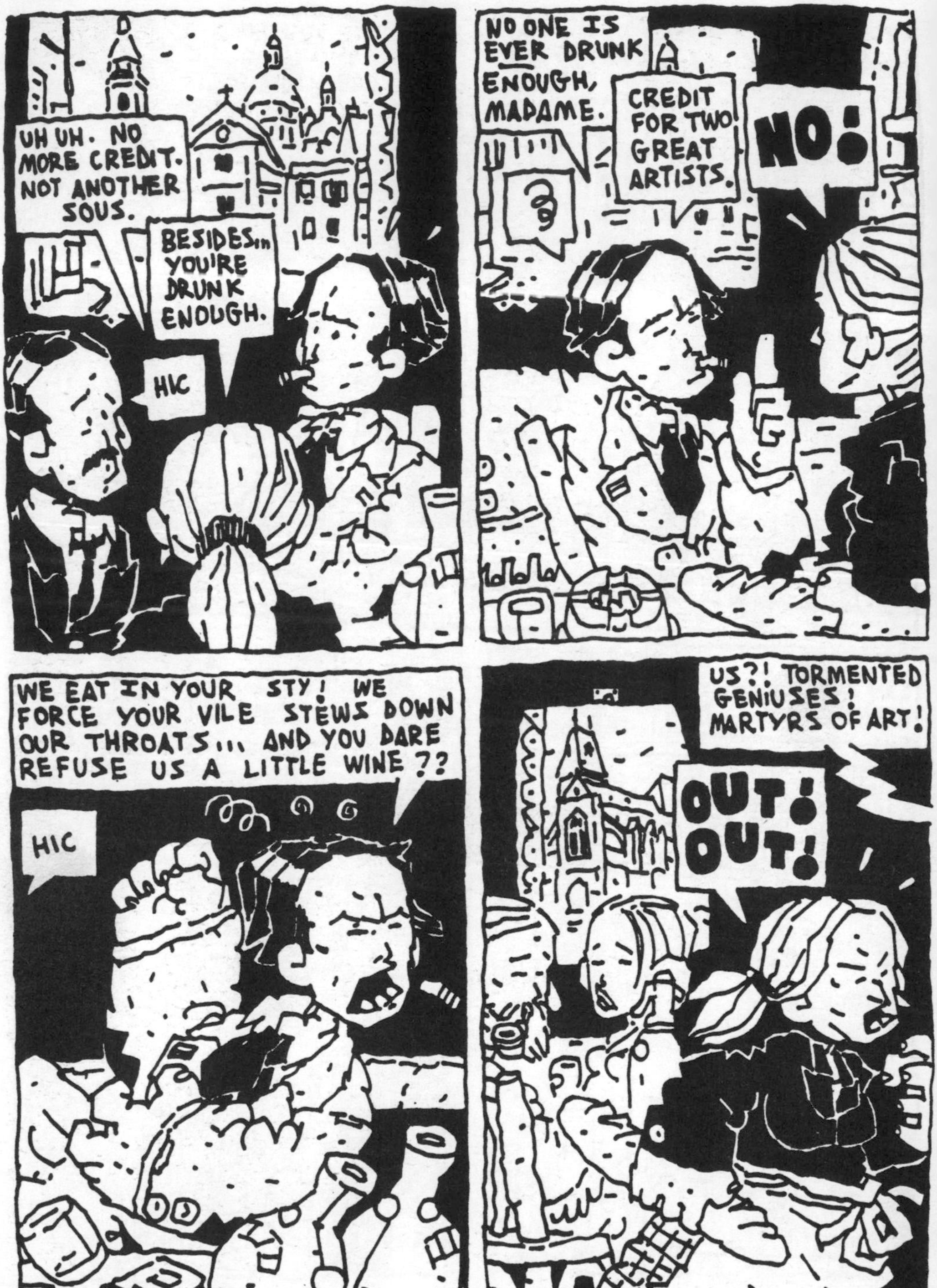
UH UH. NO MORE CREDIT. NOT ANOTHER SOUS.
BESIDES... YOU'RE DRUNK ENOUGH.
HIC
NO ONE IS EVER DRUNK ENOUGH, MADAME.
CREDIT FOR TWO GREAT ARTISTS.
NO!
WE EAT IN YOUR STY! WE FORCE YOUR VILE STEWS DOWN OUR THROATS... AND YOU DARE REFUSE US A LITTLE WINE?
HIC
US?! TORMENTED GENIUSES! MARTYRS OF ART!
OUT! OUT!
VI

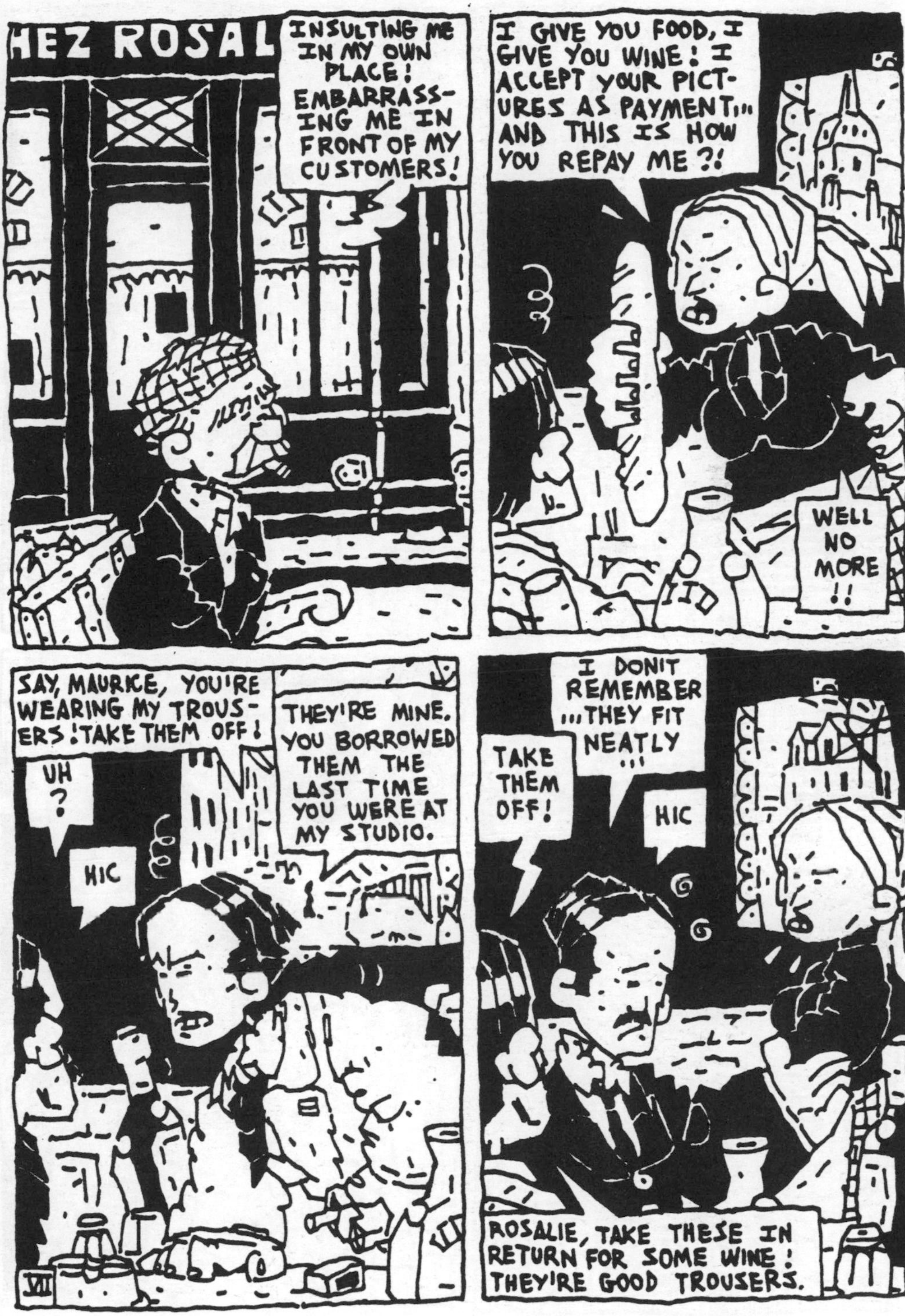
HEZ ROSAL
INSULTING ME IN MY OWN PLACE! EMBARRASSING ME IN FRONT OF MY CUSTOMERS!
I GIVE YOU FOOD, I GIVE YOU WINE! I ACCEPT YOUR PICTURES AS PAYMENT... AND THIS IS HOW YOU REPAY ME?!
WELL NO MORE !!
SAY, MAURICE, YOU'RE WEARING MY TROUSERS! TAKE THEM OFF!
UH ?
HIC
THEY'RE MINE. YOU BORROWED THEM THE LAST TIME YOU WERE AT MY STUDIO.
VII
I DON'T REMEMBER ...THEY FIT NEATLY ...
TAKE THEM OFF!
HIC
ROSALIE, TAKE THESE IN RETURN FOR SOME WINE! THEY'RE GOOD TROUSERS.

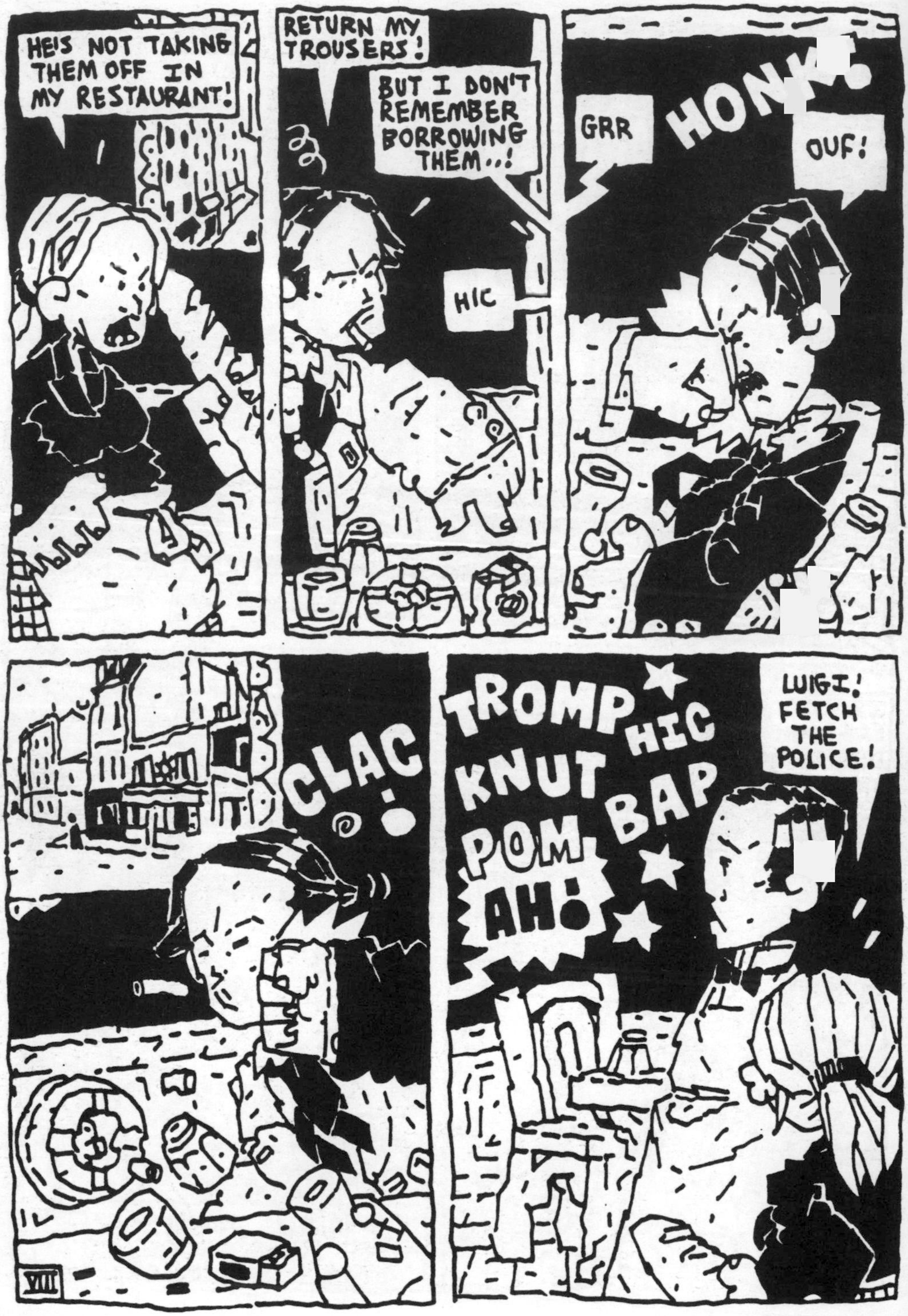

HE'S NOT TAKING THEM OFF IN MY RESTAURANT!
RETURN MY TROUSERS!
BUT I DON'T REMEMBER BORROWING THEM..!
HIC
GRR
HONK!
OUF!
CLAC
VIII
TROMP
HIC
KNUT
BAP
POM
AH!
LUIGI! FETCH THE POLICE!

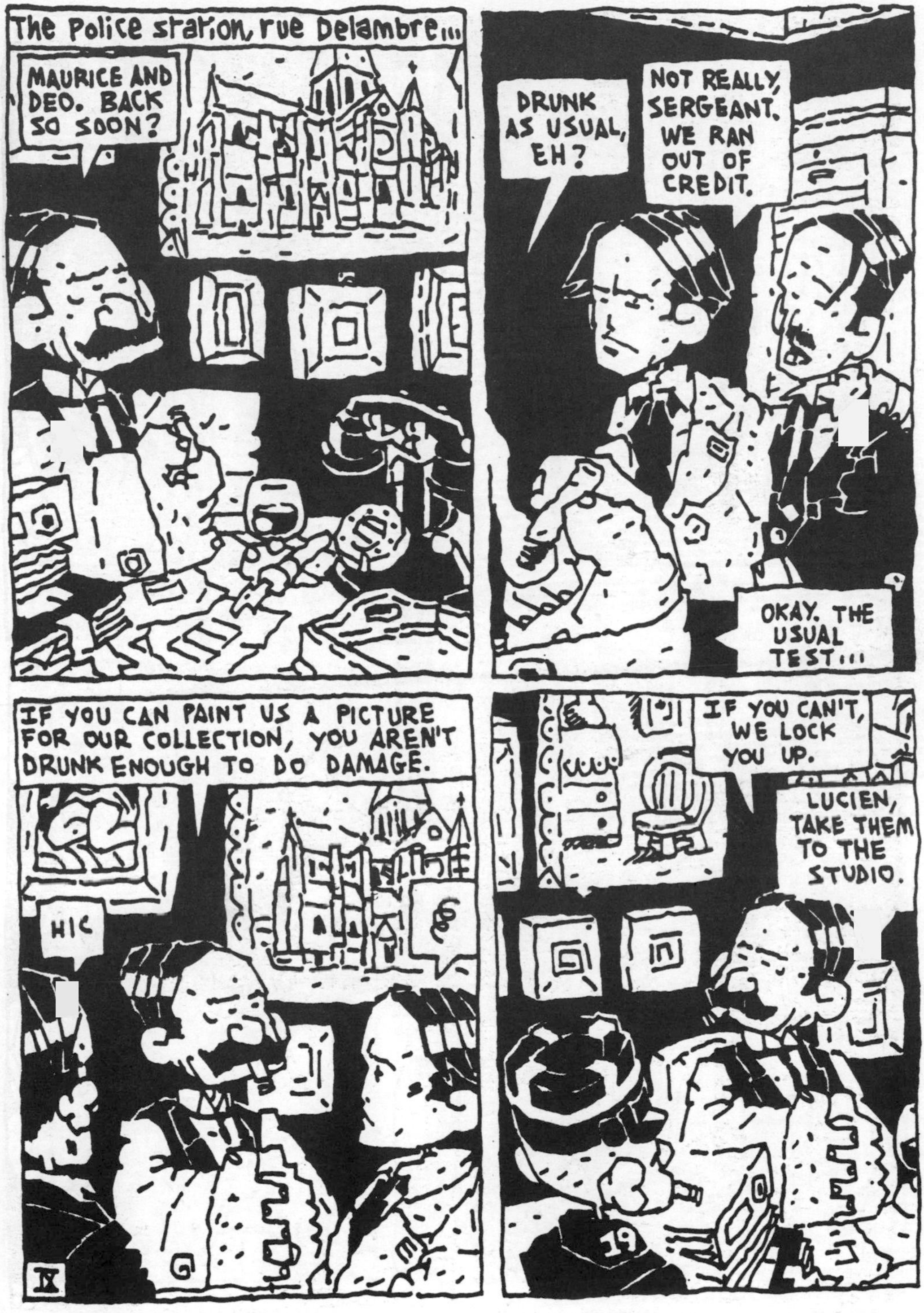
The Police station, rue Delambre...
MAURICE AND DEO. BACK SO SOON?
DRUNK AS USUAL, EH?
NOT REALLY, SERGEANT. WE RAN OUT OF CREDIT.
OKAY. THE USUAL TEST...
IF YOU CAN PAINT US A PICTURE FOR OUR COLLECTION, YOU AREN'T DRUNK ENOUGH TO DO DAMAGE.
HIC
IX
IF YOU CAN'T, WE LOCK YOU UP.
LUCIEN, TAKE THEM TO THE STUDIO.
19

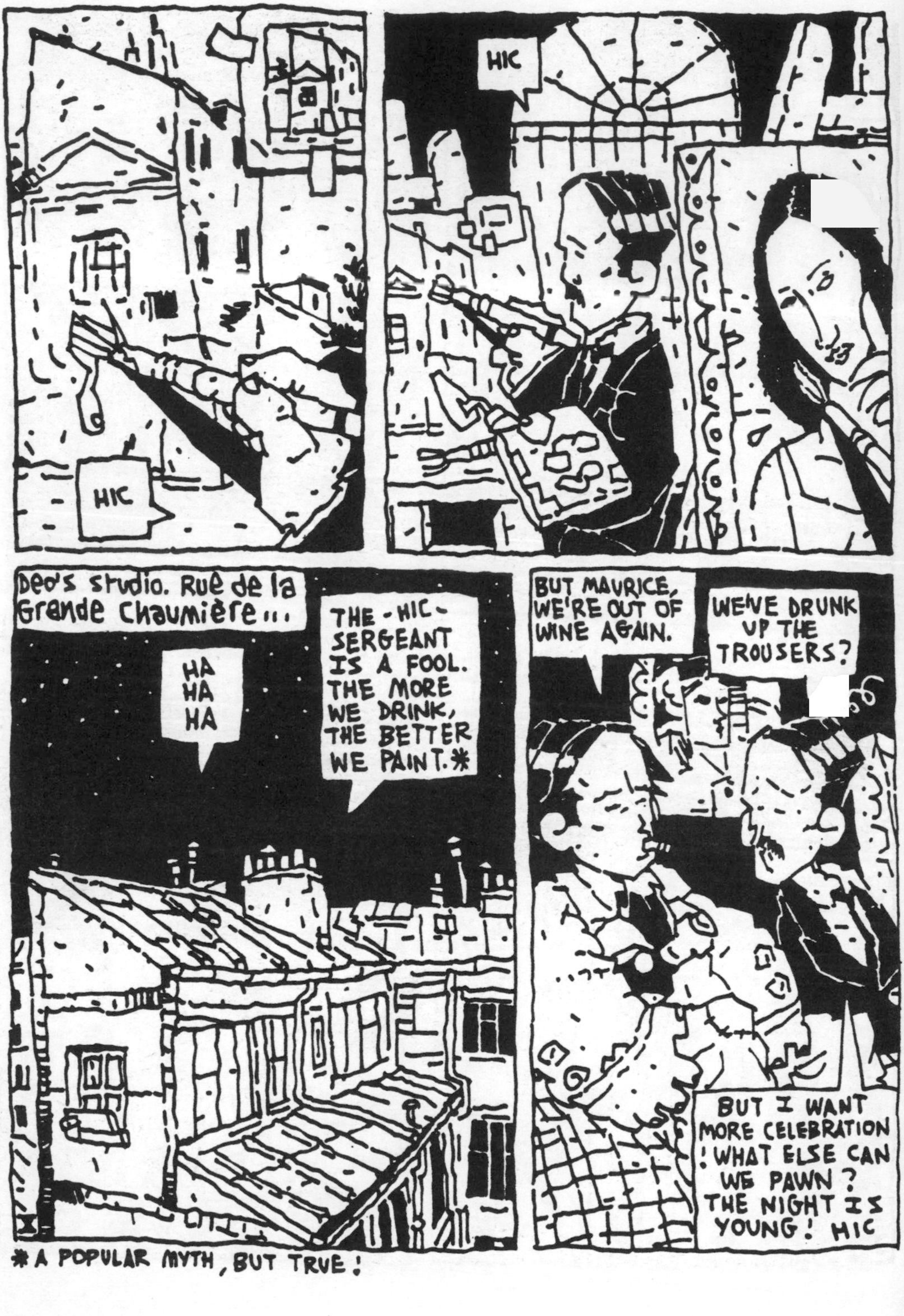
HIC
HIC
Deo's studio. Rue de la Grande Chaumière...
HA HA HA
THE -HIC- SERGEANT IS A FOOL. THE MORE WE DRINK, THE BETTER WE PAINT.*
BUT MAURICE, WE'RE OUT OF WINE AGAIN.
WE'VE DRUNK UP THE TROUSERS?
BUT I WANT MORE CELEBRATION! WHAT ELSE CAN WE PAWN? THE NIGHT IS YOUNG! HIC

* A POPULAR MYTH, BUT TRUE!

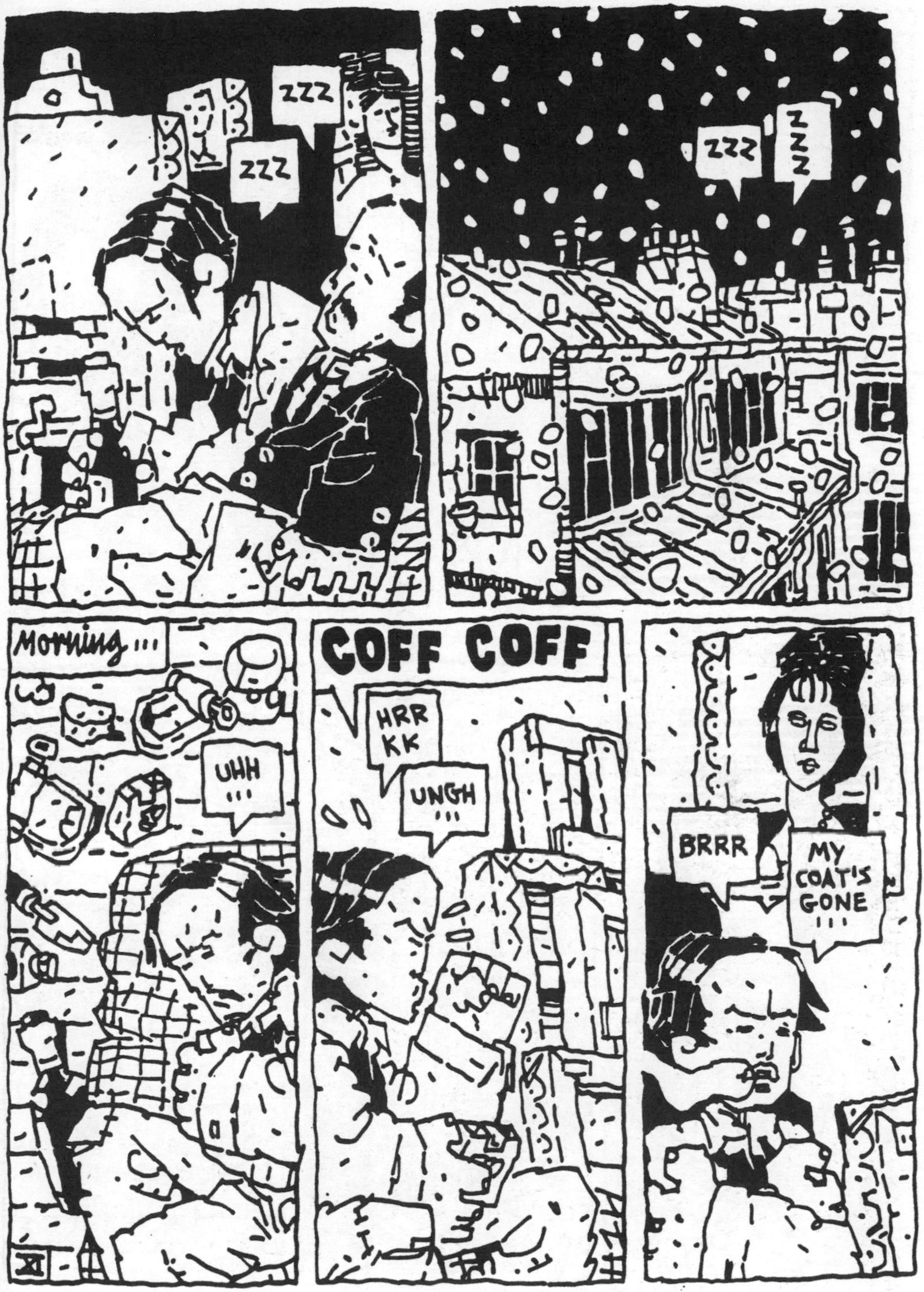

ZZZ
ZZZ
ZZZ
ZZZ
Morning...
UHH ...
COFF COFF
HRR KK
UNGH ...
BRRR
MY COAT'S GONE ...

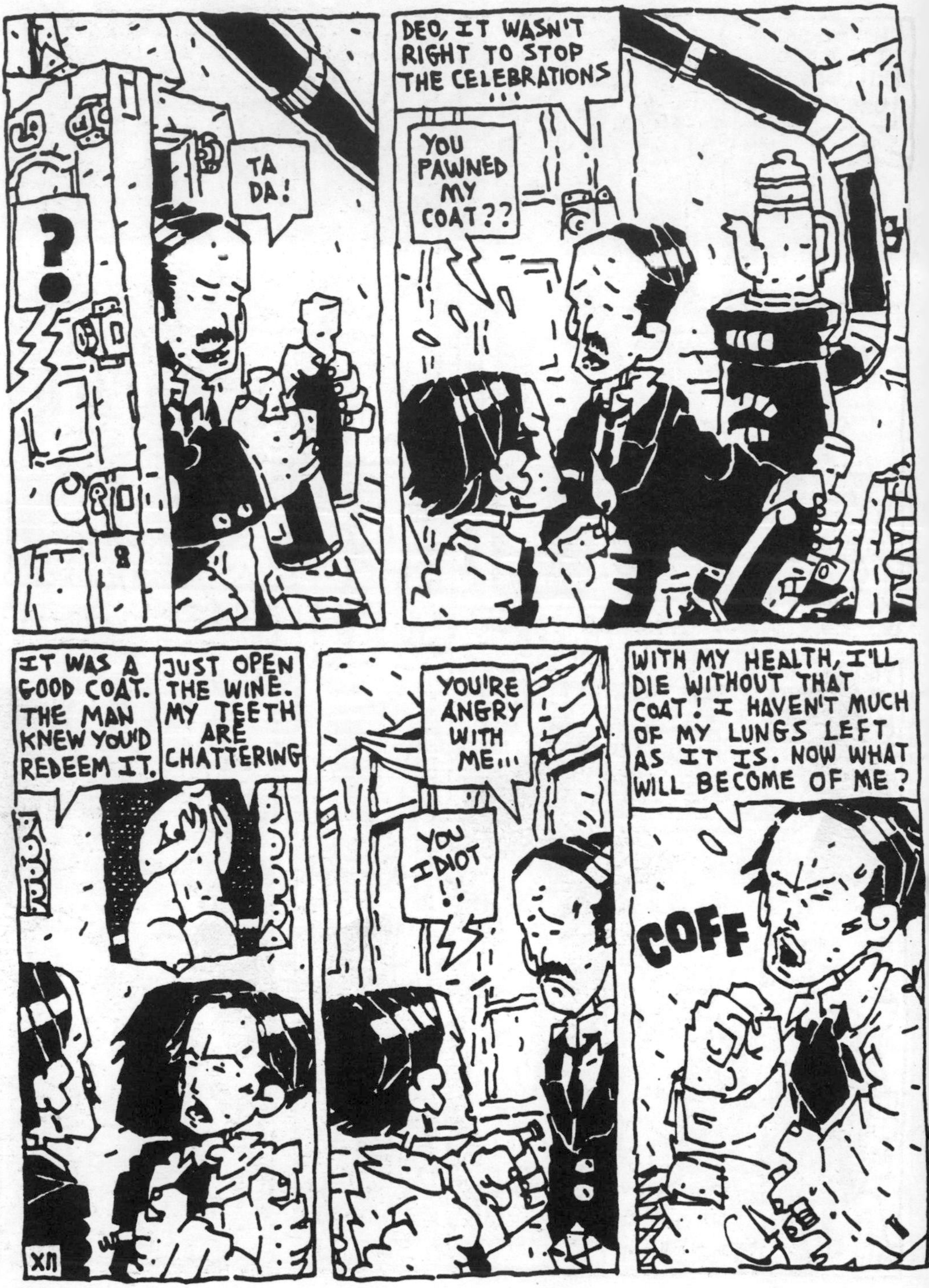
TA DA!
?
DEO, IT WASN'T RIGHT TO STOP THE CELEBRATIONS ...
YOU PAWNED MY COAT??
IT WAS A GOOD COAT. THE MAN KNEW YOU'D REDEEM IT.
JUST OPEN THE WINE. MY TEETH ARE CHATTERING
YOU'RE ANGRY WITH ME...
YOU IDIOT !!
WITH MY HEALTH, I'LL DIE WITHOUT THAT COAT! I HAVEN'T MUCH OF MY LUNGS LEFT AS IT IS. NOW WHAT WILL BECOME OF ME?
COFF
XII

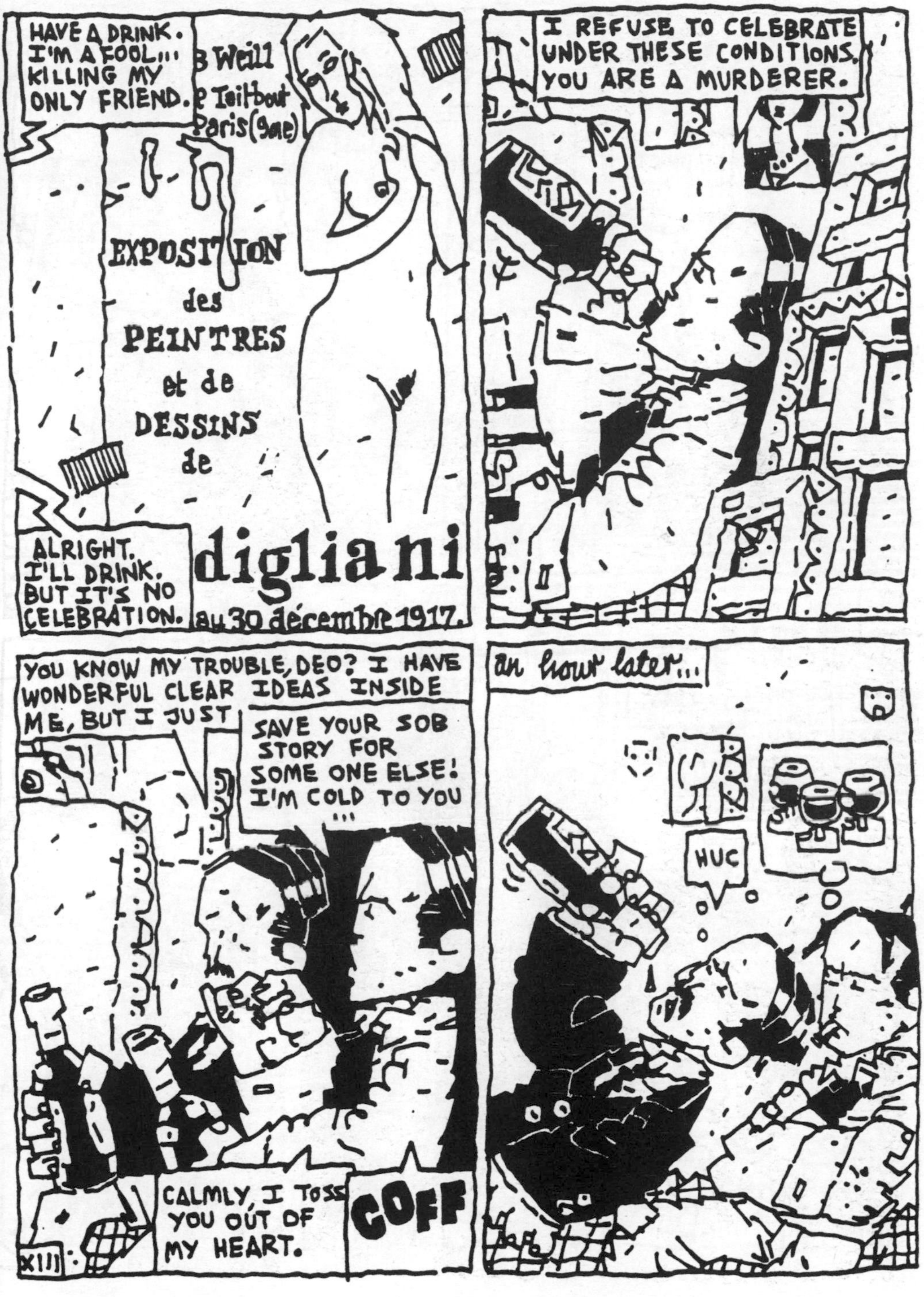

HAVE A DRINK. I'M A FOOL... KILLING MY ONLY FRIEND.
B Weill
Taitbout
Paris (9me)
EXPOSITION des PEINTRES et de DESSINS de
digliani
au 30 décembre 1917.
ALRIGHT. I'LL DRINK. BUT IT'S NO CELEBRATION.
I REFUSE TO CELEBRATE UNDER THESE CONDITIONS. YOU ARE A MURDERER.
YOU KNOW MY TROUBLE, DEO? I HAVE WONDERFUL CLEAR IDEAS INSIDE ME, BUT I JUST
SAVE YOUR SOB STORY FOR SOME ONE ELSE! I'M COLD TO YOU ...
CALMLY, I TOSS YOU OUT OF MY HEART.
COFF
XIII
an hour later...
HUC

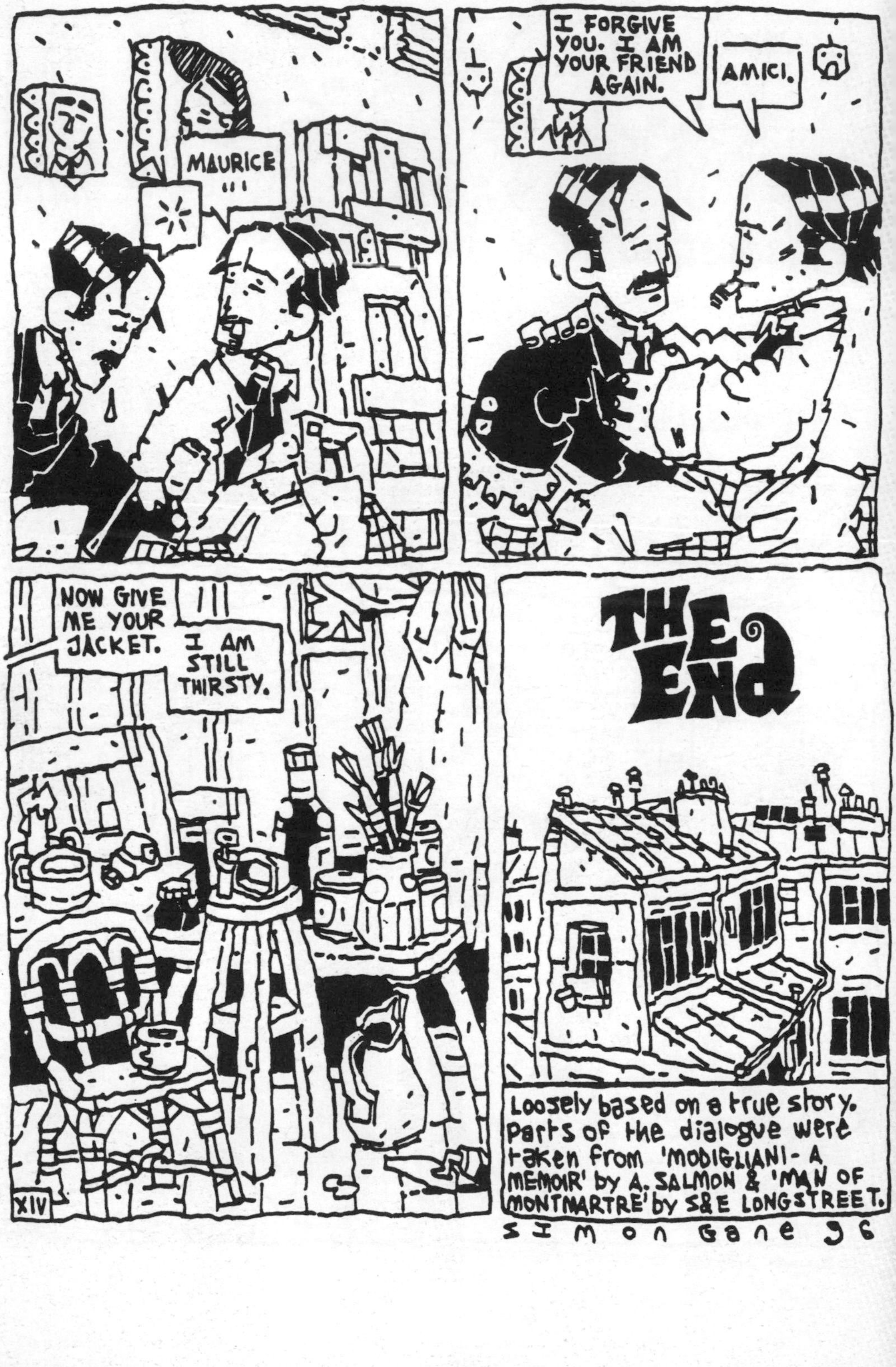
MAURICE ...
I FORGIVE YOU. I AM YOUR FRIEND AGAIN.
AMICI.
NOW GIVE ME YOUR JACKET.
I AM STILL THIRSTY.
XIV
THE END
Loosely based on a true story. Parts of the dialogue were taken from 'MODIGLIANI - A MEMOIR' by A. SALMON & 'MAN OF MONTMARTRE' by S&E LONGSTREET.
SIMON GANE 96

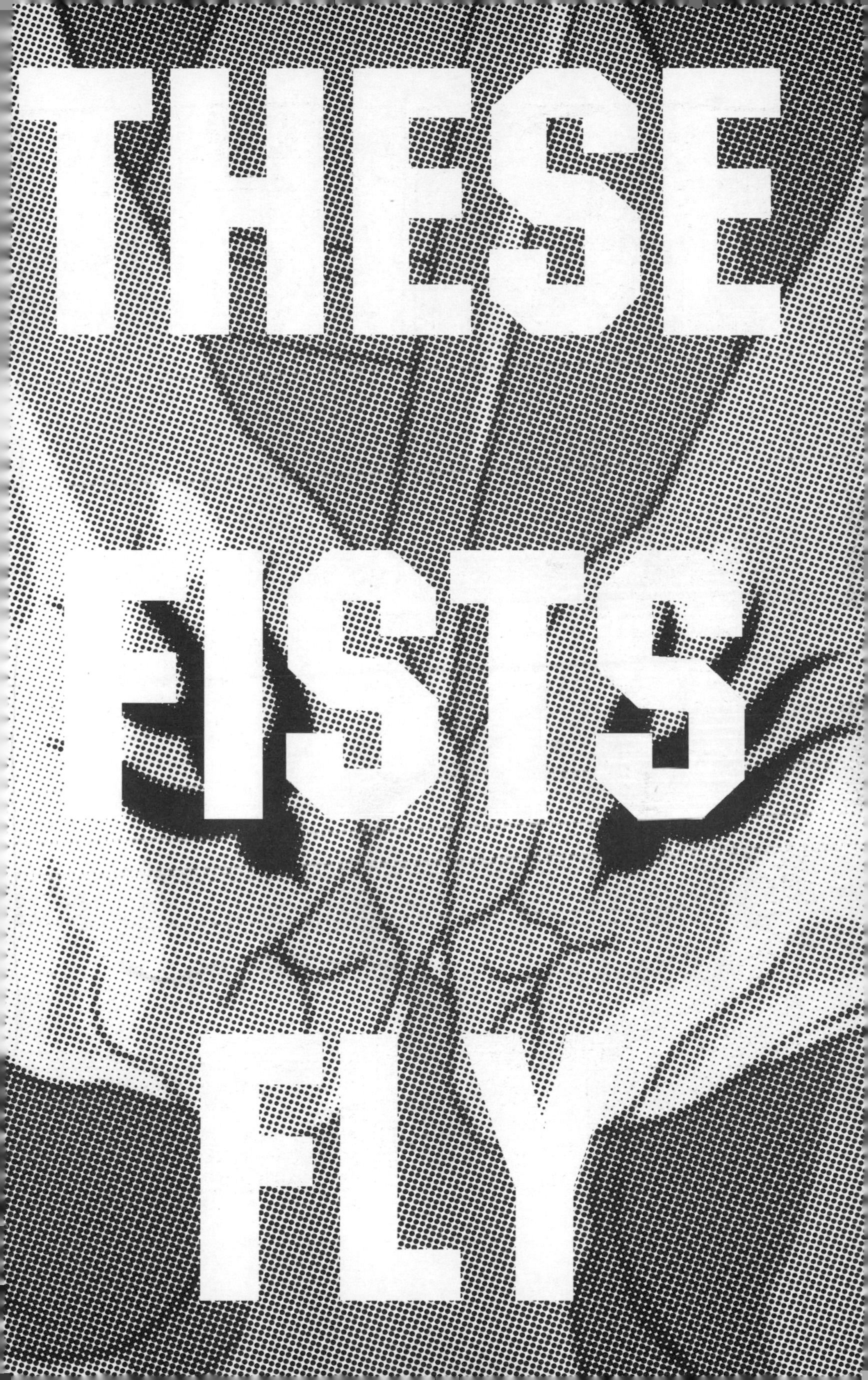
THESE
FISTS
FLY

Daniel Locke

THESE FISTS FLY
Green #4, self-published, 2007

Having previously worked with video and sculpture, fine artist Daniel Locke only settled on comics as his chosen medium in 2006. *Green* was his print venue for various narrative experiments, no two alike in style or approach, from sci-fi to character portraits.

"The subject of this piece is a fictional character based on a number of people I had known when I was young. Growing up, holidays and weekends were spent in pub gardens, working men's clubs, football and golf course clubhouses. Dad would stand at the bar with his mates whilst my sister and I played in the family saloon or outside. Occasionally I'd go up to Dad and the men, to try and get a Coke or a bag of crisps – always fascinated by the huge, loud talkers, earwigging on their conversations." – DL

Daniel's work features in the *Open Day Book* and *A Graphic Cosmogony* from Nobrow Press, among many anthologies of contemporary comics. He is currently working on his first full-length graphic novel, *Going Home*, as well as a portrait in comics of a young autistic musician, with video artist Laura Malacart. In 2013 he collaborated with artist David Blandy and scientist Dr Adam Rutherford on an illustrated history of DNA for the Wellcome Trust.

www.daniellocke.com

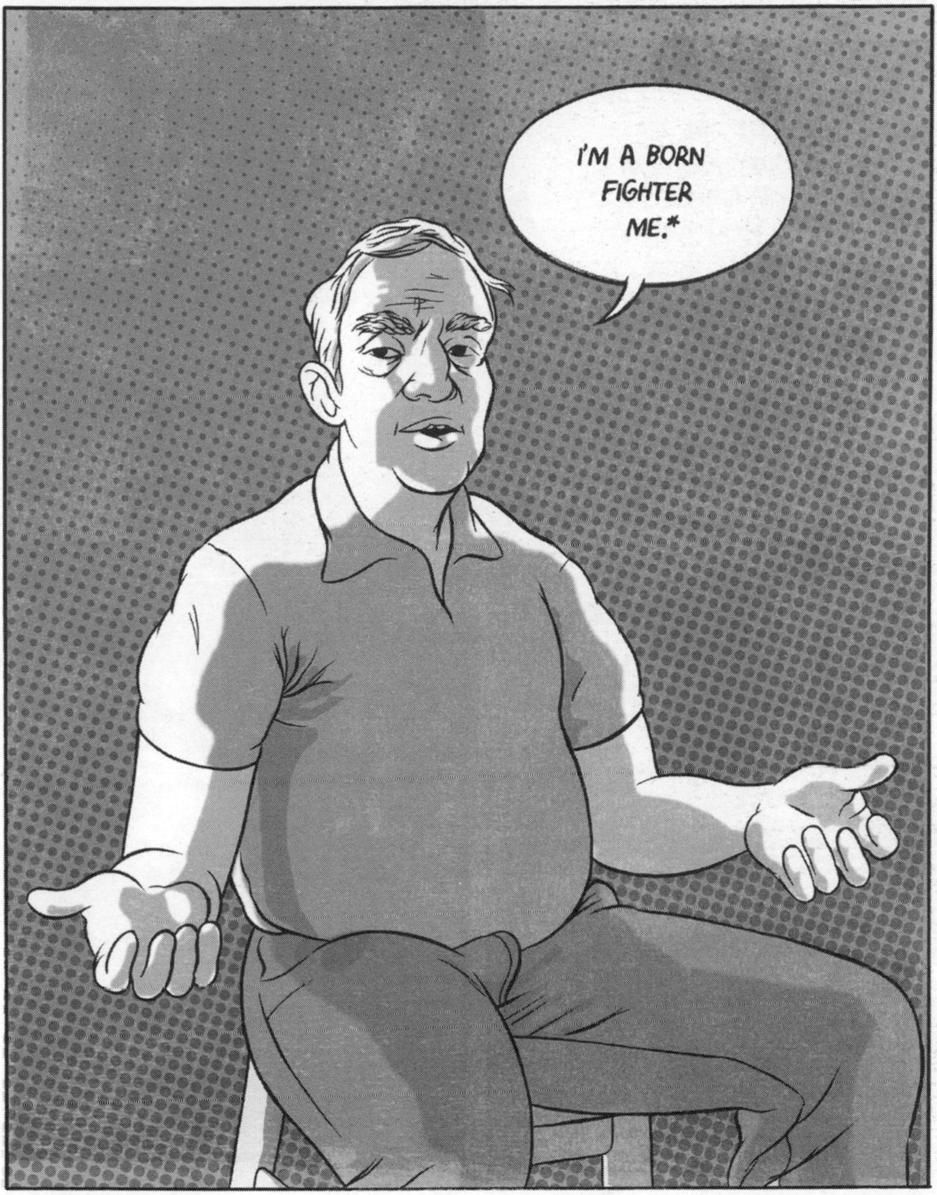
I'M A BORN FIGHTER ME.*

* MR JAMES TERRENCE COOPER.

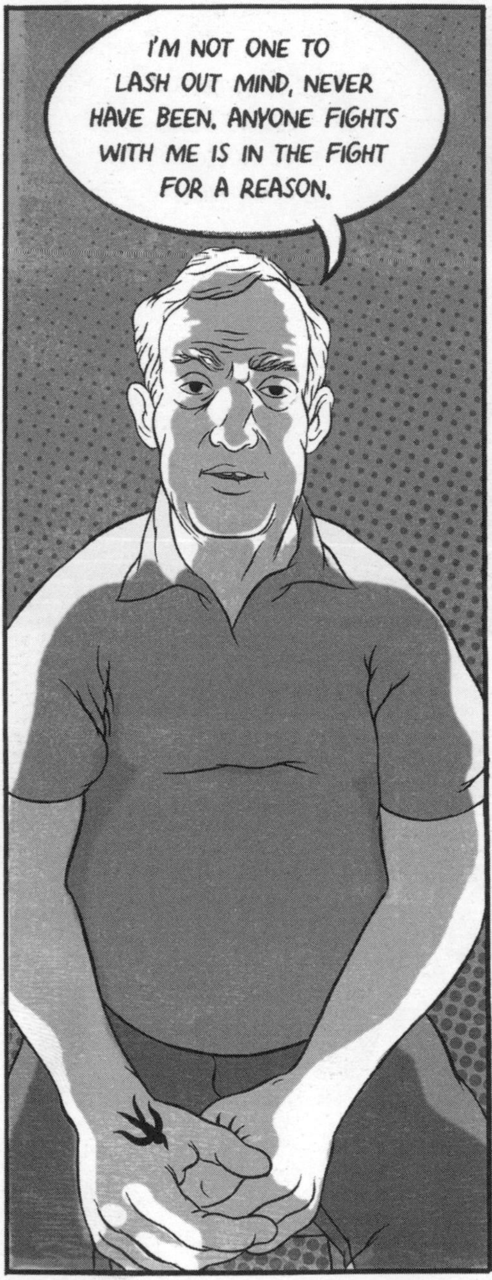
I'M NOT ONE TO LASH OUT MIND, NEVER HAVE BEEN. ANYONE FIGHTS WITH ME IS IN THE FIGHT FOR A REASON.

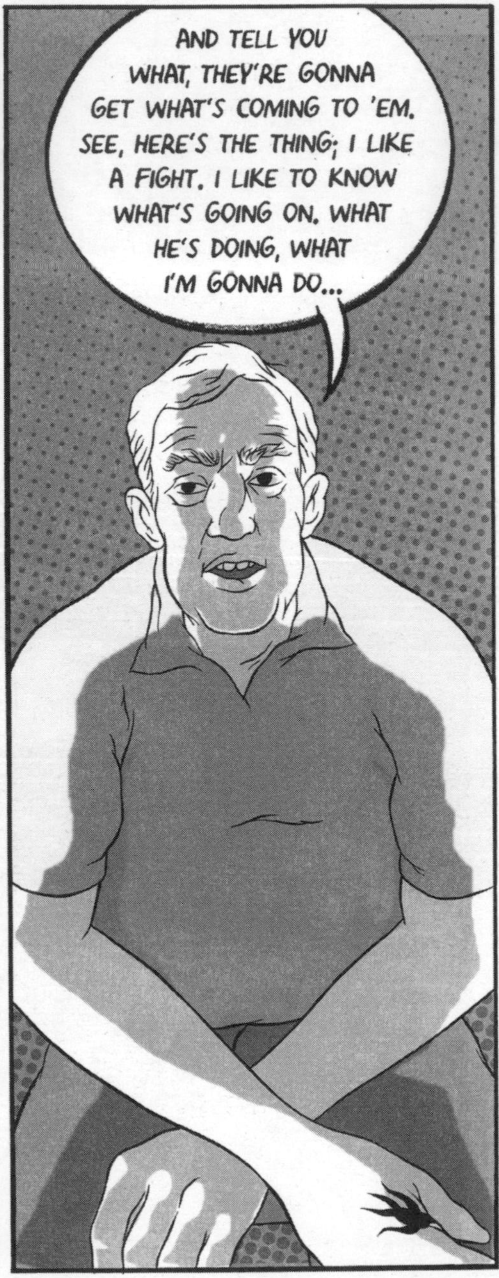
AND TELL YOU WHAT, THEY'RE GONNA GET WHAT'S COMING TO 'EM. SEE, HERE'S THE THING; I LIKE A FIGHT. I LIKE TO KNOW WHAT'S GOING ON. WHAT HE'S DOING, WHAT I'M GONNA DO...

1. THIS IS NOT ENTIRELY TRUE. ON A NUMBER OF OCCASIONS IT WOULD HAVE BEEN FAIR TO LABEL MR COOPER'S ACTIONS AS AN EXAMPLE OF "LASHING OUT", SOMETIMES IN AN EXTREMELY VIOLENT MANNER. THIS WAS MOST OFTEN THE CASE AFTER HE HAD CONSUMED LARGE QUANTITIES OF ALCOHOL.

2. THIS IS ENTIRELY TRUE. AMONGST OTHER THINGS, MR COOPER WAS ADDICTED TO THE RUSH OF EPINEPHRINE (ADRENALINE) THAT WAS RELEASED BY HIS ADRENAL GLAND AT THE OUTSET OF A FIGHT. THIS, COMBINED WITH HIS ACCELERATED HEART BEAT, AND THE INCREASED FIRING OF NEUTRONS IN HIS BRAIN, MADE FIGHTING ONE OF THE MOST STIMULATING ACTIVITIES IN HIS LIFE.

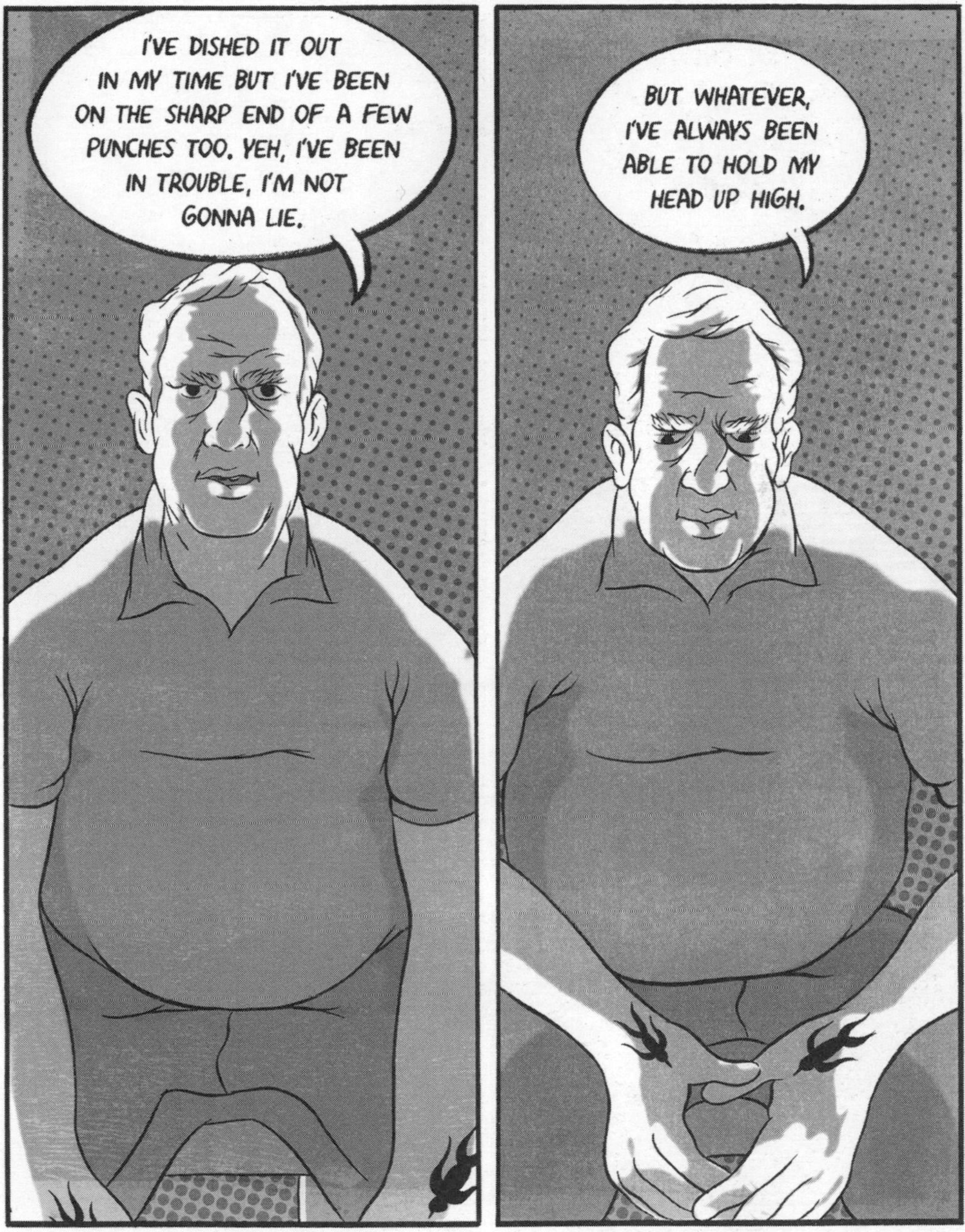
I'VE DISHED IT OUT IN MY TIME BUT I'VE BEEN ON THE SHARP END OF A FEW PUNCHES TOO. YEH, I'VE BEEN IN TROUBLE, I'M NOT GONNA LIE.
BUT WHATEVER, I'VE ALWAYS BEEN ABLE TO HOLD MY HEAD UP HIGH.

3. SEPT.1963–OCT.1964, HM PRISON HIGHDOWN. AUG. 1974–NOV. 1976, HM PRISON LEWES. THREE POLICE CAUTIONS.

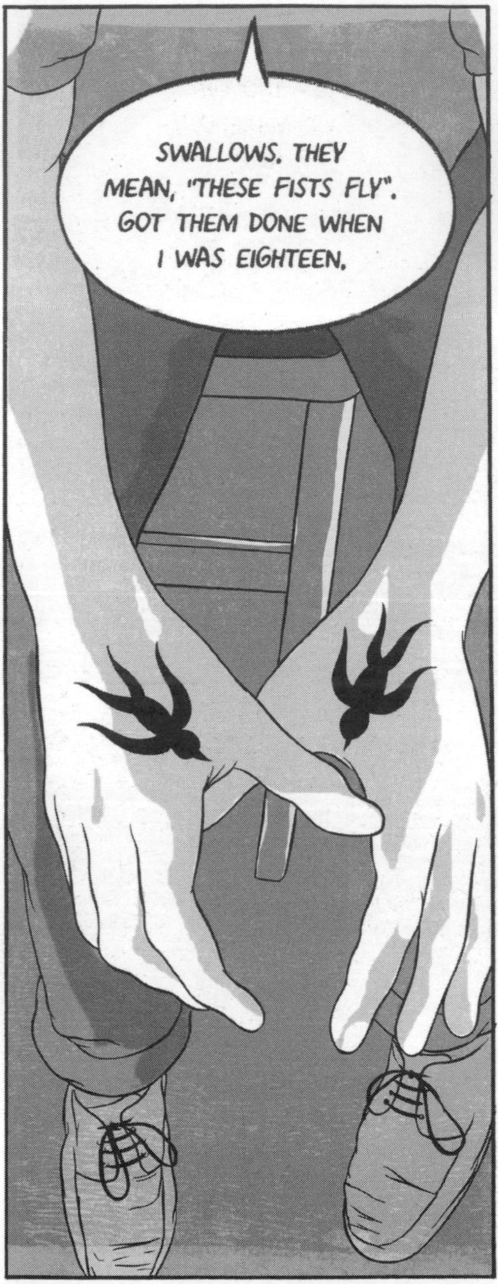
SWALLOWS. THEY MEAN, "THESE FISTS FLY". GOT THEM DONE WHEN I WAS EIGHTEEN.

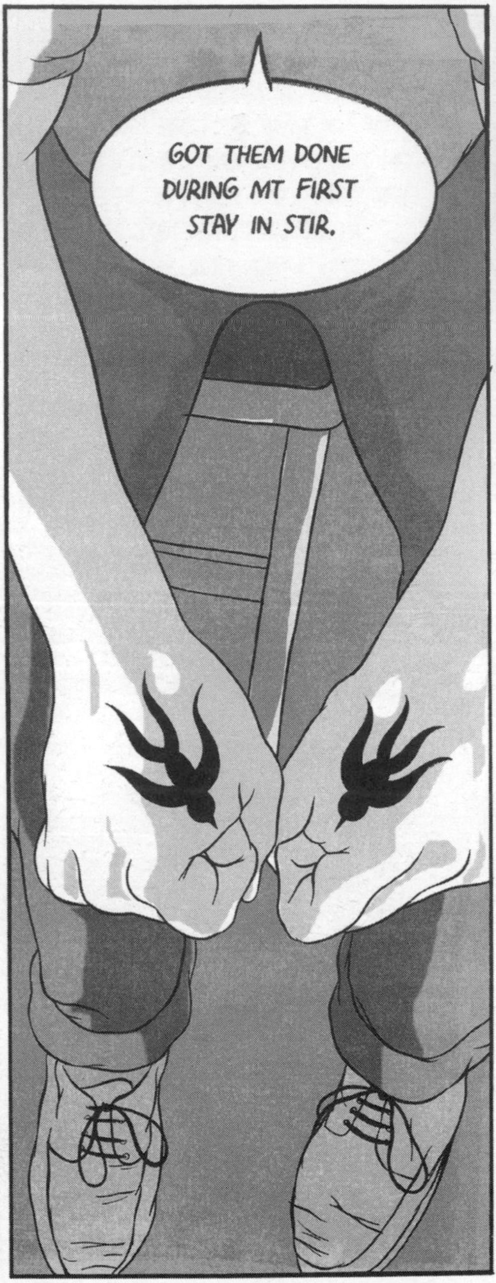
GOT THEM DONE DURING MT FIRST STAY IN STIR.

4. SWALLOWS ARE COMMON INTERNATIONALLY AS A MOTIF FOR PRISON TATTOOS. THE MEANINGS THEY CARRY VARY ACCORDING TO LOCAL CONNOTATIONS, AND WHERE ON THE BODY THEY ARE PLACED. IN SOUTH AFRICAN PRISONS, SWALLOWS ARE APPLIED FORCIBLY BY INMATES ON THOSE WHO ARE SERVING SENTENCES FOR CHILD ABUSE. IN THE SOUTH OF ENGLAND AND LONDON, SWALLOWS ARE WORN OUT OF CHOICE, AS A WAY OF CONVEYING THE 'HARDMAN' STATUS OF THE WEARER.

5. STIR, SHORT FOR STIRPEND, A ROMANI WORD MEANING PRISON. IN THIS CASE HM PRISON HIGHDOWN. MR COOPER WAS SENT THERE TO COMPLETE A SENTENCE FOR AGGRAVATED ASSAULT ON A MR JOSEPH WALTER TULLY.

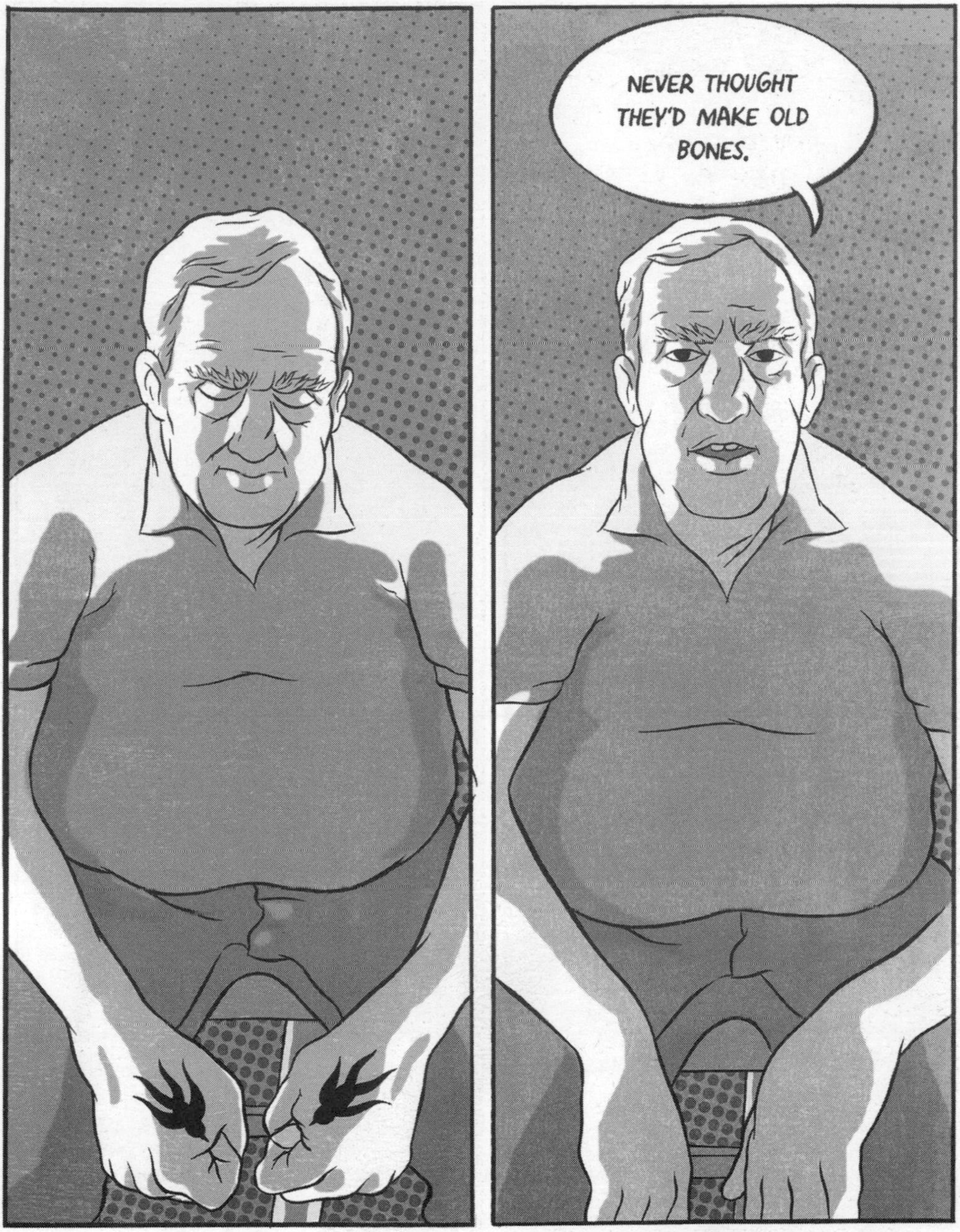
NEVER THOUGHT THEY'D MAKE OLD BONES.

6. MR COOPER HAS GROWN OLD. HE WILL BE 71 THIS COMING DECEMBER. ALTHOUGH WHEN SPEAKING ABOUT FIGHTING HE USES THE PRESENT TENSE, HE HAS NOT ACTUALLY BEEN IN A FIGHT SINCE 1982; A PUB FIGHT IN WHICH HE SUSTAINED A BROKEN NOSE AND BRUISED KNUCKLES.

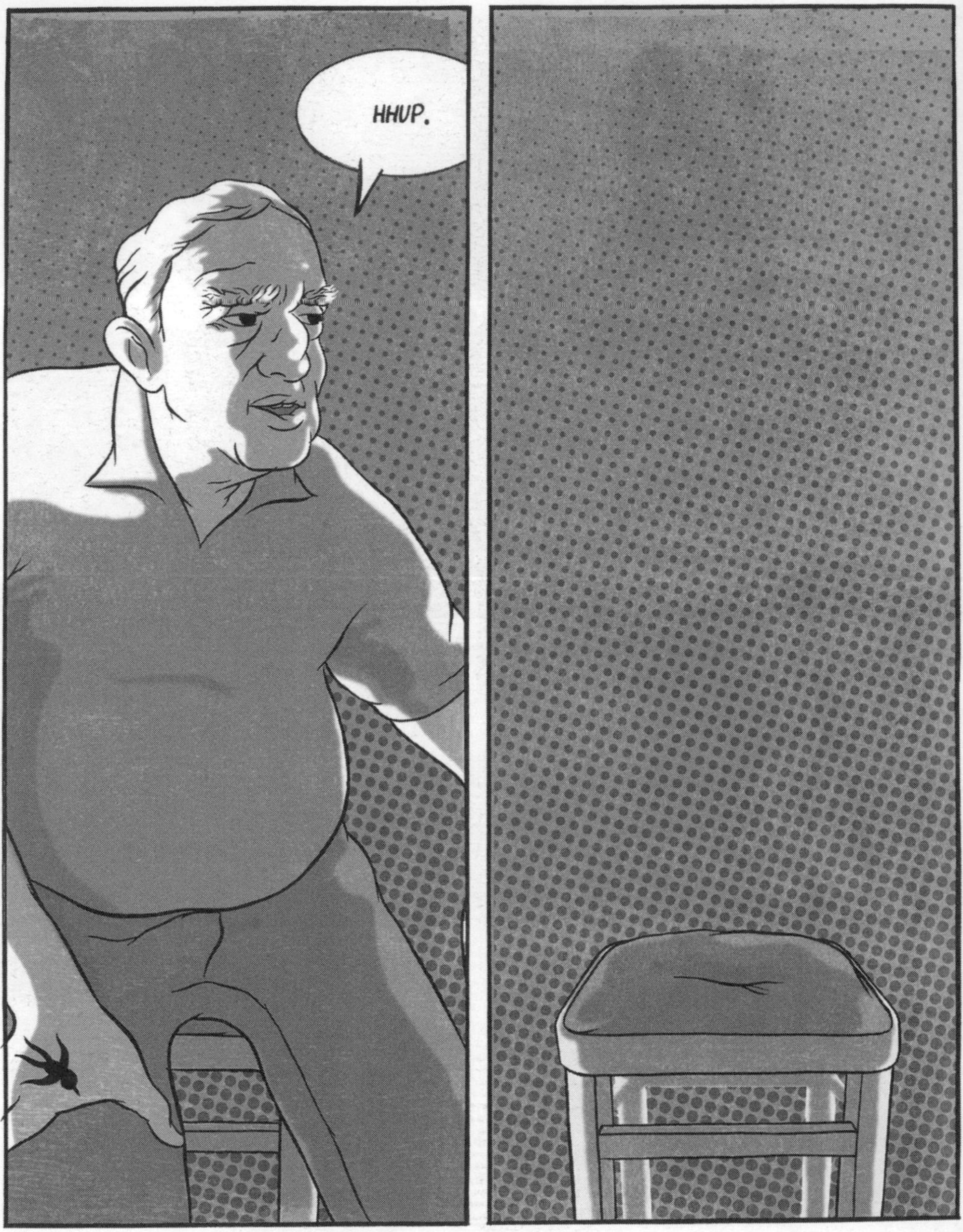
HHUP.

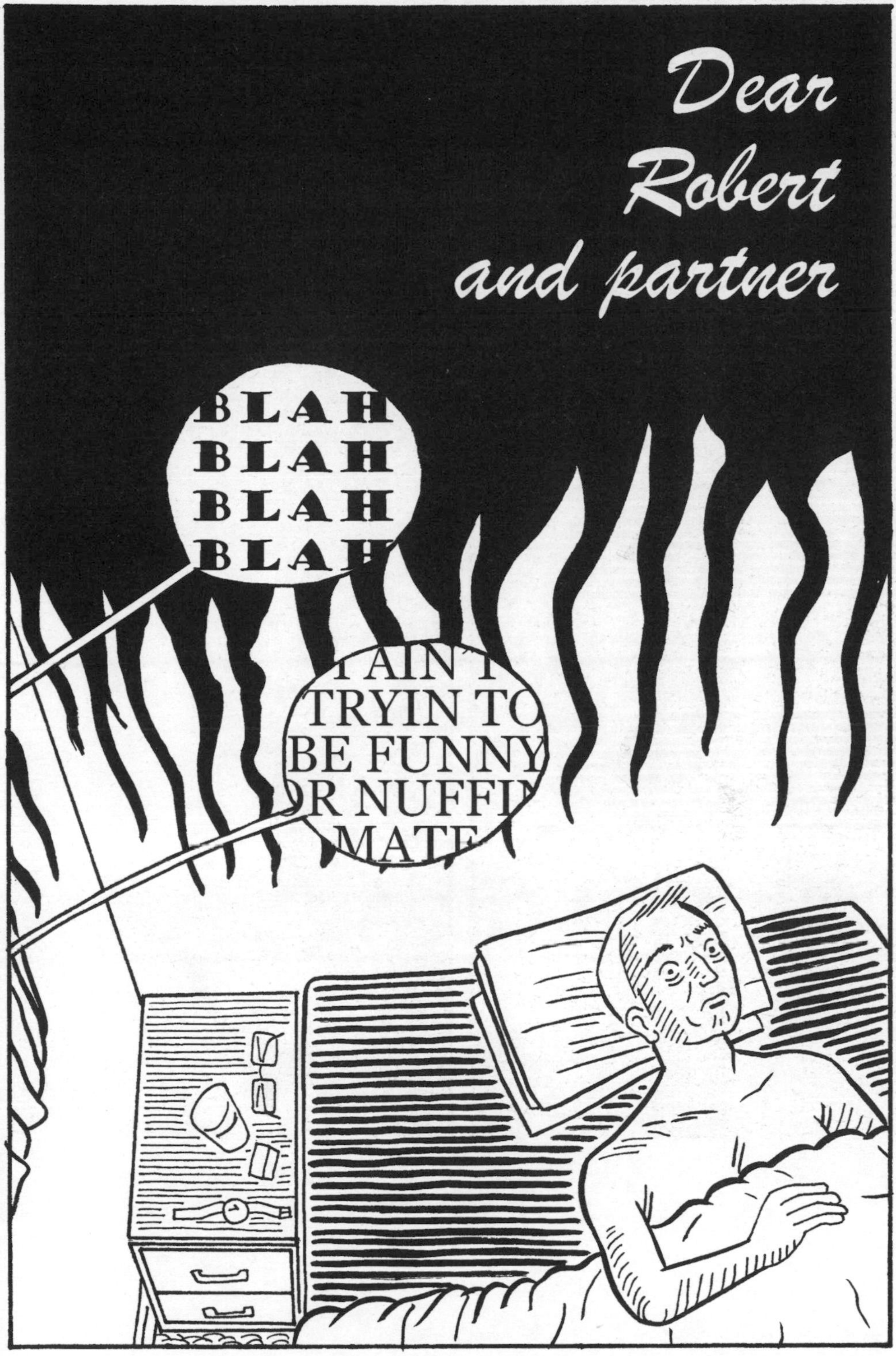
Dear Robert and partner
BLAH BLAH BLAH BLAH
AIN'T TRYIN TO BE FUNNY R NUFFI MATE

Paul B. Rainey

DEAR ROBERT AND PARTNER
Self-published, 2007

Dear Robert began life as a competition entry for the UK's annual Graphic Short Story Prize, the scenario based on a real incident involving troublesome neighbours. We've all been there.

During this same period, writer and artist Paul B. Rainey was hard at work on his magnum opus, the graphic novel *There's No Time Like The Present. TNTLTP* took seven years to complete and is due to be collected in a single volume by Escape Books.

Since that time Paul has self-published six issues of *Thunder Brother: Soap Division*, in which everyone's favourite (or least favourite) TV soap operas turn out, in fact, to be real. He also creates various strips for long-running UK humour comic *Viz*, including *14 Year Old Stand-Up Comedian*, *Peter The Slow Eater* and *The Charlie Brooker Story*, plus strip content exclusive to his website. Clearly, PBR's neighbourly troubles are not over since this includes *Man V Van*, inspired by a mysterious giant van parked outside his flat for days at a time.

www.pbrainey.com

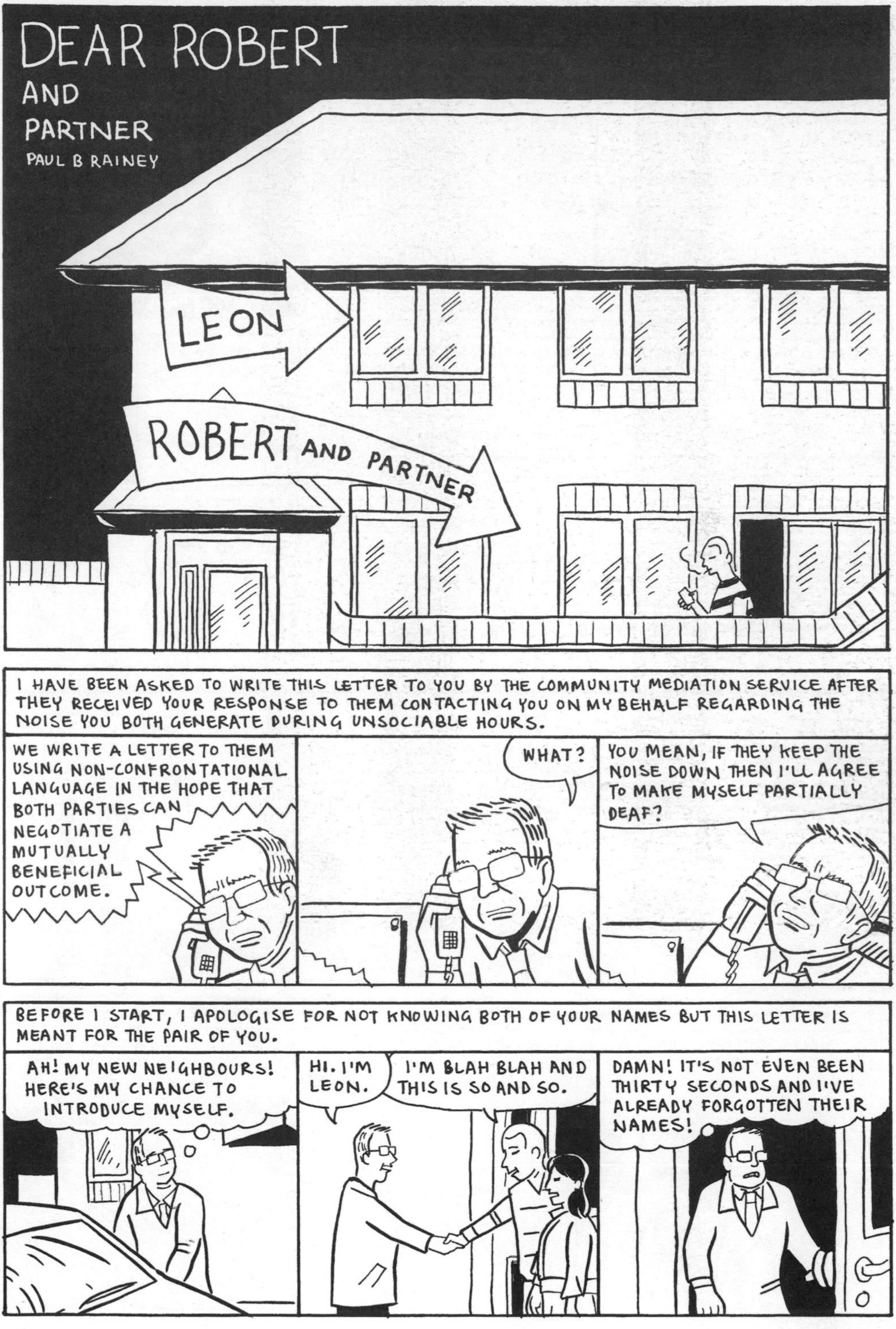
DEAR ROBERT
AND
PARTNER
PAUL B RAINEY
LEON
ROBERT AND PARTNER
I HAVE BEEN ASKED TO WRITE THIS LETTER TO YOU BY THE COMMUNITY MEDIATION SERVICE AFTER THEY RECEIVED YOUR RESPONSE TO THEM CONTACTING YOU ON MY BEHALF REGARDING THE NOISE YOU BOTH GENERATE DURING UNSOCIABLE HOURS.
WE WRITE A LETTER TO THEM USING NON-CONFRONTATIONAL LANGUAGE IN THE HOPE THAT BOTH PARTIES CAN NEGOTIATE A MUTUALLY BENEFICIAL OUTCOME.
WHAT?
YOU MEAN, IF THEY KEEP THE NOISE DOWN THEN I'LL AGREE TO MAKE MYSELF PARTIALLY DEAF?
BEFORE I START, I APOLOGISE FOR NOT KNOWING BOTH OF YOUR NAMES BUT THIS LETTER IS MEANT FOR THE PAIR OF YOU.
AH! MY NEW NEIGHBOURS! HERE'S MY CHANCE TO INTRODUCE MYSELF.
HI. I'M LEON.
I'M BLAH BLAH AND THIS IS SO AND SO.
DAMN! IT'S NOT EVEN BEEN THIRTY SECONDS AND I'VE ALREADY FORGOTTEN THEIR NAMES!

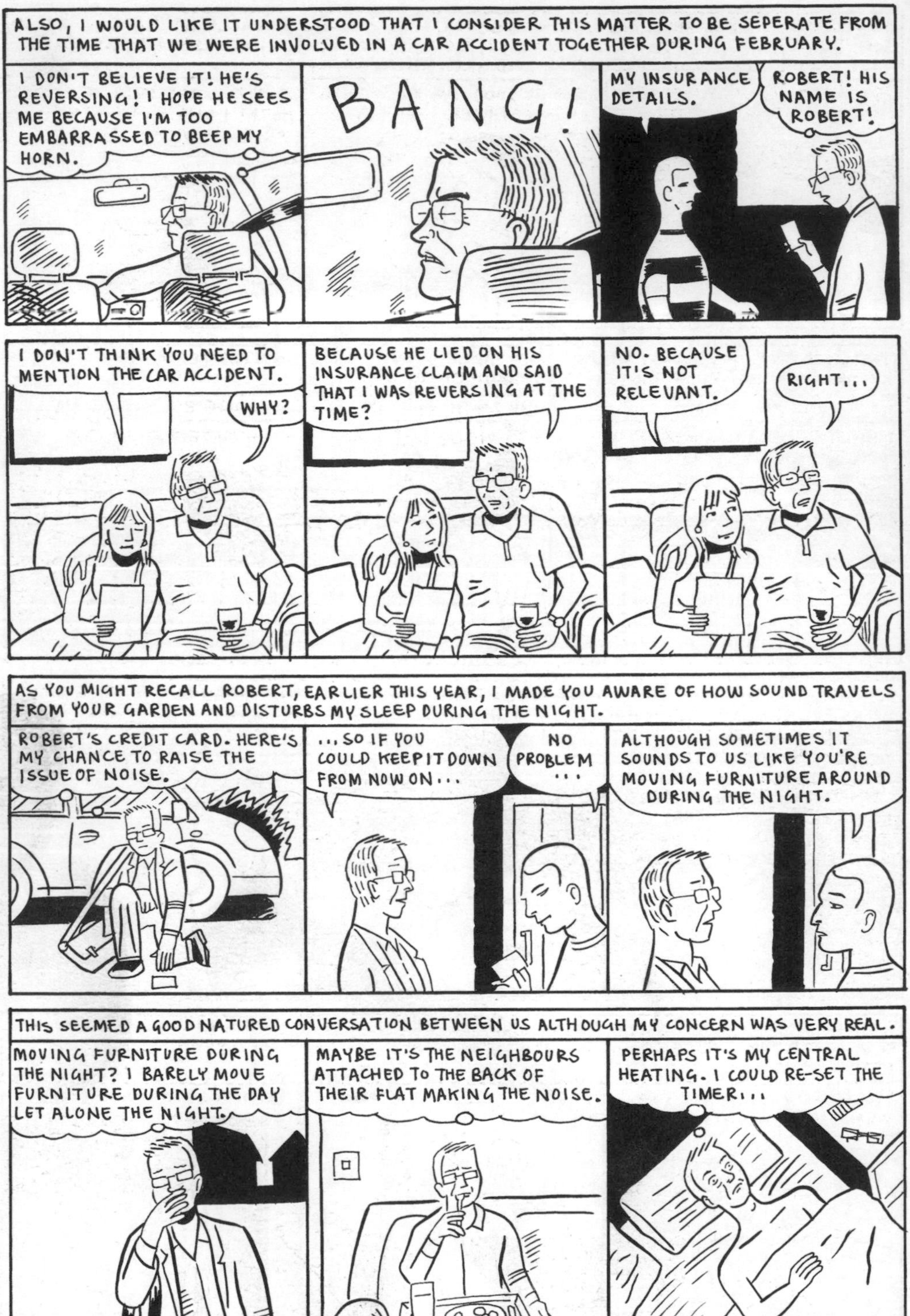

ALSO, I WOULD LIKE IT UNDERSTOOD THAT I CONSIDER THIS MATTER TO BE SEPERATE FROM THE TIME THAT WE WERE INVOLVED IN A CAR ACCIDENT TOGETHER DURING FEBRUARY.
I DON'T BELIEVE IT! HE'S REVERSING! I HOPE HE SEES ME BECAUSE I'M TOO EMBARRASSED TO BEEP MY HORN.
BANG!
MY INSURANCE DETAILS.
ROBERT! HIS NAME IS ROBERT!
I DON'T THINK YOU NEED TO MENTION THE CAR ACCIDENT.
WHY?
BECAUSE HE LIED ON HIS INSURANCE CLAIM AND SAID THAT I WAS REVERSING AT THE TIME?
NO. BECAUSE IT'S NOT RELEVANT.
RIGHT...
AS YOU MIGHT RECALL ROBERT, EARLIER THIS YEAR, I MADE YOU AWARE OF HOW SOUND TRAVELS FROM YOUR GARDEN AND DISTURBS MY SLEEP DURING THE NIGHT.
ROBERT'S CREDIT CARD. HERE'S MY CHANCE TO RAISE THE ISSUE OF NOISE.
...SO IF YOU COULD KEEP IT DOWN FROM NOW ON...
NO PROBLEM...
ALTHOUGH SOMETIMES IT SOUNDS TO US LIKE YOU'RE MOVING FURNITURE AROUND DURING THE NIGHT.
THIS SEEMED A GOOD NATURED CONVERSATION BETWEEN US ALTHOUGH MY CONCERN WAS VERY REAL.
MOVING FURNITURE DURING THE NIGHT? I BARELY MOVE FURNITURE DURING THE DAY LET ALONE THE NIGHT.
MAYBE IT'S THE NEIGHBOURS ATTACHED TO THE BACK OF THEIR FLAT MAKING THE NOISE.
PERHAPS IT'S MY CENTRAL HEATING. I COULD RE-SET THE TIMER...

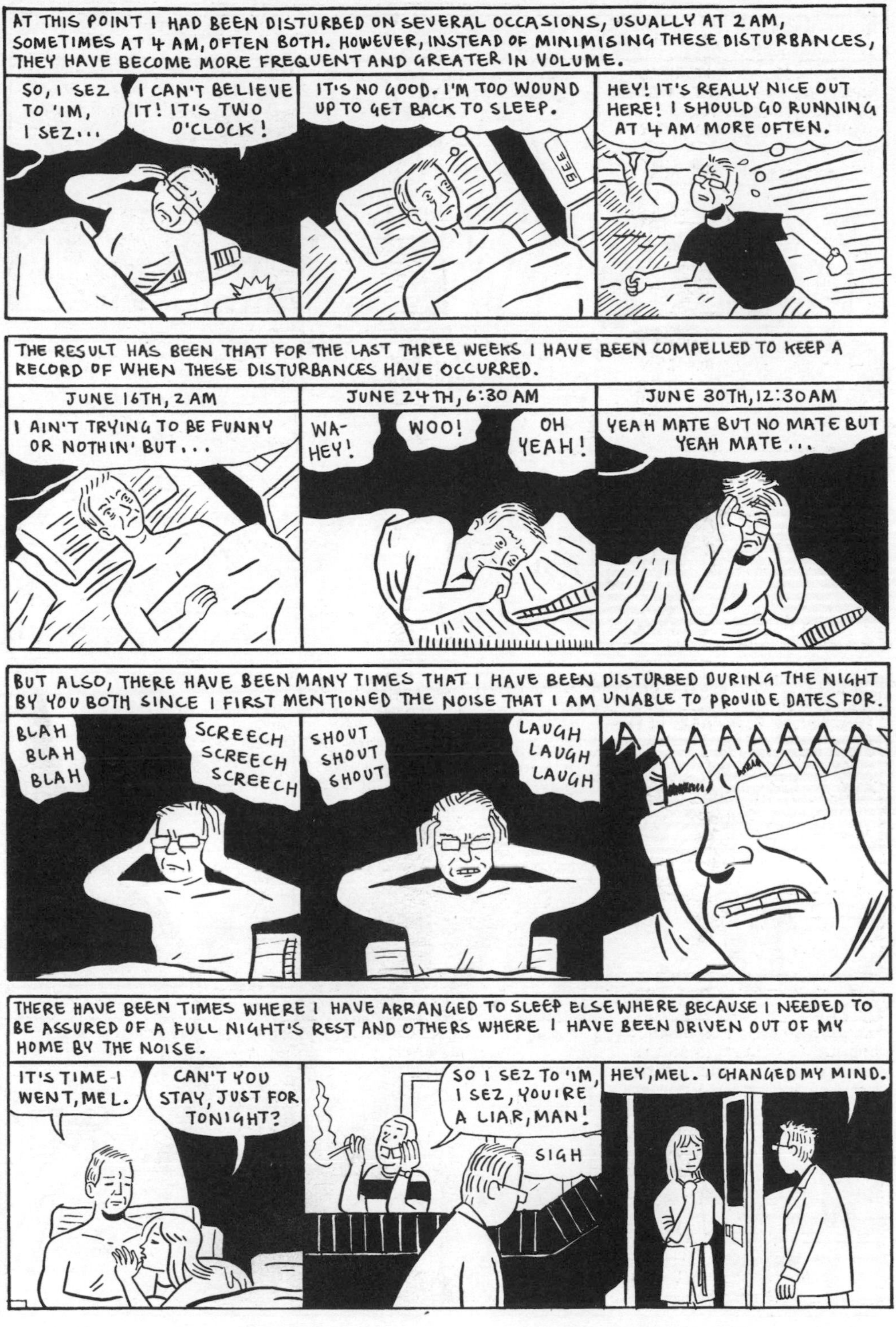

AT THIS POINT I HAD BEEN DISTURBED ON SEVERAL OCCASIONS, USUALLY AT 2 AM, SOMETIMES AT 4 AM, OFTEN BOTH. HOWEVER, INSTEAD OF MINIMISING THESE DISTURBANCES, THEY HAVE BECOME MORE FREQUENT AND GREATER IN VOLUME.
SO, I SEZ TO 'IM, I SEZ...
I CAN'T BELIEVE IT! IT'S TWO O'CLOCK!
IT'S NO GOOD. I'M TOO WOUND UP TO GET BACK TO SLEEP.
HEY! IT'S REALLY NICE OUT HERE! I SHOULD GO RUNNING AT 4 AM MORE OFTEN.
THE RESULT HAS BEEN THAT FOR THE LAST THREE WEEKS I HAVE BEEN COMPELLED TO KEEP A RECORD OF WHEN THESE DISTURBANCES HAVE OCCURRED.
JUNE 16TH, 2 AM
I AIN'T TRYING TO BE FUNNY OR NOTHIN' BUT...
JUNE 24TH, 6:30 AM
WA-HEY!
WOO!
OH YEAH!
JUNE 30TH, 12:30 AM
YEAH MATE BUT NO MATE BUT YEAH MATE...
BUT ALSO, THERE HAVE BEEN MANY TIMES THAT I HAVE BEEN DISTURBED DURING THE NIGHT BY YOU BOTH SINCE I FIRST MENTIONED THE NOISE THAT I AM UNABLE TO PROVIDE DATES FOR.
BLAH BLAH BLAH
SCREECH SCREECH SCREECH
SHOUT SHOUT SHOUT
LAUGH LAUGH LAUGH
AAAAAAAA
THERE HAVE BEEN TIMES WHERE I HAVE ARRANGED TO SLEEP ELSEWHERE BECAUSE I NEEDED TO BE ASSURED OF A FULL NIGHT'S REST AND OTHERS WHERE I HAVE BEEN DRIVEN OUT OF MY HOME BY THE NOISE.
IT'S TIME I WENT, MEL.
CAN'T YOU STAY, JUST FOR TONIGHT?
SO I SEZ TO 'IM, I SEZ, YOU'RE A LIAR, MAN!
SIGH
HEY, MEL. I CHANGED MY MIND.

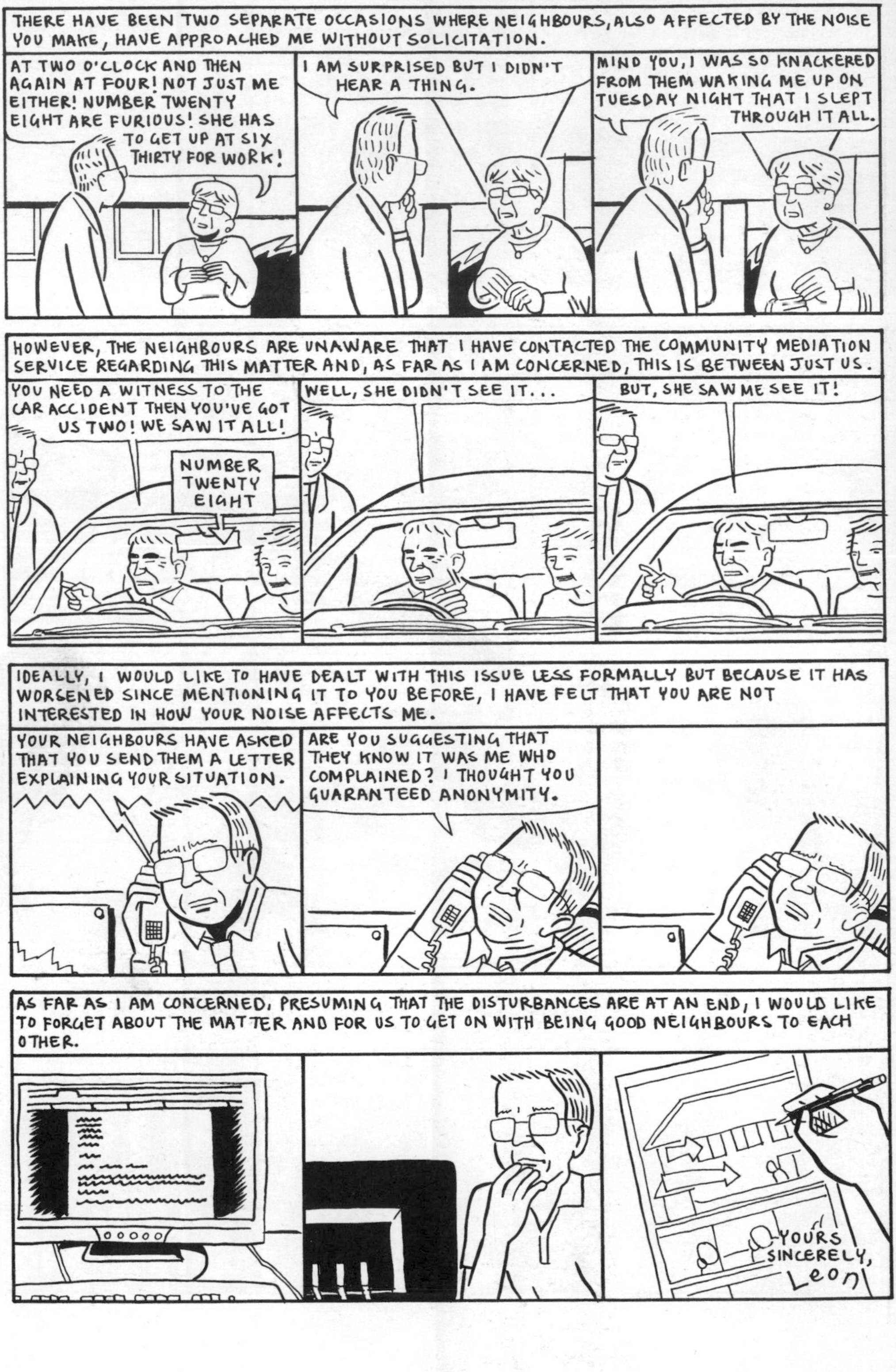
THERE HAVE BEEN TWO SEPARATE OCCASIONS WHERE NEIGHBOURS, ALSO AFFECTED BY THE NOISE YOU MAKE, HAVE APPROACHED ME WITHOUT SOLICITATION.
AT TWO O'CLOCK AND THEN AGAIN AT FOUR! NOT JUST ME EITHER! NUMBER TWENTY EIGHT ARE FURIOUS! SHE HAS TO GET UP AT SIX THIRTY FOR WORK!
I AM SURPRISED BUT I DIDN'T HEAR A THING.
MIND YOU, I WAS SO KNACKERED FROM THEM WAKING ME UP ON TUESDAY NIGHT THAT I SLEPT THROUGH IT ALL.
HOWEVER, THE NEIGHBOURS ARE UNAWARE THAT I HAVE CONTACTED THE COMMUNITY MEDIATION SERVICE REGARDING THIS MATTER AND, AS FAR AS I AM CONCERNED, THIS IS BETWEEN JUST US.
YOU NEED A WITNESS TO THE CAR ACCIDENT THEN YOU'VE GOT US TWO! WE SAW IT ALL!
NUMBER TWENTY EIGHT
WELL, SHE DIDN'T SEE IT...
BUT, SHE SAW ME SEE IT!
IDEALLY, I WOULD LIKE TO HAVE DEALT WITH THIS ISSUE LESS FORMALLY BUT BECAUSE IT HAS WORSENED SINCE MENTIONING IT TO YOU BEFORE, I HAVE FELT THAT YOU ARE NOT INTERESTED IN HOW YOUR NOISE AFFECTS ME.
YOUR NEIGHBOURS HAVE ASKED THAT YOU SEND THEM A LETTER EXPLAINING YOUR SITUATION.
ARE YOU SUGGESTING THAT THEY KNOW IT WAS ME WHO COMPLAINED? I THOUGHT YOU GUARANTEED ANONYMITY.
AS FAR AS I AM CONCERNED, PRESUMING THAT THE DISTURBANCES ARE AT AN END, I WOULD LIKE TO FORGET ABOUT THE MATTER AND FOR US TO GET ON WITH BEING GOOD NEIGHBOURS TO EACH OTHER.
YOURS SINCERELY,
Leon

HOLIDAY SKETCHBOOK

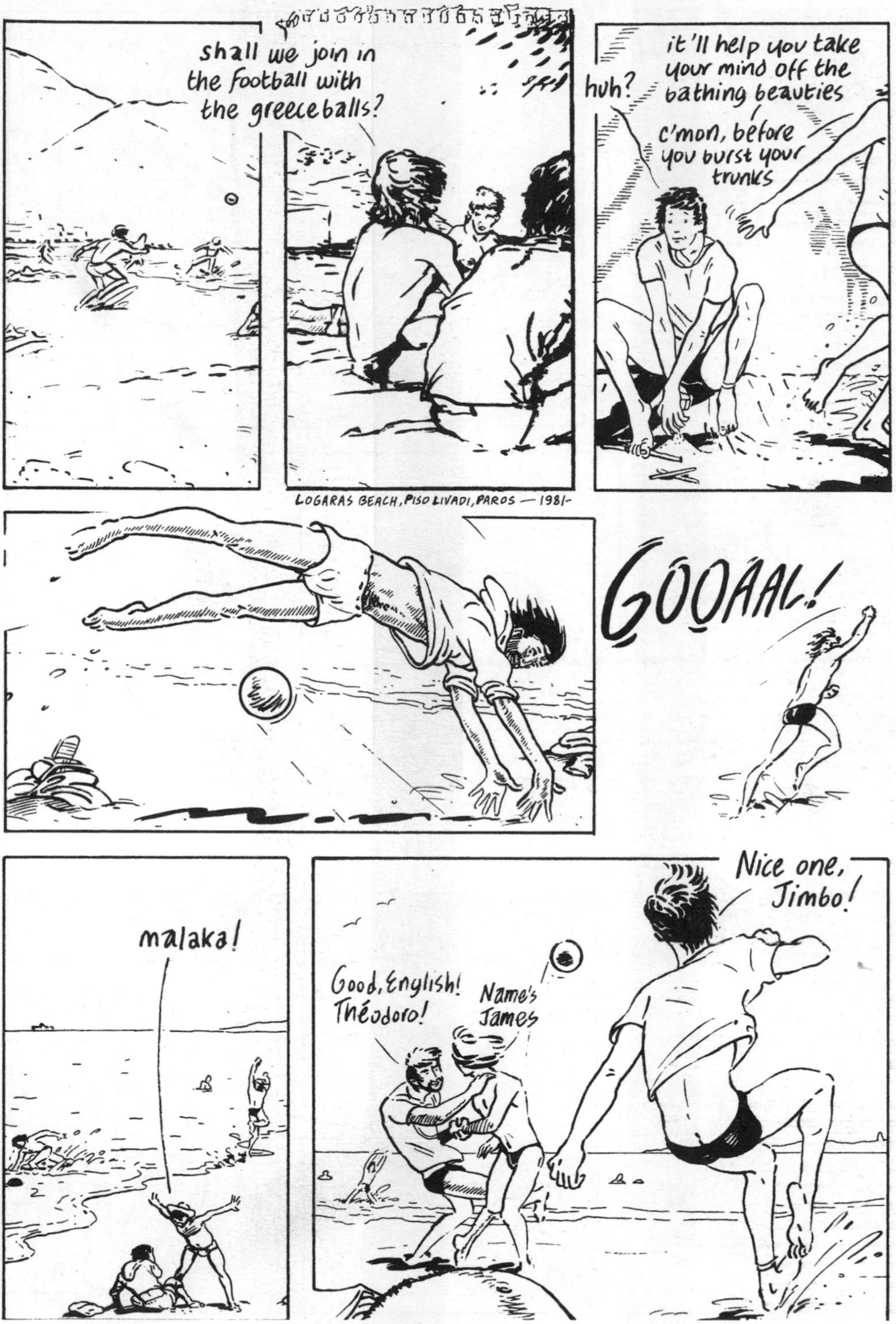
shall we join in the football with the greeceballs?
huh?
it'll help you take your mind off the bathing beauties
c'mon, before you burst your trunks
LOGARAS BEACH, PISO LIVADI, PAROS — 1981 —
GOOAAL!
malaka!
Good, English! Théodoro!
Name's James
Nice one, Jimbo!

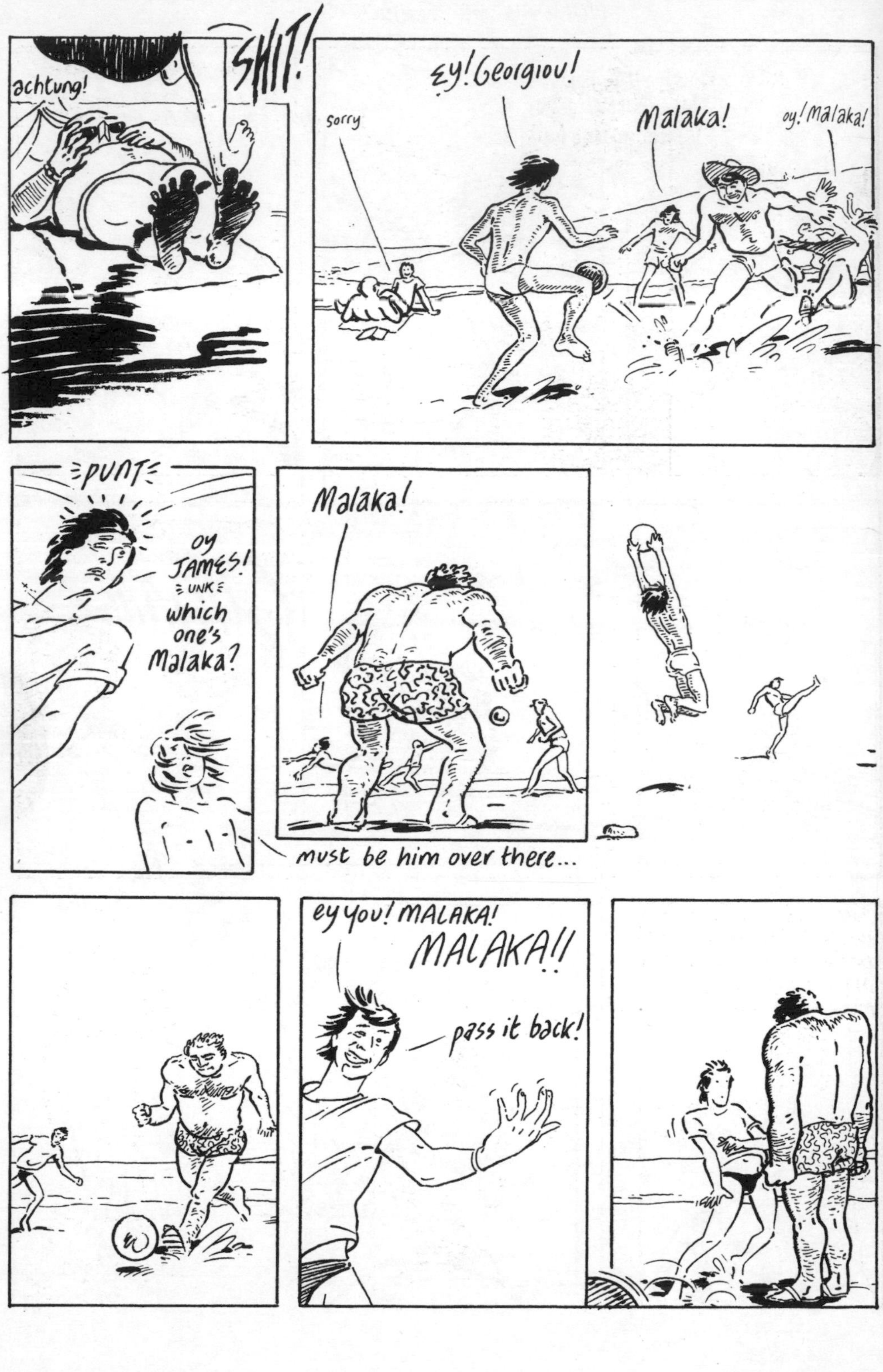
achtung!
SHIT!
ey! Georgiou!
sorry
Malaka!
oy! Malaka!
PUNT
oy JAMES!
UNK
which one's Malaka?
Malaka!
must be him over there...
ey you! MALAKA!
MALAKA!!
pass it back!

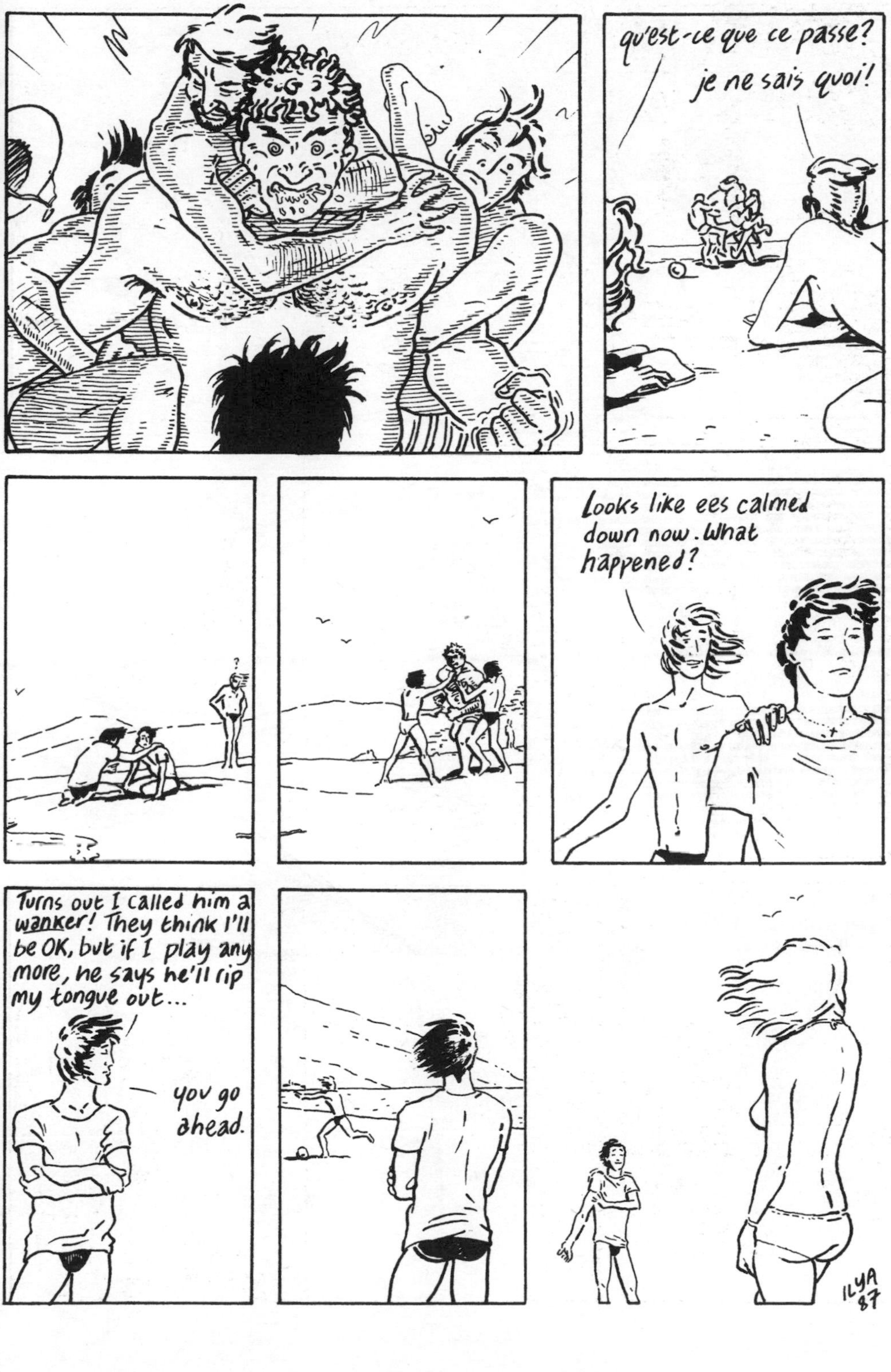
qu'est-ce que ce passe?
je ne sais quoi!
Looks like ees calmed down now. What happened?
Turns out I called him a wanker! They think I'll be OK, but if I play any more, he says he'll rip my tongue out...
you go ahead.
ILYA 87

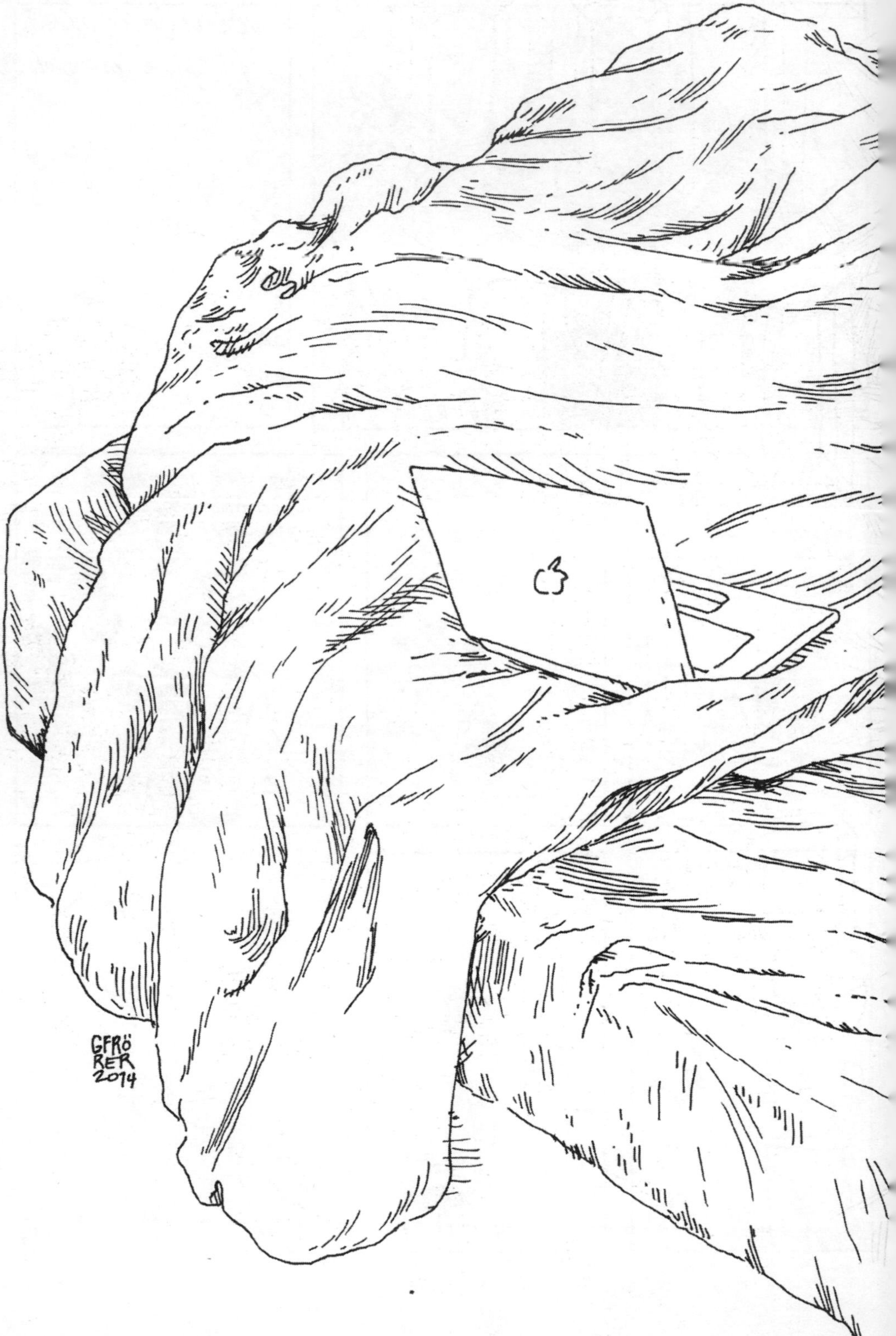
GFRÖRER
2014

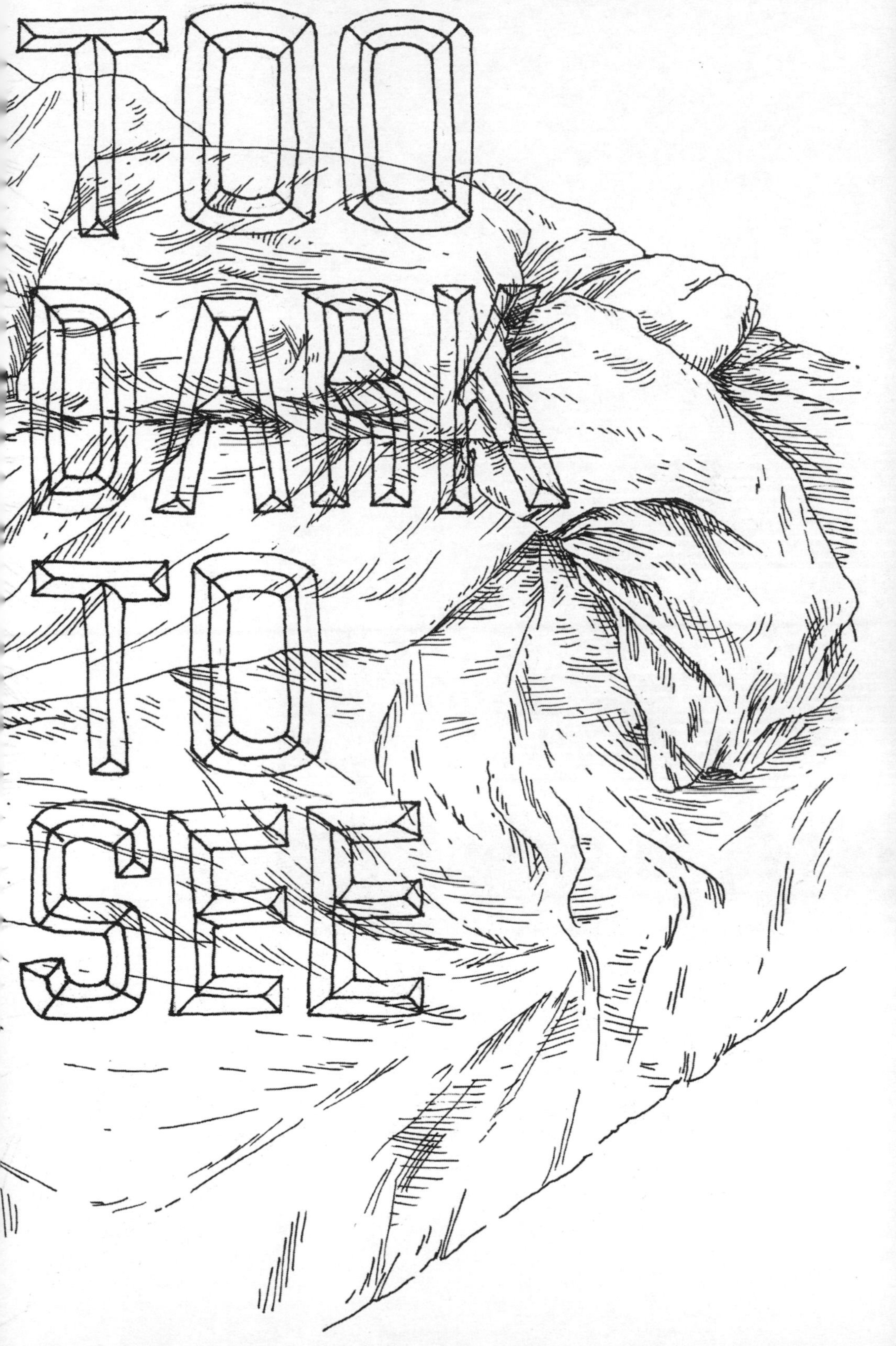
TOO
DARK
TO
SEE

Julia Gfrörer

TOO DARK TO SEE
Self-published, 2011

Her last name rhymes with despair, and her heart is
black as jet.

Born in 1982 in Concord, NH, Julia's work has appeared
in *Thickness*, *Black Eye*, the magazines *Arthur* and *Study
Group*, and *Best American Comics*.

"*Too Dark to See* wasn't inspired by incubus/succubus
mythology but the experience of a relationship breaking
down, for reasons that are unclear or unspeakable. The
pain of it is palpable enough but not linked to a manifest
cause, yet reason insists that a cause must exist,
somewhere just out of sight. A persistent theme in my
work links involuntary physical responses to suppressed
emotional responses, and the semen, tears and blood
that punctuate the story serve as inadequate avatars
for the permanently unnamed source of the characters'
pain.

"It took me a month to draw, and I've reprinted it
sporadically in different forms. I still consider it one of
the most frightening and painful stories I've ever written.
I've since made several more horror mini-comics, lots of
anthology pieces, and a graphic novel (*Black is the Color*,
published by Fantagraphics in 2013). My blog previews my
latest work and original drawings for sale." – JG

www.thorazos.net

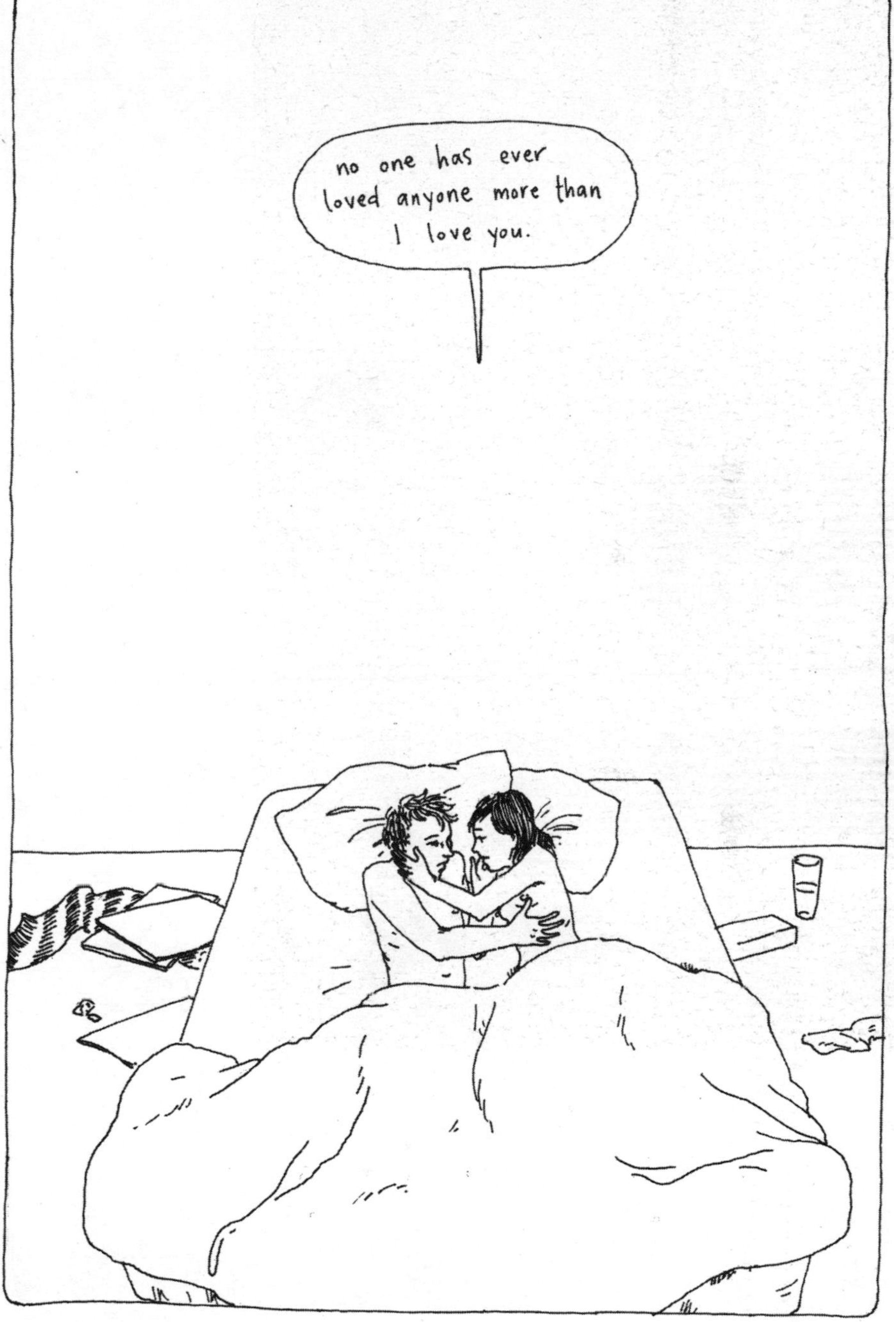
no one has ever loved anyone more than I love you.

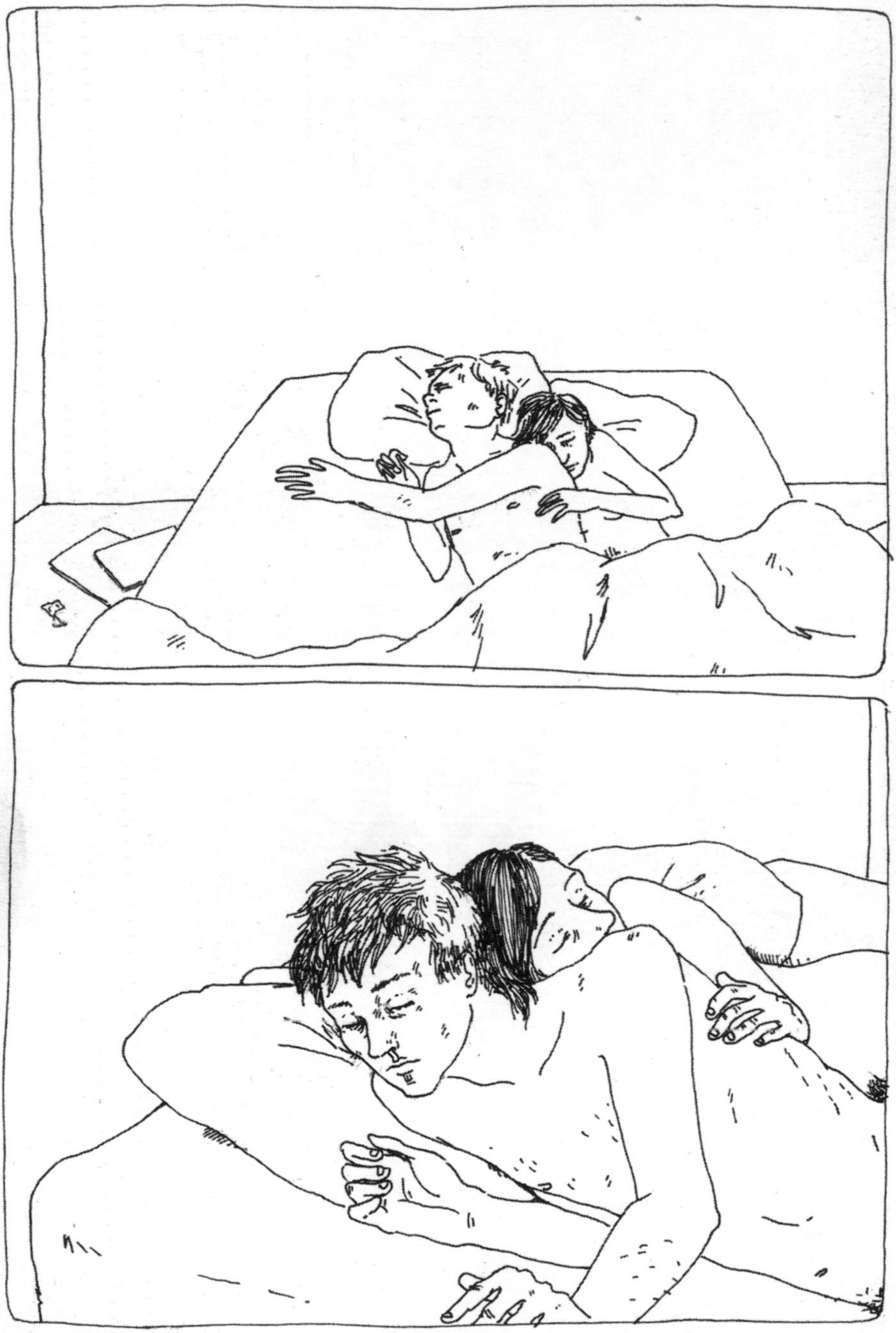

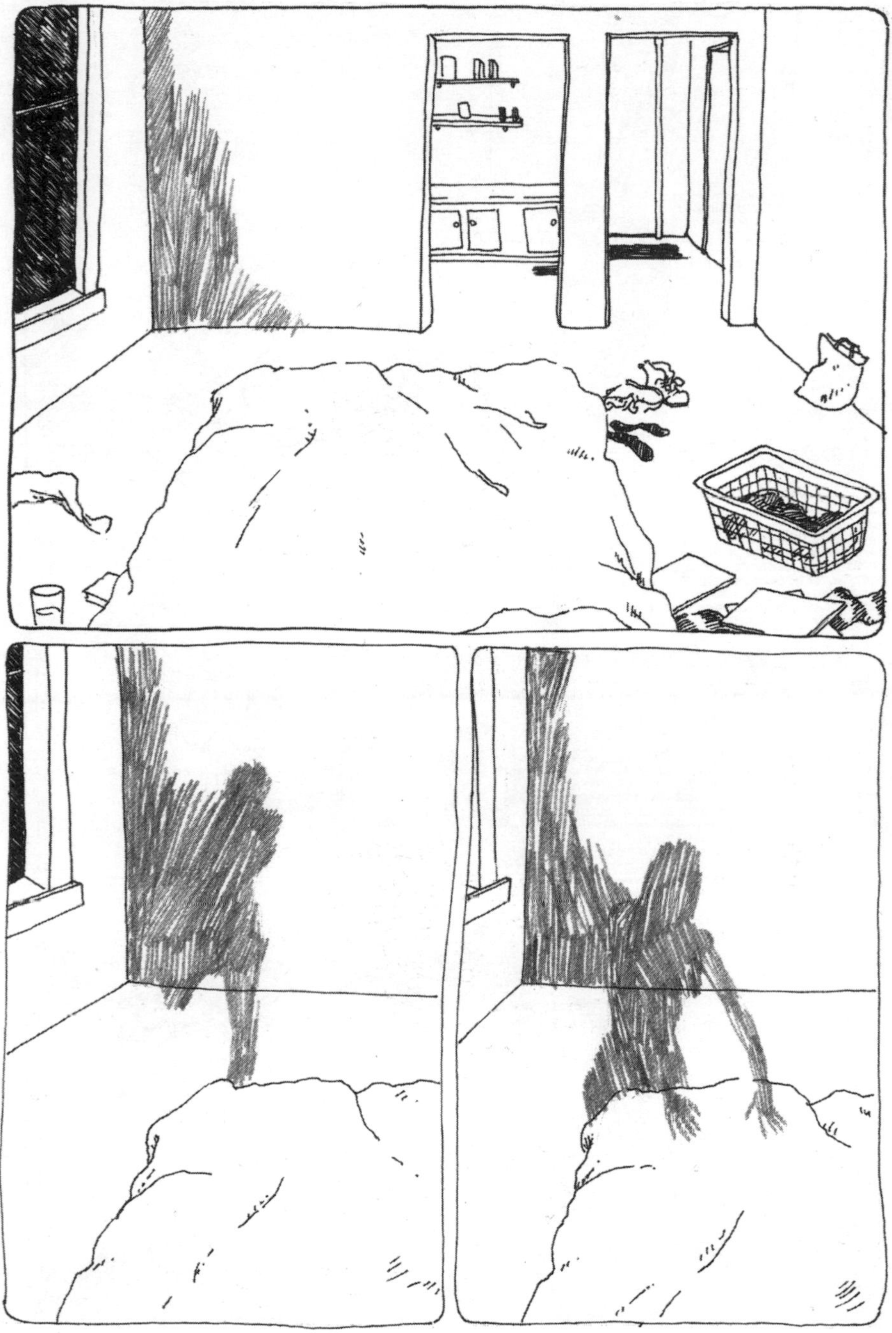

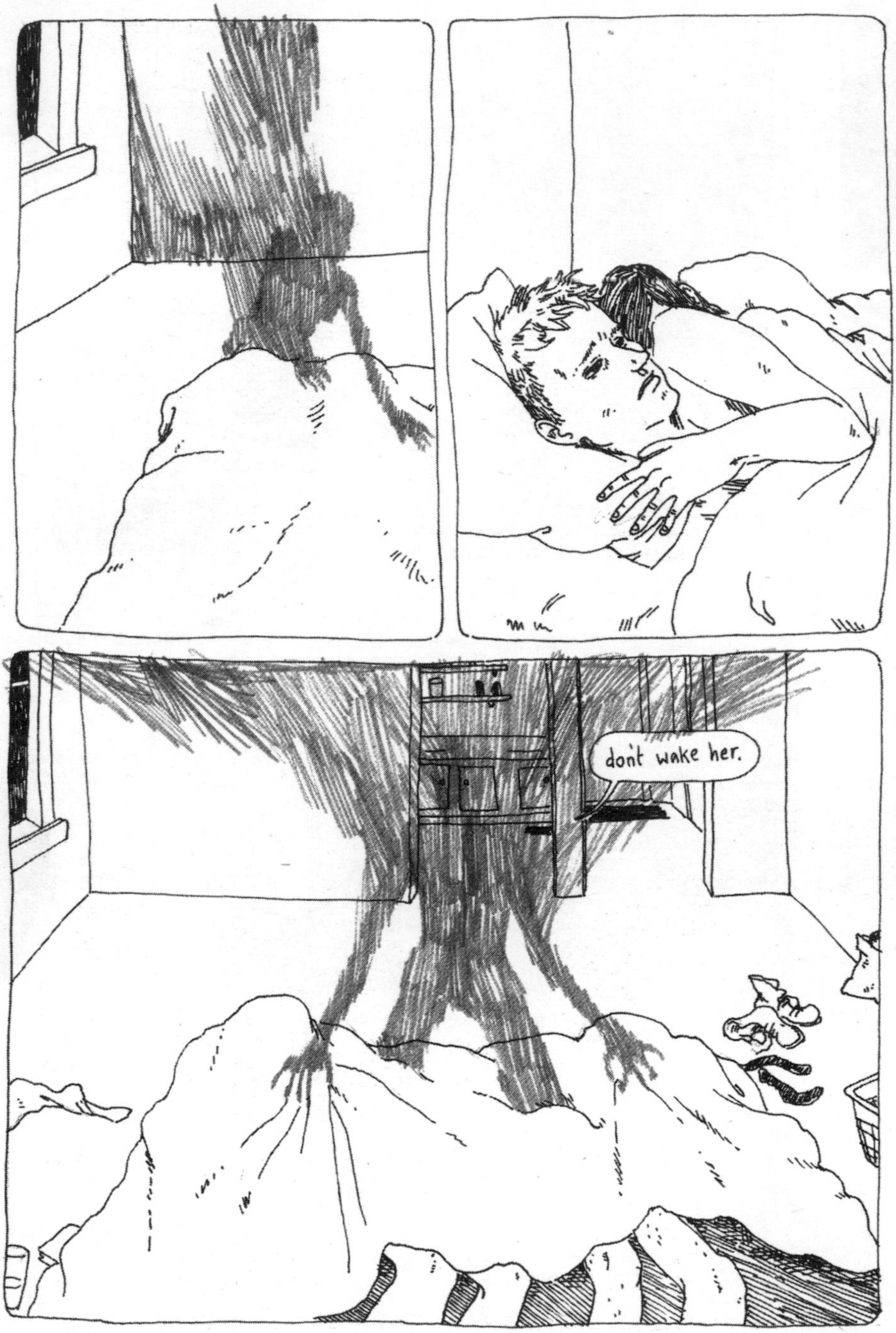
don't wake her.

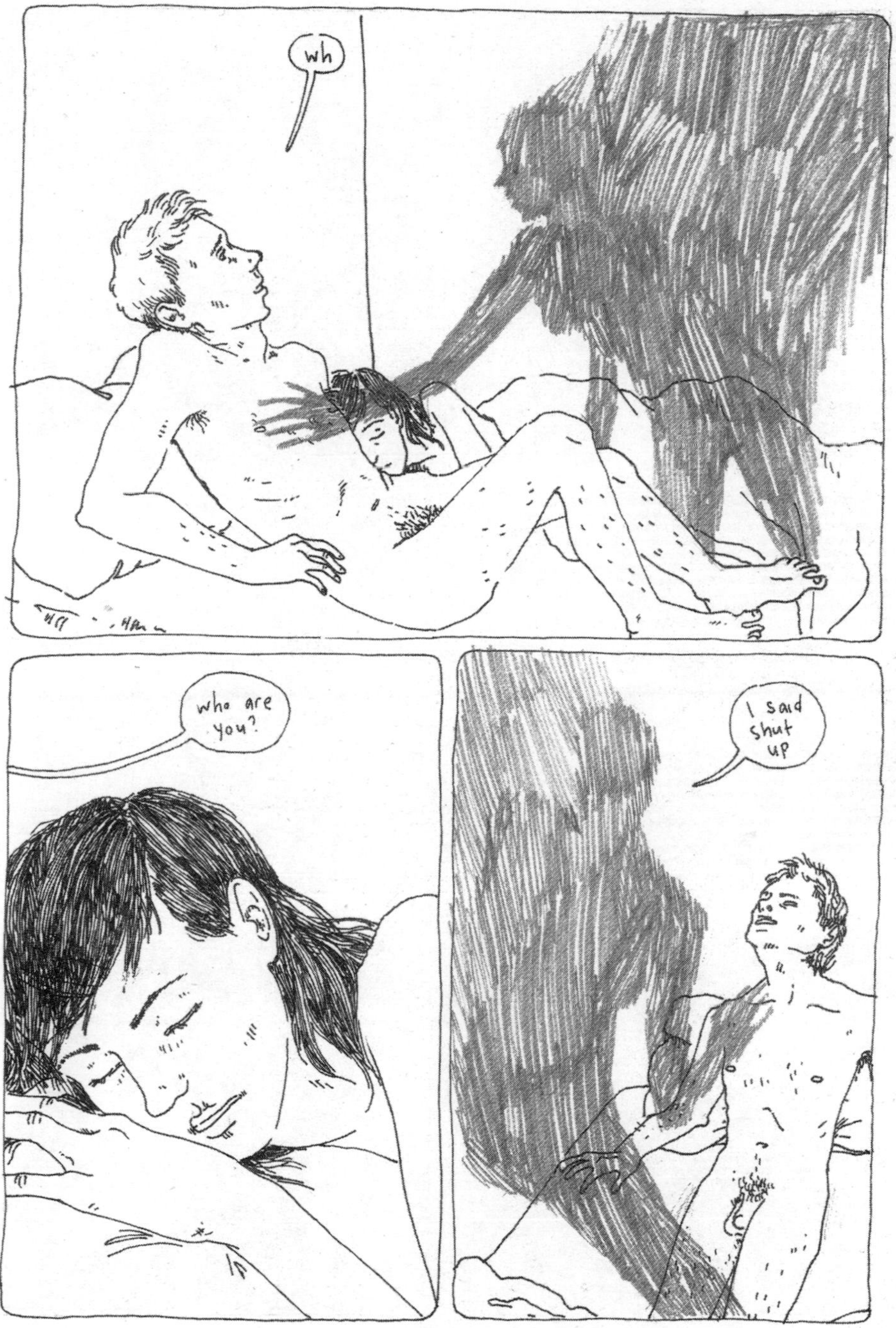
wh
who are you?
I said shut up

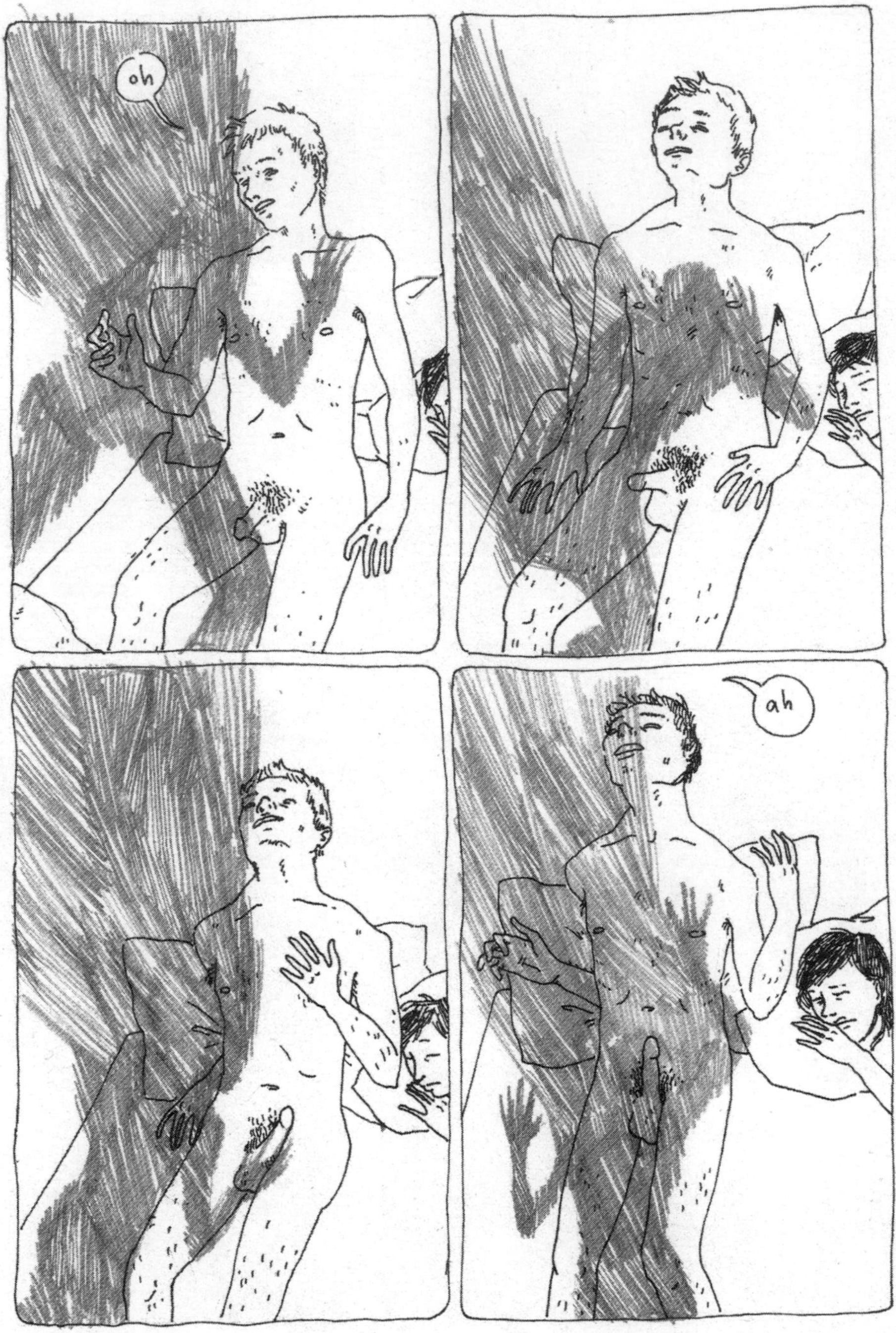
oh
ah

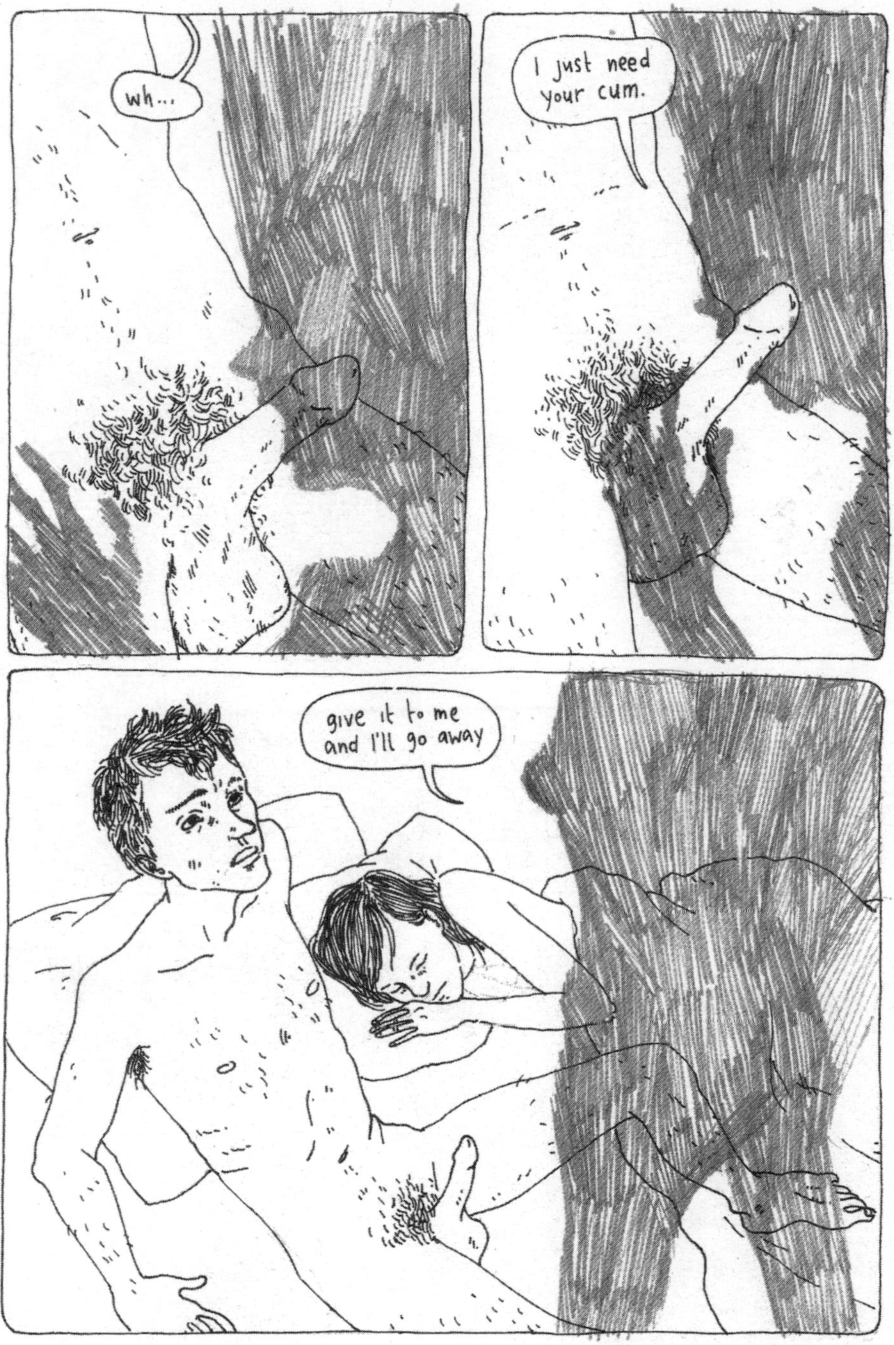
wh...
I just need your cum.
give it to me and I'll go away

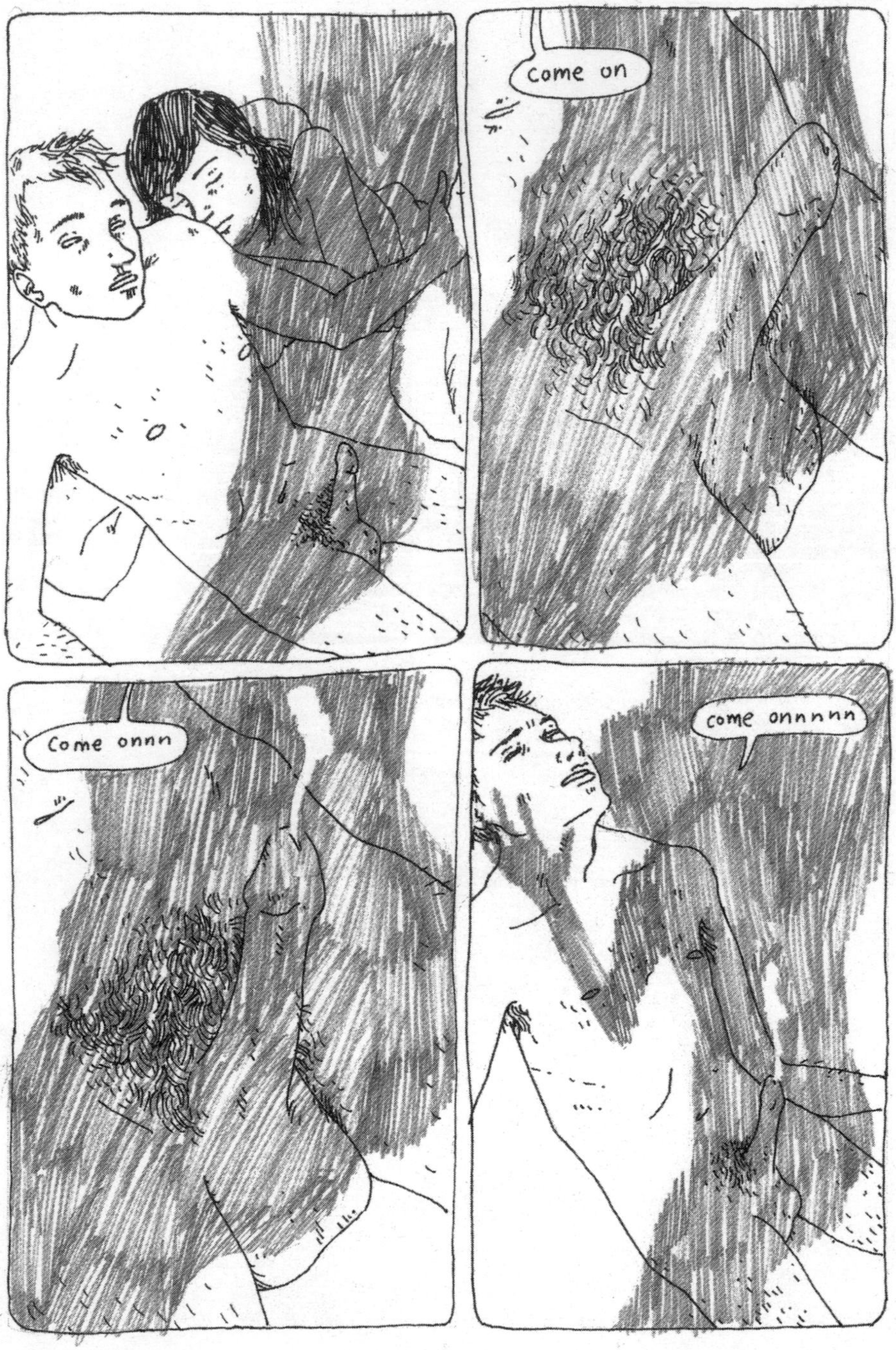
come on
Come onnn
come onnnnn

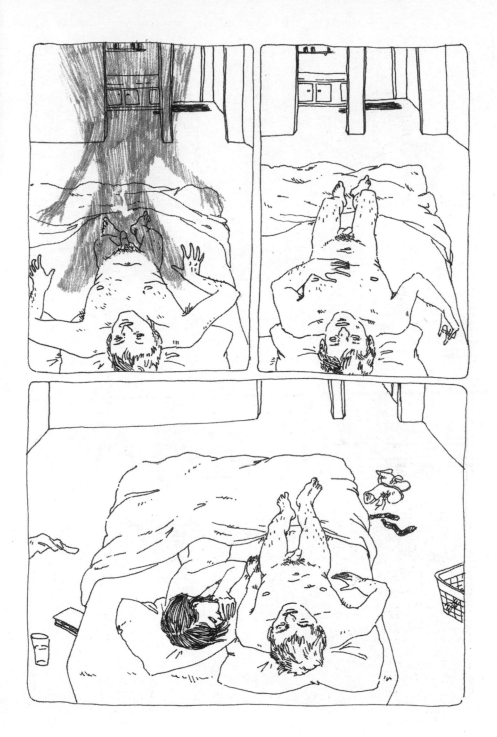

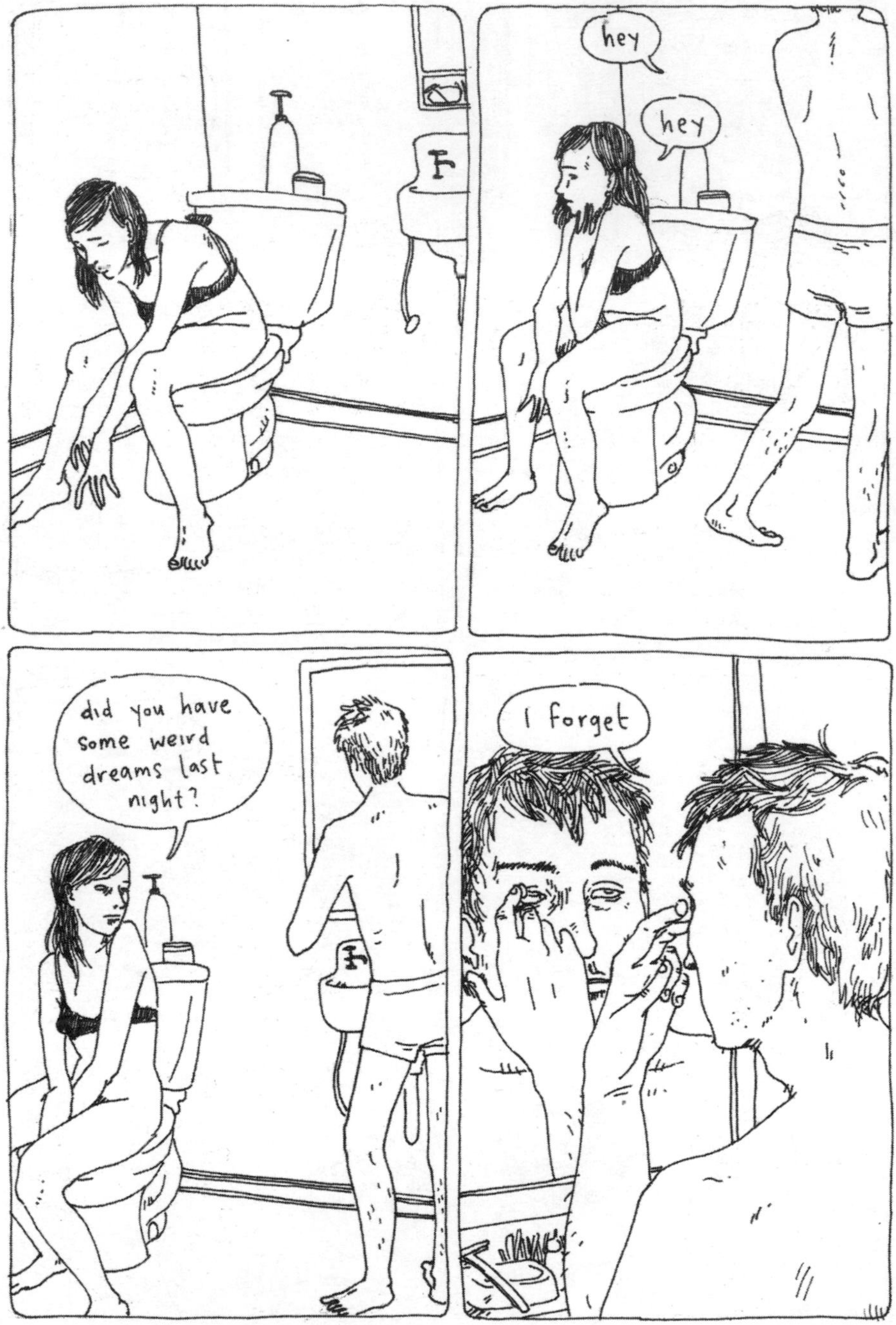
hey
hey
did you have some weird dreams last night?
I forget

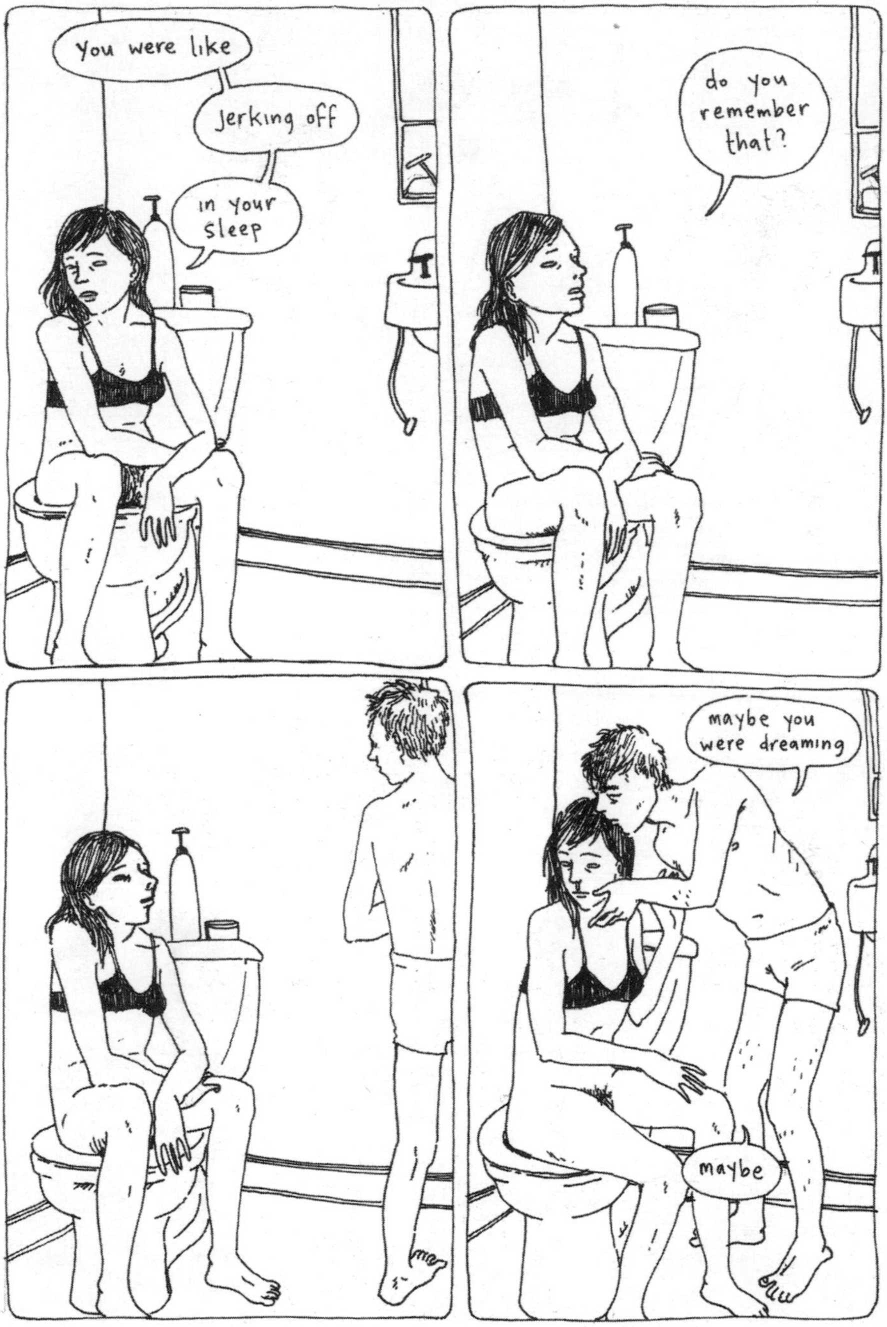
you were like
jerking off
in your sleep
do you remember that?
maybe you were dreaming
maybe

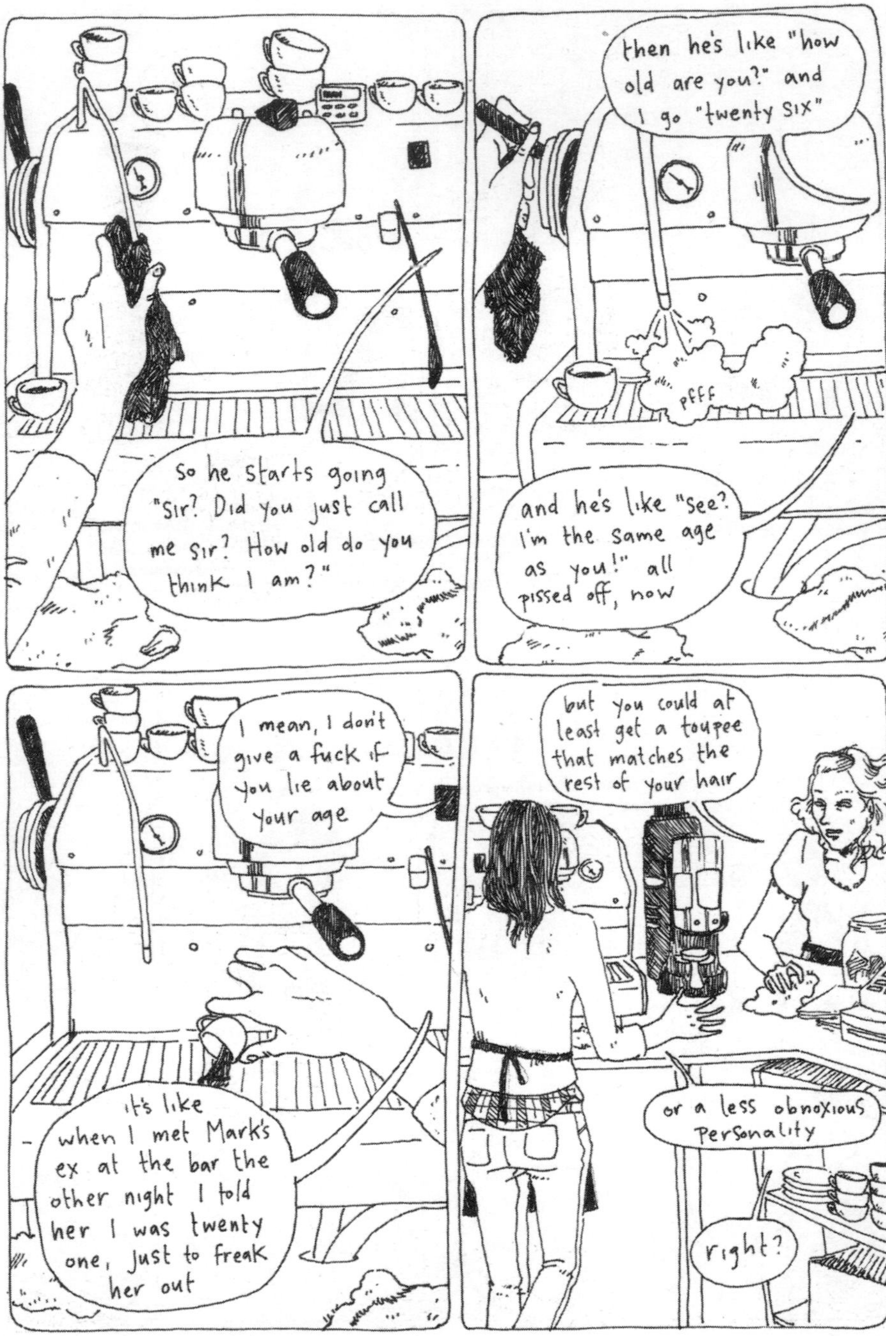
so he starts going "sir? Did you just call me sir? How old do you think I am?"
then he's like "how old are you?" and I go "twenty six"
pfff
and he's like "see? I'm the same age as you!" all pissed off, now
I mean, I don't give a fuck if you lie about your age
it's like when I met Mark's ex at the bar the other night I told her I was twenty one, just to freak her out
but you could at least get a toupee that matches the rest of your hair
or a less obnoxious personality
right?

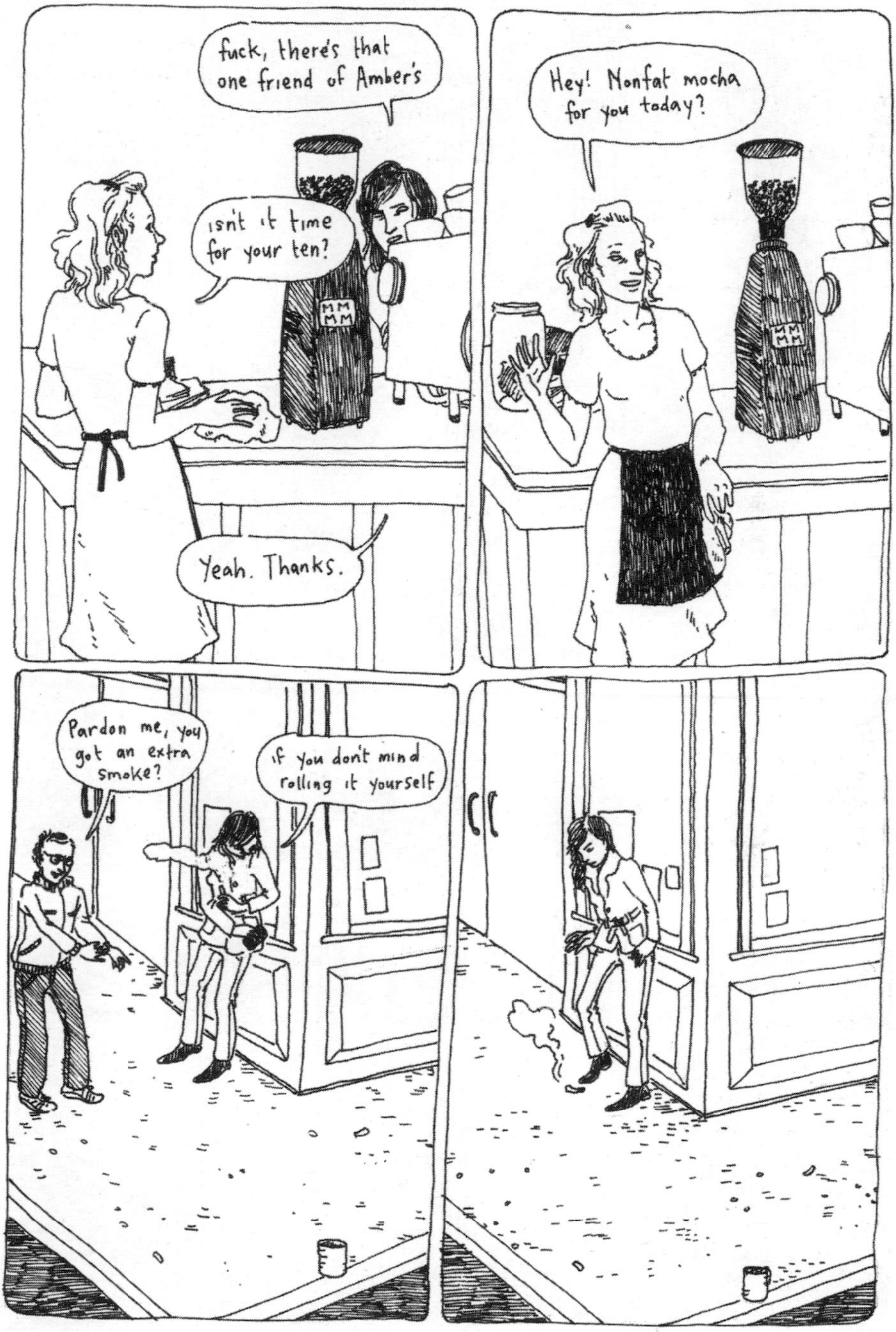
fuck, there's that one friend of Amber's
isn't it time for your ten?
Yeah. Thanks.
Hey! Nonfat mocha for you today?
Pardon me, you got an extra smoke?
if you don't mind rolling it yourself

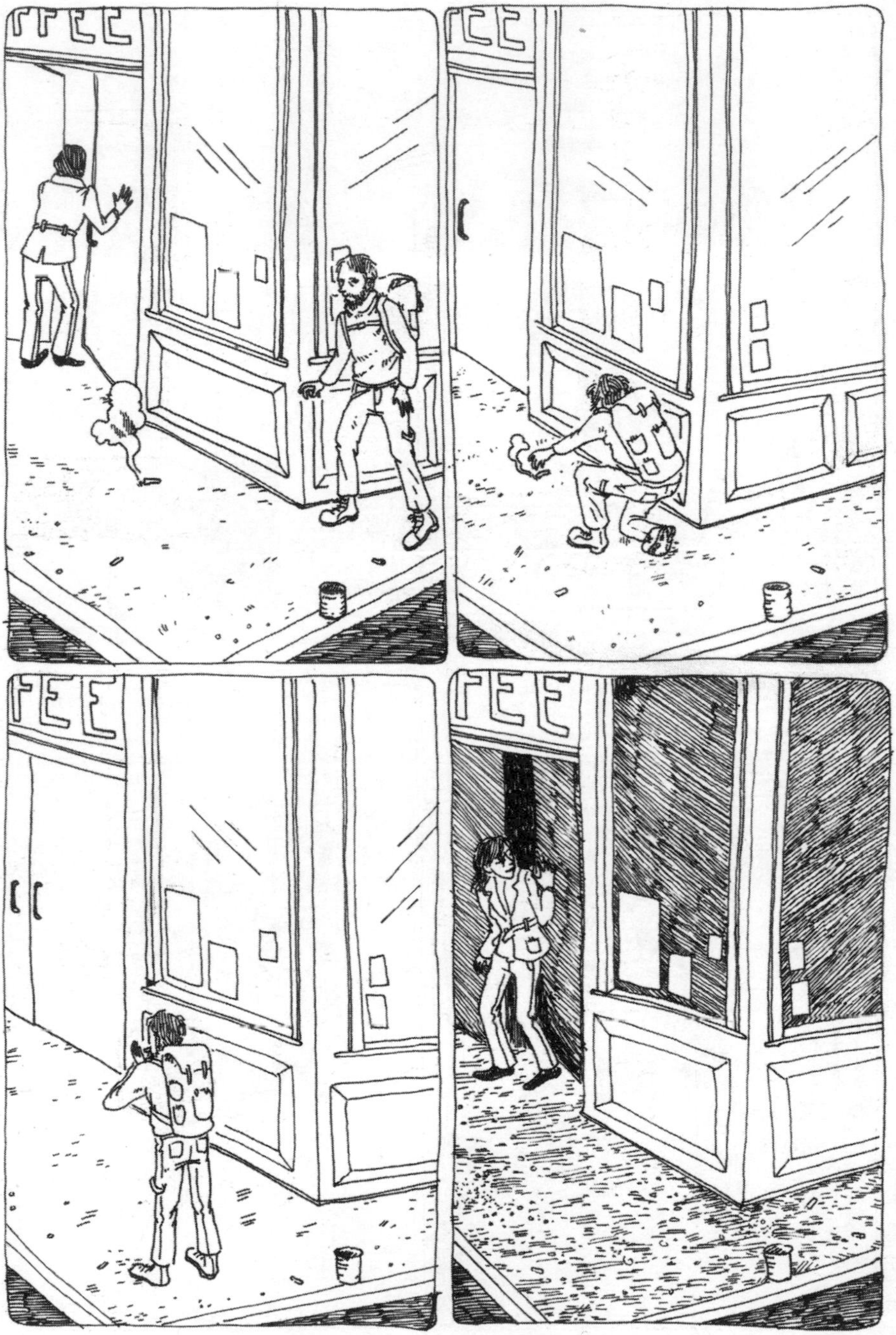

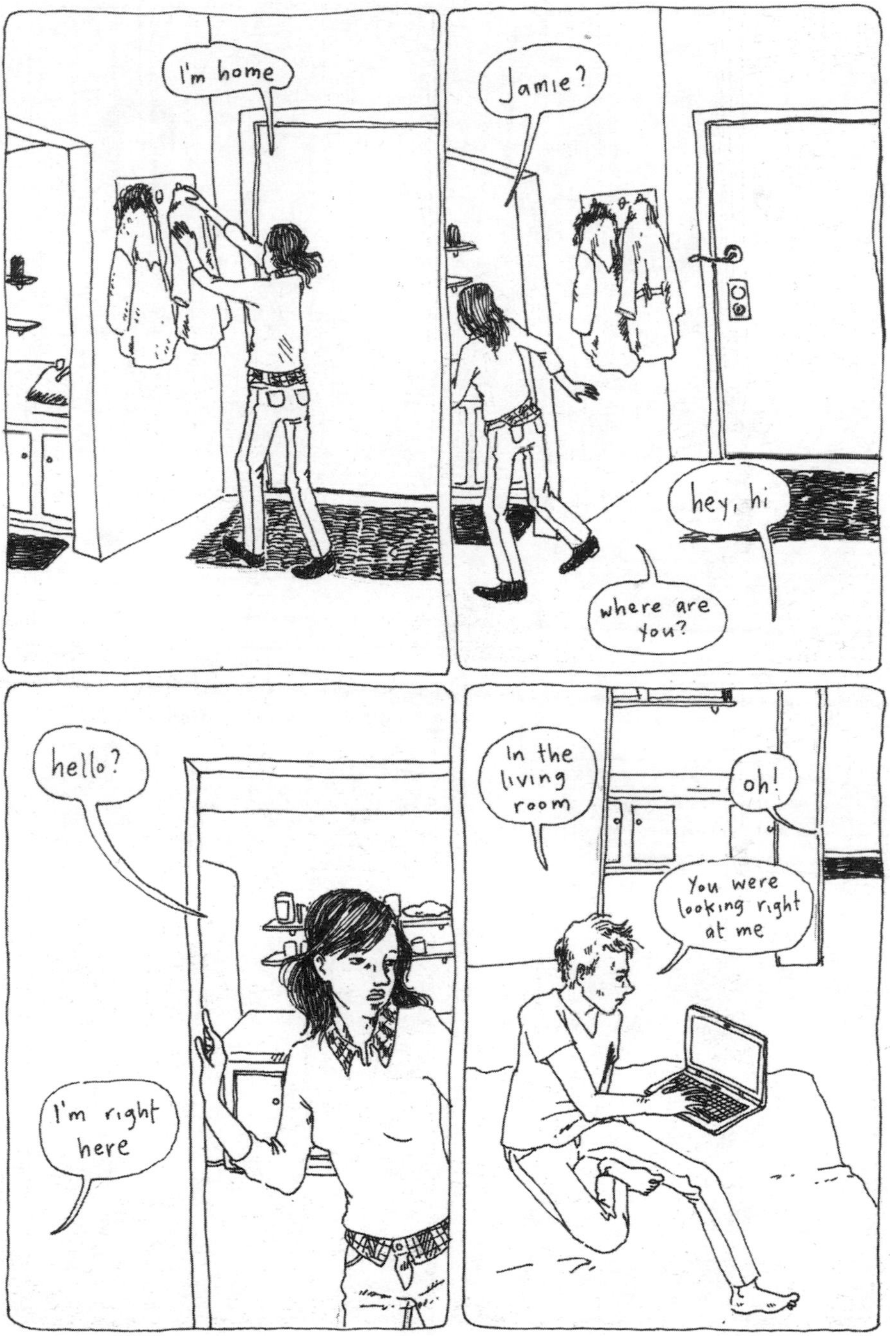
I'm home
Jamie?
hey, hi
where are you?
hello?
I'm right here
In the living room
oh!
You were looking right at me

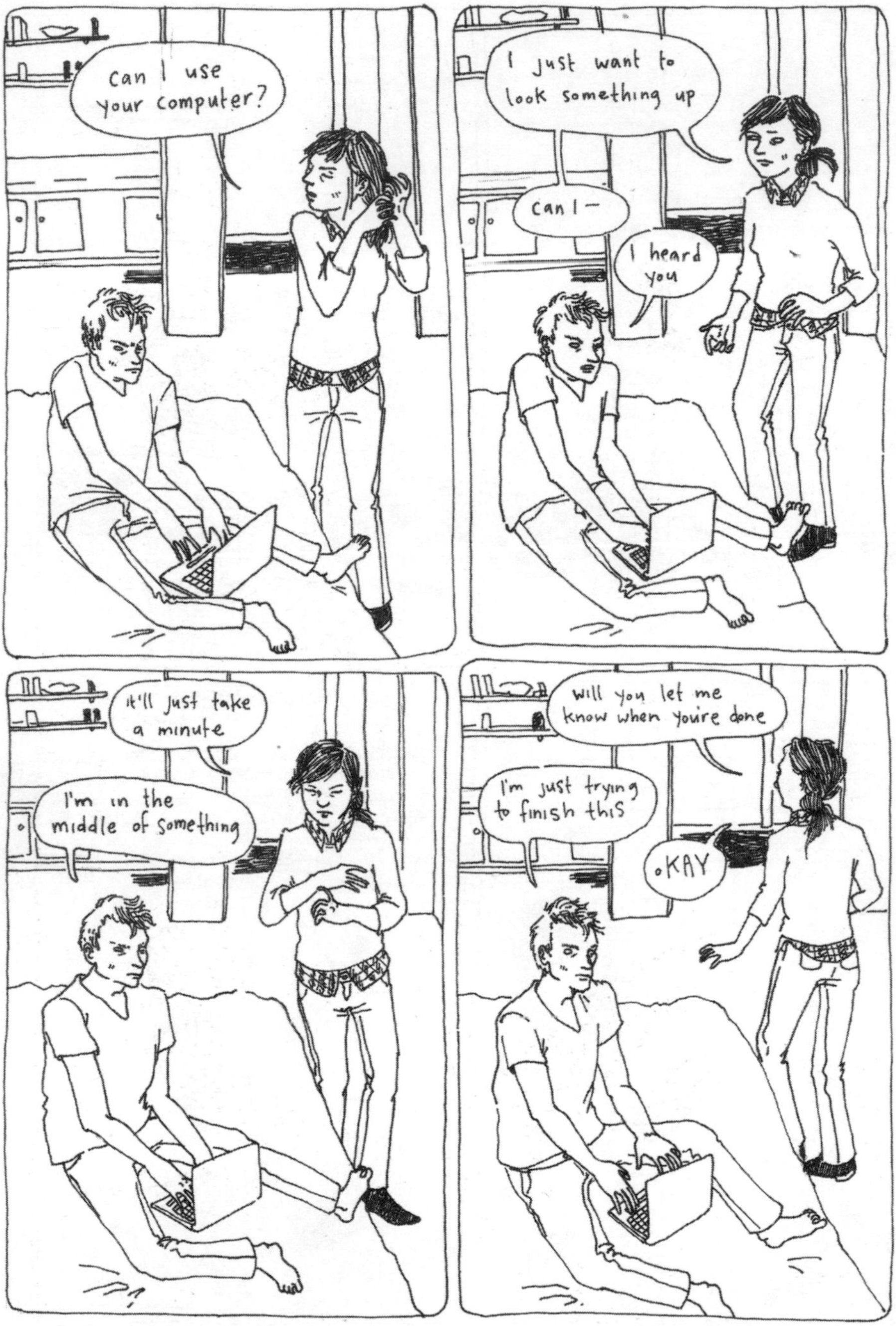
Can I use your computer?
I just want to look something up
Can I—
I heard you
it'll just take a minute
I'm in the middle of something
will you let me know when you're done
I'm just trying to finish this
OKAY

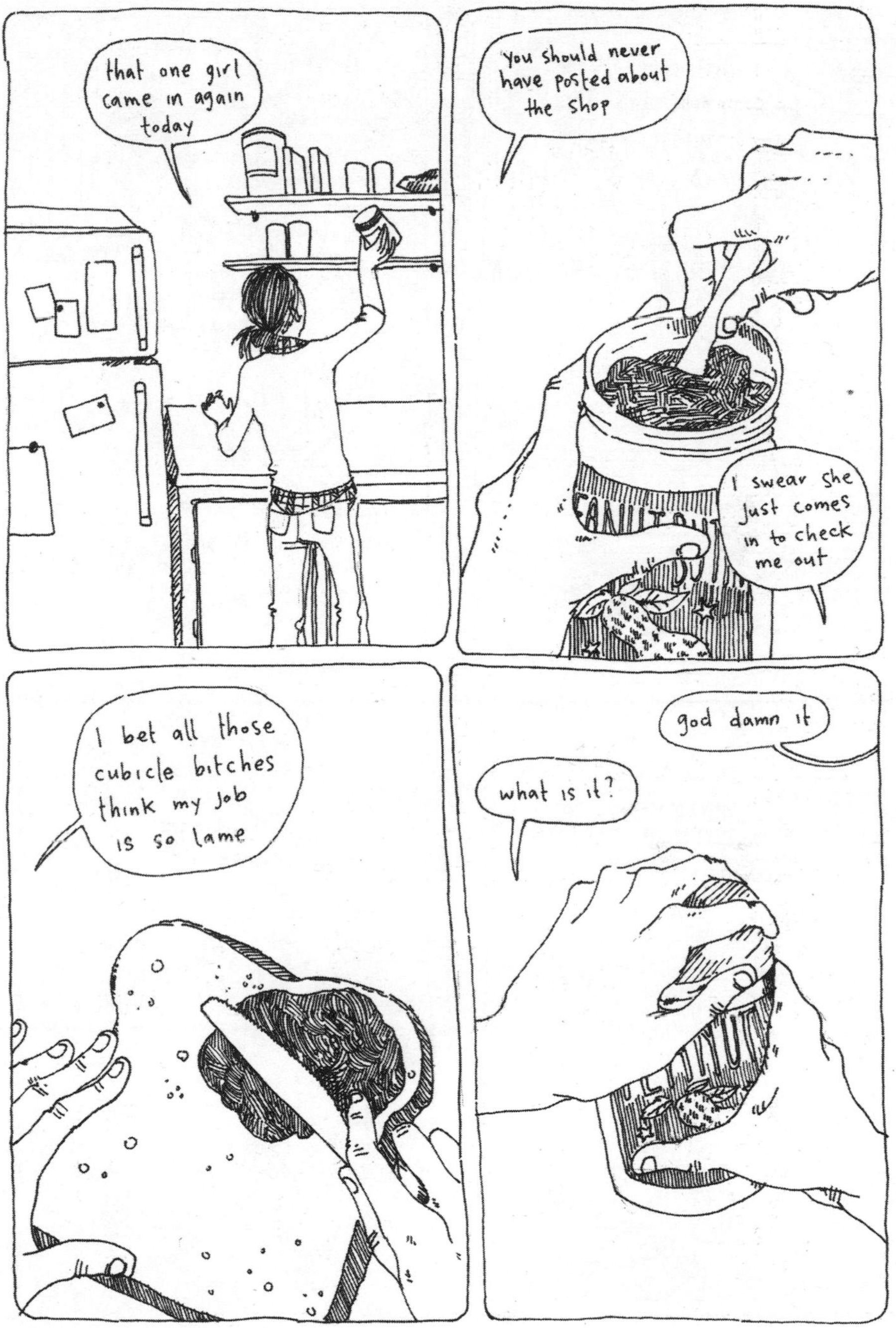
that one girl came in again today
You should never have posted about the shop
I swear she just comes in to check me out
I bet all those cubicle bitches think my job is so lame
god damn it
what is it?

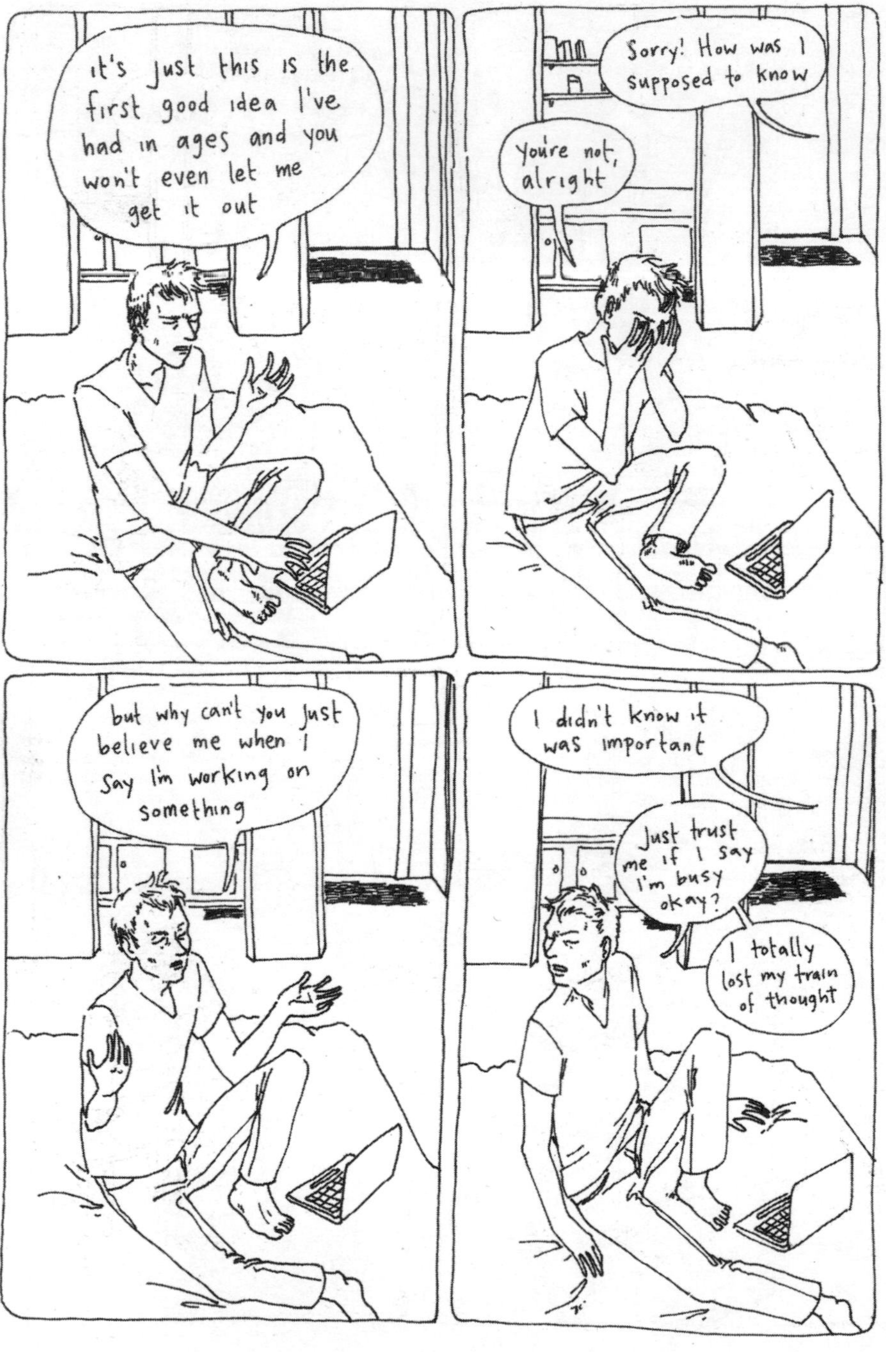
it's just this is the first good idea I've had in ages and you won't even let me get it out
Sorry! How was I supposed to know
You're not, alright
but why can't you just believe me when I say I'm working on something
I didn't know it was important
Just trust me if I say I'm busy okay?
I totally lost my train of thought

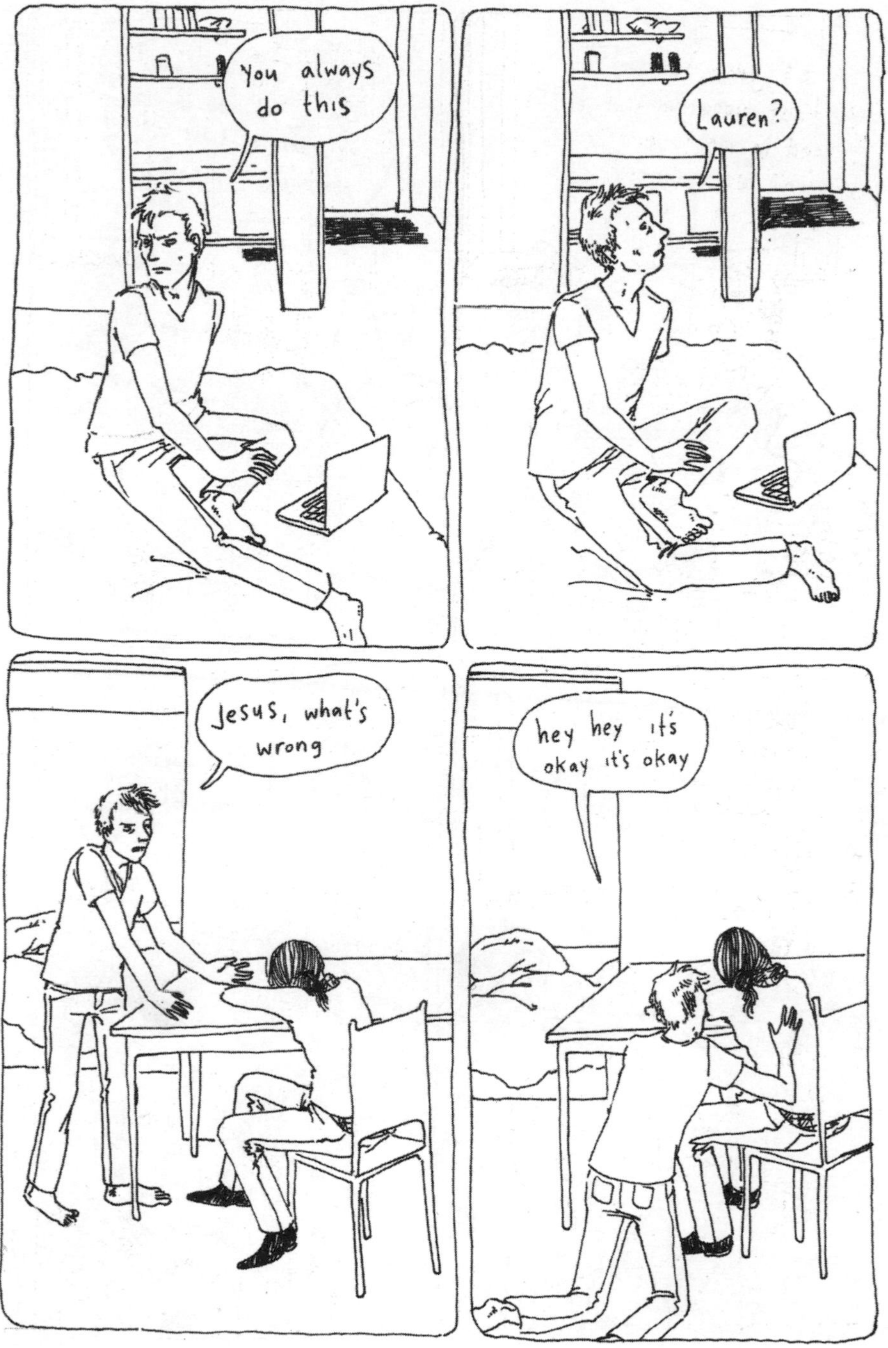
you always do this
Lauren?
Jesus, what's wrong
hey hey it's okay it's okay

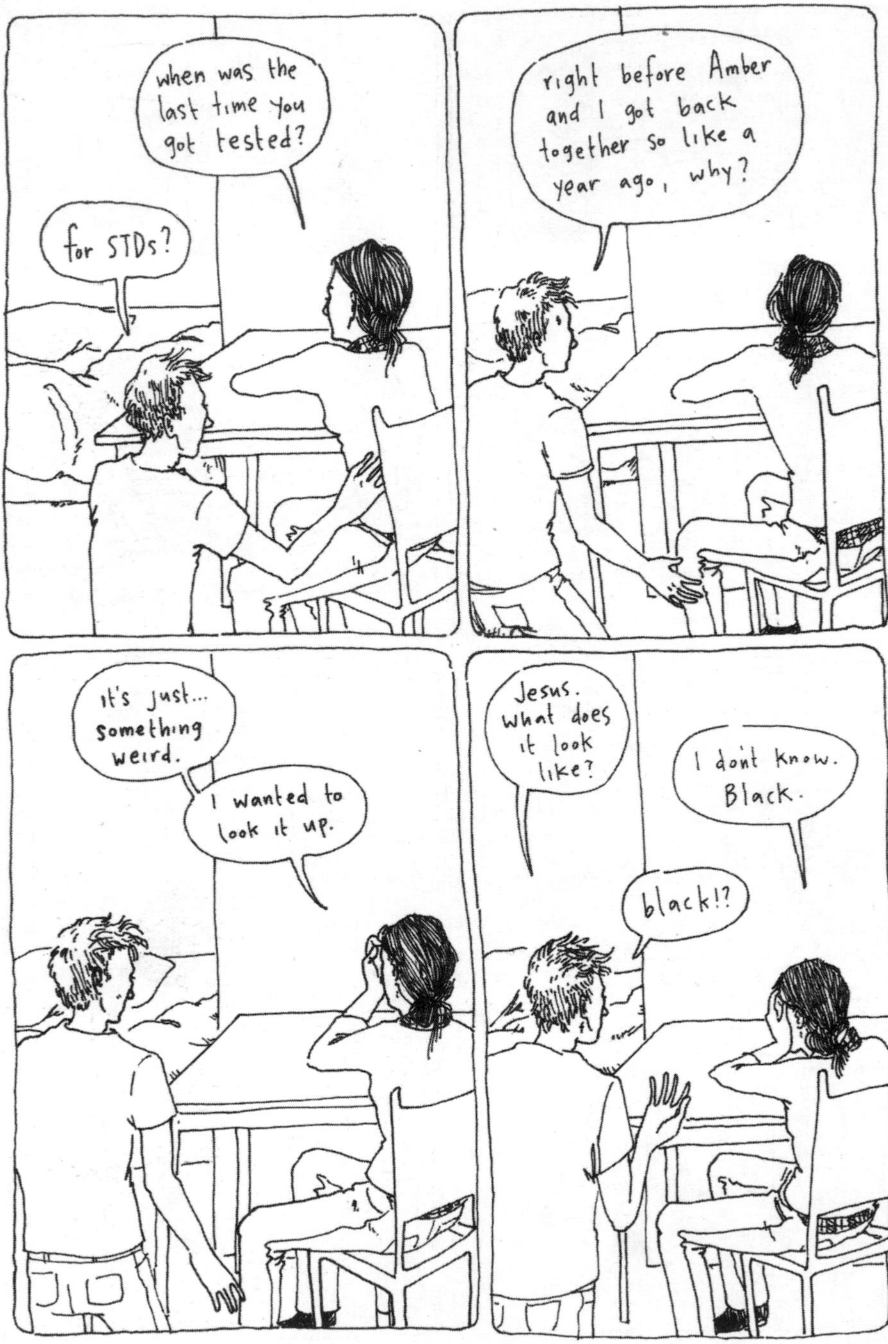
when was the last time you got tested?
for STDs?
right before Amber and I got back together so like a year ago, why?
it's just... something weird.
I wanted to look it up.
Jesus. what does it look like?
I don't know. Black.
black!?

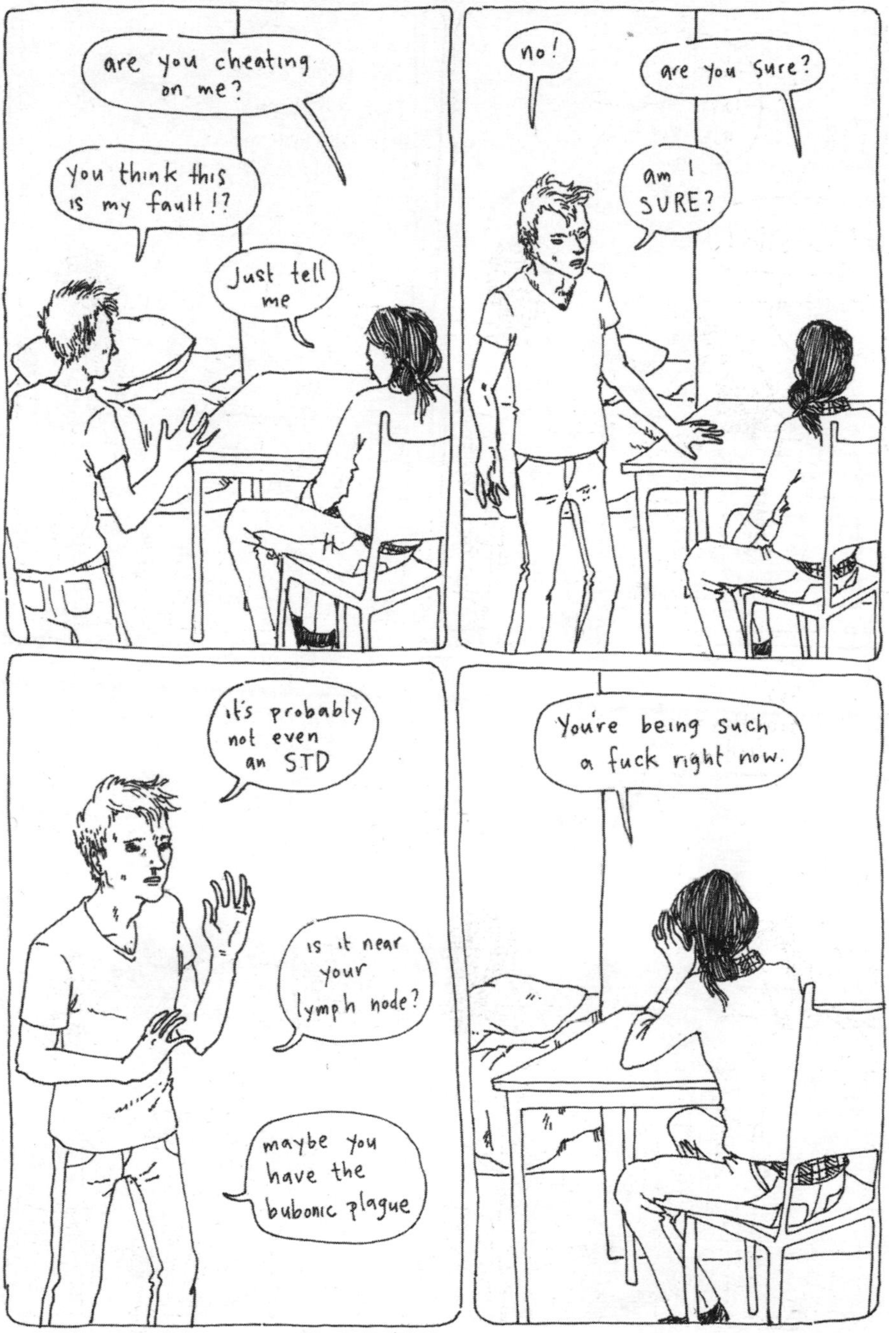
are you cheating on me?
You think this is my fault!?
Just tell me
no!
are you sure?
am I SURE?
it's probably not even an STD
is it near your lymph node?
maybe you have the bubonic plague
You're being such a fuck right now.

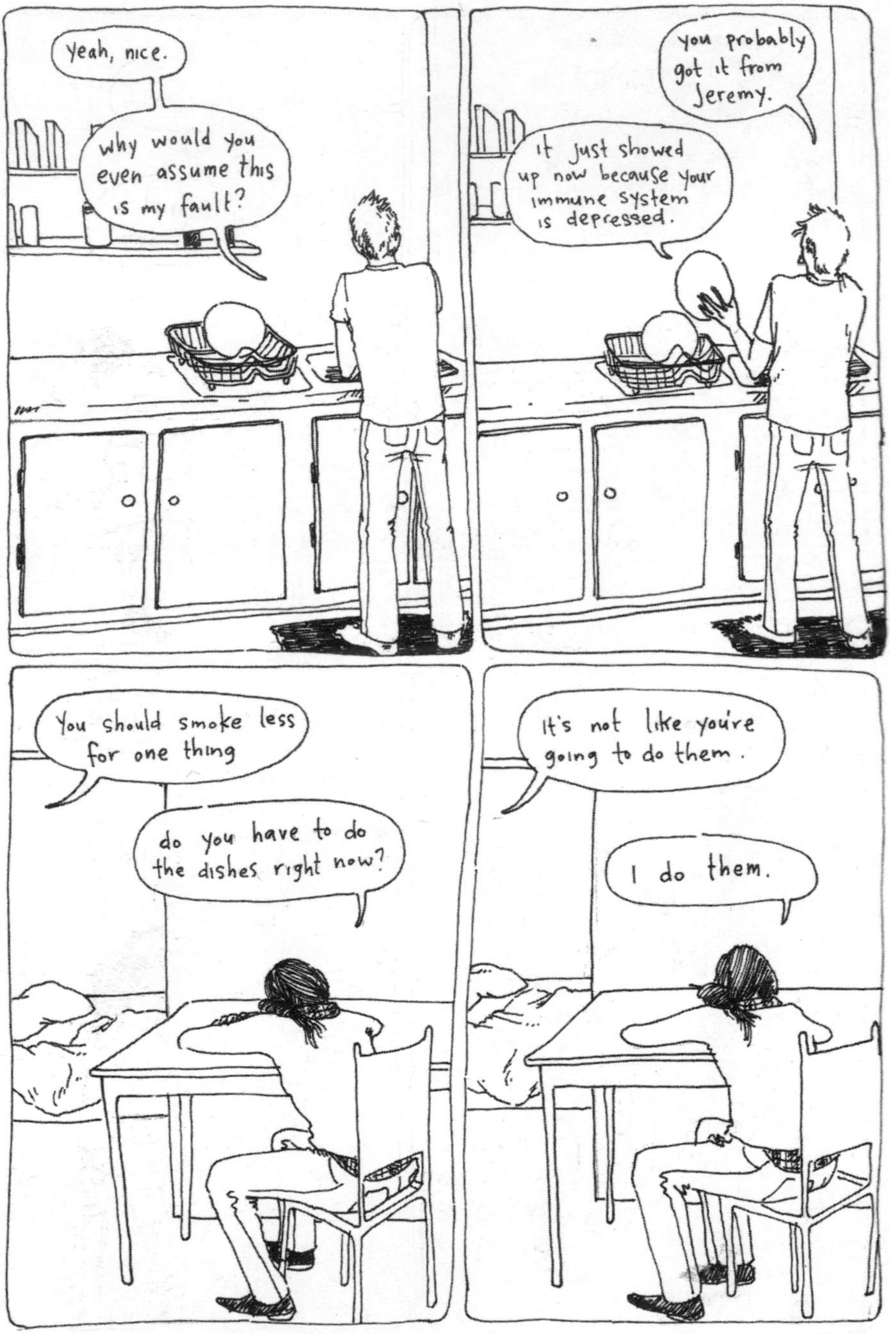
Yeah, nice.
why would you even assume this is my fault?
you probably got it from Jeremy.
It just showed up now because your immune system is depressed.
You should smoke less for one thing
do you have to do the dishes right now?
It's not like you're going to do them.
I do them.

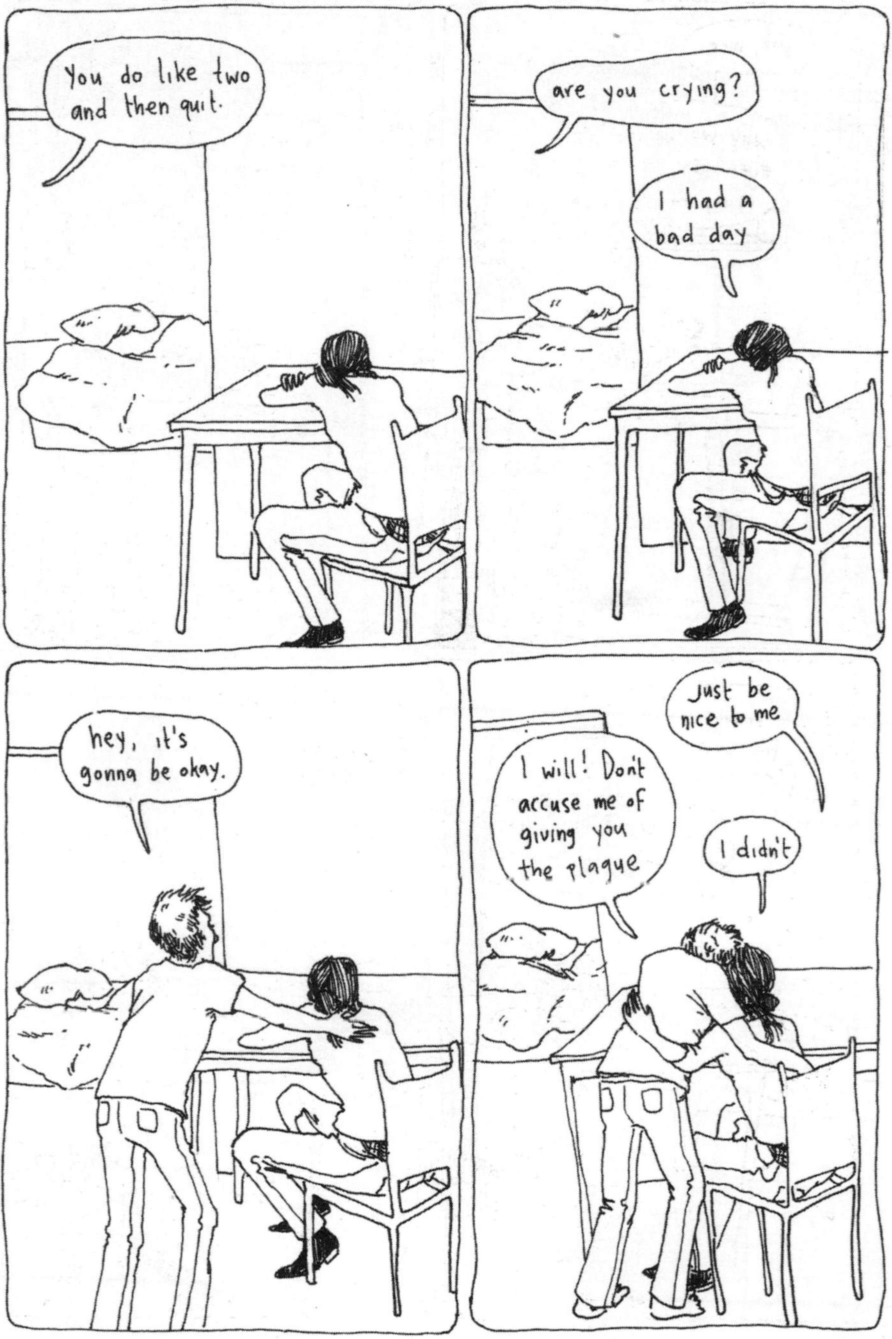
You do like two and then quit.
are you crying?
I had a bad day
hey, it's gonna be okay.
Just be nice to me
I will! Don't accuse me of giving you the plague
I didn't

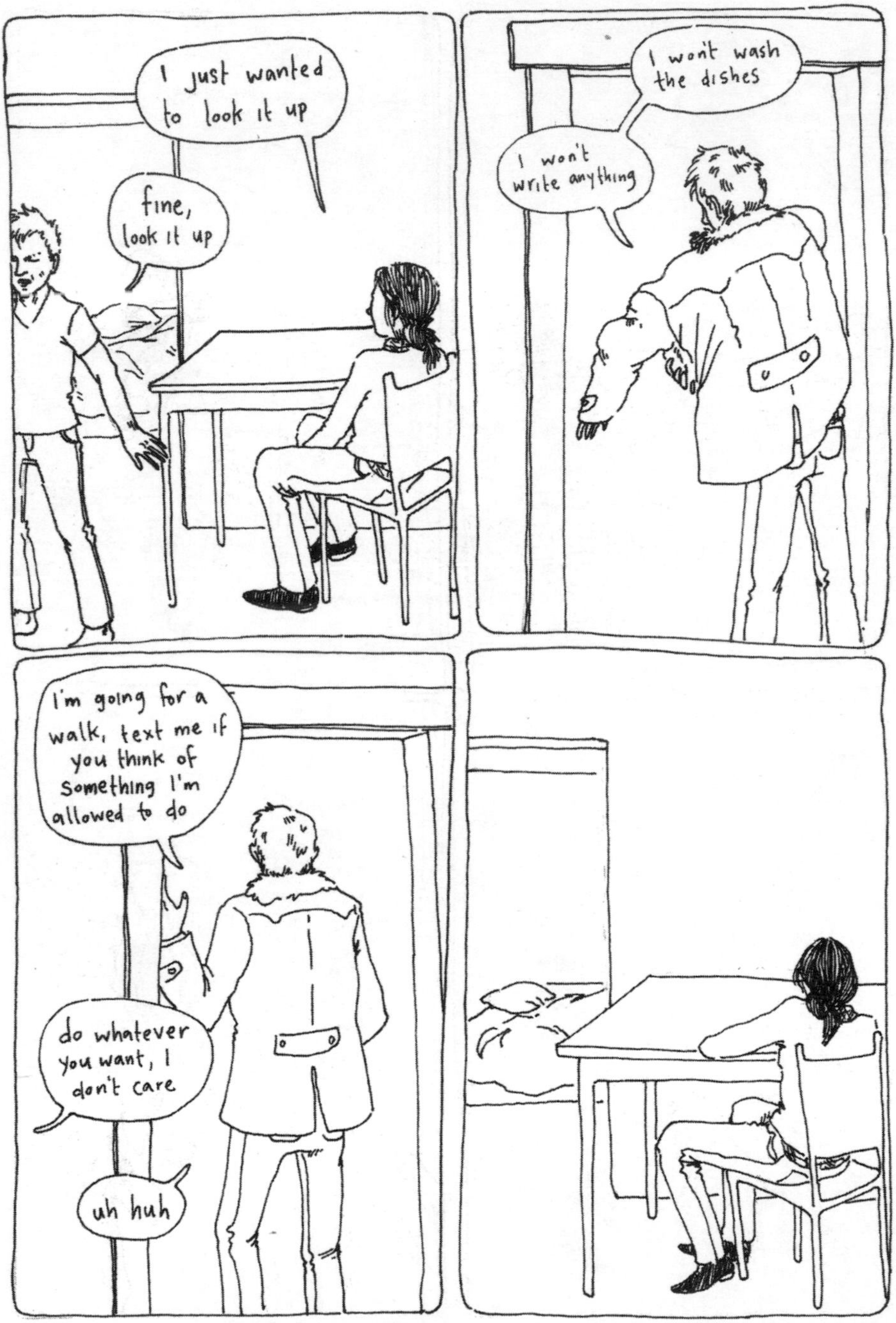
I just wanted to look it up
fine, look it up
I won't wash the dishes
I won't write anything
I'm going for a walk, text me if you think of something I'm allowed to do
do whatever you want, I don't care
uh huh

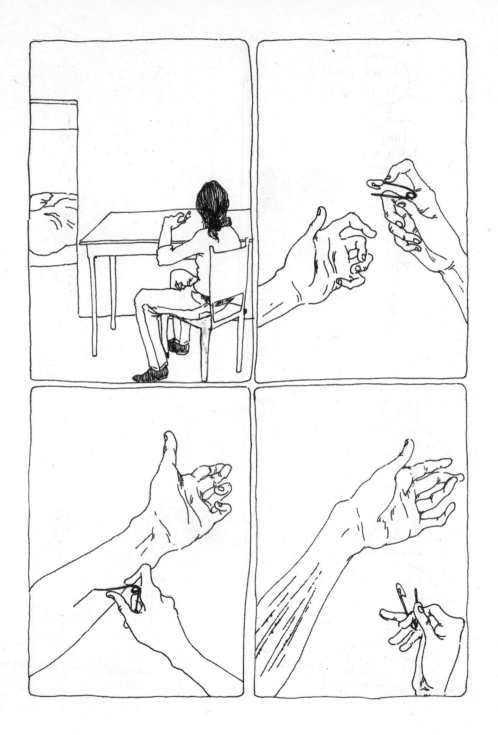

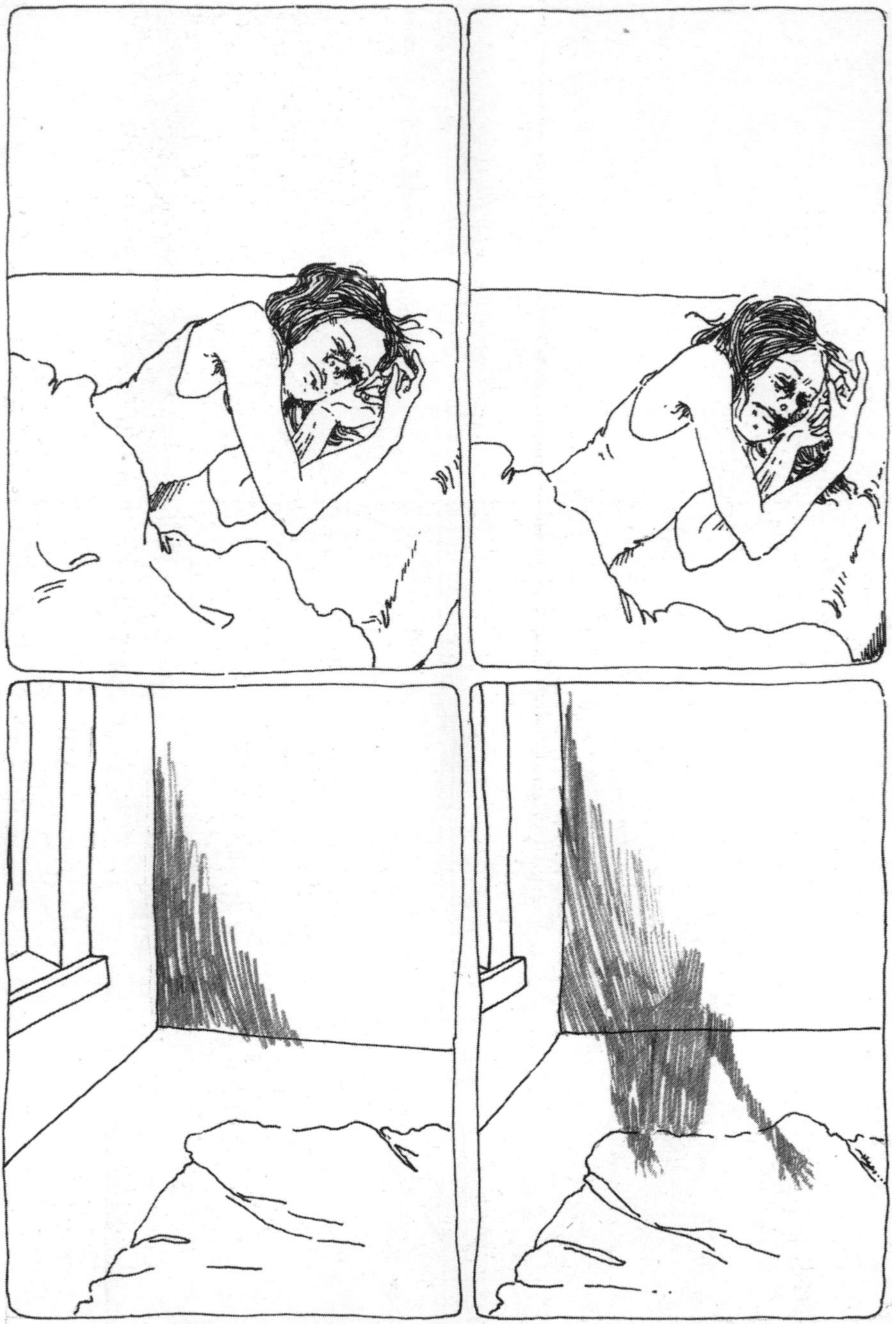

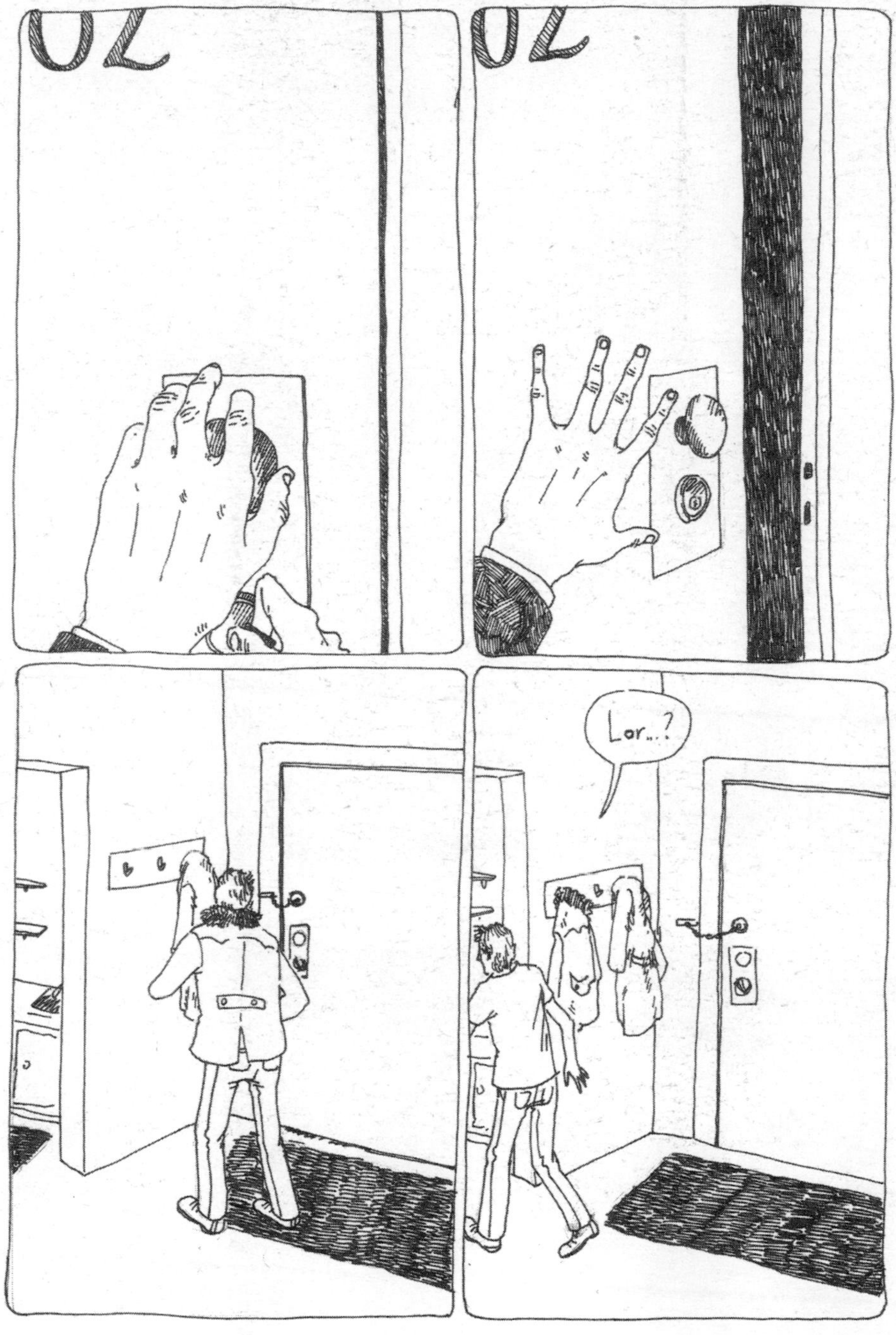
Lor...?

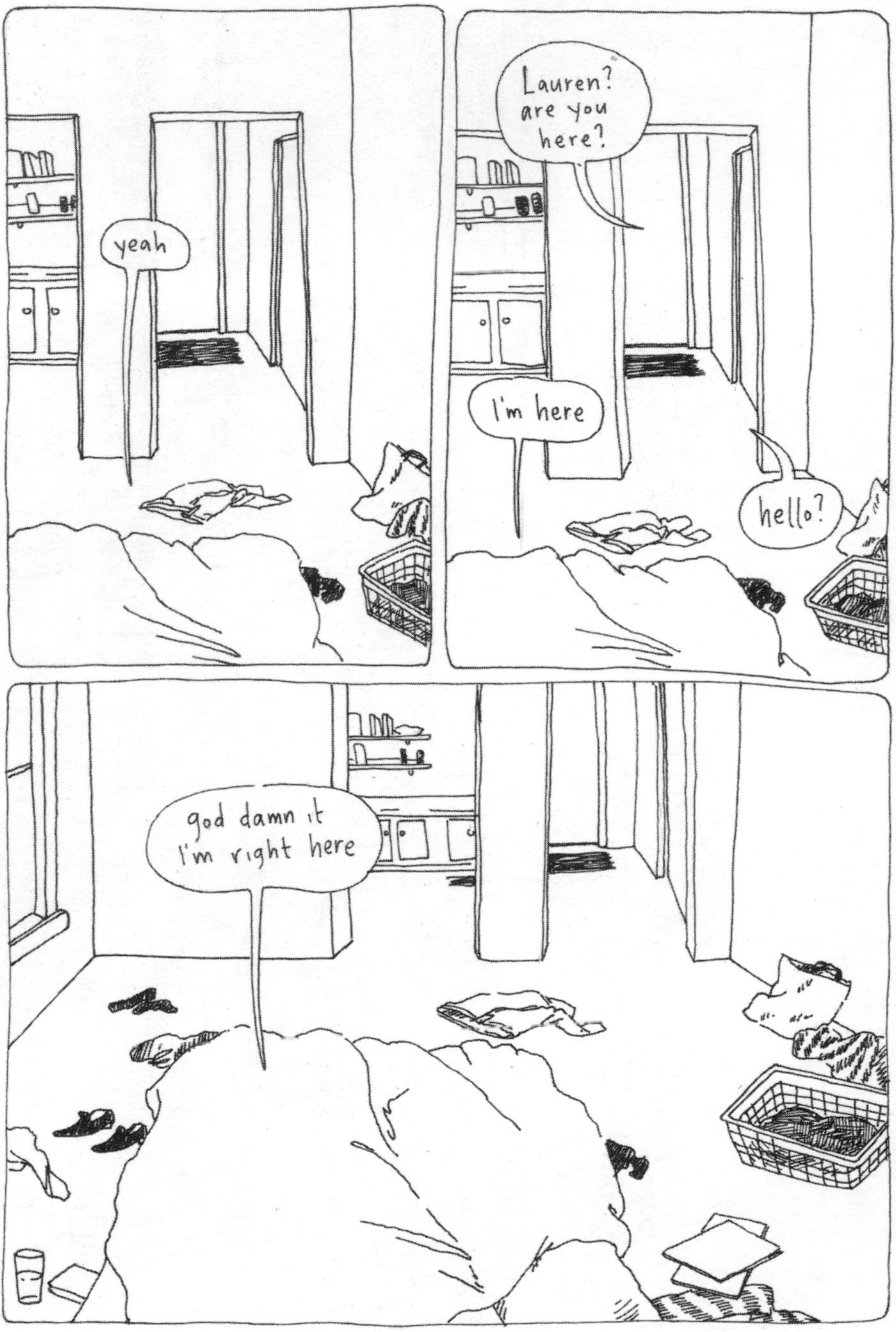
yeah
Lauren? are you here?
I'm here
hello?
god damn it I'm right here

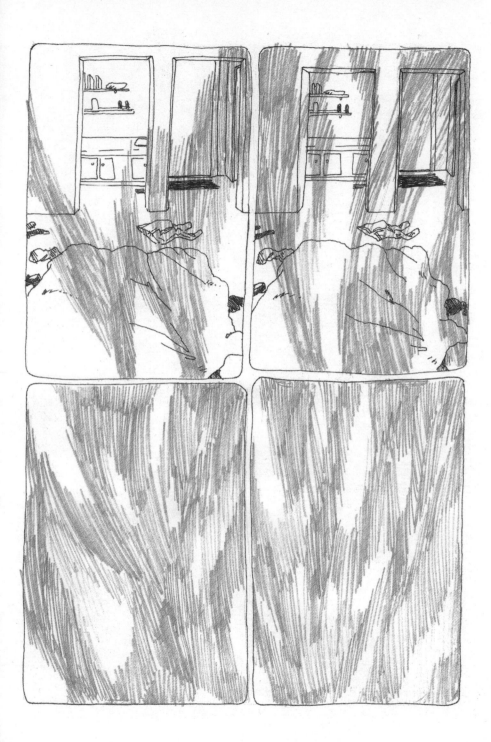

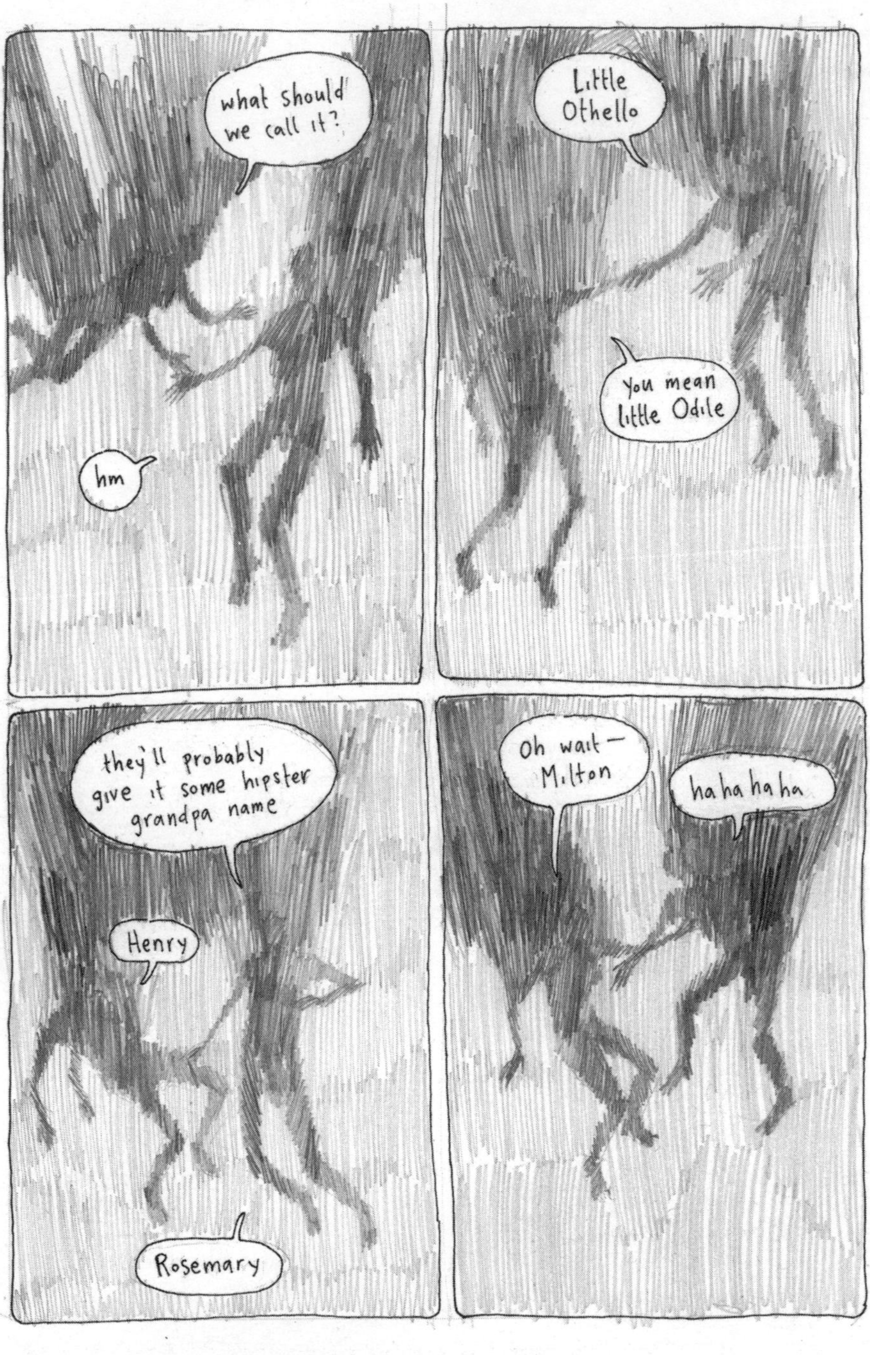
what should we call it?
hm
Little Othello
you mean little Odile
they'll probably give it some hipster grandpa name
Henry
Rosemary
Oh wait— Milton
ha ha ha ha

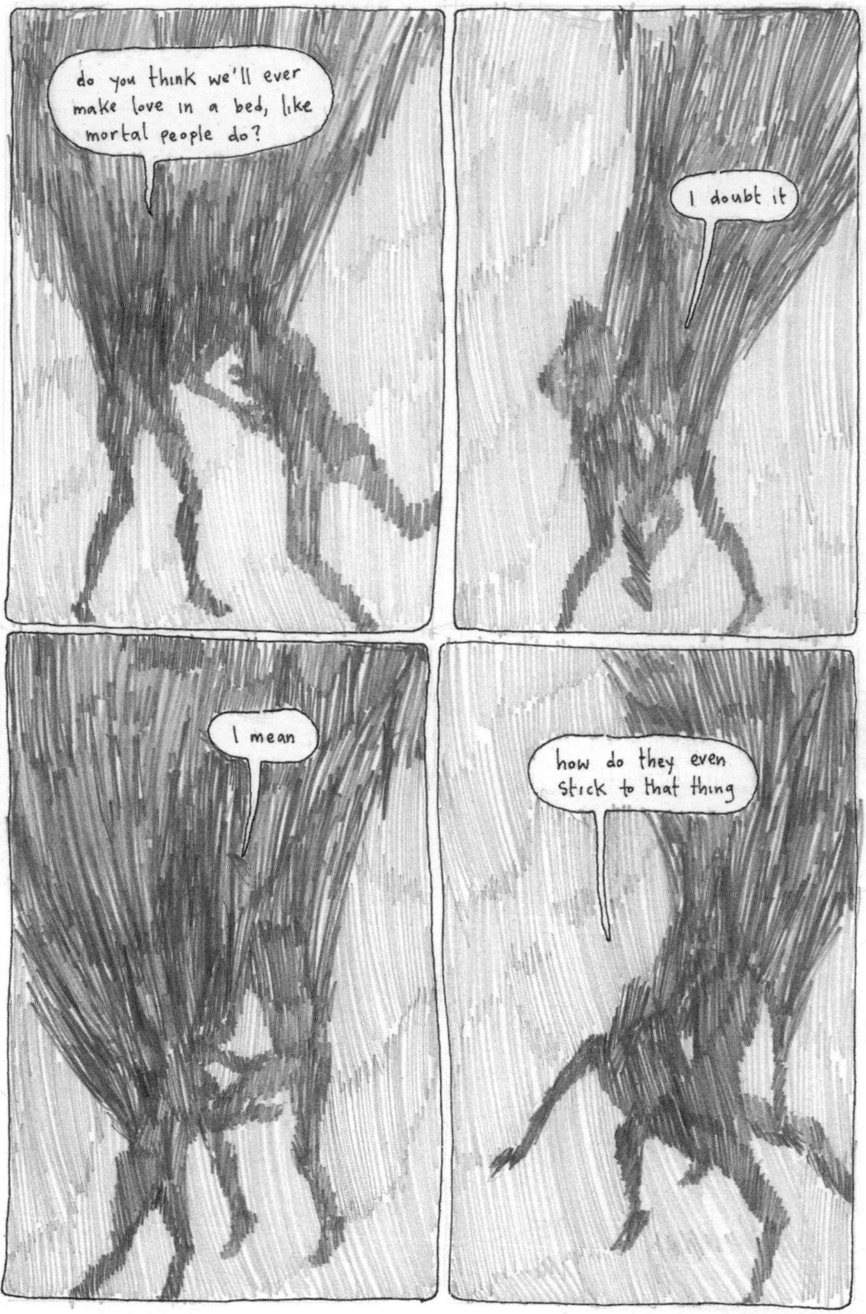
do you think we'll ever make love in a bed, like mortal people do?
I doubt it
I mean
how do they even stick to that thing

Too Dark to See by Julia Gfrörer © 2011

thank you Babyhawke, Knightrider, Neptune,
Zaphod, Renfro, Renfro, and Coffeehouse Northwest
for the inspiration, encouragement and support.

www. thorazos. net

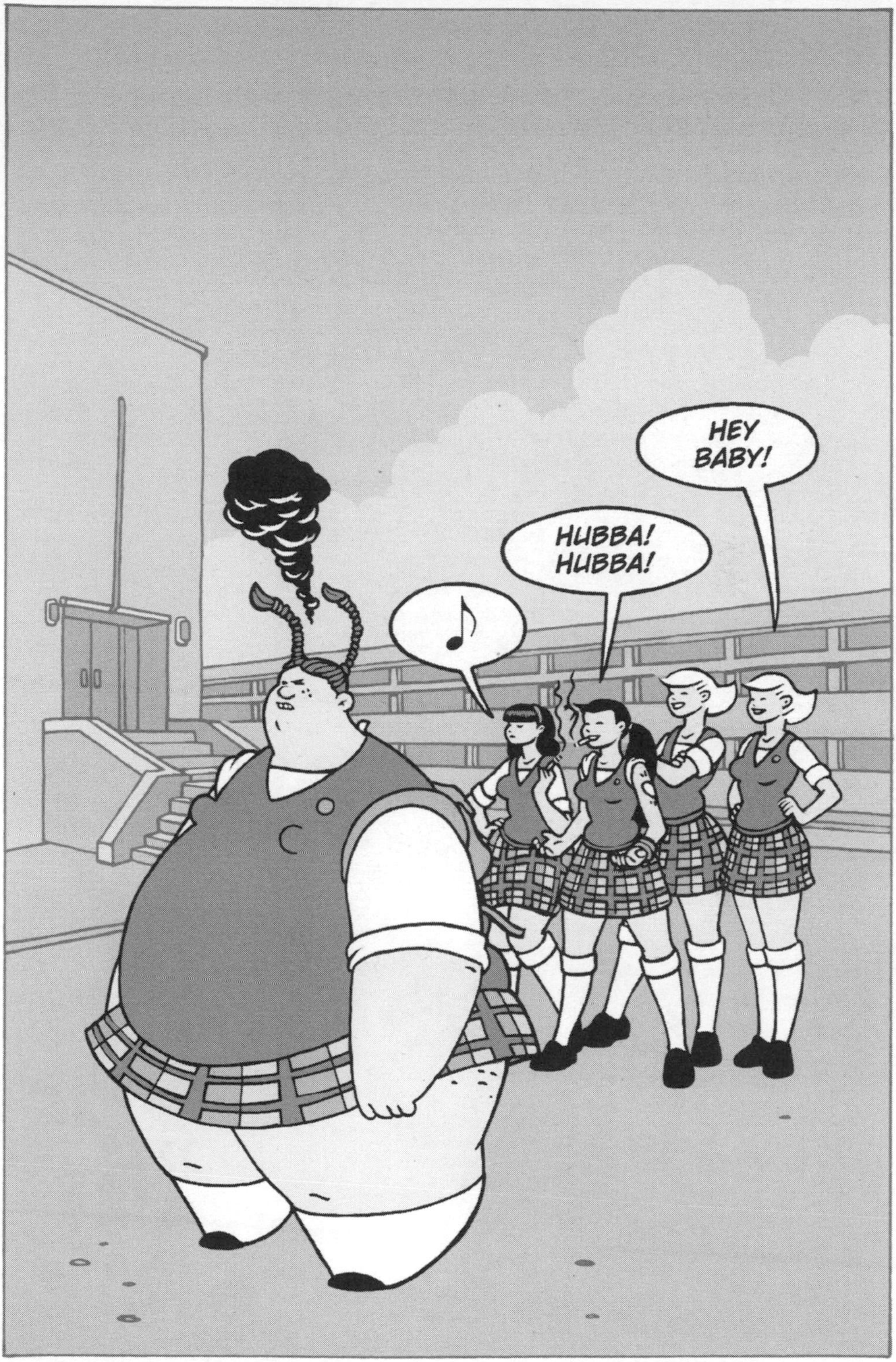
♪
HUBBA!
HUBBA!
HEY
BABY!

Karl Wills

JESSICA OF THE SCHOOLYARD

Self-published, 2001–06

"*Jessica* was created in 1995 when I was drawing a regular comic strip for a free monthly music magazine. It was a different character every month, whatever I felt like doing at the time: I had the idea to do *Tarzan of the Apes* crossed with *Grange Hill* (a TV drama set in a British state school from the early eighties), something totally over the top and silly. When I did the first strip, the character came out as a thug so I just went with that. She proved very popular so I did a few more then expanded it into a series of mini-comics based on the Tijuana Bible format.

"There were twelve books in total, all sold well, and in 2006 the last one, a special thirteenth book, came with an original music CD, where Jessica forms a pop band, The Jawbreakers. In 2008 I went [from New Zealand] to Los Angeles, to pitch it as an animated show, but that couldn't be done without turning it into something more palatable. There are no current plans to make new *Jessica* comics but I'm sorting out making a collected book.

"My main project now is drawing and co-writing (with Tim Kidd) a medieval fantasy comic called *Holocaust Rex*, using the same format. It's an ongoing storyline and will eventually be released as a complete, 100-page plus graphic novel. There's more about that, and other stuff I work on, at my website." – KW

www.comicbookfactory.net

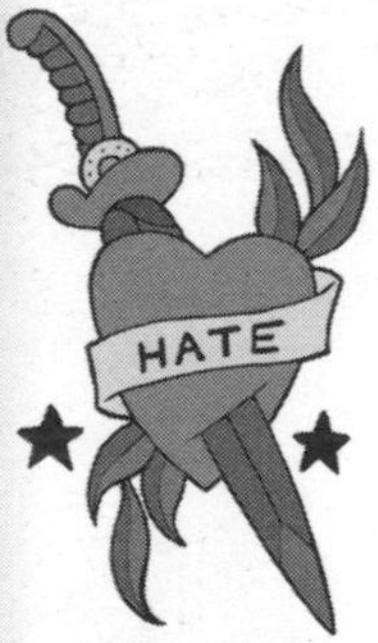
HATE

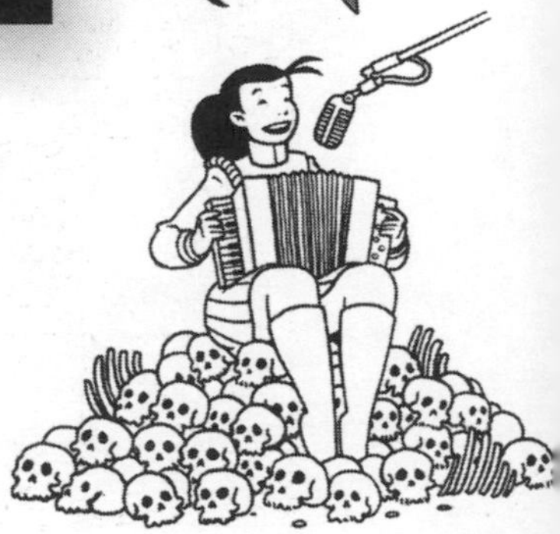

424 ☛ 433

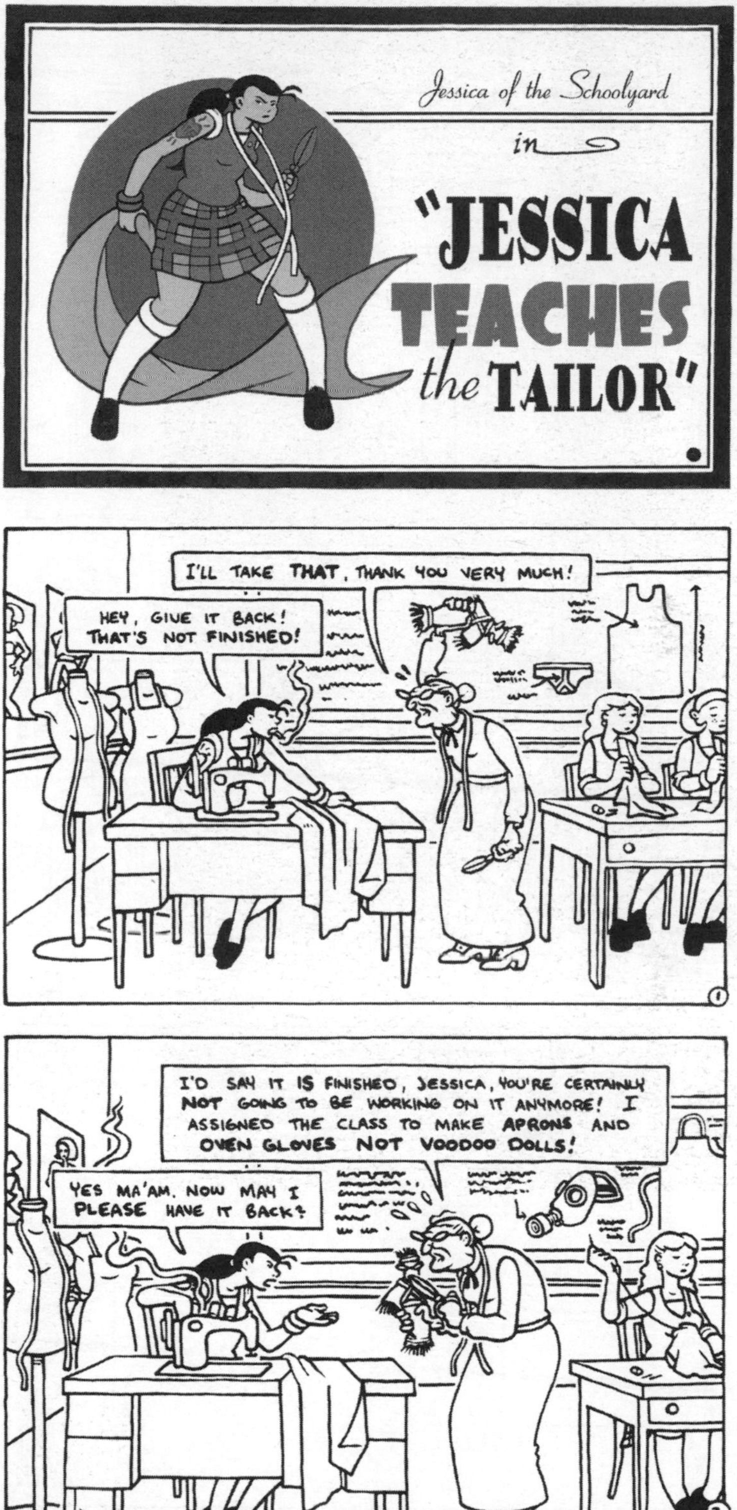
Jessica of the Schoolyard
in
"JESSICA TEACHES the TAILOR"
I'LL TAKE THAT, THANK YOU VERY MUCH!
HEY, GIVE IT BACK! THAT'S NOT FINISHED!
1
I'D SAY IT IS FINISHED, JESSICA, YOU'RE CERTAINLY NOT GOING TO BE WORKING ON IT ANYMORE! I ASSIGNED THE CLASS TO MAKE APRONS AND OVEN GLOVES NOT VOODOO DOLLS!
YES MA'AM. NOW MAY I PLEASE HAVE IT BACK?
2

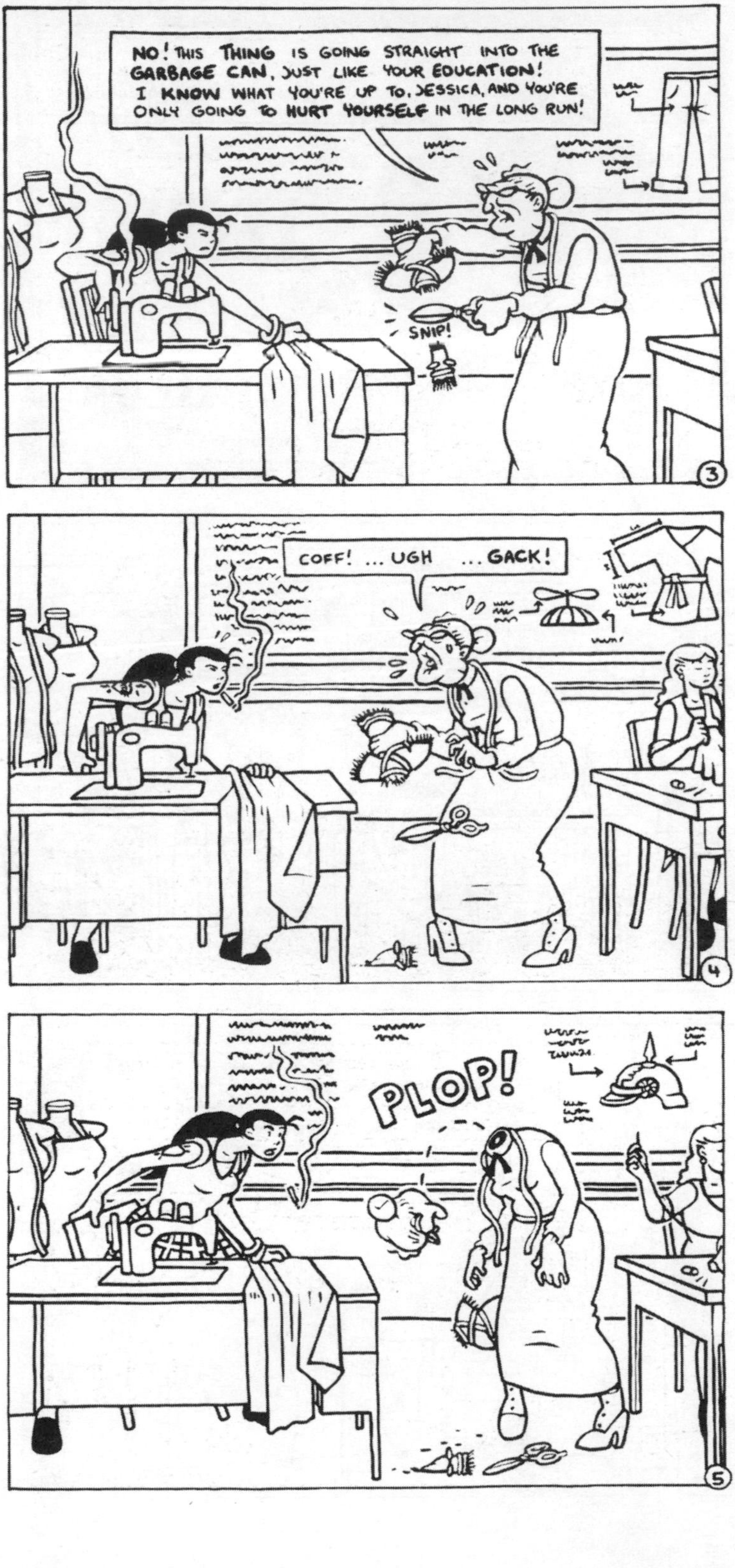
NO! THIS THING IS GOING STRAIGHT INTO THE GARBAGE CAN, JUST LIKE YOUR EDUCATION! I KNOW WHAT YOU'RE UP TO, JESSICA, AND YOU'RE ONLY GOING TO HURT YOURSELF IN THE LONG RUN!
SNIP!
3
COFF! ... UGH ... GACK!
4
PLOP!
5

SAY, I WONDER IF I CAN FIND THE ANSWERS TO NEXT WEEKS TEST IN HERE!
HOORAY FOR JESSICA!
HULLY GEE!
6
HOW ABOUT THAT! ...A NOTE FROM MY MOTHER!
AS THANKS FOR LIBERATING US FROM MISS STUDEBAKERS OPPRESIVE REGIME HERE IS A MILLION DOLLARS!
7
MEANWHILE --
THESE ARE THE WORST LOOKING OVEN GLOVES I HAVE EVER SEEN! THEY LOOK MORE LIKE BOXING GLOVES! JESSICA, ARE YOU DELIBERATELY TRYING TO FAIL MY CLASS?! JESSICA?!
©KUTTLS 25·05·02
8

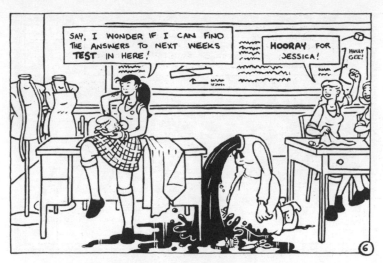

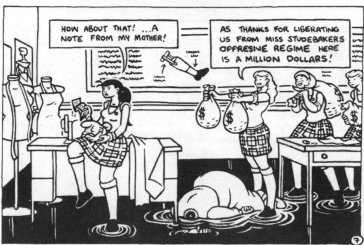

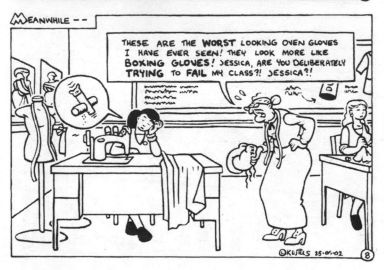

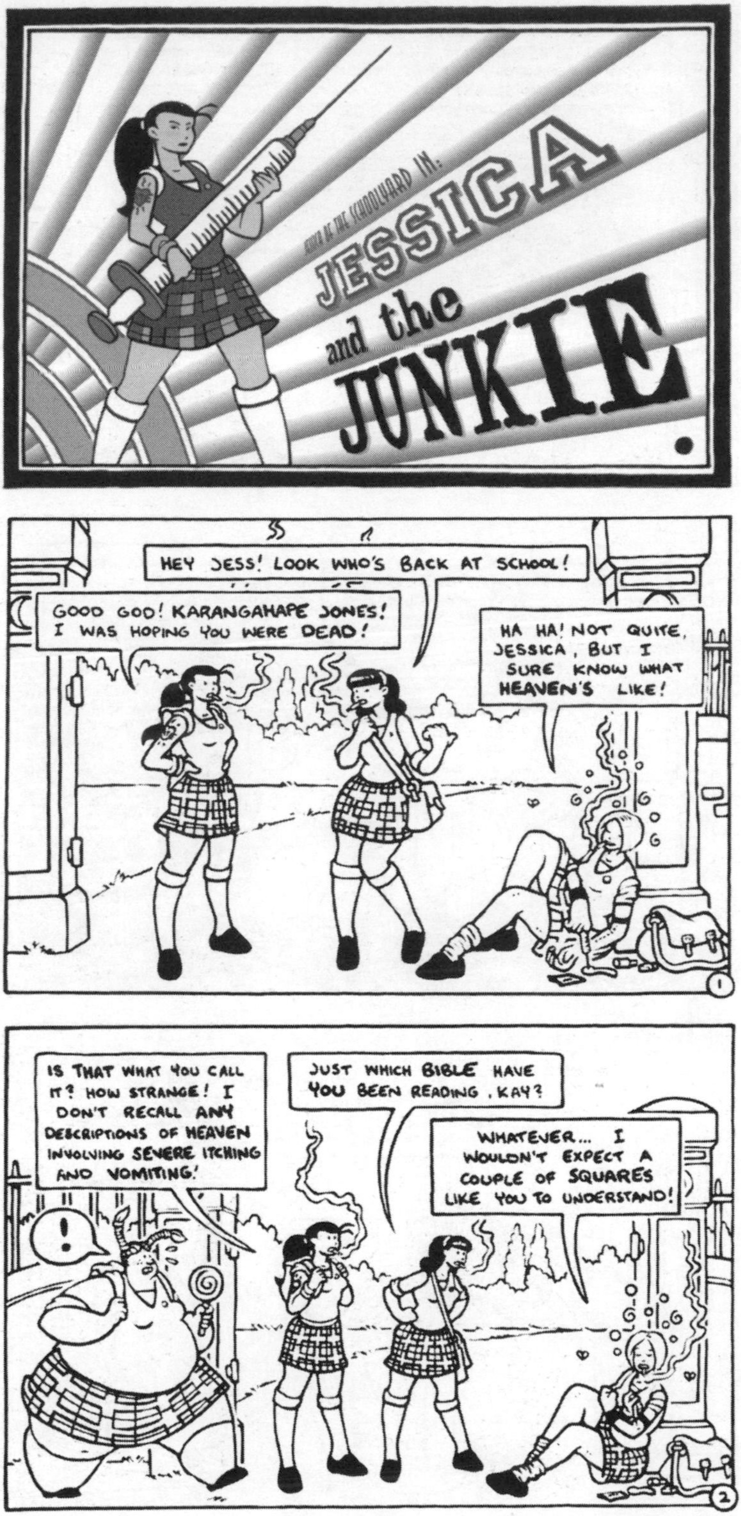
OF THE SCHOOLYARD IN:
JESSICA
and the
JUNKIE.
HEY JESS! LOOK WHO'S BACK AT SCHOOL!
GOOD GOD! KARANGAHAPE JONES! I WAS HOPING YOU WERE DEAD!
HA HA! NOT QUITE, JESSICA, BUT I SURE KNOW WHAT HEAVEN'S LIKE!
1
IS THAT WHAT YOU CALL IT? HOW STRANGE! I DON'T RECALL ANY DESCRIPTIONS OF HEAVEN INVOLVING SEVERE ITCHING AND VOMITING!
JUST WHICH BIBLE HAVE YOU BEEN READING, KAY?
WHATEVER... I WOULDN'T EXPECT A COUPLE OF SQUARES LIKE YOU TO UNDERSTAND!
!
2

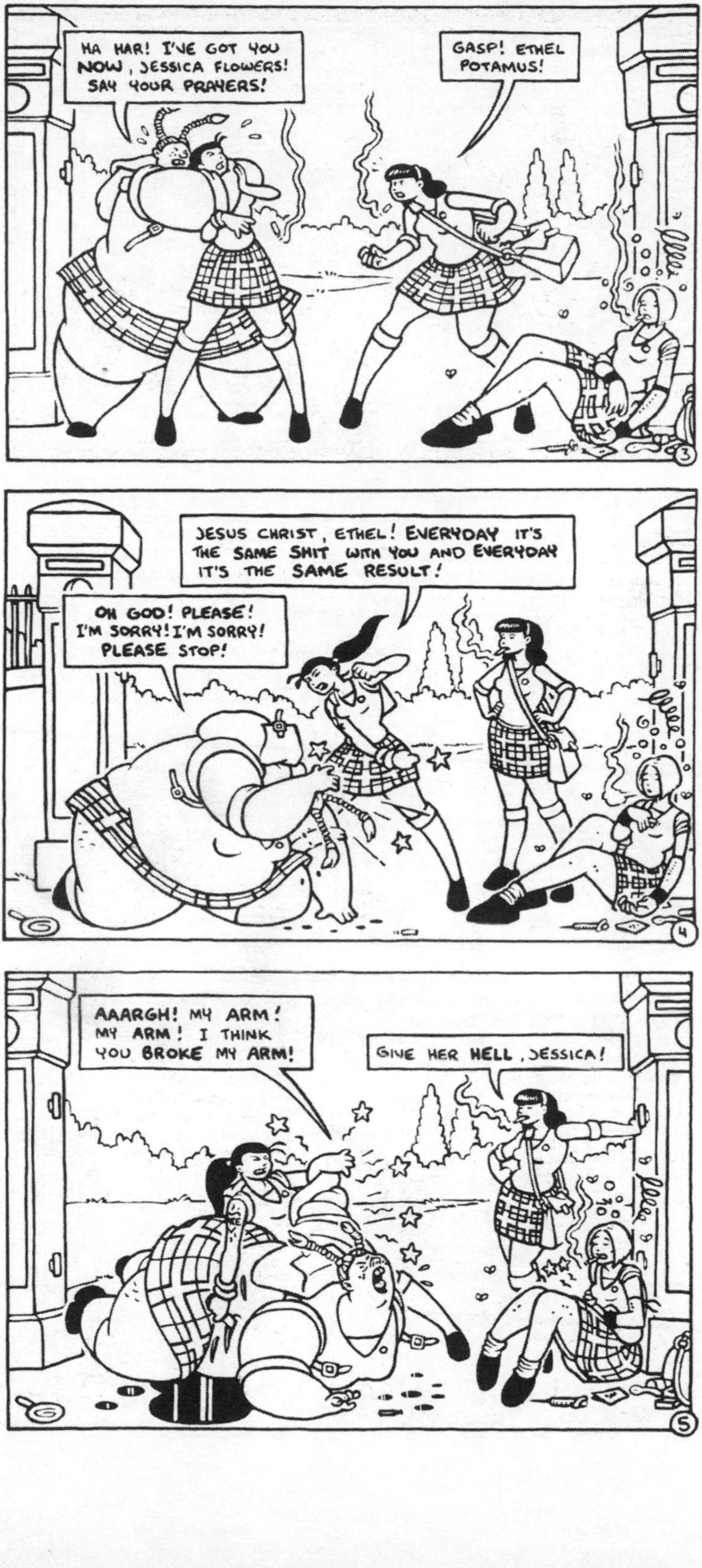
HA HAR! I'VE GOT YOU NOW, JESSICA FLOWERS! SAY YOUR PRAYERS!
GASP! ETHEL POTAMUS!
3
JESUS CHRIST, ETHEL! EVERYDAY IT'S THE SAME SHIT WITH YOU AND EVERYDAY IT'S THE SAME RESULT!
OH GOD! PLEASE! I'M SORRY! I'M SORRY! PLEASE STOP!
4
AAARGH! MY ARM! MY ARM! I THINK YOU BROKE MY ARM!
GIVE HER HELL, JESSICA!
5

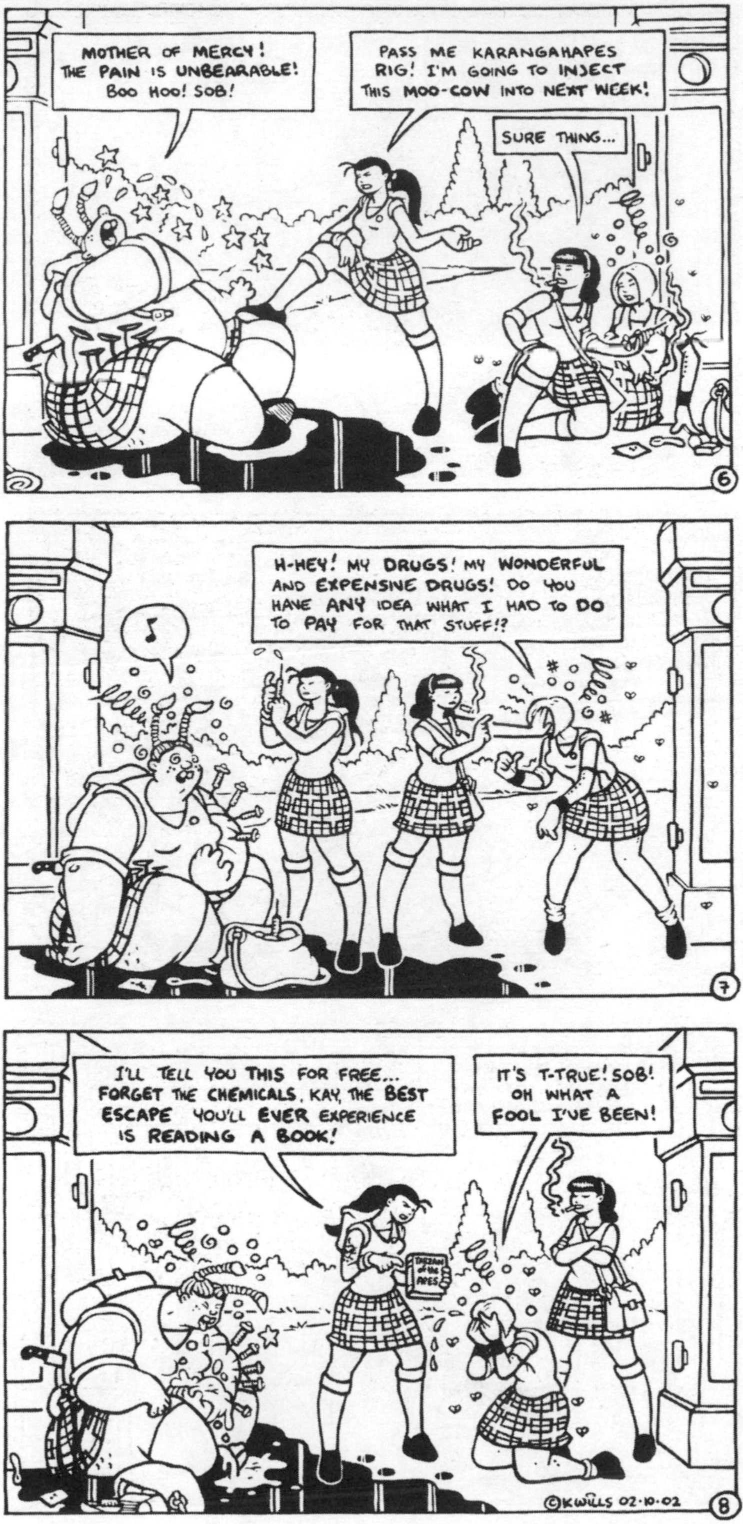
MOTHER OF MERCY! THE PAIN IS UNBEARABLE! BOO HOO! SOB!
PASS ME KARANGAHAPES RIG! I'M GOING TO INJECT THIS MOO-COW INTO NEXT WEEK!
SURE THING...
6
H-HEY! MY DRUGS! MY WONDERFUL AND EXPENSIVE DRUGS! DO YOU HAVE ANY IDEA WHAT I HAD TO DO TO PAY FOR THAT STUFF!?
7
I'LL TELL YOU THIS FOR FREE... FORGET THE CHEMICALS, KAY, THE BEST ESCAPE YOU'LL EVER EXPERIENCE IS READING A BOOK!
IT'S T-TRUE! SOB! OH WHAT A FOOL I'VE BEEN!
TARZAN of the APES
©KWILLS 02·10·02
8

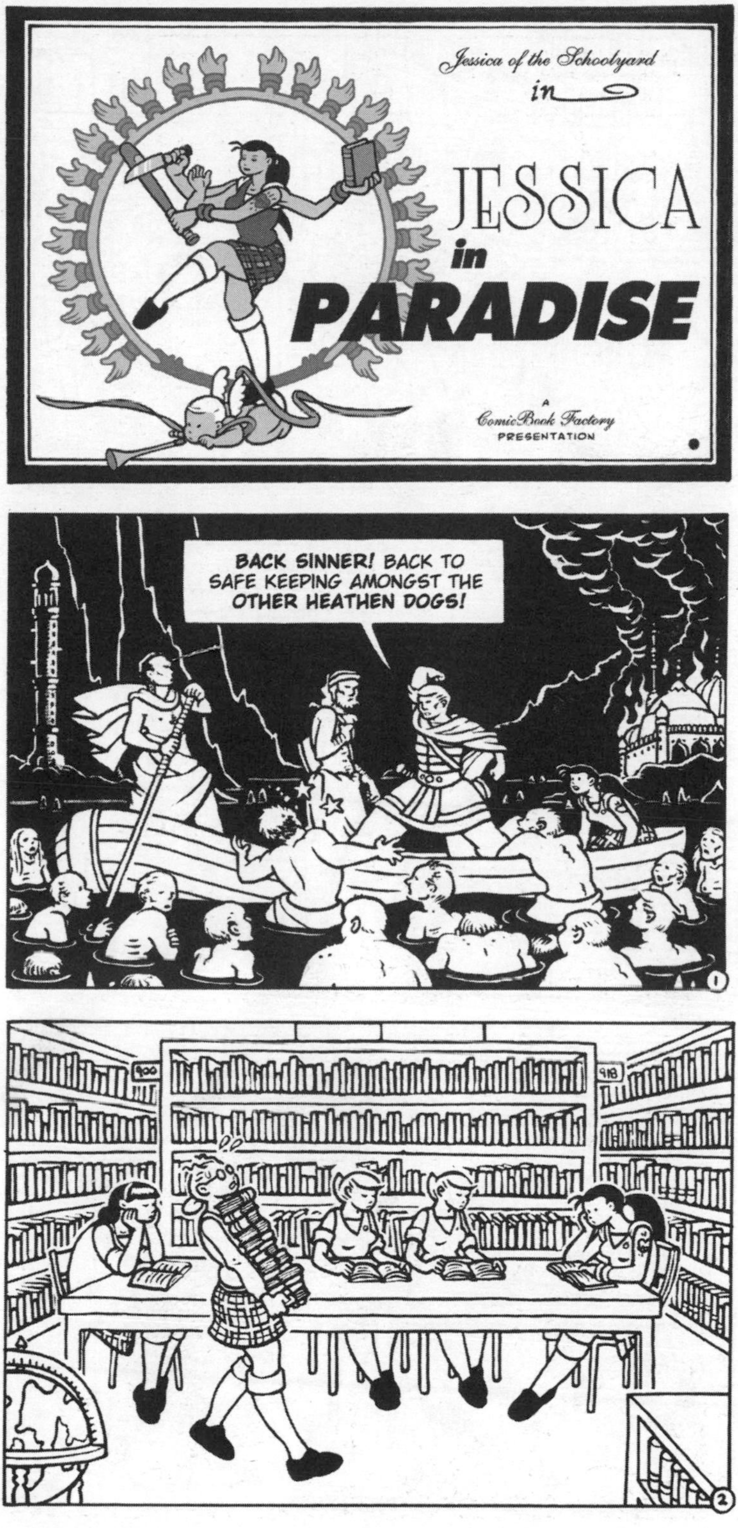
Jessica of the Schoolyard
in
JESSICA
in
PARADISE
A
ComicBook Factory
PRESENTATION
BACK SINNER! BACK TO SAFE KEEPING AMONGST THE OTHER HEATHEN DOGS!

OH!
HEY! SHUT UP DOWN THERE!
THIS IS A LIBRARY...
...NOT A NURSERY!
WHAT A PERFORMANCE!
BOO HOO HOO! BOO HOO HOO!
OKAY... YOU CAN TAKE IT OUTSIDE NOW FOUR-EYES, YOUR FIFTEEN SECONDS IS UP!

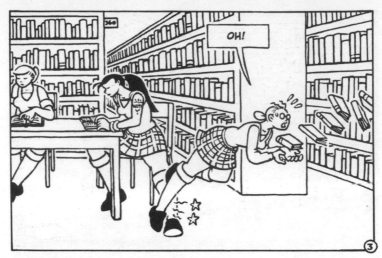

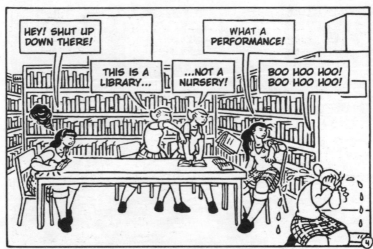

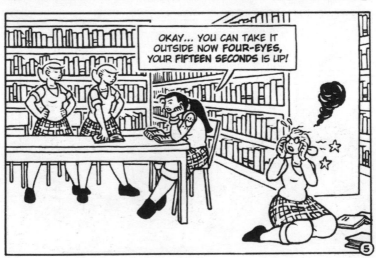

599-73
PTUH!
6
6 MONTHS LATER --
HEY JESSICA! LOOK WHO'S FINALLY OUT OF HOSPITAL AND BACK AT SCHOOL!
PLEASE DON'T HURT ME!
HALLELUJAH!
SNAP!
7
©Kwilus 15.09.03
POOR WENDY! DO YOU THINK WE SHOULD HELP HER?
I'M HELPING BY NOT HELPING!
8

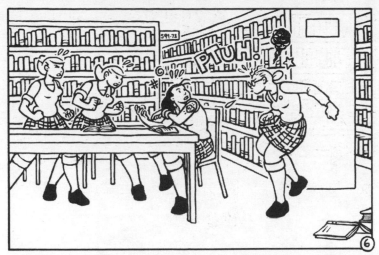

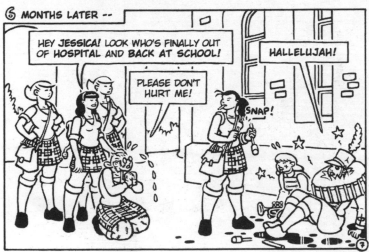

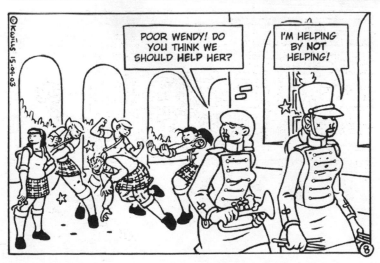

Tomasz Kaczynski

VAGUE CITIES
Cartoon Dialectics volume 2, self-published, 2011

Then: "2006. Brooklyn, NY. I'd been living in New York for a few years, working in advertising. I was part of a group of cartoonists that met weekly (Gabrielle Bell, Jon Lewis, Vanessa Davis ...). After completing three mini-comics (*Trans Alaska*, *Trans Siberia* and *Trans Atlantis*), I wanted to produce something new and very different for the next Alternative Press Expo in San Francisco. I came up with *Vague Cities*. I had recently re-read Italo Calvino's *Invisible Cities* and that was on my mind. The art pairs clean drafted lines (used for architecture and backgrounds) with a more organic brushed line (for the characters). This became my preferred mode of working for quite some time – a trial run for all of my future stories that ran in the *MOME* anthology, now collected in *Beta Testing The Apocalypse* (Fantagraphics, 2013)." – TK

Now: As founder of Uncivilized Books, Tom K has published Gabrielle Bell, David B., Jon Lewis, James Romberger, Joann Sfar, Sam Alden and many more – plus his new book, *Trans Terra*. He lives in Minneapolis with partner Nikki, two black cats and a golden retriever.

www.tomkaczynski.com
www.uncivilizedbooks.com

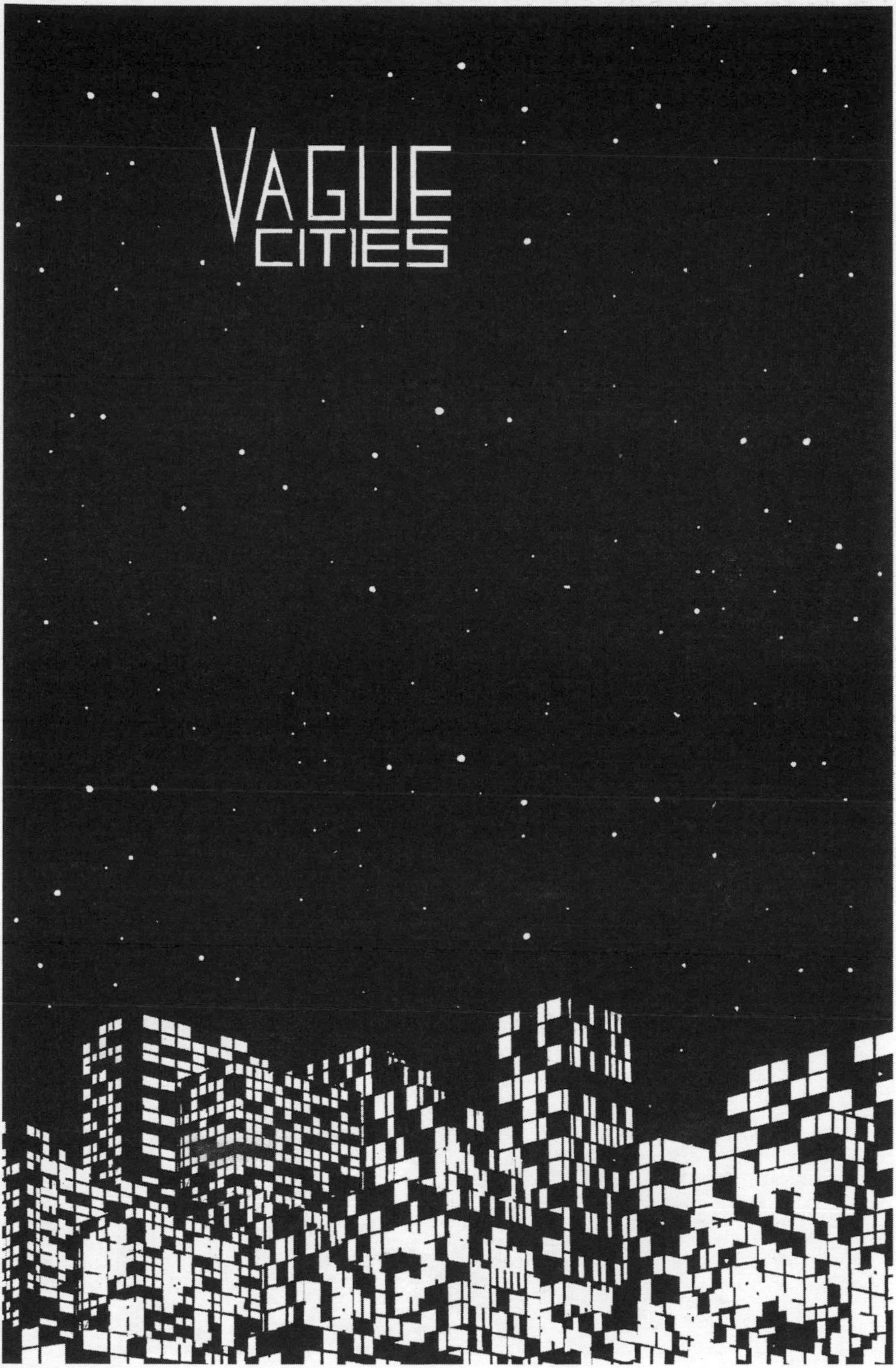
VAGUE
CITIES

FOR AEONS HUMANS HAVE BELIEVED THEIR LIVES TO BE AFFECTED BY THE SUBTLE INTERPLAY OF THE MYSTERIOUS FORCES THAT DETERMINE THE PATHS AND PATTERNS OF THE COUNTLESS STARS AND PLANETS THAT LIGHT UP THE NIGHT SKY.

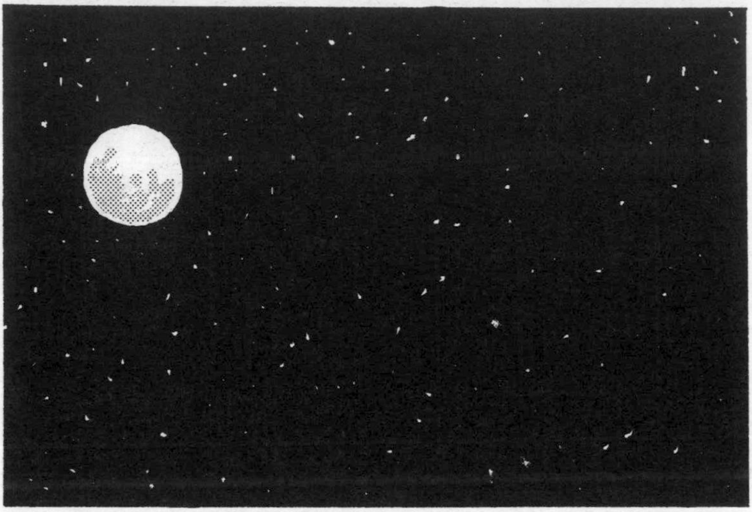

THE CITIZENS OF THE CURRENT AEON DON'T BELIEVE IN THE POWER OF STARS. THE STARS FOLLOW THEIR OWN RATIONAL COURSE AND ARE UNCONCERNED BY THE AFFAIRS OF MERE HUMANS.

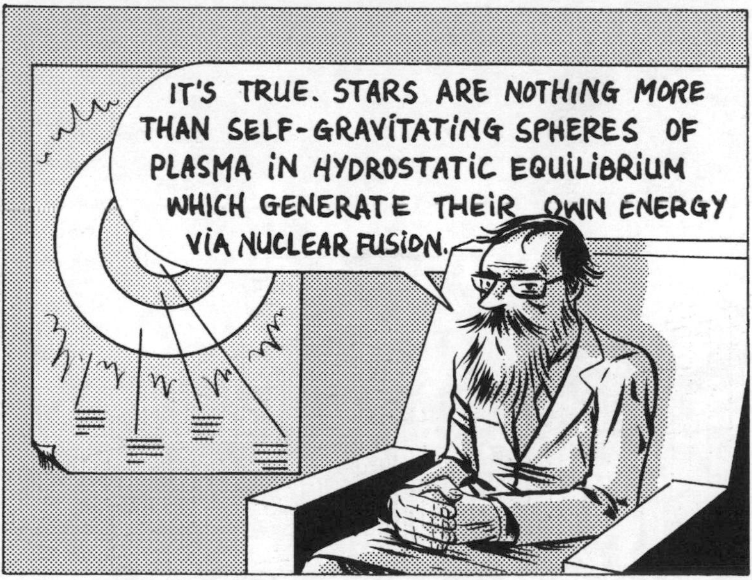
IT'S TRUE. STARS ARE NOTHING MORE THAN SELF-GRAVITATING SPHERES OF PLASMA IN HYDROSTATIC EQUILIBRIUM WHICH GENERATE THEIR OWN ENERGY VIA NUCLEAR FUSION.

THE CITIES THEY BUILD COMPETE WITH THE
HEAVENLY GLOW. AN ELECTRIC GAZE ILLUMINATES
THE DARKNESS WITH DESIRE AND AMBITION.
TOWERS OF LIGHT SCRAPE THE SKY.

THE NOCTURNAL DISPLAY DISSIPATES AT DAWN.
HUMBLED BY THE SUN, THE CITY RESUMES ITS
MUNDANE EXISTENCE.

BY DAY, BILLS HAVE TO BE PAID, MONEY HAS TO BE MADE, FOOD MUST BE EATEN, APPOINTMENTS KEPT. ALL TASKS ARE DIVIDED INTO SMALL PIECES. THE GARGANTUAN EFFORT OF CIVILIZATION IS MAPPED ONTO THE SMALLEST OF ACTIVITIES.

WHAT TASK WERE YOU ASSIGNED BY CIVILIZATION?

I CREATE JOBS.
I UPHOLD THE LAW.
I HAVE SEX.
I MAKE FOOD.
BUT I'M NOT DEFINED BY MY JOB!

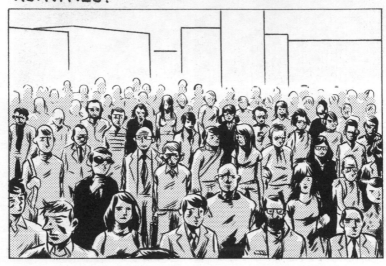

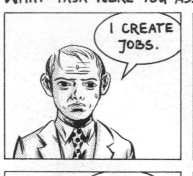

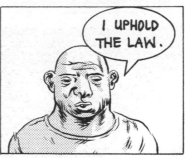

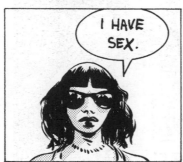

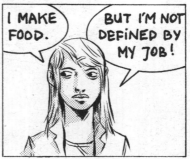

BY NIGHT THE MUNDANE GIVES WAY TO DREAM.
THE CITY IS RECREATED AS A SPECTRAL
LUMINESCENCE. FLICKERING ONTO THE
COLLECTIVE IMAGINATION.

ELECTRIFIED DESIRE DELUGES THE STREETS
SOME CITIZENS TRANSFORM. SATURATED BY
FLOURESCENT ENERGY THEY BECOME RADIANT
ENTITIES. STARS.

OTHERS, SEDUCED BY THE INTIMATE WARMTH OF CATHODE RAYS, DIODES, LEDs AND PLASMA EMISSIONS, ENTER HYPNOGOGIC REALMS OF THE UNREAL. ANOTHER KIND OF TRANSFORMATION.

HA
HA
HA

WHAT DO YOU DREAM OF BECOMING?

A STAR.
A MILLIONAIRE.
A WIZARD.
AN ARTIST.

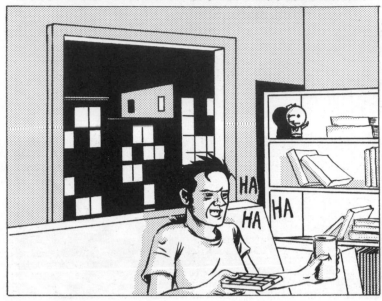

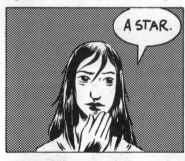

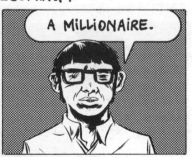

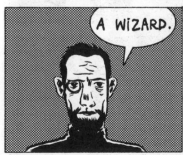

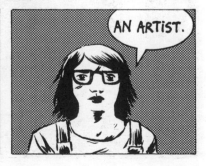

IN THE LIMINAL LIGHT OF THE EARLY MORNING THE NOCTURNAL EVENTS ACQUIRE THE PATINA OF MEMORY. TINGED WITH UNCERTAIN REGRET THE REVERIE OF THE MOMENT COLLIDES WITH REALITY.

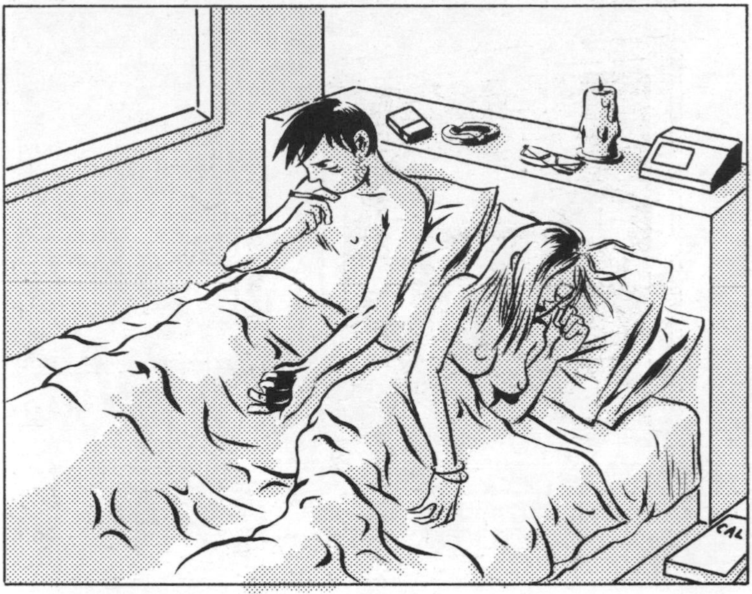
CAL

THE STUPOR OF A DAY'S LABOR DISSOLVES UNDER THE SPECTACULAR (THOUGH RARELY SEEN IN THE CITY) DISPLAY OF THE SETTING SUN. THIS IS THE MOMENT WHEN THE CITIZENS OF THE CITY QUESTION THEIR COMMITMENT TO CIVILIZATION.

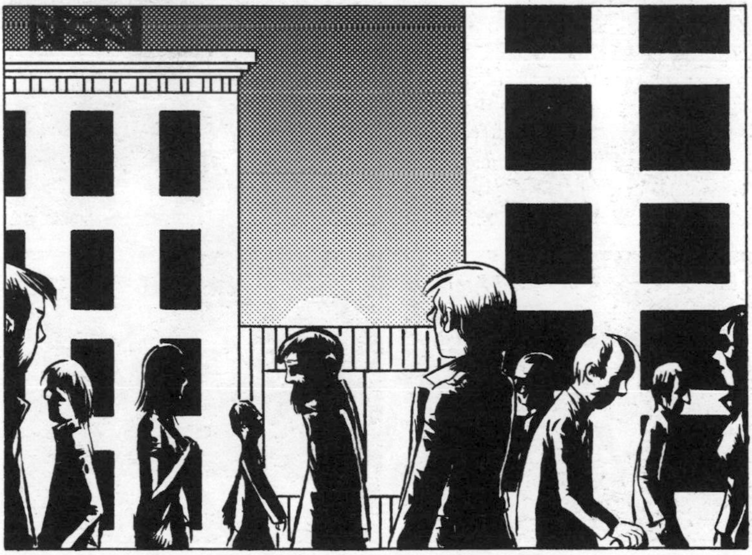

THESE MOMENTS OF TWILIGHT REFLECTION AND QUESTIONING UNCOVER THE FISSURES IN THE RATIONAL FOUNDATIONS OF DAILY ROUTINE. THE CITY IS REVEALED TO BE MEANINGLESS AND FORMLESS.

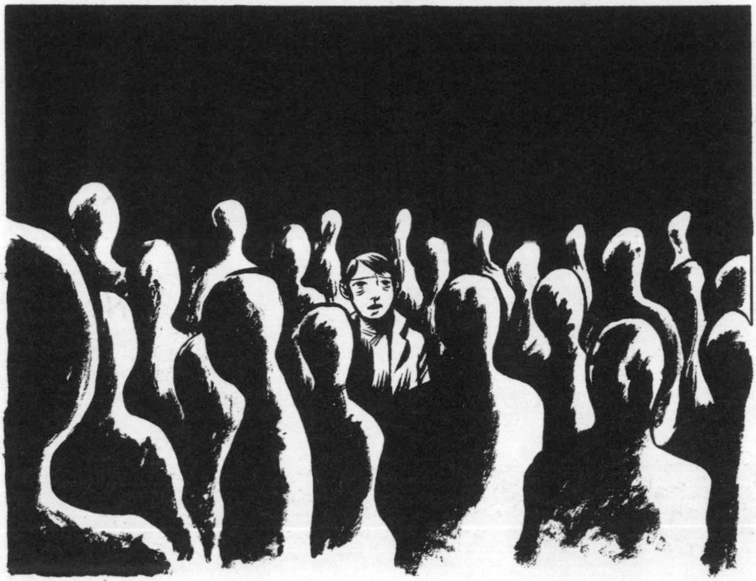

AS WHOLE NEW TERRITORIES OF THE IRRATIONAL BECOME ILLUMINATED, THE ARTIFICIAL SPECTACLE OF THE CITY DIMS BY COMPARISON. THE CITIZENS ONCE AGAIN TURN THEIR GAZE TO THE STARS.

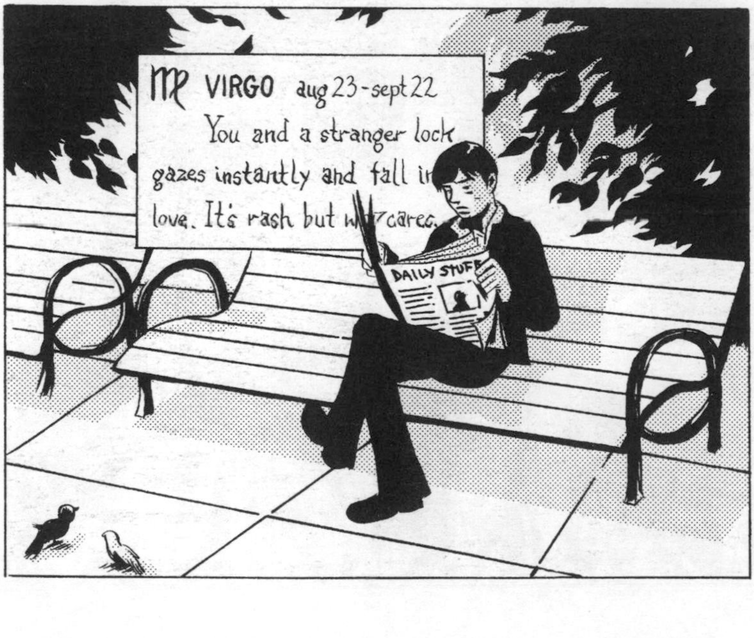
VIRGO aug 23-sept 22
You and a stranger lock gazes instantly and fall i
love. It's rash but
cares.
DAILY STUFF

DO YOU WANT TO LEAVE THE CITY?

AFTER YEARS IN THE GLARING CITY LIGHT, THE CITIZENS BEGIN TO PLAN THEIR ESCAPE. SOME TRAVEL TO DISTANT LOCATIONS, SEDUCED BY THE PROSPECT OF AN UNSPOILED INFINITE HORIZON.

BY THE TIME THEY RETURN TO SETTLE IN SOLITUDE THEY FIND THE HORIZON GONE, REPLACED BY ANOTHER CITY, IDENTICAL TO THE ONE THEY LEFT.

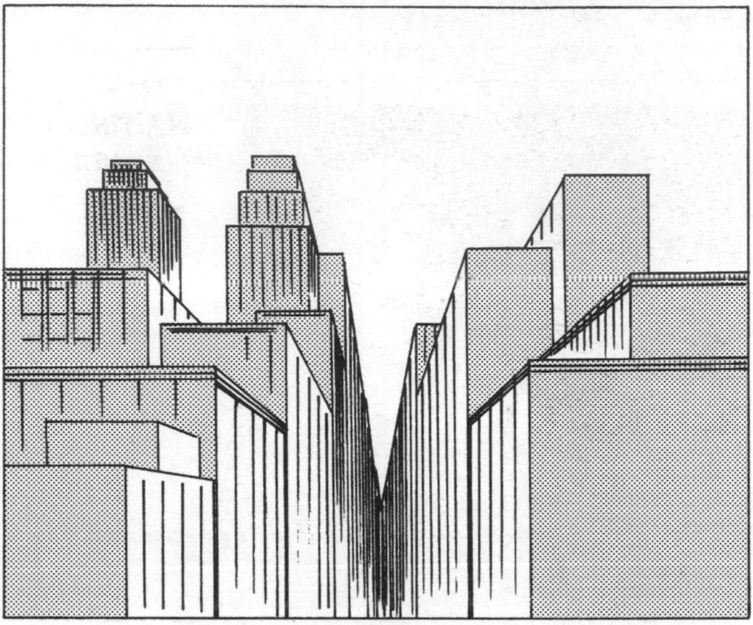

AND THE STARS ARE EVEN FEWER THAN BEFORE.

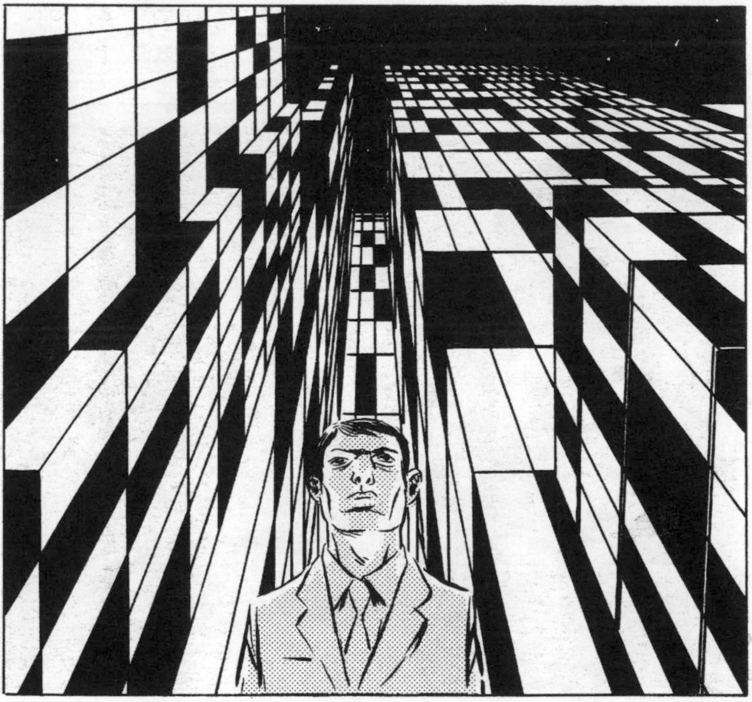

OTHERS REMAIN IN PLACE AND WAIT WITH UNCERTAIN FATALISM FOR SOMETHING TO HAPPEN, FOR SOMETHING TO EXTRACT THEM FROM THIS EMPTY ENLIGHTMENT.

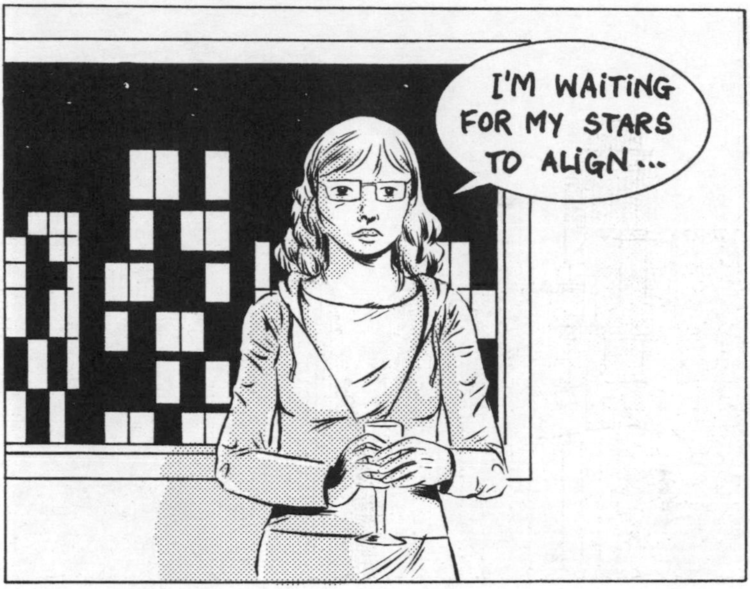
I'M WAITING FOR MY STARS TO ALIGN...

BUT THE STARS, REDUCED TO BLOBS OF PLASMA, HAVE LOST THEIR ANCIENT ABILITY TO ALIGN. THE ON/OFF FLICKER OF LIGHT BULBS IS NOT A SUBSTITUTE.

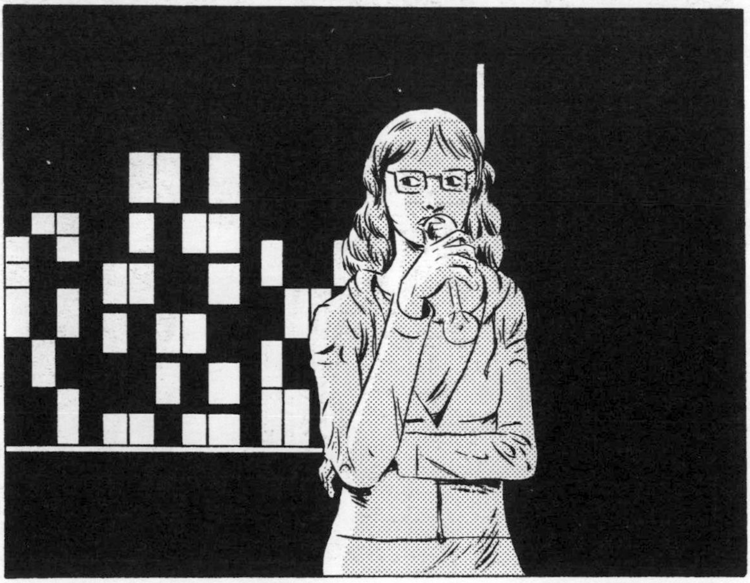

OCCASIONALLY, DUE TO THE INEFFICIENCIES OF ITS HYPER-EFFICIENT SYSTEM OF ORGANIZATION, OR DUE TO PURE ACCIDENT, THE CITY PLUNGES INTO A PRIMORDIAL DARKNESS.

OH...

THE UNDILUTED NIGHT IS AN UNEXPECTED PLEASURE.

WOW...
THIS IS NICE BUT I'VE SEEN BETTER
IT'S BEAUTIFUL
AWESOME

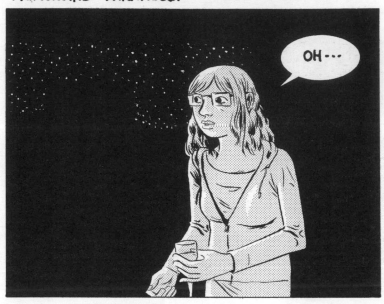

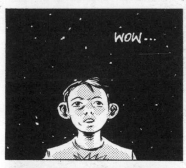

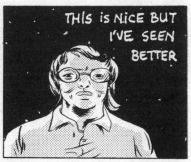

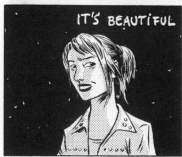

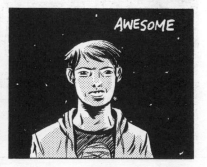

ONCE THE CITIZENS' EYES ADJUST TO THE ASTRAL DARKNESS, A NEW KIND OF VISION EMERGES. CHANCE, MYTH, MYSTERY AND DESTINY ARE THE FALLOUT OF THE COSMIC RADIANCE. STARS ALIGN ONCE AGAIN IN NEW AND UNUSUAL PATTERNS. ANYTHING IS POSSIBLE...

...AT LEAST UNTIL THE LIGHTS RETURN.

end

Howard Stangroom – with (1) Eddie Campbell, (2) Pete Martin and (3) Steve Whitaker

PANDORA

Howard Stangroom has been writing comics criticism, journalism and occasionally even strips since reform school in 1972. Nowadays he sells them, from 30th Century Comics in Putney.

Page-length *Pandora* appeared in dozens of fanzines, small-press and occasionally even mainstream comics (such as Charlton's *Scary Tales* # 38) throughout the 1980s and early 1990s. American reviewer Cara Sherman Tereno observed, "It's a neat play on her name – all-gifted, she gives, but what she gives is not necessarily what the seeker wants." Her creator sums it up more simply: "She's Bizarro Mary Poppins" – HS

ILYA

HERR SHITE
Speakeasy sexologist, as according to ILYA

ILYA

HOLIDAY SKETCHBOOK
Speech Defects, self-published, 1987

Steve Whitaker

SHANE & GAIL
Dream Logic, co-publication with Nick Abadzis, 1991

Inside front cover illustrations: Clockwise from top left – Gregory Benton's *Hummingbird*, the never-released second issue; *Jessica of the Schoolyard* rules the world, according to NZ's Karl Wills; Daniel Locke's *Green*; Eddie Campbell's hand-coloured and Tippex-lathered original cover to *Gencomics 2: Blues* – a little dab'll do ya.

Inside back cover illustrations: Clockwise from top left – Peter Rigg and Paul "Mooncat" Schroeder's seminal *Lee Butler* (complete in two issues – the second named for Lee's wife, Jenny); Christ-mas-on-a-bike! It's a very jolly *Sadist* come to rule your yule; Butler and Hogg's one-shot, *Tick-Tock Follies*.